EDITORIAL

Editor	Jean Dale
Editorial Assistant	Susan Cross
Graphic Technician	Davina Rowan
Cover Figurine	The Moor, HN 3642

ACKNOWLEDGEMENTS

The Charlton Press wishes to thank those who have helped with past editions of *The Charlton Standard Catalogue of Royal Doulton Figurines*. Over 100,000 copies of this catalogue are now in print, and the success is by no small measure, a credit to those who have helped.

SPECIAL THANKS

The publisher would like to thank: **Louise Irvine** for writing the introduction to this publication. Louise is an independent writer and lecturer on Royal Doulton's history and products and is not connected with the pricing of this catalogue.

Our thanks go to the staff of Royal Doulton, who have helped with additional technical information and images, especially **Sarah Williams,** Senior Product Manager, **Chetna Luthar,** Production Manager (U.K.); **Marion Proctor,** Marketing Manager (Canada); **Tricia Clemens**, Public Relations Manager (Canada); **Paula Bell**, Product Manager (Canada); **Janet Drift**, Director Retail Sales (U.S.A.) and Joseph **Schmidt**, Associate Product Manager.

CONTRIBUTORS TO THE TENTH EDITION

The publisher would like to thank the following individuals or companies who graciously supplied photographs, date and other valuable information for the ninth edition. We offer sincere thanks to:

Mary Dolph of Marcus and Company, Newmarket, Ontario, Canada; **Melissa Dysart and Paul Pound**, Precious Memories Fine China Gifts and Collectables, P.E.I.; **Ed Pascoe**, Pascoe and Company, Florida; **Stan Worrey**, Colonial House of Collectibles, Ohio, and all the past contributors who over the years have supplied so much important information that has helped establish this catalogue as the standard reference.

A SPECIAL NOTE TO COLLECTORS

We welcome and would appreciate any comments or suggestions in regard to *The Charlton Standard Catalogue of Royal Doulton Figurines*. If any errors or omissions come to your attention, please write to us, or if you would like to participate in pricing or supply previously unavailable data or information, please contact Jean Dale at (416) 488-1418 or e-mail us at chpress@charltonpress.com.

DISCLAIMER

While every care has been taken to ensure accuracy in the compilation of the data in this catalogue, the publisher cannot accept responsibility for typographical errors.

The Charlton Press

Editorial Office
P. O. Box 820, Station Willowdale B
North York, Ontario M2K 2R1 Canada
Telephone: (416) 488-1418 Fax: (416) 488-4656
Telephone: (800) 442-6042 Fax: (800) 442-1542
www.charltonpress.com
e-mail: chpress@charltonpress.com

PRICING, OLD, NEW AND THE INTERNET

Over the past thirty years we have gathered pricing information from auctions, dealer submissions, direct mail catalogues and newsletters. All contributed prices on one of two levels, wholesale or retail. We, at the Charlton Press, consider auctions basically a dealer affair, while price lists, naturally retail. To equate both prices, we needed to adjust the auction results upward, by a margin of 30% to 40%, allowing for dealer markups, before comparing and then looking for a consensus on a retail price.

The marketplace has changed, the Internet on-line auctions are growing at such a rate that all other pricing sources we used are being completely overwhelmed by the sheer volume of items being offered for sale

At a moment in time on December 9th, 2004, under the Royal Doulton category over 10,300 individual items were posted for sale on e-Bay. Assuming this is an average day, then for the week 72,100 items are offered, and for the year nearly 3,750,000 will be offered for sale. The "Economist," a weekly news magazine, projected the on-line auctions with over 100,000,000 registered users.

The impact the Internet will have on collectables has yet to be appreciated by collectors and dealers alike. All the old avenues such as fairs, shows, dealer stores, retail outlets, direct mail houses and auction rooms are being forced to change due to the extreme pressure of this new marketing force. Margins have come under pressure, wholesale and retail prices are starting to blend, and competition for the collectors' budget will intensify. However, through it all one point remains, a price guide is just that, a guide, and the final say is between the buyer and the seller.

HOW TO USE THIS CATALOGUE

THE PURPOSE

As with the other catalogues in Charlton's Royal Doulton reference and pricing library, this publication has been designed to serve two specific purposes. First, to furnish the Royal Doulton enthusiast with accurate listings containing vital information, and photographs to aid in the building of a rewarding collection. Secondly, this publication provides Royal Doulton collectors and dealers with current market prices for Royal Doulton Figurines. Jugs are covered in "The Charlton Standard Catalogue of Royal Doulton Jugs," and animals are covered in "The Charlton Standard Catalogue of Royal Doulton Animals."

STYLES AND VARIATIONS

On the pages that follow, Royal Doulton figurines are listed, illustrated and described in **HN** and **M** number order. Stoneware, Vellum and Earthenware figures are listed by modeller and then alphabetically.

STYLES: When two or more figures have the same name but different physical modelling characteristics, they are listed as **Style One**, **Style Two**, and so on. Such figurines will also have a different HN number.

VARIATIONS: Slight design alterations in a mould for any reason is considered a variation. In variations the HN number assigned will not change. Colourways (change in colouring) are also termed variations.

STATISTICS

D Number: D numbers are the design numbers assigned to items manufactured by Royal Doulton. This number carries throughout the early part of figurine production for Stoneware, Vellum and Earthenware.

HN Number: The figurines with HN numbers flow from 1 to almost 5000.

Height: Stated in inches and centimetres

Issue Date: Dates of production

Colourway: Colours of the figurine

Backstamp: Maker's marks

Pricing: Market pricing in three currencies, U.K. Pounds, U.S. dollars, and Canadian dollars.

Images: Although the publisher has made every attempt to obtain and photograph all figures and their varieties, several pieces, naturally, have not come into the publishers view and thus original images are not available. In this case, if an image of another colourway is available, that image will be used for shape recognition purposes.

CONTENTS

PRICING, OLD NEW AND THE INTERNET..iv

INTRODUCTION

    The History of Royal Doulton Figures xi

    Building a Collection xi

    Making Doulton Figurines xi

    Year Cyphers..xi

DOULTON LAMBETH FIGURINES

    John Broad Figures 2

    Leslie Harradine Figures 6

    Leslie Harradine Dickens Figures 10

    Mark Marshall Figures 11

    Charles Noke Vellum Figures 12

    Charles Noke Wall Pockets and Lights..16

    George Tinworth Figures..17

HN SERIES..21

AIL SERIES...447

CLASSIQUE SERIES 449

M SERIES..455

COLLECTING BY TYPE OR SERIES...469

ALPHABETICAL INDEX...477

ADVERTISERS...492

THE HISTORY OF ROYAL DOULTON FIGURES

The Doulton company was founded in 1815 and the first figures were produced at Lambeth in London and Burslem in Stoke-on-Trent during the 1880s. Charles Noke, who became Royal Doulton's Art Director, was responsible for modelling many of the early figures and for developing the company's famous HN collection which was launched in 1913. The 'HN' numbering system refers to Harry Nixon, who was in charge of the new figure painting department at the Burslem factory. At first, Noke commissioned figures from a number of independent sculptors but in 1920 he secured the talents of Leslie Harradine, who became the mainstay of the collection for more than thirty years. From the 1950s to the 1970s nearly all the figures were produced by either Peggy Davies, who specialised in pretty ladies, or Mary Nicholl, who contributed a wide range of character figures. Doulton's modelling team was expanded considerably in the 1970s and 80s to cope with increased demand from collectors and a Club magazine called 'Gallery' was established in 1980 to keep members informed of new developments in the HN collection.

BUILDING A COLLECTION

Since the 1890s, more than 2,500 figures have been added to the range and these are now avidly collected in many parts of the world. It would be virtually impossible to aquire them all, even if space and budget allowed, but there is plenty of scope to build interesting collections, based on artist, period, style or theme.

Collecting Lambeth Figures

Royal Doulton's famous HN series is known and appreciated all over the world, but few collectors are aware of the other types of Royal Doulton figures made at their Lambeth factory in London. They are quite different in appearance from their Burslem counterparts, being made of salt glaze stoneware or terracotta, and they are scarce in the market place as they were produced in very limited numbers.

George Tinworth, Doulton's first resident sculptor, often included human figures in practical items, such as candlesticks, menu holders and spill vases, but in the 1890s he produced an extensive collection of free-standing figures featuring boys playing musical instruments. These **Merry Musicians** have been recorded playing about 40 different instruments. They stand around 5 inches high and are executed in a plain brown stoneware body, although some have white faces. Occasionally, Tinworth produced other figurative subjects, such as the teatime group, **Scandal,** and a portrait of his favourite Dickens character, **Mr. Pickwick,** but these seem to have been unique pieces. A notable exception is the terracotta figure of a jester that he made for the Art Union of London in an edition of 12, around 1900.

One of the most versatile figure modellers at the Lambeth factory was **John Broad,** who was equally at home producing small studies with the aid of a magnifying glass and huge monumental commissions that required scaffolding. He particularly enjoyed working in terracotta and one of his first small-scale figures in this medium was a study of a **Thrower** in 1883. Later terracotta figures by Broad include a devotional statuette of **Our Lady** and a study of **Pomona,** the classical goddess of fruit.

Broad also modelled some delightful studies of classical maidens in salt glaze stoneware, and these were reproduced in limited numbers before and after the First World War, as denoted by their X pattern numbers. The different numbers for **Atalanta** (X7910 and X8707) and the **Bather** (X7912 and X8706) denote different types of stoneware, either plain brown or fully coloured (also known as Doultonware).

Important national events in the early 1900s, such as the Boer War, Nelson's Centenary, the death of Queen Victoria and the coronation of her son, inspired Broad to produce a number of commemorative figures, including handsome terracotta portraits of **King Edward** and **Queen Alexandra,** a faience figure of **Nelson** and imposing salt glaze stoneware studies of **Queen Victoria** and the **Boer War Soldier.**

During the First World War, Doulton developed a hard paste porcelain body for making laboratory ware, and John Broad used this new medium, with either a biscuit or glost finish, for some delicate figures of pretty ladies. His porcelain figures, particularly the portraits of the American actress **Doris Keane,** were a major influence on the HN collection in Burslem, as indeed were the pretty lady figures by **Mark Marshall.** Although Marshall is best known for his art nouveau style vases, adorned with grotesque dragons and reptiles, he dabbled occasionally in figurative sculpture, producing fashionable ladies in white glazed stoneware, accented in blue. His **Crinoline** of 1910 is almost identical to the figure of the same name (HN13) introduced a few years later in Burslem.

Marshall, Broad and Tinworth all helped train the young **Leslie Harradine** when he joined the Lambeth studio in 1902. Unlike his mentors, Harradine's special interest was modelling ornamental figures and animals and he disliked having to design vases for reproduction. Broad's **Boer War soldier** inspired him to produce a group of contemporary soldiers in salt glaze stoneware, including a **British Tommy,** a **French Legionaire,** a **North African Spahi** and a **Cossack,** whilst Marshall's pretty ladies prompted elegant figures such as **Polly Peachum.**

Most importantly, Tinworth's enthusiasm for The Pickwick Papers led Harradine to discover all the colourful characters created by Charles Dickens, and he modelled a selection of stoneware figures in time for the centenary of Dickens' birth in 1912. These were made of slip cast stoneware on square bases and were available in brown, buff or coloured Doultonware. Harradine also modelled different versions of the Dickens characters in rich brown stoneware, and these were reproduced in the HN collection (HN553-558) in 1923. He also modelled a set of miniature Dickens figures as prototypes for the HN collection and these were introduced in 1922.

Harradine spent little time in London after he completed his apprenticeship, preferring to work in his country studio in Hertfordshire, where he produced some powerful studies of farm workers, notably **The Harvester, The Peat Cutter** and **The Reaper.** This last character was available in three different effects, plain brown stoneware, coloured Doultonware and brighter 'toby' colours. European peasants were also favourite subjects, and he modelled a very striking group of two Brittany peasants gossiping, a mother with her baby and some Dutch characters.

Several of Harradine's models were reproduced in white slip cast stoneware, sometimes with blue detailing, and these were allocated H pattern numbers along with his animal models and vase designs. They remained in production long after Harradine had left Doulton to emigrate to Canada. After serving in the First World War, Harradine returned to the UK and worked on a freelance basis for Charles Noke, the art director of the Burslem studio, where he became better known as the star modeller of the HN collection.

Harradine's departure from London virtually marked the end of purely ornamental figures at the Lambeth studio. Harry Simeon did some sterling work reviving the Staffordshire toby jug tradition, and little stoneware figures of Toby Philpotts and related characters were incorporated in match stands and ashtrays during the mid 1920s. At the same time, he also included models of a pixie and Pan playing his pipes in a range of bibelots or trinket trays.

Occasionally freelance artists contributed designs for reproduction at the Lambeth studio, but these are even harder to find than the work of the resident modellers. Around 1912, the successful sculptor Stanley Nicholson Babb contributed a figure of a **Lute Player**, which was issued in salt glaze stoneware in a small edition. Twenty years later, Richard Garbe, a professor at the Royal College of Art, produced several designs in conjunction with the Lambeth studio, including a salt glaze stoneware figure of a **Sea Sprite**, which was based on a bronze original.

Another twenty years elapsed before figures were made again at Lambeth, this time by Helen Walters, who worked at the studio between 1953 and 1956. Two of her salt glaze stoneware figures were exhibited at the Royal Academy, and her study of **Demeter** was purchased by Stoke City Art Gallery. It was probably the last figure model to be fired in the Lambeth kilns, as the factory closed down in 1956, thus ending another remarkable chapter in the story of Royal Doulton figures.

Collecting Vellum Figures

In the 1890s, some twenty years before the HN collection was launched, Charles Noke was experimenting with a very different style of Doulton figures. Known as the Vellum figures, because of their parchment colour, they are very similar to the work he was doing at the Worcester factory in the 1880s.

Usually the Vellum figures are tinted with soft sheens of pink and green, but occasionally bolder on-glaze colours are used, such as scarlet or black. Gold highlights were often added and sometimes intricate printed patterns of flowers. Each figure is slightly different, thanks to the varied talents of the prestige artists who worked in Robert Allen's decorating studio. Generally the Vellum figures are much larger than the HN models, ranging from 10 to 20 inches in height, and they were made in very small editions.

In the past, collectors tended to overlook these early Noke designs as they do not come onto the market very often and information was scarce. However, there has been a new awareness of the Vellum models ever since they were catalogued in the classic reference book, Royal Doulton Figures. Their pioneering status is now fully recognised, and connoisseurs around the world appreciate the quality of Noke's early modelling and the decorative skills of Robert Allen's artists.

Most of the themes explored in the Vellum figure range preoccupied Noke throughout his modelling career. There are jesters, pierrots and other entertainers from the Victorian stage. His admiration for the acting talents of Henry Irving and Ellen Terry led to several models of them in famous roles, including **Shylock** and **Portia** from "The Merchant of Venice," **Mephistopheles** and **Marguerite** from "Faust" and **Cardinal Wolsey** and **Queen Catharine** from "Henry VIII." This last pair was the most popular, as they turn up most frequently today.

It would appear that **The Devil** was also based on Henry Irving's role in Faust. New discoveries are still being made in the Vellum range, notably an imposing figure of Lily Langtry as **Cleopatra**, which was not recorded in the Doulton archives. More recently **The Moorish Minstrel** has come to light as part of a candlestick.

Many of the Vellum figures also served practical purposes, either being incorporated into light fittings or flower holders. **The Lady Jester**, **The Sorceress** and **The Geisha** were all made with flat backs for wall mounting as vases, whilst **The Witch** was a wall mounted electric light, with the bulb at the end of her broomstick!

Charles Noke showed his first Vellum figures at the Chicago exhibition of 1893, but the reception was luke-warm. Perhaps the colouring was too bland for the taste of the times and they were very expensive. Noke continued to exhibit the figures in Paris (1900), St. Louis (1904) and Christchurch (1906), and it is likely that they continued to be made in small numbers until work on the HN collection began in 1909.

Some of the most successful Vellum models were later reissued in brighter colours as HN figures, notably The **Jester**, **Jack Point**, **Cardinal Wolsey** and **Queen Catharine**. Other Vellum designs can also be found with on-glaze enamel colours, even though they were never assigned HN numbers, for example, The **Kneeling Jester** and **The Witch**.

In all, 21 free-standing Vellum figures have been recorded in a variety of colourways, plus four wall mounted pieces. Perhaps there are even more models waiting to be discovered. Forming a complete collection would be a challenging but rewarding experience if patience and purse strings allow.

Collecting The HN Series By Artist

New collectors quickly gravitate towards a particular style of figure and often discover that they favour the work of a specific artist. In the early years the artist was acknowledged on the base of the figures and collectors could appreciate the diverse modelling skills of artists such as Charles Noke, Harry Tittensor and others. After a gap of many years, this practice was revived in 1984 when the artist's facsimile signature was incorporated into the backstamp, making identification as easy as it had been previously.

The work of each Doulton artist has a distinctive quality, even though their figures might be classified with many others as 'fair ladies' or 'character studies.' An experienced eye can quickly spot the difference between a Peggy Davies crinoline lady and one by Leslie Harradine. Similarly Mary Nicoll's nautical figures are quite distinct from Bill Harper's. Each of these artists has a wide following and the scope for collecting their work is often vast and varied, particularly in the case of Peggy Davies, who produced about 250 figures in her 40 year career with Royal Doulton.

Collecting By Period

It has been said of Royal Doulton figures that they are a reflection of the times in which they are made. Certainly, with many of the subjects it is possible to attribute them to a particular period, based on costume, fabric designs and hair styles. The bright young things of the 1920s, such as **Lido Lady** (HN1200) and **Angela** (HN1204) with their negligees and lounging pyjamas, are amongst the most appealing of these period figures but collections can also be formed from other decades. The glamorous style of the 1930s, inspired by the Hollywood stars, is represented in figures such as **Gloria** (HN1488) and **Clothilde** (HN1598) whilst the teenage trends of the 1950s can be seen in **Faraway** (HN2133) and **Sweet Sixteen** (HN2231).

For the fashion conscious, it is possible to create a cat-walk of costumes through the ages from the Medieval period to the 20th century. Some collectors focus exclusively on 18th century style costumes, as worn by **Antoinette** (HN1850) and **Kate Hardcastle** (HN1861), which were notable for their wide hooped skirts adorned with ribbons, bows and ruffles of lace. Others prefer Victorian dresses with their flounced skirts and frothy petticoats, represented by such pieces as **Spring Morning** (HN1922) and **Chloe** (HN1470). Whether it be hats (from wimples to poke bonnets), or fluttering fans, even ladies' fashionable accessories have inspired collections.

Collecting By Subject

Child Studies

Darling, the first figure in the HN collection, was so successful that it was soon followed by many more child studies. Consequently, there is plenty of scope to form a delightful collection, whether it includes the sort of children who were 'seen but not heard' in Victorian times, like **Monica** (HN1467) or **Lily** (HN1798), or the mischievous kids of today like **Pillow Fight** (HN2270) and **Lights Out** (HN2262). There are many popular series inspired by childhood, including Leslie Harradine's **Nursery Rhymes** figures and the **Age of Innocence** series. Many of the latest child studies incorporate animals and the special relationship young children enjoy with their pets would be an interesting theme to explore with both new and discontinued figures. As well as puppies and kittens, Doulton children also play with teddies, dolls and other toys. It would be fun to track down a representative collection, although there will be competition from serious Teddy Bear collectors. **Sleepyhead** (HN2114), cuddling her teddy, would be a very exciting discovery whilst **Nanny** (HN2221), mending her charge's teddy, is more readily available.

Fair Ladies

There are more fair ladies than any other type of Doulton figure so it is a good idea to specialize at an early stage. Collecting by artist has already been discussed and, as well as the great names of the past, such as Leslie Harradine and Peggy Davies, there are many talented modellers to look for today. Pauline Parsons has portrayed many famous **Queens of the Realm** and Peter Gee has been inspired by the famous paintings of **Gainsborough** and **Reynolds** ladies. More recent artists, Nada Pedley and Valerie Annand, have given us romantic interpretations of Victorian and Edwardian fashions.

Faced with this wide choice, a popular approach is to collect by colour, choosing only shades which harmonize with the furnishings of particular rooms. For example, ladies dressed in pastel shades might be suitable for a bedroom whilst richer colours might be more appropriate for the lounge or dining room. Displays could be changed to match the seasons, with all the ladies dressed in yellow and green featured in the spring and all the red outfits at Christmas time. There are many Doulton figures which celebrate the festive season, including **Noelle** (HN2179) with her ermine trimmed cloak and muff and **Santa Claus** himself (HN2725).

Figures can also be used effectively as table centres, whatever the season, or as feature displays with flower arrangements. Some of the figures are even portrayed arranging bowls of tiny hand-made flowers, whilst others carry baskets of blooms, lavish bouquets or a single red rose, so a fair ladies collection could be 'all a blooming'.

Swirling voluminous gowns have inspired many collections of dancing ladies, most of them the work of Peggy Davies who excelled at conveying movement in the folds of the fabric. Peggy's talent in this area can be seen in **Ninette** (HN2379) and **Elaine** (HN2791). **Minuet** (HN2019), one of her earliest figures was inspired by the stately minuet and over the years she added **Polka** (HN2156), **First Waltz** (HN2862) and the flamboyant **Gypsy Dance** (HN2230). She also studied many national dances and costumes for her **Dancers of the World** collection.

Many collectors are influenced by the names of the figures, whether it be the sentiment conveyed or the name of a loved one.

In some cases it has been possible to put together a 'family' of figures representing children, grandchildren, and so on. 'Fair ladies,' of course, can form part of much wider theme collections of the types suggested below.

Character Figures

As with the fair ladies there is a huge choice of character figures from all walks of life and most collectors look for a particular artist or theme. Art director Charles Noke specialised in character modelling and many of his personal interests can be seen in his range, including literature, history and the theatre. Leslie Harradine, renowned for his beautiful lady figures, was equally at home with characters, contributing country folk, such as **Lambing Time** (HN1890), and colourful street vendors selling balloons, silks and ribbons or fruit and flowers. One such example is **The Orange Seller** (HN1325).

Mary Nicoll dominated the character collection from the mid 1950s to the 1970s and she also launched the nautical figures, which are so popular with sea lovers today. She also developed a collection of figures featuring traditional crafts and professions, for example **The Clockmaker** (HN2279) and **The Judge** (HN2443) and she celebrated the twilight years in her studies of Old Dears, notably **Family Album** (HN2321) and **Teatime** (HN2255). All these successful sub-collections have been continued in recent years by Bill Harper, who has also expanded the London collection of characters with **The Lifeguard** (HN2781) and **The Guardsman** (HN2784). Former Art Director Eric Griffiths portrayed many members of the British Royal family before his retirement in 1991 and he was also responsible for the **Soldiers of the Revolution** collection of military figures.

Younger modellers are also making their mark. Robert Tabbenor produced some fine sporting characters, such as **Teeing Off** (HN3276) and Alan Maslankowski has excelled with his limited edition historical subjects, notably **Christopher Columbus** (HN3392).

Any one of these themes can form the basis of a fascinating collection, which can become even more rewarding by researching the characters behind the figures.

The World of Entertainment

Collecting Royal Doulton figures can literally be an 'entertaining' hobby as many of the stars of stage and screen have been portrayed by Doulton modellers. From the pierrots of pantomime and seaside concerts, to the great Shakespearean roles played by Henry Irving and Ellen Terry, many of the earliest figures reflect Charles Noke's fascination with the theatre. A taste for the exotic is particularly evident in his work, stemming from the fashionable oriental flavour of many operas, musicals and ballets of the time. Examples are the **Mandarin** (HN84) and the **Eastern Cobbler** (HN542).

An interesting collection could include famous stage personalities of the past, such as the American actress **Doris Keane** (HN90), and more recent stars from the silver screen such as **Groucho Marx** (HN2777) and **Charlie Chaplin** (HN2771). As well as these classic clowns of the cinema, there are also lots of circus clowns by Mary Nicoll and Bill Harper to collect. Their ancestors of mirth, the court jesters, have also been popular characters in the figures collection since the earliest days, notably **Jack Point** (HN85) and **The Wandering Minstrel** (HN1224) from Gilbert and Sullivan's famous operettas.

The ballet has been a fertile source of inspiration for Doulton modellers from the great **Pavlova** (HN487) in her most famous role as 'The Dying Swan' to aspiring young dancers practising in frilly tutus, such as **Little Ballerina** (HN3395). Like many young girls, Peggy Davies had ambitions to be a ballerina and as a result she contributed many delightful studies of dancers, including **Coppelia** (HN2115) and **Giselle** (HN2140).

Music lovers can seek out figures playing instruments, whether they be an elegant orchestra of **Lady Musicians** or a precocious violinist such as **The Young Master** (HN2872). Even street performers, such as **The Organ Grinder** (HN2173) and **The Punch and Judy Man** (HN2765), could be included in this colourful revue of the world of entertainment.

Literature

Book lovers will enjoy all of the characters from literature that have been portrayed in the figure collection over the years. Classical myths, Eastern romances, European folklore and English classics have all provided inspiration for individual figures and series. Art Director Charles Noke was a great admirer of Shakespeare and he modelled the great bard himself for the Vellum range, as well as several of his characters. The novels of Charles Dickens were an even greater influence and there are several sets of his famous characters, including the very collectable miniatures. Children's books have also been a fertile source of ideas and, as well as the obvious collection of **Characters from Children's Literature**, there have been figures based on nursery rhymes, Kate Greenaway's picture books and Victorian classics, such as Treasure Island. The figure of this name depicts a young boy poring over the pages of Stevenson's great adventure yarn and pages from the book can be enjoyed with the aid of a magnifying glass. There are many other 'readers' in the figures range, including several others with legible books and this has become a particularly popular collecting theme. A representative display might include the scholarly **Professor** (HN2281) with his nose in a book, **The Wizard** (HN2877) who is consulting his book of spells, or some of the daydreaming fair ladies who rest closed books on their laps.

History

The figures collection is like a historical pageant with famous people from all ages commemorated in clay. It is to be expected that an English company would pay homage to British national heroes and heroines such as **Florence Nightingale** (HN3144) and more recently **Winston Churchill** (HN3057), but there are also many historical personalities from other countries. It would be possible for patriotic Americans to form a 'Stars and Stripes' collection, which might include the **Soldiers of the Revolution** or the **Characters from Williamsburg** series. Canadians can look for the unusual Mountie busts of **R.C.M.P. 1973** (HN2547) and **R.C.M.P. 1873** (HN2555) or the portrait figure of **Sir John A. MacDonald** (HN2860).

Those interested in military history could seek out the rare First World War soldiers, **Digger** (HN321-2) and **Blighty** (HN323) or the **Drummer Boy** (HN2679) from the Napoleonic Wars whilst naval historians could add **Captain Cook** (HN2889) or **The Captain** (HN2260) to a general seafaring collection.

The current British royal family has proved to be a popular collection in recent years and many of the Queen's illustrious ancestors have also been portrayed as Doulton figures. **Henry VIII** (HN370, 1792 and 3350) and **King Charles I** (HN404) are good examples. As well as the reigning monarchs, there have also been portraits of their consorts, courtiers and even one of their courtesans, **Nell Gwynne** (HN1882)!

Collecting By Size

For collectors with limited display space miniature figures are particularly appealing. The M series was launched in 1932 but there had been miniature figures in the HN range before that, notably the tiny Dickens characters which were re-numbered in line with all the new introductions. By 1949, there were 24 Dickens characters in the M series and they continued in production with minor alterations until 1981-3.

The majority of the miniature fair ladies were scaled down versions of existing figures by Leslie Harradine. Although only three to four inches tall, the detailing of the costumes and accessories is exceptional, with tiny flower baskets ¾ inch across and parasols less than an inch long. As in the standard range of the 1930s, there was also a wide range of colourways and **Polly Peachum** has been found in at least 15 different costumes. Unfortunately, rising labour costs led to the withdrawal of the miniature ladies by 1949 and, as many had only been made for about 10 years, they are very elusive for today's collector. Consequently, their prices do not match their diminutive size and they can cost as much, or more, than their standard size counterparts.

Miniature figures were revived in 1988 when the Royal Doulton International Collectors Club commissioned a tiny version of the ever popular **Top o' the Hill** (HN2126). More fair ladies followed in quick succession, with special rich colourways produced exclusively for Michael Doulton's signature collection. All have been allocated HN numbers and are reduced versions of popular figures in the current range. A selection of miniature character figures was introduced in 1989 but these were not well received. Several were quickly withdrawn so they will no doubt become hard to find in the future.

Also easily accommodated in a small display area are the figures of young girls dressed in fashions of the past. These range in size from four to six inches tall and some, such as **Dinky Do** (HN1678) and **Monica** (HN1467) were in continuous production for over 50 years testifying to the appeal of this scale and subject matter.

Today, the average Doulton fair lady stands around eight inches tall, whilst seated subjects in proportion measure around six inches. Limited editions and character figures tend to be a little larger, averaging nine inches for standing subjects. Eric Griffiths, the former director of Sculpture, favoured larger scale figures, particularly for character portraits, as he believed a better likeness could be achieved. Consequently his figure of Lord Olivier as **Richard III** (HN2881) is above average size. He also introduced the **Haute Ensemble** series of tall, slender ladies and the attenuated **Images** and **Reflections** series.

In the past, there was much more variety of scale in the collection and figures of more than 12 inches in height were not unusual. **The Welsh Girl** (HN39) and **Lady With Shawl** (HN447) are good examples. Some large scale figures from the past now form the Prestige collection and **Princess Badoura** (HN2081), at 20 inches in height, is the largest in the range.

Collecting By Series

Numerous collectors subscribe to Royal Doulton's established series of figures, many of which are limited editions. In these cases the company has already chosen all the characters to fit a specific theme and has defined the limits of the collection so there are fewer decisions required than with the more general themes already discussed. This method also allows collectors to budget for forthcoming annual introductions in the more expensive limited edition series.

Some of the recently discontinued series are becoming increasingly difficult to find and it could take some time to find all

18 of the **Kate Greenaway** figures or all 24 **Dickens** miniatures. There always seems to be one or two figures in a series which are rarer than the others and prices rise accordingly. For example, **Tom Bombadil** (HN2924) is a particularly elusive model in the now desirable **Tolkien** series. Occasionally complete series come up for sale but for some collectors that spoils the fun of the chase.

Limited Editions, Prestige Figures and Special Editions

In 1933, discerning customers were offered a range of specially commissioned figures by Richard Garbe RA, a distinguished sculptor of the day. Inspired by his sculptures in other media, the new figures were larger than most others in the HN collection and many were embellished with gold. In order to emphasise their prestige status, it was announced that only a limited number of each model would be produced and the edition size was marked on the base. The editions ranged from 25 to 150 pieces and took several years to sell out. Not surprisingly, they are now very desirable on the secondary market. At the same time, Charles Noke introduced a limited edition figure of **King Henry VIII**, which is more typical of Doulton's later limited editions in terms of subject matter, scale and decoration.

During the 1950s, some of the largest and most impressive figures in the range were revamped to form the basis of a Prestige collection. Three of these subjects were originally modelled by Charles Noke, **The Moor** (HN2082), **Jack Point** (HN2080), and **King Charles** (HN2084), and the first two are still produced today, although in very limited quantities to special order. The most expensive prestige figure of all, **Princess Badoura** (HN2081), was introduced in 1952. The painting and gilding on this figure take about eight weeks to complete, hence the high cost. Repeated kiln firings and complex model assembly also add to the expense of producing prestige pieces, as with the spectacular **Matador and Bull** (HN2324), which was modelled by Peggy Davies in 1964. Two more of Peggy's ambitious large scale sculptures were produced in limited editions of 500 each, **The Indian Brave** (HN2376) produced in 1967 and **The Palio** (HN2428) of 1971. However, she is better known today for her limited edition collections of **Lady Musicians** (1970-76) and **Dancers of the World** (1977-82). These highly detailed and richly decorated models were each limited to 750 pieces and were introduced at the rate of one or two each year, complete with presentation boxes and certificates of authenticity. This has become the pattern for most of the company's limited editions today, although edition sizes have grown to reflect increased demand.

Special occasions have also inspired limited editions and there are portrait figures celebrating Royal weddings, birthdays and coronation anniversaries. Expo'92 in Seville, for example prompted a limited edition colourway of **Mantilla** (HN3192) and a special edition of **Discovery** (HN3428), a reduced version of the symbolic sculpture in the British Pavilion. This piece was offered exclusively to members of the Royal Doulton International Collectors Club. The opportunity to purchase limited editions and special editions of figures is one of the benefits of joining the Club. Generally speaking, special editions are limited by the offer period, which in the case of the early Doulton Club commissions was six months. The term is also used more widely to describe special products commissioned by independent companies which are not individually numbered on their bases nor accompanied by a certificate of authenticity.

For the collector looking for something extra special, Royal Doulton limited and special editions are in great demand today and popular subjects are often quickly oversubscribed. It is important,

therefore, to respond quickly to the announcements for new releases. Discontinued limited editions command premium prices in the secondary market, particularly if they are sold with their original literature and packaging and the first of a collection of six or twelve figures is usually the hardest to find.

Collecting Colourways and Variations

From the earliest days of the figures collection, some of the most popular models have been produced in alternative colourways. The first fair lady figure, **The Crinoline**, was originally offered in a plain lilac dress or with a floral design. Each colourway was assigned a different HN number to distinguish the decorative treatment. Charles Noke's study of **A Jester** has been available in 12 different coloured suits as well as in Parian and Vellum finishes. Noke also experimented with different glaze effects on figures, including a lustrous red flambé, a mottled blue green Titanian, a glittering gold and a dark brown to simulate bronze. These were produced only in very limited numbers and were not given HN references.

During the 1920s, when more master painters joined the figure painting department, colour effects and patterns became more ambitious. The lady figures were dressed in all of the fashionable fabrics of the day with floral designs, polka dots, stripes, diapers and checks painted by hand. It was unusual to have a lady figure in just one colourway and in the case of **Victorian Lady**, there was a choice of 15 varied designs.

After the Second World War the collection was rationalised and alternative colourways became less common. However, the idea was revived during the 1980s, initially for special occasions such as Michael Doulton tours. A new colourway of **Wistful** (HN2472) was devised exclusively for his personal appearances in 1985. Colourways have also been commissioned by independent retailers and in some cases the name has been changed as well as the colours. For example, a variation of **Adrienne** (HN2304) was commissioned to promote Joan's Gift Shop in Scotland and was renamed **Joan** (HN3217).

Alternative colourways now appear regularly in the general range, sometimes with a new name, and it is not just fair ladies which ring the changes. Character figures have also been given a fresh new look from time to time. **The Lobster Man**, for instance, is available with two different coloured sweaters (HN2317 and HN2323).

During the 1970s, former Art Director Eric Griffiths experimented with matte glazes but these were not a commercial success and most of the models were quickly withdrawn. An exception is **The Judge** (HN2443) which was changed from a matte to a glossy finish because it was so popular.

From time to time alterations have been made to models after they have been introduced, usually to decrease the risk of damage during production or in transit. In early models of **The Carpet Seller** (HN1464) for example, the character's hand is outstretched, whereas in later models the fingers are clasped around the carpet, making them less vulnerable to breakage. The figure of **Masque** (HN2554) also had to be modified as the long metal handle of the mask was easily broken. It was removed and the hand was remodelled. Eagle eyed collectors will also notice that early models of **Autumn Breezes** (HN1911) have two feet peeping out from under the dress whilst later models have only one.

There are some keen collectors who enjoy tracking down the different model and colour variations but the majority take advantage of the wide choice of shades and patterns to co-ordinate a new purchase with an existing display.

MAKING DOULTON FIGURES

Threr are many people involved in the creation of each Royal Doulton figure, beginning with the artist who works with modelling clay to transform an image in his head, or on paper, into three dimensional sculpture.

When the original model is complete it is taken to the mould maker, whose years of experience enable him to cut up the figure into separate parts so that a master mould, known as a block, can be produced. Complex figures are divided into many parts and a palster of Paris mould is made from the original head, torso, arms, skirts and so on. Working moulds are made as required during production so that the crisp detail of the original is maintained.

Liquid clay, known as slip, is gently poured into each mould by the caster and once the body has set to the required thickness the excess slip is poured out. At this stage the parts of the figure are carefully removed from the mould and, as the clay is still very fragile, they are pieced together using slip as an adhesive.

Before the complete figure has been thoroughly dried, the seams are sponged away in a process known as fettling. The piece is then ready for its first firing. It is removed from the kiln, having shrunk to its 'biscuit' state and then, if it is a character figure, it is ready for painting. Painting takes place at this stage because pieces are coloured under-glaze to give the more rugged effect expected of these subjects.

Fair lady figures in their biscuit state are dipped into a vat of glaze and fired again before decorating begins. The dresses and accessories are painted with on-glaze colours and to achieve the rich colour effects, like the deep red, several applications of colour are needed. Each layer requires a separate firing. When the costume decoration is complete, the faces of the fair ladies are painted by the most experienced artists and a final firing ensures that the colours are permanently sealed under the glaze.

Bodies and Glazes

The fair lady figures are made from bone china which is a traditionally British body, composed of China clay, Cornish stone and bone ash. Most character figures are made from English Porcelain, a whiter coloured body formerly known as English Translucent China, which was pioneered by Royal Doulton chemists in 1959. Before the invention of English Porcelain, many Doulton figures were produced in an earthenware body, which is fired to a lower temperature than china and is more porous. There are slight differences in size between figures made of earthenware and those made of porcelain and colours often look different on the two bodies.

Most Royal Doulton figures have a brilliant glossy glaze. In the early 1970s, however, some matt figures were produced and this matt finish was also used for limited edition subjects as it enhanced the intricate modelling and gave a distinctive effect. A matt glazed black basalt body has been used more recently in the Images range of modern style sculptures.

CURRENT AND DISCONTINUED FIGURES

Figures which are produced at the Royal Doulton factories today are generally referred to as 'current' whilst models which are no longer made are variously described as 'withdrawn', 'retired' or 'discontinued'. A current figure might have been in the range for a long time and one or two have been in continuous production for over fifty years, for example **The Balloon Man**. Because this figure is still generally available today, a 1930s version is unlikely to be worth more than the current model, even though it is older and probably differs slightly in appearance, due to changes in body and paint formulations over the years. It is worth remembering, however, that originally it would have been purchased for just a few pounds or dollars.

Figures are discontinued on an annual basis in order to make way for new introductions. There is a limit to the number of models the factory can produce, or the retailer can display, so eventually some have to go. In some cases the choice is easy as it is apparent that all the collectors who want a particular model have already purchased it and world-wide sales are decreasing. Occasionally figures disappear after only a couple of years in the range and these short-lived models often become very desirable on the secondary market.

The number of figures withdrawn each year varies enormously. Sometimes it is less than 12 a year and other times, after a major reassessment of the range, there might be 50 or so. The first withdrawals took place during the Second World War and it is unlikely that more than 2,000 of each of the early models were produced. This is less than many limited editions, so it is not surprising that these pieces are amongst the most desirable figures on the secondary market today. Older figures with short production runs are obviously less likely to appear in the market-place than those that were made for many years. However, this alone does not affect the price, which will probably also be governed by aesthetic considerations and market awareness.

In 1990, the company introduced a system of marking the bases of retiring figures 'last year of issue' but this practice ceased in 1993.

YEAR CYPHERS

Beginning in 1998, a cypher was added to the base of each figurine to denote the year of production. For information on historical backstamps please see the introduction of previous editions.

| 1998 Umbrella | 1999 Top Hat | 2000 Fob Watch | 2001 Waistcoat | 2002 Boot | 2003 Gloves | 2004 Bottle Oven | 2005 Henry Doulton |

INTERNATIONAL COLLECTORS CLUB

Founded in 1980 The Royal Doulton International Collectors Club provides an information service on all aspects of the company's products, past and present. A Club magazine, "Gallery," is published four times per year with information on new products and current events that will keep the collector up-to-date on the happenings in the world of Royal Doulton. Upon joining the club, each new member will receive a free gift and invitations to special events and exclusive offers throughout the year. To join the Royal Doulton Collectrors Club, please contact the club directly by writing to the address opposite or calling the appropriate number.

International Collectors Club
Sir Henry Doulton House
Forge Lane, Etruria
Stoke-on-Trent
Staffordshire, ST1 5NN, England
Telephone:
U.K.: 8702 412696
Overseas: +44 (0) 1782 404045
On-line at www.doulton-direct.co.uk
E-mail: icc@royal-doulton.com

WEBSITE AND E-MAIL ADDRESS

Websites:
www.royal-doulton.com
www.doulton-direct.com.au
www.royal-doulton-brides.com

E-mail Addresses:
Consumer Enquiries: enquiries@royal-doulton.com
Museum Curator: heritage@royal-doulton.com
Doulton-Direct: direct@royal-doulton.com

DOULTON CHAPTERS

Detroit Chapter
Ronald Griffin, President
629 Lynne Avenue
Ypsilanti, MI., 48198-3829

Edmonton Chapter
Mildred's Collectibles
6813 104 Street
Edmonton, AB

New England Chapter
Lee Piper, President
Meridith Nelson, Vice President
Michael Lynch, Secretary
Scott Reichenberg, Treasurer
E-mail: doingantiq@aol.com

Northern California Chapter
Edward L. Khachadourian, President
P.O. Box 214, Moraga, CA 94556-0214
Tel.: (925) 376-2221
Fax (925) 376-3581
Email: khach@pacbell.net

Northwest, Bob Haynes Chapter
Alan Matthew, President
15202 93rd Place NE,
Bothell, WA 98011
Tel.: (425) 488-9604

Rochester Chapter
Judith L. Trost, President
103 Garfield Street, Rochester
NY 14611 Tel.: (716) 436-3321

Ohio Chapter
David Harris
15 Lucy Lane
Northfield, Ohio 44067-1821
Tel.: (330) 467-4532

Western Pennyslvania Chapter
John Re, President
9589 Parkedge Drive
Allison Park, PA 15101
Tel.: (412) 366-0201
Fax: (412) 366-2558

THE DOULTON MARKETS
Land Auctions

AUSTRALIA

Goodman's
7 Anderson Street
Double Bay, Sydney, 2028, N.S.W., Australia
Tel.: +61 (0) 2 9327 7311; Fax: +61 (0) 2 9327 2917
Enquiries: Suzanne Brett
www.goodmans.com.au
E-mail: info@goodmans.com.au

Sotheby's
118-122 Queen Street, Woollahra
Sydney, 2025, N.S.W., Australia
Tel.: +61 (0) 2 9362 1000; Fax: +61 (0) 2 9362 1100

CANADA

Empire Auctions
Montreal
5500 Paré Street, Montreal, Quebec H4P 2M1
Tel.: (514) 737-6586; Fax: (514) 342-1352
Enquiries: Isadore Rubinfeld
E-mail: montreal@empireauctions.com
Ottawa
1380 Cyrville Road, Gloucester, Ontario
Tel.: (613) 748-5343; Fax: (613) 748-0354
Enquiries: Elliot Melamed
E-mail: ottawa@empireauctions.com
Toronto
165 Tycos Drive
Toronto, Ontario, M6B 1W6
Tel.: (416) 784-4261; Fax: (416) 784-4262
Enquiries: Michael Rogozinsky
www.empireauctions.com
E-mail: toronto@empireauctions.com

Maynard's Industries Ltd.
Arts / Antiques
415 West 2nd Avenue, Vancouver, BC, V5Y 1E3
Tel.: (604) 876-1311; Fax: (604) 876-1323
www.maynards.com
E-mail: antiques@maynards.com

Ritchie's
Montreal
1980 Rue Sherbrooke
Suite 100, Montreal
Tel.: (514) 934-1864; Fax: (514) 934-1860

Toronto
288 King Street East, Toronto, Ontario M5A 1K4
Tel.: (416) 364-1864; Fax: (416) 364-0704
Enquiries: Caroline Kaiser
www.ritchies.com
E-mail: auction@ritchies.com

Waddington's
Brighton
101 Applewood Dr.,
Brighton, Ontario, K0K 1H0
Tel.: (613) 475-6223; Fax: (613) 475-6224
Enquiries: David Simmons
www.waddingtonsauctions.ca/brighton

Toronto
111 Bathurst Street, Toronto, Ontario M5V 2R1
Tel.: (416) 504-9100; Fax: (416) 504-0033
Enquiries: Bill Kime
www.waddingtonsauctions.com
E-mail: info@waddingtonsauctions.com

UNITED KINGDOM

Bonhams
Bond Street:
101 New Bond Street, London. W15 1SR, England

Chelsea:
65-69 Lots Road, Chelslea, London, SW10 0RN, England

Knightsbridge:
Montpelier Street, Knightsbridge, London, SW7 1HH
Enquiries: Tel.: +44 (0) 20 7393 3900
www.bonhams.com
E-mail: info@bonhams.com

Christie's
London
8 King Street, London, SW1 England
Tel.: +44 (0) 20 7839 9060; Fax: +44 (0) 20 7839 1611

South Kensington
85 Old Brompton Road, London SW7 3LD, England
Tel.: +44 (0) 20 7581 7611; Fax: +44 (0) 20 7321 3321
Enquiries: Tel.: +44 (0) 20 7321 3237
www.christies.com
E-mail: info@christies.com

Potteries Specialist Auctions
271 Waterloo Road, Cobridge, Stoke-on-Trent
Staffordshire, ST6 3HR, England
Tel.: +44 (0) 1782 286622; Fax: +44 (0) 1782 201518
Enquiries: Martyn Bullock
www.potteriesauctions.com
E-mail: enquiries@potteriesauctions.com

Sotheby's
London
34-35 New Bond Street, London, W1A 2AA, England
Tel.: +44 (0) 20 7293 5000; Fax: +44 (0) 20 7293 5989

Olympia
Hammersmith Road, London, W14 8UX, England
Tel.: +44 (0) 20 7293 5555; Fax: +44 (0) 20 7293 6939

Sussex
Summers Place, Billingshurst
Sussex, RH14 9AF, England
Tel.: +44 (0) 1403 833500; Fax: +44 (0) 1403 833699
www.sothebys.com
E-mail: info@sothebys.com

Louis Taylor
Britannia House
10 Town Road, Hanley
Stoke-on-Trent, Staffordshire, England
Tel.: +44 (0) 1782 214111; Fax: +44 (0) 1782 215283
Enquiries: Clive Hillier

Thomson Roddick & Medcalf
60 Whitesands
Dumfries DG1 2RS
Scotland
Tel.: +44 (0) 1387 279879; Fax: +44 (0) 1387 266236
Enquiries: C. R. Graham-Campbell

Peter Wilson Auctioneers
Victoria Gallery
Market Street
Nantwich, Cheshire, CW5 5DG, England
Tel.: +44 (0) 1270 610508; Fax: +44 (0) 1270 610508
Enquiries: Peter Wilson

UNITED STATES

Christie's East
219 East 67th Street, New York, NY 10012
Tel.: +1 212 606 0400
Enquiries: Timothy Luke
www.christies.com

William Doyle Galleries
175 East 87th Street, New York, NY 10128
Tel.: +1 212 427 2730; Fax: +1 212 369 0892

Sotheby's Arcade Auctions
1334 York Avenue, New York, NY 10021
Tel.: +1 212 606 7000
Enquiries: Andrew Cheney
www.sothebys.com

VIRTUAL AUCTIONS

Amazon.com ® Auctions
Main site: www.amazon.com
Plus 4 International sites

AOL.com Auctions ®
Main site: www.aol.com
Links to – E-bay.com
– U-bid.com

E-BAY ® The World's On-Line Market Place ™
Main Site: www.ebay.com
Plus 20 International sites

YAHOO! Auctions ®
Main site: www.yahoo.com
Plus 15 International auction sites

FAIRS, MARKETS AND SHOWS

AUSTRALIA

Royal Doulton and Antique Collectable Fair
Marina Hall, Civic Centre,
Hurstville, Sydney

UNITED KINGDOM

20th Century Fairs
266 Glossop Road, Sheffield S10 2HS, England
Usually in May or June
For information on times and dates:
Tel.: +44 (0) 114 275 0333; Fax: +44 (0) 114 275 4443

DGM Antiques Fairs Ltd.
Newark, the largest in the UK with usually six fairs
annually. For information on times and dates for this
and many other fairs contact:
DMG
Newark, P.O. Box 100, Newark
Nottinghamshire, NG2 1DJ
Tel.: +44 (0) 1636 702326; Fax: +44 (0) 1636 707923
www.antiquesdirectory.co.uk

U.K. Fairs
Doulton and Beswick Fair for Collectors
River Park Leisure Centre, Winchester
Usually held in October. For information on times and
dates contact:
Enquiries U.K. Fairs; Tel.: 44 (0) 20 8500 3505
www.portia.co.uk
E-mail: ukfairs@portia.co.uk

LONDON MARKETS

Alfie's Antique Market
13-25 Church Street, London; Tuesday to Saturday
Camden Passage Market
London; Wednesday and Saturday
New Caledonia Market
Bermondsey Square, London; Friday morning
Portobello Road Market
Portobello Road, London; Saturday

UNITED STATES

Atlantique City
Atlantic City Convention Centre
One Miss America Way
Atlantic City, NJ 08401
Tel.: (609) 449-2000; Fax: (609) 449-2090
info@accenter.com

International Gift and Collectible Expo
Donald E. Stephens Convention Centre
Rosemont, Illinois

For information on the above two shows contact:
Krause Publications
700 East State Street, Iola, WI 54990-9990
Tel.: (877) 746-9757; Fax: (715) 445-4389
www.collectibleshow.com
E-mail: iceshow@krause.com

Doulton Convention and Sale International
Fort Lauderdale, Florida, U.S.A.
Usually February. For information on times and dates:
Pascoe & Company
575 S.W. 22nd Ave., Miami, Florida 33135
Tel.: (305) 643-2550; Fax: (305) 643-2123
www.pascoeandcompany.com
E-mail: sales@pascoeandcompany.com

Royal Doulton Convention & Sale
Cleveland, Ohio
Usually August. For information on times and dates:
Colonial House Productions
182 Front Street, Berea, Ohio 44308
Tel.: (440) 826-4169; Fax: (440) 826-0839
www.Colonial-House-Collectibles.com
E-mail: yworry@aol.com

DOULTON LAMBETH FIGURINES

JOHN BROAD

Atalanta (Headband)
Designer: John Broad
Height: 9", 23.0 cm
Colour: 1. X7910, Brown stoneware
2. X8707, Coloured Doultonware
Issued: 1. 1912
2. 1928

Description	U.S.$	Can. $	U.K. £
1. Brown	4,000.	4,750.	2,250.
2. Coloured	4,000.	4,750.	2,250.

Photograph not
available
at press time

Atalanta (Flowers)
Designer: John Broad
Height: 9", 23.0 cm
Colour: 1. X7910, Brown stoneware
2. X8707, Coloured Doultonware
Issued: 1. 1912
2. 1928

Description	U.S. $	Can. $	U.K. £
1. Brown		Extremely Rare	
2. Coloured		Extremely Rare	

Bather
Designer: John Broad
Height: 13 ½", 34.0 cm
Colour: 1. X7912, Brown stoneware
2. X8706, Coloured Doultonware
Issued: 1. 1912
2. 1928

Description	U.S. $	Can. $	U.K. £
1. Brown	6,000.	7,250.	3,250.
2. Coloured	6,000.	7,250.	3,250.

Boer War Soldier
Designer: John Broad
Height: 12 ½", 32.0 cm
Colour: Brown stoneware
Issued: 1901
Series: Soldiers

Description	U.S. $	Can. $	U.K. £
Brown	4,000.	4,750.	2,250.

Diana
Designer: John Broad
Height: 11 ½", 29.7 cm
Colour: Terracotta
Issued: c. 1880

Description	U.S. $	Can. $	U.K. £
Terracotta		Rare	

Doris Keane
(also called The Minuet)
Designer: John Broad
Height: 9", 23.0 cm
Colour: White glost porcelain
Issued: c.1918

Description	U.S. $	Can. $	U.K. £
White glost	2,000.	2,400.	1,100.

**Doris Keane
(also called Romance)**
Designer: John Broad
Height: 8 ¾", 22.5 cm
Colour: White biscuit porcelain
Issued: c.1918

Description	U.S. $	Can. $	U.K. £
White biscuit	2,000.	2,400.	1,100.

Girl Holding Vase
Designer: John Broad
Height: 13 ¼", 33 cm
Colour: X8708, Coloured Doultonware
Issued: 1928

Description	U.S. $	Can. $	U.K. £
Coloured	5,000.	6,000.	2,750.

Photograph not
available
at press time

King Edward VII
Designer: John Broad
Height: 16 ¾", 42.0 cm
Colour: Terracotta
Issued: 1901

Description	U.S. $	Can. $	U.K. £
Terracotta		Extremely Rare	

Lady in Elizabethan Dress
Designer: John Broad
Height: 8", 20.5 cm
Colour: White biscuit porcelain
Issued: c.1918

Description	U.S. $	Can. $	U.K. £
White biscuit		Extremely Rare	

Lady with Dog
Designer: John Broad
Height: 7 ½", 19.0 cm
Colour: White biscuit porcelain
Issued: c.1918

Description	U.S. $	Can. $	U.K. £
White biscuit	2,500.	3,000.	1,350.

Lady with Muff
Designer: John Broad
Height: 7 ¼", 18.5 cm
Colour: White biscuit porcelain
Issued: c.1918

Description	U.S. $	Can. $	U.K. £
White biscuit	1,500.	1,800.	800.

Lady with Rose

Designer: John Broad
Height: 8", 20.5 cm
Colour: White biscuit porcelain
Issued: c.1918

Description	U.S. $	Can. $	U.K. £
White biscuit	2,000.	2,400.	1,100.

Lady with Tall Hat

Designer: John Broad
Height: 8", 20.5 cm
Colour: White biscuit porcelain
Issued: c.1918

Description	U.S. $	Can. $	U.K. £
White biscuit	2,000.	2,400.	1,100.

Madame Pompadour

Designer: John Broad
Height: 8 ½", 21.5 cm
Colour: 1. X8754, Coloured Doultonware
       2. White biscuit porcelain
Issued: c.1918

Description	U.S. $	Can. $	U.K. £
1. Coloured	2,000.	2,400.	1,100.
2. White	2,000.	2,400.	1,100.

Nelson

Designer: John Broad
Height: 8", 20.5 cm
Colour: 1. X6426, Brown stoneware
       2. Green faience
Issued: 1905

Description	U.S. $	Can. $	U.K. £
1. Brown	1,800.	2,150.	975.
2. Green	1,800.	2,150.	975.

Our Lady

Designer: John Broad
Height: Unknown
Colour: Terracotta
Issued: c.1910

Description	U.S. $	Can. $	U.K. £
Terracitta		Extremely Rare	

Pomona

Designer: John Broad
Height: 14", 35.0 cm
Colour: X7911, Terracotta
Issued: 1912

Description	U.S. $	Can. $	U.K. £
Terracotta		Extremely Rare	

Photograph not
available
at press time

Queen Alexndra

Designer: John Broad
Height: 16 ½", 42.0 cm
Colour: Terracotta
Issued: 1901

Description	U.S. $	Can. $	U.K. £
Terracotta		Extremely Rare	

Queen Victoria

Designer: John Broad
Height: 11 ¾, 29.75 cm
Colour: Brown salt glaze stoneware
Issued: 1901

Description	U.S.$	Can. $	U.K. £
Brown	6,000.	7,250.	3,250.

Thrower

Designer: John Broad
Height: 7", 18.0 cm
Colour: 1. Brown stoneware
2. Terracotta
Issued: 1883

Description	U.S. $	Can. $	U.K. £
1. Brown Stone		Extremely Rare	
2. Terracotta		Extremely Rare	

LESLIE HARRADINE

Amused Child Study
Model No.: H48
Designer: Leslie Harradine
Height: 6", 15.5 cm
Colour: Slip cast buff stoneware on either a green base or a blue base
Issued: c.1912

Description	U.S. $	Can. $	U.K. £
Slip cast		Extremely Rare	

Breton Women Gossiping
Model No.: H64
Designer: Leslie Harradine
Height: 10", 25.5 cm
Colour: Black and white stoneware
Issued: c.1912

Description	U.S. $	Can. $	U.K. £
Black and white		Extremely Rare	

British Soldier
Model No.: Unknown
Designer: Leslie Harradine
Height: 9 ½", 24.0 cm
Colour: Brown stoneware
Issued: 1910
Series: Soldiers

Description	U.S. $	Can. $	U.K. £
Brown	3,500.	4,250.	1,900.

Cossack
Model No.: H78
Designer: Leslie Harradine
Height: 9 ½", 24.0 cm
Colour: Brown stoneware
Issued: c.1910
Series: Soldiers

Description	U.S. $	Can. $	U.K. £
Brown	2,500.	3,000.	1,350.

Dutch Man
Model No.: H10
Designer: Leslie Harradine
Height: 8 ½", 21.5 cm
Colour: White slip cast stoneware with blue detailing
Issued: 1912
Varieties: Also called 'The Toiler'

Description	U.S. $	Can. $	U.K. £
White slip cast	1,000.	1,300.	500.

Dutch Woman
Model No.: H3 (X7728)
Designer: Leslie Harradine
Height: 7 ¾", 19.5 cm
Colour: White slip cast stoneware with blue detailing
Issued: 1912

Description	U.S. $	Can. $	U.K. £
White slip cast	1,000.	1,300.	500.

Dutch Woman
Model No.: H9
Designer: Leslie Harradine
Height: 4 ½", 11.5 cm
Colour: White slip cast stoneware with blue or green detailing
Issued: 1912

Description	U.S. $	Can. $	U.K. £
White slip cast	700.	950.	400.

French Legionnaire
Model No.: H72
Designer: Leslie Harradine
Height: 9 ½", 24.0 cm
Colour: Brown stoneware
Issued: c.1910
Series: Soldiers

Description	U.S. $	Can. $	U.K. £
Brown	2,500.	3,000.	1,350.

Harvester (with Scythe)
Model No.: H66
Designer: Leslie Harradine
Height: 7", 18.0 cm
Colour: Brown stoneware
Issued: c.1910

Description	U.S. $	Can. $	U.K. £
Brown	1,200.	1,500.	700.

Hunched Figure on Pedestal
Model No.: H45
Designer: Leslie Harradine
Height: Unknown
Colour: White slip cast stoneware on brown base
Issued: c.1910

Description	U.S. $	Can. $	U.K. £
White slip cast	850.	1,000.	450.

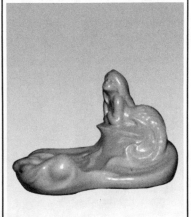

Mermaids
Model No.: H29
Designer: Leslie Harradine
Height: 7", 18.0 cm
Colour: White slip cast stoneware
Issued: 1912

Description	U.S. $	Can. $	U.K. £
White slip cast	1,000.	1,300.	550.

Mother and Child Standing
Model No.: H24
Designer: Leslie Harradine
Height: 8 ¾", 23.0 cm
Colour: 1. Brown stoneware
2. White slip cast stoneware
Issued: 1912

Description	U.S. $	Can. $	U.K. £
1. Brown		Extremely Rare	
2. White slip cast		Extremely Rare	

Motherhood

Model No.: H4 (X7729)
Designer: Leslie Harradine
Height: 5", 12.5 cm
Colour: White slip cast stoneware
Issued: 1912

Description	U.S. $	Can. $	U.K. £
White slip cast		Extremely Rare	

North African Spahi

Model No.: Unknown
Designer: Leslie Harradine
Height: 9 ½", 24.0 cm
Colour: Brown stoneware
Issued: c.1910
Series: Soldiers

Description	U.S. $	Can. $	U.K. £
Brown	2,500.	3,000.	1,350.

Peasant Girl

Model No.: H8
Designer: Leslie Harradine
Height: 8", 21.0 cm
Colour: White slip cast stoneware
Issued: 1912

Description	U.S. $	Can. $	U.K. £
White slip cast	1,000.	1,300.	500.

Peat Cutter

Model No.: Unknown
Designer: Leslie Harradine
Height: 7", 18.0 cm
Colour: Brown stoneware
Issued: c.1912

Description	U.S. $	Can. $	U.K. £
Brown	1,350.	1,625.	725.

Reaper

Model No.: H68
Designer: Leslie Harradine
Height: 7 ½", 19.0 cm
Colour: 1. X8666, Brown stoneware
           2. Coloured Doultonware and toby
              colours
Issued: 1. c.1912; 2. 1927

Description	U.S. $	Can. $	U.K. £
1. Brown	1,500.	1,800.	800.
2. Coloured	1,500.	1,800.	800.

Soldier

Model No.: H78
Designer: Leslie Harradine
Height: 9 ½", 24.0 cm
Colour: Brown stoneware
Issued: 1910
Series: Soldiers

Description	U.S. $	Can. $	U.K. £
Brown	2,500.	3,000.	1,350.

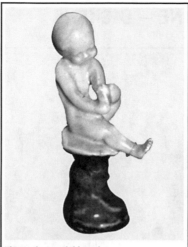

This Little Pig Child Study
Model No.: H49
Designer: Leslie Harradine
Height: 5", 13.0 cm
Colour: Slip cast buff and brown stoneware
Issued: c.1912

Description	U.S. $	Can. $	U.K. £
Slip cast buff stoneware		Extremely Rare	

Worker (with Bucket)
Model No.: Unknown
Designer: Leslie Harradine
Height: 7", 18.0 cm
Colour: Brown stoneware
Issued: c.1912

Description	U.S. $	Can. $	U.K. £
Brown stoneware		Extremely Rare	

LESLIE HARRADINE – DICKENS

Mr. Micawber
Model No.: H20
Designer: Leslie Harradine
Height: 9 ¼", 24.0 cm
Colour: 1. Brown
            2. Buff slip cast stoneware
            3. Coloured Doultonware
Issued: 1912

Description	U.S. $	Can. $	U.K. £
Brown	1,750.	2,100.	950.
Buff slipcast	1,750.	2,100.	950.
Coloured	1,750.	2,100.	950.

Mr. Pickwick
Model No.: H19
Designer: Leslie Harradine
Height: 8 ¾", 22.0 cm
Colour: 1. Brown
            2. Buff slip cast stoneware
Issued: 1912

Description	U.S. $	Can. $	U.K. £
Brown	2,000.	2,400.	1,100.
Buff slipcast	2,000.	2,400.	1,100.

Mr. Squeers
Model No.: Unknown
Designer: Leslie Harradine
Height: 9 ¼", 23.5 cm
Colour: 1. Brown
            2. Buff slip cast stoneware
Issued: 1912

Description	U.S. $	Can. $	U.K. £
Brown	1,750.	2,100.	950.
Buff slipcast	1,750.	2,100.	950.

Pecksniff
Model No.: H21
Designer: Leslie Harradine
Height: 9", 23.0 cm
Colour: 1. Brown
            2. Buff slip cast stoneware
Issued: 1912

Description	U.S. $	Can. $	U.K. £
Brown	1,750.	2,100.	950.
Buff slip cast	1,750.	2,100.	950.

Sairey Gamp
Model No.: Unknown
Designer: Leslie Harradine
Height: 7 ½", 20.0 cm
Colour: 1. Brown
            2. Buff slip cast stoneware
Issued: 1912

Description	U.S. $	Can. $	U.K. £
Brown	2,000.	2,400.	1,100.
Buff slip cast	2,000.	2,400.	1,100.

Sam Weller
Model No.: H23
Designer: Leslie Harradine
Height: 9 ½", 24.5 cm
Colour: 1. Brown
            2. Buff slip cast stoneware
Issued: 1912

Description	U.S. $	Can. $	U.K. £
Brown	1,750.	2,100.	950.
Buff slip cast	1,750.	2,100.	950.

MARK MARSHALL

Bear Stripper

Designer:	Mark Marshall
Height:	5 ½", 14.0 cm
Colour:	White stoneware
Issued:	c.1910

Description	U.S. $	Can. $	U.K. £
White stoneware		Extremely Rare	

Crinoline (as HN 13)

Designer:	Mark Marshall
Height:	7", 18.0 cm
Colour:	Matt white stoneware with blue details
Issued:	1910

Description	U.S. $	Can. $	U.K. £
Matt white stoneware	1,500.00	1,800.00	800.00

18th Century Figure with Fan

Designer:	Mark Marshall
Height:	8", 20.5 cm
Colour:	Matt white stoneware with blue details
Issued:	c.1890

Description	U.S. $	Can. $	U.K. £
Matt white stoneware	1,200.00	1,450.00	650.00

Old Woman Figure

Designer:	Mark Marshall
Height:	9 ½", 24.3 cm
Colour:	Unknown
Issued:	c.1900

Description	U.S. $	Can. $	U.K. £
Old Woman Figure		Extremely Rare	

CHARLES NOKE — VELLUM

Beefeater Toasting the Queen
Designer: Charles Noke
Height: 12 ¾", 32.5 cm
Colour: 1. Ivory with pink and blue tints
               2. Scarlet
Issued: 1899

Description	U.S. $	Can. $	U.K. £
1. Ivory	8,000.	9,000.	4,500.
2. Scarlet	8,000.	9,000.	4,500.

Cleopatra
Designer: Charles Noke
Height: 12", 30.5 cm
Colour: Ivory with pink and green tints
Issued: c.1892

Description	U.S. $	Can. $	U.K. £
Ivory	8,000.	9,000.	4,500.

Note: Only three pieces known.

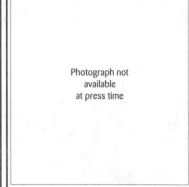

Photograph not
available
at press time

Columbus
Designer: Charles Noke
Height: 20", 51.0 cm
Colour: 1. Gold printed pattern
               2. Ivory
               3. Parian
Issued: 1893

Description	U.S. $	Can. $	U.K. £
1. Gold		Extremely Rare	
2. Ivory		Extremely Rare	
3. Parian		Extremely Rare	

Devil
Designer: Charles Noke
Height: 20", 51.0 cm
Colour: 1. Ivory with pink and green tints
               2. Scarlet and gold
Issued: 1893

Description	U.S. $	Can. $	U.K. £
1. Ivory		Extremely Rare	
2. Scarlet		Extremely Rare	

Diana
Designer: Charles Noke
Height: 11 ½", 29.5 cm
Colour: 1. Ivory with pink and green tints
               2. Printed flowers
               3. Printed scroll pattern
Issued: 1893

Description	U.S. $	Can. $	U.K. £
1. Coloured	6,500.	7,750.	3,500.
2. Flowers	6,500.	7,750.	3,500.
3. Scroll	6,500.	7,750.	3,500.

Ellen Terry as Queen Catharine
Designer: Charles Noke
Height: 1. 12 ½", 31.0 cm
               2. 9", 23.0 cm
Colour: 1. Ivory
               2. Ivory with green and gold tints
Issued: 1893

Height	U.S. $	Can. $	U.K. £
1. 12 ½"	2,750.	3,250.	1,400.
2. 9"	1,800.	2,150.	1,000.

Henry Irving as Cardinal Wolsey
Designer: Charles Noke
Height: 1. 13", 33.0 cm
2. 9 ¼", 23.5 cm
Colour: 1. Ivory
2. Ivory with green and pink sheen
Issued: 1899

Height	U.S. $	Can. $	U.K. £
1. 13"	2,750.	3,250.	1,400.
2. 9 ¼"	1,800.	2,150.	1,000.

Photograph not
available
at press time

Jack Point
Designer: Charles Noke
Height: 16", 40.5 cm
Colour: Ivory
Issued: 1893

Description	U.S. $	Can. $	U.K. £
Ivory		Extremely Rare	

Jester
Designer: Charles Noke
Height: 9 ½", 23.5 cm
Colour: 1. Ivory
2. Ivory with pink and green tints
3. Parian
Issued: 1892
Varieties: Also found on lamp base

Description	U.S. $	Can. $	U.K. £
1. Ivory	5,500.	6,750.	3,000.
2. Ivory/tints	5,500.	6,750.	3,000.
3. Parian	5,500.	6,750.	3,000.

Jester (Kneeling)
Designer: Charles Noke
Height: 4 ½", 14.0 cm
Colour: Scarlet with gold, flambé
Issued: Vellum c.1900, Flambé c.1938

Description	U.S. $	Can. $	U.K. £
1. Scarlet	9,500.	11,500.	5,250.
2. Flambé	9,500.	11,500.	5,250.

Mephistopheles and Marguerite
This is a double-sided figure

Designer: Charles Noke
Height: 12 ½", 32.0 cm
Colour: 1. Deep blue with printed dragon
design
2. Ivory
3. Ivory with pink and green tints
4. Purple and gold
5. Scarlet
6. Scarlet and gold
Issued: 1891

Description	U.S. $	Can. $	U.K. £
1. Blue / dragon design	5,500.	6,750.	3,000.
2. Ivory	5.500.	6,750.	3,000.
3. Ivory/ pink / green	5,500.	6,750.	3,000.
4. Purple/ gold	5,500.	6,750.	3,000.
5. Scarlet	5,500.	6,750.	3,000.
6. Scarlet / gold	5,500.	6,750.	3,000.

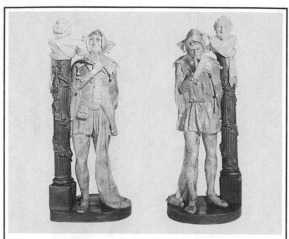

Mirth and Melancholy
This is a double-sided figure.
Designer: Charles Noke
Height: 16", 40.5 cm
Colour: 1. Gold printed pattern
  2. Ivory
  3. Ivory with pink and green tint
Issued: 1892

Description	U.S. $	Can. $	U.K. £
1. Gold printed pattern	9,500.	11,500.	5,250.
2. Ivory	9,500.	11,500.	5,250.
3. Ivory/pink/green	9,500.	11,500.	5,250.

Moorish Minstrel
Designer: Charles Noke
Height: Unknown
Colour: 1. Blue and grey; scarlet and blue
  2. Ivory with green and pink tints
  3. Ivory with green and pink tints, white and gold flowers
Issued: 1892
Varieties: Also found on lamp base

Description	U.S. $	Can. $	U.K. £
1. Ivory/green/pink	5,500.	6,750.	3,000.
2. Ivory/green/pink/white/gold	5,500.	6,750.	3,000.
3. Blue/grey/scarlet/blue	5,500.	6,750.	3,000.

Oh! Law
This is a double-sided figure
Designer: Charles Noke
Height: 8 ½ ", 21.5 cm
Colour: 1. Gold printed pattern
  2. Ivory
  3. Ivory with green and pink tints
Issued: 1893

Description	U.S. $	Can. $	U.K. £
1. Gold printed pattern	6,000.	7,500.	3,250.
2. Ivory	6,000.	7,500.	3,250.
3. Ivory / green / pink	6,000.	7,500.	3,250.

Pierrot
Designer: Charles Noke
Height: 6 ½", 16.5 cm
Colour: 1. Ivory with black details
  2. Ivory with green and gold details
Issued: 1899

Description	U.S. $	Can. $	U.K. £
1. Ivory / black	6,000.	7,500.	3,250.
2. Ivory / green / gold	6,000.	7,500.	3,250.

Portia

Designer: Charles Noke
Height: 16 ¾", 42.5 cm
Colour: 1. Green and pink with flowers
2. Green and pink with scrolls and flowers
3. Ivory
Issued: 1893

Description	U.S.$	Can.$	U.K. £
Green/flowers	8,500.	10,000.	4,500.
Green/scrolls	8,500.	10,000.	4,500.
Ivory	8,500.	10,000.	4,500.

St. Mark's Birds

Designer: Charles Noke
Height: 17 ½", 44.0 cm
Colour: 1. Ivory and gold
2. Ivory with pink tints
3. Printed flowers
Issued: 1892

Description	U.S.$	Can.$	U.K.£
Ivory/gold	8,500.	10,000.	4,500.
Ivory/pink tints	8,500.	10,000.	4,500.
Printed flowers	8,500.	10,000.	4,500.

Photograph not
available
at press time

Sentimental Pierrot

Designer: Charles Noke
Height: 6", 15.0 cm
Colour: 1. Ivory
2. Ivory with pink and green tints
Issued: 1899

Description	U.S.$	Can.$	U.K.£
Ivory	8,000.	9,500.	4,500.
Ivory/tints	8,000.	9,500.	4,500.

Shakespeare

Designer: Charles Noke
Height: 12 ½", 31.0 cm
Colour: 1. Ivory
2. Ivory/pink/green
Issued: c.1899

Description	U.S.$	Can.$	U.K.£
Ivory	7,000.	8,500.	3,750.
Ivory/tints	7,000.	8,500.	3,750.

Shylock

Designer: Charles Noke
Height: 16", 40.5 cm
Colour: 1. Brown, gold printed pattern
2. Ivory
Issued: 1893

Description	U.S.$	Can.$	U.K.£
Brown/gold	16,500.	20,000.	10,000.
Ivory	7,500.	9,000.	4,000.

Water Carrier

Designer: Charles Noke
Height: 20 ¾", 52.0 cm
Colour: Ivory with pink and green tints
Issued: 1893

Description	U.S.$	Can.$	U.K.£
	Extremely Rare		

CHARLES NOKE — WALL POCKETS AND LIGHTS

Geisha Wall Pocket

Designer: Charles Noke
Height: 9 ¼", 23.5 cm
Colour: 1. Gold printed pattern
2. Ivory
3. Ivory with pink tints
Issued: 1893

Description	U.S. $	Can. $	U.K. £
1. Gold printed pattern	5,000.	6,000.	2,700.
2. Ivory	5,000.	6,000.	2,700.
3. Ivory / pink	5,000.	6,000.	2,700.

Lady Jester Wall Pocket

Designer: Charles Noke
Height: 9 ¾", 24.5 cm
Colour: 1. Ivory with green and pink tints
2. Printed floral pattern
Issued: 1892

Description	U.S. $	Can. $	U.K. £
1. Ivory / green / pink	5,500.	6,750.	3,000.
2. Printed floral pattern	5,500.	6,750.	3,000.

Sorceress Wall Pocket

Designer: Charles Noke
Height: 10 ¾, 27.5 cm
Colour: 1. Green tint with white floral pattern
2. Ivory
Issued: 1892

Description	U.S. $	Can. $	U.K. £
1. Green / white floral	5,500.	6,750.	3,000.
2. Ivory	5,500.	6,750.	3,000.

The Witch Wall Light

Designer: Charles Noke
Height: Unknown
Colour: Green and scarlet with gold floral pattern
Issued: 1897

Description	U.S. $	Can. $	U.K. £
Green / scarlet / gold		Extremely Rare	

GEORGE TINWORTH

Designer: George Tinworth
Height: 5", 13.0 cm
Colour: 1. Brown Siliconware
2. Coloured Doultonware
Issued: c.1890

Description	U.S. $	Can. $	U.K. £
1. Brown	6,000.	7,500.	3,250.
2. Coloured	6,000.	7,500.	3,250.

Boy Jester
Designer: George Tinworth
Height: 5", 13.0 cm
Colour: Brown stoneware
Issued: c.1890

Description	U.S. $	Can. $	U.K. £
Brown	2,500.	3,000.	1,350.

Boy with Melon
Designer: George Tinworth
Height: 3 ½", 9.0 cm
Colour: Brown stoneware
Issued: c.1890

Description	U.S. $	Can. $	U.K. £
Brown	2,500.	3,000.	1,350.

Boy with Vase
Designer: George Tinworth
Height: Unknown
Colour: Coloured Doultonware
Issued: c.1890

Description	U.S. $	Can. $	U.K. £
Coloured	6,000.	7,500.	3,250.

Drunken Husband
Designer: George Tinworth
Height: 5 ¼", 12.0 cm
Colour: Coloured Doultonware
Issued: 1881

Description	U.S. $	Can. $	U.K. £
Coloured	17,500.	20,000.	9,500.

Note: A number of variations of this figurine exist.
Mainly in the placement of the small figures.

Five Miles to London
Designer: George Tinworth
Height: 9", 23.0 cm
Colour: Coloured Doultonware
Issued: c.1885

Description	U.S. $	Can. $	U.K. £
Coloured	12,500.	15,000.	6,750.

Photograph not
available
at press time

Girl with Tambourine

Designer:	George Tinworth
Height:	9", 23.0 cm
Colour:	Coloured Doultonware
Issued:	c.1885

Description	U.S. $	Can. $	U.K. £
Coloured	9,000.	11,000.	4,750.

Jester

Designer:	George Tinworth
Height:	12 ½", 31.5 cm
Colour:	Terracotta
Issued:	1900
	Produced for the Art Union in an edition of 12

Description	U.S. $	Can. $	U.K. £
Terracotta	12,500.	15,000.	6,750.

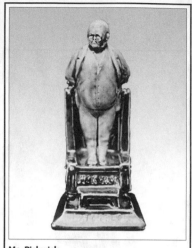

Mr. Pickwick

Designer:	George Tinworth
Height:	5", 12.5 cm
Colour:	Coloured Doultonware
Issued:	c.1895

Description	U.S. $	Can. $	U.K. £
Coloured		Extremely Rare	

Scandal

Designer:	George Tinworth
Height:	6 ¼", 16.0 cm
Colour:	Coloured Doultonware
Issued:	1891

Description	U.S. $	Can. $	U.K. £
Coloured	15,000.	18,000.	8,000.

Young Carpenter

Designer:	George Tinworth
Height:	5 ¼", 13.0 cm
Colour:	Brown stoneware
Issued:	c.1892

Description	U.S. $	Can. $	U.S.£
Coloured	5,000.	6,000.	2,700.

Note: These early Doulton Lambeth figures are all rare with limited examples known. Prices will vary widely depending on supply and demand at the time of sale. Prices listed are indications only.

The Merry Musicians

The exact number of Merry Musicians is not recorded but there are probably around a hundred different figures, playing at least forty different instruments, some of which are listed on page 20. The figures can be found with endless variations of poses, expressions, hats and instruments, many of which are very obscure. The Musicians were produced from the 1890s until the early 1900s in small numbers. Around 1910 a set was produced with white faces for the Australian agent, John Shorter. Many of the Musicians have Tinworth's monogram although some were produced entirely by assistants.

A List of Recorded Merry Musicians to Date

Bagpipes	Cymbals	Military Bass Type	Sousaphone
Banjo	Flageolet	Drum	Scottish Bagpipes
Barrel drum	Flute	Military Side	Spiral Horn
Bass Clarinet	French Horn	One Man Band	Tambourine
Bells	Harp	Organ	Trombone
Botuto	Horn	Organistrum	Trumpet
Carillon	Hurdy Gurdy	Piano	Tuba
Cello	Kettle Drum	Piccolo	Tympanum
Cittern	Lute	Positive Organ	Ukulele
Concertina	Lyre	Rebec	Viola
Conductor	Mandolin	Barrel Drum	Violin
Cornet	Marimba	Saxophone	Whistle

Pricing: The Merry Musicians can only be priced with indicating ranges. Within the series there will be rare figures, so that any demand for a scarce ro rare musician could easily double or triple the price. We also find that the more complicated the musician the higher the price. An example of this is the organ which sold at the Harriman Judd Part Two Sotheby's auction for $2,700.00 US including premium.

U.S.: $2,000.00 - $2,700.00   Can.: $2,400.00 - $3,250.00   U.K.: £1,100.00 - $1,500.00

Note: We would appreciate any new information, and/or photographs, of the Merry Musicians. Please refer to our editorial office address in the front of the catalogue as to where to send the information.

BAGPIPES

BOTUTO

CONCERTINA

LUTE

ORGAN

PIANO

PICCOLO

SCOTTISH BAGPIPES

SCOTTISH BAGPIPES

VIOLIN

ROYAL DOULTON
FIGURINES

HN SERIES

Jessica HN 4763 from the 2005 Chic Trends Series

HN 1
Darling
Style One
Designer: C. Vyse
Height: 7 ¾", 19.5 cm
Issued: 1913-1928
Colour: Light grey
Varieties: HN 1319, 1371, 1372, 4140

U.S.:	$3,750.00
Can.:	$4,500.00
U.K.:	£2,000.00

HN 2
Elizabeth Fry
Designer: C. Vyse
Height: 17", 43.2 cm
Issued: 1913-1936
Colour: Light blue, green base
Varieties: HN 2A

U.S.:	$ 8,500.00
Can.:	$11,000.00
U.K.:	£ 4,750.00

HN 2A
Elizabeth Fry
Designer: C. Vyse
Height: 17", 43.2 cm
Issued: 1913-1936
Colour: Light blue, blue base
Varieties: HN 2

U.S.:	$ 8,500.00
Can.:	$11,000.00
U.K.:	£ 4,750.00

HN 3
Milking Time
Designer: P. Stabler
Height: 6 ½", 16.5 cm
Colour: Blue dress, white apron
Issued: 1913-1938
Varieties: HN 306

U.S.:	Only
Can.:	three
U.K.:	known

HN 4
Picardy Peasant (woman)
Designer: P. Stabler
Height: 9 ¼", 23.5 cm
Colour: Blue and white
Issued: 1913-1938
Varieties: HN 5, 17A, 351, 513

U.S.:	$5,500.00
Can.:	$6,500.00
U.K.:	£3,000.00

HN 5
Picardy Peasant (woman)
Designer: P. Stabler
Height: 9 ½", 24.0 cm
Colour: Grey
Issued: 1913-1938
Varieties: HN 4, 17A, 351, 513

U.S.:	
Can.:	Extremely rare
U.K.:	

HN 6
Dunce
Designer: C. J. Noke
Height: 10 ½", 26.7 cm
Colour: Light blue
Issued: 1913-1936
Varieties: HN 310, 357

U.S.:	Only
Can.:	three
U.K.:	known

HN 7
Pedlar Wolf
Designer: C. J. Noke
Height: 5 ½", 14.0 cm
Colour: Blue and black
Issued: 1913-1938
Varieties: Also known in flambé

U.S.:	Only
Can.:	two
U.K.:	known

HN 8
The Crinoline
Designer: G. Lambert
Height: 6 ¼", 15.8 cm
Colour: Lavender
Issued: 1913-1938
Varieties: HN 9, 9A, 21, 21A,
            413, 566, 628

U.S.:	**$4,000.00**
Can.:	**$4,750.00**
U.K.:	**£2,150.00**

HN 9
The Crinoline
Designer: G. Lambert
Height: 6 ¼", 15.8 cm
Colour: Light green, flowers
            on skirt
Issued: 1913-1938
Varieties: HN 8, 9A, 21, 21A,
            413, 566, 628

U.S.:	**$4,000.00**
Can.:	**$4,750.00**
U.K.:	**£2,150.00**

HN 9A
The Crinoline
Designer: G. Lambert
Height: 6 ¼", 15.8 cm
Colour: Light green,
            no flowers
Issued: 1913-1938
Varieties: HN 8, 9, 21, 21A,
            413, 566, 628

U.S.:	
Can.:	**Extremely rare**
U.K.:	

HN 10
Madonna of the Square
Designer: P. Stabler
Height: 7", 17.8 cm
Colour: Lavender
Issued: 1913-1936
Varieties: HN 10A, 11, 14, 27,
            326, 573, 576, 594,
            613, 764, 1968, 1969,
            2034

U.S.:	**$2,750.00**
Can.:	**$3,250.00**
U.K.:	**£1,500.00**

HN 10A
Madonna of the Square
Designer: P. Stabler
Height: 7", 17.8 cm
Colour: Green and blue
Issued: 1913-1936
Varieties: HN 10, 11, 14, 27,
            326, 573, 576, 594,
            613, 764, 1968,
            1969, 2034

U.S.:	
Can.:	**Extremely rare**
U.K.:	

HN 11
Madonna of the Square
Designer: P. Stabler
Height: 7", 17.8 cm
Colour: Grey
Issued: 1913-1936
Varieties: HN 10, 10A, 14, 27,
            326, 573, 576, 594,
            613, 764, 1968,
            1969, 2034

U.S.:	
Can.:	**Extremely rare**
U.K.:	

HN 12
Baby
Designer: C. J. Noke
Height: 4 ¾" 12.0 cm
Colour: Pale pink
Issued: 1913-1938

U.S.:	**Only**
Can.:	**two**
U.K.:	**known**

HN 13
Picardy Peasant (man)
Designer: P. Stabler
Height: 9", 22.9 cm
Colour: Blue costume
            with white cap
Issued: 1913-1938
Varieties: HN 17, 19

U.S.:	
Can.:	**Extremely rare**
U.K.:	

HN 14
Madonna of the Square
Designer: P. Stabler
Height: 7", 17.8 cm
Colour: Blue
Issued: 1913-1936
Varieties: HN 10, 10A, 11, 27,
326, 573, 576, 594,
613, 764, 1968,
1969, 2034

U.S.: $2,750.00
Can.: $3,250.00
U.K.: £1,500.00

HN 15
The Sleepy Scholar
Designer: W. White
Height: 6 ¾", 17.2 cm
Colour: Blue
Issued: 1913-1938
Varieties: HN 16, 29

U.S.: $ 9,000.00
Can.: $11,000.00
U.K.: £ 5,000.00

HN 16
The Sleepy Scholar
Designer: W. White
Height: 6 ¾", 17.2 cm
Colour: Green
Issued: 1913-1938
Varieties: HN 15, 29

U.S.: $ 9,000.00
Can.: $11,000.00
U.K.: £ 5,000.00

HN 17
Picardy Peasant (man)
Designer: P. Stabler
Height: 9 ½", 24.0 cm
Colour: Green
Issued: 1913-1938
Varieties: HN 13, 19,

U.S.:
Can.: **Extremely rare**
U.K.:

HN 17A
Picardy Peasant (woman)
Designer: P. Stabler
Height: 9 ½", 24.0 cm
Colour: Green
Issued: 1913-1938
Varieties: HN 4, 5, 351, 513

U.S.:
Can.: **Extremely rare**
U.K.:

HN 18
Pussy
Designer: F. C. Stone
Height: 7 ¾", 19.7 cm
Colour: Light blue
Issued: 1913-1938
Varieties: HN 325, 507; also
called 'The Black Cat'

U.S.: **Only**
Can.: **six**
U.K.: **known**

Also known with white dress.

HN 19
Picardy Peasant (man)
Designer: P. Stabler
Height: 9 ½", 24.0 cm
Colour: Green
Issued: 1913-1938
Varieties: HN 13, 17

U.S.:
Can.: **Extremely rare**
U.K.:

HN 20
The Coquette
Designer: W. White
Height: 9 ¼", 23.5 cm
Colour: Blue
Issued: 1913-1938
Varieties: HN 20A, 37

U.S.: $ 9,000.00
Can.: $11,000.00
U.K.: £ 5,000.00

HN 20A
The Coquette
Designer: W. White
Height: 9 ¼", 23.5 cm
Colour: Green
Issued: 1913-1938
Varieties: HN 20, 37

U.S.:	**$ 9,000.00**
Can.:	**$11,000.00**
U.K.:	**£ 5,000.00**

HN 21
The Crinoline
Designer: G. Lambert
Height: 6 ¼", 15.8 cm
Colour: Yellow, with rosebuds
Issued: 1913-1938
Varieties: HN 8, 9, 9A, 21A, 413,
566, 628

U.S.:	**$4,000.00**
Can.:	**$4,750.00**
U.K.:	**£2,150.00**

HN 21A
The Crinoline
Designer: G. Lambert
Height: 6 ¼", 15.8 cm
Colour: Yellow, no rosebuds
Issued: 1913-1938
Varieties: HN 8, 9, 9A, 21, 413,
566, 628

U.S.:	
Can.:	**Extremely rare**
U.K.:	

HN 22
The Lavender Woman
Designer: P. Stabler
Height: 8 ¼", 21.0 cm
Colour: Light blue
Issued: 1913-1936
Varieties: HN 23, 23A, 342,
569, 744

U.S.:	**$6,000.00**
Can.:	**$7,250.00**
U.K.:	**£3,250.00**

HN 23
The Lavender Woman
Designer: P. Stabler
Height: 8 ¼", 21.0 cm
Colour: Green
Issued: 1913-1936
Varieties: HN 22, 23A, 342,
569, 744

U.S.:	
Can.:	**Extremely rare**
U.K.:	

HN 23A
The Lavender Woman
Designer: P. Stabler
Height: 8 ¼", 21.0 cm
Colour: Blue and green
Issued: 1913-1936
Varieties: HN 22, 23, 342,
569, 744

U.S.:	
Can.:	**Extremely rare**
U.K.:	

HN 24
Sleep
Designer: P. Stabler
Height: 8 ¼", 21.0 cm
Colour: Light green
Issued: 1913-1936
Varieties: HN 24A, 25, 25A,
424, 692, 710

U.S.:	**$3,750.00**
Can.:	**$4,500.00**
U.K.:	**£2,000.00**

HN 24A
Sleep
Designer: P. Stabler
Height: 8 ¼", 21.0 cm
Colour: Dark blue
Issued: 1913-1936
Varieties: HN 24, 25, 25A,
424, 692, 710

U.S.:	**$3,750.00**
Can.:	**$4,500.00**
U.K.:	**£2,000.00**

HN 25
Sleep
Designer: P. Stabler
Height: 8 ¼", 21.0 cm
Colour: Dark green
Issued: 1913-1936
Varieties: HN 24, 24A, 25A, 424, 692, 710

U.S.:	**$3,750.00**
Can.:	**$4,500.00**
U.K.:	**£2,000.00**

HN 25A
Sleep
Designer: P. Stabler
Height: 8 ¼", 21.0 cm
Colour: Dark green
Issued: 1913-1936
Varieties: HN 24, 24A, 25, 424, 692, 710

U.S.:	
Can.:	**Extremely rare**
U.K.:	

HN 26
The Diligent Scholar
Designer: W. White
Height: 7", 17.8 cm
Colour: Mottled brown and green
Issued: 1913-1936
Varieties: Also called 'The Attentive Scholar'

U.S.:	**$ 9,000.00**
Can.:	**$11,000.00**
U.K.:	**£ 5,000.00**

HN 27
Madonna of the Square
Designer: P. Stabler
Height: 7", 17.8 cm
Colour: Blue
Issued: 1913-1936
Varieties: HN 10, 10A, 11, 14, 326, 573, 576, 594, 613, 764, 1968, 1969, 2034

U.S.:	
Can.:	**Extremely rare**
U.K.:	

HN 28
Motherhood
Style One
Designer: P. Stabler
Height: 8", 20.3 cm
Colour: Light blue
Issued: 1913-1936
Varieties: HN 30, 303

U.S.:	**$ 8,500.00**
Can.:	**$10,500.00**
U.K.:	**£ 4,750.00**

HN 29
The Sleepy Scholar
Designer: W. White
Height: 6 ¾", 17.2 cm
Colour: Brown
Issued: 1913-1938
Varieties: HN 15, 16

U.S.:	**$ 9,000.00**
Can.:	**$11,000.00**
U.K.:	**£ 5,000.00**

HN 30
Motherhood
Style One
Designer: P. Stabler
Height: 8", 20.3 cm
Colour: White, blue and yellow
Issued: 1913-1936
Varieties: HN 28, 303

U.S.:	**None**
Can.:	**known**
U.K.:	**to exist**

HN 31
The Return of Persephone
Designer: C. Vyse
Height: 16", 40.6 cm
Colour: Light and dark blue
Issued: 1913-1938

U.S.:	**Only**
Can.:	**two**
U.K.:	**known**

HN 32
Child on Crab
Designer: C. J. Noke.
Height: 5 ¼", 13.3 cm
Colour: Pale blue, green
            and brown
Issued: 1913-1938
Varieties: Also known in flambé

U.S.:	$ 9,500.00
Can.:	$11,750.00
U.K.:	£ 5,250.00

HN 33
An Arab
Designer: C. J. Noke
Height: 16 ½", 41.9 cm
Colour: Dark blue, green
Issued: 1913-1938
Varieties: HN 343, 378; also
            called 'The Moor'
            HN 1308, 1366, 1425,
            1657, 2082, 3642,
            3926

U.S.:	$5,500.00
Can.:	$6,500.00
U.K.:	£3,000.00

HN 34
A Moorish Minstrel
Designer: C. J. Noke
Height: 13 ½", 34.3 cm
Colour: Deep purple
Issued: 1913-1938
Varieties: HN 364, 415, 797

U.S.:	$5,500.00
Can.:	$6,500.00
U.K.:	£3,000.00

Derived from Burslem figure
produced in 1890s.

HN 35
Charley's Aunt
Style One
Designer: A. Toft
Height: 7", 17.8 cm
Colour: Black and white
Issued: 1913-1936
Varieties: HN 640

U.S.:	$1,275.00
Can.:	$1,550.00
U.K.:	£ 700.00

HN 36
The Sentimental Pierrot
Designer: C. J. Noke
Height: 5 ½", 14.0 cm
Colour: Grey
Issued: 1914-1936
Varieties: HN 307

U.S.:	$ 9,500.00
Can.:	$11,750.00
U.K.:	£ 5,250.00

HN 37
The Coquette
Designer: W. White
Height: 9 ¼", 23.5 cm
Colour: Green flowered dress
Issued: 1914-1938
Varieties: HN 20, 20A

U.S.:	$ 9,000.00
Can.:	$11,000.00
U.K.:	£ 5,000.00

HN 38
The Carpet Vendor
Style One
Designer: C. J. Noke
Height: 5 ½", 14.0 cm
Colour: Blue, yellow and green
Issued: 1914-1936
Varieties: HN 76, 350; also
            known in flambé

U.S.:	
Can.:	Extremely rare
U.K.:	

HN 38A
The Carpet Vendor
Style Two
Designer: C. J. Noke
Height: 6 ¼", 15.9 cm
Colour: Blue and yellow,
            patterned long carpet
Issued: 1914-1936
Varieties: HN 348

U.S.:	
Can.:	Extremely rare
U.K.:	

HN 39
Myfanwy Jones
Designer: E. W. Light
Height: 12", 30.5 cm
Colour: Red, black, purple
Issued: 1914-1936
Varieties: HN 92, 456, 514, 516,
519, 520, 660, 668,
669, 701, 792; also
called 'The Welsh Girl'

U.S.: $ 9,000.00
Can.: $11,000.00
U.K.: £ 5,000.00

HN 40
A Lady of the Elizabethan Period
Style One
Designer: E. W. Light
Height: 9 ½", 24.1 cm
Colour: Orange and brown
with pattern
Issued: 1914-1938
Varieties: HN 40A, 73, 411; also
called 'Elizabethan
Lady' (Style One)

U.S.:
Can.: **Extremely rare**
U.K.:

HN 40A
A Lady of the Elizabethan Period
Style One
Designer: E. W. Light
Height: 9 ½", 24.1 cm
Colour: Orange and brown
Issued: 1914-1938
Varieties: HN 40, 73, 411; also
called 'Elizabethan
Lady' (Style One)

U.S.:
Can.: **Extremely rare**
U.K.:

HN 41
A Lady of the Georgian Period
Designer: E. W. Light
Height: 10 ¼", 26.0 cm
Colour: Gold and blue
Issued: 1914-1936
Varieties: HN 331, 444, 690,
702

U.S.: $5,500.00
Can.: $6,500.00
U.K.: £3,000.00

HN 42
Robert Burns
Style One
Designer: E. W. Light
Height: 14", 35.5 cm
Colour: Brown, green
and yellow
Issued: 1914-1938

U.S.: **Only**
Can.: **one**
U.K.: **known**

HN 43
A Woman of the Time of
Henry VI
Designer: E. W. Light
Height: 9 ¼", 23.5 cm
Colour: Green and yellow
Issued: 1914-1938

U.S.: **Only**
Can.: **three**
U.K.: **known**

HN 44
A Lilac Shawl
Designer: C. J. Noke
Height: 8 ¾", 22.2 cm
Colour: Cream and blue
Issued: 1915-1938
Varieties: HN 44A; also called
'In Grandma's Days'
HN 339, 340, 388,
442; 'The Poke Bonnet'
HN 362, 612, 765

U.S.: $4,000.00
Can.: $4,750.00
U.K.: £2,150.00

HN 44A
A Lilac Shawl
Designer: C. J. Noke
Height: 8 ¾", 22.2 cm
Colour: White and lilac
Issued: 1915-1938
Varieties: HN 44; also called
'In Grandma's Days'
HN 339, 340, 388,
442; 'The Poke Bonnet'
HN 362, 612, 765

U.S.: $4,000.00
Can.: $4,750.00
U.K.: £2,150.00

HN 45
A Jester
Style One
Designer: C. J. Noke
Height: 9 ½", 24.1 cm
Colour: Black and white
Issued: 1915-1938
Varieties: HN 71, 71A, 320, 367, 412, 426, 446, 552, 616, 627, 1295, 1702, 2016, 3922

U.S.: $ 8,500.00
Can.: $10,500.00
U.K.: £ 4,750.00

HN 45A
A Jester
Style Two
Designer: C. J. Noke
Height: 10 ¼", 26.0 cm
Colour: Green and white
Issued: 1915-1938
Varieties: HN 45B, 55, 308, 630, 1333; also known in black and white

U.S.: $ 8,500.00
Can.: $10,500.00
U.K.: £ 4,750.00

HN 45B
A Jester
Style Two
Designer: C. J. Noke
Height: 10 ¼", 26.0 cm
Colour: Red and white
Issued: 1915-1938
Varieties: HN 45A, 55, 308, 630, 1333; also known in black and white

U.S.: $ 8,500.00
Can.: $10,500.00
U.K.: £ 4,750.00

HN 46
The Gainsborough Hat
Designer: H. Tittensor
Height: 8 ¾", 22.2 cm
Colour: Lavender
Issued: 1915-1936
Varieties: HN 46A, 47, 329, 352, 383, 453, 675, 705

U.S.: $5,500.00
Can.: $6,500.00
U.K.: £3,000.00

HN 46A
The Gainsborough Hat
Designer: H. Tittensor
Height: 8 ¾", 22.2 cm
Colour: Lavender with black collar
Issued: 1915-1936
Varieties: HN 46, 47, 329, 352, 383, 453, 675, 705

U.S.: None
Can.: known
U.K.: to exist

HN 47
The Gainsborough Hat
Designer: H. Tittensor
Height: 8 ¾", 22.2 cm
Colour: Green
Issued: 1915-1936
Varieties: HN 46, 46A, 329, 352, 383, 453, 675, 705

U.S.: $5,500.00
Can.: $6,500.00
U.K.: £3,000.00

HN 48
Lady of the Fan
Designer: E. W. Light
Height: 9 ½", 24.1 cm
Colour: Lavender
Issued: 1916-1936
Varieties: HN 52, 53, 53A, 335, 509

U.S.: None
Can.: known
U.K.: to exist

HN 48A
Lady with Rose
Designer: E. W. Light
Height: 9 ½", 24.1 cm
Colour: Cream and orange
Issued: 1916-1936
Varieties: HN 52A, 68, 304, 336, 515, 517, 584, 624

U.S.: $5,000.00
Can.: $6,000.00
U.K.: £2,750.00

HN 49
Under the Gooseberry Bush
Designer: C. J. Noke
Height: 3 ½", 8.9 cm
Colour: Green and brown
Issued: 1916-1938
U.S.: $4,500.00
Can.: $5,500.00
U.K.: £2,500.00

HN 50
A Spook
Style One
Designer: H. Tittensor
Height: 7", 17.8 cm
Colour: Green robe, black cap
Issued: 1916-1936
Varieties: HN 51, 51A, 51B, 58, 512, 625; also known in flambé
U.S.: $5,500.00
Can.: $6,500.00
U.K.: £3,000.00

HN 51
A Spook
Style One
Designer: H. Tittensor
Height: 7", 17.8 cm
Colour: Green robe, red cap
Issued: 1916-1936
Varieties: HN 50, 51A, 51B, 58, 512, 625; also known in flambé
U.S.: $5,500.00
Can.: $6,500.00
U.K.: £3,000.00

HN 51A
A Spook
Style One
Designer: H. Tittensor
Height: 7", 17.8 cm
Colour: Green robe, black cap
Issued: 1916-1936
Varieties: HN 50, 51, 51B, 58, 512, 625; also known in flambé
U.S.: $5,500.00
Can.: $6,500.00
U.K.: £3,000.00

HN 51B
A Spook
Designer: H. Tittensor
Height: 7", 17.8 cm
Colour: Blue robe, red cap
Issued: 1916-1936
Varieties: HN 50, 51, 51A, 58, 512, 625; also known in flambé
U.S.: None
Can.: known
U.K.: to exist

HN 52
Lady of the Fan
Designer: E. W. Light
Height: 9 ½", 24.1 cm
Colour: Green
Issued: 1916-1936
Varieties: HN 48, 53, 53A, 335, 509
U.S.: $5,500.00
Can.: $6,500.00
U.K.: £3,000.00

HN 52A
Lady with Rose
Designer: E. W. Light
Height: 9 ½", 24.1 cm
Colour: Yellow
Issued: 1916-1936
Varieties: HN 48A, 68, 304, 336, 515, 517, 584, 624
U.S.: None
Can.: known
U.K.: to exist

HN 53
Lady of the Fan
Designer: E. W. Light
Height: 9 ½", 24.1 cm
Colour: Dark purple
Issued: 1916-1936
Varieties: HN 48, 52, 53A, 335, 509
U.S.: $5,500.00
Can.: $6,500.00
U.K.: £3,000.00

HN 53A
Lady of the Fan
Designer: E. W. Light
Height: 9", 22.9 cm
Colour: Green
Issued: 1916-1936
Varieties: HN 48, 52, 53, 335, 509

U.S.:	**Only**
Can.:	**one**
U.K.:	**known**

HN 54
The Ermine Muff
Designer: C. J. Noke
Height: 8 ½", 21.6 cm
Colour: Grey coat, pale green dress
Issued: 1916-1938
Varieties: HN 332, 671; also called 'Lady Ermine' and 'Lady With Ermine Muff'

U.S.:	**$4,500.00**
Can.:	**$5,500.00**
U.K.:	**£2,500.00**

HN 55
A Jester
Style Two
Designer: C. J. Noke
Height: 10 ¼", 26.0 cm
Colour: Black and lavender
Issued: 1916-1938
Varieties: HN 45A, 45B, 308, 630, 1333; also known in black and white

U.S.:	**$ 9,000.00**
Can.:	**$11,000.00**
U.K.:	**£ 5,000.00**

HN 56
The Land of Nod
First Version
Designer: H. Tittensor
Height: 9 ½", 24.1 cm
Colour: Ivory, green candlestick
Issued: 1916-1938
Varieties: HN 56A, 56B

U.S.:	**$ 9,500.00**
Can.:	**$11,750.00**
U.K.:	**£ 5,500.00**

The owl was produced as animal figure HN 169.

HN 56A
The Land of Nod
First Version
Designer: H. Tittensor
Height: 9 ½", 24.1 cm
Colour: Light grey, green candlestick
Issued: 1916-1938
Varieties: HN 56, 56B

U.S.:	**$ 9,500.00**
Can.:	**$11,750.00**
U.K.:	**£ 5,500.00**

HN 56B
The Land of Nod
First Version
Designer: H. Tittensor
Height: 9 ½", 24.1 cm
Colour: Light grey, red candlestick
Issued: 1916-1938
Varieties: HN 56, 56A

U.S.:	**$ 9,500.00**
Can.:	**$11,750.00**
U.K.:	**£ 5,500.00**

HN 57
The Curtsey
Designer: E. W. Light
Height: 11", 27.9 cm
Colour: Orange
Issued: 1916-1936
Varieties: HN 57B, 66A, 327, 334, 363, 371, 518, 547, 629, 670

U.S.:	**None**
Can.:	**known**
U.K.:	**to exist**

HN 57A
The Flounced Skirt
Designer: E. W. Light
Height: 9 ¾", 24.7 cm
Colour: Orange
Issued: 1916-1938
Varieties: HN 66, 77, 78, 333; also called 'The Bow'

U.S.:	**None**
Can.:	**known**
U.K.:	**to exist**

HN 57B
The Curtsey
Designer: E. W. Light
Height: 11", 27.9 cm
Colour: Lavender
Issued: 1916-1936
Varieties: HN 57, 66A, 327, 334,
             363, 371, 518, 547,
             629, 670

U.S.: $4,750.00
Can.: $5,500.00
U.K.:   £2,500.00

HN 58
A Spook
Style One
Designer: H. Tittensor
Height: 7", 17.8 cm
Colour: Unknown
Issued: 1916-1936
Varieties: HN 50, 51, 51A, 51B,
             512, 625; also known
             in flambé

U.S.:   None
Can.:   known
U.K.:   to exist

HN 59
Upon Her Cheeks She Wept
Designer: L. Perugini
Height: 9", 22.8 cm
Colour: Grey dress
Issued: 1916-1938
Varieties: HN 511, 522

U.S.: $ 9,500.00
Can.: $11,750.00
U.K.:   £ 5,500.00

HN 60
Shy Anne
Designer: L. Perugini
Height: 7 ¾", 19.7 cm
Colour: Blue dress with flowers,
             blue bow in hair
Issued: 1916-1936
Varieties: HN 64, 65, 568

U.S.:
Can.:   Extremely rare
U.K.:

HN 61
Katharine
Style One
Designer: C. J. Noke
Height: 5 ¾", 14.6 cm
Colour: Green
Issued: 1916-1938
Varieties: HN 74, 341, 471,
             615, 793

U.S.: $4,000.00
Can.: $4,800.00
U.K.:   £2,250.00

HN 62
A Child's Grace
Designer: L. Perugini
Height: 9 ¼", 23.5 cm
Colour: Green and yellow
             coat, yellow dress
Issued: 1916-1938
Varieties: HN 62A, 510

U.S.:   Only
Can.:   two
U.K.:   known

HN 62A
A Child's Grace
Designer: L. Perugini
Height: 9 ¼", 23.5 cm
Colour: Green coat,
             yellow dress
Issued: 1916-1938
Varieties: HN 62, 510

U.S.:
Can.:   Extremely rare
U.K.:

HN 63
The Little Land
Designer: H. Tittensor
Height: 7 ½", 19.1 cm
Colour: Green and yellow
Issued: 1916-1936
Varieties: HN 67

U.S.: $ 9,000.00
Can.: $11,000.00
U.K.:   £ 5,000.00

HN 64
Shy Anne
Designer: L. Perugini
Height: 7 ¾", 19.7 cm
Colour: Pale blue, white bow
            in hair
Issued: 1916-1936
Varieties: HN 60, 65, 568

   U.S.:   **$ 8,500.00**
   Can.:   **$10,500.00**
   U.K.:   **£ 4,750.00**

HN 65
Shy Anne
Designer: L. Perugini
Height: 7 ¾", 19.7 cm
Colour: Pale blue, dark blue
            stripe around hem of
            skirt, white bow in hair
Issued: 1916-1936
Varieties: HN 60, 64, 568

   U.S.:   **$ 8,500.00**
   Can.:   **$10,500.00**
   U.K.:   **£ 4,750.00**

HN 66
The Flounced Skirt
Designer: E. W. Light
Height: 9 ¾", 24.7 cm
Colour: Lavender
Issued: 1916-1938
Varieties: HN 57A, 77, 78, 333;
            also called 'The Bow'.

   U.S.:   **$4,750.00**
   Can.:   **$5,700.00**
   U.K.:   **£2,550.00**

HN 66A
The Curtsey
Designer: E. W. Light
Height: 11", 27.9 cm
Colour: Lavender
Issued: 1916-1936
Varieties: HN 57, 57B, 327, 334,
            363, 371, 518, 547,
            629, 670

   U.S.:   **$4,750.00**
   Can.:   **$5,700.00**
   U.K.:   **£2,500.00**

HN 67
The Little Land
Designer: H. Tittensor
Height: 7 ½", 19.1 cm
Colour: Lilac and yellow
Issued: 1916-1936
Varieties: HN 63

   U.S.:   **$ 9,000.00**
   Can.:   **$11,000.00**
   U.K.:   **£ 5,000.00**

HN 68
Lady With Rose
Designer: E. W. Light
Height: 9 ½", 24.1 cm
Colour: Green and yellow
Issued: 1916-1936
Varieties: HN 48A, 52A, 304,
            336, 515, 517, 584,
            624

   U.S.:   **$5,000.00**
   Can.:   **$6,000.00**
   U.K.:   **£2,750.00**

HN 69
Pretty Lady
Designer: H. Tittensor
Height: 9 ½", 24.1 cm
Colour: Blue dress with flowers
Issued: 1916-1936
Varieties: HN 70, 302, 330, 361,
            384, 565, 700, 763,
            783

   U.S.:   **None**
   Can.:   **known**
   U.K.:   **to exist**

HN 70
Pretty Lady
Designer: H. Tittensor
Height: 9 ½", 24.1 cm
Colour: Grey
Issued: 1916-1938
Varieties: HN 69, 302, 330, 361,
            384, 565, 700, 763,
            783

   U.S.:   **$4,000.00**
   Can.:   **$4,750.00**
   U.K.:   **£2,150.00**

HN 71
A Jester
Style One
Designer: C. J. Noke
Height: 9", 22.9 cm
Colour: Light green checks
Issued: 1917-1938
Varieties: HN 45, 71A, 320, 367,
412, 426, 446, 552,
616, 627, 1295, 1702,
2016, 3922

U.S.: **$7,500.00**
Can.: **$9,000.00**
U.K.: **£4,000.00**

HN 71A
A Jester
Style One
Designer: C. J. Noke
Height: 9½", 24.1 cm
Colour: Dark green checks
Issued: 1917-1938
Varieties: HN 45, 71, 320, 367,
412, 426, 446, 552,
616, 627, 1295, 1702,
2016, 3922

U.S.: **$7,500.00**
Can.: **$9,000.00**
U.K.: **£4,000.00**

HN 72
An Orange Vendor
Designer: C. J. Noke
Height: 6 ¼", 15.9 cm
Colour: Green, white
and orange
Issued: 1917-1938
Varieties: HN 508, 521, 1966

U.S.: **$2,750.00**
Can.: **$3,250.00**
U.K.: **£1,500.00**

HN 73
A Lady of the Elizabethan Period
Style One
Designer: E. W. Light
Height: 9 ½", 24.1 cm
Colour: Dark turquoise
Issued: 1917-1938
Varieties: HN 40, 40A, 411;
also called 'Elizabethan
Lady' (Style One)

U.S.:
Can.: **Extremely rare**
U.K.:

HN 74
Katharine
Style One
Designer: C. J. Noke
Height: 5 ¾", 14.6 cm
Colour: Light blue dress with
green spots
Issued: 1917-1938
Varieties: HN 61, 341, 471,
615, 793

U.S.: **None**
Can.: **known**
U.K.: **to exist**

HN 75
Blue Beard
(With Plume on Turban)
Style One
Designer: E. W. Light
Height: 11", 27.9 cm
Colour: Light blue
Issued: 1917-1936
Varieties: HN 410

U.S.: **$12,000.00**
Can.: **$14,500.00**
U.K.: **£ 6,500.00**

HN 76
The Carpet Vendor
Style One
Designer: C. J. Noke
Height: 5 ½", 14.0 cm
Colour: Blue and orange
Issued: 1917-1936
Varieties: HN 38, 350; also
known in flambé

U.S.: **$6,000.00**
Can.: **$7,250.00**
U.K.: **£3,250.00**

HN 77
The Flounced Skirt
Style One
Designer: E. W. Light
Height: 9 ¾", 24.7 cm
Colour: Yellow dress with
black trim
Issued: 1917-1938
Varieties: HN 57A, 66, 78, 333;
also called 'The Bow'

U.S.: **$4,750.00**
Can.: **$5,700.00**
U.K.: **£2,500.00**

HN 78
The Flounced Skirt
Designer: E. W. Light
Height: 9 ¾", 24.7 cm
Colour: Yellow dress with flowers
Issued: 1917-1938
Varieties: HN 57A, 66, 77, 333; also called 'The Bow'

U.S.: $4,750.00
Can.: $5,700.00
U.K.: £2,500.00

HN 79
Shylock
Designer: C. J. Noke
Height: Unknown
Colour: Multicoloured robe, yellow sleeves
Issued: 1917-1938
Varieties: HN 317; also known with Titanian glaze

U.S.: **Only**
Can.: **one**
U.K.: **known**

HN 80
Fisherwomen
Designer: C. J. Noke
Height: 11 ¾", 29.8 cm
Colour: Lavender, pink and green
Issued: 1917-1938
Varieties: HN 349, 359, 631; also called 'Looking for the Boats' and 'Waiting for the Boats'

U.S.: **None**
Can.: **known**
U.K.: **to exist**

HN 81
A Shepherd
Style One
Designer: C. J. Noke
Height: 13 ¼", 33.6 cm
Colour: Brown
Issued: 1918-1938
Varieties: HN 617, 632

U.S.:
Can.: **Extremely rare**
U.K.:

Earthenware

HN 82
Lady with an Ermine Muff
Designer: E. W. Light
Height: 6 ¾", 17.2 cm
Colour: Grey and cream, grey hat
Issued: 1918-1938
Varieties: Also called 'Afternoon Call' and ''Making a Call'

U.S.: $ 8,500.00
Can.: $10,000.00
U.K.: £ 4,600.00

HN 83
The Lady Anne
Designer: E. W. Light
Height: 9 ½", 24.0 cm
Colour: Yellow
Issued: 1918-1938
Varieties: HN 87, 93

U.S.: $8,000.00
Can.: $9,750.00
U.K.: £4,500.00

HN 84
A Mandarin
Style One
Designer: C. J. Noke
Height: 10 ¼", 26.0 cm
Colour: Mauve and green
Issued: 1918-1936
Varieties: HN 316, 318, 382, 611, 746, 787, 791; 'Chinese Mandarin' and 'The Mikado'

U.S.: **None**
Can.: **known**
U.K.: **to exist**

HN 85
Jack Point
Designer: C. J. Noke
Height: 16 ¼", 41.2 cm
Colour: Red checks, green base
Issued: 1918-1938
Varieties: HN 91, 99, 2080, 3920, 3925

U.S.: **None**
Can.: **known**
U.K.: **to exist**

HN 86
Out For a Walk
Designer: E. W. Light
Height: 10", 25.4 cm
Colour: Grey, white and black
Issued: 1918-1936
Varieties: HN 443, 748

U.S.: **$6,750.00**
Can.: **$8,000.00**
U.K.: **£3,650.00**

HN 87
The Lady Anne
Designer: E. W. Light
Height: 9 ½", 24.0 cm
Colour: Green
Issued: 1918-1938
Varieties: HN 83, 93

U.S.: **$8,000.00**
Can.: **$9,750.00**
U.K.: **£4,500.00**

HN 88
Spooks
Designer: C. J. Noke
Height: 7 ¼", 18.4 cm
Colour: Green robes,
        black caps
Issued: 1918-1936
Varieties: HN 89, 372; also
        called 'Double Spook'

U.S.: **$8,000.00**
Can.: **$9,750.00**
U.K.: **£4,500.00**

HN 89
Spooks
Designer: C. J. Noke
Height: 7 ¼", 18.4 cm
Colour: Green robes, red caps
Issued: 1918-1936
Varieties: HN 88, 372; also
        called 'Double Spook'

U.S.: **$8,000.00**
Can.: **$9,750.00**
U.K.: **£4,500.00**

HN 90
Doris Keene as Cavallini
Style One
Designer: C. J. Noke
Height: 11", 27.9 cm
Colour: Dark green
Issued: 1918-1936
Varieties: HN 467

U.S.: **$4,500.00**
Can.: **$5,500.00**
U.K.: **£2,500.00**

HN 91
Jack Point
Designer: C. J. Noke
Height: 16 ¼", 41.2 cm
Colour: Green and black
        checked suit
Issued: 1918-1938
Varieties: HN 85, 99, 2080,
        3920, 3925

U.S.: **$8,000.00**
Can.: **$9,750.00**
U.K.: **£4,500.00**

HN 92
Myfanwy Jones
Designer: E. W. Light
Height: 12", 30.5 cm
Colour: White
Issued: 1918-1936
Varieties: HN 39, 456, 514, 516,
        519, 520, 660, 668,
        669, 701, 792; also
        called 'The Welsh Girl'

U.S.: **Only**
Can.: **two**
U.K.: **known**

HN 93
The Lady Anne
Designer: E. W. Light
Height: 9 ½", 24.0 cm
Colour: Blue
Issued: 1918-1938
Varieties: HN 83, 87

U.S.: **$8,000.00**
Can.: **$9,750.00**
U.K.: **£4,500.00**

HN 94
The Young Knight
Designer: C. J. Noke
Height: 9 ½", 24.1 cm
Colour: Purple, green and black
Issued: 1918-1936

U.S.:   **Only**
Can.:   **one**
U.K.:   **known**

HN 95
Europa and the Bull
Style One
Designer: E. W. Light
Height: 9 ¾", 24.7 cm
Colour: Lavender with browns
Issued: 1918-1936

U.S.:   **$10,000.00**
Can.:   **$12,250.00**
U.K.:   **£ 5,700.00**

HN 96
Doris Keene as Cavallini
Style Two
Designer: C. J. Noke
Height: 10 ¾", 27.8 cm
Colour: Black and white
Issued: 1918-1936
Varieties: HN 345; also called
             'Romance' (Style One)

U.S.:   **$5,500.00**
Can.:   **$6,500.00**
U.K.:   **£3,000.00**

HN 97
The Mermaid
Designer: H. Tittensor
Height: 7", 17.8 cm
Colour: Green and cream
Issued: 1918-1936
Varieties: HN 300

U.S.:   **$1,650.00**
Can.:   **$2,000.00**
U.K.:   **£   900.00**

HN 98
Guy Fawkes
Style One
Designer: C. J. Noke
Height: 10 ½", 26.7 cm
Colour: Red cloak, black hat
             and robes
Issued: 1918-1949
Varieties: HN 347, 445; also
             known in Sung

U.S.:   **$3,500.00**
Can.:   **$4,500.00**
U.K.:   **£1,875.00**

HN 99
Jack Point
Designer: C. J. Noke
Height: 16 ¼", 41.2 cm
Colour: Purple and green
Issued   1918-1938
Varieties: HN 85, 91, 2080,
             3920, 3925

U.S.:   **$6,750.00**
Can.:   **$8,000.00**
U.K.:   **£3,600.00**

HN 100 - 299 Animal, Bird figures,
except HN 174, 177 and 230, not
issued.

HN 300
The Mermaid
Designer: H. Tittensor
Height: 7", 17.8 cm
Colour: Green and cream,
             red berries in hair
Issued: 1918-1936
Varieties: HN 97

U.S.:   **Only**
Can.:   **two**
U.K.:   **known**

HN 301
Moorish Piper Minstrel
Designer: C. J. Noke
Height: 13 ½", 34.3 cm
Colour: Purple
Issued: 1918-1938
Varieties: HN 328, 416

U.S.:   **$5,000.00**
Can.:   **$6,000.00**
U.K.:   **£2,700.00**

HN 302
Pretty Lady
Designer: H. Tittensor
Height: 9 ½", 24.1 cm
Colour: Green and lavender
Issued: 1918-1938
Varieties: HN 69, 70, 330, 361,
384, 565, 700, 763, 783

U.S.:	**$3,500.00**
Can.:	**$4,250.00**
U.K.:	**£2,000.00**

HN 303
Motherhood
Style One
Designer: P. Stabler
Height: 8", 20.3 cm
Colour: White dress with black
Issued: 1918-1936
Varieties: HN 28, 30

U.S.:	**None**
Can.:	**known**
U.K.:	**to exist**

HN 304
Lady with Rose
Designer: E. W. Light
Height: 9 ½", 24.1 cm
Colour: Patterned lavender
dress
Issued: 1918-1936
Varieties: HN 48A, 52A, 68, 336,
515, 517, 584, 624

U.S.:	**Only**
Can.:	**one**
U.K.:	**known**

HN 305
A Scribe
Designer: C. J. Noke
Height: 6", 15.2 cm
Colour: Green, blue and orange
Issued: 1918-1936
Varieties: HN 324, 1235

U.S.:	**$3,000.00**
Can.:	**$3,500.00**
U.K.:	**£1,650.00**

HN 306
Milking Time
Designer: P. Stabler
Height: 6 ½", 16.5 cm
Colour: Light blue dress with
black
Issued: 1913-1938
Varieties: HN 3

U.S.:	
Can.:	**Extremely rare**
U.K.:	

HN 307
The Sentimental Pierrot
Designer: C. J. Noke
Height: 5 ½", 14.0 cm
Colour: Black, white
Issued: 1918-1936
Varieties: HN 36

U.S.:	**$ 9,500.00**
Can.:	**$11,750.00**
U.K.:	**£ 5,500.00**

HN 308
A Jester
Style Two
Designer: C. J. Noke
Height: 10 ¼", 26.0 cm
Colour: Black and lavender
Issued: 1918-1938
Varieties: HN 45A, 45B, 55, 630;
also known in black
and white

U.S.:	**Only**
Can.:	**two**
U.K.:	**known**

HN 309
An Elizabethan Lady
Style Two
Designer: E. W. Light
Height: 9 ½", 24.1 cm
Colour: Dark green-blue,
green and black
Issued: 1918-1938
Varieties: Also called 'A Lady of
the Elizabethan Period'
(Style Two)

U.S.:	**$5,500.00**
Can.:	**$6,600.00**
U.K.:	**£3,000.00**

HN 310
Dunce
Designer: C. J. Noke
Height: 10 ½", 26.7 cm
Colour: Black and white
           with green base
Issued: 1918-1936
Varieties: HN 6, 357

U.S.:	**None**
Can.:	**known**
U.K.:	**to exist**

HN 311
Dancing Figure
Designer: Unknown
Height: 17 ¾", 45.0 cm
Colour: Pink
Issued: 1918-1938

U.S.:	**Only**
Can.:	**two**
U.K.:	**known**

HN 312
Spring
Style One
Designer: Unknown
Height: 7 ½"; 19.1 cm
Colour: Yellow
Issued: 1918-1938
Varieties: HN 472
Series: The Seasons
           (Series One)

U.S.:	**$2,750.00**
Can.:	**$3,250.00**
U.K.:	**£1,500.00**

HN 313
Summer
Style One
Designer: Unknown
Height: 7 ½", 19.1 cm
Colour: Pale green
Issued: 1918-1938
Varieties: HN 473
Series: The Seasons
           (Series One)

U.S.:	**$2,750.00**
Can.:	**$3,250.00**
U.K.:	**£1,500.00**

HN 314
Autumn
Style One
Designer: Unknown
Height: 7 ½", 19.1 cm
Colour: Lavender
Issued: 1918-1938
Varieties: HN 474
Series: The Seasons
           (Series One)

U.S.:	**$2,750.00**
Can.:	**$3,250.00**
U.K.:	**£1,500.00**

HN 315
Winter
Style One
Designer: Unknown
Height: 7 ½", 19.1 cm
Colour: Pale green
Issued: 1918-1938
Varieties: HN 475
Series: The Seasons
           (Series One)

U.S.:	**$2,750.00**
Can.:	**$3,250.00**
U.K.:	**£1,500.00**

HN 316
A Mandarin
Style One
Designer: C. J. Noke
Height: 10 ¼", 26.0 cm
Colour: Black and yellow
Issued: 1918-1936
Varieties: HN 84, 318, 382, 611,
           746, 787, 791; also
           called 'Chinese
           Mandarin' and 'The
           Mikado'

U.S.:	**$ 9,500.00**
Can.:	**$11,000.00**
U.K.:	**£ 5,000.00**

HN 317
Shylock
Designer: C. J. Noke
Height: Unknown
Colour: Brown and green
Issued: 1918-1938
Varieties: HN 79; also known
           with Titanian glaze

U.S.:	
Can.:	**Extremely rare**
U.K.:	

HN 318
A Mandarin
Style One
Designer: C. J. Noke
Height: 10 ¼", 26.0 cm
Colour: Gold
Issued: 1918-1936
Varieties: HN 84, 316, 382, 611, 746, 787, 791; also called 'Chinese Mandarin' and 'The Mikado'

U.S.:	$ 9,500.00
Can.:	$11,000.00
U.K.:	£ 5,000.00

HN 319
A Gnome
Designer: H. Tittensor
Height: 6 ¼", 15.9 cm
Colour: Light blue
Issued: 1918-1938
Varieties: HN 380, 381; also known in flambé

U.S.:	
Can.:	**Extremely rare**
U.K.:	

A Titanian 4½" model is known to exist.

HN 320
A Jester
Style One
Designer: C. J. Noke
Height: 10", 25.4 cm
Colour: Green and black
Issued: 1918-1938
Varieties: HN 45, 71, 71A, 367, 412, 426, 446, 552, 616, 627, 1295, 1702, 2016, 3922

U.S.:	$ 9,000.00
Can.:	$11,000.00
U.K.:	£ 5,000.00

HN 321
Digger (New Zealand)
Designer: E. W. Light
Height: 11 ¼", 28.5 cm
Colour: Mottled green
Issued: 1918-1938

U.S.:	**$7,500.00**
Can.:	**$9,000.00**
U.K.:	**£4,000.00**

HN 322
Digger (Australian)
Designer: E. W. Light
Height: 11 ¼", 28.5 cm
Colour: Brown
Issued: 1918-1938
Varieties: HN 353

U.S.:	**$4,000.00**
Can.:	**$4,800.00**
U.K.:	**£2,150.00**

HN 323
Blighty
Designer: E. W. Light
Height: 11 ¼", 28.5 cm
Colour: Green
Issued: 1918-1938
Varieties: Khaki version

U.S.:	**$5,000.00**
Can.:	**$6,000.00**
U.K.:	**£2,700.00**

HN 324
A Scribe
Designer: C. J. Noke
Height: 6", 15.2 cm
Colour: Brown, green and orange
Issued: 1918-1938
Varieties: HN 305, 1235

U.S.:	**$2,750.00**
Can.:	**$3,250.00**
U.K.:	**£1,500.00**

HN 325
Pussy
Designer: F. C. Stone
Height: 7 ½", 19.1 cm
Colour: White patterned dress with black
Issued: 1918-1938
Varieties: HN 18, 507; also called 'The Black Cat'

U.S.:	**Only**
Can.:	**one**
U.K.:	**known**

HN 326
Madonna of the Square
Designer: P. Stabler
Height: 7", 17.8 cm
Colour: Grey
Issued: 1918-1936
Varieties: HN 10, 10A, 11, 14, 27,
            573, 576, 594, 613,
            764, 1968, 1969, 2034
  U.S.: $2,500.00
  Can.: $3,000.00
  U.K.:   £1,350.00

HN 327
The Curtsey
Designer: E. W. Light
Height: 11", 27.9 cm
Colour: Blue
Issued: 1918-1936
Varieties: HN 57, 57B, 66A, 334,
            363, 371, 518, 547,
            629 670
  U.S.: $4,500.00
  Can.: $5,500.00
  U.K.:   £2,500.00

HN 328
Moorish Piper Minstrel
Designer: C. J. Noke
Height: 13 ½", 34.3 cm
Colour: Green and brown
            stripes
Issued: 1918-1938
Varieties: HN 301, 416
  U.S.:   None
  Can.:   known
  U.K.:   to exist

HN 329
The Gainsborough Hat
Designer: H. Tittensor
Height: 8 ¾", 22.2 cm
Colour: Patterned blue dress
Issued: 1918-1936
Varieties: HN 46, 46A, 47, 352,
            383, 453, 675, 705
  U.S.:   None
  Can.:   known
  U.K.:   to exist

HN 330
Pretty Lady
Designer: H. Tittensor
Height: 9 ½", 24.1 cm
Colour: Patterned blue dress
Issued: 1918-1938
Varieties: HN 69, 70, 302, 361,
            384, 565, 700, 763,
            783
  U.S.:   None
  Can.:   known
  U.K.:   to exist

HN 331
A Lady of the Georgian Period
Designer: E. W. Light
Height: 10 ¼", 26.0 cm
Colour: Mottled green overskirt,
            yellow underskirt
Issued: 1918-1936
Varieties: HN 41, 444, 690, 702
  U.S.: $5,500.00
  Can.: $6,500.00
  U.K.:   £3,000.00

HN 332
The Ermine Muff
Designer: C. J. Noke
Height: 8 ½", 21.6 cm
Colour: Red coat, green and
            yellow skirt
Issued: 1918-1938
Varieties: HN 54, 671; also called
            'Lady Ermine' and 'Lady
            with Ermine Muff'
  U.S.:   Only
  Can.:   one
  U.K.:   known

HN 333
The Flounced Skirt
Designer: E. W. Light
Height: 9 ¾", 24.7 cm
Colour: Mottled green and blue
Issued: 1918-1938
Varieties: HN 57A, 66, 77, 78;
            also called 'The Bow'
  U.S.: $4,500.00
  Can.: $5,500.00
  U.K.:   £2,500.00

HN 334
The Curtsey
Designer: E. W. Light
Height: 11", 27.9 cm
Colour: Purple
Issued: 1918-1936
Varieties: HN 57, 57B, 66A, 327, 363, 371, 518, 547, 629, 670

U.S.: $4,500.00
Can.: $5,500.00
U.K.: £2,500.00

HN 335
Lady of the Fan
Designer: E. W. Light
Height: 9 ½", 24.1 cm
Colour: Blue
Issued: 1919-1936
Varieties: HN 48, 52, 53, 53A, 509

U.S.: $5,000.00
Can.: $6,000.00
U.K.: £2,700.00

HN 336
Lady with Rose
Designer: E. W. Light
Height: 9 ½", 24.1 cm
Colour: Multicoloured
Issued: 1919-1936
Varieties: HN 48A, 52A, 68, 304, 515, 517, 584, 624

U.S.: None
Can.: known
U.K.: to exist

HN 337
The Parson's Daughter
Designer: H. Tittensor
Height: 10", 25.4 cm
Colour: Lavender dress with brown flowers
Issued: 1919-1938
Varieties: HN 338, 441, 564, 790, 1242, 1356, 2018

U.S.: $3,000.00
Can.: $3,600.00
U.K.: £1,600.00

HN 338
The Parson's Daughter
Designer: H. Tittensor
Height: 10", 25.4 cm
Colour: Green and red
Issued: 1919-1938
Varieties: HN 337, 441, 564, 790, 1242, 1356, 2018

U.S.: $3,000.00
Can.: $3,600.00
U.K.: £1,600.00

HN 339
In Grandma's Days
Designer: C. J. Noke
Height: 8 ¾", 22.2 cm
Colour: Green and yellow
Issued: 1919-1938
Varieties: HN 340, 388, 442; also called 'A Lilac Shawl' HN 44, 44A; 'The Poke Bonnet' HN 362, 612, 765

U.S.: $4,500.00
Can.: $5,500.00
U.K.: £2,500.00

HN 340
In Grandma's Days
Designer: C. J. Noke
Height: 8 ¾", 22.2 cm
Colour: Yellow and lavender
Issued: 1919-1938
Varieties: HN 339, 388, 442; also called 'A Lilac Shawl' HN 44, 44A; 'The Poke Bonnet' HN 362, 612, 765

U.S.: $4,500.00
Can.: $5,500.00
U.K.: £2,500.00

HN 341
Katharine
Style One
Designer: C. J. Noke
Height: 5 ¾", 14.6 cm
Colour: Red
Issued: 1919-1938
Varieties: HN 61, 74, 471, 615, 793

U.S.: $3,750.00
Can.: $4,500.00
U.K.: £2,000.00

HN 342
The Lavender Woman
Designer: P. Stabler
Height: 8 ¼", 21.0 cm
Colour: Multicoloured dress,
             lavender shawl
Issued: 1919-1938
Varieties: HN 22, 23, 23A, 569,
             744

U.S.: $6,500.00
Can.: $7,750.00
U.K.:   £3,500.00

HN 343
An Arab
Designer: C. J. Noke
Height: 16 ½", 41.9 cm
Colour: Yellow and purple
Issued: 1919-1938
Varieties: HN 33, 378; also called
             'The Moor' HN 1308,
             1366, 1425, 1657,
             2082, 3642, 3926

U.S.:   None
Can.:   known
U.K.:   to exist

HN 344
Henry Irving as Cardinal Wolsey
Designer: C. J. Noke
Height: 13 ¼", 33.7 cm
Colour: Red
Issued: 1919-1949

U.S.: $5,500.00
Can.: $6,500.00
U.K.:   £3,000.00

HN 345
Doris Keene as Cavallini
Style Two
Designer: C. J. Noke
Height: 10 ½", 26.6 cm
Colour: Black and white, dark
             collar and striped muff
Issued: 1919-1949
Varieties: HN 96; Also called
             'Romance' (Style One)

U.S.: $5,500.00
Can.: $6,500.00
U.K.:   £3,000.00

HN 346
Tony Weller
Style One
Designer: C. J. Noke
Height: 10 ½", 26.7 cm
Colour: Green, blue and brown
Issued: 1919-1938
Varieties: HN 368, 684

U.S.:   None
Can.:   known
U.K.:   to exist

HN 347
Guy Fawkes
Style One
Designer: C. J. Noke
Height: 10 ½", 26.7 cm
Colour: Brown-red cloak
Issued: 1919-1938
Varieties: HN 98, 445; also
             known in Sung

U.S.:
Can.:   Extremely rare
U.K.:

HN 348
The Carpet Vendor
Style Two
Designer: C. J. Noke
Height: 6 ¼", 15.9 cm
Colour: Turquoise, long
             patterned carpet
Issued: 1919-1936
Varieties: HN 38A

U.S.:   One
Can.:   known
U.K.:   to exist

HN 349
Fisherwomen
Designer: C. J. Noke
Height: 11 ¾", 29.8 cm
Colour: Lavender, yellow
             and green
Issued: 1919-1938
Varieties: HN 80, 359, 631;
             also called 'Looking
             for the Boats' and
             'Waiting for the Boats'

U.S.:   None
Can.:   known
U.K.:   to exist

HN 350
The Carpet Vendor
Style One
Designer: C. J. Noke
Height: 5 ½", 14.0 cm
Colour: Blue and mottled green
Issued: 1919-1936
Varieties: HN 38, 76; also known
in flambé

U.S.:	$6,000.00
Can.:	$7,250.00
U.K.:	£3,250.00

HN 351
Picardy Peasant (woman)
Designer: P. Stabler
Height: 9 ½", 24.0 cm
Colour: Blue striped skirt,
spotted hat
Issued: 1919-1938
Varieties: HN 4, 5, 17A, 513

U.S.:	$8,000.00
Can.:	$9,500.00
U.K.:	£4,500.00

HN 352
The Gainsborough Hat
Designer: H. Tittensor
Height: 8 ¾", 22.2 cm
Colour: Yellow dress, purple hat
Issued: 1919-1936
Varieties: HN 46, 46A, 47, 329,
383, 453, 675, 705

U.S.:	None
Can.:	known
U.K.:	to exist

HN 353
Digger (Australian)
Designer: E. W. Light
Height: 11 ¼", 28.5 cm
Colour: Brown
Issued: 1919-1938
Varieties: HN 322

U.S.:	
Can.:	Extremely rare
U.K.:	

HN 354
A Geisha
Style One
Designer: H. Tittensor
Height: 10 ¾", 27.3 cm
Colour: Yellow, pink, blue
Issued: 1919-1938
Varieties: HN 376, 376A, 387,
634, 741, 779, 1321,
1322; also called 'The
Japanese Lady'

U.S.:	$ 8,500.00
Can.:	$10,000.00
U.K.:	£ 4,500.00

HN 355
Dolly
Style One
Designer: C. J. Noke
Height: 7 ¼", 18.4 cm
Colour: Blue
Issued: 1919-1938

U.S.:	$ 9,000.00
Can.:	$11,000.00
U.K.:	£ 5,000.00

HN 356
Sir Thomas Lovell
Designer: C. J. Noke
Height: 7 ¾", 19.7 cm
Colour: Brown and green
Issued: 1919-1936

U.S.:	$7,000.00
Can.:	$8,500.00
U.K.:	£3,750.00

HN 357
Dunce
Designer: C. J. Noke
Height: 10 ½", 26.7 cm
Colour: Light brown
Issued: 1919-1936
Varieties: HN 6, 310

U.S.:	
Can.:	Extremely rare
U.K.:	

HN 358
An Old King
Designer: C. J. Noke
Height: 9 ¾", 24.7 cm
Colour: Green, blue, red
            and gold
Issued: 1919-1938
Varieties: HN 623, 1801, 2134

U.S.:   One
Can.:   known
U.K.:   to exist

HN 359
Fisherwomen
Designer: C. J. Noke
Height: 11 ¾", 29.8 cm
Colour: Lavender, red
            and green
Issued: 1919-1938
Varieties: HN 80, 349, 631; also
            called 'Looking for the
            Boats' and 'Waiting for
            the Boats'

U.S.:
Can.:   Extremely rare
U.K.:

HN 360 not issued.

HN 361
Pretty Lady
Designer: H. Tittensor
Height: 9 ½", 24.1 cm
Colour: Turquoise
Issued: 1919-1938
Varieties: HN 69, 70, 302, 330,
            384, 565, 700, 763,
            783

U.S.: $3,500.00
Can.: $4,250.00
U.K.:   £2,000.00

HN 362
The Poke Bonnet
Designer: C. J. Noke
Height: 8 ¾", 22.2 cm
Colour: Green, yellow, red
Issued: 1919-1938
Varieties: HN 612, 765; also
            called 'A Lilac Shawl'
            HN 44, 44A; 'In
            Grandma's Days'
            HN 339, 340, 388, 442

U.S.: $4,500.00
Can.: $5,500.00
U.K.:   £2,500.00

HN 363
The Curtsey
Designer: E. W. Light
Height: 11", 27.9 cm
Colour: Lavender and peach
Issued: 1919-1936
Varieties: HN 57, 57B, 66A, 327,
            334, 371, 518, 547,
            629, 670

U.S.:   None
Can.:   known
U.K.:   to exist

HN 364
A Moorish Minstrel
Designer: C. J. Noke
Height: 13 ½", 34.3 cm
Colour: Blue, green and orange
Issued: 1920-1938
Varieties: HN 34, 415, 797

U.S.: $5,500.00
Can.: $6,500.00
U.K.:   £3,000.00

HN 365
Double Jester
Designer: C. J. Noke
Height: Unknown
Colour: Brown, green and
            purple
Issued: 1920-1938

U.S.:   Only
Can.:   two
U.K.:   known

HN 366
A Mandarin
Style Two
Designer: C. J. Noke
Height: 8 ¼" 21.0 cm
Colour: Yellow and blue
Issued: 1920-1938
Varieties: HN 455, 641

U.S.:   Only
Can.:   one
U.K.:   known

HN 367
A Jester
Style One
Designer: C. J. Noke
Height: 10", 25.4 cm
Colour: Green and red
Issued: 1920-1938
Varieties: HN 45, 71, 71A, 320,
             412, 426, 446, 552,
             616, 627, 1295, 1702,
             2016, 3922

U.S.:	$ 9,500.00
Can.:	$11,500.00
U.K.:	£ 5,000.00

HN 368
Tony Weller
Style One
Designer: C. J. Noke
Height: 10 ½", 26.7 cm
Colour: Green and brown
Issued: 1920-1938
Varieties: HN 346, 684

U.S.:	$2,750.00
Can.:	$3,250.00
U.K.:	£1,500.00

Photograph
Not
Available

HN 369
Cavalier
Style One
Designer: Unknown
Height: Unknown
Colour: Turquoise
Issued: 1920-1936

U.S.:	None
Can.:	known
U.K.:	to exist

Photograph
Not
Available

HN 370
Henry VIII
Style One
Designer: C. J. Noke
Height: Unknown
Colour: Brown, green
             and purple
Issued: 1920-1938
Varieties: HN 673

U.S.:	Only
Can.:	one
U.K.:	known

HN 371
The Curtsey
Designer: E. W. Light
Height: 11", 27.9 gm
Colour: Yellow
Issued: 1920-1936
Varieties: HN 57, 57B, 66A, 327,
             334, 363, 518, 547,
             629, 670

U.S.:	None
Can.:	known
U.K.:	to exist

HN 372
Spooks
Designer: C. J. Noke
Height: 7 ¼", 18.4 cm
Colour: Brown
Issued: 1920-1936
Varieties: HN 88, 89; also called
             'Double Spook'

U.S.:	$8,000.00
Can.:	$9,750.00
U.K.:	£4,500.00

HN 373
Boy on Crocodile
Designer: C. J. Noke
Height: 5", 12.7 cm
Length: 14 ½, 36.8 cm
Colour: Green-brown
Issued: 1920-1936
Varieties: Also known in flambé

U.S.:	Only
Can.:	two
U.K.:	known

Photograph
Not
Available

HN 374
Lady and Blackamoor
Style One
Designer: H. Tittensor
Height: Unknown
Colour: Blue and green
Issued: 1920-1936

U.S.:	Only
Can.:	one
U.K.:	known

HN 375
Lady and Blackamoor
Style Two
Designer: H. Tittensor
Height: 7 ¼", 18.4 cm
Colour: Purple and yellow
Issued: 1920-1936
Varieties: HN 377, 470

U.S.:	**Only**
Can.:	**one**
U.K.:	**known**

HN 376
A Geisha
Style One
Designer: H. Tittensor
Height: 10 ¾", 27.3 cm
Colour: Lilac and yellow
Issued: 1920-1936
Varieties: HN 354, 376A, 387,
            634, 741, 779, 1321,
            1322; also called
            'The Japanese Lady'

U.S.:	**$ 9,000.00**
Can:	**$11,000.00**
U.K.:	**£ 5,000.00**

HN 376A
A Geisha
Style One
Designer: H. Tittensor
Height: 10 ¾", 27.3 cm
Colour: Blue
Issued: 1920-1936
Varieties: HN 354, 376, 387,
            634, 741, 779, 1321,
            1322; also called
            'The Japanese Lady'

U.S.:	**$ 9,000.00**
Can:	**$11,000.00**
U.K.:	**£ 5,000.00**

HN 377
Lady and Blackamoor
Style Two
Designer: H. Tittensor
Height: 7 ¼", 18.4 cm
Colour: Pink and green
Issued: 1920-1936
Varieties: HN 375, 470

U.S.:	**None**
Can.:	**known**
U.K.:	**to exist**

HN 378
An Arab
Designer: C. J. Noke
Height: 16 ½", 41.9 cm
Colour: Green, brown and
            yellow
Issued: 1920-1938
Varieties: HN 33, 343; also called
            'The Moor' HN 1308,
            1366, 1425, 1657,
            2082, 3642, 3926

U.S.:	**$5,500.00**
Can.:	**$6,500.00**
U.K.:	**£3,000.00**

HN 379
Ellen Terry as Queen Catharine
Designer: C. J. Noke
Height: 12 ½", 31.7 cm
Colour: Purple and blue
Issued: 1920-1949

U.S.:	**$5,000.00**
Can.:	**$6,000.00**
U.K.:	**£2,700.00**

HN 380
A Gnome
Designer: H. Tittensor
Height: 6 ¼", 15.9 cm
Colour: Purple
Issued: 1920-1938
Varieties: HN 319, 381; also
            known in flambé

U.S.:	**None**
Can.:	**known**
U.K.:	**to exist**

A Titanian 4½" model is known to
exist.

HN 381
A Gnome
Designer: H. Tittensor
Height: 6 ¼", 15.9 cm
Colour: Green
Issued: 1920-1938
Varieties: HN 319, 380; also
            known in flambé

U.S.:	**Only**
Can.:	**one**
U.K.:	**known**

A Titanian 4½" model is known to
exist.

HN 382
A Mandarin
Style One
Designer:	C. J. Noke
Height:	10 ¼", 26.0 cm
Colour:	Green
Issued:	1920-1936
Varieties:	HN 84, 316, 318, 611, 746, 787, 791; also called 'Chinese Mandarin' and 'The Mikado'

U.S.:	$ 9,500.00
Can.:	$11,000.00
U.K.:	£ 5,000.00

HN 383
The Gainsborough Hat
Designer:	H. Tittensor
Height:	8 ¾", 22.2 cm
Colour:	Green stripes
Issued:	1920-1936
Varieties:	HN 46, 46A, 47, 329, 352, 453, 675, 705

U.S.:	None
Can.:	known
U.K.:	to exist

HN 384
Pretty Lady
Designer:	H. Tittensor
Height:	9 ½", 24.1 cm
Colour:	Red
Issued:	1920-1938
Varieties:	HN 69, 70, 302, 330, 361, 565, 700, 763, 783

U.S.:	$4,000.00
Can.:	$4,750.00
U.K.:	£2,150.00

HN 385
St. George
Style One
Designer:	S. Thorogood
Height:	16", 40.6 cm
Colour:	Grey, purple and gold
Issued:	1920-1938
Varieties:	HN 386, 1800, 2067

U.S.:	$ 8,000.00
Can.:	$10,000.00
U.K.:	£ 4,500.00

HN 386
St. George
Style One
Designer:	S. Thorogood
Height:	16", 40.6 cm
Colour:	Blue and white
Issued:	1920-1938
Varieties:	HN 385, 1800, 2067

U.S.:	$ 8,000.00
Can.:	$10,000.00
U.K.:	£ 4,500.00

HN 387
A Geisha
Style One
Designer:	H. Tittensor
Height:	10 ¾", 27.3 cm
Colour:	Blue and yellow
Issued:	1920-1936
Varieties:	HN 354, 376, 376A, 634, 741, 779, 1321, 1322; also called 'The Japanese Lady'

U.S.:	$ 8,000.00
Can.:	$10,000.00
U.K.:	£ 4,500.00

HN 388
In Grandma's Days
Designer:	C. J. Noke
Height:	8 ¾", 22.2 cm
Colour:	Blue
Issued:	1920-1938
Varieties:	HN 339, 340, 442; also called 'A Lilac Shawl 'HN 44, 44A; 'The Poke Bonnet' HN 362, 612, 765

U.S.:	None
Can.:	known
U.K.:	to exist

HN 389
Dolly
Style Two
Designer:	H. Tittensor
Height:	11", 27.9 cm
Colour:	Pink dress, blonde hair
Issued:	1920-1938
Varieties:	HN 390; also called 'The Little Mother' (Style One) HN 469

U.S.:	Only
Can.:	two
U.K.:	known

HN 390
Dolly
Style Two
Designer: H. Tittensor
Height: 11", 27.9 cm
Colour: Pink dress, brown hair
Issued: 1920-1938
Varieties: HN 389; also called
            'The Little Mother'
            (Style One) HN 469

U.S.:	Only
Can.:	one
U.K.:	known

HN 391
The Princess
Designer: L. Harradine
Height: 9 ¼", 23.5 cm
Colour: Green and purple
Issued: 1920-1936
Varieties: HN 392, 420, 430,
            431, 633

U.S.:	Only
Can.:	one
U.K.:	known

HN 392
The Princess
Designer: L. Harradine
Height: 9 ¼", 23.5 cm
Colour: Multicoloured
Issued: 1920-1936
Varieties: HN 391, 420, 430,
            431, 633

U.S.:	Only
Can.:	one
U.K.:	known

Photograph
Not
Available

HN 393
The Necklace
Designer: G. Lambert
Height: 9", 22.9 cm
Colour: Yellow, green and
            purple
Issued: 1920-1936
Varieties: HN 394

U.S.:	Only
Can.:	one
U.K.:	known

Photograph
Not
Available

HN 394
The Necklace
Designer: G. Lambert
Height: 9", 22.9 cm
Colour: Green and yellow
Issued: 1920-1936
Varieties: HN 393

U.S.:	
Can.:	Extremely rare
U.K.:	

HN 395
Contentment
Designer: L. Harradine
Height: 7 ¼", 18.4 cm
Colour: Yellow and lilac
Issued: 1920-1938
Varieties: HN 396, 421, 468, 572,
            685, 686, 1323

U.S.:	$4,500.00
Can.:	$5,500.00
U.K.:	£2,500.00

HN 396
Contentment
Designer: L. Harradine
Height: 7 ¼", 18.4 cm
Colour: Blue, yellow and pink
Issued: 1920-1938
Varieties: HN 395, 421, 468, 572,
            685, 686, 1323

U.S.:	$4,500.00
Can.:	$5,500.00
U.K.:	£2,500.00

HN 397
Puff and Powder
Designer: L. Harradine
Height: 6 ½", 16.5 cm
Colour: Yellow skirt, brown
            bodice
Issued: 1920-1936
Varieties: HN 398, 400, 432,
            433

U.S.:	$6,000.00
Can.:	$7,500.00
U.K.:	£3,300.00

HN 398
Puff and Powder
Designer: L. Harradine
Height: 6 ½", 16.5 cm
Colour: Lavender
Issued: 1920-1936
Varieties: HN 397, 400, 432, 433

U.S.:	**None**
Can.:	**known**
U.K.:	**to exist**

HN 399
Japanese Fan
Designer: H. Tittensor
Height: 4 ¾", 12.1 cm
Colour: Dark blue and yellow
Issued: 1920-1936
Varieties: HN 405, 439, 440; also known in flambé

U.S.:	**$5,500.00**
Can.:	**$6,500.00**
U.K.:	**£3,000.00**

Unpainted model illustrated.

HN 400
Puff and Powder
Designer: L. Harradine
Height: 6 ½", 16.5 cm
Colour: Green, blue and yellow
Issued: 1920-1936
Varieties: HN 397, 398, 432, 433

U.S.:	**None**
Can.:	**known**
U.K.:	**to exist**

HN 401
Marie
Style One
Designer: L. Harradine
Height: 7", 17.8 cm
Colour: Pink, cream and blue
Issued: 1920-1938
Varieties: HN 434, 502, 504, 505, 506

U.S.:	
Can.:	**Extremely rare**
U.K.:	

HN 402
Betty
Style One
Designer: L. Harradine
Height: 7 ½", 19.1 cm
Colour: Pink and black
Issued: 1920-1938
Varieties: HN 403, 435, 438, 477, 478

U.S.:	
Can.:	**Extremely rare**
U.K.:	

Unpainted model illustrated.

HN 403
Betty
Style One
Designer: L. Harradine
Height: 7 ½", 19.1 cm
Colour: Green, blue and yellow
Issued: 1920-1938
Varieties: HN 402, 435, 438, 477, 478

U.S.:	
Can.:	**Extremely rare**
U.K.:	

Unpainted model illustrated.

HN 404
King Charles
Designer: C. J. Noke and H. Tittensor
Height: 16 ¾", 42.5 cm
Colour: Black, pink base
Issued: 1920-1951
Varieties: HN 2084, 3459

U.S.:	**$5,000.00**
Can.:	**$6,000.00**
U.K.:	**£2,700.00**

HN 405
Japanese Fan
Designer: H. Tittensor
Height: 5", 12.7 cm
Colour: Light yellow
Issued: 1920-1936
Varieties: HN 399, 439, 440; also known in flambé

U.S.:	**None**
Can.:	**known**
U.K.:	**to exist**

Unpainted model illustrated.

HN 406
The Bouquet
Designer: G. Lambert
Height: 9", 22.9 cm
Colour: Yellow and blue
Issued: 1920-1936
Varieties: HN 414, 422, 428,
            429, 567, 794; also
            called 'The Nosegay'

U.S.:	$6,000.00
Can.:	$7,250.00
U.K.:	£3,250.00

HN 407
Omar Khayyam and the Beloved
(With base)
Style One
Designer: C. J. Noke
Height: 10", 25.4 cm
Colour: Purple and pink
Issued: 1920-Unknown

U.S.:	**Only**
Can.:	**one**
U.K.:	**known**

HN 408
Omar Khayyam
Style One
Designer: C. J. Noke
Height: 6", 15.2 cm
Colour: Blue, green and brown
Issued: 1920-1938
Varieties: HN 409

U.S.:	**Only**
Can.:	**one**
U.K.:	**known**

HN 409
Omar Khayyam
Style One
Designer: C. J. Noke
Height: 6", 15.2 cm
Colour: Black and yellow
Issued: 1920-1938
Varieties: HN 408

U.S.:	**Only**
Can.:	**one**
U.K.:	**known**

HN 410
Blue Beard
(Without plume on turban)
Style One
Designer: E. W. Light
Height: 11", 27.9 cm
Colour: Green and blue
Issued: 1920-1936
Varieties: HN 75

U.S.:	**$11,000.00**
Can.:	**$13,000.00**
U.K.:	£ 6,000.00

HN 411
A Lady of the Elizabethan Period
Style One
Designer: E. W. Light
Height: 9 ¾", 24.7 cm
Colour: Purple
Issued: 1920-1938
Varieties: HN 40, 40A, 73; also
            called 'Elizabethan Lady'

U.S.:	**$5,000.00**
Can.:	**$6,000.00**
U.K.:	**£2,700.00**

HN 412
A Jester
Style One
Designer: C. J. Noke
Height: 10", 25.4 cm
Colour: Green and red
Issued: 1920-1938
Varieties: HN 45, 71, 71A, 320,
            367, 426, 446, 552,
            616, 627, 1295, 1702,
            2016, 3922

U.S.:	
Can.:	**Extremely rare**
U.K.:	

HN 413
The Crinoline
Designer: G. Lambert
Height: 6 ¼" 15.8 cm
Colour: Light blue and lemon
Issued: 1920-1938
Varieties: HN 8, 9, 9A, 21, 21A,
            566, 628

U.S.:	**$4,000.00**
Can.:	**$4,750.00**
U.K.:	**£2,150.00**

HN 414
The Bouquet
Designer: G. Lambert
Height: 9", 22.9 cm
Colour: Pink and yellow
Issued: 1920-1936
Varieties: HN 406, 422, 428, 429, 567, 794; also called 'The Nosegay'

U.S.: None
Can.: known
U.K.: to exist

HN 415
A Moorish Minstrel
Designer: C. J. Noke
Height: 13 ½", 34.3 cm
Colour: Green and yellow
Issued: 1920-1938
Varieties: HN 34, 364, 797

U.S.: $5,500.00
Can.: $6,500.00
U.K.: £3,000.00

HN 416
Moorish Piper Minstrel
Designer: C. J. Noke
Height: 13 ½", 34.3 cm
Colour: Green and yellow stripes
Issued: 1920-1938
Varieties: HN 301, 328

U.S.: None
Can.: known
U.K.: to exist

HN 417
One of the Forty
Style One
Designer: H. Tittensor
Height: 8 ¼", 21.0 cm
Colour: Green and blue
Issued: 1920-1936
Varieties: HN 490, 495, 501, 528, 648, 677, 1351, 1352

U.S.: None
Can.: known
U.K.: to exist

HN 418
One of the Forty
Style Two
Designer: H. Tittensor
Height: 7 ¼", 18.4 cm
Colour: Striped green robes
Issued: 1920-1936
Varieties: HN 494, 498, 647, 666, 704, 1353

U.S.: None
Can.: known
U.K.: to exist

HN 419
Omar Khayyam and the Beloved
(Without base)
Style Two
Designer: C. J. Noke
Height: 10", 25.4 cm
Colour: Green and turquoise
Issued: 1920-1936
Varieties: HN 459, 598

U.S.: Only
Can.: two
U.K.: known

HN 420
The Princess
Designer: L. Harradine
Height: 9 ¼", 23.5 cm
Colour: Pink and green striped skirt, blue cape
Issued: 1920-1936
Varieties: HN 391, 392, 430, 431, 633

U.S.: Only
Can.: one
U.K.: known

HN 421
Contentment
Designer: L. Harradine
Height: 7 ¼", 18.4 cm
Colour: Light green
Issued: 1920-1938
Varieties: HN 395, 396, 468, 572, 685, 686, 1323

U.S.: $4,500.00
Can.: $5,500.00
U.K.: £2,500.00

HN 422
The Bouquet
Designer: G. Lambert
Height: 9", 22.9 cm
Colour: Yellow and pink
Issued: 1920-1936
Varieties: HN 406, 414, 428,
             429, 567, 794; also
             called 'The Nosegay'

U.S.:	**None**
Can.:	**known**
U.K.:	**to exist**

HN 423
One of the Forty
Style Three
Designer: H. Tittensor
Height: 3", 7.6 cm
Colour: Varied
Issued: 1921-1936

U.S.:	**$1,650.00**
Can.:	**$2,000.00**
U.K.:	**£ 900.00**

HN 423A
One of the Forty
Style Four
Designer: H. Tittensor
Height: 2 ¾", 6.9 cm
Colour: Varied
Issued: 1921-1936

U.S.:	**$1,650.00**
Can.:	**$2,000.00**
U.K.:	**£ 900.00**

HN 423B
One of the Forty
Style Five
Designer: H. Tittensor
Height: 2 ¾", 6.9 cm
Colour: Varied
Issued: 1921-1936

U.S.:	**$1,650.00**
Can.:	**$2,000.00**
U.K.:	**£ 900.00**

HN 423C
One of the Forty
Style Six
Designer: H. Tittensor
Height: 2 ¾", 6.9 cm
Colour: Varied
Issued: 1921-1936

U.S.:	**$1,650.00**
Can.:	**$2,000.00**
U.K.:	**£ 900.00**

HN 423D
One of the Forty
Style Seven
Designer: H. Tittensor
Height: 2 ¾", 6.9 cm
Colour: Varied
Issued: 1921-1936

U.S.:	**$1,650.00**
Can.:	**$2,000.00**
U.K.:	**£ 900.00**

Also known in all-white.

HN 423E
One of the Forty
Style Eight
Designer: H. Tittensor
Height: 2 ¾", 6.9 cm
Colour: Varied
Issued: 1921-1936

U.S.:	**$1,650.00**
Can.:	**$2,000.00**
U.K.:	**£ 900.00**

HN 423F
One of the Forty
Style Nine
Designer: H. Tittensor
Height: 2 ¾", 6.9 cm
Colour: Olive green and yellow
Issued: 1921-1938

U.S.:	**$1,650.00**
Can.:	**$2,000.00**
U.K.:	**£ 900.00**

HN 424
Sleep
Designer: P. Stabler
Height: 6", 15.2 cm
Colour: Blue
Issued: 1921-1936
Varieties: HN 24, 24A, 25, 25A,
692, 710

U.S.:	$3,500.00
Can.:	$4,250.00
U.K.:	£1,950.00

HN 425
The Goosegirl
Style One
Designer: L. Harradine
Height: 8", 20.3 cm
Colour: Blue
Issued: 1921-1936
Varieties: HN 436, 437, 448,
559, 560

U.S.:	None
Can.:	known
U.K.:	to exist

HN 426
A Jester
Style One
Designer: C. J. Noke
Height: 10", 25.4 cm
Colour: Pink and black
Issued: 1921-1938
Varieties: HN 45, 71, 71A, 320,
367, 412, 446, 552,
616, 627, 1295, 1702,
2016, 3922

U.S.:	$ 9,500.00
Can.:	$11,000.00
U.K.:	£ 5,000.00

Photograph
Not
Available

HN 427
One of the Forty
Style Ten
Designer: H. Tittensor
Height: Unknown
Colour: Green
Issued: 1921-1936

U.S.:	
Can.:	**Extremely rare**
U.K.:	

HN 428
The Bouquet
Designer: G. Lambert
Height: 9", 22.9 cm
Colour: Blue and green
Issued: 1921-1936
Varieties: HN 406, 414, 422, 429,
567, 794; also called
'The Nosegay'

U.S.:	$6,500.00
Can.:	$7,750.00
U.K.:	£3,500.00

HN 429
The Bouquet
Designer: G. Lambert
Height: 9", 22.9 cm
Colour: Green and red
Issued: 1921-1936
Varieties: HN 406, 414, 422, 428,
567, 794; also called
'The Nosegay'

U.S.:	$6,500.00
Can.:	$7,750.00
U.K.:	£3,500.00

HN 430
The Princess
Designer: L. Harradine
Height: 9 ¼", 23.5 cm
Colour: Green
Issued: 1921-1936
Varieties: HN 391, 392, 402,
431, 633

U.S.:	Only
Can.:	one
U.K.:	known

HN 431
The Princess
Designer: L. Harradine
Height: 9 ¼", 23.5 cm
Colour: Yellow and white
Issued: 1921-1936
Varieties: HN 391, 392, 420,
430, 633

U.S.:	Only
Can.:	one
U.K.:	known

HN 432
Puff and Powder
Designer: L. Harradine
Height: 6 ½", 16.5 cm
Colour: Lavender and orange
Issued: 1921-1936
Varieties: HN 397, 398, 400, 433

U.S.:	None
Can.:	known
U.K.:	to exist

HN 433
Puff and Powder
Designer: L. Harradine
Height: 6 ½", 16.5 cm
Colour: Lilac and green
Issued: 1921-1936
Varieties: HN 397, 398, 400, 432

U.S.:	$6,000.00
Can.:	$7,500.00
U.K.:	£3,300.00

Photograph
Not
Available

HN 434
Marie
Style One
Designer: L. Harradine
Height: 7", 17.8 cm
Colour: Yellow and orange
Issued: 1921-1938
Varieties: HN 401, 502, 504,
            505, 506

U.S.:	None
Can.:	known
U.K.:	to exist

HN 435
Betty
Style One
Designer: L. Harradine
Height: 7 ½", 19.1 cm
Colour: Blue and yellow
Issued: 1921-1938
Varieties: HN 402, 403, 438,
            477, 478

U.S.:	None
Can.:	known
U.K.:	to exist

Unpainted model illustrated.

HN 436
The Goosegirl
Style One
Designer: L. Harradine
Height: 8", 20.3 cm
Colour: Green and blue
Issued: 1921-1936
Varieties: HN 425, 437, 448,
            559, 560

U.S.:	$6,500.00
Can.:	$7,750.00
U.K.:	£3,500.00

HN 437
The Goosegirl
Style One
Designer: L. Harradine
Height: 8", 20.3 cm
Colour: Brown and blue
Issued: 1921-1936
Varieties: HN 425, 436, 448,
            559, 560

U.S.:	$6,500.00
Can.:	$7,750.00
U.K.:	£3,500.00

HN 438
Betty
Style One
Designer: L. Harradine
Height: 7 ½", 19.1 cm
Colour: Blue and cream
Issued: 1921-1938
Varieties: HN 402, 403, 435,
            477, 478

U.S.:	Only
Can.:	one
U.K.:	known

Unpainted model illustrated.

HN 439
Japanese Fan
Designer: H. Tittensor
Height: 4 ¾", 12.1 cm
Colour: Blue with green spots
Issued: 1921-1936
Varieties: HN 399, 405, 440;
            also known in flambé

U.S.:	None
Can.:	known
U.K.:	to exist

Unpainted model illustrated.

HN 440
Japanese Fan
Designer: H. Tittensor
Height: 4 ¾", 12.1 cm
Colour: Cream and orange
Issued: 1921-1936
Varieties: HN 399, 405, 439;
also known in flambé

U.S.:	**$5,500.00**
Can.:	**$6,500.00**
U.K.:	**£3,000.00**

Unpainted model illustrated.

HN 441
The Parson's Daughter
Designer: H. Tittensor
Height: 10", 25.4 cm
Colour: Yellow and orange
Issued: 1921-1938
Varieties: HN 337, 338, 564, 790,
1242, 1356, 2018

U.S.:	**$3,000.00**
Can.:	**$3,600.00**
U.K.:	**£1,600.00**

HN 442
In Grandma's Days
Designer: C. J. Noke
Height: 8 ¾", 22.2 cm
Colour: White and green
Issued: 1921-1938
Varieties: HN 339, 340, 388; also
called 'A Lilac Shawl'
HN 44, 44A; 'The Poke
Bonnet' HN 362, 612,
765

U.S.:	**None**
Can.:	**known**
U.K.:	**to exist**

HN 443
Out For a Walk
Designer: E. W. Light
Height: 10", 25.4 cm
Colour: Brown check
Issued: 1921-1936
Varieties: HN 86, 748

U.S.:	**None**
Can.:	**known**
U.K.:	**to exist**

HN 444
A Lady of the Georgian Period
Designer: E. W. Light
Height: 10 ¼", 26.0 cm
Colour: Blue-green spotted
dress
Issued: 1921-1936
Varieties: HN 41, 331, 690, 702

U.S.:	**None**
Can.:	**known**
U.K.:	**to exist**

HN 445
Guy Fawkes
Style One
Designer: C. J. Noke
Height: 10 ½", 26.7 cm
Colour: Green cloak
Issued: 1921-1938
Varieties: HN 98, 347; also
known in Sung

U.S.:	
Can.:	**Extremely rare**
U.K.:	

HN 446
A Jester
Style One
Designer: C. J. Noke
Height: 10", 25.4 cm
Colour: Black, green, and blue
Issued: 1921-1938
Varieties: HN 45, 71, 71A, 320,
367, 412, 426, 552,
616, 627, 1295, 1702,
2016, 3922

U.S.:	**$ 9,000.00**
Can.:	**$11,000.00**
U.K.:	**£ 5,000.00**

HN 447
Lady with Shawl
Designer: L. Harradine
Height: 13 ¼", 33.7 cm
Colour: Green and cream
striped dress
Issued: 1921-1936
Varieties: HN 458, 626, 678, 679

U.S.:	**$ 8,500.00**
Can.:	**$10,000.00**
U.K.:	**£ 4,600.00**

HN 448
The Goosegirl
Style One
Designer: L. Harradine
Height: 8", 20.3 cm
Colour: Blue
Issued: 1921-1936
Varieties: HN 425, 436, 437,
             559, 560

U.S.:   **None**
Can.:   **known**
U.K.:   **to exist**

HN 449
Fruit Gathering
Designer: L. Harradine
Height: 7 ¾", 19.7 cm
Colour: Blue
Issued: 1921-1936
Varieties: HN 476, 503, 561,
             562, 706, 707

U.S.:   **None**
Can.:   **known**
U.K.:   **to exist**

Photograph
Not
Available

HN 450
Chu Chin Chow
Style One
Designer: C. J. Noke
Height: 6 ½", 16.5 cm
Colour: Red coat and green cap
Issued: 1921-1936
Varieties: HN 460, 461

U.S.:
Can.:   **Extremely rare**
U.K.:

HN 451
An Old Man
Designer: Unknown
Height: 3", 7.5 cm
Colour: Blue, green and red
Issued: 1921-1938

U.S.:   **Only**
Can.:   **Two**
U.K.:   **known**

HN 452 not issued.

HN 453
The Gainsborough Hat
Designer: H. Tittensor
Height: 8 ¾", 22.2 cm
Colour: Red, blue and green
Issued: 1921-1936
Varieties: HN 46, 46A, 47, 329,
             352, 383, 675, 705

U.S.:   **None**
Can.:   **known**
U.K.:   **to exist**

HN 454
The Smiling Buddha
Designer: C. J. Noke
Height: 6 ¼", 15.9 cm
Colour: Green-blue
Issued: 1921-1936
Varieties: Also known in flambé
             and Sung

U.S.:   **$7,500.00**
Can.:   **$9,000.00**
U.K.:   **£4,000.00**

HN 455
A Mandarin
Style Two
Designer: C. J. Noke
Height: 8 ¼", 21.0 cm
Colour: Green
Issued: 1921-1938
Varieties: HN 366, 641

U.S.:   **None**
Can.:   **known**
U.K.:   **to exist**

HN 456
Myfanwy Jones
Designer: E. W. Light
Height: 12", 30.5 cm
Colour: Green and brown
Issued: 1921-1936
Varieties: HN 39, 92, 514, 516,
             519, 520, 660, 668,
             669, 701, 792; also
             called 'The Welsh Girl'

U.S: **$ 9,000.00**
Can.:   **$11,000.00**
U.K.:   **£ 5,000.00**

HN 457
Crouching Nude
Designer: Unknown
Height: 5 ½", 14.0 cm
Colour: Cream, green base
Issued: 1921-1936

U.S.:	**$5,500.00**
Can.:	**$6,500.00**
U.K.:	**£3,000.00**

HN 458
Lady with Shawl
Designer: L. Harradine
Height: 13 ¼", 33.7 cm
Colour: Pink
Issued: 1921-1936
Varieties: HN 447, 626, 678, 679

U.S.:	**None**
Can.:	**known**
U.K.:	**to exist**

HN 459
Omar Khayyam and the Beloved
(Without base)
Style Two
Designer: C. J. Noke
Height: 10", 25.4 cm
Colour: Purple, green, orange
and blue
Issued: 1921-1936
Varieties: HN 419, 598

U.S.:	
Can.:	**Extremely rare**
U.K.:	

Photograph
Not
Available

HN 460
Chu Chow Chin
Style One
Designer: C. J. Noke
Height: 6 ½", 16.5 cm
Colour: Blue and green
Issued: 1921-1936
Varieties: HN 450, 461

U.S.:	**Only**
Can.:	**one**
U.K.:	**known**

Photograph
Not
Available

HN 461
Chu Chow Chin
Style One
Designer: C. J. Noke
Height: 6 ½", 16.5 cm
Colour: Red
Issued: 1921-1936
Varieties: HN 450, 460

U.S.:	**Only**
Can.:	**one**
U.K.:	**known**

HN 462
Motherhood
Style Two
Designer: Unknown
Height: 9 ¼", 23.5 cm
Colour: Green and white
Issued: 1921-1938
Varieties: HN 570, 703, 743

U.S.:	**$ 9,000.00**
Can.:	**$11,000.00**
U.K.:	**£ 5,000.00**

HN 463
Polly Peachum
Style One
Designer: L. Harradine
Height: 6 ¼", 15.9 cm
Colour: Pale blue
Issued: 1921-1949
Varieties: HN 465, 550, 589,
614, 680, 693
Series: Beggar's Opera

U.S.:	**$1,500.00**
Can.:	**$1,750.00**
U.K.:	**£ 800.00**

HN 464
Captain MacHeath
Designer: L. Harradine
Height: 7", 17.8 cm
Colour: Red, yellow and black
Issued: 1921-1949
Varieties: HN 590, 1256
Series: Beggar's Opera

U.S.:	**$1,650.00**
Can.:	**$2,000.00**
U.K.:	**£ 900.00**

HN 465
Polly Peachum
Style One
Designer: L. Harradine
Height: 6 ¼", 15.9 cm
Colour: Red
Issued: 1921-1949
Varieties: HN 463, 550, 589,
            614, 680, 693
Series: Beggar's Opera

U.S.:	**$1,600.00**
Can.:	**$2,000.00**
U.K.:	**£ 900.00**

HN 466
Tulips
Designer: Unknown
Height: 9 ½", 24.1 cm
Colour: Green
Issued: 1921-1936
Varieties: HN 488, 672, 747,
            1334

U.S.:	**None**
Can.:	**known**
U.K.:	**to exist**

HN 467
Doris Keene as Cavallini
Style One
Designer: C. J. Noke
Height: 11", 27.9 cm
Colour: Dark green with
            gold jewellery
Issued: 1921-1936
Varieties: HN 90

U.S.:	
Can.:	**Extremely rare**
U.K.:	

HN 468
Contentment
Designer: L. Harradine
Height: 7 ¼", 18.4 cm
Colour: Green spotted dress
Issued: 1921-1938
Varieties: HN 395, 396, 421, 572,
            685, 686, 1323

U.S.:	**$5,000.00**
Can.:	**$6,000.00**
U.K.:	**£2,750.00**

HN 469
Little Mother
Style One
Designer: H. Tittensor
Height: 11", 27.9 cm
Colour: White
Issued: 1921-1938
Varieties: Also called 'Dolly'
            (Style Two) HN 389,
            390

U.S.:	**Only**
Can.:	**one**
U.K.:	**known**

HN 470
Lady and Blackamoor
Style Two
Designer: H. Tittensor
Height: 7 ¼", 18.4 cm
Colour: Green patterned dress
            lilac bodice; boy with
            red turban and blue
            coat
Issued: 1921-1936
Varieties: HN 375, 377

U.S.:	**Only**
Can.:	**one**
U.K.:	**known**

HN 471
Katharine
Style One
Designer: C. J. Noke
Height: 5 ¾", 14.6 cm
Colour: Patterned green dress
Issued: 1921-1938
Varieties: HN 61, 74, 341, 615,
            793

U.S.:	**$3,750.00**
Can.:	**$4,500.00**
U.K.:	**£2,000.00**

HN 472
Spring
Style One
Designer: Unknown
Colour: Patterned lavender
            robe
Height: 7 ½", 19.1 cm
Issued: 1921-1938
Varieties: HN 312
Series: The Seasons
            (Series One)

U.S:	**$3,000.00**
Can.:	**$3,500.00**
U.K.:	**£1,600.00**

HN 473
Summer
Style One
Designer: Unknown
Height: 7 ½", 19.1 cm
Colour: Patterned light green
            robes
Issued: 1921-1938
Varieties: HN 313
Series: The Seasons
            (Series One)

U.S.:   **None**
Can.:   **known**
U.K.:   **to exist**

HN 474
Autumn
Style One
Designer: Unknown
Height: 7 ½", 19.1 cm
Colour: Patterned pink robes
Issued: 1921-1938
Varieties: HN 314
Series: The Seasons
            (Series One)

U.S.:   **None**
Can.:   **known**
U.K.:   **to exist**

HN 475
Winter
Style One
Designer: Unknown
Height: 7 ½", 19.1 cm
Colour: Patterned pale green
            robes
Issued: 1921-1938
Varieties: HN 315
Series: The Seasons
            (Series One)

U.S.:   **None**
Can.:   **known**
U.K.:   **to exist**

HN 476
Fruit Gathering
Designer: L. Harradine
Height: 8" 20.3 cm
Colour: Lavender and yellow
Issued: 1921-1936
Varieties: HN 449, 503, 561,
            562, 706, 707

U.S.:   **$5,000.00**
Can.:   **$6,000.00**
U.K.:   **£2,750.00**

HN 477
Betty
Style One
Designer: L. Harradine
Height: 7 ½", 19.1 cm
Colour: Green
Issued: 1921-1938
Varieties: HN 402, 403, 435,
            438, 478

U.S.:   **Only**
Can.:   **one**
U.K.:   **known**

HN 478
Betty
Style One
Designer: L. Harradine
Height: 7 ½", 19.1 cm
Colour: White
Issued: 1921-1938
Varieties: HN 402, 403, 435,
            438, 477

U.S.:
Can.:   **Extremely rare**
U.K.:

HN 479
The Balloon Seller
Style One
Designer: L. Harradine
Height: 9", 22.9 cm
Colour: Dark blue and lavender
Issued: 1921-1938
Varieties: HN 486, 548, 583,
            697; also called 'The
            Balloon Woman'

U.S.:   **$5,000.00**
Can.:   **$6,000.00**
U.K.:   **£2,750.00**

HN 480
One of the Forty
Style Eleven
Designer: H. Tittensor
Height: 7", 17.8 cm
Colour: Brown, yellow and blue
Issued: 1921-1938
Varieties: HN 493, 497, 499,
            664, 714

U.S.:   **$6,750.00**
Can.:   **$8,000.00**
U.K.:   **£3,600.00**

Unpainted model illustrated.

Unpainted model illustrated.

HN 481
One of the Forty
Style Twelve
Designer: H. Tittensor
Height: Unknown
Colour: Dark colour
Issued: 1921-1936
Varieties: HN 483, 491, 646,
            667, 712, 1336, 1350;
            also known in flambé

U.S.:	**None**
Can.:	**known**
U.K.:	**to exist**

Photograph
Not
Available

HN 482
One of the Forty
Style Thirteen
Designer: H. Tittensor
Height: 6", 15.2 cm
Colour: White
Issued: 1921-1938
Varieties: HN 484, 492, 645,
            663, 713

U.S.:	**None**
Can.:	**known**
U.K.:	**to exist**

HN 483
One of the Forty
Style Twelve
Designer: H. Tittensor
Height: Unknown
Colour: Brown and green
Issued: 1921-1938
Varieties: HN 481, 491, 646, 667,
            712, 1336, 1350; also
            known in flambé

U.S.:	**None**
Can.:	**known**
U.K.:	**to exist**

Photograph
Not
Available

HN 484
One of the Forty
Style Thirteen
Designer: H. Tittensor
Height: 6", 15.2 cm
Colour: Green
Issued: 1921-1938
Varieties: HN 482, 492, 645,
            663, 713

U.S.:	**None**
Can.:	**known**
U.K.:	**to exist**

Photograph
Not
Available

HN 485
Lucy Lockett
Style One
Designer: L. Harradine
Height: 6", 15.2 cm
Colour: Green
Issued: 1921-1949
Series: Beggar's Opera

U.S.:	**$2,750.00**
Can.:	**$3,500.00**
U.K.:	**£1,500.00**

HN 486
The Balloon Seller
Style One
Designer: L. Harradine
Height: 9", 22.9 cm
Colour: Blue dress, no hat
Issued: 1921-1938
Varieties: HN 479, 548, 583, 697;
            also called 'The Balloon
            Woman'

U.S.:	**None**
Can.:	**known**
U.K.:	**to exist**

HN 487
Pavlova
Designer: C. J. Noke
Height: 4 ¼", 10.8 cm
Colour: White tutu, black base
Issued: 1921-1938
Varieties: HN 676; also called
            'Swan Song'

U.S.:	**Only**
Can.:	**two**
U.K.:	**known**

HN 488
Tulips
Designer: Unknown
Height: 9 ½", 24.1 cm
Colour: Cream
Issued: 1921-1936
Varieties: HN 466, 672, 747,
            1334

U.S.:	**None**
Can.:	**known**
U.K.:	**to exist**

Photograph
Not
Available

HN 489
Polly Peachum
Style Two
Designer: L. Harradine
Height: 4 ¼", 10.8 cm
Colour: Turquoise
Issued: 1921-1938
Varieties: HN 549, 620, 694, 734
Series: Beggar's Opera
  U.S.:   **$1,400.00**
  Can.:   **$1,675.00**
  U.K.:   **£   750.00**

HN 490
One of the Forty
Style One
Dsigner: H. Tittensor
Height: 8 ¼", 21.0 cm
Colour: Blue and brown
Issued: 1921-1938
Varieties: HN 417, 495, 501, 528,
            648, 677, 1351, 1352
  U.S.:   **None**
  Can.:   **known**
  U.K.:   **to exist**

HN 491
One of the Forty
Style Twelve
Designer: H. Tittensor
Height: Unknown
Colour: Green and white
Issued: 1921-1936
Varieties: HN 481, 483, 646,
            667, 712, 1336, 1350;
            also known in flambé
  U.S.:   **None**
  Can.:   **known**
  U.K.:   **to exist**

HN 492
One of the Forty
Style Thirteen
Designer: H. Tittensor
Height: 6", 15.2 cm
Colour: Yellow and white
Issued: 1921-1938
Varieties: HN 482, 484, 645,
            663, 713
  U.S.:   **None**
  Can.:   **known**
  U.K.:   **to exist**

Photograph
Not
Available

HN 493
One of the Forty
Style Eleven
Designer: H. Tittensor
Height: 6 ¾", 17.1 cm
Colour: Blue and black
Issued: 1921-1938
Varieties: HN 480, 497, 499,
            664, 714
  U.S.:   **None**
  Can.:   **known**
  U.K.:   **to exist**

HN 494
One of the Forty
Style Two
Designer: H. Tittensor
Height: 7 ¼", 18.4 cm
Colour: Cream and blue
Issued: 1921-1936
Varieties: HN 418, 498, 647, 666,
            704, 1353
  U.S.:   **None**
  Can.:   **known**
  U.K.:   **to exist**

HN 495
One of the Forty
Style One
Designer: H. Tittensor
Height: 8 ¼", 21.0 cm
Colour: Brown and blue
Issued: 1921-1938
Varieties: HN 417, 490, 501, 528,
            648, 677, 1351, 1352
  U.S.:   **None**
  Can.:   **known**
  U.K.:   **to exist**

HN 496
One of the Forty
Style Fourteen
Designer: H. Tittensor
Height: 7 ¾", 19.6 cm
Colour: Orange and yellow
            checks
Issued: 1921-1938
Varieties: HN 500, 649, 665,
            1354
  U.S.:   **None**
  Can.:   **known**
  U.K.:   **to exist**

HN 497
One of the Forty
Style Eleven
Designer: H. Tittensor
Height: 6 ¾", 17.1 cm
Colour: Brown and green
Issued: 1921-1938
Varieties: HN 480, 493, 499,
             664, 714

U.S.:	
Can.:	**Extremely rare**
U.K.:	

HN 498
One of the Forty
Style Two
Designer: H. Tittensor
Height: 7 ¼", 18.4 cm
Colour: Dark colours
Issued: 1921-1936
Varieties: HN 418, 494, 647, 666,
             704, 1353

U.S.:	**None**
Can.:	**known**
U.K.:	**to exist**

HN 499
One of the Forty
Style Eleven
Designer: H. Tittensor
Height: 6 ¾", 17.1 cm
Colour: Cream and green
Issued: 1921-1938
Varieties: HN 480, 493, 497,
             664, 714

U.S.:	**None**
Can.:	**known**
U.K.:	**to exist**

Photograph
Not
Available

HN 500
One of the Forty
Style Fourteen
Designer: H. Tittensor
Height: 7 ¾", 19.6 cm
Colour: Orange checks and
             red turban
Issued: 1921-1938
Varieties: HN 496, 649, 665, 1354

U.S.:	**None**
Can.:	**known**
U.K.:	**to exist**

HN 501
One of the Forty
Style One
Designer: H. Tittensor
Height: 8 ¼", 21.0 cm
Colour: Green stripes
Issued: 1921-1938
Varieties: HN 417, 490, 495, 528,
             648, 677, 1351, 1352

U.S.:	**None**
Can.:	**known**
U.K.:	**to exist**

Photograph
Not
Available

HN 502
Marie
Style One
Designer: L. Harradine
Height: 7", 17.8 cm
Colour: White, red and blue
Issued: 1921-1938
Varieties: HN 401, 434, 504,
             505, 506

U.S.:	**None**
Can.:	**known**
U.K.:	**to exist**

HN 503
Fruit Gathering
Designer: L. Harradine
Height: 7 ¾", 19.7 cm
Colour: Brown and blue
Issued: 1921-1936
Varieties: HN 449, 476, 561,
             562, 706, 707

U.S.:	**$5,000.00**
Can.:	**$6,000.00**
U.K.:	**£2,750.00**

Photograph
Not
Available

HN 504
Marie
Style One
Designer: L. Harradine
Height: 7", 17.8 cm
Colour: Green, blue and red
Issued: 1921-1938
Varieties: HN 401, 434, 502,
             505, 506

U.S.:	**None**
Can.:	**known**
U.K.:	**to exist**

Photograph
Not
Available

HN 505
Marie
Style One
Designer: L. Harradine
Height: 7", 17.8 cm
Colour: Blue bodice, green
            and lavender skirt
Issued: 1921-1938
Varieties: HN 401, 434, 502,
            504, 506

U.S.:	None
Can.:	known
U.K.:	to exist

Photograph
Not
Available

HN 506
Marie
Style One
Designer: L. Harradine
Height: 7", 17.8 cm
Colour: Blue and green bodice,
            lavender skirt
Issued: 1921-1938
Varieties: HN 401, 434, 502,
            504, 505

U.S.:	None
Can.:	known
U.K.:	to exist

HN 507
Pussy
Designer: F. C. Stone
Height: 7 ½", 19.1 cm
Colour: Spotted blue dress
Issued: 1921-1938
Varieties: HN 18, 325; also called
            'The Black Cat'

U.S.:	None
Can.:	known
U.K.:	to exist

HN 508
An Orange Vendor
Designer: C. J. Noke
Height: 6 ¼", 15.9 cm
Colour: Red, cream and orange
Issued: 1921-1938
Varieties: HN 72, 521, 1966

U.S.:	$4,000.00
Can.:	$4,750.00
U.K.:	£2,150.00

HN 509
Lady of the Fan
Designer: E. W. Light
Height: 9 ½", 24.1 cm
Colour: Green and lavender
Issued: 1921-1936
Varieties: HN 48, 52, 53, 53A,
            335

U.S.:	None
Can.:	known
U.K.:	to exist

HN 510
A Child's Grace
Designer: L. Perugini
Height: 9 ¼", 23.5 cm
Colour: Green and yellow
Issued: 1921-1938
Varieties: HN 62, 62A

U.S.:	None
Can.:	known
U.K.:	to exist

HN 511
Upon Her Cheeks She Wept
Designer: L. Perugini
Height: 9", 22.8 cm
Colour: Lavender
Issued: 1921-1938
Varieties: HN 59, 522

U.S.:	None
Can.:	known
U.K.:	to exist

HN 512
A Spook
Style Two
Designer: H. Tittensor
Height: 7", 17.8 cm
Colour: Purple
Issued: 1921-1936
Varieties: HN 50, 51, 51A, 51B,
            58, 625; also known in
            flambé

U.S.:	
Can.:	Extremely rare
U.K.:	

HN 513
Picardy Peasant (woman)
Designer: P. Stabler
Height: 9 ½", 24.0 cm
Colour: Blue
Issued: 1921-1938
Varieties: HN 4, 5, 17A, 351

U.S.: None
Can.: known
U.K.: to exist

HN 514
Myfanwy Jones
Designer: E. W. Light
Height: 12", 30.5 cm
Colour: Green and red
Issued: 1921-1936
Varieties: HN 39, 92, 456, 516, 519, 520, 660, 668, 669, 701, 792; also called 'The Welsh Girl'

U.S.: None
Can.: known
U.K.: to exist

HN 515
Lady with Rose
Designer: E. W. Light
Height: 9 ½", 24.1 cm
Colour: Lavender, green
Issued: 1921-1936
Varieties: HN 48A, 52A, 68, 304, 336, 517, 584, 624

U.S.: None
Can.: known
U.K.: to exist

HN 516
Myfanwy Jones
Designer: E. W. Light
Height: 12", 30.5 cm
Colour: Black and lavender
Issued: 1921-1936
Varieties: HN 39, 92, 456, 514, 519, 520, 660, 668, 669, 701, 792; also called 'The Welsh Girl'

U.S.: None
Can.: known
U.K.: to exist

HN 517
Lady with Rose
Designer: E. W. Light
Height: 9 ½", 24.1 cm
Colour: Lavender with orange spots
Issued: 1921-1936
Varieties: HN 48A, 52A, 68, 304, 336, 515, 584, 624

U.S.: None
Can.: known
U.K.: to exist

HN 518
The Curtsey
Designer: E. W. Light
Height: 11", 27.9 cm
Colour: Lavender
Issued: 1921-1936
Varieties: HN 57, 57B, 66A, 327, 334, 363, 371, 547, 629, 670

U.S.: None
Can.: known
U.K.: to exist

HN 519
Myfanwy Jones
Designer: E. W. Light
Height: 12", 30.5 cm
Colour: Blue and lavender
Issued: 1921-1936
Varieties: HN 39, 92, 456, 514, 516, 520, 660, 668, 669, 701, 792; also called 'The Welsh Girl'

U.S.: None
Can.: known
U.K.: to exist

HN 520
Myfanwy Jones
Designer: E. W. Light
Height: 12", 30.5 cm
Colour: Black and lavender
Issued: 1921-1936
Varieties: HN 39, 92, 456, 514, 516, 519, 660, 668, 669, 701, 792; also called 'The Welsh Girl'

U.S.: None
Can.: known
U.K.: to exist

HN 521
An Orange Vendor
Designer: C. J. Noke
Height: 6 ¼", 15.9 cm
Colour: Pale blue, black
             and purple
Issued: 1921-1938
Varieties: HN 72, 508, 1966

U.S.:	**None**
Can.:	**known**
U.K.:	**to exist**

HN 522
Upon Her Cheeks She Wept
Designer: L. Perugini
Height: 9", 22.8 cm
Colour: Lavender
Issued: 1921-1938
Varieties: HN 59, 511

U.S.:	**None**
Can.:	**known**
U.K.:	**to exist**

HN 523
Sentinel
Designer: Unknown
Height: 17 ½", 44.4 cm
Colour: Red, blue and black
Issued: 1921-1938

U.S.:	**Only**
Can.:	**three**
U.K.:	**known**

HN 524
Lucy Lockett
Style Two
Designer: L. Harradine
Height: 6", 15.2 cm
Colour: Orange
Issued: 1921-1949
Varieties: Earthenware and China
Series: Beggar's Opera

U.S.:	**$1,100.00**
Can.:	**$1,325.00**
U.K.:	**£ 600.00**

HN 525
The Flower Seller's Children
Designer: L. Harradine
Height: 8 ¼", 21.0 cm
Colour: Green and blue
Issued: 1921-1949
Varieties: HN 551, 1206, 1342,
             1406

U.S.:	**None**
Can.:	**known**
U.K.:	**to exist**

HN 526
The Beggar
Style One
Designer: L. Harradine
Height: 6 ½", 16.5 cm
Colour: Green and blue
Issued: 1921-1949
Varieties: HN 591
Series: Beggar's Opera

U.S.:	**$1,400.00**
Can.:	**$1,700.00**
U.K.:	**£ 775.00**

HN 527
The Highwayman
Designer: L. Harradine
Height: 6 ½", 16.5 cm
Colour: Green and red
Issued: 1921-1949
Varieties: HN 592, 1257
Series: Beggar's Opera

U.S.:	**$1,400.00**
Can.:	**$1,700.00**
U.K.:	**£ 775.00**

HN 528
One of the Forty
Style One
Designer: H. Tittensor
Height: 8 ¼", 21.0 cm
Colour: Brown
Issued: 1921-1938
Varieties: HN 417, 490, 495, 501,
             648, 677, 1351, 1352

U.S.:	**None**
Can.:	**known**
U.K.:	**to exist**

HN 529
Mr. Pickwick
Style One
Designer: L. Harradine
Height: 3 ¾", 9.5 cm
Colour: Black and tan
Issued: 1922-1932
Varieties: M41
Series: Dickens (Series One)

U.S.:	**$125.00**
Can.:	**$150.00**
U.K.:	**£ 70.00**

HN 530
Fat Boy
Style One
Designer: L. Harradine
Height: 3 ½", 8.9 cm
Colour: Blue and white
Issued: 1922-1932
Varieties: M44
Series: Dickens (Series One)

U.S.:	**$140.00**
Can.:	**$170.00**
U.K.:	**£ 75.00**

HN 531
Sam Weller
Designer: L. Harradine
Height: 4", 10.1 cm
Colour: Yellow and brown
Issued: 1922-1932
Varieties: M48
Series: Dickens (Series One)

U.S.:	**$140.00**
Can.:	**$170.00**
U.K.:	**£ 75.00**

HN 532
Mr. Micawber
Style One
Designer: L. Harradine
Height: 3 ½", 8.9 cm
Colour: Tan and black
Issued: 1922-1932
Varieties: M42
Series: Dickens (Series One)

U.S.:	**$125.00**
Can.:	**$150.00**
U.K.:	**£ 70.00**

HN 533
Sairey Gamp
Style One
Designer: L. Harradine
Height: 4", 10.1 cm
Colour: Light and dark green
Issued: 1922-1932
Varieties: M46
Series: Dickens (Series One)

U.S.:	**$140.00**
Can.:	**$170.00**
U.K.:	**£ 75.00**

HN 534
Fagin
Style One
Designer: L. Harradine
Height: 4", 10.1 cm
Colour: Dark brown
Issued: 1922-1932
Varieties: M49
Series: Dickens (Series One)

U.S.:	**$140.00**
Can.:	**$170.00**
U.K.:	**£ 75.00**

HN 535
Pecksniff
Style One
Designer: L. Harradine
Height: 3 ¾", 9.5 cm
Colour: Brown
Issued: 1922-1932
Varieties: M43
Series: Dickens (Series One)

U.S.:	**$140.00**
Can.:	**$170.00**
U.K.:	**£ 75.00**

HN 536
Stiggins
Designer: L. Harradine
Height: 3 ¾", 9.5 cm
Colour: Black
Issued: 1922-1932
Varieties: M50
Series: Dickens (Series One)

U.S.:	**$140.00**
Can.:	**$170.00**
U.K.:	**£ 75.00**

HN 537
Bill Sykes
Designer:	L. Harradine
Height:	3 ¾", 9.5 cm
Colour:	Black and brown
Issued:	1922-1932
Varieties:	M54
Series:	Dickens (Series One)
U.S.:	**$140.00**
Can.:	**$170.00**
U.K.:	**£ 75.00**

HN 538
Buz Fuz
Designer:	L. Harradine
Height:	3 ¾", 9.5 cm
Colour:	Black and brown
Issued:	1922-1932
Varieties:	M53
Series:	Dickens (Series One)
U.S.:	**$140.00**
Can.:	**$170.00**
U.K.:	**£ 75.00**

HN 539
Tiny Tim
Designer:	L. Harradine
Height:	3 ½", 8.9 cm
Colour:	Black, brown and blue
Issued:	1922-1932
Varieties:	M56
Series:	Dickens (Series One)
U.S.:	**$125.00**
Can.:	**$150.00**
U.K.:	**£ 70.00**

HN 540
Little Nell
Designer:	L. Harradine
Height:	4", 10.1 cm
Colour:	Pink
Issued:	1922-1932
Varieties:	M51
Series:	Dickens (Series One)
U.S.:	**$140.00**
Can.:	**$170.00**
U.K.:	**£ 75.00**

HN 541
Alfred Jingle
Designer:	L. Harradine
Height:	3 ¾", 9.5 cm
Colour:	Brown and black
Issued:	1922-1932
Varieties:	M52
Series:	Dickens (Series One)
U.S.:	**$140.00**
Can.:	**$170.00**
U.K.:	**£ 75.00**

HN 542
The Cobbler
Style One
Designer:	C. J. Noke
Height:	7 ½", 19.1 cm
Colour:	Green and brown
Issued:	1922-1939
Varieties:	HN 543, 682
U.S.:	**$2,000.00**
Can.:	**$2,500.00**
U.K.:	**£1,050.00**

HN 543
The Cobbler
Style One
Designer:	C. J. Noke
Height:	7 ½", 19.1 cm
Colour:	Green and brown
Issued:	1922-1938
Varieties:	HN 542, 682
U.S.:	**Only**
Can.:	**two**
U.K.:	**known**

HN 544
Tony Weller
Style Two
Designer:	L. Harradine
Height:	3 ½", 8.9 cm
Colour:	Green and yellow
Issued:	1922-1932
Varieties:	M47
Series:	Dickens (Series One)
U.S.:	**$140.00**
Can.:	**$170.00**
U.K.:	**£ 75.00**

HN 545
Uriah Heep
Style One
Designer: L. Harradine
Height: 4", 10.1 cm
Colour: Black
Issued: 1922-1932
Varieties: M45
Series: Dickens (Series One)
  U.S.:   **$140.00**
  Can.:   **$170.00**
  U.K.:   **£ 75.00**

HN 546
Artful Dodger
Designer: L. Harradine
Height: 3 ¾", 9.5 cm
Colour: Black and brown
Issued: 1922-1932
Varieties: M55
Series: Dickens (Series One)
  U.S.:   **$140.00**
  Can.:   **$170.00**
  U.K.:   **£ 75.00**

HN 547
The Curtsey
Designer: E. W. Light
Height: 11", 27.9 cm
Colour: Blue, green
             and yellow
Issued: 1922-1936
Varieties: HN 57, 57B, 66A, 327,
             334, 363, 371, 518,
             629, 670
  U.S.:
  Can.:   **Extremely rare**
  U.K.:

HN 548
The Balloon Seller
Style One
Designer: L. Harradine
Height: 9", 22.9 cm
Colour: Blue and black
Issued: 1922-1938
Varieties: HN 479, 486, 583, 697;
             also called 'The
             Balloon Woman'
  U.S.:
  Can.:   **Extremely rare**
  U.K.:

HN 549
Polly Peachum
Style Two
Designer: L. Harradine
Height: 4 ¼", 10.8 cm
Colour: Rose pink
Issued: 1922-1949
Varieties: HN 489, 620, 694,
             734
Series: Beggar's Opera
  U.S.:   **$1,000.00**
  Can.:   **$1,200.00**
  U.K.:   **£ 550.00**

HN 550
Polly Peachum
Style One
Designer: L. Harradine
Height: 6 ½", 16.5 cm
Colour: Rose pink
Issued: 1922-1949
Varieties: HN 463, 465, 589,
             614, 680, 693
Series: Beggar's Opera
  U.S.:   **$1,400.00**
  Can.:   **$1,675.00**
  U.K.:   **£ 750.00**

HN 551
The Flower Seller's Children
Designer: L. Harradine
Height: 8 ¼", 21.0 cm
Colour: Blue, orange and
             yellow
Issued: 1922-1949
Varieties: HN 525, 1206, 1342,
             1406
  U.S.:   **None**
  Can.:   **known**
  U.K.:   **to exist**

HN 552
A Jester
Style One
Designer: C. J. Noke
Height: 10", 25.4 cm
Colour: Black and red
Issued: 1922-1938
Varieties: HN 45, 71, 71A, 320,
             367, 412, 426, 446,
             616, 627, 1295, 1702,
             2016, 3922
  U.S.:   **$ 9,500.00**
  Can.:   **$11,500.00**
  U.K.:   **£ 5,200.00**

HN 553
Pecksniff
Style Two
Designer: L. Harradine
Height: 7", 17.8 cm
Colour: Black and brown
Issued: 1923-1939
Varieties: HN 1891
Series: Dickens (Series Two)

U.S.:	**$ 875.00**
Can.:	**$1,050.00**
U.K.:	**£ 475.00**

HN 554
Uriah Heep
Style Two
Designer: L. Harradine
Height: 7 ¼", 18.4 cm
Colour: Black
Issued: 1923-1939
Varieties: HN 1892
Series: Dickens (Series Two)

U.S.:	**$ 875.00**
Can.:	**$1,050.00**
U.K.:	**£ 475.00**

HN 555
Fat Boy
Style Two
Designer: L. Harradine
Height: 7", 17.8 cm
Colour: Blue and cream
Issued: 1923-1939
Varieties: HN 1893
Series: Dickens (Series Two)

U.S.:	**$ 875.00**
Can.:	**$1,050.00**
U.K.:	**£ 475.00**

HN 556
Mr. Pickwick
Style Two
Designer: L. Harradine
Height: 7", 17.8 cm
Colour: Blue, yellow and tan
Issued: 1923-1939
Varieties: HN 1894
Series: Dickens (Series Two)

U.S.:	**$ 875.00**
Can.:	**$1,050.00**
U.K.:	**£ 475.00**

HN 557
Mr. Micawber
Style Two
Designer: L. Harradine
Height: 7", 17.8 cm
Colour: Brown, black and tan
Issued: 1923-1939
Varieties: HN 1895
Series: Dickens (Series Two)

U.S.:	**$ 875.00**
Can.:	**$1,050.00**
U.K.:	**£ 475.00**

HN 558
Sairey Gamp
Style Two
Designer: L. Harradine
Height: 7", 17.8 cm
Colour: Black
Issued: 1923-1939
Varieties: HN 1896
Series: Dickens (Series Two)

U.S.:	**$1,200.00**
Can.:	**$1,500.00**
U.K.:	**£ 650.00**

HN 559
The Goosegirl
Style One
Designer: L. Harradine
Height: 8", 20.3 cm
Colour: Pink
Issued: 1923-1936
Varieties: HN 425, 436, 437, 448, 560

U.S.:	**$6,500.00**
Can.:	**$7,750.00**
U.K.:	**£3,500.00**

Earthenware

HN 560
The Goosegirl
Style One
Designer: L. Harradine
Height: 8", 20.3 cm
Colour: Pink and white
Issued: 1923-1936
Varieties: HN 425, 436, 437, 448, 559

U.S.:	
Can.:	**Extremely rare**
U.K.:	

HN 561
Fruit Gathering
Designer: L. Harradine
Height: 7 ¾", 19.7 cm
Colour: Green, white and pink
Issued: 1923-1936
Varieties: HN 449, 476, 503, 562,
           706, 707

U.S.:	None
Can.:	known
U.K.:	to exist

HN 562
Fruit Gathering
Designer: L. Harradine
Height: 7 ¾", 19.7 cm
Colour: Pink, white and green
Issued: 1923-1936
Varieties: HN 449, 476, 503, 561,
           706, 707

U.S.:	$5,000.00
Can.:	$6,000.00
U.K.:	£2,750.00

HN 563
Man in Tudor Costume
Designer: Unknown
Height: 3 ¾", 9.5 cm
Colour: Orange striped tunic,
           black cloak
Issued: 1923-1938

U.S.:	$5,500.00
Can.:	$6,500.00
U.K.:	£3,000.00

HN 564
The Parson's Daughter
Designer: H. Tittensor
Height: 9 ½", 24.1 cm
Colour: Red, yellow and green
Issued: 1923-1949
Varieties: HN 337, 338, 441, 790,
           1242, 1356, 2018

U.S.:	$750.00
Can.:	$900.00
U.K.:	£400.00

HN 565
Pretty Lady
Designer: H. Tittensor
Height: 10", 25.4 cm
Colour: Yellow and green
Issued: 1923-1938
Varieties: HN 69, 70, 302, 330,
           361, 384, 700, 763,
           783; appears in two
           colours, yellow and
           orange

U.S.:	$3,000.00
Can.:	$3,600.00
U.K.:	£1,650.00

HN 566
The Crinoline
Designer: G. Lambert
Height: 6 ¼", 15.8 cm
Colour: Cream and green
Issued: 1923-1938
Varieties: HN 8, 9, 9A, 21,
           21A, 413, 628

U.S.:	$4,000.00
Can.:	$4,750.00
U.K.:	£2,150.00

HN 567
The Bouquet
Designer: G. Lambert
Height: 9 ½", 24.1 cm
Colour: Pink dress, beige
           patterned shawl
Issued: 1923-1936
Varieties: HN 406, 414, 422,
           428, 429, 794; also
           called 'The Nosegay'

U.S.:	$5,500.00
Can.:	$6,500.00
U.K.:	£3,000.00

HN 568
Shy Anne
Designer: L. Perugini
Height: 7 ½", 19.1 cm
Colour: Green dress with
           black spots
Issued: 1923-1936
Varieties: HN 60, 64, 65

U.S.:	$ 8,500.00
Can.:	$10,500.00
U.K.:	£ 4,750.00

Earthenware and China

HN 569
The Lavender Woman
Designer: P. Stabler
Height: 8 ¼", 21.0 cm
Colour: Lavender
Issued: 1924-1936
Varieties: HN 22, 23, 23A,
342, 744

U.S.:	**$6,000.00**
Can.:	**$7,250.00**
U.K.:	**£3,250.00**

HN 570
Motherhood
Style Two
Designer: Unknown
Height: 9 ¼", 23.5 cm
Colour: Pink and green
Issued: 1923-1938
Varieties: HN 462, 703, 743

U.S.:	**$ 9,000.00**
Can.:	**$11,000.00**
U.K.:	**£ 5,000.00**

HN 571
Falstaff
Style One
Designer: C. J. Noke
Height: 7", 17.8 cm
Colour: Brown and green
Issued: 1923-1938
Varieties: HN 575, 608, 609,
619, 638, 1216, 1606

U.S.:	**$4,000.00**
Can.:	**$4,750.00**
U.K.:	**£2,150.00**

HN 572
Contentment
Designer: L. Harradine
Height: 7 ¼", 18.4 cm
Colour: Cream and orange
Issued: 1923-1938
Varieties: HN 395, 396, 421,
468, 685, 686, 1323

U.S.:	**$4,000.00**
Can.:	**$4,750.00**
U.K.:	**£2,150.00**

HN 573
Madonna of the Square
Designer: P. Stabler
Height: 7", 17.8 cm
Colour: Orange
Issued: 1923-1936
Varieties: HN 10, 10A, 11, 14, 27,
326, 576, 594, 613,
764, 1968, 1969, 2034

U.S.:	**None**
Can.:	**known**
U.K.:	**to exist**

HN 575
Falstaff
Style One
Designer: C. J. Noke
Height: 7", 17.8 cm
Colour: Brown and yellow
Issued: 1923-1938
Varieties: HN 571, 608, 609,
619, 638, 1216, 1606

U.S.:	**$4,000.00**
Can.:	**$4,750.00**
U.K.:	**£2,150.00**

HN 576
Madonna of the Square
Designer: P. Stabler
Height: 7", 17.8 cm
Colour: Green and black
Issued: 1923-1936
Varieties: HN 10, 10A, 11, 14, 27,
326, 573, 594, 613,
764, 1968, 1969, 2034

U.S.:	**$3,000.00**
Can.:	**$3,600.00**
U.K.:	**£1,650.00**

HN 577
The Chelsea Pair (woman)
Designer: L. Harradine
Height: 6", 15.2 cm
Colour: White dress, blue
flowers
Issued: 1923-1938
Varieties: HN 578

U.S.:	**$1,150.00**
Can.:	**$1,375.00**
U.K.:	**£ 620.00**

HN 574 not issued.

HN 578
The Chelsea Pair (woman)
Designer: L. Harradine
Height: 6", 15.2 cm
Colour: White dress, yellow
            flowers
Issued: 1923-1938
Varieties: HN 577

U.S.:	**$1,150.00**
Can.:	**$1,375.00**
U.K.:	**£ 620.00**

HN 579
The Chelsea Pair (man)
Designer: L. Harradine
Height: 6", 15.2 cm
Colour: Red and black, yellow
            flowers
Issued: 1923-1938
Varieties: HN 580

U.S.:	**$1,150.00**
Can.:	**$1,375.00**
U.K.:	**£ 620.00**

HN 580
The Chelsea Pair (man)
Designer: L. Harradine
Height: 6", 15.2 cm
Colour: Red and black, blue
            flowers
Issued: 1923-1938
Varieties: HN 579

U.S.:	**$1,150.00**
Can.:	**$1,375.00**
U.K.:	**£ 620.00**

HN 581
The Perfect Pair
Designer: L. Harradine
Height: 6 ¾", 17.2 cm
Colour: Pink and red
Issued: 1923-1938

U.S.:	**$1,650.00**
Can.:	**$2,000.00**
U.K.:	**£ 900.00**

HN 582
Grossmith's 'Tsang Ihang'
Perfume of Thibet
Designer: Unknown
Height: 11 ½", 29.2 cm
Colour: Yellow, black and blue
Issued: 1923-Unknown

U.S.:	**$1,500.00**
Can.:	**$1,800.00**
U.K.:	**£ 800.00**

HN 583
The Balloon Seller
Style One
Designer: L. Harradine
Height: 9", 22.9 cm
Colour: Green and cream
Issued: 1923-1949
Varieties: HN 479, 486, 548,697;
            also called 'The Balloon
            Woman'

U.S.:	**$1,650.00**
Can.:	**$1,950.00**
U.K.:	**£ 900.00**

HN 584
Lady with Rose
Designer: E.W. Light
Height: 9 ½", 24.1 cm
Colour: Green and pink
Issued: 1923-1936
Varieties: HN 48A, 52A, 68, 304,
            336, 515, 517, 624

U.S.:	**None**
Can.:	**known**
U.K.:	**to exist**

HN 585
Harlequinade
Designer: L. Harradine
Height: 6 ½", 16.5 cm
Colour: Blue, yellow, white,
            green and purple
Issued: 1923-1940
Varieties: HN 635, 711, 780

U.S.:	**$6,500.00**
Can.:	**$7,750.00**
U.K.:	**£3,500.00**

Earthenware

HN 586
Boy with Turban
Designer: L. Harradine
Height: 3 ¾", 9.5 cm
Colour: Blue and green
Issued: 1923-1936
Varieties: HN 587, 661, 662,
1210, 1212, 1213,
1214, 1225

U.S.: **$2,000.00**
Can.: **$2,500.00**
U.K.: **£1,100.00**

HN 587
Boy with Turban
Designer: L. Harradine
Height: 3 ¾", 9.5 cm
Colour: Green, red and blue
Issued: 1923-1936
Varieties: HN 586, 661, 662,
1210, 1212, 1213,
1214, 1225

U.S.: **$2,000.00**
Can.: **$2,500.00**
U.K.: **£1,100.00**

HN 588
Spring
Style Two
Designer: L. Harradine
Height: 6 ¼", 15.9 cm
Colour: Pink or yellow dress
Issued: 1923-1938
U.S.:
Can.: **Extremely rare**
U.K.:

HN 589
Polly Peachum
Style One
Designer: L. Harradine
Height: 6 ½", 16.5 cm
Colour: Pink and yellow
Issued: 1924-1949
Varieties: HN 463, 465, 550,
614, 680, 693
Series: Beggar's Opera

U.S.:
Can.: **Extremely rare**
U.K.:

HN 590
Captain MacHeath
Designer: L. Harradine
Height: 7", 17.8 cm
Colour: Red, black and yellow
Issued: 1924-1949
Varieties: HN 464, 1256
Series: Beggar's Opera

U.S.: **$1,650.00**
Can.: **$2,000.00**
U.K.: **£ 900.00**

HN 591
The Beggar
Style One
Designer: L. Harradine
Height: 6 ¾", 17.2 cm
Colour: Green and blue
Issued: 1924-1949
Varieties: HN 526
Series: Beggar's Opera

U.S.: **$1,400.00**
Can.: **$1,700.00**
U.K.: **£ 775.00**

Earthenware

HN 592
The Highwayman
Designer: L. Harradine
Height: 6 ½", 16.5 cm
Colour: Green and red
Issued: 1924-1949
Varieties: HN 527, 1257
Series: Beggar's Opera

U.S.: **$1,400.00**
Can.: **$1,700.00**
U.K.: **£ 775.00**

HN 593
Nude on Rock
Designer: Unknown
Height: 6 ¾", 17.1 cm
Colour: Blue
Issued: 1924-1938

U.S.: **Only**
Can.: **one**
U.K.: **known**

HN 594
Madonna of the Square
Designer: P. Stabler
Height: 7", 17.8 cm
Colour: Green and brown
Issued: 1924-1936
Varieties: HN 10, 10A, 11, 14, 27,
           326, 573, 576, 613,
           764, 1968, 1969, 2034

U.S.:   **None**
Can.:   **known**
U.K.:   **to exist**

HN 595
Grief
Designer: C. J. Noke
Height: 1 ¾", 4.5 cm
Colour: Blue
Issued: 1924-1938

U.S.:   **$3,500.00**
Can.:   **$4,250.00**
U.K.:   **£1,875.00**

Photograph
Not
Available

HN 596
Despair
Designer: C. J. Noke
Height: 4 ¾", 9.5 cm
Colour: Mottled blue
Issued: Unknown
Varieties: Also known in flambé

U.S.:   **Only**
Can.:   **one**
U.K.:   **known**

HN 597
The Bather
Style One, First Version
Designer: L. Harradine
Height: 7 ¾", 19.7 cm
Colour: Grey
Issued: 1924-1938
Varieties: HN 687, 781, 782,
           1238, 1708

U.S.:   **$5,250.00**
Can.:   **$6,300.00**
U.K.:   **£2,800.00**

HN 598
Omar Khayyam and the Beloved
(Without base)
Style Two
Designer: C. J. Noke
Height: 10", 25.4 cm
Colour: Green, pink and blue
Issued: 1924-1936
Varieties: HN 419, 459

U.S.:   **None**
Can.:   **known**
U.K.:   **to exist**

HN 599
Masquerade (man)
Style One
Designer: L. Harradine
Height: 6 ¾", 17.2 cm
Colour: Red
Issued: 1924-1936
Varieties: HN 636, 683

U.S.:   **$1,650.00**
Can.:   **$2,000.00**
U.K.:   **£ 900.00**

HN 600
Masquerade (woman)
Style One
Designer: L. Harradine
Height: 6 ¾", 17.2 cm
Colour: Pink
Issued: 1924-1949
Varieties: HN 637, 674

U.S.:   **$1,650.00**
Can.:   **$2,000.00**
U.K.:   **£ 900.00**

Photograph
Not
Available

HN 601
A Mandarin
Style Three
Designer: C. J. Noke
Height: 10", 25.4 cm
Colour: Red
Issued: 1924-1938

U.S.:   **$ 9,000.00**
Can.:   **$11,000.00**
U.K.:   **£ 5,000.00**

HN 602 not issued.

HN 603A
A Child Study
Style One
Designer:	L. Harradine
Height:	4 ¾", 12.0 cm
Colour:	White, primroses around base
Issued:	1924-1938
Varieties:	HN 603B, 1441; also known in flambé
U.S.:	**$1,400.00**
Can.:	**$1,650.00**
U.K.:	**£ 750.00**

HN 603B
A Child Study
Style One
Designer:	L. Harradine
Height:	4 ¾", 12.0 cm
Colour:	White, kingcups around base
Issued:	1924-1938
Varieties:	HN 603A, 1441; also known in flambé
U.S.:	**$1,400.00**
Can.:	**$1,650.00**
U.K.:	**£ 750.00**

HN 604A
A Child Study
Style Two
Designer:	L. Harradine
Height:	5 ½", 14.0 cm
Colour:	White, primroses around base
Issued:	1924-1938
Varieties:	HN 604B, 1442, 1443
U.S.:	**$1,400.00**
Can.:	**$1,650.00**
U.K.:	**£ 750.00**

HN 604B
A Child Study
Style Two
Designer:	L. Harradine
Height:	5 ½", 14.0 cm
Colour:	White, kingcups around base
Issued:	1924-1938
Varieties:	HN 604A, 1442, 1443
U.S.:	**$1,400.00**
Can.:	**$1,650.00**
U.K.:	**£ 750.00**

HN 605A
A Child Study
Style Three
Designer:	L. Harradine
Height:	Unknown
Colour:	White, primroses around base
Issued:	1924-1938
Varieties:	HN 605B
U.S.:	**$1,600.00**
Can.:	**$1,900.00**
U.K.:	**£ 850.00**

HN 605B
A Child Study
Style Three
Designer:	L. Harradine
Height:	Unknown
Colour:	White, kingcups around base
Issued:	1924-1938
Varieties:	HN 605A
U.S.:	**$1,600.00**
Can.:	**$1,900.00**
U.K.:	**£ 850.00**

HN 606A
Female Study
Designer:	L. Harradine
Height:	5", 12.7 cm
Colour:	White, primroses around base
Issued:	1924-1936
Varieties:	HN 606B; also known in flambé
U.S.:	**$1,400.00**
Can.:	**$1,650.00**
U.K.:	**£ 750.00**

HN 606B
Female Study
Designer:	L. Harradine
Height:	5", 12.7 cm
Colour:	White, kingcups around base
Issued:	1924-1936
Varieties:	HN 606A; also known in flambé
U.S.:	**$1,400.00**
Can.:	**$1,650.00**
U.K.:	**£ 750.00**

HN 607 not issued.

HN 608
Falstaff
Style One
Designer: C. J. Noke
Height: 7", 17.8 cm
Colour: Red
Issued: 1924-1938
Varieties: HN 571, 575, 609, 619, 638, 1216, 1606

U.S.: **None**
Can.: **known**
U.K.: **to exist**

HN 609
Falstaff
Style One
Designer: C. J. Noke
Height: 7", 17.8 cm
Colour: Green
Issued: 1924-1938
Varieties: HN 571, 575, 608, 619, 638, 1216, 1606

U.S.: **None**
Can.: **known**
U.K.: **to exist**

HN 610
Henry Lytton as Jack Point
Designer: C. J. Noke
Height: 6 ½", 16.5 cm
Colour: Blue, black and brown
Issued: 1924-1949

U.S.: **$1,750.00**
Can.: **$2,000.00**
U.K.: **£ 950.00**

HN 611
A Mandarin
Style One
Designer: C. J. Noke
Height: 10 ¼", 26.0 cm
Colour: Gold and yellow
Issued: 1924-1936
Varieties: HN 84, 316, 318, 382, 746, 787, 791; also called 'Chinese Mandarin' and 'The Mikado'

U.S.: **$ 9,500.00**
Can.: **$11,500.00**
U.K.: **£ 5,200.00**

HN 612
The Poke Bonnet
Designer: C. J. Noke
Height: 9 ½", 24.1 cm
Colour: Yellow and green
Issued: 1924-1938
Varieties: HN 362, 765; also called 'A Lilac Shawl' HN 44, 44A; 'In Grandma's Days' HN 339, 340, 388, 442

U.S.: **$4,000.00**
Can.: **$4,750.00**
U.K.: **£2,150.00**

HN 613
Madonna of the Square
Designer: P. Stabler
Height: 7", 17.8 cm
Colour: Pink and orange
Issued: 1924-1936
Varieties: HN 10, 10A, 11, 14, 27, 326, 573, 576, 594, 764, 1968, 1969, 2034

U.S.: **$3,000.00**
Can.: **$3,600.00**
U.K.: **£1,650.00**

HN 614
Polly Peachum
Style One
Designer: L. Harradine
Height: 6 ½", 16.5 cm
Colour: Pale pink and blue
Issued: 1924-1949
Varieties: HN 463, 465, 550, 589, 680, 693
Series: Beggar's Opera

U.S.: **$1,600.00**
Can.: **$2,000.00**
U.K.: **£ 900.00**

HN 615
Katharine
Designer: C. J. Noke
Height: 5 ¾", 14.6 cm
Colour: Red with green spots
Issued: 1924-1938
Varieties: HN 61, 74, 341, 471, 793

U.S.: **$3,750.00**
Can.: **$4,500.00**
U.K.: **£2,000.00**

HN 616
A Jester
Style One
Designer: C. J. Noke
Height: 10", 25.4 cm
Colour: Black and white
Issued: 1924-1938
Varieties: HN 45, 71, 71A, 320, 367,
                 412, 426, 446, 552,
                 627, 1295, 1702, 2016,
                 3922

U.S.:   None
Can.:   known
U.K.:   to exist

HN 617
A Shepherd
Style One
Designer: C. J. Noke
Height: 13 ¼", 33.6 cm
Colour: Dark blue
Issued: 1924-1938
Varieties: HN 81, 632

U.S.:
Can.:   Extremely rare
U.K.:

China

HN 618
Falstaff
Style Two
Designer: C. J. Noke
Height: 7", 17.8 cm
Colour: Black, red and green
Issued: 1924-1938
Varieties: HN 2054

U.S.:
Can.:   Extremely rare
U.K.:

HN 619
Falstaff
Style One
Designer: C. J. Noke
Height: 7", 17.8 cm
Colour: Brown, green
                 and yellow
Issued: 1924-1938
Varieties: HN 571, 575, 608,
                 609, 638, 1216, 1606

U.S.:
Can.:   Extremely rare
U.K.:

HN 620
Polly Peachum
Style Two
Designer: L. Harradine
Height: 4 ¼", 10.8 cm
Colour: Pink
Issued: 1924-1938
Varieties: HN 489, 549, 694, 734
Series: Beggar's Opera

U.S.: $1,400.00
Can.: $1,675.00
U.K.:   £   750.00

HN 621
Pan on Rock
Designer: Unknown
Height: 5 ¼", 13.3 cm
Colour: Cream, green base
Issued: 1924-1936
Varieties: HN 622

U.S.:
Can.:   Extremely rare
U.K.:

HN 622
Pan on Rock
Designer: Unknown
Height: 5 ¼", 13.3 cm
Colour: Cream, black base
Issued: 1924-1938
Varieties: HN 621

U.S.:
Can.:   Extremely rare
U.K.:

HN 623
An Old King
Designer: C. J. Noke
Height: 9 ¾", 24.7 cm
Colour: Grey, red and green
Issued: 1924-1938
Varieties: HN 358, 1801, 2134

U.S.:   None
Can.:   known
U.K.:   to exist

HN 624
Lady with Rose
Designer: E. W Light
Height: 9 ½", 24.1 cm
Colour: Turquoise
Issued: 1924-1936
Varieties: HN 48A, 52A, 68, 304,
              336, 515, 517, 584

U.S.:   **None**
Can.:   **known**
U.K.:   **to exist**

HN 625
A Spook
Style One
Designer: H. Tittensor
Height: 7", 17.8 cm
Colour: Yellow
Issued: 1924-1936
Varieties: HN 50, 51, 51A, 51B,
              58, 512; also known
              in flambé

U.S.:   **$6,000.00**
Can.:   **$7,250.00**
U.K.:   **£3,300.00**

HN 626
Lady with Shawl
Designer: L. Harradine
Height: 13 ¼", 33.6 cm
Colour: Yellow and white
Issued: 1924-1936
Varieties: HN 447, 458, 678,
              679

U.S.:   **None**
Can.:   **known**
U.K.:   **to exist**

HN 627
A Jester
Style One
Designer: C. J. Noke
Height: 10", 25.4 cm
Colour: Brown checks
Issued: 1924-1938
Varieties: HN 45, 71, 71A, 320,
              367, 412, 426, 446,
              552, 616, 1295, 1702,
              2016, 3922

U.S.:   **$ 9,500.00**
Can.:   **$11,500.00**
U.K.:   **£ 5,200.00**

HN 628
The Crinoline
Designer: G. Lambert
Height: 6 ¼", 15.8 cm
Colour: Yellow and blue
Issued: 1924-1938
Varieties: HN 8, 9, 9A, 21, 21A,
              413, 566

U.S.:   **None**
Can.:   **known**
U.K.:   **to exist**

HN 629
The Curtsey
Designer: E. W. Light
Height: 11", 27.9 cm
Colour: Green and black
Issued: 1924-1936
Varieties: HN 57, 57B, 66A, 327,
              334, 363, 371, 518,
              547, 670

U.S.:   **None**
Can.:   **known**
U.K.:   **to exist**

HN 630
A Jester
Style Two
Designer: C. J. Noke
Height: 10 ¼", 26.0 cm
Colour: Brown
Issued: 1924-1938
Varieties: HN 45A, 45B, 55, 308,
              1333; also known in
              black and white

U.S.:   **$ 9,500.00**
Can.:   **$11,500.00**
U.K.:   **£ 5,200.00**

HN 631
Fisherwomen
Designer: C. J. Noke
Height: 11 ¾", 29.8 cm
Colour: Mauve and green
Issued: 1924-1938
Varieties: HN 80, 349, 359; also
              called 'Looking for the
              Boats' and 'Waiting
              For The Boats'

U.S.:
Can.:   **Extremely rare**
U.K.:

HN 632
A Shepherd
Style One
Designer: C. J. Noke
Height: 13 ¼", 33.6 cm
Colour: Blue and white
Issued: 1924-1938
Varieties: HN 81, 617

U.S.:	None
Can.:	known
U.K.:	to exist

China

HN 633
The Princess
Style One
Designer: L. Harradine
Height: 9 ¼", 23.5 cm
Colour: Black and white
Issued: 1924-1936
Varieties: HN 391, 392, 420, 430, 431

U.S.:	None
Can.:	known
U.K.:	to exist

HN 634
A Geisha
Style One
Designer: H. Tittensor
Height: 10 ¾", 27.3 cm
Colour: Black and white
Issued: 1924-1936
Varieties: HN 354, 376, 376A, 387, 741, 779, 1321, 1322; also called 'The Japanese Lady'

U.S.:	$ 8,500.00
Can.:	$10,000.00
U.K.:	£ 4,500.00

HN 635
Harlequinade
Designer: L. Harradine
Height: 6 ½", 16.5 cm
Colour: Gold
Issued: 1924-1940
Varieties: HN 585, 711, 780

U.S.:	$6,000.00
Can.:	$7,250.00
U.K.:	£3,250.00

HN 636
Masquerade (man)
Style One
Designer: L. Harradine
Height: 6 ¾", 17.2 cm
Colour: Gold
Issued: 1924-1936
Varieties: HN 599, 683

U.S.:	$1,750.00
Can.:	$2,100.00
U.K.:	£ 950.00

HN 637
Masquerade (woman)
Style One
Designer: L. Harradine
Height: 6 ¾", 17.2 cm
Colour: Gold
Issued: 1924-1938
Varieties: HN 600, 674

U.S.:	$1,750.00
Can.:	$2,100.00
U.K.:	£ 950.00

HN 638
Falstaff
Style One
Designer: C. J. Noke
Height: 7", 17.8 cm
Colour: Red and cream
Issued: 1924-1938
Varieties: HN 571, 575, 608, 609, 619, 1216, 1606

U.S.:	
Can.:	Extremely Rare
U.K.:	

HN 639
Elsie Maynard
Style One
Designer: C. J. Noke
Height: 7", 17.8 cm
Colour: Mauve and pink
Issued: 1924-1949

U.S.:	$1,900.00
Can.:	$2,275.00
U.K.:	£1,000.00

HN 640
Charley's Aunt
Style One
Designer: A. Taft
Height: 7", 17.8 cm
Colour: Green and lavender
Issued: 1924-1936
Varieties: HN 35

U.S.:	**$2,750.00**
Can.:	**$3,250.00**
U.K.:	**£1,500.00**

HN 641
A Mandarin
Style Two
Designer: C. J. Noke
Height: 8 ¼", 21.0 cm
Colour: Yellow and blue
Issued: 1924-1938
Varieties: HN 366, 455

U.S.:	**Only**
Can.:	**two**
U.K.:	**known**

HN 642
Pierrette
Style One
Designer: L. Harradine
Height: 7 ¼", 18.4 cm
Colour: Red
Issued: 1924-1938
Varieties: HN 643, 644, 691,
             721, 731, 732, 784

U.S.:	**$5,250.00**
Can.:	**$6,250.00**
U.K.:	**£2,800.00**

HN 643
Pierrette
Style One
Designer: L. Harradine
Height: 7 ¼", 18.4 cm
Colour: Red, black and white
Issued: 1924-1938
Varieties: HN 642, 644, 691,
             721, 731, 732, 784

U.S.:	**$5,250.00**
Can.:	**$6,250.00**
U.K.:	**£2,800.00**

HN 644
Pierrette
Style One
Designer: L. Harradine
Height: 7 ¼", 18.4 cm
Colour: White and black
Issued: 1924-1938
Varieties: HN 642, 643, 691,
             721, 731, 732, 784

U.S.:	**$4,500.00**
Can.:	**$5,500.00**
U.K.:	**£2,500.00**

Photograph
Not
Available

HN 645
One of the Forty
Style Thirteen
Designer: H. Tittensor
Height: 6", 15.2 cm
Colour: Blue, black and white
Issued: 1924-1938
Varieties: HN 482, 484, 492,
             663, 713

U.S.:	**None**
Can.:	**known**
U.K.:	**to exist**

HN 646
One of the Forty
Style Twelve
Designer: H. Tittensor
Height: Unknown
Colour: Cream, blue and black
Issued: 1924-1936
Varieties: HN 481, 483, 491,
             667, 712, 1336, 1350;
             also known in flambé

U.S.:	
Can.:	**Extremely rare**
U.K.:	

HN 647
One of the Forty
Style Two
Designer: H. Tittensor
Height: 7 ¼", 18.4 cm
Colour: Blue, black and white
Issued: 1924-1936
Varieties: HN 418, 494, 498, 666,
             704, 1353

U.S.:	**None**
Can.:	**known**
U.K.:	**to exist**

HN 648
One of the Forty
Style One
Designer: H. Tittensor
Height: 8 ¼", 21.0 cm
Colour: Blue, black and white
Issued: 1924-1938
Varieties: HN 417, 490, 495, 501, 528, 677, 1351, 1352

U.S.:	None
Can.:	known
U.K.:	to exist

Photograph
Not
Available

HN 649
One of the Forty
Style Fourteen
Designer: H. Tittensor
Height: 7 ¾", 19.7 cm
Colour: Blue, black and white
Issued: 1924-1938
Varieties: HN 496, 500, 665, 1354

U.S.:	None
Can.:	known
U.K.:	to exist

HN 650
Crinoline Lady
Designer: Unknown
Height: 3", 7.6 cm
Colour: Green and white
Issued: 1924-1938
Varieties: HN 651, 652, 653, 654, 655

U.S.:	$3,500.00
Can.:	$4,250.00
U.K.:	£1,950.00

HN 651
Crinoline Lady
Designer: Unknown
Height: 3", 7.6 cm
Colour: Orange and white
Issued: 1924-1938
Varieties: HN 650, 652, 653, 654, 655

U.S.:	$3,500.00
Can.:	$4,250.00
U.K.:	£1,950.00

HN 652
Crinoline Lady
Designer: Unknown
Height: 3", 7.6 cm
Colour: Purple
Issued: 1924-1938
Varieties: HN 650, 651, 653, 654, 655

U.S.:	$3,500.00
Can.:	$4,250.00
U.K.:	£1,950.00

HN 653
Crinoline Lady
Designer: Unknown
Height: 3", 7.6 cm
Colour: Black and white
Issued: 1924-1938
Varieties: HN 650, 651, 652, 654, 655

U.S.:	$3,500.00
Can.:	$4,250.00
U.K.:	£1,950.00

HN 654
Crinoline Lady
Designer: Unknown
Height: 3", 7.6 cm
Colour: Red and purple
Issued: 1924-1938
Varieties: HN 650, 651, 652, 653, 655

U.S.:	$3,500.00
Can.:	$4,250.00
U.K.:	£1,950.00

HN 655
Crinoline Lady
Designer: Unknown
Height: 3", 7.6 cm
Colour: Blue and black
Issued: 1924-1938
Varieties: HN 650, 651, 652, 653, 654

U.S.:	$3,500.00
Can.:	$4,250.00
U.K.:	£1,950.00

HN 656
The Mask
Style One
Designer: L. Harradine
Height: 6 ¾", 17.2 cm
Colour: Blue and purple
Issued: 1924-1938
Varieties: HN 657, 729, 733,
             785, 1271

U.S.:   **$6,000.00**
Can.:   **$7,250.00**
U.K.:   **£3,250.00**

HN 657
The Mask
Style One
Designer: L. Harradine
Height: 6 ¾", 17.2 cm
Colour: Black and white
Issued: 1924-1938
Varieties: HN 656, 729, 733,
             785, 1271

U.S.:   **$6,000.00**
Can.:   **$7,250.00**
U.K.:   **£3,250.00**

HN 658
Mam'selle
Designer: L. Harradine
Height: 7", 17.8 cm
Colour: Black and white
Issued: 1924-1938
Varieties: HN 659, 724, 786

U.S.:   **$6,500.00**
Can.:   **$7,750.00**
U.K.:   **£3,500.00**

HN 659
Mam'selle
Designer: L. Harradine
Height: 7", 17.8 cm
Colour: Dark blue
Issued: 1924-1938
Varieties: HN 658, 724, 786

U.S.:   **$6,500.00**
Can.:   **$7,750.00**
U.K.:   **£3,500.00**

HN 660
Myfanwy Jones
Designer: E. W. Light
Height: 12", 30.5 cm
Colour: White and blue
Issued: 1924-1936
Varieties: HN 39, 92, 456,514,
             516, 519, 520, 668,
             669, 701, 792; also
             called 'The Welsh Girl'

U.S.:
Can.:   **Extremely rare**
U.K.:

HN 661
Boy with Turban
Designer: L. Harradine
Height: 3 ¾", 9.5 cm
Colour: Blue
Issued: 1924-1936
Varieties: HN 586, 587, 662,
             1210, 1212, 1213,
             1214, 1225

U.S.:   **$2,000.00**
Can.:   **$2,500.00**
U.K.:   **£1,100.00**

HN 662
Boy with Turban
Designer: L. Harradine
Height: 3 ¾", 9.5 cm
Colour: Black and white
Issued: 1924-1936
Varieties: HN 586, 587, 661,
             1210, 1212, 1213,
             1214, 1225

U.S.:   **$2,000.00**
Can.:   **$2,500.00**
U.K.:   **£1,100.00**

Photograph
Not
Available

HN 663
One of the Forty
Style Thirteen
Designer: H. Tittensor
Height: 6", 15.2 cm
Colour: Yellow
Issued: 1924-1938
Varieties: HN 482, 484, 492,
             645, 713,

U.S.:
Can.:   **Extremely rare**
U.K.:

HN 664
One of the Forty
Style Eleven
Designer: H. Tittensor
Height: 7 ¾", 19.7 cm
Colour: Yellow, green and black
Issued: 1924-1938
Varieties: HN 480, 493, 497, 499, 714

U.S.:	$5,000.00
Can.:	$6,000.00
U.K.:	£2,750.00

Photograph
Not
Available

HN 665
One of the Forty
Style Fourteen
Designer: H. Tittensor
Height: 7 ¾", 19.7 cm
Colour: Yellow
Issued: 1924-1938
Varieties: HN 496, 500, 649, 1354

U.S.:	
Can.:	Extremely rare
U.K.:	

HN 666
One of the Forty
Style Two
Designer: H. Tittensor
Height: 7 ¼", 18.4 cm
Colour: Yellow
Issued: 1924-1936
Varieties: HN 418, 494, 498, 647, 704, 1353

U.S.:	
Can.:	Extremely rare
U.K.:	

HN 667
One of the Forty
Style Twelve
Designer: H. Tittensor
Height: Unknown
Colour: Yellow and black
Issued: 1924-1936
Varieties: HN 481, 483, 491, 646, 712, 1336, 1350; also known in flambé

U.S.:	
Can.:	Extremely rare
U.K.:	

HN 668
Myfanwy Jones
Designer: E. W. Light
Height: 12", 30.5 cm
Colour: Yellow and pink
Issued: 1924-1936
Varieties: HN 39, 92, 456, 514, 516, 519, 520, 660, 669, 701, 792; also called 'The Welsh Girl'

U.S.:	$ 9,500.00
Can.:	$11,500.00
U.K.:	£ 5,200.00

HN 669
Myfanwy Jones
Designer: E. W. Light
Height: 8 ½", 21.5 cm
Colour: Yellow and green
Issued: 1924-1936
Varieties: HN 39, 92, 456, 514, 516, 519, 520, 660, 668, 701, 792; also called 'The Welsh Girl'

U.S.:	$ 9,500.00
Can.:	$11,500.00
U.K.:	£ 5,200.00

HN 670
The Curtsey
Designer: E. W. Light
Height: 11", 27.9 cm
Colour: Pink and yellow
Issued: 1924-1936
Varieties: HN 57, 57B, 66A, 327, 334, 363, 371, 518, 547, 629

U.S.:	$4,500.00
Can.:	$5,500.00
U.K.:	£2,500.00

HN 671
The Ermine Muff
Designer: C. J. Noke
Height: 8 ½", 21.6 cm
Colour: Green and yellow
Issued: 1924-1938
Varieties: HN 54, 332; also called 'Lady Ermine' and 'Lady with the Ermine Muff'

U.S.:	None
Can.:	known
U.K.:	to exist

HN 672
Tulips
Designer: Unknown
Height: 9 ½" 24.1 cm
Colour: Green and blue
Issued: 1924-1936
Varieties: HN 466, 488, 747,
            1334

U.S.:   **$5,500.00**
Can.:   **$6,500.00**
U.K.:   **£3,000.00**

Earthenware

Photograph
Not
Available

HN 673
Henry VIII
Style One
Designer: C. J. Noke
Height: Unknown
Colour: Brown and lavender
Issued: 1924-1938
Varieties: HN 370

U.S.:   **None**
Can.:   **known**
U.K.:   **to exist**

HN 674
Masquerade (woman)
Style One
Designer: L. Harradine
Height: 6 ¾", 17.2 cm
Colour: Orange and yellow
Issued: 1924-1938
Varieties: HN 600, 637

U.S.:   **$1,900.00**
Can.:   **$2,275.00**
U.K.:   **£1,000.00**

HN 675
The Gainsborough Hat
Designer: H. Tittensor
Height: 8 ¾", 22.2 cm
Colour: Cream
Issued: 1924-1936
Varieties: HN 46, 46A, 47, 329,
            352, 383, 453, 705

U.S.:   **$6,000.00**
Can.:   **$7,250.00**
U.K.:   **£3,250.00**

HN 676
Pavlova
Designer: C. J. Noke
Height: 4 ¼", 10.8 cm
Colour: White and blue tutu,
            black base
Issued: 1924-1938
Varieties: HN 487; also called
            'Swan Song'

U.S.:
Can.:   **Extremely rare**
U.K.:

HN 677
One of the Forty
Style One
Designer: H. Tittensor
Height: 8 ¼", 21.0 cm
Colour: Orange, yellow and red
Issued: 1924-1938
Varieties: HN 417, 490, 495, 501,
            528, 648, 1351, 1352

U.S.:
Can.:   **Extremely rare**
U.K.:

HN 678
Lady with Shawl
Designer: L. Harradine
Height: 13 ¼", 33.7 cm
Colour: Black, yellow and white
Issued: 1924-1936
Varieties: HN 447, 458, 626, 679

U.S.:   **$ 8,500.00**
Can.:   **$10,000.00**
U.K.:   **£ 4,600.00**

HN 679
Lady with Shawl
Designer: L. Harradine
Height: 13 ¼", 33.7 cm
Colour: Black, yellow, blue
            and white
Issued: 1924-1936
Varieties: HN 447, 458, 626, 678

U.S.:   **None**
Can.:   **known**
U.K.:   **to exist**

HN 680
Polly Peachum
Style One
Designer: L. Harradine
Height: 6 ½", 16.5 cm
Colour: White
Issued: 1924-1949
Varieties: HN 463, 465, 550, 589, 614, 693
Series: Beggar's Opera

U.S.:	**None**
Can.:	**known**
U.K.:	**to exist**

HN 681
The Cobbler
Style Two
Designer: C. J. Noke
Height: 8 ½", 21.6 cm
Colour: Green and red
Issued: 1924-1938
Varieties: HN 1251, 1283

U.S.:	**None**
Can.:	**known**
U.K.:	**to exist**

HN 682
The Cobbler
Style One
Designer: C. J. Noke
Height: 7 ½", 19.1 cm
Colour: Red and green
Issued: 1924-1938
Varieties: HN 542, 543

U.S.:	**None**
Can.:	**known**
U.K.:	**to exist**

HN 683
Masquerade (man)
Style One
Designer: L. Harradine
Height: 7 ¼", 18.4 cm
Colour: Green
Issued: 1924-1936
Varieties: HN 599, 636

U.S.:	**$1,750.00**
Can.:	**$2,100.00**
U.K.:	**£ 950.00**

Earthenware

HN 684
Tony Weller
Style One
Designer: C. J. Noke
Height: 10 ¼", 26.0 cm
Colour: Green and brown
Issued: 1924-1938
Varieties: HN 346, 368

U.S.:	**$2,500.00**
Can.:	**$3,000.00**
U.K.:	**£1,350.00**

HN 685
Contentment
Designer: L. Harradine
Height: 7 ¼", 18.4 cm
Colour: Black and white
Issued: 1924-1938
Varieties: HN 395, 396, 421, 468, 572, 686, 1323

U.S.:	**Only**
Can.:	**one**
U.K.:	**known**

HN 686
Contentment
Designer: L. Harradine
Height: 7 ¼", 18.4 cm
Colour: Black and white
Issued: 1924-1938
Varieties: HN 395, 396, 421, 468, 572, 685, 1323

U.S.:	**None**
Can.:	**known**
U.K.:	**to exist**

HN 687
The Bather
Style One, First Version
Designer: L. Harradine
Height: 7 ¾", 19.7 cm
Colour: Blue
Issued: 1924-1949
Varieties: HN 597, 781, 782, 1238, 1708

U.S.:	**$2,750.00**
Can.:	**$3,250.00**
U.K.:	**£1,500.00**

HN 688
A Yeoman of the Guard
Designer:	L. Harradine
Height:	5 ¾", 14.6 cm
Colour:	Red, gold and brown
Issued:	1924-1938
Varieties:	HN 2122
U.S.:	**$1,500.00**
Can.:	**$1,800.00**
U.K.:	**£ 800.00**

HN 689
A Chelsea Pensioner
Designer:	L. Harradine
Height:	5 ¾", 14.6 cm
Colour:	Red
Issued:	1924-1938
U.S.:	**$3,500.00**
Can.:	**$4,250.00**
U.K.:	**£1,900.00**

Also produced as a miniature
figurine, but without an M number.

HN 690
A Lady of the Georgian Period
Designer:	E. W. Light
Height:	10 ¼", 26.0 cm
Colour:	Pink, white and
	yellow overdress
Issued:	1925-1936
Varieties:	HN 41, 331, 444, 702
U.S.:	**None**
Can.:	**known**
U.K.:	**to exist**

HN 691
Pierrette
Style One
Designer:	L. Harradine
Height:	7 ¼", 18.4 cm
Colour:	Gold
Issued:	1925-1938
Varieties:	HN 642, 643, 644,
	721, 731, 732, 784
U.S.:	**$6,000.00**
Can.:	**$7,250.00**
U.K.:	**£3,250.00**

HN 692
Sleep
Designer:	P. Stabler
Height:	6", 15.2 cm
Colour:	Gold
Issued:	1925-1936
Varieties:	HN 24, 24A, 25, 25A,
	424, 710
U.S.:	**$3,750.00**
Can.:	**$4,500.00**
U.K.:	**£2,000.00**

HN 693
Polly Peachum
Style One
Designer:	L. Harradine
Height:	6 ½", 16.5 cm
Colour:	Pink and green
Issued:	1925-1949
Varieties:	HN 463, 465, 550,
	589, 614, 680
Series:	Beggar's Opera
U.S.:	**$1,600.00**
Can.:	**$2,000.00**
U.K.:	**£ 900.00**

HN 694
Polly Peachum
Style Two
Designer:	L. Harradine
Height:	4 ¼", 10.8 cm
Colour:	Pink and green
Issued:	1925-1949
Varieties:	HN 489, 549, 620, 734
Series:	Beggar's Opera
U.S.:	**$1,600.00**
Can.:	**$2,000.00**
U.K.:	**£ 900.00**

HN 695
Lucy Lockett
Style Three
Designer:	L. Harradine
Height:	6", 15.2 cm
Colour:	Orange
Issued:	1925-1949
Varieties:	HN 696
Series:	Beggar's Opera
U.S.:	**$1,600.00**
Can.:	**$2,000.00**
U.K.:	**£ 900.00**

HN 696
Lucy Lockett
Style Three
Designer: L. Harradine
Height: 6", 15.2 cm
Colour: Pale blue
Issued: 1925-1949
Varieties: HN 695
Series: Beggar's Opera

U.S.:	**None**
Can.:	**known**
U.K.:	**to exist**

HN 697
The Balloon Seller
Style One
Designer: L. Harradine
Height: 9", 22.9 cm
Colour: Red and blue
Issued: 1925-1938
Varieties: HN 479, 486, 548, 583; also called 'The Balloon Woman'

U.S.:	**None**
Can.:	**known**
U.K.:	**to exist**

HN 698
Polly Peachum
Style Three
Designer: L. Harradine
Height: 2 ¼", 5.7 cm
Colour: Rose pink
Issued: 1925-1949
Varieties: HN 699, 757, 758, 759, 760, 761, 762, M21, M22, M23
Series: Beggar's Opera

U.S.:	**$1,750.00**
Can.:	**$2,100.00**
U.K.:	**£ 950.00**

HN 699
Polly Peachum
Style Three
Designer: L. Harradine
Height: 2 ¼", 5.7 cm
Colour: Pale blue
Issued: 1925-1949
Varieties: HN 698, 757, 758, 759, 760, 761, 762, M21, M22, M23
Series: Beggar's Opera

U.S.:	**$1,750.00**
Can.:	**$2,100.00**
U.K.:	**£ 950.00**

HN 700
Pretty Lady
Designer: H. Tittensor
Height: 9 ½", 24.1 cm
Colour: Yellow and green
Issued: 1925-1938
Varieties: HN 69, 70, 302, 330, 361, 384, 565, 763, 783

U.S.:	**$3,500.00**
Can.:	**$4,500.00**
U.K.:	**£2,000.00**

HN 701
Myfanwy Jones
Designer: E. W. Light
Height: 12", 30.5 cm
Colour: Multicoloured
Issued: 1925-1936
Varieties: HN 39, 92, 456, 514, 516, 519, 520, 660, 668, 669, 792; also called 'The Welsh Girl'

U.S.:	**None**
Can.:	**known**
U.K.:	**to exist**

HN 702
A Lady of the Georgian Period
Designer: E. W. Light
Height: 10 ¼", 26.0 cm
Colour: Pink and green
Issued: 1925-1936
Varieties: HN 41, 331, 444, 690

U.S.:	**None**
Can.:	**known**
U.K.:	**to exist**

HN 703
Motherhood
Style Two
Designer: Unknown
Height: 9 ¼" 23.5 cm
Colour: Purple, black and red
Issued: 1925-1938
Varieties: HN 462, 570, 743

U.S.:	**None**
Can.:	**known**
U.K.:	**to exist**

HN 704
One of the Forty
Style Two
Designer: H. Tittensor
Height: 7 ¼", 18.4 cm
Colour: Red
Issued: 1925-1936
Varieties: HN 418, 494, 498, 647, 666, 1353

U.S.:	None
Can.:	known
U.K.:	to exist

HN 705
The Gainsborough Hat
Designer: H. Tittensor
Height: 9", 22.9 cm
Colour: Blue
Issued: 1925-1936
Varieties: HN 46, 46A, 47, 329, 352, 383, 453, 675

U.S.:	$6,000.00
Can.:	$7,250.00
U.K.:	£3,250.00

Earthenware

HN 706
Fruit Gathering
Designer: L. Harradine
Height: 7 ¼", 18.4 cm
Colour: Purple and yellow
Issued: 1925-1936
Varieties: HN 449, 476, 503, 561, 562, 707

U.S.:	
Can.:	Extremely rare
U.K.:	

HN 707
Fruit Gathering
Designer: L. Harradine
Height: 7 ¼", 18.4 cm
Colour: Red
Issued: 1925-1936
Varieties: HN 449, 476, 503, 561, 562, 706

U.S.:	$5,000.00
Can.:	$6,000.00
U.K.:	£2,750.00

Earthenware

HN 708
Shepherdess
Style One
Designer: L. Harradine
Height: 3 ½", 8.8 cm
Colour: Red, yellow and pink
Issued: 1925-1938
Varieties: M18, M20

U.S.:	$4,000.00
Can.:	$4,750.00
U.K.:	£2,150.00

HN 709
Shepherd
Style Two
Designer: L. Harradine
Height: 3 ½", 8.8 cm
Colour: Green, red and black
Issued: 1925-1938
Varieties: M17, M19

U.S.:	$4,000.00
Can.:	$4,750.00
U.K.:	£2,150.00

HN 710
Sleep
Designer: P. Stabler
Height: 6", 15.2 cm
Colour: Blue
Issued: 1925-1936
Varieties: HN 24, 24A, 25, 25A, 424, 692

U.S.:	$3,750.00
Can.:	$4,500.00
U.K.:	£2,000.00

HN 711
Harlequinade
Designer: L. Harradine
Height: 7", 17.8 cm
Colour: White and black
Issued: 1925-1940
Varieties: HN 585, 635, 780

U.S.:	$6,500.00
Can.:	$7,750.00
U.K.:	£3,500.00

HN 712
One of the Forty
Style Twelve
Designer: H. Tittensor
Height: Unknown
Colour: Red and black
Issued: 1925-1936
Varieties: HN 481, 483, 491,
646, 667, 1336, 1350;
also known in flambé

U.S.:
Can.: **Extremely rare**
U.K.:

Photograph
Not
Available

HN 713
One of the Forty
Style Thirteen
Designer: H. Tittensor
Height: 6", 15.2 cm
Colour: Red
Issued: 1925-1938
Varieties: HN 482, 484, 492,
645, 663

U.S.: **None**
Can.: **known**
U.K.: **to exist**

HN 714
One of the Forty
Style Eleven
Designer: H. Tittensor
Height: 6 ¾", 17.2 cm
Colour: Red and blue
Issued: 1925-1938
Varieties: HN 480, 493, 497,
499, 664

U.S.: **$5,000.00**
Can.: **$6,000.00**
U.K.: **£2,750.00**

HN 715
Proposal (woman)
Designer: L. Harradine
Height: 5 ¾", 14.6 cm
Colour: Burgundy and black
Issued: 1925-1940
Varieties: HN 716, 788

U.S.: **$2,750.00**
Can.: **$3,250.00**
U.K.: **£1,500.00**

HN 716
Proposal (woman)
Designer: L. Harradine
Height: 5 ¾", 14.6 cm
Colour: White and black
Issued: 1925-1940
Varieties: HN 715, 788

U.S.: **$4,000.00**
Can.: **$5,000.00**
U.K.: **£2,250.00**

HN 717
Lady Clown
Designer: L. Harradine
Height: 7 ½", 19.1 cm
Colour: White, red and black
Issued: 1925-1938
Varieties: HN 718, 738, 770;
also called 'Clownette'
HN 1263

U.S.: **$10,000.00**
Can.: **$12,000.00**
U.K.: **£ 5,250.00**

HN 718
Lady Clown
Designer: L. Harradine
Height: 7 ½", 19.1 cm
Colour: White, red and black
Issued: 1925-1938
Varieties: HN 717, 738, 770;
also called 'Clownette'
HN1263

U.S.: **One**
Can.: **known**
U.K.: **to exist**

HN 719
Butterfly
Designer: L. Harradine
Height: 6 ½", 16.5 cm
Colour: Pink, yellow and black
Issued: 1925-1940
Varieties: HN 720, 730, 1203;
also called 'Butterfly
Woman' HN 1456

U.S.: **$5,500.00**
Can.: **$6,500.00**
U.K.: **£3,000.00**

HN 720
Butterfly
Designer: L. Harradine
Height: 6 ½", 16.5 cm
Colour: Red, white and black
Issued: 1925-1940
Varieties: HN 719, 730, 1203;
             also called 'Butterfly
             Woman' HN 1456

U.S.:   **$5,500.00**
Can.:   **$6,500.00**
U.K.:   **£3,000.00**

HN 721
Pierrette
Style One
Designer: L. Harradine
Height: 7 ¼", 18.4 cm
Colour: Black and white
Issued: 1925-1938
Varieties: HN 642, 643, 644,
             691, 731, 732, 784

U.S.:   **$5,500.00**
Can.:   **$6,500.00**
U.K.:   **£3,000.00**

HN 722
Mephisto
Designer: L. Harradine
Height: 6 ½", 16.5 cm
Colour: Black and red
Issued: 1925-1938
Varieties: HN 723

U.S.:   **$7,500.00**
Can.:   **$9,000.00**
U.K.:   **£4,250.00**

HN 723
Mephisto
Designer: L. Harradine
Height: 6 ½", 16.5 cm
Colour: Red and black
Issued: 1925-1938
Varieties: HN 722

U.S.:   **$7,500.00**
Can.:   **$9,000.00**
U.K.:   **£4,250.00**

HN 724
Mam'selle
Designer: L. Harradine
Height: 7", 17.8 cm
Colour: White, red and yellow
Issued: 1925-1938
Varieties: HN 658, 659, 786

U.S.:   **$6,500.00**
Can.:   **$7,750.00**
U.K.:   **£3,500.00**

HN 725
The Proposal (man)
Designer: Unknown
Height: 5 ½", 14.0 cm
Colour: Red and black
Issued: 1925-1938
Varieties: HN 1209

U.S.:   **$4,000.00**
Can.:   **$5,000.00**
U.K.:   **£2,250.00**

HN 726
A Victorian Lady
Style One
Designer: L. Harradine
Height: 7 ½", 19.1 cm
Colour: Purple and yellow
Issued: 1925-1938
Varieties: HN 727, 728, 736,
             739, 740, 742, 745,
             1208, 1258, 1276,
             1277, 1345, 1452,
             1529

U.S.:   **$1,750.00**
Can.:   **$2,100.00**
U.K.:   **£ 950.00**

HN 727
A Victorian Lady
Style One
Designer: L. Harradine
Height: 7 ½", 19.1 cm
Colour: Pink and green
Issued: 1925-1938
Varieties: HN 726, 728, 736, 739,
             740, 742, 745, 1208,
             1258, 1276, 1277,
             1345, 1452, 1529

U.S.:   **$1,000.00**
Can.:   **$1,200.00**
U.K.:   **£ 550.00**

HN 728
A Victorian Lady
Style One
Designer: L. Harradine
Height: 7 ¾", 19.7 cm
Colour: Pink and purple
Issued: 1925-1952
Varieties: HN 726, 727, 736, 739,
           740, 742, 745, 1208,
           1258, 1276, 1277,
           1345, 1452, 1529
  U.S.: $ 900.00
  Can.: $1,100.00
  U.K.:   £   500.00

HN 729
The Mask
Style One
Designer: L. Harradine
Height: 6 ¾", 17.2 cm
Colour: Red and black
Issued: 1925-1938
Varieties: HN 656, 657, 733,
           785, 1271
  U.S.: $6,000.00
  Can.: $7,250.00
  U.K.:   £3,250.00

HN 730
Butterfly
Designer: L. Harradine
Height: 6 ½", 16.5 cm
Colour: Yellow , blue and black
Issued: 1925-1940
Varieties: HN 719, 720, 1203;
           also called 'Butterfly
           Woman' HN 1456
  U.S.: $6,000.00
  Can.: $7,250.00
  U.K.:   £3,250.00

HN 731
Pierrette
Style One
Designer: L. Harradine
Height: 7 ¼", 18.4 cm
Colour: Black and white
Issued: 1925-1938
Varieties: HN 642, 643, 644,
           691, 721, 732, 784
  U.S.: $6,000.00
  Can.: $7,250.00
  U.K.:   £3,250.00

HN 732
Pierrette
Style One
Designer: L. Harradine
Height: 7 ¼", 18.4 cm
Colour: Black and white
Issued: 1925-1938
Varieties: HN 642, 643, 644,
           691, 721, 731, 784
  U.S.: $6,000.00
  Can.: $7,250.00
  U.K.:   £3,250.00

HN 733
The Mask
Style One
Designer: L. Harradine
Height: 6 ¾", 17.2 cm
Colour: White and black
Issued: 1925-1938
Varieties: HN 656, 657, 729,
           785, 1271
  U.S.: $6,000.00
  Can.: $7,250.00
  U.K.:   £3,250.00

HN 734
Polly Peachum
Style Two
Designer: L. Harradine
Height: 4 ¼", 10.8 cm
Colour: Black and white
Issued: 1925-1949
Varieties: HN 489, 549, 620, 694
Series: Beggar's Opera
  U.S.: $2,750.00
  Can.: $3,250.00
  U.K.:   £1,500.00

HN 735
Shepherdess
Style Two
Designer: L. Harradine
Height: 7", 17.8 cm
Colour: Blue and black
Issued: 1925-1938
Varieties: HN 750; also called
           'Milkmaid' (Style One)
  U.S.: $4,500.00
  Can.: $5,250.00
  U.K.:   £2,500.00

HN 736
A Victorian Lady
Style One
Designer: L. Harradine
Height: 7 ¾", 19.7 cm
Colour: Pink and purple
Issued: 1925-1938
Varieties: HN 726, 727, 728, 739,
            740, 742, 745, 1208,
            1258, 1276, 1277,
            1345, 1452, 1529

U.S.: $1,000.00
Can.: $1,200.00
U.K.:   £ 550.00

HN 737 not issued.

HN 738
Lady Clown
Designer: L. Harradine
Height: 7 ½", 19.1 cm
Colour: Black, white and red
Issued: 1925-1938
Varieties: HN 717, 718, 770;
            also called 'Clownette'
            HN 1263

U.S.:   None
Can.:   known
U.K.:   to exist

HN 739
A Victorian Lady
Style One
Designer: L. Harradine
Height: 7 ¾", 19.7 cm
Colour: Red, blue, yellow
Issued: 1925-1938
Varieties: HN 726, 727, 728, 736,
            740, 742, 745, 1208,
            1258, 1276, 1277,
            1345, 1452, 1529

U.S.: $1,850.00
Can.: $2,250.00
U.K.:   £1,000.00

HN 740
A Victorian Lady
Style One
Designer: L. Harradine
Height: 7 ¾", 19.7 cm
Colour: Pink
Issued: 1925-1938
Varieties: HN 726, 727, 728, 736,
            739, 742, 745, 1208,
            1258, 1276, 1277,
            1345, 1452, 1529

U.S.: $1,650.00
Can.: $2,000.00
U.K.:   £ 900.00

HN 741
A Geisha
Style One
Designer: H. Tittensor
Height: 10 ¾", 27.3 cm
Colour: Multicoloured
Issued: 1925-1936
Varieties: HN 354, 376, 376A,
            387, 634, 779, 1321,
            1322; also called 'The
            Japanese Lady'

U.S.:   None
Can.:   known
U.K.:   to exist

HN 742
A Victorian Lady
Style One
Designer: L. Harradine
Height: 7 ¾", 19.7 cm
Colour: Black and white
Issued: 1925-1938
Varieties: HN 726, 727, 728, 736,
            739, 740, 745, 1208,
            1258, 1276, 1277,
            1345, 1452, 1529

U.S.: $1,850.00
Can.: $2,250.00
U.K.:   £1,000.00

HN 743
Motherhood
Style Two
Designer: Unknown
Height: 9 ¼", 23.5 cm
Colour: Blue and yellow
Issued: 1925-1938
Varieties: HN 462, 570, 703

U.S.:   None
Can.:   known
U.K.:   to exist

HN 744
The Lavender Woman
Designer: P. Stabler
Height: 8 ¼", 21.0 cm
Colour: Blue
Issued: 1925-1936
Varieties: HN 22, 23, 23A, 342,
            569

U.S.: $6,000.00
Can.: $7,250.00
U.K.:   £3,250.00

HN 745
A Victorian Lady
Style One
Designer:	L. Harradine
Height:	7 ¾", 19.7 cm
Colour:	Pink and green
Issued:	1925-1938
Varieties:	HN 726, 727, 728, 736, 739, 740, 742, 1208, 1258, 1276, 1277, 1345, 1452, 1529
U.S.:	**$ 1,650.00**
Can.:	**$ 2,000.00**
U.K.:	**£ 900.00**

HN 746
A Mandarin
Style One
Designer:	C. J. Noke
Height:	10 ¼", 26.0 cm
Colour:	Yellow, black and blue
Issued:	1925-1936
Varieties:	HN 84, 316, 318, 382, 611, 787, 791; also 'Chinese Mandarin' and 'The Mikado'
U.S.:	**$ 9,500.00**
Can.:	**$11,000.00**
U.K.:	**£ 5,000.00**

HN 747
Tulips
Designer:	Unknown
Height:	9 ½", 24.1 cm
Colour:	Blue and green
Issued:	1925-1936
Varieties:	HN 466, 488, 672, 1334
U.S.:	**$6,000.00**
Can.:	**$7,250.00**
U.K.:	**£3,250.00**

HN 748
Out For a Walk
Designer:	E. W. Light
Height:	10", 25.4 cm
Colour:	Green, red and white
Issued:	1925-1936
Varieties:	HN 86, 443
U.S.:	**$7,500.00**
Can.:	**$9,000.00**
U.K.:	**£4,000.00**

HN 749
London Cry, Strawberries
Designer:	L. Harradine
Height:	6 ¾", 17.2 cm
Colour:	Red and cream
Issued:	1925-1936
Varieties:	HN 772
U.S.:	**$4,000.00**
Can.:	**$4,750.00**
U.K.:	**£2,200.00**

HN 750
Shepherdess
Style Two
Designer:	L. Harradine
Height:	7", 17.8 cm
Colour:	Pink and yellow
Issued:	1925-1938
Varieties:	HN 735; also called 'Milkmaid' (Style One)
U.S.:	**$4,500.00**
Can.:	**$5,500.00**
U.K.:	**£2,500.00**

HN 751
Shepherd
Style Three
Designer:	L. Harradine
Height:	7", 17.8 cm
Colour:	Green, black, red and white
Issued:	1925-1938
U.S.:	**$4,500.00**
Can.:	**$5,500.00**
U.K.:	**£2,500.00**

HN 752
London Cry, Turnips and Carrots
Designer:	L. Harradine
Height:	6 ¾", 17.2 cm
Colour:	Purple, red, black and green
Issued:	1925-1938
Varieties:	HN 771
U.S.:	**$4,000.00**
Can.:	**$4,750.00**
U.K.:	**£2,200.00**

HN 753
The Dandy
Designer: L. Harradine
Height: 6 ¾", 17.2 cm
Colour: Red, white, black
and green
Issued: 1925-1936

U.S.: $3,000.00
Can.: $3,600.00
U.K.: £1,650.00

HN 754
The Belle
Style One
Designer: L. Harradine
Height: 6 ½", 16.5 cm
Colour: Multicoloured
Issued: 1925-1938
Varieties: HN 776

U.S.: $2,750.00
Can.: $3,250.00
U.K.: £1,500.00

HN 755
Mephistopheles and Marguerite
Designer: C. J. Noke
Height: 7 ¾", 19.7 cm
Colour: Orange and purple
Issued: 1925-1949
Varieties: HN 775

U.S.: $4,000.00
Can.: $5,000.00
U.K.: £2,250.00

HN 756
The Modern Piper
Designer: L. Harradine
Height: 8 ½", 21.6 cm
Colour: Lavender and green
Issued: 1925-1940

U.S.: $6,500.00
Can.: $7,750.00
U.K.: £3,500.00

HN 757
Polly Peachum
Style Three
Designer: L. Harradine
Height: 2 ¼", 5.7 cm
Colour: Red
Issued: 1925-1949
Varieties: HN 698, 699, 758, 759,
760, 761, 762; M21,
M22, M23
Series: Beggar's Opera

U.S.: $1,800.00
Can.: $2,150.00
U.K.: £ 975.00

HN 758
Polly Peachum
Style Three
Designer: L. Harradine
Height: 2 ¼", 5.7 cm
Colour: Pink and orange
Issued: 1925-1949
Varieties: HN 698, 699, 757,
759, 760, 761, 762;
M21, M22, M23
Series: Beggar's Opera

U.S.: $2,000.00
Can.: $2,500.00
U.K.: £1,100.00

HN 759
Polly Peachum
Style Three
Designer: L. Harradine
Height: 2 ¼", 5.7 cm
Colour: Yellow, white and black
Issued: 1925-1949
Varieties: HN 698, 699, 757,
758, 760, 761, 762;
M21, M22, M23
Series: Beggar's Opera

U.S.: $2,000.00
Can.: $2,500.00
U.K.: £1,100.00

HN 760
Polly Peachum
Style Three
Designer: L. Harradine
Height: 2 ¼", 5.7 cm
Colour: Multicoloured
Issued: 1925-1949
Varieties: HN 698, 699, 757,
758, 759, 761, 762;
M21, M22, M23
Series: Beggar's Opera

U.S.: $2,000.00
Can.: $2,500.00
U.K.: £1,100.00

HN 761
Polly Peachum
Style Three
Designer: L. Harradine
Height: 2 ¼", 5.7 cm
Colour: Blue and purple
Issued: 1925-1949
Varieties: HN 698, 699, 757,
758, 759, 760, 762
M21, M22, M23
Series: Beggar's Opera
U.S.:	**$2,000.00**
Can.:	**$2,500.00**
U.K.:	**£1,100.00**

HN 762
Polly Peachum
Style Three
Designer: L. Harradine
Height: 2 ¼", 5.7 cm
Colour: Red and white
Issued: 1925-1949
Varieties: HN 698, 699, 757,
758, 759, 760, 761;
M21, M22, M23
Series: Beggar's Opera
U.S.:	**$2,000.00**
Can.:	**$2,500.00**
U.K.:	**£1,100.00**

HN 763
Pretty Lady
Designer: H. Tittensor
Height: 9 ½", 24.1 cm
Colour: Orange, white and
green
Issued: 1925-1938
Varieties: HN 69, 70, 302, 330,
361, 384, 565, 700,
783
U.S.:	**None**
Can.:	known
U.K.:	to exist

HN 764
Madonna of the Square
Designer: P. Stabler
Height: 7", 17.8 cm
Colour: Blue, purple and yellow
Issued: 1925-1936
Varieties: HN 10, 10A, 11, 14, 27,
326, 573, 576, 594,
613, 1968, 1969,
2034
U.S.:	
Can.:	**Extremely rare**
U.K.:	

HN 765
The Poke Bonnet
Designer: C. J. Noke
Height: 8 ¾", 22.2 cm
Colour: Green, blue, purple
Issued: 1925-1938
Varieties: HN 362, 612; also
called 'A Lilac Shawl'
HN 44, 44A; and
'In Grandma's Days'
HN 339, 340, 388, 442
U.S.:	**None**
Can.:	known
U.K.:	to exist

HN 766
Irish Colleen
Designer: L. Harradine
Height: 6 ½", 16.5 cm
Colour: Red, black, white
and grey
Issued: 1925-1936
Varieties: HN 767
U.S.:	**$6,750.00**
Can.:	**$8,000.00**
U.K.:	**£3,650.00**

HN 767
Irish Colleen
Designer: L. Harradine
Height: 6 ½", 16.5 cm
Colour: Black, red and green
Issued: 1925-1936
Varieties: HN 766
U.S.:	**$6,750.00**
Can.:	**$8,000.00**
U.K.:	**£3,650.00**

HN 768
Harlequinade Masked
Designer: L. Harradine
Height: 6 ½", 16.5 cm
Colour: Blue, red and green
Issued: 1925-1938
Varieties: HN 769, 1274, 1304
U.S.:	
Can.:	**Extremely rare**
U.K.:	

HN 769
Harlequinade Masked
Designer:	L. Harradine
Height:	6 ½", 16.5 cm
Colour:	Yellow, orange blue and beige
Issued:	1925-1938
Varieties:	HN 768, 1274, 1304

U.S.:	**$ 9,000.00**
Can.:	**$11,000.00**
U.K.:	**£ 5,000.00**

HN 770
Lady Clown
Designer:	L. Harradine
Height:	7 ½", 19.1 cm
Colour:	White and green
Issued:	1925-1938
Varieties:	HN 717, 718, 738; also called 'Clownette' HN 1263

U.S.:	**$10,000.00**
Can.:	**$12,000.00**
U.K.:	**£ 5,250.00**

HN 771
London Cry, Turnips and Carrots
Designer:	L. Harradine
Height:	6 ¾", 17.2 cm
Colour:	Lavender, cream and brown
Issued:	1925-1938
Varieties:	HN 752

U.S.:	**$4,000.00**
Can.:	**$4,750.00**
U.K.:	**£2,200.00**

HN 772
London Cry, Strawberries
Designer:	L. Harradine
Height:	6 ¾", 17.2 cm
Colour:	Lavender and cream
Issued:	1925-1936
Varieties:	HN 749

U.S.:	**$4,000.00**
Can.:	**$4,750.00**
U.K.:	**£2,200.00**

HN 773
The Bather
Style Two
Designer:	L. Harradine
Height:	7 ½", 19.1 cm
Colour:	Pink, purple and black
Issued:	1925-1938
Varieties:	HN 774, 1227

U.S.:	**$6,000.00**
Can.:	**$7,250.00**
U.K.:	**£3,250.00**

HN 774
The Bather
Style Two
Designer:	L. Harradine
Height:	7 ¾", 19.7 cm
Colour:	Blue, red and black
Issued:	1925-1938
Varieties:	HN 773, 1227

U.S.:	**$6,000.00**
Can.:	**$7,250.00**
U.K.:	**£3,250.00**

HN 775
Mephistopheles and Marguerite
Designer:	C. J. Noke
Height:	7 ¾", 19.7 cm
Colour:	Orange and cream
Issued:	1925-1949
Varieties:	HN 755

U.S.:	**$3,500.00**
Can.:	**$4,250.00**
U.K.:	**£1,900.00**

HN 776
The Belle
Style One
Designer:	L. Harradine
Height:	6 ½", 16.5 cm
Colour:	Unknown
Issued:	1925-1938
Varieties:	HN 754

U.S.:	
Can.:	**Extremely rare**
U.K.:	

HN 777
Bo-Peep
Style One
Designer: L. Harradine
Height: 6 ¾", 17.2 cm
Colour: Dark blue
Issued: 1926-1936
Varieties: HN 1202, 1327, 1328

U.S.:	**$6,000.00**
Can.:	**$7,250.00**
U.K.:	**£3,250.00**

HN 778
Captain
Style One
Designer: L. Harradine
Height: 7", 17.8 cm
Colour: Red and white
Issued: 1926-1936

U.S.:	**$4,750.00**
Can.:	**$5,750.00**
U.K.:	**£2,550.00**

HN 779
Geisha
Style One
Designer: H. Tittensor
Height: 10 ¾", 27.3 cm
Colour: Red and purple
Issued: 1926-1936
Varieties: HN 354, 376, 376A,
387, 634, 741, 1321,
1322; also called
'The Japanese Lady'

U.S.:	**$ 9,000.00**
Can.:	**$11,000.00**
U.K.:	**£ 5,000.00**

HN 780
Harlequinade
Designer: L. Harradine
Height: 6 ½", 16.5 cm
Colour: Pink, blue, orange
and black
Issued: 1926-1940
Varieties: HN 585, 635, 711

U.S.:	**$6,500.00**
Can.:	**$7,750.00**
U.K.:	**£3,500.00**

HN 781
The Bather
Style One, First Version
Designer: L. Harradine
Height: 7 ¾", 19.7 cm
Colour: Blue and green
Issued: 1926-1938
Varieties: HN 597, 687, 782,
1238, 1708

U.S.:	
Can.:	**Extremely rare**
U.K.:	

HN 782
The Bather
Style One, First Version
Designer: L. Harradine
Height: 7 ¾", 19.7 cm
Colour: Purple and black
Issued: 1926-1938
Varieties: HN 597, 687, 781,
1238, 1708

U.S.:	
Can.:	**Extremely rare**
U.K.:	

HN 783
Pretty Lady
Designer: H. Tittensor
Height: 9 ½", 24.1 cm
Colour: Blue
Issued: 1926-1938
Varieties: HN 69, 70, 302, 330,
361, 384, 565, 700, 763

U.S.:	**$3,750.00**
Can.:	**$4,500.00**
U.K.:	**£2,000.00**

HN 784
Pierrette
Style One
Designer: L. Harradine
Height: 7 ¼", 18.4 cm
Colour: Pink and black
Issued: 1926-1938
Varieties: HN 642, 643, 644,
691, 721, 731, 732

U.S.:	**$6,000.00**
Can.:	**$7,250.00**
U.K.:	**£3,250.00**

HN 785
The Mask
Style One
Designer: L. Harradine
Height: 6 ¾", 17.2 cm
Colour: Blue, black and pink
Issued: 1926-1938
Varieties: HN 656, 657, 729,
             733, 1271

U.S.:	$6,500.00
Can.:	$7,750.00
U.K.:	£3,500.00

HN 786
Mam'selle
Designer: L. Harradine
Height: 7", 17.8 cm
Colour: Pink and black
Issued: 1926-1938
Varieties: HN 658, 659, 724

U.S.:	$6,500.00
Can.:	$7,750.00
U.K.:	£3,500.00

HN 787
A Mandarin
Style One
Designer: C. J. Noke
Height: 10 ¼", 26.0 cm
Colour: Pink and orange
Issued: 1926-1936
Varieties: HN 84, 316, 318, 382,
             611, 746, 791; also
             called 'Chinese
             Mandarin' and 'The
             Mikado'

U.S.:	
Can.:	Extremely rare
U.K.:	

HN 788
Proposal (woman)
Designer: L. Harradine
Height: 5 ¾", 14.6 cm
Colour: Pink
Issued: 1926-1940
Varieties: HN 715, 716

U.S.:	
Can.:	Extremely rare
U.K.:	

HN 789
The Flower Seller
Designer: L. Harradine
Height: 8 ¾", 22.2 cm
Colour: Green, cream
             and white
Issued: 1926-1938

U.S.:	$2,750.00
Can.:	$3,250.00
U.K.:	£1,500.00

Earthenware

HN 790
The Parson's Daughter
Designer: H. Tittensor
Height: 10", 25.4 cm
Colour: Multicoloured
Issued: 1926-1938
Varieties: HN 337, 338, 441,
             564, 1242, 1356, 2018

U.S.:	$3,250.00
Can.:	$4,000.00
U.K.:	£1,750.00

HN 791
A Mandarin
Style One
Designer: C. J. Noke
Height: 10 ¼", 26.0 cm
Colour: Black and purple
Issued: 1926-1936
Varieties: HN 84, 316, 318, 382,
             611, 746, 787; also
             called 'Chinese
             Mandarin' and 'The
             Mikado'

U.S.:	$ 9,500.00
Can.:	$11,000.00
U.K.:	£ 5,000.00

HN 792
Myfanwy Jones
Designer: E. W. Light
Height: 12", 30.5 cm
Colour: Pink and blue
Issued: 1926-1936
Varieties: HN 39, 92, 456, 514,
             516, 519, 520, 660,
             668, 669, 701; also
             called 'The Welsh Girl'

U.S.:	
Can.:	Extremely rare
U.K.:	

HN 793
Katharine
Style One
Designer: C. J. Noke
Height: 5 ¾", 14.6 cm
Colour: Lavender and green
Issued: 1926-1938
Varieties: HN 61, 74, 341, 471, 615

U.S.:	$3,750.00
Can.:	$4,500.00
U.K.:	£2,000.00

HN 794
The Bouquet
Designer: G. Lambert
Height: 9", 22.9 cm
Colour: Blue, red and green
Issued: 1926-1936
Varieties: HN 406, 414, 422, 428, 429, 567; also called 'The Nosegay'

U.S.:	
Can.:	Extremely rare
U.K.:	

HN 795
Pierrette
Style Two
Designer: L. Harradine
Height: 3 ½", 8.9 cm
Colour: Pink
Issued: 1926-1938
Varieties: HN 796

U.S.:	
Can.:	Extremely rare
U.K.:	

HN 796
Pierrette
Style Two
Designer: L. Harradine
Height: 3 ½", 8.9 cm
Colour: White and silver
Issued: 1926-1938
Varieties: HN 795

U.S.:	
Can.:	Extremely rare
U.K.:	

HN 797
Moorish Minstrel
Designer: C. J. Noke
Height: 13 ½", 34.3 cm
Colour: Purple
Issued: 1926-1949
Varieties: HN 34, 364, 415

U.S.:	$5,500.00
Can.:	$6,500.00
U.K.:	£3,000.00

HN 798
Tete-a-Tete
Style One
Designer: L. Harradine
Height: 5 ¾", 14.6 cm
Colour: Pink and red
Issued: 1926-1938
Varieties: HN 799

U.S.:	$4,500.00
Can.:	$5,500.00
U.K.:	£2,500.00

HN 799
Tete-a-Tete
Style One
Designer: L. Harradine
Height: 5 ¾", 14.6 cm
Colour: Blue and red
Issued: 1926-1940
Varieties: HN 798

U.S.:	$4,500.00
Can.:	$5,500.00
U.K.:	£2,500.00

HN 800 - 1200 Animal and Bird figures, except HN 816, 817, 830, 887, 959, 1006, 1060, 1061, 1122, 1123, 1124, 1200 not issued.

HN 1201
Hunts Lady
Designer: L. Harradine
Height: 8 ¼", 21.0 cm
Colour: Grey-blue and cream
Issued: 1926-1938

U.S.:	$5,000.00
Can.:	$6,500.00
U.K.:	£3,000.00

HN 1202
Bo-Peep
Style One
Designer:　L. Harradine
Height:　6 ¾", 17.2 cm
Colour:　Purple, green and pink
Issued:　1926-1936
Varieties:　HN 777, 1327, 1328

U.S.:
Can.:　**Extremely rare**
U.K.:

HN 1203
Butterfly
Designer:　L. Harradine
Height:　6 ½", 16.5 cm
Colour:　Black and gold
Issued:　1926-1940
Varieties:　HN 719, 720, 730;
　　　　　also called 'Butterfly
　　　　　Woman' HN 1456

U.S.:
Can.:　**Extremely rare**
U.K.:

HN 1204
Angela
Style One
Designer:　L. Harradine
Height:　7 ¼", 18.4 cm
Colour:　Purple and pink
Issued:　1926-1940
Varieties:　HN 1303; also called
　　　　　'Fanny'

U.S.:　$4,000.00
Can.:　$4,750.00
U.K.:　£2,000.00

HN 1205
Miss 1926
Designer:　L. Harradine
Height:　7 ¼", 18.4 cm
Colour:　Black and white
Issued:　1926-1938
Varieties:　HN 1207

U.S.:　$10,000.00
Can.:　$12,000.00
U.K.:　£ 5,500.00

HN 1206
The Flower Seller's Children
Designer:　L. Harradine
Height:　8 ¼", 21.0 cm
Colour:　Blue and purple
Issued:　1926-1949
Varieties:　HN 525, 551, 1342,
　　　　　1406

U.S.:　$3,500.00
Can.:　$4,250.00
U.K.:　£1,900.00

HN 1207
Miss 1926
Designer:　L. Harradine
Height:　7 ¼", 18.4 cm
Colour:　Black
Issued:　Unknown
Varieties:　HN 1205

U.S.:
Can.:　**Extremely rare**
U.K.:

HN 1208
A Victoria Lady
Style One
Designer:　L. Harradine
Height:　7 ¾", 19.7 cm
Colour:　Green and purple
Issued:　1926-1938
Varieties:　HN 726, 727, 728,
　　　　　736, 739, 740, 742,
　　　　　745, 1258, 1276,
　　　　　1277, 1345, 1452,
　　　　　1529

U.S.:　$1,650.00
Can.:　$2,000.00
U.K.:　£ 900.00

HN 1209
The Proposal (Man)
Designer:　Unknown
Height:　5 ½", 14.0 cm
Colour:　Blue and pink
Issued:　1926-1938
Varieties:　HN 725

U.S.:　$4,000.00
Can.:　$5,000.00
U.K.:　£2,250.00

HN 1210
Boy with Turban
Designer: L. Harradine
Height: 3 ¾", 9.5 cm
Colour: Orange, black and
white
Issued: 1926-1936
Varieties: HN 586, 587, 661, 662,
1212, 1213, 1214, 1225

U.S.: $2,000.00
Can.: $2,500.00
U.K.: £1,100.00

HN 1211
Quality Street
Designer: Unknown
Height: 7 ¼", 18.4 cm
Colour: Red
Issued: 1926-1936
Varieties: HN 1211A

U.S.: $2,500.00
Can.: $3,000.00
U.K.: £1,350.00

HN 1211A
Quality Street
Designer: Unknown
Height: 7 ¼", 18.4 cm
Colour: Lavender
Issued: 1926-1936
Varieties: HN 1211

U.S.: $4,000.00
Can.: $4,750.00
U.K.: £2,150.00

HN 1212
Boy with Turban
Designer: L. Harradine
Height: 3 ¾", 9.5 cm
Colour: Purple and green
Issued: 1926-1936
Varieties: HN 586, 587, 661, 662,
1210, 1213, 1214, 1225

U.S.: $2,000.00
Can.: $2,500.00
U.K.: £1,100.00

HN 1213
Boy with Turban
Designer: L. Harradine
Height: 3 ¾", 9.5 cm
Colour: White and black
Issued: 1926-1936
Varieties: HN 586, 587, 661, 662,
1210, 1212, 1214, 1225

U.S.: $2,000.00
Can.: $2,500.00
U.K.: £1,100.00

HN 1214
Boy with Turban
Designer: L. Harradine
Height: 3 ½", 8.9 cm
Colour: Black, white
and green
Issued: 1926-1936
Varieties: HN 586, 587, 661, 662,
1210, 1212, 1213, 1225

U.S.: $2,000.00
Can.: $2,500.00
U.K.: £1,100.00

HN 1215
The Pied Piper
Style One
Designer: L. Harradine
Height: 8 ¼", 21.0 cm
Colour: Red, black and yellow
Issued: 1926-1938
Varieties: HN 2102

U.S.: $4,000.00
Can.: $4,750.00
U.K.: £2,150.00

HN 1216
Falstaff
Style One
Designer: C. J. Noke
Height: 7", 17.8 cm
Colour: Multicoloured
Issued: 1926-1949
Varieties: HN 571, 575, 608,
609, 619, 638, 1606

U.S.: $3,500.00
Can.: $4,250.00
U.K.: £1,900.00

HN 1217
The Prince of Wales
Designer: L. Harradine
Height: 7 ½", 19.1 cm
Colour: Red and white
Issued: 1926-1938
U.S.: $3,000.00
Can.: $3,600.00
U.K.: £1,625.00

HN 1218
A Spook
Style Two
Designer: H. Tittensor
Height: 3", 7.6 cm
Colour: Multicoloured
Issued: 1926-1936
Varieties: Colourway: Red
cloak, black cap
U.S.: $4,000.00
Can.: $4,750.00
U.K.: £2,200.00

HN 1219
Negligée
Designer: L. Harradine
Height: 5", 12.7 cm
Colour: Bluish-yellow, blue
hair band
Issued: 1927-1936
Varieties: HN 1228, 1272,
1273, 1454
U.S.: $3,750.00
Can.: $4,500.00
U.K.: £2,000.00

HN 1220
Lido Lady
First Version
Designer: L. Harradine
Height: 6 ¾", 17.2 cm
Colour: Pink
Issued: 1927-1936
Varieties: HN 1229
U.S.: $3,000.00
Can.: $3,600.00
U.K.: £1,625.00

HN 1221
Lady Jester
Style One
Designer: L. Harradine
Height: 7", 17.8 cm
Colour: Multicoloured
Issued: 1927-1938
Varieties: HN 1222, 1332
U.S.: $6,000.00
Can.: $7,250.00
U.K.: £3,250.00

HN 1222
Lady Jester
Style One
Designer: L. Harradine
Height: 7", 17.8 cm
Colour: Black and white
Issued: 1927-1938
Varieties: HN 1221, 1332
U.S.: $6,000.00
Can.: $7,250.00
U.K.: £3,250.00

HN 1223
A Geisha
Style Two
Designer: C. J. Noke
Height: 6 ¾", 17.2 cm
Colour: Black and orange
Issued: 1927-1938
Varieties: HN 1234, 1292, 1310
U.S.: $3,000.00
Can.: $3,600.00
U.K.: £1,625.00

HN 1224
The Wandering Minstrel
Designer: L. Harradine
Height: 7", 17.8 cm
Colour: Purple and red
Issued: 1927-1936
U.S.: $6,000.00
Can.: $7,250.00
U.K.: £3,250.00

HN 1225
Boy with Turban
Designer: L. Harradine
Height: 3 ¾", 9.5 cm
Colour: Yellow and blue
Issued: 1927-1936
Varieties: HN 586, 587, 661, 662,
1210, 1212, 1213, 1214

U.S.:	**$2,250.00**
Can.:	**$2,750.00**
U.K.:	**£1,200.00**

HN 1226
The Huntsman
Style One
Designer: L. Harradine
Height: 8 ¾", 22.2 cm
Colour: Red and white
Issued: 1927-1938

U.S.:	**$5,000.00**
Can.:	**$6,000.00**
U.K.:	**£2,700.00**

HN 1227
The Bather
Style Two
Designer: L. Harradine
Height: 7 ½", 19.1 cm
Colour: Pink and black
Issued: 1927-1938
Varieties: HN 773, 774

U.S.:	**$7,500.00**
Can.:	**$9,000.00**
U.K.:	**£4,000.00**

HN 1228
Negligée
Designer: L. Harradine
Height: 5", 12.7 cm
Colour: Bluish-yellow, red
hair band
Issued: 1927-1936
Varieties: HN 1219, 1272,
1273, 1454

U.S.:	**$3,750.00**
Can.:	**$4,500.00**
U.K.:	**£2,000.00**

HN 1229
Lido Lady
First Version
Designer: L. Harradine
Height: 6 ¾", 17.2 cm
Colour: Blue
Issued: 1927-1936
Varieties: HN 1220

U.S.:	**$6,000.00**
Can.:	**$7,250.00**
U.K.:	**£3,250.00**

HN 1230
Baba
Designer: L. Harradine
Height: 3 ¼", 8.3 cm
Colour: Blue, yellow and purple
Issued: 1927-1938
Varieties: HN 1243, 1244, 1245,
1246, 1247, 1248

U.S.:	**$2,250.00**
Can.:	**$2,750.00**
U.K.:	**£1,225.00**

HN 1231
Cassim
Style One
Designer: L. Harradine
Height: 3", 7.6 cm
Colour: Blue, yellow and
turquoise
Issued: 1927-1938
Varieties: HN 1232

U.S.:	**$2,250.00**
Can.:	**$2,750.00**
U.K.:	**£1,225.00**

HN 1232
Cassim
Style One
Designer: L. Harradine
Height: 3", 7.6 cm
Colour: Orange and black
Issued: 1927-1938
Varieties: HN 1231

U.S.:	**$2,000.00**
Can.:	**$2,500.00**
U.K.:	**£1,100.00**

HN 1233
Susanna
Designer: L. Harradine
Height: 6", 15.2 cm
Colour: Pink
Issued: 1927-1936
Varieties: HN 1288, 1299

U.S.:	**$3,500.00**
Can.:	**$4,250.00**
U.K.:	**£1,900.00**

HN 1234
A Geisha
Style Two
Designer: C. J. Noke
Height: 6 ¾", 17.2 cm
Colour: Green and red
Issued: 1927-1938
Varieties: HN 1223, 1292, 1310

U.S.:	**$2,750.00**
Can.:	**$3,250.00**
U.K.:	**£1,500.00**

HN 1235
A Scribe
Designer: C. J. Noke
Height: 6", 15.2 cm
Colour: Brown, blue and orange
Issued: 1927-1938
Varieties: HN 305, 324

U.S.:	**$3,000.00**
Can.:	**$3,500.00**
U.K.:	**£1,650.00**

HN 1236
Tete-a-Tete
Style Two
Designer: C. J. Noke
Height: 3", 7.6 cm
Colour: Purple and red
Issued: 1927-1938
Varieties: HN 1237

U.S.:	**$4,750.00**
Can.:	**$5,750.00**
U.K.:	**£2,550.00**

HN 1237
Tete-a-Tete
Style Two
Designer: C. J. Noke
Height: 3", 7.6 cm
Colour: Pink
Issued: 1927-1938
Varieties: HN 1236

U.S.:	**$4,750.00**
Can.:	**$5,750.00**
U.K.:	**£2,550.00**

HN 1238
The Bather
Style One, First Version
Designer: L. Harradine
Height: 7 ¾", 19.7 cm
Colour: Red and black
Issued: 1927-1938
Varieties: HN 597, 687, 781,
           782, 1708

U.S.:	**$4,500.00**
Can.:	**$5,500.00**
U.K.:	**£2,500.00**

HN 1242
The Parson's Daughter
Designer: H. Tittesnor
Height: 10", 25.4 cm
Colour: Lavender and yellow
Issued: 1927-1938
Varieties: HN 337, 338, 441, 564,
           790, 1356, 2018

U.S.:	**$3,000.00**
Can.:	**$3,600.00**
U.K.:	**£1,600.00**

HN 1243
Baba
Designer: L. Harradine
Height: 3 ¼", 8.3 cm
Colour: Orange
Issued: 1927-1938
Varieties: HN 1230, 1244,1245,
           1246, 1247, 1248

U.S.:	**$2,250.00**
Can.:	**$2,750.00**
U.K.:	**£1,225.00**

HN 1239 - 1241 not issued.

EARLY HN FIGURINES

HN 1
Darling
1913-1928

HN 56
The Land of Nod
1916-1938

HN 355
Dolly, Style One
1919-1938

Colourways of Shy Anne

HN 60
1916-1936

HN 64
1916-1936

HN 65
1916-1936

HN 568
1923-1936

EARLY HN FIGURINES

HN 42
Robert Burns, Style One
1914-1938

HN 347
Guy Fawkes, Style One
1919-1938

HN 364
A Moorish Minstrel
1920-1938

HN 2
Elizabeth Fry
1913-1936

HN 31
The Return of Persephone
1913-1938

Colourways of The Mask

HN 656
1924-1938

HN 729
1925-1938

HN 733
1925-1938

Colourways of Harlequinade

HN 585
1923-1940

HN 635
1924-1940

HN 780
1926-1940

PERIOD COSTUMES

HN 87
The Lady Anne
1918-1938

HN 43
A Woman of the Time of Henry VI
1914-1938

HN 41
A Lady of the Georgian Period
1914-1936

HN 309
An Elizabethan Lady
Style Two, 1918-1938

HN 411
A Lady of the Elizabethan Period
Style One, 1920-1938

Colourways of Omar Khayyam and the Beloved

HN 407
Style One
1920-Unknown

HN 419
Style Two
1920-1936

HN 459
Style Two
1921-1936

Colourways of An Old King

HN 358
1919-1938

HN 2134
1954-1992

Colourways of A Jester

HN 45
1915-1938

HN 1295
1928-1949

HN 1702
1935-1949

Colourways of A Mandarin

HN 316
1918-1936

HN 746
1925-1936

HN 791
1926-1936

Pavlova

HN 487
1921-1938

Crinoline Lady

HN 654
1924-1938

Colourways

HN 676
1924-1938

HN 655
1924-1938

Colourways of Butterfly / The Butterfly Woman

HN 719
1925-1940

HN 720
1925-1940

HN 1456
1931-1940

HN FIGURINES FROM THE 1920s AND 1930s

HN 1201
Hunts Lady

HN 1217
The Prince of Wales

HN 1226
The Huntsman, Style One

HN 1301
Young Mother with Child
1928-1938

HN 562
Fruit Gathering
1923-1936

HN 1302
The Gleaner
1928-1936

HN 1244
Baba
Designer: L. Harradine
Height: 3 ¼", 8.3 cm
Colour: Yellow and green
Issued: 1927-1938
Varieties: HN 1230, 1243,1245,
             1246, 1247, 1248

U.S.:   **$2,500.00**
Can.:   **$3,000.00**
U.K.:   **£1,350.00**

HN 1245
Baba
Designer: L. Harradine
Height: 3 ¼", 8.3 cm
Colour: White and black
Issued: 1927-1938
Varieties: HN 1230, 1243, 1244,
             1246, 1247, 1248

U.S.:   **$2,500.00**
Can.:   **$3,000.00**
U.K.:   **£1,350.00**

HN 1246
Baba
Designer: L. Harradine
Height: 3 ¼", 8.3 cm
Colour: Green
Issued: 1927-1938
Varieties: HN 1230, 1243,1244,
             1245, 1247, 1248

U.S.:   **$2,500.00**
Can.:   **$3,000.00**
U.K.:   **£1,350.00**

HN 1247
Baba
Designer: L. Harradine
Height: 3 ¼", 8.3 cm
Colour: Black, white and
             orange
Issued: 1927-1938
Varieties: HN 1230, 1243, 1244,
             1245, 1246, 1248

U.S.:   **$2,500.00**
Can.:   **$3,000.00**
U.K.:   **£1,350.00**

HN 1248
Baba
Designer: L. Harradine
Height: 3 ¼", 8.3 cm
Colour: Green and orange
Issued: 1927-1938
Varieties: HN 1230, 1243, 1244,
             1245, 1246, 1247

U.S.:   **$2,500.00**
Can.:   **$3,000.00**
U.K.:   **£1,350.00**

HN 1249
Circe
Designer: L. Harradine
Height: 7 ¾", 19.7 cm
Colour: Green, orange and pink
Issued: 1927-1936
Varieties: HN 1250, 1254, 1255

U.S.:   **$5,500.00**
Can.:   **$6,500.00**
U.K.:   **£3,000.00**

HN 1250
Circe
Designer: L. Harradine
Height: 7 ½", 19.1 cm
Colour: Orange and black
Issued: 1927-1936
Varieties: HN 1249, 1254, 1255

U.S.:   **$5,500.00**
Can.:   **$6,500.00**
U.K.:   **£3,000.00**

HN 1251
The Cobbler
Style Two
Designer: C. J. Noke
Height: 8 ½", 21.6 cm
Colour: Black and red
Issued: 1927-1938
Varieties: HN 681, 1283

U.S.:   **$3,000.00**
Can.:   **$3,750.00**
U.K.:   **£1,650.00**

HN 1252
Kathleen
Style One
Designer: L. Harradine
Height: 7 ¾", 19.7 cm
Colour: Lavender, pink,
           purple and blue
Issued: 1927-1938
Varieties: HN 1253, 1275, 1279,
           1291, 1357, 1512

  U.S.: $1,500.00
  Can.: $1,875.00
  U.K.:   £ 850.00

HN 1253
Kathleen
Style One
Designer: L. Harradine
Height: 7 ½", 19.1 cm
Colour: Red and purple
Issued: 1927-1938
Varieties: HN 1252, 1275, 1279,
           1291, 1357, 1512

  U.S.: $1,500.00
  Can.: $1,875.00
  U.K.:   £ 850.00

HN 1254
Circe
Designer: L. Harradine
Height: 7 ½", 19.1 cm
Colour: Orange and red
Issued: 1927-1936
Varieties: HN 1249, 1250, 1255

  U.S.:
  Can.:   **Extremely rare**
  U.K.:

HN 1255
Circe
Designer: L. Harradine
Height: 7 ½", 19.1 cm
Colour: Blue
Issued: 1927-1938
Varieties: HN 1249, 1250, 1254

  U.S.:
  Can.:   **Extremely rare**
  U.K.:

HN 1256
Captain MacHeath
Designer: L. Harradine
Height: 7", 17.8 cm
Colour: Red, yellow and black
Issued: 1927-1949
Varieties: HN 464, 590
Series: Beggar's Opera

  U.S.: $1,600.00
  Can.: $2,000.00
  U.K.:   £ 900.00

Earthenware

HN 1257
Highwayman
Designer: L. Harradine
Height: 6 ½", 16.5 cm
Colour: Green and red
Issued: 1927-1949
Varieties: HN 527, 592
Series: Beggar's Opera

  U.S.: $1,300.00
  Can.: $1,550.00
  U.K.:   £ 725.00

Earthenware

HN 1258
A Victorian Lady
Style One
Designer: L. Harradine
Height: 7 ¾", 19.7 cm
Colour: Purple and blue
Issued: 1927-1938
Varieties: HN 726, 727, 728, 736,
           739, 740, 742, 745,
           1208, 1276,1277,
           1345, 1452, 1529

  U.S.: $1,550.00
  Can.: $1,850.00
  U.K.:   £ 850.00

HN 1259
The Alchemist
Designer: L. Harradine
Height: 11 ½", 29.2 cm
Colour: Green and red
Issued: 1927-1938
Varieties: HN 1282

  U.S.: $3,500.00
  Can.: $4,250.00
  U.K.:   £1,900.00

HN 1260
Carnival
Designer: L. Harradine
Height: 8 ¼", 21.0 cm
Colour: Red, black and purple
Issued: 1927-1936
Varieties: HN 1278
    U.S.: $10,000.00
    Can.: $12,000.00
    U.K.:   £ 5,250.00

HN 1261
Sea Sprite
Style One
Designer: L. Harradine
Height: 5", 12.7 cm
Colour: Red, purple and black
Issued: 1927-1938
    U.S.: $1,500.00
    Can.: $1,800.00
    U.K.:   £ 820.00

HN 1262
Spanish Lady
Designer: L. Harradine
Height: 8 ½", 21.6 cm
Colour: Black with red flowers
Issued: 1927-1940
Varieties: HN 1290, 1293, 1294,
            1309
    U.S.: $2,500.00
    Can.: $3,000.00
    U.K.:   £1,350.00

HN 1263
Clownette
Designer: L. Harradine
Height: 7 ¼", 18.4 cm
Colour: Mottled purple
Issued: 1927-1938
Varieties: Also called 'Lady
            Clown' HN 717, 718,
            738, 770
    U.S.: $10,000.00
    Can.: $12,000.00
    U.K.:   £ 5,250.00

HN 1264
Judge and Jury
Designer: J. G. Hughes
Height: 6", 15.2 cm
Colour: Red and white
Issued: 1927-1938
    U.S.:
    Can.:   **Extremely rare**
    U.K.:

HN 1265
Lady Fayre
Designer: L. Harradine
Height: 5 ¼", 13.3 cm
Colour: Lavender and red
Issued: 1928-1938
Varieties: HN 1557
    U.S.: $1,500.00
    Can.: $1,800.00
    U.K.:   £ 820.00

HN 1266
Ko-Ko
Style One
Designer: L. Harradine
Height: 5", 12.7 cm
Colour: Black, white and yellow
Issued: 1928-1936
Varieties: HN 1286
    U.S.: $2,400.00
    Can.: $3,000.00
    U.K.:   £1,300.00

HN 1267
Carmen
Style One
Designer: L. Harradine
Height: 7", 17.8 cm
Colour: Red and black
Issued: 1928-1938
Varieties: HN 1300
    U.S.: $2,250.00
    Can.: $2,750.00
    U.K.:   £1,200.00

HN 1268
Yum-Yum
Style One
Designer: L. Harradine
Height: 5", 12.7 cm
Colour: Pink and cream
Issued: 1928-1936
Varieties: HN 1287

U.S.:	**$2,400.00**
Can.:	**$3,000.00**
U.K.:	**£1,300.00**

HN 1269
Scotch Girl
Designer: L. Harradine
Height: 7 ½", 19.1 cm
Colour: Red and green
Issued: 1928-1938

U.S.:	**$5,000.00**
Can.:	**$6,000.00**
U.K.:	**£2,700.00**

HN 1270
The Swimmer
First Version
Designer: L. Harradine
Height: 7 ¼", 18.4 cm
Colour: Mottled blue,
             red and black
Issued: 1928-1938
Varieties: HN 1326, 1329

U.S.:	**$5,250.00**
Can.:	**$6,500.00**
U.K.:	**£3,000.00**

HN 1271
The Mask
Style One
Designer: L. Harradine
Height: 6 ¾", 17.2 cm
Colour: Black, blue and red
Issued: 1928-1938
Varieties: HN 656, 657, 729,
             733, 785

U.S.:	**$5,500.00**
Can.:	**$6,750.00**
U.K.:	**£3,000.00**

HN 1272
Negligée
Designer: L. Harradine
Height: 5", 12.7 cm
Colour: Red and black
Issued: 1928-1936
Varieties: HN 1219, 1228,
             1273, 1454,

U.S.:	**$3,500.00**
Can.:	**$4,500.00**
U.K.:	**£2,000.00**

HN 1273
Negligée
Designer: L. Harradine
Height: 5", 12.7 cm
Colour: White and pink
Issued: 1928-1936
Varieties: HN 1219, 1228,
             1272, 1454

U.S.:	**$3,500.00**
Can.:	**$4,500.00**
U.K.:	**£2,000.00**

HN 1274
Harlequinade Masked
Designer: L. Harradine
Height: 6 ½", 16.5 cm
Colour: Orange and black
Issued: 1928-1938
Varieties: HN 768, 769, 1304

U.S.:	**$6,750.00**
Can.:	**$8,000.00**
U.K.:	**£3,650.00**

HN 1275
Kathleen
Style One
Designer: L. Harradine
Height: 7 ½", 19.1 cm
Colour: Pink and black
Issued: 1928-1938
Varieties: HN 1252, 1253, 1279,
             1291, 1357, 1512

U.S.:	
Can.:	**Extremely rare**
U.K.:	

HN 1276
A Victorian Lady
Style One
Designer: L. Harradine
Height: 7 ½", 19.1 cm
Colour: Purple, red, yellow
Issued: 1928-1938
Varieties: HN 726, 727, 728, 736, 739, 740, 742, 745, 1208, 1258, 1277, 1345, 1452, 1529

U.S.: $1,800.00
Can.: $2,250.00
U.K.: £ 975.00

HN 1277
A Victorian Lady
Style One
Designer: L. Harradine
Height: 7 ¾", 19.7 cm
Colour: Red, yellow, blue
Issued: 1928-1938
Varieties: HN 726, 727, 728, 736, 739, 740, 742, 745, 1208, 1258, 1276, 1345, 1452, 1529

U.S.: $1,800.00
Can.: $2,250.00
U.K.: £ 975.00

HN 1278
Carnival
Designer: L. Harradine
Height: 8 ½", 21.6 cm
Colour: Blue, orange and purple
Issued: 1928-1936
Varieties: HN 1260

U.S.: $12,000.00
Can.: $14,500.00
U.K.: £ 6,000.00

HN 1279
Kathleen
Style One
Designer: L. Harradine
Height: 7 ¾", 19.7 cm
Colour: Red
Issued: 1928-1938
Varieties: HN 1252, 1253, 1275, 1291, 1357, 1512

U.S.: $1,500.00
Can.: $1,875.00
U.K.: £ 850.00

HN 1280
Blue Bird
Designer: L. Harradine
Height: 4 ¾", 12.0 cm
Colour: Pink base
Issued: 1928-1938

U.S.: $1,800.00
Can.: $2,250.00
U.K.: £ 975.00

HN 1281
Scotties
Designer: L. Harradine
Height: 5 ½", 14.0 cm
Colour: Red and black
Issued: 1928-1936
Varieties: HN 1349

U.S.: $3,500.00
Can.: $4,250.00
U.K.: £1,900.00

HN 1282
The Alchemist
Designer: L. Harradine
Height: 11 ¼", 28.5 cm
Colour: Purple and red
Issued: 1928-1938
Varieties: HN 1259

U.S.: $3,500.00
Can.: $4,250.00
U.K.: £1,900.00

Earthenware

HN 1283
The Cobbler
Style Two
Designer: C. J. Noke
Height: 8 ½", 21.6 cm
Colour: Light green
Issued: 1928-1949
Varieties: HN 681, 1251

U.S.: $1,650.00
Can.: $2,000.00
U.K.: £ 900.00

HN 1284
Lady Jester
Style Two
Designer: L. Harradine
Height: 4 ¼", 10.8 cm
Colour: Purple and red
Issued: 1928-1938
Varieties: HN 1285

U.S.:	$5,000.00
Can.:	$6,000.00
U.K.:	£2,700.00

HN 1285
Lady Jester
Style Two
Designer: L. Harradine
Height: 4 ¼", 10.8 cm
Colour: Red, pink and blue
Issued: 1928-1938
Varieties: HN 1284

U.S.:	$5,000.00
Can.:	$6,000.00
U.K.:	£2,700.00

HN 1286
Ko-Ko
Style One
Designer: L. Harradine
Height: 5", 12.7 cm
Colour: Red and purple
Issued: 1938-1949
Varieties: HN 1266

U.S.:	$2,250.00
Can.:	$2,750.00
U.K.:	£1,200.00

HN 1287
Yum-Yum
Style One
Designer: L. Harradine
Height: 5", 12.7 cm
Colour: Purple and cream
Issued: 1928-1936
Varieties: HN 1268

U.S.:	$2,250.00
Can.:	$2,750.00
U.K.:	£1,200.00

HN 1288
Susanna
Designer: L. Harradine
Height: 6", 15.2 cm
Colour: Red
Issued: 1928-1936
Varieties: HN 1233, 1299

U.S.:	$3,500.00
Can.:	$4,250.00
U.K.:	£1,900.00

HN 1289
Midinette
Style One
Designer: L. Harradine
Height: 9", 22.9 cm
Colour: Purple and pink
Issued: 1928-1938
Varieties: HN 1306

U.S.:	$ 9,000.00
Can.:	$11,000.00
U.K.:	£ 5,000.00

HN 1290
Spanish Lady
Designer: L. Harradine
Height: 8 ¼", 21.0 cm
Colour: Lavender, yellow
           and black
Issued: 1928-1940
Varieties: HN 1262, 1293,
           1294, 1309

U.S.:	$2,250.00
Can.:	$2,750.00
U.K.:	£1,200.00

HN 1291
Kathleen
Style One
Designer: L. Harradine
Height: 7 ½", 19.1 cm
Colour: Red and yellow
Issued: 1928-1938
Varieties: HN 1252, 1253, 1275,
           1279, 1357, 1512

U.S.:	$1,650.00
Can.:	$2,000.00
U.K.:	£ 920.00

HN 1292
A Geisha
Style Two
Designer: C. J. Noke
Height: 6 ¾", 17.2 cm
Colour: Pink and lavender
Issued: 1928-1938
Varieties: HN 1223, 1234, 1310

U.S.:	**$2,500.00**
Can.:	**$3,000.00**
U.K.:	**£1,350.00**

HN 1293
Spanish Lady
Designer: L. Harradine
Height: 8 ¼", 21.0 cm
Colour: Black with yellow
flowers
Issued: 1928-1940
Varieties: HN 1262, 1290,
1294, 1309

U.S.:	**$2,500.00**
Can.:	**$3,000.00**
U.K.:	**£1,350.00**

HN 1294
Spanish Lady
Designer: L. Harradine
Height: 8 ¼", 21.0 cm
Colour: Red and black
Issued: 1928-1940
Varieties: HN 1262, 1290,
1293, 1309

U.S.:	**$2,000.00**
Can.:	**$2,400.00**
U.K.:	**£1,100.00**

HN 1295
A Jester
Style One
Designer: C. J. Noke
Height: 10", 25.4 cm
Colour: Brown and purple
Issued: 1928-1949
Varieties: HN 45, 71, 71A, 320,
367, 412, 426, 446,
552, 616, 627, 1702,
2016, 3922

U.S.:	**$2,500.00**
Can.:	**$3,000.00**
U.K.:	**£1,350.00**

HN 1296
Columbine
Style One
Designer: L. Harradine
Height: 6", 15.2 cm
Colour: Orange and lavender
Issued: 1928-1940
Varieties: HN 1297, 1439

U.S.:	**$2,250.00**
Can.:	**$2,750.00**
U.K.:	**£1,200.00**

HN 1297
Columbine
Style One
Designer: L. Harradine
Height: 6", 15.2 cm
Colour: Pink and purple
Issued: 1928-1940
Varieties: HN 1296, 1439

U.S.:	**$2,250.00**
Can.:	**$2,750.00**
U.K.:	**£1,200.00**

HN 1298
Sweet and Twenty
Style One
Designer: L. Harradine
Height: 5 ¾", 14.6 cm
Colour: Red and blue-green
Issued: 1928-1969
Varieties: HN 1360, 1437, 1438,
1549, 1563, 1649

U.S.:	**$450.00**
Can.:	**$550.00**
U.K.:	**£250.00**

HN 1299
Susanna
Designer: L. Harradine
Height: 6", 15.2 cm
Colour: Black, red and blue
Issued: 1928-1936
Varieties: HN 1233, 1288

U.S.:	**$3,500.00**
Can.:	**$4,250.00**
U.K.:	**£1,900.00**

HN 1300
Carmen
Style One
Designer: L. Harradine
Height: 7", 17.8 cm
Colour: Pale blue-lavender
Issued: 1928-1938
Varieties: HN 1267

U.S.:	$5,500.00
Can.:	$6,500.00
U.K.:	£3,000.00

HN 1301
Young Mother with Child
Designer: Unknown
Height: 14 ½", 37.0 cm
Colour: Green, red, white
            and blue
Issued: 1928-1938

U.S.:	Only
Can.:	one
U.K.:	known

HN 1302
The Gleaner
Designer: Unknown
Height: 14 ½", 36.2 cm
Colour: Red and cream
Issued: 1928-1936

U.S.:	Only
Can.:	one
U.K.:	known

HN 1303
Angela
Style One
Designer: L. Harradine
Height: 7 ¼", 18.4 cm
Colour: Blue
Issued: 1928-1940
Varieties: HN 1204; also called
            'Fanny'

U.S.:	$ 8,500.00
Can.:	$10,000.00
U.K.:	£ 4,250.00

HN 1304
Harlequinade Masked
Designer: L. Harradine
Height: 6 ½", 16.5 cm
Colour: Mottled blue
Issued: 1928-1938
Varieties: HN 768, 769, 1274

U.S.:	$7,500.00
Can.:	$9,000.00
U.K.:	£4,000.00

HN 1305
Siesta
Designer: L. Harradine
Height: 4 ¾", 12.0 cm
Colour: Red
Issued: 1928-1940

U.S.:	$7,000.00
Can.:	$8,500.00
U.K.:	£3,750.00

HN 1306
Midinette
Style One
Designer: L. Harradine
Height: 9", 22.9 cm
Colour: Red and green
Issued: 1928-1938
Varieties: HN 1289

U.S.:	$ 9,000.00
Can.:	$11,000.00
U.K.:	£ 5,000.00

HN 1307
An Irishman
Designer: H. Fenton
Height: 6 ¾", 17.2 cm
Colour: Green coat with
            brown striped trousers
Issued: 1928-1938

U.S.:	$5,500.00
Can.:	$6,500.00
U.K.:	£3,000.00

HN 1308
The Moor
Designer: C. J. Noke
Height: 16 ½", 41.9 cm
Colour: Blue and mottled red
Issued: 1929-1938
Varieties: HN 1366, 1425, 1657,
             2082, 3642, 3926;
             also called 'An Arab'
             HN 33, 343, 378
U.S.:   **$5,000.00**
Can.:   **$6,000.00**
U.K.:   **£2,700.00**

HN 1309
Spanish Lady
Designer: L. Harradine
Height: 8 ¼", 21.0 cm
Colour: Black and
             multicoloured
Issued: 1929-1940
Varieties: HN 1262, 1290, 1293,
             1294
U.S.:   **$3,500.00**
Can.:   **$4,250.00**
U.K.:   **£1,900.00**

HN 1310
A Geisha
Style Two
Designer: C. J. Noke
Height: 6 ¾", 17.2 cm
Colour: Green
Issued: 1929-1938
Varieties: HN 1223, 1234, 1292
U.S.:   **$2,500.00**
Can.:   **$3,000.00**
U.K.:   **£1,350.00**

Photograph
Not
Available

HN 1311
Cassim
Style Two
Designer: L. Harradine
Height: 3 ¾", 9.5 cm
Colour: Unknown
Issued: 1929-1938
Varieties: HN 1312
U.S.:
Can.:   **Very Rare**
U.K.:

Photograph
Not
Available

HN 1312
Cassim
Style Two
Designer: L. Harradine
Height: 3 ¾", 9.5 cm
Colour: Unknown
Issued: 1929-1938
Varieties: HN 1311
U.S.:
Can.:   **Very Rare**
U.K.:

HN 1313
Sonny
Designer: L. Harradine
Height: 3 ½", 8.9 cm
Colour: Pink
Issued: 1929-1938
Varieties: HN 1314
U.S.:   **$1,750.00**
Can.:   **$2,250.00**
U.K.:   **£1,000.00**

HN 1314
Sonny
Designer: L. Harradine
Height: 3 ½", 8.9 cm
Colour: Blue
Issued: 1929-1938
Varieties: HN 1313
U.S.:   **$1,750.00**
Can.:   **$2,250.00**
U.K.:   **£1,000.00**

HN 1315
Old Balloon Seller
Style One
Designer: L. Harradine
Height: 7 ½", 19.1 cm
Colour: Green, purple
             and white
Issued: 1929-1998
Varieties: HN 3737
U.S.:   **$250.00**
Can.:   **$300.00**
U.K.:   **£135.00**

Earthenware and china

Photograph
Not
Available

HN 1316
Toys
Designer:	L. Harradine
Height:	Unknown
Colour:	Green, red and yellow
Issued:	1929-1938

U.S.:	
Can.:	**Extremely rare**
U.K.:	

HN 1317
The Snake Charmer
Designer:	Unknown
Height:	4", 10.1 cm
Colour:	Green and black
Issued:	1929-1938

U.S.:	**$2,750.00**
Can.:	**$3,300.00**
U.K.:	**£1,500.00**

HN 1318
Sweet Anne
Style One
Designer:	L. Harradine
Height:	7 ½", 19.1 cm
Colour:	Blue and green
Issued:	1929-1949
Varieties:	HN 1330, 1331, 1453, 1496, 1631, 1701

U.S.:	**$375.00**
Can.:	**$450.00**
U.K.:	**£200.00**

HN 1319
Darling
Style One
Designer:	C. Vyse
Height:	7 ½", 19.1 cm
Colour:	White, black base
Issued:	1929-1959
Varieties:	HN 1, 1371, 1372, 4140

U.S.:	**$275.00**
Can.:	**$350.00**
U.K.:	**£150.00**

HN 1320
Rosamund
Style One
Designer:	L. Harradine
Height:	7 ¼", 18.4 cm
Colour:	Lavender
Issued:	1929-1937

U.S.:	**$4,000.00**
Can.:	**$5,000.00**
U.K.:	**£2,250.00**

HN 1321
A Geisha
Style One
Designer:	H. Tittensor
Height:	10 ¾", 27.3 cm
Colour:	Green
Issued:	1929-1936
Varieties:	HN 354, 376, 376A, 387, 634, 741, 779, 1322; also called 'The Japanese Lady'

U.S.:	
Can.:	**Extremely rare**
U.K.:	

HN 1322
A Geisha
Style One
Designer:	H. Tittensor
Height:	10 ¾", 27.3 cm
Colour:	Pink and blue
Issued:	1929-1936
Varieties:	HN 354, 376, 376A, 387, 634, 741, 779, 1321; also called 'The Japanese Lady'

U.S.:	
Can.:	**Extremely rare**
U.K.:	

HN 1323
Contentment
Designer:	L. Harradine
Height:	7 ¼", 18.4 cm
Colour:	Red and blue
Issued:	1929-1938
Varieties:	HN 395, 396, 421, 468, 572, 685, 686

U.S.:	**$3,250.00**
Can.:	**$4,000.00**
U.K.:	**£1,750.00**

HN 1324
Fairy
Style One
Designer: L. Harradine
Height: 6 ½", 16.5 cm
Colour: Multicoloured
Issued: 1929-1938

U.S.:   **$3,250.00**
Can.:   **$4,000.00**
U.K.:   **£1,750.00**

HN 1325
The Orange Seller
Designer: L. Harradine
Height: 7", 17.8 cm
Colour: Green and lavender
Issued: 1929-1940

U.S.:   **$2,250.00**
Can.:   **$2,750.00**
U.K.:   **£1,225.00**

HN 1326
The Swimmer
First Version
Designer: L. Harradine
Height: 7 ½", 19.1 cm
Colour: Pink and purple
Issued: 1929-1938
Varieties: HN 1270, 1329

U.S.:   **$6,500.00**
Can.:   **$7,750.00**
U.K.:   **£3,500.00**

HN 1327
Bo-Peep
Style One
Designer: L. Harradine
Height: 6 ¾", 17.2 cm
Colour: Multicoloured
Issued: 1929-1936
Varieties: HN 777, 1202, 1328

U.S.:   **$5,000.00**
Can.:   **$6,000.00**
U.K.:   **£2,750.00**

HN 1328
Bo-Peep
Style One
Designer: L. Harradine
Height: 6 ¾", 17.2 cm
Colour: Purple and cream
Issued: 1929-1936
Varieties: HN 777, 1202, 1327

U.S.:   **$5,000.00**
Can.:   **$6,000.00**
U.K.:   **£2,750.00**

HN 1329
The Swimmer
First Version
Designer: L. Harradine
Height: 7 ½", 19.1 cm
Colour: Pink
Issued: 1929-1938
Varieties: HN 1270, 1326

U.S.:   **$6,500.00**
Can.:   **$7,750.00**
U.K.:   **£3,500.00**

HN 1330
Sweet Anne
Style One
Designer: L. Harradine
Height: 7 ¼", 18.4 cm
Colour: Blue, pink-yellow
Issued: 1929-1949
Varieties: HN 1318, 1331, 1453,
            1496, 1631, 1701

U.S.:   **$550.00**
Can.:   **$675.00**
U.K.:   **£300.00**

HN 1331
Sweet Anne
Style One
Designer: L. Harradine
Height: 7 ¼", 18.4 cm
Colour: Red, blue-yellow
Issued: 1929-1949
Varieties: HN 1318, 1330, 1453,
            1496, 1631, 1701

U.S.:   **$550.00**
Can.:   **$675.00**
U.K.:   **£300.00**

HN 1332
Lady Jester
Style One
Designer: L. Harradine
Height: 7", 17.8 cm
Colour: Red, blue and black
Issued: 1929-1938
Varieties: HN 1221, 1222

  U.S.:   **$6,000.00**
  Can.:   **$7,250.00**
  U.K.:   **£3,250.00**

HN 1333
A Jester
Style Two
Designer: C. J. Noke
Height: 10 ¼", 26.0 cm
Colour: Blue, yellow and black
Issued: 1929-1949
Varieties: HN 45A, 45B, 55, 308,
             630; also known in
             black and white

  U.S.:   **$ 9,000.00**
  Can.:   **$11,000.00**
  U.K.:   **£ 5,000.00**

HN 1334
Tulips
Designer: Unknown
Height: 9 ½", 24.1 cm
Colour: Lavender and pink
Issued: 1929-1936
Varieties: HN 466, 488, 672, 747

  U.S.:   **$4,000.00**
  Can.:   **$4,750.00**
  U.K.:   **£2,150.00**

HN 1335
Folly
Designer: L. Harradine
Height: 9", 22.9 cm
Colour: Lavender with orange
             and yellow balloons
Issued: 1929-1938
Varieties: HN 1750

  U.S.:   **$4,000.00**
  Can.:   **$4,750.00**
  U.K.:   **£2,150.00**

China

HN 1336
One of the Forty
Style Eleven
Designer: H. Tittensor
Height: Unknown
Colour: Red, orange and blue
Issued: 1929-1938
Varieties: HN 481, 483, 491, 646,
             667, 712, 1350; also
             known in flambé

  U.S.:   **$7,000.00**
  Can.:   **$8,500.00**
  U.K.:   **£3,750.00**

HN 1337
Priscilla
Style One
Designer: L. Harradine
Height: 8", 20.3 cm
Colour: Lavender and yellow
Issued: 1929-1938
Varieties: HN 1340, 1495,
             1501, 1559

  U.S.:   **$1,500.00**
  Can.:   **$1,800.00**
  U.K.:   **£ 800.00**

HN 1338
The Courtier
Designer: L. Harradine
Height: 4 ½", 11.4 cm
Colour: Red and white
Issued: 1929-1938

  U.S.:   **$5,000.00**
  Can.:   **$6,000.00**
  U.K.:   **£2,700.00**

HN 1339
Covent Garden
Style One
Designer: L. Harradine
Height: 9", 22.9 cm
Colour: Green and lavender
Issued: 1929-1938

  U.S.:   **$4,000.00**
  Can.:   **$4,750.00**
  U.K.:   **£2,150.00**

HN 1340
Priscilla
Style One
Designer: L. Harradine
Height: 8", 20.3 cm
Colour: Red and purple
Issued: 1929-1949
Varieties: HN 1337, 1495,
             1501, 1559

   U.S.: $750.00
   Can.: $900.00
   U.K.:   £400.00

HN 1341
Marietta
Designer: L. Harradine
Height: 8", 20.3 cm
Colour: Red and black
Issued: 1929-1940
Varieties: HN 1446, 1699

   U.S.: $2,500.00
   Can.: $3,000.00
   U.K.:   £1,350.00

HN 1342
The Flower Seller's Children
Designer: L. Harradine
Height: 8", 20.3 cm
Colour: Purple, red and yellow
Issued: 1929-1993
Varieties: HN 525, 551, 1206,
             1406

   U.S.: $700.00
   Can.: $875.00
   U.K.:   £380.00

HN 1343
Dulcinea
Designer: L. Harradine
Height: 5 ½", 14.0 cm
Colour: Red, black, green
             and blue
Issued: 1929-1936
Varieties: HN 1419

   U.S.: $5,000.00
   Can.: $6,000.00
   U.K.:   £2,750.00

HN 1344
Sunshine Girl
First Version
Designer: L. Harradine
Height: 5", 12.7 cm
Colour: Green, black and red
Issued: 1929-1938
Varieties: HN 1348

   U.S.: $ 9,500.00
   Can.: $11,500.00
   U.K.:   £ 5,150.00

HN 1345
A Victorian Lady
Style One
Designer: L. Harradine
Height: 7 ¾", 19.7 cm
Colour: Green and purple
Issued: 1929-1949
Varieties: HN 726, 727, 728,
             736, 739, 740, 742,
             745, 1208, 1258, 1276,
             1277, 1452, 1529

   U.S.: $800.00
   Can.: $975.00
   U.K.:   £450.00

HN 1346
Iona
Designer: L. Harradine
Height: 7 ½", 19.1 cm
Colour: Green, black and
             lavender
Issued: 1929-1938

   U.S.: $7,000.00
   Can.: $8,500.00
   U.K.:   £3,750.00

HN 1347
Moira
Designer: L. Harradine
Height: 6 ½", 16.5 cm
Colour: Lavender, pink and
             green
Issued: 1929-1938

   U.S.: $7,000.00
   Can.: $8,500.00
   U.K.:   £3,750.00

HN 1348
Sunshine Girl
First Version
Designer: L. Harradine
Height: 5", 12.7 cm
Colour: Black and orange
Issued: 1929-1937
Varieties: HN 1344

U.S.:	$ 9,500.00
Can.:	$11,500.00
U.K.:	£ 5,150.00

HN 1349
Scotties
Designer: L. Harradine
Height: 5 ¼", 13.3 cm
Colour: Blue
Issued: 1929-1936
Varieties: HN 1281

U.S.:	$6,000.00
Can.:	$7,500.00
U.K.:	£3,250.00

HN 1350
One of the Forty
Style Twelve
Designer: H. Tittensor
Height: Unknown
Colour: Multicoloured
Issued: 1929-1949
Varieties: HN 481, 483, 491,
            646, 667, 712, 1336,
            also known in flambé

U.S.:	None
Can.:	known
U.K.:	to exist

HN 1351
One of the Forty
Style One
Designer: H. Tittensor
Height: 8 ¼", 21.0 cm
Colour: Mottled red
            and purple
Issued: 1929-1949
Varieties: HN 417, 490, 495, 501,
            528, 648, 677, 1352

U.S.:	$7,000.00
Can.:	$8,500.00
U.K.:	£3,750.00

HN 1352
One of the Forty
Style One
Designer: H. Tittensor
Height: 8 ¼", 21.0 cm
Colour: Multicoloured
Issued: 1929-1949
Varieties: HN 417, 490, 495, 501,
            528, 648, 677, 1351

U.S.:	$7,000.00
Can.:	$8,500.00
U.K.:	£3,750.00

HN 1353
One of the Forty
Style Two
Designer: H. Tittensor
Height: 7 ¼", 18.4 cm
Colour: Orange and purple
Issued: 1929-1936
Varieties: HN 418, 494, 498,
            647, 666, 704

U.S.:	$7,000.00
Can.:	$8,500.00
U.K.:	£3,750.00

Photograph
Not
Available

HN 1354
One of the Forty
Style Fourteen
Designer: H. Tittensor
Height: 7 ¾", 19.7 cm
Colour: Multicoloured
Issued: 1929-1949
Varieties: HN 496, 500, 649, 665

U.S.:	$7,000.00
Can.:	$8,500.00
U.K.:	£3,750.00

HN 1355
The Mendicant
Designer: L. Harradine
Height: 8 ¼", 21.0 cm
Colour: Brown
Issued: 1929-1938
Varieties: HN 1365 (minor glaze
            difference)

U.S.:	$400.00
Can.:	$475.00
U.K.:	£200.00

Earthenware

HN 1356
The Parson's Daughter
Designer: H. Tittensor
Height: 9 ¼", 23.5 cm
Colour: Multicoloured
Issued: 1929-1938
Varieties: HN 337, 338, 441,
           564, 790, 1242, 2018

U.S.:	**$1,500.00**
Can.:	**$1,850.00**
U.K.:	**£ 850.00**

HN 1357
Kathleen
Style One
Designer: L. Harradine
Height: 7 ½", 19.1 cm
Colour: Pink, lavender and blue
Issued: 1929-1938
Varieties: HN 1252, 1253, 1275,
           1279, 1291, 1512

U.S.:	**$1,500.00**
Can.:	**$1,875.00**
U.K.:	**£ 850.00**

HN 1358
Rosina
Designer: L. Harradine
Height: 5 ¾", 14.6 cm
Colour: Red
Issued: 1929-1937
Varieties: HN 1364, 1556

U.S.:	**$2,000.00**
Can.:	**$2,400.00**
U.K.:	**£1,100.00**

HN 1359
Two-A-Penny
Designer: L. Harradine
Height: 8 ¼", 21.0 cm
Colour: Red and green
Issued: 1929-1938

U.S.:	**$8,000.00**
Can.:	**$9,500.00**
U.K.:	**£4,300.00**

Earthenware

HN 1360
Sweet and Twenty
Style One
Designer: L. Harradine
Height: 6", 15.2 cm
Colour: Blue and green
Issued: 1929-1938
Varieties: HN 1298, 1437, 1438,
           1549, 1563, 1649

U.S.:	**$1,300.00**
Can.:	**$1,450.00**
U.K.:	**£ 700.00**

HN 1361
Mask Seller
Designer: L. Harradine
Height: 8 ½", 21.6 cm
Colour: Black, white and red
Issued: 1929-1938
Varieties: HN 2103

U.S.:	**$3,500.00**
Can.:	**$4,250.00**
U.K.:	**£1,900.00**

HN 1362
Pantalettes
Style One
Designer: L. Harradine
Height: 7 ¾", 19.7 cm
Colour: Green and blue
Issued: 1929-1942
Varieties: HN 1412, 1507, 1709

U.S.:	**$700.00**
Can.:	**$900.00**
U.K.:	**£400.00**

HN 1363
Doreen
Designer: L. Harradine
Height: 5 ¼", 13.3 cm
Colour: Red
Issued: 1929-1940
Varieties: HN 1389, 1390

U.S.:	**$2,250.00**
Can.:	**$2,750.00**
U.K.:	**£1,200.00**

HN 1364
Rosina
Designer: L. Harradine
Height: 5 ¼", 13.3 cm
Colour: Purple and red
Issued: 1929-1937
Varieties: HN 1358, 1556
  U.S.:   **$2,000.00**
  Can.:   **$2,400.00**
  U.K.:   **£1,100.00**

HN 1365
The Mendicant
Designer: L. Harradine
Height: 8 ¼", 21.0 cm
Colour: Brown
Issued: 1929-1969
Varieties: HN 1355 (minor glaze
             differences)
  U.S.:   **$400.00**
  Can.:   **$475.00**
  U.K.:   **£200.00**

Earthenware

HN 1366
The Moor
Designer: C. J. Noke
Height: 16 ½", 41.9 cm
Colour: Multicoloured
Issued: 1930-1949
Varieties: HN 1308, 1425, 1657,
             2082, 3642, 3926;
             also called 'An Arab'
             HN 33, 343, 378
  U.S.:   **$5,000.00**
  Can.:   **$6,000.00**
  U.K.:   **£2,700.00**

Photograph
Not
Available

HN 1367
Kitty
Style One
Designer: Unknown
Height: 4", 10.1 cm
Colour: White, yellow
             and purple
Issued: 1930-1938
  U.S.:
  Can.:   **Extremely rare**
  U.K.:

HN 1368
Rose
Style One
Designer: L. Harradine
Height: 4 ½", 11.4 cm
Colour: Pink
Issued: 1930-1995
Varieties: HN 1387, 1416, 1506,
             1654, 2123
  U.S.:   **$100.00**
  Can.:   **$125.00**
  U.K.:   **£ 50.00**

Photograph
Not
Available

HN 1369
Boy on Pig
Designer: C. J. Noke
Height: 4", 10.1 cm
Colour: Green and brown
Issued: 1930-1938
Varieties: Also known in flambé
  U.S.:
  Can.:   **Extremely rare**
  U.K.:

HN 1370
Marie
Style Two
Designer: L. Harradine
Height: 4 ¾", 12.0 cm
Colour: Purple
Issued: 1930-1988
Varieties: HN 1388, 1417, 1489,
             1531, 1635, 1655
  U.S.:   **$150.00**
  Can.:   **$175.00**
  U.K.:   **£ 75.00**

HN 1371
Darling
Style One
Designer: C. Vyse
Height: 7 ½", 19.1 cm
Colour: Green
Issued: 1930-1938
Varieties: HN 1, 1319, 1372,
             4140
  U.S.:   **$1,750.00**
  Can.:   **$2,250.00**
  U.K.:   **£ 950.00**

HN 1372
Darling
Style One
Designer: C. Vyse
Height: 7 ¾", 19.7 cm
Colour: Pink, black base
Issued: 1930-1938
Varieties: HN 1, 1319, 1371, 4140

U.S.:	**$1,750.00**
Can.:	**$2,250.00**
U.K.:	**£ 950.00**

HN 1373
Sweet Lavender
Designer: L. Harradine
Height: 9", 22.8 cm
Colour: Green, red and black
Issued: 1930-1949
Varieties: Also called 'Any Old Lavender'

U.S.:	**$1,250.00**
Can.:	**$1,500.00**
U.K.:	**£ 675.00**

Earthenware

HN 1374
Fairy
Style Two
Designer: L. Harradine
Height: 4", 10.1 cm
Colour: Yellow flowers
Issued: 1930-1938
Varieties: HN 1380, 1532

U.S.:	**$3,500.00**
Can.:	**$4,250.00**
U.K.:	**£2,000.00**

HN 1375
Fairy
Style Three
Designer: L. Harradine
Height: 3", 7.6 cm
Colour: Yellow flowers
Issued: 1930-1938
Varieties: HN 1395, 1533

U.S.:	**$3,500.00**
Can.:	**$4,250.00**
U.K.:	**£2,000.00**

HN 1376
Fairy
Style Four
Designer: L. Harradine
Height: 2 ½", 6.3 cm
Colour: Yellow flowers
Issued: 1930-1938
Varieties: HN 1536

U.S.:	**$1,750.00**
Can.:	**$2,250.00**
U.K.:	**£1,000.00**

Photograph
Not
Available

HN 1377
Fairy
Style Five
Designer: L. Harradine
Height: 1 ½", 3.8 cm
Colour: Lavender and yellow
Issued: 1930-1938

U.S.:	
Can.:	**Extremely Rare**
U.K.:	

HN 1378
Fairy
Style Six
Designer: L. Harradine
Height: 2 ½", 6.3 cm
Colour: Orange flowers
Issued: 1930-1938
Varieties: HN 1396, 1535

U.S.:	**$1,850.00**
Can.:	**$2,250.00**
U.K.:	**£1,000.00**

HN 1379
Fairy
Style Seven
Designer: L. Harradine
Height: 2 ½", 6.3 cm
Colour: Blue flowers
Issued: 1930-1938
Varieties: HN 1394, 1534

U.S.:	**$1,850.00**
Can.:	**$2,250.00**
U.K.:	**£1,000.00**

HN 1380
Fairy
Style Two
Designer: L. Harradine ·
Height: 4", 10.1 cm
Colour: Black, red, blue
                 and purple
Issued: 1930-1938
Varieties: HN 1374, 1532

U.S.:   **$3,500.00**
Can.:   **$4,250.00**
U.K.:   **£2,000.00**

HN 1381 - 1386 not issued.

HN 1387
Rose
Style One
Designer: L. Harradine
Height: 4 ½", 11.4 cm
Colour: Blue, pink and orange
Issued: 1930-1938
Varieties: HN 1368, 1416, 1506,
                 1654, 2123

U.S.:   **$350.00**
Can.:   **$425.00**
U.K.:   **£200.00**

HN 1388
Marie
Style Two
Designer: L. Harradine
Height: 4 ½", 11.4 cm
Colour: Pink
Issued: 1930-1938
Varieties: HN 1370, 1417, 1489,
                 1531, 1635, 1655

U.S.:   **$350.00**
Can.:   **$425.00**
U.K.:   **£200.00**

HN 1389
Doreen
Designer: L. Harradine
Height: 5 ¼", 13.3 cm
Colour: Green
Issued: 1930-1940
Varieties: HN 1363, 1390

U.S.:   **$2,250.00**
Can.:   **$2,750.00**
U.K.:   **£1,200.00**

HN 1390
Doreen
Designer: L. Harradine
Height: 5 ¾", 14.6 cm
Colour: Lavender
Issued: 1929-1940
Varieties: HN 1363, 1389

U.S.:   **$2,250.00**
Can.:   **$2,750.00**
U.K.:   **£1,200.00**

HN 1391
Pierrette
Style Three
Designer: L. Harradine
Height: 8 ½", 21.6 cm
Colour: Red
Issued: 1930-1938
Varieties: HN 1749

U.S.:   **$3,250.00**
Can.:   **$4,000.00**
U.K.:   **£1,800.00**

Earthenware

HN 1392
Paisley Shawl
Style One
Designer: L. Harradine
Height: 8 ¼", 21.0 cm
Colour: Red shawl, flowered
                 cream dress
Issued: 1930-1949
Varieties: HN 1460, 1707,
                 1739, 1987

U.S.:   **$600.00**
Can.:   **$725.00**
U.K.:   **£325.00**

HN 1393
Fairy
Style Eight
Designer: L. Harradine
Height: 2 ½", 6.3 cm
Colour: Yellow flowers
Issued: 1930-1938

U.S.:   **$1,750.00**
Can.:   **$2,250.00**
U.K.:   **£1,000.00**

HN 1394
Fairy
Style Seven
Designer: L. Harradine
Height: 2 ½", 6.3 cm
Colour: Yellow flowers
Issued: 1930-1938
Varieties: HN 1379, 1534

U.S.:	$1,850.00
Can.:	$2,250.00
U.K.:	£1,000.00

HN 1395
Fairy
Style Three
Designer: L. Harradine
Height: 3", 7.6 cm
Colour: Blue flowers
Issued: 1930-1938
Varieties: HN 1375, 1533

U.S.:	$3,500.00
Can.:	$4,250.00
U.K.:	£2,000.00

HN 1396
Fairy
Style Six
Designer: L. Harradine
Height: 2 ½", 6.3 cm
Colour: Blue flowers
Issued: 1930-1938
Varieties: HN 1378, 1535

U.S.:	$1,850.00
Can.:	$2,250.00
U.K.:	£1,000.00

HN 1397
Gretchen
Designer: L. Harradine
Height: 7 ¾", 19.7 cm
Colour: Blue and white
Issued: 1930-1940
Varieties: HN 1562

U.S.:	$1,375.00
Can.:	$1,650.00
U.K.:	£ 750.00

HN 1398
Derrick
Designer: L. Harradine
Height: 8", 20.3 cm
Colour: Blue and white
Issued: 1930-1940

U.S.:	$1,375.00
Can.:	$1,650.00
U.K.:	£ 750.00

HN 1399
The Young Widow
Designer: L. Harradine
Height: 8", 20.3 cm
Colour: Purple
Issued: 1930-1930
Varieties: Also called 'Little
Mother' (Style Two)
HN 1418, 1641

U.S.:	$5,500.00
Can.:	$6,750.00
U.K.:	£3,000.00

HN 1400
The Windmill Lady
Designer: L. Harradine
Height: 8 ½", 21.6 cm
Colour: Green, yellow and
orange
Issued: 1930-1937

U.S.:	$ 8,500.00
Can.:	$10,000.00
U.K.:	£ 4,600.00

HN 1401
Chorus Girl
Designer: L. Harradine
Height: 8 ½", 21.6 cm
Colour: Red and orange
Issued: 1930-1936

U.S.:	$4,500.00
Can.:	$5,500.00
U.K.:	£2,500.00

HN 1402
Miss Demure
Designer: L. Harradine
Height: 7 ½", 19.1 cm
Colour: Lavender and pink
Issued: 1930-1975
Varieties: HN 1440, 1463, 1499,
             1560

U.S.:	**$350.00**
Can.:	**$425.00**
U.K.:	**£200.00**

HN 1404
Betty
Style Two
Designer: L. Harradine
Height: 4 ½", 11.4 cm
Colour: Lavender
Issued: 1930-1936
Varieties: HN 1405, 1435, 1436

U.S.:	**$4,500.00**
Can.:	**$5,500.00**
U.K.:	**£2,450.00**

HN 1405
Betty
Style Two
Designer: L. Harradine
Height: 4 ½", 11.4 cm
Colour: Green
Issued: 1930-1936
Varieties: HN 1404, 1435, 1436

U.S.:	**$4,500.00**
Can.:	**$5,500.00**
U.K.:	**£2,450.00**

HN 1406
The Flower Seller's Children
Designer: L. Harradine
Height: 8 ¼", 21.0 cm
Colour: Yellow and blue
Issued: 1930-1938
Varieties: HN 525, 551, 1206,
             1342

U.S.:	**$3,500.00**
Can.:	**$4,250.00**
U.K.:	**£1,900.00**

HN 1403 not issued.

HN 1407
The Winner
Designer: Unknown
Height: 6 ¾", 17.2 cm
Colour: Red, blue and grey
Issued: 1930-1938

U.S.:	
Can.:	**Very rare**
U.K.:	

HN 1408
John Peel
Designer: Unknown
Height: 9 ½", 24.1 cm
Colour: Red and brown
Issued: 1930-1937
Varieties: Also called
             'The Huntsman'
             (Style Two) HN 1815

U.S.:	**$6,000.00**
Can.:	**$7,500.00**
U.K.:	**£3,500.00**

HN 1409
Hunting Squire
Designer: Unknown
Height: 9 ¾", 24.7 cm
Colour: Red and grey
Issued: 1930-1938
Varieties: Also called 'The Squire'
             HN 1814

U.S.:	**$6,000.00**
Can.:	**$7,500.00**
U.K.:	**£3,500.00**

HN 1410
Abdullah
Designer: L. Harradine
Height: 5 ¾", 14.6 cm
Colour: Blue, lavender
             and green
Issued: 1930-1937
Varieties: HN 2104

U.S.:	**$3,000.00**
Can.:	**$3,600.00**
U.K.:	**£1,625.00**

HN 1411
Charley's Aunt
Style Two
Designer: H. Fenton
Height: 8", 20.3 cm
Colour: Black
Issued: 1930-1938
Varieties: HN 1554

U.S.: $2,250.00
Can.: $2,750.00
U.K.: £1,200.00

HN 1412
Pantalettes
Style One
Designer: L. Harradine
Height: 7 ¾", 19.7 cm
Colour: Blue and pink
Issued: 1930-1949
Varieties: HN 1362, 1507, 1709

U.S.: $750.00
Can.: $900.00
U.K.: £400.00

HN 1413
Margery
Designer: L. Harradine
Height: 11", 27.9 cm
Colour: Maroon and purple
Issued: 1930-1949

U.S.: $750.00
Can.: $900.00
U.K.: £400.00

Earthenware

HN 1414
Patricia
Style One
Designer: L. Harradine
Height: 8 ½", 21.6 cm
Colour: Yellow and green
Issued: 1930-1949
Varieties: HN 1431, 1462, 1567

U.S.: $1,500.00
Can.: $1,750.00
U.K.: £ 750.00

HN 1415 not issued.

HN 1416
Rose
Style One
Designer: L. Harradine
Height: 4 ½", 11.4 cm
Colour: Lavender
Issued: 1930-1949
Varieties: HN 1368, 1387, 1506, 1654, 2123

U.S.: $350.00
Can.: $425.00
U.K.: £200.00

HN 1417
Marie
Style Two
Designer: L. Harradine
Height: 4 ¾", 12.0 cm
Colour: Rose-pink
Issued: 1930-1949
Varieties: HN 1370, 1388, 1489, 1531, 1635, 1655

U.S.: $350.00
Can.: $425.00
U.K.: £200.00

HN 1418
The Little Mother
Style Two
Designer: L. Harradine
Height: 8", 20.3 cm
Colour: Purple
Issued: 1930-1938
Varieties: HN 1641; also called 'Young Widow' HN 1399

U.S.: $6,500.00
Can.: $7,750.00
U.K.: £3,500.00

HN 1419
Dulcinea
Designer: L. Harradine
Height: 5 ½", 14.0 cm
Colour: Red
Issued: 1930-1938
Varieties: HN 1343

U.S.: $5,000.00
Can.: $6,000.00
U.K.: £2,750.00

HN 1420
Phyllis
Style One
Designer: L. Harradine
Height: 9", 22.9 cm
Colour: Purple and green
Issued: 1930-1949
Varieties: HN 1430, 1486, 1698

U.S.:	**$1,500.00**
Can.:	**$1,800.00**
U.K.:	**£ 800.00**

HN 1421
Barbara
Style One
Designer: L. Harradine
Height: 7 ¾", 19.7 cm
Colour: Cream and lavender
Issued: 1930-1937
Varieties: HN 1432, 1461

U.S.:	**$2,250.00**
Can.:	**$2,750.00**
U.K.:	**£1,200.00**

HN 1422
Joan
Style One
Designer: L. Harradine
Height: 5 ½", 14.0 cm
Colour: Blue
Issued: 1930-1949
Varieties: HN 2023 (minor
              glaze difference)

U.S.:	**$500.00**
Can.:	**$625.00**
U.K.:	**£275.00**

HN 1423
Babette
Designer: L. Harradine
Height: 5", 12.7 cm
Colour: Yellow, green and red
Issued: 1930-1938
Varieties: HN 1424

U.S.:	**$2,500.00**
Can.:	**$3,000.00**
U.K.:	**£1,350.00**

HN 1424
Babette
Designer: L. Harradine
Height: 5", 12.7 cm
Colour: Blue
Issued: 1930-1938
Varieties: HN 1423

U.S.:	**$2,250.00**
Can.:	**$2,750.00**
U.K.:	**£1,200.00**

HN 1425
The Moor
Designer: C. J. Noke
Height: 16 ½", 41.9 cm
Colour: Multicoloured
Issued: 1930-1949
Varieties: HN 1308, 1366, 1657,
              2082, 3642, 3926;
              also called 'An Arab'
              HN 33, 343, 378

U.S.:	**$5,000.00**
Can.:	**$6,000.00**
U.K.:	**£2,700.00**

HN 1426
The Gossips
Designer: L. Harradine
Height: 5 ¾", 14.6 cm
Colour: Turquoise and pink
Issued: 1930-1949
Varieties: HN 1429, 2025

U.S.:	**$2,500.00**
Can.:	**$3,000.00**
U.K.:	**£1,350.00**

HN 1427
Darby
Designer: L. Harradine
Height: 5 ½", 14.0 cm
Colour: Pink and blue
Issued: 1930-1949
Varieties: HN 2024 (minor
              glaze difference)

U.S.:	**$500.00**
Can.:	**$625.00**
U.K.:	**£275.00**

HN 1428
Calumet
Designer: C. J. Noke
Height: 6", 15.2 cm
Colour: Brown, blue
 and yellow
Issued: 1930-1949
Varieties: HN 1689, 2068

U.S.:	**$3,000.00**
Can.:	**$3,600.00**
U.K.:	**£1,600.00**

HN 1429
The Gossips
Designer: L. Harradine
Height: 5 ¾", 14.6 cm
Colour: Red and cream
Issued: 1930-1949
Varieties: HN 1426, 2025

U.S.:	**$1,600.00**
Can.:	**$1,950.00**
U.K.:	**£ 900.00**

HN 1430
Phyllis
Style One
Designer: L. Harradine
Height: 9", 22.9 cm
Colour: Blue and pink
Issued: 1930-1938
Varieties: HN 1420, 1486, 1698

U.S.:	**$2,250.00**
Can.:	**$2,750.00**
U.K.:	**£1,200.00**

HN 1431
Patricia
Style One
Designer: L. Harradine
Height: 8 ½", 21.6 cm
Colour: Lavender and blue
Issued: 1930-1949
Varieties: HN 1414, 1462, 1567

U.S.:	**$1,750.00**
Can.:	**$1,950.00**
U.K.:	**£ 900.00**

HN 1432
Barbara
Style One
Designer: L. Harradine
Height: 7 ¾", 19.7 cm
Colour: Lavender
Issued: 1930-1937
Varieties: HN 1421, 1461

U.S.:	**$2,250.00**
Can.:	**$2,750.00**
U.K.:	**£1,200.00**

HN 1433
The Little Bridesmaid
Style One
Designer: L. Harradine
Height: 5 ¼", 13.3 cm
Colour: Lavender and pink
Issued: 1930-1951
Varieties: HN 1434, 1530

U.S.:	**$250.00**
Can.:	**$350.00**
U.K.:	**£140.00**

HN 1434
The Little Bridesmaid
Style One
Designer: L. Harradine
Height: 5", 12.7 cm
Colour: Yellow-green
Issued: 1930-1949
Varieties: HN 1433, 1530

U.S.:	**$400.00**
Can.:	**$500.00**
U.K.:	**£225.00**

HN 1435
Betty
Style Two
Designer: L. Harradine
Height: 4 ½", 11.4 cm
Colour: Multicoloured
Issued: 1930-1936
Varieties: HN 1404, 1405, 1436

U.S.:	**$4,750.00**
Can.:	**$5,750.00**
U.K.:	**£2,550.00**

HN 1436
Betty
Style Two
Designer: L. Harradine
Height: 4 ½", 11.4 cm
Colour: Green
Issued: 1930-1936
Varieties: HN 1404, 1405, 1435

  U.S.:   **$4,750.00**
  Can.:   **$5,750.00**
  U.K.:   **£2,550.00**

HN 1437
Sweet and Twenty
Style One
Designer: L. Harradine
Height: 6", 15.2 cm
Colour: Red
Issued: 1930-1938
Varieties: HN 1298, 1360, 1438,
              1549, 1563, 1649

  U.S.:   **$1,650.00**
  Can.:   **$1,950.00**
  U.K.:   **£ 900.00**

HN 1438
Sweet and Twenty
Style One
Designer: L. Harradine
Height: 6", 15.2 cm
Colour: Multicoloured
Issued: 1930-1938
Varieties: HN 1298, 1360, 1437,
              1549, 1563, 1649

  U.S.:   **$1,750.00**
  Can.:   **$2,100.00**
  U.K.:   **£ 950.00**

HN 1439
Columbine
Style One
Designer: L. Harradine
Height: 6", 15.2 cm
Colour: Mottled lavender
              and cream
Issued: 1930-1940
Varieties: HN 1296, 1297

  U.S.:   **$2,250.00**
  Can.:   **$2,750.00**
  U.K.:   **£1,200.00**

HN 1440
Miss Demure
Designer: L. Harradine
Height: 7", 17.8 cm
Colour: Blue
Issued: 1930-1949
Varieties: HN 1402, 1463,
              1499, 1560

  U.S.:   **$1,500.00**
  Can.:   **$1,800.00**
  U.K.:   **£ 800.00**

HN 1441
Child Study
Style One
Designer: L. Harradine
Height: 5", 12.7 cm
Colour: Cream, green
              flowered base
Issued: 1931-1938
Varieties: HN 603A, 603B; also
              known in flambé

  U.S.:   **$2,000.00**
  Can.:   **$2,500.00**
  U.K.:   **£1,000.00**

HN 1442
Child Study
Style Two
Designer: L. Harradine
Height: 6 ¼", 15.9 cm
Colour: Cream, green
              flowered base
Issued: 1931-1938
Varieties: HN 604A, 604B, 1443

  U.S.:   **$2,000.00**
  Can.:   **$2,500.00**
  U.K.:   **£1,000.00**

HN 1443
Child Study
Style Two
Designer: L. Harradine
Height: 5", 12.7 cm
Colour: Cream, green
              flowered base
Issued: 1931-1938
Varieties: HN 604A, 604B, 1442

  U.S.:   **$2,000.00**
  Can.:   **$2,500.00**
  U.K.:   **£1,000.00**

HN 1444
Pauline
Style One
Designer: L. Harradine
Height: 6", 15.2 cm
Colour: Blue
Issued: 1931-1940
   U.S.: $825.00
   Can.: $975.00
   U.K.:   £450.00

HN 1445
Biddy
Designer: L. Harradine
Height: 5 ½", 14.0 cm
Colour: Yellow-green
Issued: 1931-1937
Varieties: HN 1500, 1513
   U.S.: $550.00
   Can.: $675.00
   U.K.:   £300.00

HN 1446
Marietta
Designer: L. Harradine
Height: 8", 20.3 cm
Colour: Green and lavender
Issued: 1931-1940
Varieties: HN 1341, 1699
   U.S.: $3,000.00
   Can.: $3,500.00
   U.K.:   £1,600.00

HN 1447
Marigold
Designer: L. Harradine
Height: 6", 15.2 cm
Colour: Lavender
Issued: 1931-1949
Varieties: HN 1451, 1555
   U.S.: $800.00
   Can.: $975.00
   U.K.:   £450.00

HN 1448
Rita
Designer: L. Harradine
Height: 7", 17.8 cm
Colour: Red dress with
             green shawl
Issued: 1931-1938
Varieties: HN 1450
   U.S.: $2,000.00
   Can.: $2,400.00
   U.K.:   £1,100.00

HN 1449
The Little Mistress
Designer: L. Harradine
Height: 5 ¾", 14.6 cm
Colour: Green and blue
Issued: 1931-1949
   U.S.: $ 900.00
   Can.: $1,100.00
   U.K.:   £ 500.00

HN 1450
Rita
Designer: L. Harradine
Height: 7", 17.8 cm
Colour: Blue dress with
             red shawl
Issued: 1931-1938
Varieties: HN 1448
   U.S.: $2,000.00
   Can.: $2,400.00
   U.K.:   £1,100.00

HN 1451
Marigold
Designer: L. Harradine
Height: 6", 15.2 cm
Colour: Yellow
Issued: 1931-1938
Varieties: HN 1447, 1555
   U.S.: $1,400.00
   Can.: $1,600.00
   U.K.:   £ 750.00

HN 1452
A Victorian Lady
Style one
Designer: L. Harradine
Height: 7 ¾", 19.7 cm
Colour: Green
Issued: 1931-1949
Varieties: HN 726, 727, 728,
            736, 739, 740, 742,
            745, 1208, 1258,
            1276, 1277, 1345,
            1529
  U.S.: $ 950.00
  Can.: $1,150.00
  U.K.:   £ 515.00

HN 1453
Sweet Anne
Style One
Designer: L. Harradine
Height: 7", 17.8 cm
Colour: Green
Issued: 1931-1949
Varieties: HN 1318, 1330, 1331,
            1496, 1631, 1701
  U.S.: $1,000.00
  Can.: $1,200.00
  U.K.:   £ 550.00

HN 1454
Negligée
Designer: L. Harradine
Height: 5", 12.7 cm
Colour: Pink
Issued: 1931-1936
Varieties: HN 1219, 1228,
            1272, 1273
  U.S.: $3,500.00
  Can.: $4,500.00
  U.K.:   £2,000.00

HN 1455
Molly Malone
Designer: L. Harradine
Height: 7", 17.8 cm
Colour: Red and brown
Issued: 1931-1937
  U.S.: $6,500.00
  Can.: $8,000.00
  U.K.:   £3,600.00

HN 1456
The Butterfly Woman
Designer: L. Harradine
Height: 6 ½", 16.5 cm
Colour: Lavender and green
Issued: 1931-1940
Varieties: Also called 'Butterfly'
            HN 719, 720, 730,
            1203
  U.S.: $5,500.00
  Can.: $6,500.00
  U.K.:   £3,000.00

HN 1457
All-A-Blooming
Designer: L. Harradine
Height: 6 ½", 16.5 cm
Colour: Blue
Issued: 1931-1938
Varieties: HN 1466
  U.S.: $3,250.00
  Can.: $4,000.00
  U.K.:   £1,750.00

HN 1458
Monica
Style One
Designer: L. Harradine
Height: 4", 10.1 cm
Colour: Flowered cream dress
Issued: 1931-1949
Varieties: HN 1459, 1467, 3617
  U.S.: $700.00
  Can.: $850.00
  U.K.:   £375.00

HN 1459
Monica
Style One
Designer: L. Harradine
Height: 4", 10.1 cm
Colour: Lavender
Issued: 1931-1949
Varieties: HN 1458, 1467, 3617
  U.S.: $700.00
  Can.: $850.00
  U.K.:   £375.00

HN 1460
Paisley Shawl
Style One
Designer: L. Harradine
Height: 8 ¼", 21.0 cm
Colour: Green
Issued: 1931-1949
Varieties: HN 1392, 1707,
 1739, 1987
 U.S.: $1,000.00
 Can.: $1,250.00
 U.K.: £ 550.00

HN 1461
Barbara
Style One
Designer: L. Harradine
Height: 7 ¾", 19.7 cm
Colour: Green
Issued: 1931-1937
Varieties: HN 1421, 1432
 U.S.: $2,250.00
 Can.: $2,750.00
 U.K.: £1,200.00

HN 1462
Patricia
Style One
Designer: L. Harradine
Height: 8", 20.3 cm
Colour: Green
Issued: 1931-1938
Varieties: HN 1414, 1431, 1567
 U.S.: $1,750.00
 Can.: $2,100.00
 U.K.: £ 950.00

HN 1463
Miss Demure
Designer: L. Harradine
Height: 7", 17.8 cm
Colour: Green
Issued: 1931-1949
Varieties: HN 1402, 1440,
 1499, 1560
 U.S.: $1,350.00
 Can.: $1,650.00
 U.K.: £ 750.00

HN 1464
The Carpet Seller
(Hand Open)
Style One
Designer: L. Harradine
Height: 9 ¼", 23.5 cm
Colour: Green and orange
Issued: 1929-Unknown
Varieties: HN 1464A (hand closed)
 U.S.: $1,100.00
 Can.: $1,300.00
 U.K.: £ 600.00

Earthenware

HN 1464A
The Carpet Seller
(Hand Closed)
Style One
Designer: L. Harradine
Height: 9", 22.9 cm
Colour: Green and orange
Issued: Unknown-1969
Varieties: HN 1464 (hand open)
 U.S.: $400.00
 Can.: $475.00
 U.K.: £225.00

Porcelain

HN 1465
Lady Clare
Designer: L. Harradine
Height: 7 ¾", 19.7 cm
Colour: Red
Issued: 1931-1937
 U.S.: $1,600.00
 Can.: $1,925.00
 U.K.: £ 875.00

HN 1466
All-A-Blooming
Designer: L. Harradine
Height: 6 ½", 16.5 cm
Colour: Purple, green and red
Issued: 1931-1938
Varieties: HN 1457
 U.S.: $3,250.00
 Can.: $4,000.00
 U.K.: £1,750.00

HN 1467
Monica
Style One
Designer: L. Harradine
Height: 4", 10.1 cm
Colour: Flowered purple dress
Issued: 1931-1995
Varieties: HN 1458, 1459, 3617

U.S.:	$175.00
Can.:	$210.00
U.K.:	£ 90.00

HN 1468
Pamela
Style One
Designer: L. Harradine
Height: 7 ½", 19.1 cm
Colour: Blue
Issued: 1931-1937
Varieties: HN 1469, 1564

U.S.:	$2,250.00
Can.:	$2,700.00
U.K.:	£1,200.00

HN 1469
Pamela
Style One
Designer: L. Harradine
Height: 7 ½", 19.1 cm
Colour: Yellow
Issued: 1931-1937
Varieties: HN 1468, 1564

U.S.:	$2,250.00
Can.:	$2,700.00
U.K.:	£1,200.00

HN 1470
Chloe
Style One
Designer: L. Harradine
Height: 5 ½", 14.0 cm
Colour: Yellow and purple
Issued: 1931-1949
Varieties: HN 1476, 1479,
           1498, 1765, 1956

U.S.:	$1,000.00
Can.:	$1,200.00
U.K.:	£ 525.00

HN 1471
Annette
Style One
Designer: L. Harradine
Height: 6 ¼", 15.9 cm
Colour: Blue and white
Issued: 1931-1938
Varieties: HN 1472, 1550

U.S.:	$ 950.00
Can.:	$1,150.00
U.K.:	£ 525.00

HN 1472
Annette
Style One
Designer: L. Harradine
Height: 6", 15.2 cm
Colour: Green
Issued: 1931-1949
Varieties: HN 1471, 1550

U.S.:	$ 950.00
Can.:	$1,150.00
U.K.:	£ 525.00

HN 1473
Dreamland
Designer: L. Harradine
Height: 4 ¾", 12.0 cm
Colour: Lavender, blue,
           yellow and purple
Issued: 1931-1937
Varieties: HN 1481

U.S.:	$7,500.00
Can.:	$9,000.00
U.K.:	£4,000.00

HN 1474
In the Stocks
Style One
Designer: L. Harradine
Height: 5", 12.7 cm
Colour: Red and brown
Issued: 1931-1938
Varieties: HN 1475; also called
           'Love in the Stocks'
           and 'Love Locked In'

U.S.:	$4,500.00
Can.:	$5,500.00
U.K.:	£2,450.00

HN 1475
In the Stocks
Style One
Designer: L. Harradine
Height: 5 ¼", 13.3 cm
Colour: Green
Issued: 1931-1937
Varieties: HN 1474; also called
            'Love in the Stocks'
            and 'Love Locked In'

U.S.:	**$4,500.00**
Can.:	**$5,500.00**
U.K.:	**£2,450.00**

HN 1476
Chloe
Style One
Designer: L. Harradine
Height: 5 ½", 14.0 cm
Colour: Blue
Issued: 1931-1938
Varieties: HN 1470, 1479, 1498,
            1765, 1956

U.S.:	**$500.00**
Can.:	**$600.00**
U.K.:	**£275.00**

HN 1477 not issued.

HN 1478
Sylvia
Designer: L. Harradine
Height: 10 ½", 26.7 cm
Colour: Orange and blue
Issued: 1931-1938

U.S.:	**$1,200.00**
Can.:	**$1,500.00**
U.K.:	**£ 650.00**

Earthenware

HN 1479
Chloe
Style One
Designer: L. Harradine
Height: 5 ½", 14.0 cm
Colour: Lavender
Issued: 1931-1949
Varieties: HN 1470, 1476, 1498,
            1765, 1956

U.S.:	**$1,100.00**
Can.:	**$1,450.00**
U.K.:	**£ 600.00**

HN 1480
Newhaven Fishwife
Designer: H. Fenton
Height: 7 ¾", 19.7 cm
Colour: Red, white and black
Issued: 1931-1937

U.S.:	**$8,000.00**
Can.:	**$9,500.00**
U.K.:	**£4,250.00**

HN 1481
Dreamland
Designer: L. Harradine
Height: 4 ¾", 12.0 cm
Colour: Orange and purple
Issued: 1931-1937
Varieties: HN 1473

U.S.:	**$7,500.00**
Can.:	**$9,000.00**
U.K.:	**£4,000.00**

HN 1482
Pearly Boy
Style One
Designer: L. Harradine
Height: 5 ½", 14.0 cm
Colour: Brown suit, red vest
Issued: 1931-1949
Varieties: HN 1547

U.S.:	**$400.00**
Can.:	**$475.00**
U.K.:	**£225.00**

HN 1483
Pearly Girl
Style One
Designer: L. Harradine
Height: 5 ½", 14.0 cm
Colour: Orange and brown
Issued: 1931-1949
Varieties: HN 1548

U.S.:	**$400.00**
Can.:	**$475.00**
U.K.:	**£225.00**

HN 1484
Jennifer
Style One
Designer: L. Harradine
Height: 6 ½", 16.5 cm
Colour: Yellow flowers on
             cream dress
Issued: 1931-1949
U.S.: $1,250.00
Can.: $1,500.00
U.K.:   £ 675.00

HN 1485
Greta
Designer: L. Harradine
Height: 5 ½", 14.0 cm
Colour: Lavender
Issued: 1931-1953
U.S.: $550.00
Can.: $650.00
U.K.:   £300.00

HN 1486
Phyllis
Style One
Designer: L. Harradine
Height: 9", 22.9 cm
Colour: Blue and pink
Issued: 1931-1949
Varieties: HN 1420, 1430, 1698
U.S.: $1,800.00
Can.: $2,250.00
U.K.:   £ 975.00

HN 1487
Suzette
Designer: L. Harradine
Height: 7 ½", 19.1 cm
Colour: Flowered pink dress
Issued: 1931-1950
Varieties: HN 1577, 1585,
             1696, 2026
U.S.: $750.00
Can.: $900.00
U.K.:   £400.00

HN 1488
Gloria
Style One
Designer: L. Harradine
Height: 7 ¼", 18.4 cm
Colour: Green-blue
Issued: 1932-1938
Varieties: HN 1700
U.S.: $4,000.00
Can.: $4,750.00
U.K.:   £2,000.00

HN 1489
Marie
Style Two
Designer: L. Harradine
Height: 4 ½", 11.4 cm
Colour: Pale green
Issued: 1932-1949
Varieties: HN 1370, 1388, 1417,
             1531, 1635, 1655
U.S.: $400.00
Can.: $475.00
U.K.:   £215.00

HN 1490
Dorcas
Designer: L. Harradine
Height: 7", 17.8 cm
Colour: Light blue
Issued: 1932-1938
Varieties: HN 1491, 1558
U.S.: $1,100.00
Can.: $1,300.00
U.K.:   £ 600.00

HN 1491
Dorcas
Designer: L. Harradine
Height: 6 ¾", 17.2 cm
Colour: Pale green and
             lavender
Issued: 1932-1938
Varieties: HN 1490, 1558
U.S.: $1,100.00
Can.: $1,300.00
U.K.:   £ 600.00

HN 1492
Old Lavender Seller
Designer: L. Harradine
Height: 6", 15.2 cm
Colour: Green and orange
Issued: 1932-1949
Varieties: HN 1571

U.S.:	**$1,750.00**
Can.:	**$2,100.00**
U.K.:	**£ 950.00**

Earthenware

HN 1493
The Potter
Designer: C. J. Noke
Height: 7", 17.8 cm
Colour: Brown
Issued: 1932 -1992
Varieties: HN 1518, 1522

U.S.:	**$450.00**
Can.:	**$550.00**
U.K.:	**£250.00**

HN 1494
Gwendolen
Designer: L. Harradine
Height: 6", 15.2 cm
Colour: Green and pink
Issued: 1932-1940
Varieties: HN 1503, 1570

U.S.:	**$2,250.00**
Can.:	**$2,750.00**
U.K.:	**£1,250.00**

HN 1495
Priscilla
Style One
Designer: L. Harradine
Height: 8", 20.3 cm
Colour: Blue
Issued: 1932-1949
Varieties: HN 1337, 1340,
1501, 1559

U.S.:	**$1,500.00**
Can.:	**$1,800.00**
U.K.:	**£ 800.00**

HN 1496
Sweet Anne
Style One
Designer: L. Harradine
Height: 7", 17.8 cm
Colour: Purple
Issued: 1932-1967
Varieties: HN 1318, 1330, 1331,
1453, 1631, 1701

U.S.:	**$350.00**
Can.:	**$425.00**
U.K.:	**£200.00**

HN 1497
Rosamund
Style Two
Designer: L. Harradine
Height: 8 ½", 21.6 cm
Colour: Red
Issued: 1932-1938
Varieties: HN 1551

U.S.:	**$3,750.00**
Can.:	**$4,500.00**
U.K.:	**£2,000.00**

HN 1498
Chloe
Style One
Designer: L. Harradine
Height: 6", 15.2 cm
Colour: Peach-yellow
Issued: 1932-1938
Varieties: HN 1470, 1476, 1479,
1765, 1956

U.S.:	**$1,100.00**
Can.:	**$1,300.00**
U.K.:	**£ 600.00**

HN 1499
Miss Demure
Designer: L. Harradine
Height: 7", 17.8 cm
Colour: Pink and yellow
Issued: 1932-1938
Varieties: HN 1402, 1440,
1463, 1560

U.S.:	**$1,250.00**
Can.:	**$1,500.00**
U.K.:	**£ 675.00**

HN 1500
Biddy
Designer: L. Harradine
Height: 5 ½", 14.0 cm
Colour: Yellow
Issued: 1932-1937
Varieties: HN 1445, 1513

   U.S.: $ 900.00
   Can.: $1,050.00
   U.K.:   £ 500.00

HN 1501
Priscilla
Style One
Designer: L. Harradine
Height: 8", 20.3 cm
Colour: Orange and yellow
Issued: 1932-1938
Varieties: HN 1337, 1340,
             1495, 1559

   U.S.: $1,500.00
   Can.: $1,800.00
   U.K.:   £ 800.00

HN 1502
Lucy Ann
Designer: L. Harradine
Height: 5 ¼", 13.3 cm
Colour: Lavender
Issued: 1932-1951
Varieties: HN 1565

   U.S.: $550.00
   Can.: $650.00
   U.K.:   £300.00

HN 1503
Gwendolen
Designer: L. Harradine
Height: 6", 15.2 cm
Colour: Orange and yellow
Issued: 1932-1949
Varieties: HN 1494, 1570

   U.S.: $2,250.00
   Can.: $2,750.00
   U.K.:   £1,250.00

HN 1504
Sweet Maid
Style One
Designer: L. Harradine
Height: 8", 20.3 cm
Colour: Lavender and blue
Issued: 1932-1936
Varieties: HN 1505

   U.S.: $2,500.00
   Can.: $3,000.00
   U.K.:   £1,350.00

HN 1505
Sweet Maid
Style One
Designer: L. Harradine
Height: 8", 20.3 cm
Colour: Red and green
Issued: 1932-1936
Varieties: HN 1504

   U.S.: $2,500.00
   Can.: $3,000.00
   U.K.:   £1,350.00

HN 1506
Rose
Style One
Designer: L. Harradine
Height: 4 ½", 11.4 cm
Colour: Yellow
Issued: 1932-1938
Varieties: HN 1368, 1387, 1416,
             1654, 2123

   U.S.: $400.00
   Can.: $475.00
   U.K.:   £215.00

HN 1507
Pantalettes
Style One
Designer: L. Harradine
Height: 7 ¾", 19.7 cm
Colour: Yellow
Issued: 1932-1949
Varieties: HN 1362, 1412, 1709

   U.S.: $1,600.00
   Can.: $1,900.00
   U.K.:   £ 850.00

HN 1508
Helen
Style One
Designer: L. Harradine
Height: 8", 20.3 cm
Colour: Flowered green dress
Issued: 1932-1938
Varieties: HN 1509, 1572

U.S.:	**$2,500.00**
Can.:	**$3,000.00**
U.K.:	**£1,350.00**

HN 1509
Helen
Style One
Designer: L. Harradine
Height: 8", 20.3 cm
Colour: Flowered blue-yellow dress
Issued: 1932-1938
Varieties: HN 1508, 1572

U.S.:	**$2,500.00**
Can.:	**$3,000.00**
U.K.:	**£1,350.00**

HN 1510
Constance
Style One
Designer: L. Harradine
Height: 6 ¾", 17.1 cm
Colour: Yellow-purple
Issued: 1932-1936
Varieties: HN 1511

U.S.:	**$2,500.00**
Can.:	**$3,000.00**
U.K.:	**£1,350.00**

HN 1511
Constance
Style One
Designer: L. Harradine
Height: 6 ¾", 17.1 cm
Colour: Lavender
Issued: 1932-1936
Varieties: HN 1510

U.S.:	**$2,500.00**
Can.:	**$3,000.00**
U.K.:	**£1,350.00**

HN 1512
Kathleen
Style One
Designer: L. Harradine
Height: 7 ½", 19.1 cm
Colour: Lavender and blue
Issued: 1932-1938
Varieties: HN 1252, 1253, 1275, 1279, 1291, 1357

U.S.:	**$1,600.00**
Can.:	**$2,000.00**
U.K.:	**£ 850.00**

HN 1513
Biddy
Designer: L. Harradine
Height: 5 ½", 14.0 cm
Colour: Pink dress with mauve shawl
Issued: 1932-1937
Varieties: HN 1445, 1500

U.S.:	**$400.00**
Can.:	**$475.00**
U.K.:	**£215.00**

HN 1514
Dolly Vardon
Designer: L. Harradine
Height: 8 ½", 21.6 cm
Colour: Multicoloured
Issued: 1932-1938
Varieties: HN 1515

U.S.:	**$2,500.00**
Can.:	**$3,000.00**
U.K.:	**£1,350.00**

HN 1515
Dolly Vardon
Designer: L. Harradine
Height: 8 ½", 21.6 cm
Colour: Red and lavender
Issued: 1932-1949
Varieties: HN 1514

U.S.:	**$2,250.00**
Can.:	**$2,750.00**
U.K.:	**£1,200.00**

HN 1516
Cicely
Designer: L. Harradine
Height: 5 ¾", 14.6 cm
Colour: Purple and red
Issued: 1932-1949
U.S.:   **$2,000.00**
Can.:   **$2,500.00**
U.K.:   **£1,000.00**

HN 1517
Veronica
Style One
Designer: L. Harradine
Height: 8", 20.3 cm
Colour: Red-cream
Issued: 1932-1951
Varieties: HN 1519, 1650, 1943
U.S.:   **$650.00**
Can.:   **$775.00**
U.K.:   **£350.00**

HN 1518
The Potter
Designer: C. J. Noke
Height: 6 ¾", 17.2 cm
Colour: Green
Issued: 1932-1949
Varieties: HN 1493, 1522
U.S.:   **$2,250.00**
Can.:   **$2,750.00**
U.K.:   **£1,200.00**

HN 1519
Veronica
Style One
Designer: L. Harradine
Height: 8", 20.3 cm
Colour: Blue-cream
Issued: 1932-1938
Varieties: HN 1517, 1650, 1943
U.S.:   **$1,250.00**
Can.:   **$1,500.00**
U.K.:   **£ 650.00**

HN 1520
Eugene
Designer: L. Harradine
Height: 5 ¾", 14.6 cm
Colour: Green and pink
Issued: 1932-1936
Varieties: HN 1521
U.S.:   **$2,400.00**
Can.:   **$3,000.00**
U.K.:   **£1,350.00**

HN 1521
Eugene
Designer: L. Harradine
Height: 5", 12.7 cm
Colour: Orange, yellow
           and white
Issued: 1932-1936
Varieties: HN 1520
U.S.:   **$2,400.00**
Can.:   **$3,000.00**
U.K.:   **£1,350.00**

HN 1522
The Potter
Designer: L. Harradine
Height: 6 ¾", 17.2 cm
Colour: Green and purple
Issued: 1932-1949
Varieties: HN 1493, 1518
U.S.:   **$2,000.00**
Can.:   **$2,500.00**
U.K.:   **£1,100.00**

HN 1523
Lisette
Designer: L. Harradine
Height: 5 ¼", 13.3 cm
Colour: Yellow and red
Issued: 1932-1936
Varieties: HN 1524, 1684
U.S.:   **$2,650.00**
Can.:   **$3,250.00**
U.K.:   **£1,500.00**

HN 1524
Lisette
Designer: L. Harradine
Height: 5 ¼", 13.3 cm
Colour: Blue, pink and yellow
Issued: 1932-1936
Varieties: HN 1523, 1684

U.S.:	**$2,650.00**
Can.:	**$3,250.00**
U.K.:	**£1,500.00**

HN 1525
Clarissa
Style One
Designer: L. Harradine
Height: 10", 25.4 cm
Colour: Green and red
Issued: 1932-1938
Varieties: HN 1687

U.S.:	**$1,200.00**
Can.:	**$1,450.00**
U.K.:	**£ 650.00**

Earthenware

HN 1526
Anthea
Designer: L. Harradine
Height: 6 ½", 16.5 cm
Colour: Green and blue
Issued: 1932-1940
Varieties: HN 1527, 1669

U.S.:	**$2,250.00**
Can.:	**$2,700.00**
U.K.:	**£1,200.00**

HN 1527
Anthea
Designer: L. Harradine
Height: 6 ½", 16.5 cm
Colour: Lavender
Issued: 1932-1940
Varieties: HN 1526, 1669

U.S.:	**$2,250.00**
Can.:	**$2,700.00**
U.K.:	**£1,200.00**

HN 1528
Bluebeard
Style Two
Designer: L. Harradine
Height: 11 ½", 29.2 cm
Colour: Red and purple
Issued: 1932-1949
Varieties: HN 2105

U.S.:	**$1,800.00**
Can.:	**$2,150.00**
U.K.:	**£ 950.00**

Earthenware

HN 1529
A Victorian Lady
Style One
Designer: L. Harradine
Height: 7 ¾", 19.7 cm
Colour: Green and orange
Issued: 1932-1938
Varieties: HN 726, 727, 728,
736, 739, 740, 742,
745, 1208, 1258, 1276,
1277, 1345, 1452

U.S.:	**$1,100.00**
Can.:	**$1,325.00**
U.K.:	**£ 600.00**

HN 1530
The Little Bridesmaid
Style One
Designer: L. Harradine
Height: 5", 12.7 cm
Colour: Yellow and green
Issued: 1932-1938
Varieties: HN 1433, 1434

U.S.:	**$800.00**
Can.:	**$975.00**
U.K.:	**£450.00**

HN 1531
Marie
Style Two
Designer: L. Harradine
Height: 4 ½", 11.4 cm
Colour: Yellow-green
Issued: 1932-1938
Varieties: HN 1370, 1388, 1417,
1489, 1635, 1655

U.S.:	**$450.00**
Can.:	**$550.00**
U.K.:	**£250.00**

HN 1532
Fairy
Style Two
Designer: L. Harradine
Height: 4", 10.1 cm
Colour: Yellow, red, green,
            blue, white and purple
Issued: 1932-1938
Varieties: HN 1374, 1380

U.S.:	**$3,500.00**
Can.:	**$4,250.00**
U.K.:	**£2,000.00**

HN 1533
Fairy
Style Three
Designer: L. Harradine
Height: 3", 7.6 cm
Colour: Multicoloured
Issued: 1932-1938
Varieties: HN 1375, 1395

U.S.:	**$3,500.00**
Can.:	**$4,250.00**
U.K.:	**£2,000.00**

HN 1534
Fairy
Style Seven
Designer: L. Harradine
Height: 2 ½", 6.3 cm
Colour: Yellow flowers
Issued: 1932-1938
Varieties: HN 1379, 1394

U.S.:	**$2,000.00**
Can.:	**$2,500.00**
U.K.:	**£1,100.00**

HN 1535
Fairy
Style Six
Designer: L. Harradine
Height: 2 ½", 6.3 cm
Colour: Yellow and blue flowers
Issued: 1932-1938
Varieties: HN 1378, 1396

U.S.:	**$2,000.00**
Can.:	**$2,500.00**
U.K.:	**£1,100.00**

HN 1536
Fairy
Style Four
Designer: L. Harradine
Height: 2 ½", 6.3 cm
Colour: Yellow and blue flowers
Issued: 1932-1938
Varieties: HN 1376

U.S.:	**$1,750.00**
Can.:	**$2,250.00**
U.K.:	**£1,000.00**

HN 1537
Janet
Style One
Designer: L. Harradine
Height: 6 ¼", 15.9 cm
Colour: Red
Issued: 1932-1995
Varieties: HN 1538, 1652, 1737

U.S.:	**$200.00**
Can.:	**$250.00**
U.K.:	**£110.00**

HN 1538
Janet
Style One
Designer: L. Harradine
Height: 6 ¼", 15.9 cm
Colour: Purple
Issued: 1932-1949
Varieties: HN 1537, 1652, 1737

U.S.:	**$1,150.00**
Can.:	**$1,375.00**
U.K.:	**£ 625.00**

HN 1539
A Saucy Nymph
Designer: L. Harradine
Height: 4 ½", 11.4 cm
Colour: Green base
Issued: 1933-1949
Varieties: Also with pearl glaze

U.S.:	**$ 900.00**
Can.:	**$1,050.00**
U.K.:	**£ 475.00**

HN 1540
'Little Child So Rare and Sweet'
Style One
Designer: L. Harradine
Height: 5", 12.7 cm
Colour: Green base
Issued: 1933-1949

U.S.:	$1,350.00
Can.:	$1,600.00
U.K.:	£ 725.00

HN 1541
'Happy Joy, Baby Boy'
Designer: L. Harradine
Height: 6 ¼", 15.9 cm
Colour: Green base
Issued: 1933-1949

U.S.:	$1,650.00
Can.:	$2,000.00
U.K.:	£ 900.00

HN 1542
'Little Child So Rare and Sweet'
Style Two
Designer: L. Harradine
Height: 5", 12.7 cm
Colour: Blue base
Issued: 1933-1949

U.S.:	$1,350.00
Can.:	$1,600.00
U.K.:	£ 750.00

HN 1543
'Dancing Eyes and Sunny Hair'
Style One
Designer: L. Harradine
Height: 5", 12.7 cm
Colour: Blue base
Issued: 1933-1949

U.S.:	$1,350.00
Can.:	$1,600.00
U.K.:	£ 750.00

HN 1544
'Do You Wonder Where Fairies Are That Folk Declare Have Vanished'
First Version
Designer: L. Harradine
Height: 5", 12.7 cm
Colour: Lavender with
           yellow base
Issued: 1933 1949

U.S.:	$1,750.00
Can.:	$2,000.00
U.K.:	£ 950.00

HN 1545
'Called Love, A Little Boy, Almost Naked, Wanton, Blind, Cruel Now, and Then as Kind'
Designer: L. Harradine
Height: 3 ½", 8.9 cm
Colour: Tan base
Issued: 1933-1949

U.S.:	$1,750.00
Can.:	$2,000.00
U.K.:	£ 950.00

HN 1546
'Here A Little Child I Stand'
First Version
Designer: L. Harradine
Height: 6 ¼", 15.9 cm
Colour: Lavender with
           green base
Issued: 1933-1949

U.S.:	$1,650.00
Can.:	$2,000.00
U.K.:	£ 900.00

HN 1547
Pearly Boy
Style One
Designer: L. Harradine
Height: 5 ½", 14.0 cm
Colour: Green and purple
Issued: 1933-1949
Varieties: HN 1482

U.S.:	$ 950.00
Can.:	$1,150.00
U.K.:	£ 500.00

HN 1548
Pearly Girl
Style One
Designer: L. Harradine
Height: 5 ½", 14.0 cm
Colour: Green and purple
Issued: 1933-1949
Varieties: HN 1483

U.S.:	$ 950.00
Can.:	$1,150.00
U.K.:	£ 500.00

HN 1549
Sweet and Twenty
Style One
Designer: L. Harradine
Height: 6", 15.2 cm
Colour: Multicoloured
Issued: 1933-1949
Varieties: HN 1298, 1360, 1437,
           1438, 1563, 1649

U.S.:	$1,500.00
Can.:	$1,800.00
U.K.:	£ 800.00

HN 1550
Annette
Style One
Designer: L. Harradine
Height: 6 ¼", 15.9 cm
Colour: Red and green
Issued: 1933-1949
Varieties: HN 1471, 1472

U.S.:	$ 950.00
Can.:	$1,150.00
U.K.:	£ 500.00

HN 1551
Rosamund
Style Two
Designer: L. Harradine
Height: 8 ½", 21.6 cm
Colour: Blue
Issued: 1933-1938
Varieties: HN 1497

U.S.:	$5,000.00
Can.:	$6,000.00
U.K.:	£2,750.00

HN 1552
Pinkie
Designer: L. Harradine
Height: 5", 12.7 cm
Colour: Pink
Issued: 1933-1938
Varieties: HN 1553

U.S.:	$2,200.00
Can.:	$2,600.00
U.K.:	£1,200.00

HN 1553
Pinkie
Designer: L. Harradine
Height: 5", 12.7 cm
Colour: Yellow and blue
Issued: 1933-1938
Varieties: HN 1552

U.S.:	$2,200.00
Can.:	$2,600.00
U.K.:	£1,200.00

HN 1554
Charley's Aunt
Style Two
Designer: H. Fenton
Height: 7 ½", 19.1 cm
Colour: Purple
Issued: 1933-1938
Varieties: HN 1411

U.S.:	$2,400.00
Can.:	$3,000.00
U.K.:	£1,350.00

HN 1555
Marigold
Designer: L. Harradine
Height: 6", 15.2 cm
Colour: Pink and blue
Issued: 1933-1949
Varieties: HN 1447, 1451

U.S.:	$1,000.00
Can.:	$1,200.00
U.K.:	£ 550.00

HN 1556
Rosina
Designer: L. Harradine
Height: 5 ¾", 14.6 cm
Colour: Lavender
Issued: 1933-1937
Varieties: HN 1358, 1364

U.S.:	$2,000.00
Can.:	$2,400.00
U.K.:	£1,100.00

HN 1557
Lady Fayre
Designer: L. Harradine
Height: 5 ¾", 14.6 cm
Colour: Purple
Issued: 1933-1938
Varieties: HN 1265

U.S.:	$3,000.00
Can.:	$3,500.00
U.K.:	£1,650.00

HN 1558
Dorcas
Designer: L. Harradine
Height: 6 ¾", 17.2 cm
Colour: Purple
Issued: 1933-1952
Varieties: HN 1490, 1491

U.S.:	$500.00
Can.:	$600.00
U.K.:	£275.00

HN 1559
Priscilla
Style One
Designer: L. Harradine
Height: 8", 20.3 cm
Colour: Purple
Issued: 1933-1949
Varieties: HN 1337, 1340,
1495, 1501

U.S.:	$1,750.00
Can.:	$2,100.00
U.K.:	£ 950.00

HN 1560
Miss Demure
Designer: L. Harradine
Height: 7", 17.8 cm
Colour: Blue dress with
red shawl
Issued: 1933-1949
Varieties: HN 1402, 1440,
1463, 1499

U.S.:	$1,400.00
Can.:	$1,675.00
U.K.:	£ 750.00

HN 1561
Willy-Won't He
Designer: L. Harradine
Height: 6", 15.2 cm
Colour: Blue, pink and white
Issued: 1933-1949
Varieties: HN 1584, 2150

U.S.:	$2,000.00
Can.:	$2,500.00
U.K.:	£1,100.00

HN 1562
Gretchen
Designer: L. Harradine
Height: 7 ¾", 19.7 cm
Colour: Purple and white
Issued: 1933-1940
Varieties: HN 1397

U.S.:	$1,900.00
Can.:	$2,250.00
U.K.:	£1,000.00

HN 1563
Sweet and Twenty
Style One
Designer: L. Harradine
Height: 6", 15.2 cm
Colour: Black and light pink
Issued: 1933-1938
Varieties: HN 1298, 1360, 1437,
1438, 1549, 1649

U.S.:	$1,750.00
Can.:	$2,100.00
U.K.:	£ 950.00

HN 1564
Pamela
Style One
Designer: L. Harradine
Height: 8", 20.3 cm
Colour: Pink
Issued: 1933-1937
Varieties: HN 1468, 1469

U.S.:	**$2,250.00**
Can.:	**$2,700.00**
U.K.:	**£1,200.00**

HN 1565
Lucy Ann
Designer: L. Harradine
Height: 5 ¼", 13.3 cm
Colour: Light green
Issued: 1933-1938
Varieties: HN 1502

U.S.:	**$1,000.00**
Can.:	**$1,200.00**
U.K.:	**£ 550.00**

HN 1566
Estelle
Designer: L. Harradine
Height: 8", 20.3 cm
Colour: Lavender
Issued: 1933-1940
Varieties: HN 1802

U.S.:	**$2,350.00**
Can.:	**$3,000.00**
U.K.:	**£1,275.00**

HN 1567
Patricia
Style One
Designer: L. Harradine
Height: 8 ½", 21.6 cm
Colour: Red
Issued: 1933-1949
Varieties: HN 1414, 1431, 1462

U.S.:	**$2,500.00**
Can.:	**$3,000.00**
U.K.:	**£1,350.00**

HN 1568
Charmian
Designer: L. Harradine
Height: 6 ½", 16.5 cm
Colour: Red and cream
Issued: 1933-1940
Varieties: HN 1569, 1651

U.S.:	**$2,000.00**
Can.:	**$2,400.00**
U.K.:	**£1,050.00**

HN 1569
Charmian
Designer: L. Harradine
Height: 6 ½", 16.5 cm
Colour: Cream and lavender
Issued: 1933-1940
Varieties: HN 1568, 1651

U.S.:	**$2,000.00**
Can.:	**$2,400.00**
U.K.:	**£1,050.00**

HN 1570
Gwendolen
Designer: L. Harradine
Height: 6", 15.2 cm
Colour: Rose-pink
Issued: 1933-1949
Varieties: HN 1494, 1503

U.S.:	**$2,250.00**
Can.:	**$2,750.00**
U.K.:	**£1,250.00**

HN 1571
Old Lavender Seller
Designer: L. Harradine
Height: 6 ½", 16.5 cm
Colour: Orange and black
Issued: 1933-1949
Varieties: HN 1492

U.S.:	**$1,850.00**
Can.:	**$2,250.00**
U.K.:	**£1,000.00**

HN 1572
Helen
Style One
Designer: L. Harradine
Height: 8", 20.3 cm
Colour: Red
Issued: 1933-1938
Varieties: HN 1508, 1509

U.S.:	$2,500.00
Can.:	$3,000.00
U.K.:	£1,350.00

HN 1573
Rhoda
Designer: L. Harradine
Height: 10 ¼", 26.7 cm
Colour: Green and orange
Issued: 1933-1940
Varieties: HN 1574, 1688

U.S.:	$1,150.00
Can.:	$1,375.00
U.K.:	£ 625.00

Earthenware

HN 1574
Rhoda
Designer: L. Harradine
Height: 10 ¼", 26.7 cm
Colour: Burgundy and orange
Issued: 1933-1940
Varieties: HN 1573, 1688

U.S.:	$1,150.00
Can.:	$1,375.00
U.K.:	£ 625.00

Earthenware

HN 1575
Daisy
Style One
Designer: L. Harradine
Height: 3 ¾", 9.5 cm
Colour: Blue dress with flowers
Issued: 1933-1949
Varieties: HN 1961

U.S.:	$750.00
Can.:	$900.00
U.K.:	£400.00

HN 1576
Tildy
Designer: L. Harradine
Height: 5", 12.7 cm
Colour: Red and pink-cream
Issued: 1933-1939
Varieties: HN 1859

U.S.:	$2,000.00
Can.:	$2,500.00
U.K.:	£1,100.00

HN 1577
Suzette
Designer: L. Harradine
Height: 7 ½", 19.1 cm
Colour: Flowered lavender dress
Issued: 1933-1949
Varieties: HN 1487, 1585, 1696, 2026

U.S.:	$1,500.00
Can.:	$1,800.00
U.K.:	£ 800.00

HN 1578
The Hinged Parasol
Designer: L. Harradine
Height: 6 ½", 16.5 cm
Colour: Red and yellow dress with spots
Issued: 1933-1949
Varieties: HN 1579

U.S.:	$2,000.00
Can.:	$2,500.00
U.K.:	£1,100.00

HN 1579
The Hinged Parasol
Designer: L. Harradine
Height: 6 ½", 16.5 cm
Colour: Red and purple
Issued: 1933-1949
Varieties: HN 1578

U.S.:	$2,000.00
Can.:	$2,500.00
U.K.:	£1,100.00

HN 1580
Rosebud
Style One
Designer: L. Harradine
Height: 3", 7.6 cm
Colour: Pink
Issued: 1933-1938
Varieties: HN 1581

U.S.:	**$1,500.00**
Can.:	**$1,850.00**
U.K.:	**£ 825.00**

HN 1581
Rosebud
Style One
Designer: L. Harradine
Height: 3", 7.6 cm
Colour: Blue dress with flowers
Issued: 1933-1938
Varieties: HN 1580

U.S.:	**$1,500.00**
Can.:	**$1,850.00**
U.K.:	**£ 825.00**

HN 1582
Marion
Designer: L. Harradine
Height: 6 ½", 16.5 cm
Colour: Purple
Issued: 1933-1940
Varieties: HN 1583

U.S.:	**$3,000.00**
Can.:	**$3,600.00**
U.K.:	**£1,650.00**

HN 1583
Marion
Designer: L. Harradine
Height: 6 ½", 16.5 cm
Colour: Blue dress,
             patterned shawl
Issued: 1933-1940
Varieties: HN 1582

U.S.:	**$3,000.00**
Can.:	**$3,600.00**
U.K.:	**£1,650.00**

HN 1584
Willy-Won't He
Designer: L. Harradine
Height: 6", 15.2 cm
Colour: Red, green,
             blue and white
Issued: 1933-1949
Varieties: HN 1561, 2150 (minor
             glaze difference)

U.S.:	**$800.00**
Can.:	**$950.00**
U.K.:	**£425.00**

HN 1585
Suzette
Designer: L. Harradine
Height: 7 ½", 19.1 cm
Colour: Green and yellow
Issued: 1933-1938
Varieties: HN 1487, 1577,
             1696, 2026

U.S.:	**$1,400.00**
Can.:	**$1,700.00**
U.K.:	**£ 750.00**

HN 1586
Camille
Style One
Designer: L. Harradine
Height: 6 ½", 16.5 cm
Colour: Red and pink
Issued: 1933-1949
Varieties: HN 1648, 1736

U.S.:	**$2,000.00**
Can.:	**$2,500.00**
U.K.:	**£1,100.00**

HN 1587
Fleurette
Designr: L. Harradine
Height: 6 ½", 16.5 cm
Colour: Red and pink
Issued: 1933-1949

U.S.:	**$1,100.00**
Can.:	**$1,325.00**
U.K.:	**£ 600.00**

HN 1588
The Bride
Style One
Designer: L. Harradine
Height: 8 ¾", 22.2 cm
Colour: Cream
Issued: 1933-1938
Varieties: HN 1600, 1762, 1841

U.S.:	$2,200.00
Can.:	$2,750.00
U.K.:	£1,200.00

HN 1589
Sweet and Twenty
Style Two
Designer: L. Harradine
Height: 3 ½", 8.9 cm
Colour: Red dress, pale green sofa
Issued: 1933-1949
Varieties: HN 1610

U.S.:	$650.00
Can.:	$775.00
U.K.:	£350.00

HN 1590 - 1597 Wall Masks.

HN 1598
Clothilde
Designer: L. Harradine
Height: 7 ¼", 18.4 cm
Colour: Yellow and red
Issued: 1933-1949
Varieties: HN 1599

U.S.:	$1,600.00
Can.:	$2,000.00
U.K.:	£ 900.00

HN 1599
Clothilde
Designer: L. Harradine
Height: 7 ¼", 18.4 cm
Colour: Purple and red
Issued: 1933-1949
Varieties: HN 1598

U.S.:	$1,600.00
Can.:	$2,000.00
U.K.:	£ 900.00

HN 1600
The Bride
Style One
Designer: L. Harradine
Height: 8 ¾", 22.2 cm
Colour: Pale pink
Issued: 1933-1949
Varieties: HN 1588, 1762, 1841

U.S.:	$2,200.00
Can.:	$2,600.00
U.K.:	£1,200.00

HN 1601 - 1603 Wall Masks.

HN 1604
The Emir
Designer: C. J. Noke
Height: 7 ½", 19.1 cm
Colour: Yellow and red
Issued: 1933-1949
Varieties: HN 1605; also called 'Ibrahim' HN 2095

U.S.:	$1,600.00
Can.:	$2,000.00
U.K.:	£ 875.00

Pattern design on scarf may vary.

HN 1605
The Emir
Designer: C. J. Noke
Height: 7 ¼", 18.4 cm
Colour: Yellow and purple
Issued: 1933-1949
Varieties: HN 1604; also called 'Ibrahim' HN 2095

U.S.:	$1,600.00
Can.:	$2,000.00
U.K.:	£ 875.00

Pattern design on scarf may vary.

HN 1606
Falstaff
Style One
Designer: C. J. Noke
Height: 7", 17.8 cm
Colour: Red and brown
Issued: 1933-1949
Varieties: HN 571, 575, 608, 609, 619, 638, 1216

U.S.:	$3,500.00
Can.:	$4,500.00
U.K.:	£1,950.00

HN 1607
Cerise

Designer:	L. Harradine
Height:	5 ¼", 13.3 cm
Colour:	Lavender dress with flowers
Issued:	1933-1949
U.S.:	**$700.00**
Can.:	**$850.00**
U.K.:	**£375.00**

HN 1608 - 1609 Wall Masks.

HN 1610
Sweet and Twenty
Style Two

Designer:	L. Harradine
Height:	3 ½", 8.9 cm
Colour:	Red dress, green sofa
Issued:	1933-1938
Varieties:	HN 1589
U.S.:	**$800.00**
Can.:	**$975.00**
U.K.:	**£450.00**

HN 1611 - 1616 Bookends.

HN 1617
Primroses

Designer:	L. Harradine
Height:	6 ½", 16.5 cm
Colour:	Purple, red, white and yellow
Issued:	1934-1949
U.S.:	**$1,750.00**
Can.:	**$2,100.00**
U.K.:	**£ 995.00**

Earthenware

HN 1618
Maisie

Designer:	L. Harradine
Height:	6 ¼", 15.9 cm
Colour:	Yellow and blue
Issued:	1934-1949
Varieties:	HN 1619
U.S.:	**$1,000.00**
Can.:	**$1,200.00**
U.K.:	**£ 575.00**

HN 1619
Maisie

Designer:	L. Harradine
Height:	6 ¼", 15.9 cm
Colour:	Red and pink
Issued:	1934-1949
Varieties:	HN 1618
U.S.:	**$825.00**
Can.:	**$975.00**
U.K.:	**£450.00**

HN 1620
Rosabell

Designer:	L. Harradine
Height:	6 ¾", 17.1 cm
Colour:	Red and green
Issued:	1934-1940
U.S.:	**$2,000.00**
Can.:	**$2,500.00**
U.K.:	**£1,050.00**

HN 1621
Irene

Designer:	L. Harradine
Height:	6 ½", 16.5 cm
Colour:	Yellow
Issued:	1934-1951
Varieties:	HN 1697, 1952
U.S.:	**$700.00**
Can.:	**$850.00**
U.K.:	**£350.00**

HN 1622
Evelyn

Designer:	L. Harradine
Height:	6 ¼", 15.9 cm
Colour:	Red and cream
Issued:	1934-1940
Varieties:	HN 1637
U.S.:	**$2,000.00**
Can.:	**$2,400.00**
U.K.:	**£1,000.00**

HN 1623 - 1625 Bookends.

HN 1626
Bonnie Lassie
Designer: L. Harradine
Height: 5 ¼", 13.3 cm
Colour: Red
Issued: 1934-1953
  U.S.: $ 900.00
  Can.: $1,100.00
  U.K.: £ 500.00

HN 1627
Curly Knob
Designer: L. Harradine
Height: 6", 15.2 cm
Colour: Blue and red
Issued: 1934-1949
  U.S.: $1,700.00
  Can.: $2,000.00
  U.K.: £ 900.00

HN 1628
Margot
Designer: L. Harradine
Height: 5 ½", 14.0 cm
Colour: Blue and yellow
Issued: 1934-1940
Varieties: HN 1636, 1653
  U.S.: $2,000.00
  Can.: $2,500.00
  U.K.: £1,000.00

HN 1629
Grizel
Designer: L. Harradine
Height: 6 ¾", 17.2 cm
Colour: Red and cream
Issued: 1934-1938
  U.S.: $3,500.00
  Can.: $4,000.00
  U.K.: £1,750.00

HN 1630 Wall Mask.

HN 1631
Sweet Anne
Style One
Designer: L. Harradine
Height: 7", 17.8 cm
Colour: Green, red, pink
    and yellow
Issued: 1934-1938
Varieties: HN 1318, 1330, 1331,
    1453, 1496, 1701
  U.S.: $1,600.00
  Can.: $1,900.00
  U.K.: £ 825.00

HN 1632
A Gentlewoman
Designer: L. Harradine
Height: 7 ½", 19.1 cm
Colour: Lavender dress,
    green hat
Issued: 1934-1949
  U.S.: $1,500.00
  Can.: $1,750.00
  U.K.: £ 800.00

HN 1633
Clemency
Designer: L. Harradine
Height: 7", 17.8 cm
Colour: Lavender jacket,
    cream flowered dress
Issued: 1934-1938
Varieties: HN 1634, 1643
  U.S.: $2,250.00
  Can.: $2,750.00
  U.K.: £1,200.00

HN 1634
Clemency
Designer: L. Harradine
Height: 7", 17.8 cm
Colour: Green and orange
    patterned jacket,
    green dress
Issued: 1934-1949
Varieties: HN 1633, 1643
  U.S.: $2,000.00
  Can.: $2,500.00
  U.K.: £1,100.00

HN 1635
Marie
Style Two
Designer: L. Harradine
Height: 4 ¾", 12.0 cm
Colour: Blue, pink and white,
           pink flowers
Issued: 1934-1949
Varieties: HN 1370, 1388, 1417,
           1489, 1531, 1655

U.S.:	$500.00
Can.:	$600.00
U.K.:	£250.00

HN 1636
Margot
Designer: L. Harradine
Height: 5 ¾", 14.6 cm
Colour: Red, pink and yellow
Issued: 1934-1940
Varieties: HN 1628, 1653

U.S.:	$2,250.00
Can.:	$2,750.00
U.K.:	£1,200.00

HN 1637
Evelyn
Designer: L. Harradine
Height: 6", 15.2 cm
Colour: Blue and cream
Issued: 1934-1940
Varieties: HN 1622

U.S.:	$2,250.00
Can.:	$2,750.00
U.K.:	£1,200.00

HN 1638
Ladybird
Designer: L. Harradine
Height: 7 ¾", 19.7 cm
Colour: Pink
Issued: 1934-1949
Varieties: HN 1640

U.S.:	$3,500.00
Can.:	$4,500.00
U.K.:	£2,000.00

HN 1639
Dainty May
Style One
Designer: L. Harradine
Height: 6", 15.2 cm
Colour: Red and green
Issued: 1934-1949
Varieties: HN 1656

U.S.:	$800.00
Can.:	$950.00
U.K.:	£425.00

HN 1640
Ladybird
Designer: L. Harradine
Height: 7 ¾", 19.7 cm
Colour: Blue
Issued: 1934-1938
Varieties: HN 1638

U.S.:	$5,000.00
Can.:	$6,000.00
U.K.:	£2,700.00

HN 1641
The Little Mother
Style Two
Designer: L. Harradine
Height: 8", 20.3 cm
Colour: Red, green, white
           and purple
Issued: 1934-1949
Varieties: HN 1418; also called
           'Young Widow'
           HN 1399

U.S.:	$5,500.00
Can.:	$6,750.00
U.K.:	£3,000.00

HN 1642
Granny's Shawl
Designer: L. Harradine
Height: 5 ¾", 14.6 cm
Colour: Cream dress, red shawl
Issued: 1934-1949
Varieties: HN 1647

U.S.:	$ 850.00
Can.:	$1,000.00
U.K.:	£ 450.00

HN 1643
Clemency
Designer: L. Harradine
Height: 7", 17.8 cm
Colour: Red jacket, white and green dress
Issued: 1934-1938
Varieties: HN 1633, 1634

U.S.: $2,250.00
Can.: $2,700.00
U.K.: £1,200.00

HN 1644
Herminia
Designer: L. Harradine
Height: 6 ½", 16.5 cm
Colour: Flowered cream dress
Issued: 1934-1938
Varieties: HN 1646, 1704

U.S.: $2,500.00
Can.: $3,000.00
U.K.: £1,350.00

HN 1645
Aileen
Designer: L. Harradine
Height: 6", 15.2 cm
Colour: Green dress, flowered shawl
Issued: 1934-1938
Varieties: HN 1664, 1803

U.S.: $2,500.00
Can.: $3,000.00
U.K.: £1,350.00

HN 1646
Herminia
Designer: L. Harradine
Height: 6 ½", 16.5 cm
Colour: Red dress with cream stripe
Issued: 1934-1938
Varieties: HN 1644, 1704

U.S.: $2,500.00
Can.: $3,000.00
U.K.: £1,350.00

HN 1647
Granny's Shawl
Designer: L. Harradine
Height: 5 ¾", 14.6 cm
Colour: Cream dress with blue shawl
Issued: 1934-1949
Varieties: HN 1642

U.S.: $1,000.00
Can.: $1,250.00
U.K.: £ 500.00

HN 1648
Camille
Style One
Designer: L. Harradine
Height: 6 ½", 16.5 cm
Colour: Pale green flowered dress
Issued: 1934-1949
Varieties: HN 1586, 1736

U.S.: $2,500.00
Can.: $3,000.00
U.K.: £1,350.00

HN 1649
Sweet and Twenty
Style One
Designer: L. Harradine
Height: 6", 15.2 cm
Colour: Green and cream dress, brown sofa
Issued: 1934-1936
Varieties: HN 1298, 1360, 1437, 1438, 1549, 1563

U.S.: $1,500.00
Can.: $1,800.00
U.K.: £ 800.00

HN 1650
Veronica
Style One
Designer: L. Harradine
Height: 8", 20.3 cm
Colour: Green and pink
Issued: 1934-1949
Varieties: HN 1517, 1519, 1943

U.S.: $1,650.00
Can.: $2,000.00
U.K.: £ 900.00

HN 1651
Charmian
Designer: L. Harradine
Height: 6 ½", 16.5 cm
Colour: Red and green
Issued: 1934-1940
Varieties: HN 1568, 1569

  U.S.:   **$2,250.00**
  Can.:   **$2,750.00**
  U.K.:   **£1,200.00**

HN 1652
Janet
Style One
Designer: L. Harradine
Height: 6 ½", 16.5 cm
Colour: Red with pink
             flowered skirt
Issued: 1934-1949
Varieties: HN 1537, 1538, 1737

  U.S.:   **$2,000.00**
  Can.:   **$2,500.00**
  U.K.:   **£1,100.00**

HN 1653
Margot
Designer: L. Harradine
Height: 5 ¾", 14.6 cm
Colour: White and red
Issued: 1934-1940
Varieties: HN 1628, 1636

  U.S.:   **$2,250.00**
  Can.:   **$2,750.00**
  U.K.:   **£1,200.00**

HN 1654
Rose
Style One
Designer: L. Harradine
Height: 4 ½", 11.4 cm
Colour: Green and cream
Issued: 1934-1938
Varieties: HN 1368, 1387, 1416,
             1506, 2123

  U.S.:   **$450.00**
  Can.:   **$550.00**
  U.K.:   **£225.00**

HN 1655
Marie
Style Two
Designer: L. Harradine
Height: 4 ½", 11.4 cm
Colour: Pink and white
Issued: 1934-1938
Varieties: HN 1370, 1388, 1417,
             1489, 1531, 1635

  U.S.:   **$450.00**
  Can.:   **$550.00**
  U.K.:   **£225.00**

HN 1656
Dainty May
Style One
Designer: L. Harradine
Height: 6", 15.2 cm
Colour: Lavender
Issued: 1934-1949
Varieties: HN 1639

  U.S.:   **$ 950.00**
  Can.:   **$1,100.00**
  U.K.:   **£ 500.00**

HN 1657
The Moor
Designer: C. J. Noke
Height: 16 ½", 41.9 cm
Colour: Red and black
Issued: 1934-1949
Varieties: HN 1308, 1366, 1425,
             2082, 3642, 3926;
             also called 'An Arab'
             HN 33, 343, 378

  U.S.:   **$5,000.00**
  Can.:   **$6,000.00**
  U.K.:   **£2,700.00**

HN 1658 - 1661 Wall Masks.

HN 1662
Delicia
Designer: L. Harradine
Height: 5 ¾", 14.6 cm
Colour: Pink and lavender
Issued: 1934-1938
Varieties: HN 1663, 1681

  U.S.:   **$2,250.00**
  Can.:   **$2,750.00**
  U.K.:   **£1,200.00**

HN 1663
Delicia

Designer:	L. Harradine
Height:	5 ¾", 14.6 cm
Colour:	Lavender, pink and green
Issued:	1934-1938
Varieties:	HN 1662, 1681
U.S.:	**$2,250.00**
Can.:	**$2,750.00**
U.K.:	**£1,200.00**

HN 1664
Aileen

Designer:	L. Harradine
Height:	6", 15.2 cm
Colour:	Pink dress, patterned shawl
Issued:	1934-1938
Varieties:	HN 1645, 1803
U.S.:	**$2,500.00**
Can.:	**$3,000.00**
U.K.:	**£1,350.00**

HN 1665
Miss Winsome

Designer:	L. Harradine
Height:	6 ¾", 17.2 cm
Colour:	Lavender dress, patterned shawl
Issued:	1934-1949
Varieties:	HN 1666
U.S.:	**$1,650.00**
Can.:	**$2,000.00**
U.K.:	**£ 900.00**

HN 1666
Miss Winsome

Designer:	L. Harradine
Height:	6 ¾", 17.2 cm
Colour:	Green dress, patterned shawl
Issued:	1934-1938
Varieties:	HN 1665
U.S.:	**$1,850.00**
Can.:	**$2,250.00**
U.K.:	**£1,000.00**

HN 1667
Blossom

Designer:	L. Harradine
Height:	6 ¾", 17.2 cm
Colour:	Orange and blue
Issued:	1934-1949
U.S.:	**$3,500.00**
Can.:	**$4,250.00**
U.K.:	**£1,900.00**

HN 1668
Sibell

Designer:	L. Harradine
Height:	6 ½", 16.5 cm
Colour:	Red and green
Issued:	1934-1949
Varieties:	HN 1695, 1735
U.S.:	**$2,000.00**
Can.:	**$2,500.00**
U.K.:	**£1,100.00**

HN 1669
Anthea

Designer:	L. Harradine
Height:	6 ½", 16.5 cm
Colour:	Pink dress, green shawl
Issued:	1934-1940
Varieties:	HN 1526, 1527
U.S.:	**$2,250.00**
Can.:	**$2,750.00**
U.K.:	**£1,200.00**

HN 1670
Gillian
Style One

Designer:	L. Harradine
Height:	7 ¾", 19.7 cm
Colour:	Pink
Issued:	1934-1949
Varieties:	HN 1670A
U.S.:	**$2,000.00**
Can.:	**$2,500.00**
U.K.:	**£1,100.00**

HN 1670A
Gillian
Style One
Designer: L. Harradine
Height: 7 ¾", 19.7 cm
Colour: Green jacket, white
            flowered skirt
Issued: Unknown
Varieties: HN 1670

U.S.: $2,250.00
Can.: $2,750.00
U.K.:   £1,200.00

HN 1671 - 1676 Wall Masks.

HN 1677
Tinkle Bell
Designer: L. Harradine
Height: 4 ¾", 12.0 cm
Colour: Pink
Issued: 1935-1988

U.S.: $125.00
Can.: $150.00
U.K.:   £ 65.00

HN 1678
Dinky Doo
Designer: L. Harradine
Height: 4 ¾", 12.0 cm
Colour: Lavender
Issued: 1934-1996
Varieties: HN 2120, 3618

U.S.: $125.00
Can.: $150.00
U.K.:   £ 65.00

HN 1679
Babie
Designer: L. Harradine
Height: 4 ¾", 12.0 cm
Colour: Green
Issued: 1935-1992
Varieties: HN 1842, 2121

U.S.: $125.00
Can.: $150.00
U.K.:   £ 65.00

HN 1680
Tootles
Designer: L. Harradine
Height: 4 ¾", 12.0 cm
Colour: Pink
Issued: 1935-1975

U.S.: $125.00
Can.: $150.00
U.K.:   £ 65.00

HN 1681
Delicia
Designer: L. Harradine
Height: 5 ¾", 14.6 cm
Colour: Green and purple
Issued: 1935-1938
Varieties: HN 1662, 1663

U.S.: $2,250.00
Can.: $2,750.00
U.K.:   £1,200.00

HN 1682
Teresa
Style One
Designer: L. Harradine
Height: 5 ¾", 14.6 cm
Colour: Red and brown
Issued: 1935-1949
Varieties: HN 1683

U.S.: $3,500.00
Can.: $4,250.00
U.K.:   £1,900.00

HN 1683
Teresa
Style One
Designer: L. Harradine
Height: 5 ¾", 14.6 cm
Colour: Light blue and brown
Issued: 1935-1938
Varieties: HN 1682

U.S.: $4,500.00
Can.: $5,500.00
U.K.:   £2,500.00

HN 1684
Lisette
Designer: L. Harradine
Height: 5 ¼", 13.3 cm
Colour: Rose-pink dress,
                  green trim
Issued: 1935-1936
Varieties: HN 1523, 1524

U.S.:   **$3,250.00**
Can.:   **$4,000.00**
U.K.:   **£1,750.00**

HN 1685
Cynthia
Style One
Designer: L. Harradine
Height: 5 ¾", 14.6 cm
Colour: Pink and turquoise
Issued: 1935-1949
Varieties: HN 1686, 1686A

U.S.:   **$2,000.00**
Can.:   **$2,500.00**
U.K.:   **£1,100.00**

HN 1686
Cynthia
Style One
Designer: L. Harradine
Height: 5 ¾", 14.6 cm
Colour: Blue, rose pink
                  and yellow
Issued: 1935-1949
Varieties: HN 1685, 1686A

U.S.:   **$2,000.00**
Can.:   **$2,500.00**
U.K.:   **£1,100.00**

HN 1686A
Cynthia
Style One
Designer: L. Harradine
Height: 5 ¾", 14.6 cm
Colour: Red and purple
Issued: 1935-1949
Varieties: HN 1685, 1686

U.S.:   **$2,000.00**
Can.:   **$2,500.00**
U.K.:   **£1,100.00**

HN 1687
Clarissa
Style One
Designer: L. Harradine
Height: 9 ¾", 24.8 cm
Colour: Blue, green and orange
Issued: 1935-1949
Varieties: HN 1525

U.S.:   **$1,200.00**
Can.:   **$1,450.00**
U.K.:   **£ 650.00**

Earthenware

HN 1688
Rhoda
Designer: L. Harradine
Height: 10 ¼, 26.7 cm
Colour: Orange and red
Issued: 1935-1940
Varieties: HN 1573, 1574

U.S.:   **$1,200.00**
Can.:   **$1,450.00**
U.K.:   **£ 650.00**

Earthenware

HN 1689
Calumet
Designer: C. J. Noke
Height: 6 ½", 16.5 cm
Colour: Green and brown
Issued: 1935-1949
Varieties: HN 1428, 2068

U.S.:   **$1,750.00**
Can.:   **$2,100.00**
U.K.:   **£ 950.00**

Earthenware

HN 1690
June
Style One
Designer: L. Harradine
Height: 7 ¼", 18.4 cm
Colour: Pale green and pink
Issued: 1935-1949
Varieties: HN 1691, 1947, 2027

U.S.:   **$1,650.00**
Can.:   **$2,000.00**
U.K.:   **£ 900.00**

HN 1691
June
Style One
Designer: L. Harradine
Height: 7 ¼", 18.4 cm
Colour: Yellow and pink
Issued: 1935-1949
Varieties: HN 1690, 1947, 2027

U.S.:	**$1,000.00**
Can.:	**$1,200.00**
U.K.:	**£ 550.00**

HN 1692
Sonia
Designer: L. Harradine
Height: 6 ¼", 15.9 cm
Colour: Pink, white and green
Issued: 1935-1949
Varieties: HN 1738

U.S.:	**$2,000.00**
Can.:	**$2,500.00**
U.K.:	**£1,050.00**

HN 1693
Virginia
Designer: L. Harradine
Height: 7 ½", 19.1 cm
Colour: Yellow and red
Issued: 1935-1949
Varieties: HN 1694

U.S.:	**$2,250.00**
Can.:	**$2,750.00**
U.K.:	**£1,200.00**

HN 1694
Virginia
Designer: L. Harradine
Height: 7 ½", 19.1 cm
Colour: Green
Issued: 1935-1949
Varieties: HN 1693

U.S.:	**$2,250.00**
Can.:	**$2,750.00**
U.K.:	**£1,200.00**

HN 1695
Sibell
Designer: L. Harradine
Height: 6 ½", 16.5 cm
Colour: Green and orange
Issued: 1935-1949
Varieties: HN 1668, 1735

U.S.:	**$1,650.00**
Can.:	**$2,000.00**
U.K.:	**£ 900.00**

HN 1696
Suzette
Designer: L. Harradine
Height: 7 ½", 19.1 cm
Colour: Flowered green dress
Issued: 1935-1949
Varieties: HN 1487, 1577,
             1585, 2026

U.S.:	**$1,400.00**
Can.:	**$1,675.00**
U.K.:	**£ 750.00**

HN 1697
Irene
Designer: L. Harradine
Height: 7", 17.8 cm
Colour: Pink
Issued: 1935-1949
Varieties: HN 1621, 1952

U.S.:	**$1,750.00**
Can.:	**$2,100.00**
U.K.:	**£ 950.00**

HN 1698
Phyllis
Style One
Designer: L. Harradine
Height: 9", 22.9 cm
Colour: Green
Issued: 1935-1949
Varieties: HN 1420, 1430, 1486

U.S.:	**$1,850.00**
Can.:	**$2,250.00**
U.K.:	**£1,000.00**

HN 1699
Marietta
Designer: L. Harradine
Height: 8", 20.3 cm
Colour: Green and red
Issued: 1935-1940
Varieties: HN 1341, 1446

U.S.:	$3,500.00
Can.:	$4,250.00
U.K.:	£1,900.00

HN 1700
Gloria
Style One
Designer: L. Harradine
Height: 7", 17.8 cm
Colour: Green and black
Issued: 1935-1938
Varieties: HN 1488

U.S.:	$4,500.00
Can.:	$5,500.00
U.K.:	£2,500.00

HN 1701
Sweet Anne
Style One
Designer: L. Harradine
Height: 7", 17.8 cm
Colour: Pink and blue
Issued: 1935-1938
Varieties: HN 1318, 1330, 1331, 1453, 1496, 1631

U.S.:	$1,500.00
Can.:	$1,800.00
U.K.:	£ 800.00

HN 1702
A Jester
Style One
Designer: C. J. Noke
Height: 10", 25.4 cm
Colour: Brown and mauve
Issued: 1935-1949
Varieties: HN 45, 71, 71A, 320, 367, 412, 426, 446, 552, 616, 627, 1295, 2016, 3922

U.S.:	$1,000.00
Can.:	$1,200.00
U.K.:	£ 550.00

Photograph
Not
Available

HN 1703
Charley's Aunt
Style Three
Designer: A. Toft
Height: 6", 15.2 cm
Colour: Lilac and white, no base
Issued: 1935-1938

U.S.:	$2,500.00
Can.:	$3,000.00
U.K.:	£1,350.00

HN 1704
Herminia
Designer: L. Harradine
Height: 6 ¾", 17.2 cm
Colour: Red
Issued: 1935-1938
Varieties: HN 1644, 1646

U.S.:	$2,400.00
Can.:	$2,900.00
U.K.:	£1,300.00

HN 1705
The Cobbler
Style Three
Designer: C. J. Noke
Height: 8", 20.3 cm
Colour: Purple and blue
Issued: 1935-1949
Varieties: HN 1706

U.S.:	$1,600.00
Can.:	$1,900.00
U.K.:	£ 850.00

Earthenware

HN 1706
The Cobbler
Style Three
Designer: C. J. Noke
Height: 8 ¼", 21.0 cm
Colour: Green and brown
Issued: 1935-1969
Varieties: HN 1705

U.S.:	$450.00
Can.:	$550.00
U.K.:	£250.00

Earthenware

HN 1707
Paisley Shawl
Style One
Designer: L. Harradine
Height: 8 ¼", 21.0 cm
Colour: Purple
Issued: 1935-1949
Varieties: HN 1392, 1460,
            1739, 1987
  U.S.: $1,400.00
  Can.: $1,675.00
  U.K.:   £ 750.00

HN 1708
The Bather
Style One, First Version
Designer: L. Harradine
Height: 7 ¾", 19.7 cm
Colour: Black, red and
            turquoise
Issued: 1935-1938
Varieties: HN 597, 687, 781,
            782, 1238
  U.S.: $6,500.00
  Can.: $7,750.00
  U.K.:   £3,500.00

HN 1709
Pantalettes
Style One
Designer: L. Harradine
Height: 8", 20.3 cm
Colour: Red
Issued: 1935-1938
Varieties: HN 1362, 1412, 1507
  U.S.: $2,000.00
  Can.: $2,500.00
  U.K.:   £1,100.00

HN 1710
Camilla
Style One
Designer: L. Harradine
Height: 7", 17.8 cm
Colour: Red and yellow
Issued: 1935-1949
Varieties: HN 1711
  U.S.: $2,500.00
  Can.: $3,000.00
  U.K.:   £1,350.00

HN 1711
Camilla
Style One
Designer: L. Harradine
Height: 7", 17.8 cm
Colour: Green and yellow
Issued: 1935-1949
Varieties: HN 1710
  U.S.: $2,500.00
  Can.: $3,000.00
  U.K.:   £1,350.00

HN 1712
Daffy Down Dilly
Designer: L. Harradine
Height: 7 ¾", 19.7 cm
Colour: Green
Issued: 1935-1975
Varieties: HN 1713
  U.S.: $475.00
  Can.: $575.00
  U.K.:   £260.00

HN 1713
Daffy Down Dilly
Designer: L. Harradine
Height: 8 ¼", 21.0 cm
Colour: Turquoise
Issued: 1935-1949
Varieties: HN 1712
  U.S.: $1,650.00
  Can.: $2,000.00
  U.K.:   £ 900.00

HN 1714
Millicent
Designer: L. Harradine
Height: 8", 20.3 cm
Colour: Red
Issued: 1935-1949
Varieties: HN 1715, 1860
  U.S.: $2,250.00
  Can.: $2,750.00
  U.K.:   £1,200.00

HN 1715
Millicent
Designer: L. Harradine
Height: 8", 20.3 cm
Colour: Lavender
Issued: 1935-1949
Varieties: HN 1714, 1860

U.S.:	**$2,750.00**
Can.:	**$3,250.00**
U.K.:	**£1,500.00**

HN 1716
Diana
Style One
Designer: L. Harradine
Height: 5 ¾", 14.6 cm
Colour: Pink and blue
Issued: 1935-1949
Varieties: HN 1717, 1986

U.S.:	**$ 850.00**
Can.:	**$1,050.00**
U.K.:	**£ 500.00**

HN 1717
Diana
Style One
Designer: L. Harradine
Height: 5 ¾", 14.6 cm
Colour: Turquoise
Issued: 1935-1949
Varieties: HN 1716, 1986

U.S.:	**$600.00**
Can.:	**$725.00**
U.K.:	**£325.00**

HN 1718
Kate Hardcastle
Designer: L. Harradine
Height: 8", 20.3 cm
Colour: Pink and green
Issued: 1935-1949
Varieties: HN 1719, 1734, 1861, 1919, 2028

U.S.:	**$1,500.00**
Can.:	**$1,800.00**
U.K.:	**£ 825.00**

HN 1719
Kate Hardcastle
Designer: L. Harradine
Height: 8", 20.3 cm
Colour: Red and green
Issued: 1935-1949
Varieties: HN 1718, 1734, 1861, 1919, 2028

U.S.:	**$1,500.00**
Can.:	**$1,800.00**
U.K.:	**£ 825.00**

HN 1720
Frangçon
Designer: L. Harradine
Height: 7 ½", 19.1 cm
Colour: Lavender dress with orange and red flowers
Issued: 1935-1949
Varieties: HN 1721

U.S.:	**$3,500.00**
Can.:	**$4,250.00**
U.K.:	**£1,900.00**

HN 1721
Frangçon
Designer: L. Harradine
Height: 7 ¼", 18.4 cm
Colour: Green
Issued: 1935-1949
Varieties: HN 1720

U.S.:	**$2,500.00**
Can.:	**$3,000.00**
U.K.:	**£1,350.00**

HN 1722
The Coming of Spring
Designer: L. Harradine
Height: 12 ½", 31.7 cm
Colour: Yellow-pink
Issued: 1935-1949
Varieties: HN 1723

U.S.:	**$4,500.00**
Can.:	**$5,500.00**
U.K.:	**£2,500.00**

HN 1723
The Coming of Spring
Designer: L. Harradine
Height: 12 ½", 31.7 cm
Colour: Pale green
Issued: 1935-1949
Varieties: HN 1722

U.S.:	**$4,500.00**
Can.:	**$5,500.00**
U.K.:	**£2,500.00**

HN 1724
Ruby
Style One
Designer: L. Harradine
Height: 5 ¼", 13.3 cm
Colour: Red
Issued: 1935-1949
Varieties: HN 1725

U.S.:	**$ 850.00**
Can.:	**$1,000.00**
U.K.:	**£ 460.00**

HN 1725
Ruby
Style One
Designer: L. Harradine
Height: 5 ¼", 13.3 cm
Colour: Blue
Issued: 1935-1949
Varieties: HN 1724

U.S.:	**$1,100.00**
Can.:	**$1,325.00**
U.K.:	**£ 600.00**

HN 1726
Celia
Designer: L. Harradine
Height: 11 ½", 29.2 cm
Colour: Pale lavender
Issued: 1935-1949
Varieties: HN 1727

U.S.:	**$3,250.00**
Can.:	**$4,000.00**
U.K.:	**£1,750.00**

HN 1727
Celia
Designer: L. Harradine
Height: 11 ½", 29.2 cm
Colour: Pale green
Issued: 1935-1949
Varieties: HN 1726

U.S.:	**$2,500.00**
Can.:	**$3,000.00**
U.K.:	**£1,350.00**

HN 1728
The New Bonnet
Designer: L. Harradine
Height: 7", 17.8 cm
Colour: Pink
Issued: 1935-1949
Varieties: HN 1957

U.S.:	**$1,500.00**
Can.:	**$1,800.00**
U.K.:	**£ 800.00**

HN 1729
Vera
First Version
Designer: L. Harradine
Height: 4 ¼", 10.8 cm
Colour: Pink
Issued: 1935-1940
Varieties: HN 1730

U.S.:	**$1,350.00**
Can.:	**$1,650.00**
U.K.:	**£ 750.00**

HN 1730
Vera
First Version
Designer: L. Harradine
Height: 4 ¼", 10.8 cm
Colour: Green
Issued: 1935-1938
Varieties: HN 1729

U.S.:	**$1,350.00**
Can.:	**$1,650.00**
U.K.:	**£ 750.00**

HN 1731
Daydreams
Designer: L. Harradine
Height: 5 ¾", 14.6 cm
Colour: Pale pink, blue trim
Issued: 1935-1996
Varieties: HN 1732, 1944

U.S.:	$325.00
Can.:	$400.00
U.K.:	£175.00

HN 1732
Daydreams
Designer: L. Harradine
Height: 5 ½", 14.0 cm
Colour: Pink, rose-pink trim
Issued: 1935-1949
Varieties: HN 1731, 1944

U.S.:	$1,100.00
Can.:	$1,350.00
U.K.:	£ 600.00

HN 1733 Wall Mask.

HN 1734
Kate Hardcastle
Designer: L. Harradine
Height: 8 ¼", 21.0 cm
Colour: Green and white
Issued: 1935-1949
Varieties: HN 1718, 1719, 1861, 1919, 2028

U.S.:	$2,500.00
Can.:	$3,000.00
U.K.:	£1,350.00

HN 1735
Sibell
Designer: L. Harradine
Height: 6 ½", 16.5 cm
Colour: White and blue
Issued: 1935-1949
Varieties: HN 1668, 1695

U.S.:	$1,800.00
Can.:	$2,250.00
U.K.:	£ 975.00

HN 1736
Camille
Style One
Designer: L. Harradine
Height: 6 ½", 16.5 cm
Colour: Pink and cream
Issued: 1935-1949
Varieties: HN 1586, 1648

U.S.:	$2,750.00
Can.:	$3,500.00
U.K.:	£1,500.00

HN 1737
Janet
Style One
Designer: L. Harradine
Height: 6 ¼", 15.9 cm
Colour: Green
Issued: 1935-1949
Varieties: HN 1537, 1538, 1652

U.S.:	$1,000.00
Can.:	$1,200.00
U.K.:	£ 550.00

HN 1738
Sonia
Designer: L. Harradine
Height: 6 ½", 16.5 cm
Colour: Green
Issued: 1935-1949
Varieties: HN 1692

U.S.:	$2,000.00
Can.:	$2,500.00
U.K.:	£1,100.00

HN 1739
Paisley Shawl
Style One
Designer: L. Harradine
Height: 8 ¼", 21.0 cm
Colour: Green and red
Issued: 1935-1949
Varieties: HN 1392, 1460, 1707, 1987

U.S.:	$1,250.00
Can.:	$1,500.00
U.K.:	£ 675.00

HN 1740
Gladys
First Verson
Designer:	L. Harradine
Height:	5 ¼", 13.3 cm
Colour:	Green
Issued:	1935-1949
Varieties:	HN 1741
U.S.:	**$1,350.00**
Can.:	**$1,650.00**
U.K.:	**£ 750.00**

HN 1741
Gladys
First Version
Designer:	L. Harradine
Height:	5", 12.7 cm
Colour:	Pink
Issued:	1935-1938
Varieties:	HN 1740
U.S.:	**$1,350.00**
Can.:	**$1,650.00**
U.K.:	**£ 750.00**

HN 1742
Sir Walter Raleigh
Designer:	L. Harradine
Height:	10 ½", 26.7 cm
Colour:	Green, purple and orange
Issued:	1935-1949
Varieties:	HN 1751, 2015
U.S.:	**$5,500.00**
Can.:	**$6,750.00**
U.K.:	**£3,000.00**

HN 1743
Mirabel
Style One
Designer:	L. Harradine
Height:	7 ¾", 19.7 cm
Colour:	Pale blue
Issued:	1935-1949
Varieties:	HN 1744
U.S.:	**$1,850.00**
Can.:	**$2,250.00**
U.K.:	**£1,000.00**

HN 1744
Mirabel
Style One
Designer:	L. Harradine
Height:	7 ¾", 19.7 cm
Colour:	Pink
Issued:	1935-1949
Varieties:	HN 1743
U.S.:	**$1,850.00**
Can.:	**$2,250.00**
U.K.:	**£1,000.00**

HN 1745
The Rustic Swain
Designer:	L. Harradine
Height:	5 ¼", 13.3 cm
Colour:	Green, white and brown
Issued:	1935-1949
Varieties:	HN 1746
U.S.:	**$3,250.00**
Can.:	**$4,000.00**
U.K.:	**£1,750.00**

HN 1746
The Rustic Swain
Designer:	L. Harradine
Height:	5 ¼", 13.3 cm
Colour:	Green, blue and pink
Issued:	1935-1949
Varieties:	HN 1745
U.S.:	**$3,250.00**
Can.:	**$4,000.00**
U.K.:	**£1,750.00**

HN 1747
Afternoon Tea
Designer:	P. Railston
Height:	5 ¾", 14.6 cm
Colour:	Pink and blue
Issued:	1935-1982
Varieties:	HN 1748
U.S.:	**$650.00**
Can.:	**$775.00**
U.K.:	**£350.00**

HN 1748
Afternoon Tea
Designer: P. Railston
Height: 5 ¼", 13.3 cm
Colour: Green
Issued: 1935-1949
Varieties: HN 1747

U.S.:	**$2,750.00**
Can.:	**$3,500.00**
U.K.:	**£1,500.00**

HN 1749
Pierrette
Style Three
Designer: L. Harradine
Height: 8 ½", 21.6 cm
Colour: Purple
Issued: 1936-1949
Varieties: HN 1391

U.S.:	**$3,500.00**
Can.:	**$4,500.00**
U.K.:	**£2,000.00**

Earthenware

HN 1750
Folly
Designer: L. Harradine
Height: 9 ½", 24.1 cm
Colour: Black-purple
Issued: 1936-1949
Varieties: HN 1335

U.S.:	**$3,750.00**
Can.:	**$4,500.00**
U.K.:	**£2,000.00**

Earthenware

HN 1751
Sir Walter Raleigh
Designer: L. Harradine
Height: 11 ½", 29.2 cm
Colour: Orange and purple
Issued: 1936-1949
Varieties: HN 1742, 2015

U.S.:	**$2,000.00**
Can.:	**$2,500.00**
U.K.:	**£1,100.00**

Earthenware

HN 1752
Regency
Designer: L. Harradine
Height: 8", 20.3 cm
Colour: Lavender and green
Issued: 1936-1949

U.S.:	**$2,000.00**
Can.:	**$2,500.00**
U.K.:	**£1,100.00**

HN 1753
Eleanore
Designer: L. Harradine
Height: 7", 17.8 cm
Colour: Blue, green and pink
Issued: 1936-1949
Varieties: HN 1754

U.S.:	**$2,750.00**
Can.:	**$3,500.00**
U.K.:	**£1,500.00**

HN 1754
Eleanore
Designer: L. Harradine
Height: 7", 17.8 cm
Colour: Orange and cream
Issued: 1936-1949
Varieties: HN 1753

U.S.:	**$2,750.00**
Can.:	**$3,500.00**
U.K.:	**£1,500.00**

HN 1755
The Court Shoemaker
Designer: L. Harradine
Height: 6 ¾", 17.2 cm
Colour: Purple, brown
and green
Issued: 1936-1949

U.S.:	**$4,000.00**
Can.:	**$4,750.00**
U.K.:	**£2,150.00**

HN 1756
Lizana
Designer:	L. Harradine
Height:	8 ½", 21.6 cm
Colour:	Green, pink and purple
Issued:	1936-1949
Varieties:	HN 1761
U.S.:	**$1,650.00**
Can.:	**$2,000.00**
U.K.:	**£ 900.00**

HN 1757
Romany Sue
Designer:	L. Harradine
Height:	9 ¼", 23.5 cm
Colour:	Green and red
Issued:	1936-1949
Varieties:	HN 1758
U.S.:	**$2,250.00**
Can.:	**$2,750.00**
U.K.:	**£1,250.00**

HN 1758
Romany Sue
Designer:	L. Harradine
Height:	9 ½", 24.1 cm
Colour:	Lavender
Issued:	1936-1949
Varieties:	HN 1757
U.S.:	**$2,500.00**
Can.:	**$3,000.00**
U.K.:	**£1,350.00**

HN 1759
The Orange Lady
Designer:	L. Harradine
Height:	8 ¾", 22.2 cm
Colour:	Pink
Issued:	1936-1975
Varieties:	HN 1953
U.S.:	**$375.00**
Can.:	**$450.00**
U.K.:	**£200.00**

1. Earlier pieces have holes in the oranges
2. Earthenware

HN 1760
4 O'Clock
Designer:	L. Harradine
Height:	6", 15.2 cm
Colour:	Lavender
Issued:	1936-1949
U.S.:	**$2,250.00**
Can.:	**$2,750.00**
U.K.:	**£1,200.00**

HN 1761
Lizana
Designer:	L. Harradine
Height:	8 ½", 21.6 cm
Colour:	Green
Issued:	1936-1938
Varieties:	HN 1756
U.S.:	**$1,650.00**
Can.:	**$2,000.00**
U.K.:	**£ 900.00**

HN 1762
The Bride
Style One
Designer:	L. Harradine
Height:	8 ¾", 22.2 cm
Colour:	Cream
Issued:	1936-1949
Varieties:	HN 1588, 1600, 1841
U.S.:	**$2,200.00**
Can.:	**$2,750.00**
U.K.:	**£1,200.00**

HN 1763
Windflower
Style One
Designer:	L. Harradine
Height:	7 ¼", 18.4 cm
Colour:	Pink
Issued:	1936-1949
Varieties:	HN 1764, 2029
U.S.:	**$ 850.00**
Can.:	**$1,000.00**
U.K.:	**£ 450.00**

HN 1764
Windflower
Style One
Designer: L. Harradine
Height: 7 ¼", 18.4 cm
Colour: Blue
Issued: 1936-1949
Varieties: HN 1763, 2029

U.S.:	**$1,300.00**
Can.:	**$1,600.00**
U.K.:	**£ 700.00**

HN 1765
Chloe
Style One
Designer: L. Harradine
Height: 6", 15.2 cm
Colour: Blue
Issued: 1936-1950
Varieties: HN 1470, 1476,
1479, 1498, 1956

U.S.:	**$500.00**
Can.:	**$600.00**
U.K.:	**£275.00**

HN 1766
Nana
Designer: L. Harradine
Height: 4 ¾", 12.0 cm
Colour: Pink
Issued: 1936-1949
Varieties: HN 1767

U.S.:	**$625.00**
Can.:	**$750.00**
U.K.:	**£335.00**

HN 1767
Nana
Designer: L. Harradine
Height: 4 ¾", 12.0 cm
Colour: Lavender
Issued: 1936-1949
Varieties: HN 1766

U.S.:	**$625.00**
Can.:	**$750.00**
U.K.:	**£335.00**

HN 1768
Ivy
Designer: L. Harradine
Height: 4 ¾", 12.0 cm
Colour: Purple
Issued: 1936-1979
Varieties: HN 1769

U.S.:	**$150.00**
Can.:	**$180.00**
U.K.:	**£ 80.00**

HN 1769
Ivy
Designer: L. Harradine
Height: 4 ¾", 12.0 cm
Colour: Unknown
Issued: 1936-1938
Varieties: HN 1768

U.S.:	
Can.:	**Very Rare**
U.K.:	

HN 1770
Maureen
Style One
Designer: L. Harradine
Height: 7 ½", 19.1 cm
Colour: Pink
Issued: 1936-1959
Varieties: HN 1771

U.S.:	**$525.00**
Can.:	**$650.00**
U.K.:	**£300.00**

HN 1771
Maureen
Style One
Designer: L. Harradine
Height: 7 ½", 19.1 cm
Colour: Lavender
Issued: 1936-1949
Varieties: HN 1770

U.S.:	**$1,700.00**
Can.:	**$2,000.00**
U.K.:	**£ 925.00**

HN 1772
Delight
Designer: L. Harradine
Height: 7", 17.8 cm
Colour: Red
Issued: 1936-1967
Varieties: HN 1773

U.S.:	**$375.00**
Can.:	**$450.00**
U.K.:	**£200.00**

HN 1773
Delight
Designer: L. Harradine
Height: 6 ¾", 17.2 cm
Colour: Turquoise
Issued: 1936-1949
Varieties: HN 1772

U.S.:	**$1,100.00**
Can.:	**$1,300.00**
U.K.:	**£ 600.00**

HN 1774
Spring (Matte)
Style Three
Designer: R. Garbe
Height: 21", 53.3 cm
Colour: Ivory
Issued: 1933 in a limited
           edition of 100
Varieties: HN 1827

U.S.:	**Only**
Can.:	**five**
U.K.:	**known**

HN 1775
Salome (Matte)
Style One
Designer: R. Garbe
Height: 8", 20.3 cm
Colour: Ivory
Issued: 1933 in a limited
           edition of 100
Varieties: HN 1828

U.S.:	**Only**
Can.:	**two**
U.K.:	**known**

HN 1776
West Wind (Matte)
Designer: R. Garbe
Height: 14 ½", 36.8 cm
Colour: Ivory
Issued: 1933 in a limited
           edition of 25
Varieties: HN 1826

U.S.:	**Only**
Can.:	**three**
U.K.:	**known**

Photograph
Not
Available

HN 1777
Spirit of the Wind (Matte)
Designer: R. Garbe
Height: Unknown
Colour: Ivory
Issued: 1933 in a limited
           edition of 50
Varieties: HN 1825

U.S.:	**Only**
Can.:	**one**
U.K.:	**known**

HN 1778
Beethoven (Matte)
Designer: R. Garbe
Height: 22", 55.8 cm
Colour: Ivory
Issued: 1933 In a limited
           edition of 25

U.S.:	**Only**
Can.:	**three**
U.K.:	**known**

Photograph
Not
Available

HN 1779
Macaw (Matte)
Designer: R. Garbe
Height: 14 ½", 35.6 cm
Colour: Ivory
Issued: 1933-1949
Varieties: HN 1829

U.S.:	**Only**
Can.:	**one**
U.K.:	**known**

HN 1780
Lady of the Snows
Designer: R. Garbe
Height: Unknown
Colour: Unknown
Issued: 1933 in a limited
edition of 50
Varieties: HN 1830
U.S.: **Only**
Can.: **one**
U.K.: **known**

HN 1781 - 1786 Wall Masks,
HN 1787 - 1790 Not issued.

HN 1791
Old Balloon Seller and Bulldog
Designer: L. Harradine
Height: 7", 17.8 cm
Colour: Green, red and white
Issued: 1932-1938
Varieties: HN 1912
U.S.: **Only**
Can.: **one**
U.K.: **known**

HN 1792
Henry VIII
Style Two
Designer: C. J. Noke
Height: 11 ½", 29.2 cm
Colour: Multicoloured
Issued: 1933 in a limited
edition of 200
U.S.: **$ 9,000.00**
Can.: **$11,000.00**
U.K.: **£ 5,000.00**

HN 1793
This Little Pig
Designer: L. Harradine
Height: 4", 10.1 cm
Colour: Red
Issued: 1936-1995
Varieties: HN 1794, 2125
U.S.: **$150.00**
Can.: **$180.00**
U.K.: **£ 80.00**

HN 1794
This Little Pig
Designer: L. Harradine
Height: 4", 10.1 cm
Colour: Blue
Issued: 1936-1949
Varieties: HN 1793, 2125
U.S.: **$1,100.00**
Can.: **$1,300.00**
U.K.: **£ 600.00**

HN 1795
M'Lady's Maid
Designer: L. Harradine
Height: 9", 22.9 cm
Colour: Red
Issued: 1936-1949
Varieties: HN 1822
U.S.: **$6,500.00**
Can.: **$7,750.00**
U.K.: **£3,500.00**

HN 1796
Hazel
Style One
Designer: L. Harradine
Height: 5 ¼", 13.3 cm
Colour: Green and red
Issued: 1936-1949
Varieties: HN 1797
U.S.: **$1,100.00**
Can.: **$1,300.00**
U.K.: **£ 600.00**

HN 1797
Hazel
Style One
Designer: L. Harradine
Height: 5 ¼", 13.3 cm
Colour: Pink and blue
Issued: 1936-1949
Varieties: HN 1796
U.S.: **$1,100.00**
Can.: **$1,300.00**
U.K.: **£ 600.00**

HN 1798
Lily
Style One
Designer: L. Harradine
Height: 5", 12.7 cm
Colour: Pink
Issued: 1936-1971
Varieties: HN 1799

U.S.: **$200.00**
Can.: **$250.00**
U.K.: **£110.00**

HN 1799
Lily
Style One
Designer: L. Harradine
Height: 5", 12.7 cm
Colour: Green and blue
Issued: 1936-1949
Varieties: HN 1798

U.S.: **$750.00**
Can.: **$900.00**
U.K.: **£400.00**

HN 1800
St. George
Style One
Designer: S. Thorogood
Height: 16", 40.6 cm
Colour: Purple, green
and grey
Issued: 1934-1950
Varieties: HN 385, 386, 2067

U.S.: **$5,000.00**
Can.: **$6,000.00**
U.K.: **£2,700.00**

Earthenware

HN 1801
An Old King
Designer: C. J. Noke
Height: 9 ¾", 24.7 cm
Colour: Unknown
Issued: 1937-1954
Varieties: HN 358, 623, 2134

U.S.:
Can.: **Extremely rare**
U.K.:

HN 1802
Estelle
Designer: L. Harradine
Height: 8", 20.3 cm
Colour: Pink
Issued: 1937-1940
Varieties: HN 1566

U.S.: **$2,500.00**
Can.: **$3,000.00**
U.K.: **£1,350.00**

HN 1803
Aileen
Designer: L. Harradine
Height: 6", 15.2 cm
Colour: Cream dress
with blue shawl
Issued: 1937-1949
Varieties: HN 1645, 1664

U.S.: **$3,500.00**
Can.: **$4,250.00**
U.K.: **£1,875.00**

HN 1804
Granny
Designer: L. Harradine
Height: 7", 17.8 cm
Colour: Grey, purple and brown
Issued: 1937-1949
Varieties: HN 1832

U.S.: **$6,000.00**
Can.: **$7,250.00**
U.K.: **£3,250.00**

HN 1805
To Bed
Designer: L. Harradine
Height: 6", 15.2 cm
Colour: Green
Issued: 1937-1959
Varieties: HN 1806

U.S.: **$300.00**
Can.: **$375.00**
U.K.: **£175.00**

HN 1806
To Bed

Designer:	L. Harradine
Height:	6", 15.2 cm
Colour:	Lavender
Issued:	1937-1949
Varieties:	HN 1805
U.S.:	**$800.00**
Can.:	**$950.00**
U.K.:	**£425.00**

HN 1807
Spring Flowers

Designer:	L. Harradine
Height:	7 ¼", 18.4 cm
Colour:	Green and blue
Issued:	1937-1959
Varieties:	HN 1945
U.S.:	**$675.00**
Can.:	**$800.00**
U.K.:	**£375.00**

HN 1808
Cissie

Designer:	L. Harradine
Height:	5", 12.7 cm
Colour:	Green
Issued:	1937-1951
Varieties:	HN 1809
U.S.:	**$800.00**
Can.:	**$950.00**
U.K.:	**£425.00**

HN 1809
Cissie

Designer:	L. Harradine
Height:	5", 12.7 cm
Colour:	Pink
Issued:	1937-1993
Varieties:	HN 1808
U.S.:	**$150.00**
Can.:	**$180.00**
U.K.:	**£ 80.00**

HN 1810
Bo-Peep
Style Two

Designer:	L. Harradine
Height:	5", 12.7 cm
Colour:	Blue
Issued:	1937-1949
Varieties:	HN 1811
U.S.:	**$800.00**
Can.:	**$950.00**
U.K.:	**£425.00**

HN 1811
Bo-Peep
Style Two

Designer:	L. Harradine
Height:	5", 12.7 cm
Colour:	Pink
Issued:	1937-1995
Varieties:	HN 1810
U.S.:	**$150.00**
Can.:	**$180.00**
U.K.:	**£ 80.00**

HN 1812
Forget-Me-Not
Style One

Designer:	L. Harradine
Height:	6", 15.2 cm
Colour:	Pink and green
Issued:	1937-1949
Varieties:	HN 1813
U.S.:	**$1,850.00**
Can.:	**$2,250.00**
U.K.:	**£1,000.00**

HN 1813
Forget-Me-Not
Style One

Designer:	L. Harradine
Height:	6", 15.2 cm
Colour:	Red and blue
Issued:	1937-1949
Varieties:	HN 1812
U.S.:	**$1,350.00**
Can.:	**$1,650.00**
U.K.:	**£ 750.00**

HN 1814
The Squire
Designer: Unknown
Height: 9 ¾", 24.7 cm
Colour: Red and grey
Issued: 1937-1949
Varieties: Also called ' Hunting
          Squire' HN 1409

U.S.:	**$6,000.00**
Can.:	**$7,500.00**
U.K.:	**£3,500.00**

Earthenware

HN 1815
The Huntsman
Style Two
Designer: Unknown
Height: 9 ½", 24.1 cm
Colour: Red and brown
Issued: 1937-1949
Varieties: Also called 'John
          Peel' HN 1408

U.S.:	**$6,000.00**
Can.:	**$7,500.00**
U.K.:	**£3,500.00**

Earthenware
HN 1816 - 1817 Wall Masks.

HN 1818
Miranda
Style One
Designer: L. Harradine
Height: 8 ½", 21.6 cm
Colour: Red and blue
Issued: 1937-1949
Varieties: HN 1819

U.S.:	**$3,500.00**
Can.:	**$4,500.00**
U.K.:	**£1,950.00**

HN 1819
Miranda
Style One
Designer: L. Harradine
Height: 8 ½", 21.6 cm
Colour: Green
Issued: 1937-1949
Varieties: HN 1818

U.S.:	**$3,500.00**
Can.:	**$4,500.00**
U.K.:	**£1,950.00**

HN 1820
Reflections
Designer: L. Harradine
Height: 5", 12.7 cm
Colour: Red and green
Issued: 1937-1938
Varieties: HN 1821, 1847, 1848

U.S.:	**$5,000.00**
Can.:	**$6,000.00**
U.K.:	**£2,700.00**

HN 1821
Reflections
Designer: L. Harradine
Height: 5", 12.7 cm
Colour: Green and red
Issued: 1937-1938
Varieties: HN 1820, 1847, 1848

U.S.:	**$5,000.00**
Can.:	**$6,000.00**
U.K.:	**£2,700.00**

HN 1822
M'Lady's Maid
Designer: L. Harradine
Height: 9", 22.9 cm
Colour: Multicoloured
Issued: 1937-1949
Varieties: HN 1795

U.S.:	**$7,000.00**
Can.:	**$8,500.00**
U.K.:	**£3,750.00**

HN 1823 - 1824 Wall Masks.

Photograph
Not
Available

HN 1825
Spirit of the Wind
Designer: R. Garbe
Height: Unknown
Colour: Green and ivory
Issued: 1937-1949
Varieties: HN 1777

U.S.:	**Only**
Can.:	**four**
U.K.:	**known**

HN 1826
West Wind
Designer: R. Garbe
Height: 14 ½", 36.8 cm
Colour: Antique ivory
Issued: 1937-1949
Varieties: HN 1776

U.S.:   **Only**
Can.:   **two**
U.K.:   **known**

HN 1827
Spring
Style Three
Designer: R. Garbe
Height: 21", 53.3 cm
Colour: Green and ivory
Issued: 1937-1949
Varieties: HN 1774

U.S.:   **Only**
Can.:   **four**
U.K.:   **known**

HN 1828
Salome
Style One
Designer: R. Garbe
Height: 8", 20.3 cm
Colour: Pale blue
Issued: 1937-1949
Varieties: HN 1775

U.S.:   **Only**
Can.:   **two**
U.K.:   **known**

Photograph
Not
Available

HN 1829
Macaw
Designer: R. Garbe
Height: 14 ½", 35.6 cm
Colour: Antique ivory
Issued: 1933-1949
Varieties: HN 1779

U.S.:   **Only**
Can.:   **two**
U.K.:   **known**

HN 1830
Lady of the Snows
Designer: R. Garbe
Height: Unknown
Colour: Antique ivory
Issued: 1937-1949
Varieties: HN 1780

U.S.:   **Only**
Can.:   **two**
U.K.:   **known**

Photograph
Not
Available

HN 1831
The Cloud
Designer: R. Garbe
Height: 23", 58.4 cm
Colour: Ivory and gold
Issued: 1937-1949

U.S.:   **Only**
Can.:   **two**
U.K.:   **known**

HN 1832
Granny
Designer: L. Harradine
Height: 6 ¾", 17.1 cm
Colour: Red and yellow
Issued: 1937-1949
Varieties: HN 1804

U.S.:   **$5,000.00**
Can.:   **$6,000.00**
U.K.:   **£2,700.00**

HN 1833
Top o' the Hill
Style One
Designer: L. Harradine
Height: 7", 17.8 cm
Colour: Green and blue
Issued: 1937-1971
Varieties: HN 1834, 1849,
           2127, 3735A

U.S.:   **$350.00**
Can.:   **$425.00**
U.K.:   **£190.00**

HN 1834
Top o' the Hill
Style One
Designer: L. Harradine
Height: 7", 17.8 cm
Colour: Red
Issued: 1937-2004
Varieties: HN 1833, 1849,
  2127, 3735A
  U.S.: **$300.00**
  Can.: **$350.00**
  U.K.: **£160.00**

HN 1835
Verena
Designer: L. Harradine
Height: 8 ¼", 21.0 cm
Colour: Green and peach
Issued: 1938-1949
Varieties: HN 1854
  U.S.: **$2,500.00**
  Can.: **$3,000.00**
  U.K.: **£1,350.00**

HN 1836
Vanessa
Style One
Designer: L. Harradine
Height: 7 ½", 19.1 cm
Colour: Green and blue
Issued: 1938-1949
Varieties: HN 1838
  U.S.: **$2,000.00**
  Can.: **$2,500.00**
  U.K.: **£1,100.00**

HN 1837
Mariquita
Designer: L. Harradine
Height: 8", 20.3 cm
Colour: Red and purple
Issued: 1938-1949
  U.S.: **$4,500.00**
  Can.: **$5,500.00**
  U.K.: **£2,500.00**

HN 1838
Vanessa
Style One
Designer: L. Harradine
Height: 7 ½", 19.1 cm
Colour: Pink and green
Issued: 1938-1949
Varieties: HN 1836
  U.S.: **$2,000.00**
  Can.: **$2,500.00**
  U.K.: **£1,100.00**

HN 1839
Christine
Style One
Designer: L. Harradine
Height: 7 ¾", 19.6 cm
Colour: Lavender and blue
Issued: 1938-1949
Varieties: HN 1840
  U.S.: **$1,850.00**
  Can.: **$2,250.00**
  U.K.: **£1,000.00**

HN 1840
Christine
Style One
Designer: L. Harradine
Height: 7 ¾", 19.6 cm
Colour: Pink and blue
Issued: 1938-1949
Varieties: HN 1839
  U.S.: **$1,750.00**
  Can.: **$2,100.00**
  U.K.: **£ 950.00**

HN 1841
The Bride
Style One
Designer: L. Harradine
Height: 9 ½", 24.1 cm
Colour: Blue
Issued: 1938-1949
Varieties: HN 1588, 1600, 1762
  U.S.: **$2,200.00**
  Can.: **$2,750.00**
  U.K.: **£1,200.00**

HN 1842
Babie
Designer: L. Harradine
Height: 4 ¾", 12.0 cm
Colour: Rose and green
Issued: 1938-1949
Varieties: HN 1679, 2121

U.S.: $450.00
Can.: $550.00
U.K.: £245.00

HN 1843
Biddy Penny Farthing
Designer: L. Harradine
Height: 9", 22.9 cm
Colour: Green and lavender
Issued: 1938 to the present

U.S.: $360.00
Can.: $550.00
U.K.: £175.00

Earthenware and china

HN 1844
Odds and Ends
Designer: L. Harradine
Height: 7 ¾", 19.6 cm
Colour: Orange and green
Issued: 1938-1949

U.S.: $4,000.00
Can.: $5,000.00
U.K.: £2,200.00

Earthenware

HN 1845
Modena
Designer: L. Harradine
Height: 7 ¼", 18.4 cm
Colour: Blue and pink
Issued: 1938-1949
Varieties: HN 1846

U.S.: $3,500.00
Can.: $4,250.00
U.K.: £1,900.00

HN 1846
Modena
Designer: L. Harradine
Height: 7 ¼", 18.4 cm
Colour: Red and green
Issued: 1938-1949
Varieties: HN 1845

U.S.: $3,250.00
Can.: $4,000.00
U.K.: £1,750.00

HN 1847
Reflections
Designer: L. Harradine
Height: 4 ½", 11.4 cm
Colour: Red and green
Issued: 1938-1949
Varieties: HN 1820, 1821, 1848

U.S.: $3,250.00
Can.: $4,000.00
U.K.: £1,750.00

HN 1848
Reflections
Designer: L. Harradine
Height: 5", 12.7 cm
Colour: Green, blue and pink
Issued: 1938-1949
Varieties: HN 1820, 1821, 1847

U.S.: $3,500.00
Can.: $4,250.00
U.K.: £1,900.00

HN 1849
Top o' the Hill
Style One
Designer: L. Harradine
Height: 7 ¼", 18.4 cm
Colour: Pink
Issued: 1938-1975
Varieties: HN 1833, 1834, 2127, 3735A

U.S.: $325.00
Can.: $400.00
U.K.: £175.00

HN 1850
Antoinette
Style One
Designer: L. Harradine
Height: 8 ¼", 21.0 cm
Colour: Red and pink
Issued: 1938-1949
Varieties: HN 1851

U.S.:   **$3,000.00**
Can.:   **$3,750.00**
U.K.:   **£1,650.00**

HN 1851
Antoinette
Style One
Designer: L. Harradine
Height: 8 ¼", 21.0 cm
Colour: Blue and lavender
Issued: 1938-1949
Varieties: HN 1850

U.S.:   **$3,000.00**
Can.:   **$3,750.00**
U.K.:   **£1,650.00**

HN 1852
The Mirror
Designer: L. Harradine
Height: 7 ½", 18.4 cm
Colour: Pink
Issued: 1938-1949
Varieties: HN 1853

U.S.:   **$5,000.00**
Can.:   **$6,000.00**
U.K.:   **£2,700.00**

HN 1853
The Mirror
Designer: L. Harradine
Height: 7 ½", 18.4 cm
Colour: Blue
Issued: 1938-1949
Varieties: HN 1852

U.S.:   **$5,000.00**
Can.:   **$6,000.00**
U.K.:   **£2,700.00**

HN 1854
Verena
Designer: L. Harradine
Height: 8 ¼", 21.0 cm
Colour: Blue and pink
Issued: 1938-1949
Varieties: HN 1835

U.S.:   **$3,250.00**
Can.:   **$4,000.00**
U.K.:   **£1,750.00**

HN 1855
Memories
Designer: L. Harradine
Height: 6", 15.2 cm
Colour: Green and red
Issued: 1938-1949
Varieties: HN 1856, 1857, 2030

U.S.:   **$1,100.00**
Can.:   **$1,300.00**
U.K.:   **£   600.00**

HN 1856
Memories
Designer: L. Harradine
Height: 6", 15.2 cm
Colour: Blue and white
Issued: 1938-1949
Varieties: HN 1855, 1857, 2030

U.S.:   **$1,600.00**
Can.:   **$1,900.00**
U.K.:   **£   850.00**

HN 1857
Memories
Designer: L. Harradine
Height: 6", 15.2 cm
Colour: Red and lavender
Issued: 1938-1949
Varieties: HN 1855, 1856, 2030

U.S.:   **$1,600.00**
Can.:   **$1,900.00**
U.K.:   **£   850.00**

HN 1858
Dawn
(With head-dress)
Style One
Designer: L. Harradine
Height: 10", 25.4 cm
Colour: Green
Issued: 1938-Unknown
Varieties: HN 1858A

U.S.: $3,250.00
Can.: $4,000.00
U.K.: £1,850.00

HN 1858A
Dawn
(Without head-dress)
Style One
Designer: L. Harradine
Height: 9 ¾", 24.7 cm
Colour: Green
Issued: Unknown-1949
Varieties: HN 1858

U.S.: $2,250.00
Can.: $2,750.00
U.K.: £1,250.00

HN 1859
Tildy
Designer: L. Harradine
Height: 5 ½", 14.0 cm
Colour: Red and green
Issued: 1934-1939
Varieties: HN 1576

U.S.: $2,000.00
Can.: $2,500.00
U.K.: £1,100.00

HN 1860
Millicent
Designer: L. Harradine
Height: 8", 20.3 cm
Colour: Red and blue
Issued: 1938-1949
Varieties: HN 1714, 1715

U.S.: $2,250.00
Can.: $2,750.00
U.K.: £1,200.00

HN 1861
Kate Hardcastle
Designer: L. Harradine
Height: 8", 20.3 cm
Colour: Red and blue
Issued: 1938-1949
Varieties: HN 1718, 1719, 1734,
1919, 2028

U.S.: $2,500.00
Can.: $3,000.00
U.K.: £1,350.00

HN 1862
Jasmine
Style One
Designer: L. Harradine
Height: 7 ¼", 18.4 cm
Colour: Green, blue
and orange
Issued: 1938-1949
Varieties: HN 1863, 1876

U.S.: $2,500.00
Can.: $3,000.00
U.K.: £1,350.00

HN 1863
Jasmine
Style One
Designer: L. Harradine
Height: 7 ½", 19.1 cm
Colour: Blue and green
Issued: 1938-1949
Varieties: HN 1862, 1876

U.S.: $2,500.00
Can.: $3,000.00
U.K.: £1,350.00

HN 1864
Sweet and Fair
Designer: L. Harradine
Height: 7 ½", 19.1 cm
Colour: Pink
Issued: 1938-1949
Varieties: HN 1865

U.S.: $3,500.00
Can.: $4,250.00
U.K.: £1,900.00

HN 1865
Sweet and Fair
Designer: L. Harradine
Height: 7 ¼", 18.4 cm
Colour: Green
Issued: 1938-1949
Varieties: HN 1864

U.S.:	**$3,500.00**
Can.:	**$4,250.00**
U.K.:	**£1,900.00**

HN 1866
Wedding Morn
Style One
Designer: L. Harradine
Height: 10 ½", 26.7 cm
Colour: Cream
Issued: 1938-1949
Varieties: HN 1867

U.S.:	**$4,250.00**
Can.:	**$5,250.00**
U.K.:	**£2,300.00**

HN 1867
Wedding Morn
Style One
Designer: L. Harradine
Height: 10 ½", 26.7 cm
Colour: Red and cream
Issued: 1938-1949
Varieties: HN 1866

U.S.:	**$4,250.00**
Can.:	**$5,250.00**
U.K.:	**£2,300.00**

HN 1868
Serena
Designer: L. Harradine
Height: 11", 27.9 cm
Colour: Red, pink and blue
Issued: 1938-1949

U.S.:	**$1,750.00**
Can.:	**$2,100.00**
U.K.:	**£ 950.00**

Earthenware

Photograph
Not
Available

HN 1869
Dryad of the Pines
Designer: R. Garbe
Height: 23", 58.4 cm
Colour: Ivory and gold
Issued: 1938-1949

U.S.:	
Can.:	**Extremely rare**
U.K.:	

HN 1870
Little Lady Make Believe
Designer: L. Harradine
Height: 6 ¼", 15.9 cm
Colour: Red and blue
Issued: 1938-1949

U.S.:	**$ 925.00**
Can.:	**$1,100.00**
U.K.:	**£ 500.00**

HN 1871
Annabella
Designer: L. Harradine
Height: 5 ¼", 13.3 cm
Colour: Pink and green
Issued: 1938-1949
Varieties: HN 1872, 1875

U.S.:	**$1,650.00**
Can.:	**$2,000.00**
U.K.:	**£ 900.00**

HN 1872
Annabella
Designer: L. Harradine
Height: 5 ¼", 13.3 cm
Colour: Green and blue
Issued: 1938-1949
Varieties: HN 1871, 1875

U.S.:	**$1,650.00**
Can.:	**$2,000.00**
U.K.:	**£ 900.00**

HN 1873
Granny's Heritage
Designer: L. Harradine
Height: 6 ¾", 17.2 cm
Colour: Pink, blue and grey
Issued: 1938-1949
Varieties: HN 1874, 2031

U.S.:	$1,500.00
Can.:	$1,800.00
U.K.:	£ 800.00

HN 1874
Granny's Heritage
Designer: L. Harradine
Height: 6 ¼", 15.9 cm
Colour: Blue and green
Issued: 1938-1949
Varieties: HN 1873, 2031

U.S.:	$1,750.00
Can.:	$2,100.00
U.K.:	£ 950.00

HN 1875
Annabella
Designer: L. Harradine
Height: 4 ¾", 12.0 cm
Colour: Red
Issued: 1938-1949
Varieties: HN 1871, 1872

U.S.:	$1,650.00
Can.:	$2,000.00
U.K.:	£ 900.00

HN 1876
Jasmine
Style One
Designer: L. Harradine
Height: 7 ½", 19.1 cm
Colour: Green and blue
Issued: 1938-1949
Varieties: HN 1862, 1863

U.S.:	$2,500.00
Can.:	$3,000.00
U.K.:	£1,350.00

HN 1877
Jean
Style One
Designer: L. Harradine
Height: 7 ½", 19.0 cm
Colour: Pink and purple
Issued: 1938-1949
Varieties: HN 1878, 2032

U.S.:	$1,000.00
Can.:	$1,200.00
U.K.:	£ 550.00

HN 1878
Jean
Style One
Designer: L. Harradine
Height: 7 ½", 19.0 cm
Colour: Green and red
Issued: 1938-1949
Varieties: HN 1877, 2032

U.S.:	$800.00
Can.:	$950.00
U.K.:	£430.00

HN 1879
Bon Jour
Designer: L. Harradine
Height: 6 ¾", 17.2 cm
Colour: Green
Issued: 1938-1949
Varieties: HN 1888

U.S.:	$2,250.00
Can.:	$2,750.00
U.K.:	£1,200.00

HN 1880
The Lambeth Walk
Designer: L. Harradine
Height: 10", 25.4 cm
Colour: Blue
Issued: 1938-1949
Varieties: HN 1881

U.S.:	$4,250.00
Can.:	$5,100.00
U.K.:	£2,300.00

HN 1881
The Lambeth Walk
Designer: L. Harradine
Height: 10", 25.4 cm
Colour: Pink
Issued: 1938-1949
Varieties: HN 1880

   U.S.:   **$4,250.00**
   Can.:   **$5,100.00**
   U.K.:   **£2,300.00**

HN 1882
Nell Gwynn
Designer: L. Harradine
Height: 6 ¾", 17.2 cm
Colour: Blue and pink
Issued: 1938-1949
Varieties: HN 1887

   U.S.:   **$2,250.00**
   Can.:   **$2,750.00**
   U.K.:   **£1,200.00**

HN 1883
Prudence
Designer: L. Harradine
Height: 6 ¾", 17.2 cm
Colour: Blue
Issued: 1938-1949
Varieties: HN 1884

   U.S.:   **$1,500.00**
   Can.:   **$1,800.00**
   U.K.:   **£ 825.00**

HN 1884
Prudence
Designer: L. Harradine
Height: 6 ¾", 17.2 cm
Colour: Pink
Issued: 1938-1949
Varieties: HN 1883

   U.S.:   **$1,500.00**
   Can.:   **$1,800.00**
   U.K.:   **£ 825.00**

HN 1885
Nadine
Style One
Designer: L. Harradine
Height: 7 ¾", 19.7 cm
Colour: Turquoise
Issued: 1938-1949
Varieties: HN 1886

   U.S.:   **$2,000.00**
   Can.:   **$2,500.00**
   U.K.:   **£1,100.00**

HN 1886
Nadine
Style One
Designer: L. Harradine
Height: 7 ¾", 19.7 cm
Colour: Pink
Issued: 1938-1949
Varieties: HN 1885

   U.S.:   **$2,000.00**
   Can.:   **$2,500.00**
   U.K.:   **£1,100.00**

HN 1887
Nell Gwynn
Designer: L. Harradine
Height: 6 ¾", 17.2 cm
Colour: Green and pink
Issued: 1938-1949
Varieties: HN 1882

   U.S.:   **$2,250.00**
   Can.:   **$2,750.00**
   U.K.:   **£1,200.00**

HN 1888
Bon Jour
Designer: L. Harradine
Height: 6 ¾", 17.2 cm
Colour: Red
Issued: 1938-1949
Varieties: HN 1879

   U.S.:   **$2,250.00**
   Can.:   **$2,750.00**
   U.K.:   **£1,200.00**

HN 1889
Goody Two Shoes
Style One
Designer: L. Harradine
Height: 4 ¾", 12.0 cm
Colour: Green and purple
Issued: 1938-1949
Varieties: HN 1905, 2037

U.S.:	$ 825.00
Can.:	$1,000.00
U.K.:	£ 450.00

HN 1890
Lambing Time
Style One
Designer: W. M. Chance
Height: 9 ¼", 23.5 cm
Colour: Light brown
Issued: 1938-1981

U.S.:	$300.00
Can.:	$375.00
U.K.:	£165.00

Earthenware

HN 1891
Pecksniff
Style Two
Designer: L. Harradine
Height: 7", 17.8 cm
Colour: Black and brown
Issued: 1938-1952
Varieties: HN 553
Series: Dickens (Series Two)

U.S.:	$ 875.00
Can.:	$1,050.00
U.K.:	£ 475.00

HN 1892
Uriah Heep
Style Two
Designer: L. Harradine
Height: 7", 17.8 cm
Colour: Black
Issued: 1938-1952
Varieties: HN 554
Series: Dickens (Series Two)

U.S.:	$ 875.00
Can.:	$1,050.00
U.K.:	£ 475.00

HN 1893
Fat Boy
Style Two
Designer: L. Harradine
Height: 7", 17.8 cm
Colour: Blue and cream
Issued: 1938-1952
Varieties: HN 555
Series: Dickens (Series Two)

U.S.:	$ 875.00
Can.:	$1,050.00
U.K.:	£ 475.00

HN 1894
Mr Pickwick
Style Two
Designer: L. Harradine
Height: 7", 17.8 cm
Colour: Blue, tan and cream
Issued: 1938-1952
Varieties: HN 556
Series: Dickens (Series Two)

U.S.:	$ 875.00
Can.:	$1,050.00
U.K.:	£ 475.00

Earthenware and porcelain

HN 1895
Mr Micawber
Style Two
Designer: L. Harradine
Height: 7", 17.8 cm
Colour: Brown, black and tan
Issued: 1938-1952
Varieties: HN 557
Series: Dickens (Series Two)

U.S.:	$ 875.00
Can.:	$1,050.00
U.K.:	£ 475.00

HN 1896
Sairey Gamp
Style Two
Designer: L. Harradine
Height: 7", 17.8 cm
Colour: Green
Issued: 1938-1952
Varieties: HN 558
Series: Dickens (Series Two)

U.S.:	$1,000.00
Can.:	$1,250.00
U.K.:	£ 550.00

HN 1897
Miss Fortune
Designer: L. Harradine
Height: 6", 15.2 cm
Colour: Pink and blue
Issued: 1938-1949
Varieties: HN 1898

U.S.:	$1,300.00
Can.:	$1,600.00
U.K.:	£ 700.00

HN 1898
Miss Fortune
Designer: L. Harradine
Height: 5 ¾", 14.6 cm
Colour: Blue
Issued: 1938-1949
Varieties: HN 1897

U.S.:	$1,750.00
Can.:	$2,250.00
U.K.:	£ 950.00

HN 1899
Midsummer Noon
Designer: L. Harradine
Height: 4 ¾", 12.0 cm
Colour: Pink
Issued: 1939-1949
Varieties: HN 1900, 2033

U.S.:	$1,200.00
Can.:	$1,450.00
U.K.:	£ 650.00

HN 1900
Midsummer Noon
Designer: L. Harradine
Height: 4 ¾", 12.0 cm
Colour: Blue
Issued: 1939-1949
Varieties: HN 1899, 2033

U.S.:	$3,500.00
Can.:	$4,250.00
U.K.:	£1,900.00

HN 1901
Penelope
Designer: L. Harradine
Height: 7", 17.8 cm
Colour: Red
Issued: 1939-1975
Varieties: HN 1902

U.S.:	$600.00
Can.:	$725.00
U.K.:	£325.00

HN 1902
Penelope
Designer: L. Harradine
Height: 7", 17.8 cm
Colour: Lavender and green
Issued: 1939-1949
Varieties: HN 1901

U.S.:	$2,500.00
Can.:	$3,000.00
U.K.:	£1,350.00

HN 1903
Rhythm
Designer: L. Harradine
Height: 6 ¾", 17.2 cm
Colour: Pink
Issued: 1939-1949
Varieties: HN 1904

U.S.:	$4,500.00
Can.:	$5,500.00
U.K.:	£2,500.00

HN 1904
Rhythm
Designer: L. Harradine
Height: 6 ¾", 17.2 cm
Colour: Blue
Issued: 1939-1949
Varieties: HN 1903

U.S.:	$5,500.00
Can.:	$6,500.00
U.K.:	£3,000.00

HN 1905
Goody Two Shoes
Style One
Designer: L. Harradine
Height: 4 ¾", 12.0 cm
Colour: Red and pink
Issued: 1939-1949
Varieties: HN 1889, 2037

U.S.:	$325.00
Can.:	$400.00
U.K.:	£175.00

HN 1906
Lydia
Style One
Designer: L. Harradine
Height: 4 ¼", 10.8 cm
Colour: Orange and pink
Issued: 1939-1949
Varieties: HN 1907, 1908

U.S.:	$ 850.00
Can.:	$1,000.00
U.K.:	£ 450.00

HN 1907
Lydia
Style One
Designer: L. Harradine
Height: 4 ¾", 12.0 cm
Colour: Green
Issued: 1939-1949
Varieties: HN 1906, 1908

U.S.:	$ 850.00
Can.:	$1,000.00
U.K.:	£ 450.00

HN 1908
Lydia
Style One
Designer: L. Harradine
Height: 4 ¾", 12.0 cm
Colour: Red
Issued: 1939-1995
Varieties: HN 1906, 1907

U.S.:	$200.00
Can.:	$250.00
U.K.:	£110.00

HN 1909
Honey
Designer: L. Harradine
Height: 7", 17.8 cm
Colour: Pink
Issued: 1939-1949
Varieties: HN 1910, 1963

U.S.:	$750.00
Can.:	$900.00
U.K.:	£400.00

HN 1910
Honey
Designer: L. Harradine
Height: 6 ¾", 17.2 cm
Colour: Blue
Issued: 1939-1949
Varieties: HN 1909, 1963

U.S.:	$1,500.00
Can.:	$1,800.00
U.K.:	£ 825.00

HN 1911
Autumn Breezes
Style One
Designer: L. Harradine
Height: 7 ½", 19.1 cm
Colour: Green and pink
Issued: 1939-1976
Varieties: HN 1913, 1934, 2131, 2147, 3736

U.S.:	$300.00
Can.:	$350.00
U.K.:	£165.00

HN 1912
Old Balloon Seller and Bulldog
Designer: L. Harradine
Height: 7", 17.8 cm
Colour: Unknown
Issued: 1939-1949
Varieties: HN 1791

U.S.:	Only
Can.:	one
U.K.:	known

HN 1913
Autumn Breezes
Style One
Designer: L. Harradine
Height: 7 ½", 19.1 cm
Colour: Green and blue
Issued: 1939-1971
Varieties: HN 1911, 1934, 2131,
             2147, 3736
  U.S.:   **$300.00**
  Can.:   **$350.00**
  U.K.:   **£165.00**

HN 1914
Paisley Shawl
Style Three
Designer: L. Harradine
Height: 6 ½", 16.5 cm
Colour: Green and red
Issued: 1939-1949
Varieties: HN 1988
  U.S.:   **$400.00**
  Can.:   **$500.00**
  U.K.:   **£225.00**

HN 1915
Veronica
Style Three
Designer: L. Harradine
Height: 5 ¾", 14.6 cm
Colour: Red and cream
Issued: 1939-1949
  U.S.:   **$600.00**
  Can.:   **$725.00**
  U.K.:   **£325.00**

HN 1916
Janet
Style Three
Designer: L. Harradine
Height: 5 ¼", 13.3 cm
Colour: Pink and blue
Issued: 1939-1949
Varieties: HN 1964
  U.S.:   **$375.00**
  Can.:   **$450.00**
  U.K.:   **£200.00**

HN 1917
Meryll
Designer: L. Harradine
Height: 6 ¾", 17.2 cm
Colour: Red and green
Issued: 1939-1940
Varieties: Also called 'Toinette'
             HN 1940
  U.S.:   **$4,500.00**
  Can.:   **$5,500.00**
  U.K.:   **£2,500.00**

HN 1918
Sweet Suzy
Designer: L. Harradine
Height: 6 ½", 16.5 cm
Colour: Pink and turquoise
Issued: 1939-1949
  U.S.:   **$1,600.00**
  Can.:   **$2,000.00**
  U.K.:   **£ 900.00**

HN 1919
Kate Hardcastle
Designer: L. Harradine
Height: 8 ¼", 21.0 cm
Colour: Red and green
Issued: 1939-1949
Varieties: HN 1718, 1719, 1734,
             1861, 2028
  U.S.:   **$2,500.00**
  Can.:   **$3,000.00**
  U.K.:   **£1,350.00**

HN 1920
Windflower
Style Two
Designer: L. Harradine
Height: 11", 27.9 cm
Colour: Multicoloured
Issued: 1939-1949
Varieties: HN 1939
  U.S.:   **$4,250.00**
  Can.:   **$5,250.00**
  U.K.:   **£2,250.00**

HN 1921
Roseanna
Designer: L. Harradine
Height: 8", 20.3 cm
Colour: Green
Issued: 1940-1949
Varieties: HN 1926

U.S.:	$2,750.00
Can.:	$3,250.00
U.K.:	£1,500.00

HN 1922
Spring Morning
Style One
Designer: L. Harradine
Height: 7 ½", 19.1 cm
Colour: Pink and blue
Issued: 1940-1973
Varieties: HN 1923

U.S.:	$325.00
Can.:	$400.00
U.K.:	£175.00

HN 1923
Spring Morning
Style One
Designer: L. Harradine
Height: 7 ½", 19.1 cm
Colour: Green and cream
Issued: 1940-1949
Varieties: HN 1922

U.S.:	$1,100.00
Can.:	$1,350.00
U.K.:	£ 600.00

HN 1924
Fiona
Style One
Designer: L. Harradine
Height: 5 ¾", 14.6 cm
Colour: Pink and lavender
Issued: 1940-1949
Varieties: HN 1925, 1933

U.S.:	$1,650.00
Can.:	$2,000.00
U.K.:	£ 900.00

HN 1925
Fiona
Style One
Designer: L. Harradine
Height: 5 ¾", 14.6 cm
Colour: Blue
Issued: 1940-1949
Varieties: HN 1924, 1933

U.S.:	$1,650.00
Can.:	$2,000.00
U.K.:	£ 900.00

HN 1926
Roseanna
Designer: L. Harradine
Height: 8", 20.3 cm
Colour: Pink
Issued: 1940-1959
Varieties: HN 1921

U.S.:	$700.00
Can.:	$850.00
U.K.:	£375.00

HN 1927
The Awakening
Style One
Designer: L. Harradine
Height: 10 ¼", 26.0 cm
Colour: Pale pink
Issued: 1940-1949

U.S.:	$4,750.00
Can.:	$5,750.00
U.K.:	£2,500.00

HN 1928
Marguerite
Designer: L. Harradine
Height: 8", 20.3 cm
Colour: Pink
Issued: 1940-1959
Varieties: HN 1929, 1930, 1946

U.S.:	$750.00
Can.:	$900.00
U.K.:	£400.00

HN 1929
Marguerite
Designer:	L. Harradine
Height:	8", 20.3 cm
Colour:	Pale pink and yellow
Issued:	1940-1949
Varieties:	HN 1928, 1930, 1946

U.S.:	**$2,750.00**
Can.:	**$3,250.00**
U.K.:	**£1,500.00**

HN 1930
Marguerite
Designer:	L. Harradine
Height:	8", 20.3 cm
Colour:	Blue and purple
Issued:	1940-1949
Varieties:	HN 1928, 1929, 1946

U.S.:	**$2,250.00**
Can.:	**$2,750.00**
U.K.:	**£1,200.00**

HN 1931
Meriel
Designer:	L. Harradine
Height:	7 ¼", 18.4 cm
Colour:	Pink
Issued:	1940-1949
Varieties:	HN 1932

U.S.:	**$3,500.00**
Can.:	**$4,250.00**
U.K.:	**£1,900.00**

HN 1932
Meriel
Designer:	L. Harradine
Height:	7 ¼", 18.4 cm
Colour:	Green
Issued:	1940-1949
Varieties:	HN 1931

U.S.:	**$3,500.00**
Can.:	**$4,250.00**
U.K.:	**£1,900.00**

HN 1933
Fiona
Style One
Designer:	L. Harradine
Height:	5 ¾", 14.6 cm
Colour:	Multicoloured
Issued:	1940-1949
Varieties:	HN 1924, 1925

U.S.:	**$2,000.00**
Can.:	**$2,500.00**
U.K.:	**£1,100.00**

HN 1934
Autumn Breezes
Style One
Designer:	L. Harradine
Height:	7 ½", 19.1 cm
Colour:	Red
Issued:	1940-1997
Varieties:	HN 1911, 1913, 2131, 2147, 3736

U.S.:	**$275.00**
Can.:	**$325.00**
U.K.:	**£150.00**

HN 1935
Sweeting
Designer:	L. Harradine
Height:	6", 15.2 cm
Colour:	Pink
Issued:	1940-1973
Varieties:	HN 1938

U.S.:	**$175.00**
Can.:	**$225.00**
U.K.:	**£100.00**

HN 1936
Miss Muffet
Designer:	L. Harradine
Height:	5 ½", 14.0 cm
Colour:	Red
Issued:	1940-1967
Varieties:	HN 1937

U.S.:	**$250.00**
Can.:	**$300.00**
U.K.:	**£135.00**

Colourways of The Bather and The Swimmer

HN 687
The Bather
Style One, 1924-1949

HN 773
The Bather
Style Two, 1925-1938

HN 774
The Bather
Style Two, 1925-1938

HN 1238
The Bather, Style One
1927-1938

HN 1270
The Swimmer
1928-1938

HN 1326
The Swimmer
1929-1938

FIGURINES PRODUCED DURING THE 1920s AND 1930s

HN 1233
Susanna
1927-1936

HN 1541
'Happy Joy, Baby Boy'
1933-1949

HN 1249
Circe
1927-1936

HN 1260
Carnival
1927-1936

HN 1305
Siesta
1928-1940

HN 1473
Dreamland
1931-1937

FAIRIES

HN 1393
Style Eight
1930-1938

HN 1395
Style Three
1930-1938

HN 1536
Style Four
1932-1938

HN 1378
Style Six
1930-1938

HN 1394
Style Seven
1930-1938

HN 1396
Style Six
1930-1938

HN 1324
Style One
1929-1938

HN 1380
Style Two
1930-1938

HN 1532
Style Two
1932-1938

Colourways of Kathleen

HN 1252
1927-1938

HN 1279
1928-1938

HN 1357
1929-1938

Colourways of Priscilla

HN 1337
1929-1938

HN 1340
1929-1949

HN 1501
1932-1938

Colourways of Patricia

HN 1414
1930-1949

HN 1431
1930-1949

HN 1462
1931-1938

HN 1567
1933-1949

FIGURINES PRODUCED DURING THE 1930s AND 1940s

HN 1578
The Hinged Parasol
1933-1949

HN 1607
Cerise
1933-1949

HN 1586
Camille, Style One
1933-1949

HN 1619
Maisie
1934-1949

HN 1628
Margot
1934-1940

HN 1629
Grizel
1934-1938

FIGURINES PRODUCED DURING THE 1930s AND 1940s

HN 1552
Pinkie
1933-1938

HN 1553
Pinkie
1933-1938

HN 1813
Forget-Me-Not, Style One
1937-1949

HN 1897
Miss Fortune
1938-1949

HN 1898
Miss Fortune
1938-1949

HN 1918
Sweet Suzy
1939-1949

MOUNTED RIDERS

HN 1814
The Squire
1937-1949

HN 1815
The Huntsman, Style Two
1937-1949

HN 2520
The Farmer's Boy
1938-1960

HN 2521
Dapple Grey
1938-1960

HN 1937
Miss Muffet
Designer: L. Harradine
Height: 5 ½", 14.0 cm
Colour: Green
Issued: 1940-1952
Varieties: HN 1936

U.S.:	**$500.00**
Can.:	**$600.00**
U.K.:	**£270.00**

HN 1938
Sweeting
Designer: L. Harradine
Height: 6", 15.2 cm
Colour: Purple and red
Issued: 1940-1949
Varieties: HN 1935

U.S.:	**$700.00**
Can.:	**$850.00**
U.K.:	**£375.00**

HN 1939
Windflower
Style Two
Designer: L. Harradine
Height: 11", 27.9 cm
Colour: Pink
Issued: 1940-1949
Varieties: HN 1920

U.S.:	**$4,250.00**
Can.:	**$5,250.00**
U.K.:	**£2,250.00**

HN 1940
Toinette
Designer: L. Harradine
Height: 6 ¾", 17.1 cm
Colour: Red
Issued: 1940-1949
Varieties: Also called 'Meryll'
HN 1917

U.S.:	**$3,250.00**
Can.:	**$4,000.00**
U.K.:	**£1,750.00**

HN 1941
Peggy
Designer: L. Harradine
Height: 5", 12.7 cm
Colour: Red and white
Issued: 1940-1949
Varieties: HN 2038 (minor
glaze difference)

U.S.:	**$250.00**
Can.:	**$300.00**
U.K.:	**£135.00**

HN 1942
Pyjams
Designer: L. Harradine
Height: 5 ¼", 13.3 cm
Colour: Pink
Issued: 1940-1949

U.S.:	**$1,600.00**
Can.:	**$2,000.00**
U.K.:	**£ 900.00**

HN 1943
Veronica
Style One
Designer: L. Harradine
Height: 8", 20.3 cm
Colour: Red dress and blue hat
Issued: 1940-1949
Varieties: HN 1517, 1519, 1650

U.S.:	**$1,800.00**
Can.:	**$2,200.00**
U.K.:	**£1,000.00**

HN 1944
Daydreams
Designer: L. Harradine
Height: 5 ½", 14.0 cm
Colour: Red
Issued: 1940-1949
Varieties: HN 1731, 1732

U.S.:	**$1,500.00**
Can.:	**$1,800.00**
U.K.:	**£ 825.00**

HN 1945
Spring Flowers
Designer: L. Harradine
Height: 7 ¼", 18.4 cm
Colour: Red and green
Issued: 1940-1949
Varieties: HN 1807

U.S.: $2,250.00
Can.: $2,750.00
U.K.: £1,200.00

HN 1946
Marguerite
Designer: L. Harradine
Height: 8", 20.3 cm
Colour: Pink
Issued: 1940-1949
Varieties: HN 1928, 1929, 1930

U.S.: $2,500.00
Can.: $3,000.00
U.K.: £1,350.00

HN 1947
June
Style One
Designer: L. Harradine
Height: 7 ¼", 18.4 cm
Colour: Red
Issued: 1940-1949
Varieties: HN 1690, 1691, 2027

U.S.: $1,850.00
Can.: $2,250.00
U.K.: £1,000.00

HN 1948
Lady Charmian
Designer: L. Harradine
Height: 8", 20.3 cm
Colour: Green dress with red shawl
Issued: 1940-1973
Varieties: HN 1949

U.S.: $325.00
Can.: $400.00
U.K.: £175.00

HN 1949
Lady Charmian
Designer: L. Harradine
Height: 8", 20.3 cm
Colour: Red dress with green shawl
Issued: 1940-1975
Varieties: HN 1948

U.S.: $350.00
Can.: $425.00
U.K.: £200.00

HN 1950
Claribel
Designer: L. Harradine
Height: 4 ¾", 12.0 cm
Colour: Purple and pink
Issued: 1940-1949
Varieties: HN 1951

U.S.: $700.00
Can.: $850.00
U.K.: £400.00

HN 1951
Claribel
Designer: L. Harradine
Height: 4 ¾", 12.0 cm
Colour: Red
Issued: 1940-1949
Varieties: HN 1950

U.S.: $700.00
Can.: $850.00
U.K.: £400.00

HN 1952
Irene
Designer: L. Harradine
Height: 6 ¾", 17.2 cm
Colour: Blue and purple
Issued: 1940-1950
Varieties: HN 1621, 1697

U.S.: $1,850.00
Can.: $2,250.00
U.K.: £1,000.00

HN 1953
Orange Lady
Designer: L. Harradine
Height: 8 ½", 21.6 cm
Colour: Light green dress,
dark green shawl
Issued: 1940-1975
Varieties: HN 1759

U.S.:	**$325.00**
Can.:	**$400.00**
U.K.:	**£175.00**

HN 1954
The Balloon Man
Designer: L. Harradine
Height: 7 ¼", 18.4 cm
Colour: Black and grey
Issued: 1940 to the present

U.S.:	**$360.00**
Can.:	**$550.00**
U.K.:	**£175.00**

Earthenware and China

HN 1955
Lavinia
Designer: L. Harradine
Height: 5", 12.7 cm
Colour: Red
Issued: 1940-1979

U.S.:	**$175.00**
Can.:	**$215.00**
U.K.:	**£100.00**

HN 1956
Chloe
Style One
Designer: L. Harradine
Height: 6", 15.2 cm
Colour: Red and green
Issued: 1940-1949
Varieties: HN 1470, 1476, 1479,
1498, 1765

U.S.:	**$1,200.00**
Can.:	**$1,500.00**
U.K.:	**£ 650.00**

HN 1957
The New Bonnet
Designer: L. Harradine
Height: 7", 17.8 cm
Colour: Red
Issued: 1940-1949
Varieties: HN 1728

U.S.:	**$2,250.00**
Can.:	**$2,750.00**
U.K.:	**£1,200.00**

HN 1958
Lady April
Designer: L. Harradine
Height: 7", 17.8 cm
Colour: Red and purple
Issued: 1940-1959
Varieties: HN 1965

U.S.:	**$525.00**
Can.:	**$650.00**
U.K.:	**£300.00**

HN 1959
The Choice
Designer: L. Harradine
Height: 7 ¼", 18.4 cm
Colour: Red
Issued: 1941-1949
Varieties: HN 1960

U.S.:	**$3,500.00**
Can.:	**$4,250.00**
U.K.:	**£1,900.00**

HN 1960
The Choice
Designer: L. Harradine
Height: 7 ¼", 18.4 cm
Colour: Purple
Issued: 1941-1949
Varieties: HN 1959

U.S.:	**$3,500.00**
Can.:	**$4,250.00**
U.K.:	**£1,900.00**

HN 1961
Daisy
Style One
Designer: L. Harradine
Height: 3 ½", 8.9 cm
Colour: Pink
Issued: 1941-1949
Varieties: HN 1575

U.S.:	**$ 900.00**
Can.:	**$1,100.00**
U.K.:	**£ 500.00**

HN 1962
Genevieve
Designer: L. Harradine
Height: 7", 17.8 cm
Colour: Red
Issued: 1941-1975

U.S.:	**$450.00**
Can.:	**$550.00**
U.K.:	**£250.00**

HN 1963
Honey
Designer: L. Harradine
Height: 6 ¾", 17.2 cm
Colour: Red and blue
Issued: 1941-1949
Varieties: HN 1909, 1910

U.S.:	**$1,600.00**
Can.:	**$2,000.00**
U.K.:	**£ 875.00**

HN 1964
Janet
Style Three
Designer: L. Harradine
Height: 5", 12.7 cm
Colour: Pink
Issued: 1941-1949
Varieties: HN 1916

U.S.:	**$ 950.00**
Can.:	**$1,150.00**
U.K.:	**£ 500.00**

HN 1965
Lady April
Designer: L. Harradine
Height: 7", 17.8 cm
Colour: Green and pink
Issued: 1941-1949
Varieties: HN 1958

U.S.:	**$1,350.00**
Can.:	**$1,600.00**
U.K.:	**£ 725.00**

HN 1966
An Orange Vendor
Designer: C. J. Noke
Height: 6 ¼", 15.9 cm
Colour: Purple
Issued: 1941-1949
Varieties: HN 72, 508, 521

U.S.:	**$1,500.00**
Can.:	**$1,800.00**
U.K.:	**£ 825.00**

Earthenware

HN 1967
Lady Betty
Designer: L. Harradine
Height: 6 ½", 16.5 cm
Colour: Red
Issued: 1941-1951

U.S.:	**$650.00**
Can.:	**$800.00**
U.K.:	**£375.00**

HN 1968
Madonna of the Square
Designer: P. Stabler
Height: 7", 17.8 cm
Colour: Pale green
Issued: 1941-1949
Varieties: HN 10, 10A, 11, 14,
           27, 326, 573, 576,
           594, 613, 764, 1969,
           2034

U.S.:	**$2,250.00**
Can.:	**$2,750.00**
U.K.:	**£1,250.00**

HN 1969
Madonna of the Square
Designer: P. Stabler
Height: 7", 17.8 cm
Colour: Lavender
Issued: 1941-1949
Varieties: HN 10, 10A, 11, 14,
27, 326, 573, 576,
594, 613, 764, 1968,
2034

U.S.: $2,250.00
Can.: $2,750.00
U.K.: £1,250.00

HN 1970
Milady
Designer: L. Harradine
Height: 6 ½", 16.5 cm
Colour: Pink
Issued: 1941-1949

U.S.: $2,000.00
Can.: $2,500.00
U.K.: £1,100.00

HN 1971
Springtime
Style One
Designer: L. Harradine
Height: 6", 15.2 cm
Colour: Pink and blue
Issued: 1941-1949

U.S.: $1,750.00
Can.: $2,250.00
U.K.: £1,000.00

HN 1972
Regency Beau
Designer: H. Fenton
Height: 8", 20.3 cm
Colour: Green and pink
Issued: 1941-1949

U.S.: $2,000.00
Can.: $2,500.00
U.K.: £1,100.00

HN 1973
The Corinthian
Designer: H. Fenton
Height: 7 ¾", 19.7 cm
Colour: Green, red and cream
Issued: 1941-1949

U.S.: $2,000.00
Can.: $2,500.00
U.K.: £1,100.00

HN 1974
Forty Winks
Designer: H. Fenton
Height: 6 ¾", 17.2 cm
Colour: Green and tan
Issued: 1945-1973

U.S.: $325.00
Can.: $400.00
U.K.: £175.00

HN 1975
The Shepherd
Style Four
Designer: H. Fenton
Height: 8 ½", 21.6 cm
Colour: Light brown
Issued: 1945-1975

U.S.: $300.00
Can.: $375.00
U.K.: £175.00

HN 1976
Easter Day
Designer: L. Harradine
Height: 7 ¼", 18.4 cm
Colour: White, lilac and green
Issued: 1945-1951
Varieties: HN 2039

U.S.: $ 900.00
Can.: $1,100.00
U.K.: £ 500.00

HN 1977
Her Ladyship
Designer: L. Harradine
Height: 7 ¼", 18.4 cm
Colour: Red and cream
Issued: 1945-1959

U.S.:	**$550.00**
Can.:	**$675.00**
U.K.:	**£300.00**

HN 1978
Bedtime
Style One
Designer: L. Harradine
Height: 5 ¾", 14.6 cm
Colour: White, black base
Issued: 1945-1997
Varieties: HN 2219

U.S.:	**$100.00**
Can.:	**$125.00**
U.K.:	**£ 55.00**

HN 1979
Gollywog
Designer: L. Harradine
Height: 5 ¼", 13.3 cm
Colour: Patterned white
            dungarees
Issued: 1945-1959
Varieties: HN 2040

U.S.:	**$1,500.00**
Can.:	**$1,800.00**
U.K.:	**£ 800.00**

HN 1980
Gwynneth
Designer: L. Harradine
Height: 7", 17.8 cm
Colour: Red
Issued: 1945-1952

U.S.:	**$550.00**
Can.:	**$675.00**
U.K.:	**£325.00**

HN 1981
The Ermine Coat
Designer: L. Harradine
Height: 6 ¾", 17.2 cm
Colour: White and red
Issued: 1945-1967

U.S.:	**$450.00**
Can.:	**$550.00**
U.K.:	**£250.00**

HN 1982
Sabbath Morn
Designer: L. Harradine
Height: 7 ¼", 18.4 cm
Colour: Red
Issued: 1945-1959

U.S.:	**$400.00**
Can.:	**$500.00**
U.K.:	**£215.00**

HN 1983
Rosebud
Style Two
Designer: L. Harradine
Height: 7 ½", 19.1 cm
Colour: Pink and red
Issued: 1945-1952

U.S.:	**$675.00**
Can.:	**$825.00**
U.K.:	**£375.00**

HN 1984
The Patchwork Quilt
Designer: L. Harradine
Height: 6", 15.2 cm
Colour: Multicoloured
Issued: 1945-1959

U.S.:	**$500.00**
Can.:	**$600.00**
U.K.:	**£275.00**

HN 1985
Darling
Style Two
Designer: C. Vyse
Height: 5 ¼", 13.3 cm
Colour: White, black base
Issued: 1944-1997
Varieties: HN 3613

U.S.:	**$100.00**
Can.:	**$125.00**
U.K.:	**£ 55.00**

HN 1986
Diana
Style One
Designer: L. Harradine
Height: 5 ¾", 14.6 cm
Colour: Red
Issued: 1946-1975
Varieties: HN 1716, 1717

U.S.:	**$250.00**
Can.:	**$300.00**
U.K.:	**£150.00**

HN 1987
Paisley Shawl
Style One
Designer: L. Harradine
Height: 8 ¼", 21.0 cm
Colour: Red and cream
Issued: 1946-1959
Varieties: HN 1392, 1460,
              1707, 1739

U.S.:	**$450.00**
Can.:	**$550.00**
U.K.:	**£250.00**

HN 1988
Paisley Shawl
Style Three
Designer: L. Harradine
Height: 6 ¼", 15.9 cm
Colour: Red and pink
Issued: 1946-1975
Varieties: HN 1914

U.S.:	**$275.00**
Can.:	**$325.00**
U.K.:	**£150.00**

HN 1989
Margaret
Style One
Designer: L. Harradine
Height: 7 ¼", 18.4 cm
Colour: Red and green
Issued: 1947-1959

U.S.:	**$550.00**
Can.:	**$660.00**
U.K.:	**£300.00**

HN 1990
Mary Jane
Designer: L. Harradine
Height: 7 ½", 19.1 cm
Colour: Flowered pink dress
Issued: 1947-1952

U.S.:	**$750.00**
Can.:	**$900.00**
U.K.:	**£400.00**

HN 1991
Market Day
Designer: L. Harradine
Height: 7 ¼", 18.4 cm
Colour: Blue, pink and white
Issued: 1947-1955
Varieties: Also called 'A Country
              Lass' HN 1991A

U.S.:	**$375.00**
Can.:	**$450.00**
U.K.:	**£200.00**

HN 1991A
A Country Lass
Designer: L. Harradine
Height: 7 ¼", 18.4 cm
Colour: Blue, brown and white
Issued: 1975-1981
Varieties: Also called 'Market
              Day' HN 1991

U.S.:	**$225.00**
Can.:	**$275.00**
U.K.:	**£125.00**

HN 1992
Christmas Morn
Style One
Designer: M. Davies
Height: 7", 17.8 cm
Colour: Red and white
Issued: 1947-1996
  U.S.: $250.00
  Can.: $300.00
  U.K.:   £135.00

HN 1993
Griselda
Designer: L. Harradine
Height: 5 ¾", 14.6 cm
Colour: Lavender and cream
Issued: 1947-1953
  U.S.: $650.00
  Can.: $800.00
  U.K.:   £350.00

HN 1994
Karen
Style One
Designer: L. Harradine
Height: 8", 20.3 cm
Colour: Red
Issued: 1947-1955
  U.S.: $750.00
  Can.: $900.00
  U.K.:   £400.00

HN 1995
Olivia
Style One
Designer: L. Harradine
Height: 7 ½", 19.1 cm
Colour: Red and green
Issued: 1947-1951
  U.S.: $ 900.00
  Can.: $1,100.00
  U.K.:   £ 500.00

HN 1996
Prue
Designer: L. Harradine
Height: 6 ¾", 17.2 cm
Colour: Red, white and black
Issued: 1947-1955
  U.S.: $600.00
  Can.: $725.00
  U.K.:   £325.00

HN 1997
Belle o' the Ball
Designer: R. Asplin
Height: 6", 15.2 cm
Colour: Red and white
Issued: 1947-1979
  U.S.: $525.00
  Can.: $625.00
  U.K.:   £280.00

HN 1998
Collinette
Designer: L. Harradine
Height: 7 ¼", 18.4 cm
Colour: Turquoise and cream
Issued: 1947-1949
Varieties: HN 1999
  U.S.: $ 850.00
  Can.: $1,000.00
  U.K.:   £ 460.00

HN 1999
Collinette
Designer: L. Harradine
Height: 7 ¼", 18.4 cm
Colour: Red and cream
Issued: 1947-1949
Varieties: HN 1998
  U.S.: $ 850.00
  Can.: $1,000.00
  U.K.:   £ 460.00

HN 2000
Jacqueline
Style One
Designer: L. Harradine
Height: 7 ¼", 18.4 cm
Colour: Lavender
Issued: 1947-1951
Varieties: HN 2001

U.S.:	**$775.00**
Can.:	**$950.00**
U.K.:	**£425.00**

HN 2001
Jacqueline
Style One
Designer: L. Harradine
Height: 7 ¼", 18.4 cm
Colour: Pink
Issued: 1947-1951
Varieties: HN 2000

U.S.:	**$775.00**
Can.:	**$950.00**
U.K.:	**£425.00**

HN 2002
Bess
Style One
Designer: L. Harradine
Height: 7 ¼", 18.4 cm
Colour: Red cloak, flowered
              cream dress
Issued: 1947-1969
Varieties: HN 2003

U.S.:	**$475.00**
Can.:	**$575.00**
U.K.:	**£260.00**

HN 2003
Bess
Style One
Designer: L. Harradine
Height: 7 ¼", 18.4 cm
Colour: Pink dress, purple
              cloak
Issued: 1947-1950
Varieties: HN 2002

U.S.:	**$ 975.00**
Can.:	**$1,150.00**
U.K.:	**£ 525.00**

HN 2004
A'Courting
Designer: L. Harradine
Height: 7 ¼", 18.4 cm
Colour: Red, black and grey
Issued: 1947-1953

U.S.:	**$750.00**
Can.:	**$900.00**
U.K.:	**£400.00**

HN 2005
Henrietta Maria
Style One
Designer: M. Davies
Height: 9 ½", 24.1 cm
Colour: Yellow and red
Issued: 1948-1953
Series: Period Figures in
              English History

U.S.:	**$ 950.00**
Can.:	**$1,150.00**
U.K.:	**£ 525.00**

HN 2006
The Lady Anne Nevill
Designer: M. Davies
Height: 9 ¾", 24.7 cm
Colour: Purple and white
Issued: 1948-1953
Series: Period Figures in
              English History

U.S.:	**$1,200.00**
Can.:	**$1,450.00**
U.K.:	**£ 650.00**

HN 2007
Mrs. Fitzherbert
Designer: M. Davies
Height: 9 ¼", 23.5 cm
Colour: Yellow and cream
Issued: 1948-1953
Series: Period Figures in
              English History

U.S.:	**$ 950.00**
Can.:	**$1,150.00**
U.K.:	**£ 525.00**

HN 2008
Philippa of Hainault
Style One
Designer: M. Davies
Height: 9 ¾", 24.7 cm
Colour: Blue, brown and red
Issued: 1948-1953
Series: Period Figures in
           English History

U.S.:	$ 950.00
Can.:	$1,150.00
U.K.:	£ 525.00

HN 2009
Eleanor of Provence
Designer: M. Davies
Height: 9 ½", 24.1 cm
Colour: Purple and red
Issued: 1948-1953
Series: Period Figures in
           English History

U.S.:	$ 950.00
Can.:	$1,150.00
U.K.:	£ 525.00

HN 2010
The Young Miss Nightingale
Designer: M. Davies
Height: 9 ¼", 23.5 cm
Colour: Red and green
Issued: 1948-1953
Series: Period Figures in
           English History

U.S.:	$1,200.00
Can.:	$1,400.00
U.K.:	£ 650.00

HN 2011
Matilda
Designer: M. Davies
Height: 9 ¼", 23.5 cm
Colour: Red and purple
Issued: 1948-1953
Series: Period Figures in
           English History

U.S.:	$ 900.00
Can.:	$1,100.00
U.K.:	£ 500.00

HN 2012
Margaret of Anjou
Style One
Designer: M. Davies
Height: 9 ¼", 23.5 cm
Colour: Green and yellow
Issued: 1948-1953
Series: Period Figures in
           English History

U.S.:	$1,000.00
Can.:	$1,200.00
U.K.:	£ 575.00

HN 2013
Angelina
Designer: L. Harradine
Height: 6 ¾", 17.1 cm
Colour: Red
Issued: 1948-1951

U.S.:	$1,900.00
Can.:	$2,250.00
U.K.:	£1,050.00

HN 2014
Jane
Style One
Designer: L. Harradine
Height: 6 ¼", 15.9 cm
Colour: Red and pink
Issued: 1948-1951

U.S.:	$2,250.00
Can.:	$2,750.00
U.K.:	£1,200.00

HN 2015
Sir Walter Raleigh
Designer: L. Harradine
Height: 11 ½", 29.2 cm
Colour: Orange and purple
Issued: 1948-1955
Varieties: HN 1742, 1751

U.S.:	$1,100.00
Can.:	$1,300.00
U.K.:	£ 600.00

Earthenware

HN 2016
A Jester
Style One
Designer: C. J. Noke
Height: 10", 25.4 cm
Colour: Brown and mauve
Issued: 1949-1997
Varieties: HN 45, 71, 71A, 320,
            367, 412, 426, 446,
            552, 616, 627, 1295,
            1702, 3922

U.S.: $350.00
Can.: $450.00
U.K.:   £200.00

HN 2017
Silks and Ribbons
Designer: L. Harradine
Height: 6", 15.2 cm
Colour: Green, red and white
Issued: 1949-2001

U.S.: $325.00
Can.: $400.00
U.K.:   £175.00

HN 2018
The Parson's Daughter
Designer: H. Tittensor
Height: 9 ¾", 24.7 cm
Colour: Multicoloured
Issued: 1949-1953
Varieties: HN 337, 338, 441,
            564, 790, 1242, 1356

U.S.: $1,100.00
Can.: $1,300.00
U.K.:   £ 600.00

HN 2019
Minuet
Designer: M. Davies
Height: 7 ¼", 18.4 cm
Colour: Patterned white dress
Issued: 1949-1971
Varieties: HN 2066

U.S.: $375.00
Can.: $450.00
U.K.:   £200.00

HN 2020
Deidre
Designer: L. Harradine
Height: 7", 17.8 cm
Colour: Blue and pink
Issued: 1949-1955

U.S.: $675.00
Can.: $800.00
U.K.:   £375.00

HN 2021
Blithe Morning
Designer: L. Harradine
Height: 7 ¼", 18.4 cm
Colour: Mauve and pink
Issued: 1949-1971
Varieties: HN 2065

U.S.: $325.00
Can.: $400.00
U.K.:   £175.00

HN 2022
Janice
Style One
Designer: M. Davies
Height: 7 ¼", 18.4 cm
Colour: Green and cream
Issued: 1949-1955
Varieties: HN 2165

U.S.: $675.00
Can.: $800.00
U.K.:   £375.00

HN 2023
Joan
Style One
Designer: L. Harradine
Height: 5 ¾", 14.6 cm
Colour: Blue
Issued: 1949-1959
Varieties: HN 1422 (minor
            glaze difference)

U.S.: $375.00
Can.: $450.00
U.K.:   £200.00

HN 2024
Darby
Designer: L. Harradine
Height: 5 ¾", 14.6 cm
Colour: Pink and blue
Issued: 1949-1959
Varieties: HN 1427 (minor
           glaze difference)

U.S.:	$375.00
Can.:	$450.00
U.K.:	£200.00

HN 2025
Gossips
Designer: L. Harradine
Height: 5 ½", 14.0 cm
Colour: Red and cream
Issued: 1949-1967
Varieties: HN 1426, 1429

U.S.:	$775.00
Can.:	$925.00
U.K.:	£425.00

HN 2026
Suzette
Designer: L. Harradine
Height: 7 ¼", 18.4 cm
Colour: Flowered pink dress
Issued: 1949-1959
Varieties: HN 1487, 1577,
           1585, 1696

U.S.:	$575.00
Can.:	$700.00
U.K.:	£310.00

HN 2027
June
Style One
Designer: L. Harradine
Height: 7 ¼", 18.4 cm
Colour: Yellow and pink
Issued: 1949-1952
Varieties: HN 1690, 1691, 1947

U.S.:	$ 850.00
Can.:	$1,000.00
U.K.:	£ 475.00

HN 2028
Kate Hardcastle
Designer: L. Harradine
Height: 7 ¾", 19.7 cm
Colour: Green and red
Issued: 1949-1952
Varieties: HN 1718, 1719,
           1734, 1861, 1919

U.S.:	$ 850.00
Can.:	$1,000.00
U.K.:	£ 475.00

HN 2029
Windflower
Style One
Designer: L. Harradine
Height: 7 ¼", 18.4 cm
Colour: Pink
Issued: 1949-1952
Varieties: HN 1763, 1764

U.S.:	$ 875.00
Can.:	$1,100.00
U.K.:	£ 475.00

HN 2030
Memories
Designer: L. Harradine
Height: 6", 15.2 cm
Colour: Pink and green
Issued: 1949-1959
Varieties: HN 1855, 1856, 1857

U.S.:	$775.00
Can.:	$925.00
U.K.:	£425.00

HN 2031
Granny's Heritage
Designer: L. Harradine
Height: 6 ¾", 17.2 cm
Colour: Lavender and green
Issued: 1949-1969
Varieties: HN 1873, 1874

U.S.:	$ 925.00
Can.:	$1,100.00
U.K.:	£ 500.00

HN 2032
Jean
Style One
Designer: L. Harradine
Height: 7 ½", 19.1 cm
Colour: Green and red
Issued: 1949-1959
Varieties: HN 1877, 1878

U.S.:	$475.00
Can.:	$575.00
U.K.:	£250.00

HN 2033
Midsummer Noon
Designer: L. Harradine
Height: 4 ¾", 12.0 cm
Colour: Pink
Issued: 1949-1955
Varieties: HN 1899, 1900

U.S.:	$1,000.00
Can.:	$1,250.00
U.K.:	£ 550.00

HN 2034
Madonna of the Square
Designer: P. Stabler
Height: 7", 17.8 cm
Colour: Pale green
Issued: 1949-1951
Varieties: HN 10, 10A, 11, 14,
             27, 326, 573, 576,
             594, 613, 764, 1968,
             1969

U.S.:	$1,000.00
Can.:	$1,250.00
U.K.:	£ 550.00

HN 2035
Pearly Boy
Style Two
Designer: L. Harradine
Height: 5 ¼", 13.3 cm
Colour: Reddish-brown
Issued: 1949-1959

U.S.:	$300.00
Can.:	$350.00
U.K.:	£165.00

HN 2036
Pearly Girl
Style Two
Designer: L. Harradine
Height: 5 ¼", 13.3 cm
Colour: Reddish-brown
Issued: 1949-1959

U.S.:	$300.00
Can.:	$350.00
U.K.:	£165.00

HN 2037
Goody Two Shoes
Style One
Designer: L. Harradine
Height: 5", 12.7 cm
Colour: Red and pink
Issued: 1949-1989
Varieties: HN 1889, 1905

U.S.:	$150.00
Can.:	$180.00
U.K.:	£ 90.00

HN 2038
Peggy
Designer: L. Harradine
Height: 5", 12.7 cm
Colour: Red and white
Issued: 1949-1979
Varieties: HN 1941 (minor
             glaze difference)

U.S.:	$150.00
Can.:	$180.00
U.K.:	£ 80.00

HN 2039
Easter Day
Designer: L. Harradine
Height: 7 ¼", 18.4 cm
Colour: Multicoloured
Issued: 1949-1969
Varieties: HN 1976

U.S.:	$600.00
Can.:	$725.00
U.K.:	£325.00

HN 2040
Gollywog
Designer: L. Harradine
Height: 5 ¼", 13.3 cm
Colour: Blue dungarees
Issued: 1949-1959
Varieties: HN 1979

  U.S.: $600.00
  Can.: $725.00
  U.K.:   £325.00

HN 2041
The Broken Lance
Designer: M. Davies
Height: 8 ¾", 22.2 cm
Colour: Blue, red and yellow
Issued: 1949-1975

  U.S.: $800.00
  Can.: $975.00
  U.K.:   £430.00

HN 2042
Owd Willum
Designer: L. Harradine
Height: 6 ¾", 17.2 cm
Colour: Green and brown
Issued: 1949-1973

  U.S.: $375.00
  Can.: $475.00
  U.K.:   £225.00

'Harradine' incised on figurine

HN 2043
The Poacher
Designer: L. Harradine
Height: 6", 15.2 cm
Colour: Black and brown
Issued: 1949-1959

  U.S.: $450.00
  Can.: $550.00
  U.K.:   £250.00

HN 2044
Mary, Mary
Designer: L. Harradine
Height: 5", 12.7 cm
Colour: Pink
Issued: 1949-1973
Series: Nursery Rhymes
             (Series One)

  U.S.: $325.00
  Can.: $400.00
  U.K.:   £175.00

HN 2045
She Loves Me Not
Designer: L. Harradine
Height: 5 ½", 14.0 cm
Colour: Blue
Issued: 1949-1962
Series: Nursery Rhymes
             (Series One)

  U.S.: $325.00
  Can.: $400.00
  U.K.:   £175.00

HN 2046
He Loves Me
Designer: L. Harradine
Height: 5 ½", 14.0 cm
Colour: Flowered pink dress
Issued: 1949-1962
Series: Nursery Rhymes
             (Series One)

  U.S.: $325.00
  Can.: $400.00
  U.K.:   £175.00

HN 2047
Once Upon a Time
Designer: L. Harradine
Height: 4 ¼", 10.8 cm
Colour: Pink dress with
             white spots
Issued: 1949-1955
Series: Nursery Rhymes
             (Series One)

  U.S.: $650.00
  Can.: $775.00
  U.K.:   £350.00

HN 2048
Mary Had a Little Lamb
Designer: M. Davies
Height: 3 ½", 8.9 cm
Colour: Lavender
Issued: 1949-1988
Series: Nursery Rhymes
(Series One)

U.S.: $200.00
Can.: $250.00
U.K.: £110.00

HN 2049
Curly Locks
Designer: M. Davies
Height: 4 ½", 11.4 cm
Colour: Pink flowered dress
Issued: 1949-1953
Series: Nursery Rhymes
(Series One)

U.S.: $650.00
Can.: $775.00
U.K.: £350.00

HN 2050
Wee Willie Winkie
Style One
Designer: M. Davies
Height: 5 ¼", 13.3 cm
Colour: Blue
Issued: 1949-1953
Series: Nursery Rhymes
(Series One)

U.S.: $475.00
Can.: $575.00
U.K.: £250.00

HN 2051
St. George
Style Two
Designer: M. Davies
Height: 7 ½", 19.1 cm
Colour: Green and white
Issued: 1950-1985

U.S.: $650.00
Can.: $775.00
U.K.: £350.00

HN 2052
Grandma
Designer: L. Harradine
Height: 6 ¾", 17.2 cm
Colour: Blue shawl; red
and cream dress
Issued: 1950-1959
Varieties: HN 2052A

U.S.: $500.00
Can.: $600.00
U.K.: £275.00

Earthenware

HN 2052A
Grandma
Designer: L. Harradine
Height: 6 ¾", 17.2 cm
Colour: Brown shawl; red
and cream dress
Issued: Unknown
Varieties: HN 2052

U.S.: $500.00
Can.: $600.00
U.K.: £275.00

Earthenware

HN 2053
The Gaffer
Designer: L. Harradine
Height: 7 ¾", 19.7 cm
Colour: Green and brown
Issued: 1950-1959

U.S.: $500.00
Can.: $600.00
U.K.: £275.00

Earthenware

HN 2054
Falstaff
Style Two
Designer: C. J. Noke
Height: 7", 17.8 cm
Colour: Brown
Issued: 1950-1992
Varieties: HN 618

U.S.: $200.00
Can.: $250.00
U.K.: £110.00

Earthenware and China

HN 2055
The Leisure Hour
Designer: M. Davies
Height: 7", 17.8 cm
Colour: Green, yellow
            and brown
Issued: 1950-1965
  U.S.: $600.00
  Can.: $725.00
  U.K.:   £325.00

HN 2056
Susan
Style One
Designer: L. Harradine
Height: 7", 17.8 cm
Colour: Lavender dress
            with flowered apron
Issued: 1950-1959
  U.S.: $575.00
  Can.: $700.00
  U.K.:   £325.00

HN 2057
The Jersey Milkmaid
Designer: L. Harradine
Height: 6 ½", 16.5 cm
Colour: Blue, white and red
Issued: 1950-1959
Varieties: Also called 'The
            Milkmaid' (Style Two)
            HN 2057A
  U.S.: $300.00
  Can.: $375.00
  U.K.:   £165.00

HN 2057A
The Milkmaid
Style Two
Designer: L. Harradine
Height: 6 ½", 16.5 cm
Colour: Green, white
            and brown
Issued: 1975-1981
Varieties: Also called 'The
            Jersey Milkmaid'
            HN 2057
  U.S.: $200.00
  Can.: $250.00
  U.K.:   £110.00

HN 2058
Hermione
Designer: M. Davies
Height: 7 ¾", 19.7 cm
Colour: Cream and lavender
Issued: 1950-1952
  U.S.: $2,500.00
  Can.: $3,000.00
  U.K.:   £1,250.00

HN 2059
The Bedtime Story
Designer: L. Harradine
Height: 4 ¾", 12.0 cm
Colour: Pink, white, yellow
            and blue
Issued: 1950-1996
  U.S.: $450.00
  Can.: $550.00
  U.K.:   £250.00

HN 2060
Jack
Designer: L. Harradine
Height: 5 ½", 14.0 cm
Colour: Green, white and black
Issued: 1950-1971
Series: Nursery Rhymes
            (Series One)
  U.S.: $275.00
  Can.: $350.00
  U.K.:   £150.00

HN 2061
Jill
Designer: L. Harradine
Height: 5 ½", 14.0 cm
Colour: Pink and white
Issued: 1950-1971
Series: Nursery Rhymes
            (Series One)
  U.S.: $275.00
  Can.: $350.00
  U.K.:   £150.00

HN 2062
Little Boy Blue
Style One
Designer: L. Harradine
Height: 5 ½", 14.0 cm
Colour: Blue
Issued: 1950-1973
Series: Nursery Rhymes
(Series One)

U.S.: $250.00
Can.: $300.00
U.K.: £140.00

HN 2063
Little Jack Horner
Style One
Designer: L. Harradine
Height: 4 ½", 11.4 cm
Colour: Red and white
Issued: 1950-1953
Series: Nursery Rhymes
(Series One)

U.S.: $800.00
Can.: $975.00
U.K.: £450.00

HN 2064
My Pretty Maid
Designer: L. Harradine
Height: 5 ½", 14.0 cm
Colour: Turquoise
Issued: 1950-1954
Series: Nursery Rhymes
(Series One)

U.S.: $700.00
Can.: $850.00
U.K.: £400.00

HN 2065
Blithe Morning
Designer: L. Harradine
Height: 7 ¼", 18.4 cm
Colour: Red
Issued: 1950-1973
Varieties: HN 2021

U.S.: $350.00
Can.: $425.00
U.K.: £190.00

HN 2066
Minuet
Designer: M. Davies
Height: 7 ¼", 18.4 cm
Colour: Red
Issued: 1950-1955
Varieties: HN 2019

U.S.: $1,850.00
Can.: $2,250.00
U.K.: £1,000.00

HN 2067
St. George
Style One
Designer: S. Thorogood
Height: 15 ¾", 40.0 cm
Colour: Multicoloured
Issued: 1950-1979
Varieties: HN 385, 386, 1800;
fair and dark hair

U.S.: $3,500.00
Can.: $4,250.00
U.K.: £1,950.00

HN 2068
Calumet
Designer: C. J. Noke
Height: 6 ¼", 15.9 cm
Colour: Green and brown
Issued: 1950-1953
Varieties: HN 1428, 1689

U.S.: $1,000.00
Can.: $1,200.00
U.K.: £ 550.00

Earthenware

HN 2069
Farmer's Wife
Style One
Designer: L. Harradine
Height: 9", 22.9 cm
Colour: Red, green and brown
Issued: 1951-1955

U.S.: $800.00
Can.: $975.00
U.K.: £450.00

Earthenware

HN 2070
Bridget
Designer: L. Harradine
Height: 7 ¾", 19.7 cm
Colour: Green, brown
           and lavender
Issued: 1951-1973
  U.S.: $400.00
  Can.: $475.00
  U.K.:   £225.00

Earthenware

HN 2071
Bernice
Designer: M. Davies
Height: 7 ¾", 19.7 cm
Colour: Pink and red
Issued: 1951-1953
  U.S.: $2,000.00
  Can.: $2,500.00
  U.K.:   £1,100.00

HN 2072
The Rocking Horse
Designer: L. Harradine
Height: 7", 17.8 cm
Colour: Red, white, blue
           and yellow
Issued: 1951-1953
  U.S.: $4,750.00
  Can.: $5,750.00
  U.K.:   £2,600.00

HN 2073
Vivienne
Designer: L. Harradine
Height: 7 ¾", 19.7 cm
Colour: Red
Issued: 1951-1967
  U.S.: $450.00
  Can.: $550.00
  U.K.:   £240.00

HN 2074
Marianne
Style One
Designer: L. Harradine
Height: 7 ¼", 18.4 cm
Colour: Red
Issued: 1951-1953
  U.S.: $1,800.00
  Can.: $2,200.00
  U.K.:   £1,000.00

HN 2075
French Peasant
Designer: L. Harradine
Height: 9 ¼", 23.5 cm
Colour: Brown and green
Issued: 1951-1955
  U.S.: $750.00
  Can.: $900.00
  U.K.:   £400.00

Earthenware

HN 2076
Promenade
Style One
Designer: M. Davies
Height: 8", 20.3 cm
Colour: Blue and orange
Issued: 1951-1953
  U.S.: $3,500.00
  Can.: $4,250.00
  U.K.:   £2,000.00

HN 2077
Rowena
Designer: L. Harradine
Height: 7 ¼", 18.4 cm
Colour: Red and green
Issued: 1951-1955
  U.S.: $1,000.00
  Can.: $1,200.00
  U.K.:   £ 550.00

HN 2078
Elfreda
Designer: L. Harradine
Height: 7 ¼", 18.4 cm
Colour: Red and purple
Issued: 1951-1955
U.S.:	**$1,500.00**
Can.:	**$1,800.00**
U.K.:	**£ 800.00**

HN 2079
Damaris
Designer: M. Davies
Height: 7 ¼", 18.4 cm
Colour: Green, white and purple
Issued: 1951-1952
U.S.:	**$2,750.00**
Can.:	**$3,300.00**
U.K.:	**£1,500.00**

HN 2080
Jack Point
Designer: C. J. Noke
Height: 16", 40.6 cm
Colour: Purple, green and lavender
Issued: 1952 to the present
Varieties: HN 85, 91, 99, 3920, 3925
Series: Prestige
U.S.:	**$3,750.00**
Can.:	**$4,300.00**
U.K.:	**£2,600.00**

HN 2081
Princess Badoura
Style One
Designer: H. Tittensor, H. E. Stanton and F. Van Allen Phillips
Height: 20", 50.8 cm
Colour: Multicoloured
Issued: 1952 to the present
Varieties: HN 3921
Series: Prestige
U.S.:	**$36,400.00**
Can.:	**$43,000.00**
U.K.:	**£17,000.00**

HN 2082
The Moor
Designer: C. J. Noke
Height: 16 ¼", 41.2 cm
Colour: Red and black
Issued: 1952 to the present
Varieties: HN 1308, 1366, 1425, 1657, 3642, 3926; also called 'An Arab' HN 33, 343, 378
Series: Prestige
U.S.:	**N/I**
Can.:	**$3,700.00**
U.K.:	**£2,100.00**

HN 2084
King Charles
Designer: C. J. Noke and H. Tittensor
Height: 16", 40.6 cm
Colour: Black with yellow base
Issued: 1952-1992
Varieties: HN 404, 3459
U.S.:	**$2,000.00**
Can.:	**$2,500.00**
U.K.:	**£1,100.00**

HN 2085
Spring
Style Four
Designer: M. Davies
Height: 7 ¾", 19.6 cm
Colour: Lavender and cream
Issued: 1952-1959
Series: The Seasons (Series Two)
U.S.:	**$575.00**
Can.:	**$700.00**
U.K.:	**£310.00**

HN 2086
Summer
Style Two
Designer: M. Davies
Height: 7 ¼", 18.4 cm
Colour: Red flowered dress
Issued: 1952-1959
Series: The Seasons (Series Two)
U.S.:	**$575.00**
Can.:	**$700.00**
U.K.:	**£310.00**

HN 2083 not issued.

HN 2087
Autumn
Style Two
Designer: M. Davies
Height: 7 ¼", 18.4 cm
Colour: Red and lavender
Issued: 1952-1959
Series: The Seasons
           (Series Two)

U.S.:	**$575.00**
Can.:	**$700.00**
U.K.:	**£310.00**

HN 2088
Winter
Style Two
Designer: M. Davies
Height: 6 ¼", 15.9 cm
Colour: Lavender, green
           and red
Issued: 1952-1959
Series: The Seasons
           (Series Two)

U.S.:	**$575.00**
Can.:	**$700.00**
U.K.:	**£310.00**

HN 2089
Judith
Style One
Designer: L. Harradine
Height: 7", 17.8 cm
Colour: Red and blue
Issued: 1952-1959

U.S.:	**$500.00**
Can.:	**$600.00**
U.K.:	**£275.00**

HN 2090
Midinette
Style Two
Designer: L. Harradine
Height: 7 ¼", 18.4 cm
Colour: Blue
Issued: 1952-1965

U.S.:	**$450.00**
Can.:	**$550.00**
U.K.:	**£250.00**

HN 2091
Rosemary
Style One
Designer: L. Harradine
Height: 7", 17.8 cm
Colour: Red and blue
Issued: 1952-1959

U.S.:	**$750.00**
Can.:	**$900.00**
U.K.:	**£400.00**

HN 2092
Sweet Maid
Style Two
Designer: L. Harradine
Height: 7", 17.8 cm
Colour: Lavender
Issued: 1952-1955

U.S.:	**$600.00**
Can.:	**$725.00**
U.K.:	**£325.00**

HN 2093
Georgiana
Designer: M. Davies
Height: 8 ¼", 21.0 cm
Colour: Orange and blue
Issued: 1952-1955

U.S.:	**$2,500.00**
Can.:	**$3,000.00**
U.K.:	**£1,350.00**

HN 2094
Uncle Ned
Designer: H. Fenton
Height: 6 ¾", 17.2 cm
Colour: Brown
Issued: 1952-1965

U.S.:	**$500.00**
Can.:	**$600.00**
U.K.:	**£275.00**

Earthenware

HN 2095
Ibrahim
Designer: C. J. Noke
Height: 7 ¾", 19.7 cm
Colour: Brown and yellow
Issued: 1952-1955
Varieties: Also called 'The
             Emir' HN 1604, 1605

U.S.:	**$675.00**
Can.:	**$800.00**
U.K.:	**£375.00**

Earthenware

HN 2096
Fat Boy
Style Three
Designer: L. Harradine
Height: 7 ¼", 18.4 cm
Colour: Blue and cream
Issued: 1952-1967
Series: Dickens (Series Three)

U.S.:	**$650.00**
Can.:	**$775.00**
U.K.:	**£350.00**

Earthenware

HN 2097
Mr. Micawber
Style Three
Designer: L. Harradine
Height: 7 ½", 19.1 cm
Colour: Black and brown
Issued: 1952-1967
Series: Dickens (Series Three)

U.S.:	**$650.00**
Can.:	**$775.00**
U.K.:	**£350.00**

Earthenware

HN 2098
Pecksniff
Style Three
Designer: L. Harradine
Height: 7 ¼", 18.4 cm
Colour: Black and brown
Issued: 1952-1967
Series: Dickens (Series Three)

U.S.:	**$650.00**
Can.:	**$775.00**
U.K.:	**£350.00**

Earthenware

HN 2099
Mr. Pickwick
Style Three
Designer: L. Harradine
Height: 7 ½", 19.1 cm
Colour: Blue and brown
Issued: 1952-1967
Series: Dickens (Series Three)

U.S.:	**$650.00**
Can.:	**$775.00**
U.K.:	**£350.00**

Earthenware

HN 2100
Sairey Gamp
Style Three
Designer: L. Harradine
Height: 7 ¼", 18.4 cm
Colour: Green
Issued: 1952-1967
Series: Dickens (Series Three)

U.S.:	**$750.00**
Can.:	**$900.00**
U.K.:	**£400.00**

Earthenware

HN 2101
Uriah Heep
Style Three
Designer: L. Harradine
Height: 7 ½", 19.1 cm
Colour: Black
Issued: 1952-1967
Series: Dickens (Series Three)

U.S.:	**$650.00**
Can.:	**$775.00**
U.K.:	**£350.00**

Earthenware

HN 2102
Pied Piper
Style One
Designer: L. Harradine
Height: 8 ¾", 22.2 cm
Colour: Black, red and yellow
Issued: 1953-1976
Varieties: HN 1215

U.S.:	**$400.00**
Can.:	**$500.00**
U.K.:	**£225.00**

HN 2103
Mask Seller
Designer: L. Harradine
Height: 8 ½", 21.6 cm
Colour: Green and yellow
Issued: 1953-1995
Varieties: HN 1361

U.S.:	$400.00
Can.:	$500.00
U.K.:	£225.00

Earthenware

HN 2104
Abdullah
Designer: L. Harradine
Height: 6", 15.2 cm
Colour: Multicoloured
Issued: 1953-1962
Varieties: HN 1410

U.S.:	$600.00
Can.:	$750.00
U.K.:	£325.00

HN 2105
Bluebeard
Style Two
Designer: L. Harradine
Height: 11", 27.9 cm
Colour: Purple, green
  and brown
Issued: 1953-1992
Varieties: HN 1528

U.S.:	$600.00
Can.:	$725.00
U.K.:	£325.00

HN 2106
Linda
Style One
Designer: L. Harradine
Height: 4 ¾", 12.0 cm
Colour: Red
Issued: 1953-1976

U.S.:	$275.00
Can.:	$325.00
U.K.:	£150.00

HN 2107
Valerie
Style One
Designer: M. Davies
Height: 4 ¾", 12.0 cm
Colour: Red, pink and white
Issued: 1953-1995
Varieties: HN 3620

U.S.:	$150.00
Can.:	$185.00
U.K.:	£ 85.00

HN 2108
Baby Bunting
Designer: M. Davies
Height: 5 ¼", 13.3 cm
Colour: Brown and cream
Issued: 1953-1959

U.S.:	$550.00
Can.:	$650.00
U.K.:	£295.00

HN 2109
Wendy
Designer: L. Harradine
Height: 5", 12.7 cm
Colour: Blue
Issued: 1953-1995

U.S.:	$125.00
Can.:	$150.00
U.K.:	£ 65.00

HN 2110
Christmas Time
Designer: M. Davies
Height: 6 ½", 16.5 cm
Colour: Red with white frills
Issued: 1953-1967

U.S.:	$550.00
Can.:	$650.00
U.K.:	£300.00

HN 2111
Betsy
Designer: L. Harradine
Height: 7", 17.8 cm
Colour: Lavender dress, flowered apron
Issued: 1953-1959
  U.S.: $550.00
  Can.: $650.00
  U.K.: £300.00

HN 2112
Carolyn
Style One
Designer: L. Harradine
Height: 7", 17.8 cm
Colour: White and green flowered dress
Issued: 1953-1965
  U.S.: $550.00
  Can.: $650.00
  U.K.: £300.00

HN 2113
Maytime
Designer: L. Harradine
Height: 7", 17.8 cm
Colour: Pink dress with blue scarf
Issued: 1953-1967
  U.S.: $425.00
  Can.: $525.00
  U.K.: £230.00

HN 2114
Sleepyhead
Style One
Designer: M. Davies
Height: 5", 12.7 cm
Colour: Orange, blue and white
Issued: 1953-1955
  U.S.: $3,750.00
  Can.: $4,500.00
  U.K.: £2,100.00

HN 2115
Coppelia
Designer: M. Davies
Height: 7 ¼", 18.4 cm
Colour: Blue, red and white
Issued: 1953-1959
  U.S.: $1,000.00
  Can.: $1,200.00
  U.K.: £ 550.00

HN 2116
Ballerina
Style One
Designer: M. Davies
Height: 7 ¼", 18.4 cm
Colour: Lavender
Issued: 1953-1973
  U.S.: $425.00
  Can.: $525.00
  U.K.: £230.00

HN 2117
The Skater
Style One
Designer: M. Davies
Height: 7 ¼", 18.4 cm
Colour: Red, white and brown
Issued: 1953-1971
  U.S.: $575.00
  Can.: $700.00
  U.K.: £325.00

HN 2118
Good King Wenceslas
Style One
Designer: M. Davies
Height: 8 ½", 21.6 cm
Colour: Brown and purple
Issued: 1953-1976
  U.S.: $450.00
  Can.: $550.00
  U.K.: £250.00

Earthenware

HN 2119
Town Crier
Style One
Designer: M. Davies
Height: 8 ½", 21.6 cm
Colour: Purple, green
             and yellow
Issued: 1953-1976

U.S.:	**$400.00**
Can.:	**$500.00**
U.K.:	**£225.00**

Earthenware

HN 2120
Dinky Doo
Designer: L. Harradine
Height: 4 ¾", 12.0 cm
Colour: Red
Issued: 1983-1996
Varieties: HN 1678, 3618

U.S.:	**$150.00**
Can.:	**$175.00**
U.K.:	**£ 80.00**

HN 2121
Babie
Designer: L. Harradine
Height: 4 ¾", 12.0 cm
Colour: Pink
Issued: 1983-1992
Varieties: HN 1679, 1842

U.S.:	**$150.00**
Can.:	**$175.00**
U.K.:	**£ 80.00**

HN 2122
Yeoman of the Guard
Designer: L. Harradine
Height: 5 ¾", 14.6 cm
Colour: Red, gold and brown
Issued: 1954-1959
Varieties: HN 688

U.S.:	**$1,100.00**
Can.:	**$1,325.00**
U.K.:	**£ 600.00**

HN 2123
Rose
Style One
Designer: L. Harradine
Height: 4 ½", 11.4 cm
Colour: Lavender
Issued: 1983-1995
Varieties: HN 1368, 1387, 1416,
             1506, 1654

U.S.:	**$150.00**
Can.:	**$175.00**
U.K.:	**£ 80.00**

HN 2124 not issued.

HN 2125
This Little Pig
Designer: L. Harradine
Height: 4", 10.1 cm
Colour: White
Issued: 1984-1995
Varieties: HN 1793, 1794

U.S.:	**$125.00**
Can.:	**$150.00**
U.K.:	**£ 70.00**

HN 2126
Top o' The Hill
Style Two
Designer: L. Harradine
Remodeller: P. Gee
Height: 4", 10.1 cm
Colour: Green and mauve
Issued: 1988-1988
Varieties: HN 3499
Series: 1. Miniatures
              2. R.D.I.C.C.

U.S.:	**$175.00**
Can.:	**$210.00**
U.K.:	**£100.00**

HN 2127
Top o' The Hill
Style One
Designer: L. Harradine
Height: 7", 17.8 cm
Colour: Gold
Issued: 1988-1988
Varieties: HN 1833, 1834,
             1849, 3735A

U.S.:	**$500.00**
Can.:	**$600.00**
U.K.:	**£275.00**

Commissioned for Australian
Bicentenary.

HN 2128
River Boy
Designer: M. Davies
Height: 4", 10.1 cm
Colour: Blue and green
Issued: 1962-1975

  U.S.: $250.00
  Can.: $300.00
  U.K.:   £135.00

HN 2129
The Old Balloon Seller
Style Two
Designer: L. Harradine
Remodeller: W. K. Harper
Height: 3 ½", 8.9 cm
Colour: Green and white
Issued: 1989-1991
Series: Miniatures

  U.S.: $275.00
  Can.: $325.00
  U.K.:   £150.00

HN 2130
The Balloon Seller
Style Two
Designer: L. Harradine
Remodeller: R. Tabbenor
Height: 3 ¾", 8.9 cm
Colour: Green and cream
Issued: 1989-1991
Series: Miniatures

  U.S.: $275.00
  Can.: $325.00
  U.K.:   £150.00

HN 2131
Autumn Breezes
Style One
Designer: L. Harradine
Height: 7 ½", 19.1 cm
Colour: Orange, yellow
            and black
Issued: 1990-1994
Varieties: HN 1911, 1913,
            1934, 2147, 3736

  U.S.: $400.00
  Can.: $475.00
  U.K.:   £220.00

HN 2132
The Suitor
Designer: M. Davies
Height: 7 ¼", 18.4 cm
Colour: Green, yellow and blue
Issued: 1962-1971

  U.S.: $600.00
  Can.: $725.00
  U.K.:   £325.00

HN 2133
Faraway
Designer: M. Davies
Height: 2 ½", 6.3 cm
Colour: Blue and white
Issued: 1958-1962
Series: Teenagers

  U.S.: $500.00
  Can.: $600.00
  U.K.:   £275.00

HN 2134
An Old King
Designer: C. J. Noke
Height: 10 ¾", 27.3 cm
Colour: Purple, red, green
            and brown
Issued: 1954-1992
Varieties: HN 358, 623, 1801

  U.S.: $700.00
  Can.: $850.00
  U.K.:   £380.00

HN 2135
Gay Morning
Designer: M. Davies
Height: 7", 17.8 cm
Colour: Pink
Issued: 1954-1967

  U.S.: $425.00
  Can.: $525.00
  U.K.:   £240.00

HN 2136
Delphine
Designer: M. Davies
Height: 7 ¼", 18.4 cm
Colour: Blue and lavender
Issued: 1954-1967

U.S.:	**$450.00**
Can.:	**$550.00**
U.K.:	**£250.00**

HN 2137
Lilac Time
Designer: M. Davies
Height: 7 ¼", 18.4 cm
Colour: Red
Issued: 1954-1969

U.S.:	**$450.00**
Can.:	**$550.00**
U.K.:	**£250.00**

HN 2138
La Sylphide
Designer: M. Davies
Height: 7", 17.8 cm
Colour: White and blue
Issued: 1954-1965

U.S.:	**$650.00**
Can.:	**$775.00**
U.K.:	**£350.00**

HN 2139
Giselle
Designer: M. Davies
Height: 6", 15.2 cm
Colour: Blue and white
Issued: 1954-1969

U.S.:	**$550.00**
Can.:	**$675.00**
U.K.:	**£300.00**

HN 2140
Giselle, The Forest Glade
Designer: M. Davies
Height: 7", 17.8 cm
Colour: White and blue
Issued: 1954-1965

U.S.:	**$550.00**
Can.:	**$675.00**
U.K.:	**£300.00**

HN 2141
Choir Boy
Designer: M. Davies
Height: 4 ¾", 12.0 cm
Colour: White and red
Issued: 1954-1975

U.S.:	**$175.00**
Can.:	**$200.00**
U.K.:	**£ 95.00**

HN 2142
Rag Doll
Designer: M. Davies
Height: 4 ¾", 12.0 cm
Colour: White, blue and red
Issued: 1954-1986

U.S.:	**$200.00**
Can.:	**$250.00**
U.K.:	**£110.00**

HN 2143
Friar Tuck
Designer: M. Davies
Height: 7 ½", 19.1 cm
Colour: Brown
Issued: 1954-1965

U.S.:	**$650.00**
Can.:	**$775.00**
U.K.:	**£350.00**

Earthenware

HN 2144
The Jovial Monk
Designer: M. Davies
Height: 7 ¾", 19.7 cm
Colour: Brown
Issued: 1954-1976

  U.S.: **$350.00**
  Can.: **$425.00**
  U.K.: **£200.00**

Earthenware

HN 2145
Wardrobe Mistress
Designer: M. Davies
Height: 5 ¾", 14.6 cm
Colour: Green, red, white
        and blue
Issued: 1954-1967

  U.S.: **$700.00**
  Can.: **$850.00**
  U.K.: **£400.00**

Earthenware

HN 2146
The Tinsmith
Designer: M. Nicoll
Height: 6 ½", 16.5 cm
Colour: Green and brown
Issued: 1962-1967

  U.S.: **$650.00**
  Can.: **$775.00**
  U.K.: **£350.00**

HN 2147
Autumn Breezes
Style One
Designer: L. Harradine
Height: 7 ½", 19.1 cm
Colour: Black and white
Issued: 1955-1971
Varieties: HN 1911, 1913,
          1934, 2131, 3736

  U.S.: **$450.00**
  Can.: **$550.00**
  U.K.: **£250.00**

HN 2148
The Bridesmaid
Style Three
Designer: M. Davies
Height: 5 ½", 14.0 cm
Colour: Yellow
Issued: 1955-1959

  U.S.: **$275.00**
  Can.: **$350.00**
  U.K.: **£150.00**

HN 2149
Love Letter
Style One
Designer: M. Davies
Height: 5 ½", 14.0 cm
Colour: Pink and blue
Issued: 1958-1976

  U.S.: **$600.00**
  Can.: **$725.00**
  U.K.: **£325.00**

HN 2150
Willy-Won't He
Designer: L. Harradine
Height: 5 ½", 14.0 cm
Colour: Red, green, blue
        and white
Issued: 1955-1959
Varieties: HN 1561, 1584 (minor
          glaze differences)

  U.S.: **$625.00**
  Can.: **$750.00**
  U.K.: **£335.00**

HN 2151
Mother's Help
Designer: M. Davies
Height: 5", 12.7 cm
Colour: Black and white
Issued: 1962-1969

  U.S.: **$325.00**
  Can.: **$400.00**
  U.K.: **£175.00**

HN 2152
Adrienne
Designer: M. Davies
Height: 7 ½", 19.1 cm
Colour: Purple
Issued: 1964-1976
Varieties: HN 2304; also called
            'Fiona' (Style Four)
            HN 3748; 'Joan'
            (Style Two) HN 3217

U.S.:	**$250.00**
Can.:	**$300.00**
U.K.:	**£135.00**

HN 2153
The One That Got Away
Designer: M. Davies
Height: 6 ¼", 15.9 cm
Colour: Brown
Issued: 1955-1959

U.S.:	**$550.00**
Can.:	**$675.00**
U.K.:	**£300.00**

HN 2154
A Child From Williamsburg
Designer: M. Davies
Height: 5 ½", 14.0 cm
Colour: Blue
Issued: 1964-1983
Series: Figures of Williamsburg

U.S.:	**$225.00**
Can.:	**$275.00**
U.K.:	**£125.00**

HN 2155 not issued.

HN 2156
The Polka
Designer: M. Davies
Height: 7 ½", 19.1 cm
Colour: Pink
Issued: 1955-1969

U.S.:	**$425.00**
Can.:	**$525.00**
U.K.:	**£230.00**

HN 2157
A Gypsy Dance
Style One
Designer: M. Davies
Height: 7", 17.8 cm
Colour: Lavender
Issued: 1955-1957

U.S.:	**$1,350.00**
Can.:	**$1,650.00**
U.K.:	**£ 750.00**

HN 2158
Alice
Style One
Designer: M. Davies
Height: 5", 12.7 cm
Colour: Blue
Issued: 1960-1981

U.S.:	**$250.00**
Can.:	**$300.00**
U.K.:	**£135.00**

HN 2159
Fortune Teller
Designer: L. Harradine
Height: 6 ½", 16.5 cm
Colour: Green and brown
Issued: 1955-1967

U.S.:	**$625.00**
Can.:	**$750.00**
U.K.:	**£350.00**

Earthenware

HN 2160
The Apple Maid
Designer: L. Harradine
Height: 6 ½", 16.5 cm
Colour: Blue, black
            and white
Issued: 1957-1962

U.S.:	**$525.00**
Can.:	**$650.00**
U.K.:	**£280.00**

HN 2161
The Hornpipe
Designer: M. Nicoll
Height: 9 ¼", 23.5 cm
Colour: Blue and white
Issued: 1955-1962

U.S.:	**$1,100.00**
Can.:	**$1,350.00**
U.K.:	**£ 600.00**

Earthenware

HN 2162
The Foaming Quart
Designer: M. Davies
Height: 6", 15.2 cm
Colour: Brown
Issued: 1955-1992

U.S.:	**$225.00**
Can.:	**$275.00**
U.K.:	**£125.00**

HN 2163
In The Stocks
Style Two
Designer: M. Nicoll
Height: 5 ¾", 14.6 cm
Colour: Red, brown and black
Issued: 1955-1959

U.S.:	**$1,200.00**
Can.:	**$1,500.00**
U.K.:	**£ 650.00**

HN 2164 not issued.

HN 2165
Janice
Style One
Designer: M. Davies
Height: 7 ¼", 18.4 cm
Colour: Black and pale blue
Issued: 1955-1965
Varieties: HN 2022

U.S.:	**$600.00**
Can.:	**$725.00**
U.K.:	**£325.00**

HN 2166
The Bride
Style Two
Designer: M. Davies
Height: 8", 20.3 cm
Colour: Pink
Issued: 1956-1976

U.S.:	**$275.00**
Can.:	**$350.00**
U.K.:	**£150.00**

HN 2167
Home Again
Designer: M. Davies
Height: 3 ¼", 8.3 cm
Colour: Red and white
Issued: 1956-1995

U.S.:	**$200.00**
Can.:	**$250.00**
U.K.:	**£110.00**

HN 2168
Esmeralda
Designer: M. Davies
Height: 5 ½", 14.0 cm
Colour: Yellow and red
Issued: 1956-1959

U.S.:	**$550.00**
Can.:	**$650.00**
U.K.:	**£300.00**

HN 2169
Dimity
Designer: L. Harradine
Height: 5 ¾", 14.6 cm
Colour: Green, lavender
            and cream
Issued: 1956-1959

U.S.:	**$525.00**
Can.:	**$625.00**
U.K.:	**£285.00**

HN 2170
Invitation
Designer: M. Davies
Height: 5 ½", 14.0 cm
Colour: Pink
Issued: 1956-1975

   U.S.:   **$225.00**
   Can.:   **$275.00**
   U.K.:   **£125.00**

HN 2171
The Fiddler
Designer: M. Nicoll
Height: 8 ¾", 22.2 cm
Colour: Green, cream and red
Issued: 1956-1962

   U.S.:   **$1,500.00**
   Can.:   **$1,800.00**
   U.K.:   **£ 825.00**

Earthenware

HN 2172
Jolly Sailor
Designer: M. Nicoll
Height: 6 ½", 16.5 cm
Colour: Black, brown,
             blue and white
Issued: 1956-1965

   U.S.:   **$1,200.00**
   Can.:   **$1,500.00**
   U.K.:   **£ 650.00**

Earthenware

HN 2173
The Organ Grinder
Designer: M. Nicoll
Height: 8 ¾", 22.2 cm
Colour: Green, cream
             and brown
Issued: 1956-1965

   U.S.:   **$1,500.00**
   Can.:   **$1,800.00**
   U.K.:   **£ 825.00**

Earthenware

HN 2174
The Tailor
Designer: M. Nicoll
Height: 5", 12.7 cm
Colour: Blue, cream
             and orange
Issued: 1956-1959

   U.S.:   **$1,200.00**
   Can.:   **$1,500.00**
   U.K.:   **£ 650.00**

Earthenware

HN 2175
The Beggar
Style Two
Designer: L. Harradine
Height: 6 ¾", 17.2 cm
Colour: Green
Issued: 1956-1962
Series: Beggar's Opera

   U.S.:   **$650.00**
   Can.:   **$800.00**
   U.K.:   **£350.00**

Earthenware

HN 2176
Autumn Breezes
Style Two
Designer: L. Harradine
Remodeller: D. Frith
Height: 3 ½", 8.9 cm
Colour: Red
Issued: 1991-1995
Varieties: HN 2180
Series: Miniatures

   U.S.:   **$225.00**
   Can.:   **$275.00**
   U.K.:   **£120.00**

HN 2177
My Teddy
Designer: M. Davies
Height: 3 ¼", 8.3 cm
Colour: Turquoise and brown
Issued: 1962-1967

   U.S.:   **$700.00**
   Can.:   **$850.00**
   U.K.:   **£380.00**

HN 2178
Enchantment
Designer: M. Davies
Height: 7 ½", 19.1 cm
Colour: Blue
Issued: 1957-1982

U.S.:	**$225.00**
Can.:	**$275.00**
U.K.:	**£125.00**

HN 2179
Noelle
Designer: M. Davies
Height: 6 ¾", 17.2 cm
Colour: Orange, white and black
Issued: 1957-1967

U.S.:	**$625.00**
Can.:	**$750.00**
U.K.:	**£350.00**

HN 2180
Autumn Breezes
Style Two
Designer: L. Harradine
Remodeller: D. Frith
Height: 3 ½", 8.9 cm
Colour: Red, lavender, gold trim
Issued: 1991-1995
Varieties: HN 2176
Series: 1. Miniatures
2. Signature

U.S.:	**$250.00**
Can.:	**$300.00**
U.K.:	**£135.00**

HN 2181
Summer's Day
Style One
Designer: M. Davies
Height: 5 ¾", 14.6 cm
Colour: White
Issued: 1957-1962

U.S.:	**$400.00**
Can.:	**$475.00**
U.K.:	**£225.00**

HN 2182 not issued.

HN 2183
Boy from Williamsburg
Designer: M. Davies
Height: 5 ½", 14.0 cm
Colour: Blue and pink
Issued: 1969-1983
Series: Figures of Williamsburg

U.S.:	**$250.00**
Can.:	**$300.00**
U.K.:	**£135.00**

HN 2184
Sunday Morning
Designer: M. Davies
Height: 7 ½", 19.1 cm
Colour: Red and brown
Issued: 1963-1969

U.S.:	**$500.00**
Can.:	**$600.00**
U.K.:	**£275.00**

HN 2185
Columbine
Style Two
Designer: M. Davies
Height: 7", 17.8 cm
Colour: Pink
Issued: 1957-1969
Series: Teenagers

U.S.:	**$325.00**
Can.:	**$400.00**
U.K.:	**£175.00**

HN 2186
Harlequin
Style One
Designer: M. Davies
Height: 7 ¼", 18.4 cm
Colour: Blue
Issued: 1957-1969
Series: Teenagers

U.S.:	**$325.00**
Can.:	**$400.00**
U.K.:	**£175.00**

HN 2187 - 2190 not issued.

HN 2191
Sea Sprite
Style Two
Designer: M. Davies
Height: 7", 17.8 cm
Colour: Pink and blue
Issued: 1958-1962
Series: Teenagers
  U.S.: **$525.00**
  Can.: **$625.00**
  U.K.: **£285.00**

HN 2192
Wood Nymph
Designer: M. Davies
Height: 7 ¼", 18.4 cm
Colour: Blue and white
Issued: 1958-1962
Series: Teenagers
  U.S.: **$500.00**
  Can.: **$600.00**
  U.K.: **£275.00**

HN 2193
Fair Lady
Style One
Designer: M. Davies
Height: 7 ¼", 18.4 cm
Colour: Green
Issued: 1963-1996
Varieties: HN 2832, 2835; also
  called 'Kay' HN 3340
  U.S.: **$200.00**
  Can.: **$250.00**
  U.K.: **£110.00**

HN 2194 - 2195 not issued.

HN 2196
The Bridesmaid
Style Four
Designer: M. Davies
Height: 5 ¼", 13.3 cm
Colour: Pale blue
Issued: 1960-1976
  U.S.: **$150.00**
  Can.: **$180.00**
  U.K.: **£ 80.00**

HN 2197 - 2201 not issued.

HN 2202
Melody
Style One
Designer: M. Davies
Height: 6 ¼", 15.9 cm
Colour: Blue and peach
Issued: 1957-1962
Series: Teenagers
  U.S.: **$475.00**
  Can.: **$575.00**
  U.K.: **£250.00**

HN 2203
Teenager
Designer: M. Davies
Height: 7 ¼", 18.4 cm
Colour: Orange and white
Issued: 1957-1962
Series: Teenagers
  U.S.: **$475.00**
  Can.: **$575.00**
  U.K.: **£250.00**

Also known in Flambé. Sold for
£1,035., Phillips, London May 2001.

HN 2204
Long John Silver
Style One
Designer: M. Nicoll
Height: 9", 22.9 cm
Colour: Green, black and white
Issued: 1957-1965
  U.S.: **$700.00**
  Can.: **$850.00**
  U.K.: **£385.00**

Earthenware

HN 2205
Master Sweep
Designer: M. Nicoll
Height: 8 ½", 21.6 cm
Colour: Dark turquoise,
  black and brown
Issued: 1957-1962
  U.S.: **$1,100.00**
  Can.: **$1,350.00**
  U.K.: **£ 600.00**

Earthenware

HN 2206
Sunday Best
Style One
Designer: M. Davies
Height: 7 ½", 19.1 cm
Colour: Yellow
Issued: 1979-1984
Varieties: HN 2698

U.S.:	**$250.00**
Can.:	**$300.00**
U.K.:	**£135.00**

HN 2207
Stayed at Home
Designer: M. Davies
Height: 5", 12.7 cm
Colour: Green and white
Issued: 1958-1969

U.S.:	**$275.00**
Can.:	**$325.00**
U.K.:	**£150.00**

HN 2208
Silversmith of Williamsburg
Designer: M. Davies
Height: 6 ¼", 15.9 cm
Colour: Blue, white and brown
Issued: 1960-1983
Series: Figures of Williamsburg

U.S.:	**$300.00**
Can.:	**$375.00**
U.K.:	**£175.00**

HN 2209
Hostess of Williamsburg
Designer: M. Davies
Height: 7 ¼", 18.4 cm
Colour: Pink
Issued: 1960-1983
Series: Figures of Williamsburg

U.S.:	**$300.00**
Can.:	**$375.00**
U.K.:	**£175.00**

HN 2210
Debutante
Style One
Designer: M. Davies
Height: 5", 12.7 cm
Colour: Blue
Issued: 1963-1967

U.S.:	**$375.00**
Can.:	**$450.00**
U.K.:	**£200.00**

HN 2211
Fair Maiden
Designer: M. Davies
Height: 5 ¼", 13.3 cm
Colour: Green
Issued: 1967-1994
Varieties: HN 2434

U.S.:	**$150.00**
Can.:	**$180.00**
U.K.:	**£ 80.00**

HN 2212
Rendezvous
Designer: M. Davies
Height: 7 ¼", 18.4 cm
Colour: Red and white
Issued: 1962-1971

U.S.:	**$550.00**
Can.:	**$650.00**
U.K.:	**£300.00**

HN 2213
Contemplation
Style One
Designer: M. Davies
Height: 12", 30.5 cm
Colour: White
Issued: 1982-1986
Varieties: HN 2241
Series: Images

U.S.:	**$175.00**
Can.:	**$225.00**
U.K.:	**£100.00**

HN 2214
Bunny
Designer: M. Davies
Height: 5", 12.7 cm
Colour: Turquoise
Issued: 1960-1975
U.S.:   **$250.00**
Can.:   **$300.00**
U.K.:   **£135.00**

HN 2215
Sweet April
Designer: M. Davies
Height: 7 ¼", 18.4 cm
Colour: Pink
Issued: 1965-1967
U.S.:   **$500.00**
Can.:   **$600.00**
U.K.:   **£275.00**

HN 2216
Pirouette
Designer: M. Davies
Height: 5 ¾", 14.6 cm
Colour: Pale blue
Issued: 1959-1967
U.S.:   **$275.00**
Can.:   **$325.00**
U.K.:   **£150.00**

HN 2217
Old King Cole
Designer: M. Davies
Height: 6 ½", 16.5 cm
Colour: Brown, yellow
           and white
Issued: 1963-1967
U.S.:   **$750.00**
Can.:   **$900.00**
U.K.:   **£400.00**

HN 2218
Cookie
Designer: M. Davies
Height: 4 ¾", 12.0 cm
Colour: Pink and white
Issued: 1958-1975
U.S.:   **$225.00**
Can.:   **$275.00**
U.K.:   **£125.00**

HN 2219
Bedtime
Style One
Designer: L. Harradine
Height: 5 ½", 14.0 cm
Colour: Pink
Issued: 1992
Varieties: HN 1978
Comm.by: Peter Jones China
U.S.:   **$125.00**
Can.:   **$150.00**
U.K.:   **£ 70.00**

HN 2220
Winsome
Designer: M. Davies
Height: 8", 20.3 cm
Colour: Red
Issued: 1960-1985
U.S.:   **$225.00**
Can.:   **$275.00**
U.K.:   **£150.00**

HN 2221
Nanny
Designer: M. Nicoll
Height: 6", 15.2 cm
Colour: Blue and white
Issued: 1958-1991
U.S.:   **$375.00**
Can.:   **$450.00**
U.K.:   **£200.00**

Earthenware

HN 2222
Camellia
Designer: M. Davies
Height: 7 ¾", 19.7 cm
Colour: Pink
Issued: 1960-1971

U.S.:	**$300.00**
Can.:	**$375.00**
U.K.:	**£165.00**

HN 2223
Schoolmarm
Designer: M. Davies
Height: 6 ¾", 17.2 cm
Colour: Purple, grey
           and brown
Issued: 1958-1981

U.S.:	**$375.00**
Can.:	**$450.00**
U.K.:	**£200.00**

HN 2224
Make Believe
Designer: M. Nicoll
Height: 5 ¾", 14.6 cm
Colour: White
Issued: 1984-1988
Varieties: HN 2225

U.S.:	**$175.00**
Can.:	**$225.00**
U.K.:	**£100.00**

HN 2225
Make Believe
Designer: M. Nicoll
Height: 5 ¾", 14.6 cm
Colour: Blue
Issued: 1962-1988
Varieties: HN 2224

U.S.:	**$225.00**
Can.:	**$275.00**
U.K.:	**£125.00**

HN 2226
The Cellist
Designer: M. Nicoll
Height: 8", 20.3 cm
Colour: Black and brown
Issued: 1960-1967

U.S.:	**$600.00**
Can.:	**$725.00**
U.K.:	**£325.00**

HN 2227
Gentleman from Williamsburg
Designer: M. Davies
Height: 6 ¼", 15.9 cm
Colour: Green and white
Issued: 1960-1983
Series: Figures of Williamsburg

U.S.:	**$275.00**
Can.:	**$330.00**
U.K.:	**£150.00**

HN 2228
Lady from Williamsburg
Designer: M. Davies
Height: 6", 15.2 cm
Colour: Green
Issued: 1960-1983
Series: Figures of Williamsburg

U.S.:	**$275.00**
Can.:	**$330.00**
U.K.:	**£150.00**

HN 2229
Southern Belle
Style One
Designer: M. Davies
Height: 7 ½", 19.1 cm
Colour: Red and cream
Issued: 1958-1997
Varieties: HN 2425

U.S.:	**$275.00**
Can.:	**$330.00**
U.K.:	**£150.00**

HN 2230
A Gypsy Dance
Style Two
Designer: M. Davies
Height: 7", 17.8 cm
Colour: Lavender
Issued: 1959-1971

U.S.:	**$400.00**
Can.:	**$500.00**
U.K.:	**£225.00**

HN 2231
Sweet Sixteen
Style One
Designer: M. Davies
Height: 7 ¼", 18.4 cm
Colour: Blue and white
Issued: 1958-1965
Series: Teenagers

U.S.:	**$475.00**
Can.:	**$575.00**
U.K.:	**£275.00**

HN 2232 not issued.

HN 2233
Royal Governor's Cook
Designer: M. Davies
Height: 6", 15.2 cm
Colour: Dark blue, white
            and brown
Issued: 1960-1983
Series: Figures of Williamsburg

U.S.:	**$650.00**
Can.:	**$775.00**
U.K.:	**£350.00**

HN 2234
Michele
Designer: M. Davies
Height: 7", 17.8 cm
Colour: Green
Issued: 1967-1993
Varieties: Also called 'Autumn
            Attraction' HN 3612

U.S.:	**$225.00**
Can.:	**$275.00**
U.K.:	**£125.00**

HN 2235
Dancing Years
Designer: M. Davies
Height: 6 ¾", 17.2 cm
Colour: Lavender
Issued: 1965-1971

U.S.:	**$450.00**
Can.:	**$575.00**
U.K.:	**£250.00**

HN 2236
Affection
Designer: M. Davies
Height: 4 ½", 11.4 cm
Colour: Purple
Issued: 1962-1994

U.S.:	**$175.00**
Can.:	**$225.00**
U.K.:	**£ 95.00**

HN 2237
Celeste
Style One
Designer: M. Davies
Colour: Pale blue
Height: 6 ¾", 17.2 cm
Issued: 1959-1971

U.S.:	**$275.00**
Can.:	**$350.00**
U.K.:	**£150.00**

HN 2238
My Pet
Designer: M. Davies
Height: 2 ¾", 7.0 cm
Colour: Blue and white
Issued: 1962-1975

U.S.:	**$250.00**
Can.:	**$325.00**
U.K.:	**£150.00**

HN 2239
Wigmaker of Williamsburg
Designer: M. Davies
Height: 7 ½", 19.1 cm
Colour: White and brown
Issued: 1960-1983
Series: Figures of Williamsburg

U.S.:	**$275.00**
Can.:	**$325.00**
U.K.:	**£150.00**

HN 2240
Blacksmith of Willliamsburg
Designer: M. Davies
Height: 6 ¾", 17.2 cm
Colour: Grey and white
Issued: 1960-1983
Series: Figures of Williamsburg

U.S.:	**$300.00**
Can.:	**$350.00**
U.K.:	**£175.00**

HN 2241
Contemplation
Style One
Designer: M. Davies
Height: 12", 30.5 cm
Colour: Black
Issued: 1982-1986
Varieties: HN 2213
Series: Images

U.S.:	**$175.00**
Can.:	**$225.00**
U.K.:	**£100.00**

HN 2242
First Steps
Style One
Designer: M. Davies
Height: 6 ½", 16.5 cm
Colour: Blue and yellow
Issued: 1959-1965

U.S.:	**$600.00**
Can.:	**$725.00**
U.K.:	**£325.00**

HN 2243
Treasure Island
Designer: M. Davies
Height: 4 ¾", 12.0 cm
Colour: Blue and yellow
Issued: 1962-1975

U.S.:	**$250.00**
Can.:	**$300.00**
U.K.:	**£135.00**

HN 2244
Newsboy
Designer: M. Nicoll
Height: 8 ½", 21.6 cm
Colour: Green, brown
and blue
Issued: 1959-1965
Varieties: Limited edition of 250
for Evening Sentinel

U.S.:	**$700.00**
Can.:	**$900.00**
U.K.:	**£400.00**

HN 2245
The Basket Weaver
Designer: M. Nicoll
Height: 5 ¾", 14.6 cm
Colour: Pale blue and yellow
Issued: 1959-1962

U.S.:	**$600.00**
Can.:	**$725.00**
U.K.:	**£325.00**

HN 2246
Cradle Song
Designer: M. Davies
Height: 5 ½", 14.0 cm
Colour: Green and brown
Issued: 1959-1962

U.S.:	**$625.00**
Can.:	**$750.00**
U.K.:	**£350.00**

HN 2247
Omar Khayyam
Style Two
Designer: M. Nicoll
Height: 6 ¼", 15.9 cm
Colour: Brown
Issued: 1965-1983

   U.S.:   **$275.00**
   Can.:   **$330.00**
   U.K.:   **£150.00**

Earthenware

HN 2248
Tall Story
Designer: M. Nicoll
Height: 6 ½", 16.5 cm
Colour: Blue and grey
Issued: 1968-1975
Series: Sea Characters

   U.S.:   **$450.00**
   Can.:   **$550.00**
   U.K.:   **£250.00**

HN 2249
The Favourite
Designer: M. Nicoll
Height: 7 ¾", 19.7 cm
Colour: Blue and white
Issued: 1960-1990

   U.S.:   **$275.00**
   Can.:   **$350.00**
   U.K.:   **£150.00**

HN 2250
The Toymaker
Designer: M. Nicoll
Height: 6", 15.2 cm
Colour: Brown and red
Issued: 1959-1973

   U.S.:   **$650.00**
   Can.:   **$800.00**
   U.K.:   **£350.00**

HN 2251
Masquerade
Style Two
Designer: M. Davies
Height: 8 ½", 21.6 cm
Colour: Blue and white
Issued: 1960-1965
Varieties: HN 2259

   U.S.:   **$400.00**
   Can.:   **$475.00**
   U.K.:   **£225.00**

HN 2252
The Joker
Style Two
Designer: M. Nicoll
Height: 8 ½", 21.6 cm
Colour: White
Issued: 1990-1992
Series: Clowns

   U.S.:   **$400.00**
   Can.:   **$475.00**
   U.K.:   **£220.00**

HN 2253
The Puppetmaker
Designer: M. Nicoll
Height: 8", 20.3 cm
Colour: Green, brown and red
Issued: 1962-1973

   U.S.:   **$675.00**
   Can.:   **$825.00**
   U.K.:   **£375.00**

HN 2254
Shore Leave
Designer: M. Nicoll
Height: 7 ½", 19.1 cm
Colour: Black
Issued: 1965-1979
Series: Sea Characters

   U.S.:   **$375.00**
   Can.:   **$450.00**
   U.K.:   **£200.00**

HN 2255
Teatime
Designer: M. Nicoll
Height: 7 ¼", 18.4 cm
Colour: Brown
Issued: 1972-1995

U.S.:	**$275.00**
Can.:	**$350.00**
U.K.:	**£150.00**

HN 2256
Twilight
Designer: M. Nicoll
Height: 5", 12.7 cm
Colour: Green and black
Issued: 1971-1976

U.S.:	**$350.00**
Can.:	**$425.00**
U.K.:	**£200.00**

HN 2257
Sea Harvest
Designer: M. Nicoll
Height: 7 ½", 19.1 cm
Colour: Blue and brown
Issued: 1969-1976
Series: Sea Characters

U.S.:	**$400.00**
Can.:	**$500.00**
U.K.:	**£220.00**

HN 2258
A Good Catch
Designer: M. Nicoll
Height: 7 ¼", 18.4 cm
Colour: Green and grey
Issued: 1966-1986
Series: Sea Characters

U.S.:	**$300.00**
Can.:	**$375.00**
U.K.:	**£165.00**

HN 2259
Masquerade
Style Two
Designer: M. Davies
Height: 8 ½", 21.6 cm
Colour: Red and cream
Issued: 1960-1965
Varieties: HN 2251

U.S.:	**$400.00**
Can.:	**$475.00**
U.K.:	**£225.00**

HN 2260
The Captain
Style Two
Designer: M. Nicoll
Height: 9 ½", 24.1 cm
Colour: Black and white
Issued: 1965-1982
Series: Sea Characters

U.S.:	**$450.00**
Can.:	**$550.00**
U.K.:	**£250.00**

HN 2261
Marriage of Art and Industry
Designer: M. Davies
Height: 19", 48.3 cm
Colour: Green
Issued: 1958 in a limited
edition of 12

U.S.:	
Can.:	**Very Rare**
U.K.:	

HN 2262
Lights Out
Style One
Designer: M. Davies
Height: 5", 12.7 cm
Colour: Blue trousers with
yellow spotted shirt
Issued: 1965-1969

U.S.:	**$350.00**
Can.:	**$425.00**
U.K.:	**£200.00**

HN 2263
Seashore
Designer: M. Davies
Height: 3 ½", 8.9 cm
Colour: Yellow, red and cream
Issued: 1961-1965
U.S.:   **$425.00**
Can.:   **$525.00**
U.K.:   **£235.00**

HN 2264
Elegance
Designer: M. Davies
Height: 7 ¼", 18.4 cm
Colour: Green
Issued: 1961-1985
U.S.:   **$200.00**
Can.:   **$250.00**
U.K.:   **£110.00**

HN 2265
Sara
Style One
Designer: M. Davies
Height: 7 ½", 19.1 cm
Colour: Red and white
Issued: 1981-2000
Varieties HN 3308
U.S.:   **$325.00**
Can.:   **$400.00**
U.K.:   **£175.00**

HN 2266
Ballad Seller
Designer: M. Davies
Height: 7 ½", 19.1 cm
Colour: Pink
Issued: 1968-1973
U.S.:   **$350.00**
Can.:   **$425.00**
U.K.:   **£200.00**

HN 2267
Rhapsody
Designer: M. Davies
Height: 6 ¾", 17.2 cm
Colour: Green
Issued: 1961-1973
U.S.:   **$275.00**
Can.:   **$325.00**
U.K.:   **£150.00**

HN 2268
Daphne
Designer: M. Davies
Height: 8 ¼", 21.0 cm
Colour: Pink
Issued: 1963-1975
U.S.:   **$275.00**
Can.:   **$325.00**
U.K.:   **£150.00**

HN 2269
Leading Lady
Designer: M. Davies
Height: 7 ¾", 19.7 cm
Colour: Blue and yellow
Issued: 1965-1976
U.S.:   **$250.00**
Can.:   **$325.00**
U.K.:   **£135.00**

HN 2270
Pillow Fight
Designer: M. Davies
Height: 5", 12.7 cm
Colour: Patterned pink
           nightdress
Issued: 1965-1969
U.S.:   **$350.00**
Can.:   **$425.00**
U.K.:   **£200.00**

HN 2271
Melanie
Designer: M. Davies
Height: 7 ¾", 19.7 cm
Colour: Blue
Issued: 1965-1981

U.S.: $250.00
Can.: $300.00
U.K.: £135.00

HN 2272
Repose
Designer: M. Davies
Height: 5 ¼", 13.3 cm
Colour: Pink and green
Issued: 1972-1979

U.S.: $350.00
Can.: $425.00
U.K.: £190.00

HN 2273
Denise
Style Two
Designer: M. Davies
Height: 7", 17.8 cm
Colour: Red
Issued: 1964-1971

U.S.: $425.00
Can.: $525.00
U.K.: £230.00

HN 2274
Golden Days
Designer: M. Davies
Height: 3 ¾", 9.5 cm
Colour: Yellow, white and blue
Issued: 1964-1973

U.S.: $300.00
Can.: $375.00
U.K.: £165.00

HN 2275
Sandra
Designer: M. Davies
Height: 7 ¾", 19.7 cm
Colour: Gold
Issued: 1969-1997
Varieties: HN 2401; also
called 'Annette'
(Style Two) HN 3495

U.S.: $275.00
Can.: $325.00
U.K.: £150.00

HN 2276
Heart to Heart
Designer: M. Davies
Height: 5 ½", 14.0 cm
Colour: Lavender, green
and yellow
Issued: 1961-1971

U.S.: $700.00
Can.: $850.00
U.K.: £375.00

HN 2277
Slapdash
Designer: M.Nicoll
Height: 10", 25.4 cm
Colour: Green, white and blue
Issued: 1990-1994
Series: Clowns

U.S.: $400.00
Can.: $500.00
U.K.: £225.00

HN 2278
Judith
Style Two
Designer: M. Nicoll
Height: 6 ¾", 17.2 cm
Colour: Yellow
Issued: 1986 N.America
1987 Worldwide-1989
Varieties: HN 2313

U.S.: $325.00
Can.: $400.00
U.K.: £175.00

HN 2279
The Clockmaker
Designer: M. Nicoll
Height: 7", 17.8 cm
Colour: Green and brown
Issued: 1961-1975

U.S.:	$425.00
Can.:	$525.00
U.K.:	£240.00

HN 2280
The Mayor
Designer: M. Nicoll
Height: 8 ¼", 21.0 cm
Colour: Red and white
Issued: 1963-1971
Varieties: Also known in 7 ½", 19.1 cm

U.S.:	$475.00
Can.:	$575.00
U.K.:	£270.00

HN 2281
The Professor
Designer: M. Nicoll
Height: 7 ¼", 18.4 cm
Colour: Brown and black
Issued: 1965-1981

U.S.:	$275.00
Can.:	$325.00
U.K.:	£150.00

HN 2282
The Coachman
Designer: M. Nicoll
Height: 7 ¼", 18.4 cm
Colour: Purple, grey and blue
Issued: 1963-1971

U.S.:	$650.00
Can.:	$800.00
U.K.:	£350.00

HN 2283
Dreamweaver (matte)
Designer: M. Nicoll
Height: 8 ¼", 21.0 cm
Colour: Blue, grey and brown
Issued: 1972-1976

U.S.:	$275.00
Can.:	$350.00
U.K.:	£150.00

HN 2284
The Craftsman
Designer: M. Nicoll
Height: 6", 15.2 cm
Colour: Blue, tan and brown
Issued: 1961-1965

U.S.:	$ 800.00
Can.:	$1,000.00
U.K.:	£ 450.00

HN 2285 - 2286 not issued.

HN 2287
Symphony
Designer: D.B. Lovegrove
Height: 5 ¼", 13.3 cm
Colour: Brown
Issued: 1961-1965

U.S.:	$325.00
Can.:	$400.00
U.K.:	£175.00

HN 2288 - 2303 not issued.

HN 2304
Adrienne
Designer: M. Davies
Height: 7 ½", 19.1 cm
Colour: Blue
Issued: 1964-1991
Varieties: HN 2152, also called 'Fiona' (Style Four) HN 3748; 'Joan' (Style Two) HN 3217

U.S.:	$225.00
Can.:	$275.00
U.K.:	£125.00

HN 2305
Dulcie
Designer: M. Davies
Height: 7 ¼", 18.4 cm
Colour: Blue
Issued: 1981-1984
  U.S.: **$350.00**
  Can.: **$425.00**
  U.K.: **£200.00**

HN 2306
Reverie
Designer: M. Davies
Height: 6 ½", 16.5 cm
Colour: Peach
Issued: 1964-1981
  U.S.: **$400.00**
  Can.: **$475.00**
  U.K.: **£225.00**

HN 2307
Coralie
Designer: M. Davies
Height: 7 ¼", 18.4 cm
Colour: Yellow
Issued: 1964-1988
  U.S.: **$200.00**
  Can.: **$250.00**
  U.K.: **£110.00**

HN 2308
Picnic
Designer: M. Davies
Height: 3 ¾", 9.5 cm
Colour: Yellow
Issued: 1965-1988
  U.S.: **$200.00**
  Can.: **$250.00**
  U.K.: **£110.00**

HN 2309
Buttercup
Style One
Designer: M. Davies
Height: 7", 17.8 cm
Colour: Green dress with
  yellow sleeves
Issued: 1964-1997
Varieties: HN 2399
  U.S.: **$225.00**
  Can.: **$275.00**
  U.K.: **£125.00**

HN 2310
Lisa (matte)
Style One
Designer: M. Davies
Height: 7 ¼", 18.4 cm
Colour: Blue and white
Issued: 1969-1982
Varieties: HN 2394, 3265
  U.S.: **$225.00**
  Can.: **$300.00**
  U.K.: **£135.00**

HN 2311
Lorna
Designer: M. Davies
Height: 8 ¼", 21.0 cm
Colour: Green dress,
  yellow shawl
Issued: 1965-1985
  U.S.: **$225.00**
  Can.: **$275.00**
  U.K.: **£125.00**

HN 2312
Soiree
Style One
Designer: M. Davies
Height: 7 ½", 19.1 cm
Colour: Green and cream
Issued: 1967-1984
  U.S.: **$200.00**
  Can.: **$250.00**
  U.K.: **£110.00**

HN 2313
Judith
Style Two
Designer: M. Nicholl
Height: 6 ¼", 15.9 cm
Colour: Red and cream
Issued: 1988 in a limited
                edition of 1,000
Varieties: HN 2278

U.S.:	**$375.00**
Can.:	**$450.00**
U.K.:	**£200.00**

HN 2314
Old Mother Hubbard
Designer: M. Nicholl
Height: 8", 20.3 cm
Colour: Green and white
Issued: 1964-1975

U.S.:	**$500.00**
Can.:	**$600.00**
U.K.:	**£275.00**

HN 2315
Last Waltz
Designer: M. Nicoll
Height: 7 ¾", 19.7 cm
Colour: Yellow and white
Issued: 1967-1993
Varieties: HN 2316

U.S.:	**$200.00**
Can.:	**$250.00**
U.K.:	**£110.00**

HN 2316
Last Waltz
Designer: M. Nicoll
Height: 7 ¾", 19.7 cm
Colour: Pink and cream
Issued: 1987 in a limited
                edition of 2,000
Varieties: HN 2315
Series: M. Doulton Events

U.S.:	**$375.00**
Can.:	**$450.00**
U.K.:	**£210.00**

HN 2317
The Lobster Man
Designer: M. Nicoll
Height: 7 ¼", 18.4 cm
Colour: Blue, grey and brown
Issued: 1964-1994
Varieties: HN 2323
Series: Sea Characters

U.S.:	**$250.00**
Can.:	**$300.00**
U.K.:	**£135.00**

HN 2318
Grace
Style One
Designer: M. Nicoll
Height: 7 ¾", 19.7 cm
Colour: Green
Issued: 1966-1981

U.S.:	**$300.00**
Can.:	**$400.00**
U.K.:	**£175.00**

HN 2319
The Bachelor
Designer: M. Nicoll
Height: 7", 17.8 cm
Colour: Green and brown
Issued: 1964-1975

U.S.:	**$450.00**
Can.:	**$550.00**
U.K.:	**£250.00**

HN 2320
Tuppence a Bag
Designer: M. Nicoll
Height: 5 ½", 14.0 cm
Colour: Blue and green
Issued: 1968-1995

U.S.:	**$275.00**
Can.:	**$325.00**
U.K.:	**£150.00**

HN 2321
Family Album
Designer: M. Nicholl
Height: 6 ¼", 15.9 cm
Colour: Lavender and green
Issued: 1966-1973

U.S.:	**$600.00**
Can.:	**$725.00**
U.K.:	**£325.00**

HN 2322
The Cup of Tea
Designer: M. Nicoll
Height: 7", 17.8 cm
Colour: Dark blue and grey
Issued: 1964-1983

U.S.:	**$275.00**
Can.:	**$350.00**
U.K.:	**£150.00**

HN 2323
The Lobster Man
Designer: M. Nicoll
Height: 7 ¼", 18.4 cm
Colour: Cream, blue, gold and grey
Issued: 1987-1995
Varieties: HN 2317
Series: Sea Characters

U.S.:	**$500.00**
Can.:	**$600.00**
U.K.:	**£275.00**

HN 2324
Matador and Bull
Style One
Designer: M. Davies
Height: 16", 40.6 cm
Colour: Black and yellow
Issued: 1964 to the present
Series: Prestige

U.S.:	**$27,845.00**
Can.:	**$32,700.00**
U.K.:	**£11,900.00**

HN 2325
The Master
Designer: M. Davies
Height: 6 ¼", 15.9 cm
Colour: Green and brown
Issued: 1967-1992

U.S.:	**$275.00**
Can.:	**$350.00**
U.K.:	**£150.00**

HN 2326
Antoinette
Style Two
Designer: M. Davies
Height: 6 ¼", 15.9 cm
Colour: White, white rose
Issued: 1967-1979
Varieties: Also called 'My Love' HN 2339

U.S.:	**$225.00**
Can.:	**$275.00**
U.K.:	**£125.00**

HN 2327
Katrina
Style One
Designer: M. Davies
Height: 7 ½", 19.1 cm
Colour: Red
Issued: 1965-1969

U.S.:	**$425.00**
Can.:	**$525.00**
U.K.:	**£230.00**

HN 2328
Queen of Sheba
Designer: M. Davies
Height: 9", 22.9 cm
Colour: Purple and brown with green base
Issued: 1982 in a limited edition of 750
Series: Les Femmes Fatales

U.S.:	**$1,400.00**
Can.:	**$1,700.00**
U.K.:	**£ 775.00**

HN 2329
Lynne
Style One
Designer: M. Davies
Height: 7", 17.8 cm
Colour: Green
Issued: 1971-1996
Varieties: HN 3740; also called 'Kathy' (Style Two) HN 3305

U.S.:	$225.00
Can.:	$275.00
U.K.:	£125.00

HN 2330
Meditation
Designer: M. Davies
Height: 5 ¾", 14.6 cm
Colour: Peach and cream
Issued: 1971-1983

U.S.:	$375.00
Can.:	$450.00
U.K.:	£200.00

HN 2331
Cello
Style One
Designer: M. Davies
Height: 6", 15.2 cm
Colour: Yellow and brown
Issued: 1970 in a limited edition of 750
Series: Lady Musicians

U.S.:	$1,600.00
Can.:	$2,000.00
U.K.:	£ 900.00

HN 2332
Monte Carlo
Designer: M. Davies
Height: 8 ¼", 21.0 cm
Colour: Green
Issued: 1982 in a limited edition of 1,500
Series: Sweet and Twenties

U.S.:	$500.00
Can.:	$600.00
U.K.:	£275.00

HN 2333
Jacqueline
Style Two
Designer: M. Davies
Height: 7 ½", 19.1 cm
Colour: Purple
Issued: 1982 Canada, 1983 Worldwide -1991

U.S.:	$275.00
Can.:	$325.00
U.K.:	£150.00

HN 2334
Fragrance
Style One
Designer: M. Davies
Height: 7 ¼", 18.4 cm
Colour: Blue
Issued: 1966-1995
Varieties: HN 3311

U.S.:	$200.00
Can.:	$250.00
U.K.:	£110.00

HN 2335
Hilary
Designer: M. Davies
Height: 7 ¼", 18.4 cm
Colour: Blue
Issued: 1967-1981

U.S.:	$225.00
Can.:	$275.00
U.K.:	£125.00

HN 2336
Alison
Style One
Designer: M. Davies
Height: 7 ½", 19.1 cm
Colour: Blue and white
Issued: 1966-1992
Varieties: HN 3264

U.S.:	$250.00
Can.:	$300.00
U.K.:	£135.00

HN 2337
Loretta
Designer: M. Davies
Height: 7 ¾", 19.7 cm
Colour: Purple dress,
yellow shawl
Issued: 1966-1981
U.S.: $250.00
Can.: $300.00
U.K.: £135.00

HN 2338
Penny
Designer: M. Davies
Height: 4 ¾", 12.0 cm
Colour: Green and white
Issued: 1968-1995
Varieties: HN 2424
U.S.: $100.00
Can.: $125.00
U.K.: £ 55.00

HN 2339
My Love
Style One
Designer: M. Davies
Height: 6 ¼", 15.9 cm
Colour: White, red rose
Issued: 1969-1996
Varieties: Also called 'Antoinette'
(Style Two) HN 2326
U.S.: $275.00
Can.: $330.00
U.K.: £150.00

HN 2340
Belle
Style Two
Designer: M. Davies
Height: 4 ½", 11.4 cm
Colour: Green
Issued: 1968-1988
U.S.: $100.00
Can.: $125.00
U.K.: £ 55.00

HN 2341
Cherie
Designer: M. Davies
Height: 5 ½", 14.0 cm
Colour: Blue
Issued: 1966-1992
U.S.: $125.00
Can.: $150.00
U.K.: £ 75.00

HN 2342
Lucrezia Borgia
Designer: M. Davies
Height: 8", 20.3 cm
Colour: Yellow
Issued: 1985 in a limited
edition of 750
Series: Les Femmes Fatales
U.S.: $1,400.00
Can.: $1,750.00
U.K.: £ 800.00

HN 2343
Premiere
(Hand holds cloak)
Designer: M. Davies
Height: 7 ½", 19.1 cm
Colour: Green
Issued: 1969-Unknown
Varieties: HN 2343A
U.S.: $350.00
Can.: $425.00
U.K.: £200.00

HN 2343A
Premiere
(Hand rests on cloak)
Designer: M. Davies
Height: 7 ½", 19.1 cm
Colour: Green
Issued: Unknown-1979
Varieties: HN 2343
U.S.: $225.00
Can.: $275.00
U.K.: £125.00

HN 2344
Deauville
Designer: M. Davies
Height: 8 ¼", 21.0 cm
Colour: Yellow and white
Issued: 1982 in a limited
             edition of 1,500
Series: Sweet and Twenties
  U.S.:   **$500.00**
  Can.:   **$600.00**
  U.K.:   **£280.00**

HN 2345
Clarissa
Style Two
Designer: M. Davies
Height: 7 ½", 19.1 cm
Colour: Green
Issued: 1968-1981
  U.S.:   **$225.00**
  Can.:   **$275.00**
  U.K.:   **£125.00**

HN 2346
Kathy
Style One
Designer: M. Davies
Height: 4 ¾", 12.0 cm
Colour: Cream flowered dress
Issued: 1981-1987
Series: Kate Greenaway
  U.S.:   **$275.00**
  Can.:   **$325.00**
  U.K.:   **£150.00**

HN 2347
Nina (matte)
Designer: M. Davies
Height: 7 ½", 19.1 cm
Colour: Blue
Issued: 1969-1976
  U.S.:   **$200.00**
  Can.:   **$250.00**
  U.K.:   **£110.00**

HN 2348
Geraldine (matte)
Designer: M. Davies
Height: 7 ¼", 18.4 cm
Colour: Green
Issued: 1972-1976
  U.S.:   **$200.00**
  Can.:   **$250.00**
  U.K.:   **£110.00**

HN 2349
Flora
Designer: M. Nicoll
Height: 7 ¾", 19.7 cm
Colour: Brown and white
Issued: 1966-1973
  U.S.:   **$525.00**
  Can.:   **$650.00**
  U.K.:   **£280.00**

HN 2350 - 2351 not issued.

HN 2352
A Stitch in Time
Designer: M. Nicoll
Height: 6 ¼", 15.9 cm
Colour: Purple, brown
             and turquoise
Issued: 1966-1981
  U.S.:   **$325.00**
  Can.:   **$400.00**
  U.K.:   **£175.00**

HN 2353 - 2355 not issued.

HN 2356
Ascot
Style One
Designer: M. Nicoll
Height: 5 ¾", 14.6 cm
Colour: Green dress with
             yellow shawl
Issued: 1968-1995
  U.S.:   **$250.00**
  Can.:   **$300.00**
  U.K.:   **£135.00**

HN 2357 - 2358 not issued.

HN 2359
The Detective
Designer: M. Nicoll
Height: 9 ¼", 23.5 cm
Colour: Brown
Issued: 1977-1983

U.S.:	**$450.00**
Can.:	**$550.00**
U.K.:	**£250.00**

HN 2360 not issued.

HN 2361
The Laird
(Small base)
Designer: M. Nicoll
Height: 8", 20.3 cm
Colour: Green and brown
Issued: 1969-Unknown
Varieties: HN 2361A (Large base)

U.S.:	**$350.00**
Can.:	**$425.00**
U.K.:	**£200.00**

HN 2361A
The Laird
(Large base)
Designer: M. Nicoll
Height: 8", 20.3 cm
Colour: Green and brown
Issued: Unknown-2001
Varieties: HN 2361 (Small base)

U.S.:	**$325.00**
Can.:	**$400.00**
U.K.:	**£180.00**

HN 2362
The Wayfarer
Designer: M. Nicoll
Height: 5 ½", 14.0 cm
Colour: Green, grey and brown
Issued: 1970-1976

U.S.:	**$275.00**
Can.:	**$350.00**
U.K.:	**£150.00**

HN 2363 - 2367 not issued.

HN 2368
Fleur
Style One
Designer: J. Bromley
Height: 7 ¼", 18.4 cm
Colour: Green
Issued: 1968-1995
Varieties: HN 2369; also called 'Flower of Love' HN 2460, 3970

U.S.:	**$225.00**
Can.:	**$275.00**
U.K.:	**£125.00**

HN 2369
Fleur
Style One
Designer: J. Bromley
Height: 7 ¼", 18.4 cm
Colour: Orange and blue
Issued: 1983-1986
Varieties: HN 2368; also called 'Flower of Love' HN 2460, 3970

U.S.:	**$325.00**
Can.:	**$400.00**
U.K.:	**£175.00**

HN 2370
Sir Edward
Designer: J. Bromley
Height: 11", 27.9 cm
Colour: Red and grey
Issued: 1979 in a limited edition of 500
Series: Age of Chivalry

U.S.:	**$650.00**
Can.:	**$800.00**
U.K.:	**£350.00**

HN 2371
Sir Ralph
Designer: J. Bromley
Height: 10 ¾", 27.3 cm
Colour: Turquoise and grey
Issued: 1979 in a limited edition of 500
Series: Age of Chivalry

U.S.:	**$650.00**
Can.:	**$800.00**
U.K.:	**£350.00**

HN 2372
Sir Thomas
Designer: J. Bromley
Height: 11", 27.9 cm
Colour: Black
Issued: 1979 in a limited
              edition of 500
Series: Age of Chivalry
　U.S.:   **$650.00**
　Can.:   **$800.00**
　U.K.:   **£350.00**

HN 2373
Joanne
Style One
Designer: J. Bromley
Height: 5 ¼", 13.3 cm
Colour: White
Issued: 1982-1988
Series: Vanity Fair Ladies
　U.S.:   **$300.00**
　Can.:   **$375.00**
　U.K.:   **£175.00**

HN 2374
Mary
Style One
Designer: J. Bromley
Height: 7 ¾", 19.7 cm
Colour: White
Issued: 1984-1986
Series: Vanity Fair Ladies
　U.S.:   **$300.00**
　Can.:   **$375.00**
　U.K.:   **£175.00**

HN 2375
The Viking (matte)
Designer: J. Bromley
Height: 8 ¾", 22.2 cm
Colour: Blue and brown
Issued: 1973-1976
　U.S.:   **$325.00**
　Can.:   **$400.00**
　U.K.:   **£185.00**

HN 2376
Indian Brave
Designer: M. Davies
Height: 16", 40.6 cm
Colour: Multicoloured
Issued: 1967 in a limited
              edition of 500
　U.S.:   **$5,000.00**
　Can.:   **$6,000.00**
　U.K.:   **£2,750.00**

HN 2377
Georgina
Style One
Designer: M. Davies
Height: 5 ¾", 14.6 cm
Colour: Red and yellow
Issued: 1981-1986
Series: Kate Greenaway
　U.S.:   **$275.00**
　Can.:   **$350.00**
　U.K.:   **£150.00**

HN 2378
Simone
Style One
Designer: M. Davies
Height: 7 ¼", 18.4 cm
Colour: Green
Issued: 1971-1981
　U.S.:   **$200.00**
　Can.:   **$250.00**
　U.K.:   **£110.00**

HN 2379
Ninette
Style One
Designer: M. Davies
Height: 7 ½", 19.1 cm
Colour: Yellow and cream
Issued: 1971-1997
Varieties: HN 3417; also called
              'Olivia' (Style Two)
              HN 3339
　U.S.:   **$225.00**
　Can.:   **$275.00**
　U.K.:   **£125.00**

HN 2380
Sweet Dreams
Style One
Designer: M. Davies
Height: 5", 12.7 cm
Colour: Multicoloured
Issued: 1971-1990

U.S.:	$250.00
Can.:	$300.00
U.K.:	£135.00

HN 2381
Kirsty
Style One
Designer: M. Davies
Height: 7 ½", 19.1 cm
Colour: Orange
Issued: 1971-1996
Varieties: Also called 'Janette' HN 3415

U.S.:	$250.00
Can.:	$300.00
U.K.:	£135.00

Note: This model is also known without the foot appearing at the base of the dress.

HN 2382
Secret Thoughts
Style One
Designer: M. Davies
Height: 6 ¼", 15.9 cm
Colour: Green
Issued: 1971-1988

U.S.:	$250.00
Can.:	$300.00
U.K.:	£135.00

HN 2383
Breton Dancer
Designer: M. Davies
Height: 8 ½", 21.6 cm
Colour: Blue and white
Issued: 1981 in a limited edition of 750
Series: Dancers of the World

U.S.:	$ 900.00
Can.:	$1,100.00
U.K.:	£ 500.00

HN 2384
West Indian Dancer
Designer: M. Davies
Height: 8 ¾", 22.2 cm
Colour: Yellow and white
Issued: 1981 in a limited edition of 750
Series: Dancers of the World

U.S.:	$ 900.00
Can.:	$1,100.00
U.K.:	£ 500.00

HN 2385
Debbie
Designer: M. Davies
Height: 5 ½", 14.0 cm
Colour: Blue and white
Issued: 1969-1982
Varieties: HN 2400; 'Lavender Rose' 3481; 'Memory Lane' 3746; 'Moonlight Rose' 3483; 'Old Country Roses' 3482; 'Tranquillity' 3747

U.S.:	$125.00
Can.:	$160.00
U.K.:	£ 75.00

HN 2386
HRH Prince Philip
Duke of Edinburgh
Designer: M. Davies
Height: 8 ¼", 21.0 cm
Colour: Black and gold
Issued: 1981 in a limited edition of 1500

U.S.:	$400.00
Can.:	$500.00
U.K.:	£220.00

HN 2387
Helen of Troy
Style One
Designer: M. Davies
Height: 9 ¼", 23.5 cm
Colour: Green and pink
Issued: 1981 in a limited edition of 750
Series: Les Femmes Fatales

U.S.:	$1,400.00
Can.:	$1,700.00
U.K.:	£ 750.00

HN 2388
Karen
Style Two
Designer: M. Davies
Height: 8", 20.3 cm
Colour: Red and white
Issued: 1982-1999

U.S.:   **$350.00**
Can.:   **$450.00**
U.K.:   **£200.00**

HN 2389
Angela
Style Two
Designer: M. Davies
Height: 7 ½", 19.1 cm
Colour: White
Issued: 1983-1986
Series   Vanity Fair Ladies

U.S.:   **$250.00**
Can.:   **$300.00**
U.K.:   **£135.00**

HN 2390
Spinning
Designer: M. Davies
Height: 7 ¼", 18.4 cm
Colour: Yellow, pink, blue
            and white
Issued: 1984 in a limited
            edition of 750
Series: Gentle Arts

U.S.:   **$1,750.00**
Can.:   **$2,100.00**
U.K.:   **£   950.00**

HN 2391
T'zu-hsi, Empress Dowager
Designer: M. Davies
Height: 8", 20.3 cm
Colour: Red, white and blue
Issued: 1983 in a limited
            edition of 750
Series: Les Femmes Fatales

U.S.:   **$1,400.00**
Can.:   **$1,700.00**
U.K.:   **£   775.00**

HN 2392
Jennifer
Style Two
Designer: M. Davies
Height: 7", 17.8 cm
Colour: Blue
Issued: 1982-1992

U.S.:   **$350.00**
Can.:   **$450.00**
U.K.:   **£200.00**

HN 2393
Rosalind
Designer: M. Davies
Height: 5 ½", 14.0 cm
Colour: Blue
Issued: 1970-1975

U.S.:   **$300.00**
Can.:   **$375.00**
U.K.:   **£165.00**

HN 2394
Lisa
Style One
Designer: M. Davies
Height: 7 ¼", 18.4 cm
Colour: Purple-yellow
Issued: 1983-1990
Varieties: HN 2310, 3265

U.S.:   **$225.00**
Can.:   **$275.00**
U.K.:   **£125.00**

HN 2395
Catherine
Style One
Designer: M. Davies
Height: 7 ½", 19.1 cm
Colour: Red and yellow
Issued: 1983-1984
Series: Ladies of Covent
            Garden
Comm.by: Amex

U.S.:   **$525.00**
Can.:   **$650.00**
U.K.:   **£300.00**

HN 2396
Wistful
Style One
Designer: M. Davies
Height: 6 ½", 16.5 cm
Colour: Peach and cream
Issued: 1979-1990
Varieties: HN 2472

U.S.:	**$325.00**
Can.:	**$400.00**
U.K.:	**£175.00**

HN 2397
Margaret
Style Two
Designer: M. Davies
Height: 7 ½", 19.1 cm
Colour: White dress,
blue sash
Issued: 1982-1999
Varieties: HN 3496; 'Adele'
HN 2480; 'Camille'
(Style Two) HN 3171
Series: Vanity Fair Ladies

U.S.:	**$250.00**
Can.:	**$300.00**
U.K.:	**£135.00**

HN 2398
Alexandra
Style One
Designer: M. Davies
Height: 7 ¾", 19.7 cm
Colour: Patterned green
dress, yellow cape
Issued: 1970-1976

U.S.:	**$300.00**
Can.:	**$375.00**
U.K.:	**£165.00**

HN 2399
Buttercup
Style One
Designer: M. Davies
Height: 7", 17.8 cm
Colour: Red dress with
yellow sleeves
Issued: 1983-1997
Varieties: HN 2309

U.S.:	**$300.00**
Can.:	**$375.00**
U.K.:	**£165.00**

HN 2400
Debbie
Designer: M. Davies
Height: 5 ½", 14.0 cm
Colour: Peach
Issued: 1983-1995
Varieties: HN 2385; 'Lavender
Rose', 3481;
'Memory Lane', 3746;
'Moonlight Rose' 3483;
'Old Country Roses'
(Style One) 3482;
'Tranquillity' 3747

U.S.:	**$150.00**
Can.:	**$190.00**
U.K.:	**£ 85.00**

HN 2401
Sandra
Designer: M. Davies
Height: 7 ¾", 19.7 cm
Colour: Green
Issued: 1983-1992
Varieties: HN 2275; Also
called 'Annette'
(Style Two) HN 3495

U.S.:	**$275.00**
Can.:	**$350.00**
U.K.:	**£150.00**

HN 2402 - 2407 not issued.

HN 2408
A Penny's Worth
Designer: M. Nicoll
Height: 7", 17.8 cm
Colour: Pale blue, yellow
and white
Issued: 1986-1990

U.S.:	**$275.00**
Can.:	**$325.00**
U.K.:	**£150.00**

HN 2409 not issued.

HN 2410
Lesley
Designer: M. Nicoll
Height: 8", 20.3 cm
Colour: Orange and yellow
Issued: 1986-1990

U.S.:	**$275.00**
Can.:	**$350.00**
U.K.:	**£150.00**

HN 2411 - 2416 not issued.

HN 2417
The Boatman 'Skylark'
Designer: M. Nicoll
Height: 6 ½", 16.5 cm
Colour: Yellow
Issued: 1971-1987
Varieties: HN 2417A
Series: Sea Characters

U.S.:	**$325.00**
Can.:	**$400.00**
U.K.:	**£175.00**

HN 2417A
The Boatman 'Pilot'
Designer: M. Nicoll
Height: 6 ½", 16.5 cm
Colour: Yellow
Issued: 1971-1987
Varieties: HN 2417
Series: Sea Characters
Comm.by: Pilot Insurance

U.S.:	
Can.:	**Rare**
U.K.:	

HN 2418
Country Love
Designer: J. Bromley
Height: 8", 20.3 cm
Colour: Pink flowered dress
Issued: 1990 in a limited
            edition of 12,500
Comm.by: Lawleys By Post

U.S.:	**$450.00**
Can.:	**$550.00**
U.K.:	**£250.00**

HN 2419
The Goose Girl
Style Two
Designer: J. Bromley
Height: 8", 20.3 cm
Colour: Blue and white
Issued: 1990 in a limited
            edition of 12,500
Comm.by: Lawleys By Post

U.S.:	**$450.00**
Can.:	**$550.00**
U.K.:	**£250.00**

HN 2420
The Shepherdess
Style Four
Designer: J. Bromley
Height: 9", 22.9 cm
Colour: Peach, blue and white
Issued: 1991 in a limited
            edition of 12,500
Comm.by: Lawleys By Post

U.S.:	**$450.00**
Can.:	**$550.00**
U.K.:	**£250.00**

HN 2421
Charlotte
Style One
Designer: J. Bromley
Height: 6 ½", 16.5 cm
Colour: Purple
Issued: 1972-1986
Varieties: HN 2423

U.S.:	**$250.00**
Can.:	**$300.00**
U.K.:	**£140.00**

HN 2422
Francine
(Bird's tail up)
Designer: J. Bromley
Height: 5", 12.7 cm
Colour: Green and white
Issued: 1972-Unknown
Varieties: HN 2422A (Bird's tail
            moulded to hand)

U.S.:	**$175.00**
Can.:	**$210.00**
U.K.:	**£ 95.00**

HN 2422A
Francine
(Bird's tail moulded to hand)
Designer: J. Bromley
Height: 5", 12.7 cm
Colour: Green and white
Issued: Unknown-1981
Varieties: HN 2422 (Bird's tail up)

U.S.:	**$125.00**
Can.:	**$150.00**
U.K.:	**£ 70.00**

HN 2423
Charlotte
Style One
Designer: J. Bromley
Height: 6 ½", 16.5 cm
Colour: Pale blue and pink
Issued: 1986-1992
Varieties: HN 2421

U.S.:	**$250.00**
Can.:	**$325.00**
U.K.:	**£140.00**

HN 2424
Penny
Designer: M. Davies
Height: 4 ¾", 12.0 cm
Colour: Yellow and white
Issued: 1983-1992
Varieties: HN 2338

U.S.:	**$125.00**
Can.:	**$150.00**
U.K.:	**£ 70.00**

Also known with yellow underskirt.

HN 2425
Southern Belle
Style One
Designer: M. Davies
Height: 7 ½", 19.1 cm
Colour: Pale blue and pink
Issued: 1983-1994
Varieties: HN 2229

U.S.:	**$250.00**
Can.:	**$300.00**
U.K.:	**£135.00**

HN 2426
Tranquility
Style One
Designer: M. Davies
Height: 12", 30.5 cm
Colour: Black
Issued: 1981-1986
Varieties: HN 2469
Series: Images

U.S.:	**$175.00**
Can.:	**$225.00**
U.K.:	**£100.00**

HN 2427
Virginals
Designer: M. Davies
Height: 6 ¼", 15.9 cm
Colour: Green, gold
           and brown
Issued: 1971 in a limited
           edition of 750
Series: Lady Musicians

U.S.:	**$1,750.00**
Can.:	**$2,250.00**
U.K.:	**£1,000.00**

HN 2428
The Palio
Designer: M. Davies
Height: 17 ½", 44.5 cm
Colour: Blue, yellow
           and brown
Issued: 1971 in a limited
           edition of 500

U.S.:	**$ 9,000.00**
Can.:	**$11,000.00**
U.K.:	**£ 5,000.00**

HN 2429
Elyse
Designer: M. Davies
Height: 5 ¾", 14.6 cm
Colour: Blue
Issued: 1972-1995
Varieties: HN 2474, 4131

U.S.:	**$250.00**
Can.:	**$300.00**
U.K.:	**£135.00**

HN 2430
Romance
Style Two
Designer: M. Davies
Height: 5 ¼", 13.3 cm
Colour: Gold and green
Issued: 1972-1981

U.S.:	**$250.00**
Can.:	**$300.00**
U.K.:	**£135.00**

HN 2431
Lute
Designer: M. Davies
Height: 6 ¼", 15.9 cm
Colour: Blue, white and brown
Issued: 1972 in a limited
            edition of 750
Series: Lady Musicians
    U.S.:   **$1,100.00**
    Can.:   **$1,350.00**
    U.K.:   £ **600.00**

HN 2432
Violin
Designer: M. Davies
Height: 6 ¼", 15.9 cm
Colour: Brown and gold
Issued: 1972 in a limited
            edition of 750
Series: Lady Musicians
    U.S.:   **$1,100.00**
    Can.:   **$1,350.00**
    U.K.:   £ **600.00**

HN 2433
Peace
Style One
Designer: M. Davies
Height: 8", 20.3 cm
Colour: Black
Issued: 1981-1997
Varieties: HN 2470
Series: Images
    U.S.:   **$150.00**
    Can.:   **$180.00**
    U.K.:   £ **80.00**

Flambé model known.

HN 2434
Fair Maiden
Designer: M. Davies
Height: 5 ¼", 13.3 cm
Colour: Red and white
Issued: 1983-1994
Varieties: HN 2211
    U.S.:   **$125.00**
    Can.:   **$150.00**
    U.K.:   £ **70.00**

HN 2435
Queen of the Ice
Designer: M. Davies
Height: 8", 20.3 cm
Colour: Cream
Issued: 1983-1986
Series: Enchantment
    U.S.:   **$250.00**
    Can.:   **$300.00**
    U.K.:   £**135.00**

HN 2436
Scottish Highland Dancer
Designer: M. Davies
Height: 9 ½", 24.1 cm
Colour: Red, black and white
Issued: 1978 in a limited
            edition of 750
Series: Dancers of the World
    U.S.:   **$1,750.00**
    Can.:   **$2,100.00**
    U.K.:   £ **950.00**

HN 2437
Queen of the Dawn
Designer: M. Davies
Height: 8 ½", 21.6 cm
Colour: Cream
Issued: 1983-1986
Series: Enchantment
    U.S.:   **$250.00**
    Can.:   **$300.00**
    U.K.:   £**135.00**

HN 2438
Sonata
Designer: M. Davies
Height: 6 ½", 16.5 cm
Colour: Cream
Issued: 1983-1985
Series: Enchantment
    U.S.:   **$250.00**
    Can.:   **$300.00**
    U.K.:   £**135.00**

HN 2439
Philippine Dancer
Designer: M. Davies
Height: 9 ½", 24.1 cm
Colour: Green and cream
Issued: 1978 in a limited
edition of 750
Series: Dancers of the World

U.S.:	**$1,000.00**
Can.:	**$1,250.00**
U.K.:	**£ 550.00**

HN 2440
Cynthia
Style Two
Designer: M. Davies
Height: 7 ¼", 18.4 cm
Colour: Green and yellow
Issued: 1984-1992

U.S.:	**$350.00**
Can.:	**$425.00**
U.K.:	**£200.00**

HN 2441
Pauline
Style Two
Designer: M. Davies
Height: 5", 12.7 cm
Colour: Peach
Issued: 1983 Canada,
1984 Worldwide-1989

U.S.:	**$400.00**
Can.:	**$475.00**
U.K.:	**£215.00**

HN 2442
Sailor's Holiday
Designer: M. Nicoll
Height: 6 ¼", 15.9 cm
Colour: Gold, brown and white
Issued: 1972-1979
Series: Sea Characters

U.S.:	**$475.00**
Can.:	**$575.00**
U.K.:	**£260.00**

HN 2443
The Judge (matte)
Style One
Designer: M. Nicoll
Height: 6 ½", 16.5 cm
Colour: Red and white
Issued: 1972-1976
Varieties: HN 2443A (gloss)

U.S.:	**$300.00**
Can.:	**$350.00**
U.K.:	**£165.00**

HN 2443A
The Judge (gloss)
Style One
Designer: M. Nicoll
Height: 6 ½", 16.5 cm
Colour: Red and white
Issued: 1976-1992
Varieties: HN 2443 (matte)

U.S.:	**$300.00**
Can.:	**$350.00**
U.K.:	**£165.00**

HN 2444
Bon Appetit (matte)
Designer: M. Nicoll
Height: 6", 15.2 cm
Colour: Grey and brown
Issued: 1972-1976

U.S.:	**$250.00**
Can.:	**$300.00**
U.K.:	**£135.00**

HN 2445
Parisian (matte)
Designer: M. Nicoll
Height: 8", 20.3 cm
Colour: Blue and grey
Issued: 1972-1975

U.S.:	**$250.00**
Can.:	**$300.00**
U.K.:	**£135.00**

HN 2446
Thanksgiving (matte)
Designer: M. Nicoll
Height: 8", 20.3 cm
Colour: Blue, pink and grey
Issued: 1972-1976

U.S.:	**$275.00**
Can.:	**$330.00**
U.K.:	**£150.00**

HN 2447 - 2454 not issued.

HN 2455
The Seafarer (matte)
Designer: M. Nicoll
Height: 8 ½", 21.6 cm
Colour: Gold, blue and grey
Issued: 1972-1976
Series: Sea Characters

U.S.:	**$325.00**
Can.:	**$400.00**
U.K.:	**£175.00**

HN 2456 - 2459 not issued.

HN 2460
Flower of Love
Designer: John Bromley
Height: 7 ½", 19.1 cm
Colour: White and yellow
Issued: 1991 Canada
           1992 Worldwide-1997
Varieties: HN 3970; also called
           'Fleur' (Style One)
           HN 2368, 2369
Series: Vanity Fair Ladies

U.S.:	**$225.00**
Can.:	**$275.00**
U.K.:	**£125.00**

HN 2461
Janine
Designer: J. Bromley
Height: 7 ½", 19.1 cm
Colour: Turquoise and white
Issued: 1971-1995

U.S.:	**$225.00**
Can.:	**$275.00**
U.K.:	**£125.00**

HN 2462 not issued.

HN 2463
Olga
Designer: J. Bromley
Height: 8 ¼", 21.0 cm
Colour: Turquoise and gold
Issued: 1972-1975

U.S.:	**$275.00**
Can.:	**$330.00**
U.K.:	**£150.00**

HN 2464 not issued.

HN 2465
Elizabeth
Style Two
Designer: J. Bromley
Height: 8 ½", 21.6 cm
Colour: Blue
Issued: 1990-1998

U.S.:	**$350.00**
Can.:	**$450.00**
U.K.:	**£200.00**

HN 2466
Eve
Designer: M. Davies
Height: 9 ¼", 23.5 cm
Colour: Green and brown
Issued: 1984 in a limited
           edition of 750
Series: Les Femmes Fatales

U.S.:	**$1,400.00**
Can.:	**$1,700.00**
U.K.:	**£ 750.00**

HN 2467
Melissa
Style One
Designer: M. Davies
Height: 6 ¾", 17.2 cm
Colour: Purple and cream
Issued: 1981-1994

U.S.:	**$275.00**
Can.:	**$325.00**
U.K.:	**£150.00**

HN 2468
Diana
Style Two
Designer: M. Davies
Height: 8", 20.3 cm
Colour: Flowered white dress
Issued: 1986 N. America,
 1987 Worldwide-1999
Varieties: HN 3266

U.S.:	**$225.00**
Can.:	**$275.00**
U.K.:	**£125.00**

HN 2469
Tranquility
Style One
Designer: M. Davies
Height: 12", 30.5 cm
Colour: White
Issued: 1981-1986
Varieties: HN 2426
Series: Images

U.S.:	**$150.00**
Can.:	**$175.00**
U.K.:	**£ 85.00**

HN 2470
Peace
Style One
Designer: M. Davies
Height: 8", 20.3 cm
Colour: White
Issued: 1981-2000
Varieties: HN 2433
Series: Images

U.S.:	**$100.00**
Can.:	**$125.00**
U.K.:	**£ 60.00**

Flambé model known.

HN 2471
Victoria
Style One
Designer: M. Davies
Height: 6 ½", 16.5 cm
Colour: Patterned pink dress
Issued: 1973-2000
Varieties: HN 3416

U.S.:	**$300.00**
Can.:	**$375.00**
U.K.:	**£175.00**

HN 2472
Wistful
Style One
Designer: M. Davies
Height: 6 ½", 16.5 cm
Colour: Blue and white
Issued: 1985-1985
Varieties: HN 2396
Series: M. Doulton Events

U.S.:	**$350.00**
Can.:	**$450.00**
U.K.:	**£200.00**

HN 2473
At Ease
Designer: M. Davies
Height: 6", 15.2 cm
Colour: Yellow
Issued: 1973-1979

U.S.:	**$350.00**
Can.:	**$450.00**
U.K.:	**£200.00**

HN 2474
Elyse
Designer: M. Davies
Height: 5 ¾", 14.6 cm
Colour: Patterned green dress
Issued: 1986 N. America,
 1987 Worldwide-1999
Varieties: HN 2429, 4131

U.S.:	**$400.00**
Can.:	**$500.00**
U.K.:	**£225.00**

HN 2475
Vanity
Designer: M. Davies
Height: 5 ¼", 13.3 cm
Colour: Red
Issued: 1973-1992

U.S.:	**$125.00**
Can.:	**$150.00**
U.K.:	**£ 75.00**

HN 2476
Mandy
Designer: M. Davies
Height: 4 ½", 11.4 cm
Colour: White
Issued: 1982-1992
  U.S.:   **$100.00**
  Can.: **$125.00**
  U.K.: **£ 60.00**

HN 2477
Denise
Style Three
Designer: M. Davies
Height: 7 ½", 19.1 cm
Colour: White
Issued: 1987-1996
Varieties: Also called 'Summer
         Rose' (Style Two)
         HN 3309
Series: Vanity Fair Ladies
  U.S.:   **$200.00**
  Can.: **$250.00**
  U.K.: **£110.00**

HN 2478
Kelly
Style One
Designer: M. Davies
Height: 7 ½", 19.1 cm
Colour: White with blue flowers
Issued: 1985-1992
Varieties: HN 3222
  U.S.:   **$275.00**
  Can.: **$325.00**
  U.K.: **£150.00**

HN 2479
Pamela
Style Two
Designer: M. Davies
Height: 7", 17.8 cm
Colour: White
Issued: 1986-1994
Varieties: HN 3223
Series: Vanity Fair Ladies
  U.S.:   **$200.00**
  Can.: **$250.00**
  U.K.: **£110.00**

HN 2480
Adele
Designer: M. Davies
Height: 8", 20.3 cm
Colour: Flowered white dress
Issued: 1987-1992
Varieties: Also called 'Camille'
         (Style Two) HN 3171;
         'Margaret' (Style Two)
         HN 2397, 3496
  U.S.:   **$225.00**
  Can.: **$275.00**
  U.K.: **£125.00**

HN 2481
Maureen
Style Three
Designer: M. Davies
Height: 7 ½", 19.1 cm
Colour: White dress,
         purple flowers
Issued: 1987-1992
Varieties: Also called 'Tina'
         HN 3494
Series: Vanity Fair Ladies
  U.S.:   **$225.00**
  Can.: **$275.00**
  U.K.: **£125.00**

HN 2482
Harp
Designer: M. Davies
Height: 8 ¾", 22.2 cm
Colour: Purple, green and gold
Issued: 1973 in a limited
         edition of 750
Series: Lady Musicians
  U.S.:   **$1,800.00**
  Can.: **$2,250.00**
  U.K.: **£1,000.00**

HN 2483
Flute
Designer: M. Davies
Height: 6", 15.2 cm
Colour: Red and white
Issued: 1973 in a limited
         edition of 750
Series: Lady Musicians
  U.S.:   **$1,100.00**
  Can.: **$1,325.00**
  U.K.: **£ 600.00**

HN 2484
Past Glory
Designer: M. Nicoll
Height: 7 ½", 19.1 cm
Colour: Red and black
Issued: 1973-1979

U.S.:	**$450.00**
Can.:	**$550.00**
U.K.:	**£250.00**

HN 2485
Lunchtime
Designer: M. Nicoll
Height: 8", 20.3 cm
Colour: Brown
Issued: 1973-1981

U.S.:	**$350.00**
Can.:	**$425.00**
U.K.:	**£190.00**

HN 2486 not issued.

HN 2487
Beachcomber (matte)
Designer: M. Nicoll
Height: 6 ½", 15.9 cm
Colour: Purple and grey
Issued: 1973-1976

U.S.:	**$250.00**
Can.:	**$300.00**
U.K.:	**£135.00**

HN 2488 - 2491 not issued.

HN 2492
Huntsman
Style Three
Designer: M. Nicoll
Height: 7 ½", 19.1 cm
Colour: Grey and cream
Issued: 1974-1979

U.S.:	**$400.00**
Can.:	**$475.00**
U.K.:	**£220.00**

HN 2493 not issued.

HN 2494
Old Meg (matte)
Designer: M. Nicoll
Height: 8 ¼", 21.0 cm
Colour: Blue and grey
Issued: 1974-1976

U.S.:	**$250.00**
Can.:	**$300.00**
U.K.:	**£135.00**

HN 2495 - 2498 not issued.

HN 2499
Helmsman
Designer: M. Nicoll
Height: 9", 22.9 cm
Colour: Brown
Issued: 1974-1986
Series: Sea Characters

U.S.:	**$400.00**
Can.:	**$475.00**
U.K.:	**£220.00**

HN 2500 - 2501 Animal figures.

HN 2502
Queen Elizabeth II
Style One
Designer: M. Davies
Height: 7 ¾", 19.7 cm
Colour: Pale blue
Issued: 1973 in a limited
            edition of 750

U.S.:	**$1,500.00**
Can.:	**$1,800.00**
U.K.:	**£ 850.00**

HN 2503 - 2519 Animal figures.

HN 2520
The Farmer's Boy
Designer: W. M. Chance
Height: 8 ½", 21.6 cm
Colour: White, brown
            and green
Issued: 1938-1960

U.S.:	**$2,250.00**
Can.:	**$2,750.00**
U.K.:	**£1,200.00**

HN 2521
Dapple Grey
Designer: W. M. Chance
Height: 7 ¼", 18.4 cm
Colour: White, red and brown
Issued: 1938-1960

U.S.:	**$4,000.00**
Can.:	**$4,750.00**
U.K.:	**£2,200.00**

HN 2522 - 2541 Animal and Bird figures.

HN 2542
Boudoir
Designer: E. J. Griffiths
Height: 12 ¼", 31.1 cm
Colour: Pale blue
Issued: 1974-1979
Series: Haute Ensemble

U.S.:	**$375.00**
Can.:	**$475.00**
U.K.:	**£225.00**

HN 2543
Eliza
(Handmade flowers)
Style One
Designer: E. J. Griffiths
Height: 11 ¾", 29.8 cm
Colour: Gold
Issued: 1974-1979
Varieties: HN 2543A
Series: Haute Ensemble

U.S.:	**$275.00**
Can.:	**$350.00**
U.K.:	**£150.00**

HN 2543A
Eliza
(Painted flowers)
Style One
Designer: E. J. Griffiths
Height: 11 ¾", 29.8 cm
Colour: Gold
Issued: 1974-1979
Varieties: HN 2543
Series: Haute Ensemble

U.S.:	**$225.00**
Can.:	**$275.00**
U.K.:	**£125.00**

HN 2544
A la Mode
Designer: E. J. Griffiths
Height: 12 ¼", 31.1 cm
Colour: Green
Issued: 1974-1979
Series: Haute Ensemble

U.S.:	**$275.00**
Can.:	**$350.00**
U.K.:	**£150.00**

HN 2545
Carmen
Style Two
Designer: E. J. Griffiths
Height: 11 ½", 29.2 cm
Colour: Blue
Issued: 1974-1979
Series: Haute Ensemble

U.S.:	**$300.00**
Can.:	**$375.00**
U.K.:	**£175.00**

HN 2546
Buddies (matte)
Style One
Designer: E. J. Griffiths
Height: 6", 15.2 cm
Colour: Blue and brown
Issued: 1973-1976

U.S.:	**$275.00**
Can.:	**$325.00**
U.K.:	**£150.00**

HN 2547
R.C.M.P. 1973
Designer: D. V. Tootle
Height: 8", 20.3 cm
Colour: Red
Issued: 1973 in a limited
              edition of 1,500

U.S.:	**$750.00**
Can.:	**$900.00**
U.K.:	**£400.00**

HN 2548 - 2553 Bird figures.

HN 2554
Masque
(Hand holds wand of mask)
Designer: D. V. Tootle
Height: 8 ½", 21.6 cm
Colour: Blue
Issued: 1973-1975
Varieties: HN 2554A

U.S.:	**$400.00**
Can.:	**$500.00**
U.K.:	**£220.00**

HN 2554A
Masque
(Hand holds mask to face)
Designer: D. V. Tootle
Height: 8 ½", 21.6 cm
Colour: Blue
Issued: 1975-1982
Varieties: HN 2554

U.S.:	**$275.00**
Can.:	**$330.00**
U.K.:	**£150.00**

HN 2555
R.C.M.P. 1873
Designer: D. V. Tootle
Height: 8 ¼", 21.0 cm
Colour: Red
Issued: 1973 in a limited
edition of 1,500

U.S.:	**$750.00**
Can.:	**$900.00**
U.K.:	**£400.00**

HN 2556 - 2670 Animal and Bird
figures, except HN 2627 not issued.

HN 2671
Good Morning (matte)
Designer: M. Nicoll
Height: 8", 20.3 cm
Colour: Blue, pink and brown
Issued: 1974-1976

U.S.:	**$275.00**
Can.:	**$325.00**
U.K.:	**£150.00**

HN 2672 - 2676 not issued.

HN 2677
Taking Things Easy
Designer: M. Nicoll
Height: 6 ¾", 17.2 cm
Colour: Blue, white and brown
Issued: 1975-1987
Varieties: HN 2680

U.S.:	**$325.00**
Can.:	**$400.00**
U.K.:	**£175.00**

HN 2678
The Carpenter
Designer: M. Nicoll
Height: 8", 20.3 cm
Colour: Blue, white and brown
Issued: 1986-1992

U.S.:	**$500.00**
Can.:	**$600.00**
U.K.:	**£275.00**

HN 2679
Drummer Boy
Designer: M. Nicoll
Height: 8 ½", 21.6 cm
Colour: Multicoloured
Issued: 1976-1981

U.S.:	**$500.00**
Can.:	**$600.00**
U.K.:	**£275.00**

HN 2680
Taking Things Easy
Designer: M. Nicoll
Height: 6 ¾", 17.2 cm
Colour: Cream and blue
Issued: 1987-1996
Varieties: HN 2677

U.S.:	**$325.00**
Can.:	**$400.00**
U.K.:	**£175.00**

HN 2681 - 2682 not issued.

HN 2683
Stop Press
Designer: M. Nicoll
Height: 7 ½", 19.1 cm
Colour: Brown, blue and white
Issued: 1977-1981
  U.S.:   **$275.00**
  Can.:   **$330.00**
  U.K.:   **£150.00**

HN 2684 - 2692 not issued.

HN 2693
October
Style One
Designer: M. Davies
Height: 7 ¾", 19.5 cm
Colour: White with blue dress,
           cosmos flowers
Issued: 1987-1987
Varieties: Also called 'Gillian'
           (Style Three) HN 3742
Series: Figure of the Month
  U.S.:   **$225.00**
  Can.:   **$275.00**
  U.K.:   **£125.00**

HN 2694
Fiona
Style Two
Designer: M. Davies
Height: 7 ½", 19.1 cm
Colour: Red and white
Issued: 1974-1981
  U.S.:   **$250.00**
  Can.:   **$300.00**
  U.K.:   **£135.00**

HN 2695
November
Style One
Designer: M. Davies
Height: 7 ¾", 19.7 cm
Colour: White with pink dress,
           chrysanthemum
           flowers
Issued: 1987-1987
Varieties: Also called 'Gillian'
           (Style Three) HN 3742
Series: Figure of the Month
  U.S.:   **$225.00**
  Can.:   **$275.00**
  U.K.:   **£125.00**

HN 2696
December
Style One
Designer: M. Davies
Height: 7 ¾", 19.7 cm
Colour: White with green dress,
           Christmas rose flowers
Issued: 1987-1987
Varieties: Also called 'Gillian'
           (Style Three) HN 3742
Series: Figure of the Month
  U.S.:   **$225.00**
  Can.:   **$275.00**
  U.K.:   **£125.00**

HN 2697
January
Style One
Designer: M. Davies
Height: 7 ¾", 19.7 cm
Colour: White with green dress,
           snowdrop flowers
Issued: 1987-1987
Varieties: Also called 'Gillian'
           (Style Three) HN 3742
Series: Figure of the Month
  U.S.:   **$225.00**
  Can.:   **$275.00**
  U.K.:   **£125.00**

HN 2698
Sunday Best
Style One
Designer: M. Davies
Height: 7 ½", 19.1 cm
Colour: Pink and white
Issued: 1985-1995
Varieties: HN 2206
  U.S.:   **$225.00**
  Can.:   **$275.00**
  U.K.:   **£125.00**

HN 2699
Cymbals
Designer: M. Davies
Height: 7 ½", 19.1 cm
Colour: Green and gold
Issued: 1974 in a limited
           edition of 750
Series: Lady Musicians
  U.S.:   **$ 900.00**
  Can.:   **$1,100.00**
  U.K.:   **£ 500.00**

HN 2700
Chitarrone
Designer: M. Davies
Height: 7 ½", 19.1 cm
Colour: Blue
Issued: 1974 in a limited
edition of 750
Series: Lady Musicians
U.S.: **$1,100.00**
Can.: **$1,350.00**
U.K.: **£ 600.00**

HN 2701
Deborah
Style One
Designer: M. Davies
Height: 7 ¾", 19.7 cm
Colour: Green and white
Issued: 1983-1984
Series: Ladies of Covent
Garden
Comm.by: Amex
U.S.: **$525.00**
Can.: **$650.00**
U.K.: **£300.00**

HN 2702
Shirley
Designer: M. Davies
Height: 7 ¼", 18.4 cm
Colour: White dress with
pink flowers
Issued: 1985-1997
U.S.: **$250.00**
Can.: **$300.00**
U.K.: **£135.00**

HN 2703
February
Style One
Designer: M. Davies
Height: 7 ¾", 19.7 cm
Colour: White with purple
dress, violet flowers
Issued: 1987-1987
Varieties: Also called 'Gillian'
(Style Three) HN 3742
Series: Figure of the Month
U.S.: **$225.00**
Can.: **$275.00**
U.K.: **£125.00**

HN 2704
Pensive Moments
Designer: M. Davies
Height: 5", 12.7 cm
Colour: Blue
Issued: 1975-1981
U.S.: **$325.00**
Can.: **$400.00**
U.K.: **£175.00**

HN 2705
Julia
Style One
Designer: M. Davies
Height: 7 ½", 19.1 cm
Colour: Gold
Issued: 1975-1990
Varieties: HN 2706
U.S.: **$225.00**
Can.: **$275.00**
U.K.: **£125.00**

HN 2706
Julia
Style One
Designer: M. Davies
Height: 7 ½", 19.1 cm
Colour: Pink and green
Issued: 1985-1993
Varieties: HN 2705
U.S.: **$225.00**
Can.: **$275.00**
U.K.: **£125.00**

HN 2707
March
Style One
Designer: M. Davies
Height: 7 ¾", 19.7 cm
Colour: White and green dress,
anemone flowers
Issued: 1987-1987
Varieties: Also called 'Gillian'
(Style Three) HN 3742
Series: Figure of the Month
U.S.: **$225.00**
Can.: **$275.00**
U.K.: **£125.00**

HN 2708
April
Style One
Designer: M. Davies
Height: 7 ¾", 19.7 cm
Colour: White and tan dress,
            sweet pea flowers
Issued: 1987-1987
Varieties: Also called 'Gillian'
            (Style Three) HN 3742
Series: Figure of the Month

U.S.:	**$225.00**
Can.:	**$275.00**
U.K.:	**£125.00**

HN 2709
Regal Lady
Designer: M. Davies
Height: 7 ½", 19.1 cm
Colour: Turquoise and cream
Issued: 1975-1983

U.S.:	**$275.00**
Can.:	**$350.00**
U.K.:	**£150.00**

HN 2710
Jean
Style Two
Designer: M. Davies
Height: 5 ¾", 14.6 cm
Colour: White
Issued: 1983-1986
Series: Vanity Fair Ladies

U.S.:	**$250.00**
Can.:	**$300.00**
U.K.:	**£135.00**

HN 2711
May
Style Two
Designer: M. Davies
Height: 7 ¾", 19.7 cm
Colour: White and green dress,
            lily of the valley flowers
Issued: 1987-1987
Varieties: Also called 'Gillian'
            (Style Three) HN 3742
Series: Figure of the Month

U.S.:	**$225.00**
Can.:	**$275.00**
U.K.:	**£125.00**

HN 2712
Mantilla
Designer: E. J. Griffiths
Height: 11 ½", 29.2 cm
Colour: Red, black and white
Issued: 1974-1979
Varieties: HN 3192
Series: Haute Ensemble

U.S.:	**$425.00**
Can.:	**$525.00**
U.K.:	**£230.00**

HN 2713
Tenderness
Designer: E. J. Griffiths
Height: 12", 30.5 cm
Colour: White
Issued: 1982-1997
Varieties: HN 2714
Series: Images

U.S.:	**$150.00**
Can.:	**$180.00**
U.K.:	**£ 80.00**

HN 2714
Tenderness
Designer: E. J. Griffiths
Height: 12", 30.5 cm
Colour: Black
Issued: 1982-1992
Varieties: HN 2713
Series: Images

U.S.:	**$175.00**
Can.:	**$225.00**
U.K.:	**£100.00**

HN 2715
Patricia
Style Three
Designer: M. Davies
Height: 7 ½", 19.1 cm
Colour: White
Issued: 1982-1985
Series: Vanity Fair Ladies

U.S.:	**$275.00**
Can.:	**$350.00**
U.K.:	**£150.00**

HN 2716
Cavalier
Style Two
Designer: E. J. Griffiths
Height: 9 ¾", 24.7 cm
Colour: Brown and green
Issued: 1976-1982

  U.S.: $300.00
  Can.: $350.00
  U.K.: £165.00

Flambé pilot piece known

HN 2717
Private, 2nd South Carolina
Regiment, 1781
Designer: E. J. Griffiths
Height: 11 ½", 29.2 cm
Colour: Blue and cream
Issued: 1975 in a limited
               edition of 350
Series: Soldiers of the
               Revolution

  U.S.: $1,600.00
  Can.: $2,000.00
  U.K.: £   900.00

HN 2718
Lady Pamela
Designer: D. V. Tootle
Height: 8", 20.3 cm
Colour: Purple
Issued: 1974-1981

  U.S.: $275.00
  Can.: $350.00
  U.K.: £150.00

HN 2719
Laurianne
Designer: D. V. Tootle
Height: 6 ¼", 15.9 cm
Colour: Dark blue and white
Issued: 1974-1979

  U.S.: $250.00
  Can.: $300.00
  U.K.: £135.00

HN 2720
Family
Style One
Designer: E. J. Griffiths
Height: 12", 30.5 cm
Colour: White
Issued: 1981-2002
Varieties: HN 2721
Series: Images

  U.S.: $200.00
  Can.: $250.00
  U.K.: £110.00

HN 2721
Family
Style One
Designer: E. J. Griffiths
Height: 12", 30.5 cm
Colour: Black
Issued: 1981-1992
Varieties: HN 2720
Series: Images

  U.S.: $200.00
  Can.: $250.00
  U.K.: £110.00

HN 2722
Veneta
Designer: W. K. Harper
Height: 8", 20.3 cm
Colour: Green and white
Issued: 1974-1981

  U.S.: $250.00
  Can.: $300.00
  U.K.: £135.00

HN 2723
Grand Manner
Designer: W. K. Harper
Height: 7 ¾", 19.7 cm
Colour: Lavender-yellow
Issued: 1975-1981

  U.S.: $275.00
  Can.: $350.00
  U.K.: £150.00

HN 2724
Clarinda
Designer: W. K. Harper
Height: 8 ½", 21.6 cm
Colour: Blue and white
Issued: 1975-1981

U.S.:	**$275.00**
Can.:	**$325.00**
U.K.:	**£150.00**

HN 2725
Santa Claus
Style One
Designer: W. K. Harper
Height: 9 ¾", 24.7 cm
Colour: Red and white
Issued: 1982-1993

U.S.:	**$500.00**
Can.:	**$600.00**
U.K.:	**£275.00**

HN 2726
Centurian
Designer: W. K. Harper
Height: 9 ¼", 23.5 cm
Colour: Grey and purple
Issued: 1982-1984

U.S.:	**$300.00**
Can.:	**$375.00**
U.K.:	**£175.00**

HN 2727
Little Miss Muffet
Designer: W. K. Harper
Height: 6 ¼", 15.9 cm
Colour: White and pink
Issued: 1984-1987
Series: Nursery Rhymes
             (Series Two)

U.S.:	**$225.00**
Can.:	**$275.00**
U.K.:	**£120.00**

HN 2728
Rest Awhile
Designer: W. K. Harper
Height: 8", 20.3 cm
Colour: Blue, white and purple
Issued: 1981-1984

U.S.:	**$300.00**
Can.:	**$375.00**
U.K.:	**£175.00**

HN 2729
Song of the Sea
Designer: W. K. Harper
Height: 7 ¼", 18.4 cm
Colour: Blue and grey
Issued: 1982 Canada,
             1983 Worldwide -1991
Series: Sea Characters

U.S.:	**$500.00**
Can.:	**$600.00**
U.K.:	**£275.00**

HN 2731
Thanks Doc
Designer: W. K. Harper
Height: 8 ¾", 22.2 cm
Colour: White and brown
Issued: 1975-1990

U.S.:	**$425.00**
Can.:	**$500.00**
U.K.:	**£230.00**

HN 2732
Thank You
Style One
Designer: W. K. Harper
Height: 8 ¼", 21.0 cm
Colour: White, brown and blue
Issued: 1982 Canada,
             1983 Worldwide-1986

U.S.:	**$325.00**
Can.:	**$400.00**
U.K.:	**£175.00**

HN 2730 not issued.

HN 2733
Officer of the Line
Designer:	W. K. Harper
Height:	9", 22.9 cm
Colour:	Red and yellow
Issued:	1982 Canada,
	1983 Worldwide-1986
Series:	Sea Characters
U.S.:	**$525.00**
Can.:	**$625.00**
U.K.:	**£285.00**

HN 2734
Sweet Seventeen
Designer:	D. V. Tootle
Height:	7 ½", 19.1 cm
Colour:	White with gold trim
Issued:	1975-1993
U.S.:	**$275.00**
Can.:	**$350.00**
U.K.:	**£150.00**

HN 2735
Young Love
Designer:	D. V. Tootle
Height:	10", 25.4 cm
Colour:	Cream, green,
	blue and brown
Issued:	1975-1990
U.S.:	**$650.00**
Can.:	**$800.00**
U.K.:	**£350.00**

HN 2736
Tracy
Designer:	D. V. Tootle
Height:	7 ½", 19.1 cm
Colour:	White
Issued:	1983-1994
Varieties:	HN 3291
Series:	Vanity Fair Ladies
U.S.:	**$225.00**
Can.:	**$275.00**
U.K.:	**£125.00**

HN 2737
Harlequin
Style Two
Designer:	D. V. Tootle
Height:	12 ½", 31.7 cm
Colour:	Multicoloured
Issued:	1982 to the present
Varieties:	HN 3287, 4058
Series:	Prestige
U.S.:	**$1,500.00**
Can.:	**$2,900.00**
U.K.:	**£1,900.00**

HN 2738
Columbine
Style Three
Designer:	D. V. Tootle
Height:	12 ½", 31.7 cm
Colour:	Flowered pink
	and blue dress
Issued:	1982 to the present
Varieties:	HN 3288, 4059
Series:	Prestige
U.S.:	**$1,500.00**
Can.:	**$2,900.00**
U.K.:	**£1,900.00**

HN 2739
Ann
Style One
Designer:	D. V. Tootle
Height:	7 ¾", 19.7 cm
Colour:	White
Issued:	1983-1985
Series:	Vanity Fair Ladies
U.S.:	**$250.00**
Can.:	**$300.00**
U.K.:	**£135.00**

HN 2740
Becky
Style One
Designer:	D. V. Tootle
Height:	8", 20.3 cm
Colour:	Green, yellow
	and cream
Issued:	1987-1992
U.S.:	**$275.00**
Can.:	**$350.00**
U.K.:	**£150.00**

HN 2741
Sally
Style One
Designer: D. V. Tootle
Height: 5 ½", 14.0 cm
Colour: Red and lavender
Issued: 1987-1991
   U.S.: $225.00
   Can.: $275.00
   U.K.:   £125.00

HN 2742
Sheila
Designer: D. V. Tootle
Height: 8 ¼", 21.0 cm
Colour: Pale blue flowered
            dress
Issued: 1983 Canada,
            1984 Worldwide -1991
   U.S.: $250.00
   Can.: $300.00
   U.K.:   £135.00

HN 2743
Meg
Designer: D. V. Tootle
Height: 8", 20.3 cm
Colour: Lavender and yellow
Issued: 1987-1991
   U.S.: $250.00
   Can.: $300.00
   U.K.:   £135.00

HN 2744
Modesty
Designer: D. V. Tootle
Height: 8 ½", 21.6 cm
Colour: White
Issued: 1987-1991
   U.S.: $250.00
   Can.: $300.00
   U.K.:   £135.00

HN 2745
Florence
Designer: D. V. Tootle
Height: 8", 20.3 cm
Colour: Purple
Issued: 1987-1992
   U.S.: $325.00
   Can.: $400.00
   U.K.:   £175.00

HN 2746
May
Style One
Designer: D. V. Tootle
Height: 8", 20.3 cm
Colour: Blue, red and green
Issued: 1987-1992
Varieties: HN 3251
   U.S.: $325.00
   Can.: $400.00
   U.K.:   £175.00

HN 2747
First Love
Designer: D. V. Tootle
Height: 13", 33.0 cm
Colour: White
Issued: 1987-1997
Series: Images
   U.S.: $150.00
   Can.: $200.00
   U.K.:   £ 85.00

HN 2748
Wedding Day
Designer: D. V. Tootle
Height: 12 ½", 31.7 cm
Colour: White
Issued: 1987-2003
Series: Images
   U.S.: $225.00
   Can.: $275.00
   U.K.:   £125.00

HN 2749
Lizzie
Designer: D. V. Tootle
Height: 8 ¼", 21.0 cm
Colour: Green, white and red
Issued: 1988-1991
   U.S.:   **$250.00**
   Can.:   **$300.00**
   U.K.:   **£135.00**

HN 2750
Wedding Vows
Style One
Designer: D. V. Tootle
Height: 8", 20.3 cm
Colour: White
Issued: 1988-1992
   U.S.:   **$275.00**
   Can.:   **$350.00**
   U.K.:   **£150.00**

HN 2751
Encore
Style One
Designer: D. V. Tootle
Height: 10", 25.4 cm
Colour: Lavender, white
             and blue
Issued: 1988-1989
Series: Reflections
   U.S.:   **$275.00**
   Can.:   **$350.00**
   U.K.:   **£150.00**

HN 2752
Major, 3rd New Jersey Regiment,
1776
Designer: E. J. Griffiths
Height: 10", 25.4 cm
Colour: Blue and brown
Issued: 1975 in a limited
             edition of 350
Series: Soldiers of the
             Revolution
   U.S.:   **$2,100.00**
   Can.:   **$2,500.00**
   U.K.:   **£1,150.00**

HN 2753
Serenade
Designer: E. J. Griffiths
Height: 9", 22.9 cm
Colour: Cream
Issued: 1983-1985
Series: Enchantment
   U.S.:   **$200.00**
   Can.:   **$250.00**
   U.K.:   **£110.00**

HN 2754
Private, 3rd North Carolina
Regiment, 1778
Designer: E. J. Griffiths
Height: 11", 27.9 cm
Colour: Tan
Issued: 1976 in a limited
             edition of 350
Series: Soldiers of the
             Revolution
   U.S.:   **$1,600.00**
   Can.:   **$2,000.00**
   U.K.:   **£ 900.00**

HN 2755
Captain, 2nd New York
Regiment, 1775
Designer: E. J. Griffiths
Height: 10", 25.4 cm
Colour: Brown
Issued: 1976 in a limited
             edition of 350
Series: Soldiers of the
             Revolution
   U.S.:   **$1,600.00**
   Can.:   **$2,000.00**
   U.K.:   **£ 900.00**

HN 2756
Musicale
Designer: E. J. Griffiths
Height: 9", 22.9 cm
Colour: Cream
Issued: 1983-1985
Series: Enchantment
   U.S.:   **$200.00**
   Can.:   **$250.00**
   U.K.:   **£110.00**

HN 2757
Lyric
Designer: E. J. Griffiths
Height: 6 ¼", 15.9 cm
Colour: Cream
Issued: 1983-1985
Series: Enchantment
U.S.: $175.00
Can.: $225.00
U.K.: £100.00

HN 2758
Linda
Style Two
Designer: E. J. Griffiths
Height: 7 ¾", 19.7 cm
Colour: White with pink trim
Issued: 1984-1988
Series: Vanity Fair Ladies
U.S.: $225.00
Can.: $275.00
U.K.: £125.00

HN 2759
Private, Rhode Island Regiment, 1781
Designer: E. J. Griffiths
Height: 11 ¾", 29.8 cm
Colour: Grey
Issued: 1977 in a limited edition of 350
Series: Soldiers of the Revolution
U.S.: $1,600.00
Can.: $2,000.00
U.K.: £ 900.00

HN 2760
Private, Massachusetts Regiment, 1778
Designer: E. J. Griffiths
Height: 12 ½", 31.7 cm
Colour: Blue and tan
Issued: 1977 in a limited edition of 350
Series: Soldiers of the Revolution
U.S.: $1,600.00
Can.: $2,000.00
U.K.: £ 900.00

HN 2761
Private, Delaware Regiment, 1776
Designer: E. J. Griffiths
Height: 12", 30.5 cm
Colour: Blue and tan
Issued: 1977 in a limited edition of 350
Series: Soldiers of the Revolution
U.S.: $1,600.00
Can.: $2,000.00
U.K.: £ 900.00

HN 2762
Lovers
Designer: D. V. Tootle
Height: 12", 30.5 cm
Colour: White
Issued: 1981-1997
Varieties: HN 2763
Series: Images
U.S.: $250.00
Can.: $300.00
U.K.: £135.00

Also known in flambé.

HN 2763
Lovers
Designer: D. V. Tootle
Height: 12", 30.5 cm
Colour: Black
Issued: 1981-1992
Varieties: HN 2762
Series: Images
U.S.: $250.00
Can.: $300.00
U.K.: £135.00

Also known in flambé.

HN 2764
The Lifeboat Man
Designer: W. K. Harper
Height: 9 ¼", 23.5 cm
Colour: Yellow
Issued: 1987-1991
Series: Sea Characters
U.S.: $450.00
Can.: $550.00
U.K.: £240.00

HN 2765
Punch and Judy Man
Designer: W. K. Harper
Height: 9", 22.9 cm
Colour: Green and yellow
Issued: 1981-1990

U.S.: $475.00
Can.: $575.00
U.K.: £260.00

HN 2766
Autumn Glory
Designer: W. K. Harper
Height: 11 ¾", 29.9 cm
Colour: Blue-grey and tan
Issued: 1988 in a limited
edition of 1,000
Series: Reflections
Comm.by: Home Shopping
Network, Florida

U.S.: $325.00
Can.: $400.00
U.K.: £175.00

HN 2767
Pearly Boy
Style Three
Designer: W. K. Harper
Height: 7 ½", 19.1 cm
Colour: Black, white and blue
Issued: 1988-1992

U.S.: $300.00
Can.: $350.00
U.K.: £160.00

The first year of issue 1988, was
allocated to the Guild of Specialist
China and Glass Retailers, and
carried their backstamp.

HN 2768
Pretty Polly
Designer: W. K. Harper
Height: 6", 15.2 cm
Colour: Pink and white
Issued: 1984-1986

U.S.: $275.00
Can.: $325.00
U.K.: £150.00

HN 2769
Pearly Girl
Style Three
Designer: W. K. Harper
Height: 7 ½", 19.1 cm
Colour: Black, white and blue
Issued: 1988-1992

U.S.: $300.00
Can.: $350.00
U.K.: £160.00

The first year of issue 1988, was
allocated to the Guild of Specialist
China and Glass Retailers, and
carried their backstamp.

HN 2770
New Companion
Designer: W. K. Harper
Height: 7 ¾", 19.7 cm
Colour: Purple, white
and black
Issued: 1982-1985

U.S.: $325.00
Can.: $400.00
U.K.: £175.00

HN 2771
Charlie Chaplin
Designer: W. K. Harper
Height: 9", 22.9 cm
Colour: Grey
Issued: 1989 in a limited
edition of 5,000
Series: Entertainers
Comm.by: Lawleys By Post

U.S.: $400.00
Can.: $500.00
U.K.: £225.00

HN 2772
Ritz Bell Boy
Designer: W. K. Harper
Height: 8", 20.3 cm
Colour: Black
Issued: 1989-1993

U.S.: $300.00
Can.: $375.00
U.K.: £165.00

HN 2773
Robin Hood
Style One
Designer:　W. K. Harper
Height:　7 ¾", 19.7 cm
Colour:　Green
Issued:　1985-1990

U.S.:	**$325.00**
Can.:	**$400.00**
U.K.:	**£175.00**

HN 2774
Stan Laurel
Designer:　W. K. Harper
Height:　9 ¼", 23.5 cm
Colour:　Grey-black
Issued:　1990 in a limited
　　　　edition of 9,500
Series:　Entertainers
Comm.by:　Lawleys By Post

U.S.:	**$500.00**
Can.:	**$600.00**
U.K.:	**£275.00**

HN 2775
Oliver Hardy
Designer:　W. K. Harper
Height:　10", 25.4 cm
Colour:　Black and grey
Issued:　1990 in a limited
　　　　edition of 9,500
Series:　Entertainers
Comm.by:　Lawleys By Post

U.S.:	**$500.00**
Can.:	**$600.00**
U.K.:	**£275.00**

HN 2776
Carpet Seller
(Standing)
Style Two
Designer:　W. K. Harper
Height:　9", 22.9 cm
Colour:　Flambé
Issued:　1990-1995
Series:　Flambé

U.S.:	**$625.00**
Can.:	**$775.00**
U.K.:	**£350.00**

HN 2777
Groucho Marx
Designer:　W. K. Harper
Height:　9 ½", 24.1 cm
Colour:　Black and grey
Issued:　1991 in a limited
　　　　edition of 9,500
Series:　Entertainers
Comm.by:　Lawleys By Post

U.S.:	**$525.00**
Can.:	**$650.00**
U.K.:	**£300.00**

HN 2778
The Bobby
Designer:　W. K. Harper
Height:　9", 22.9 cm
Colour:　Black
Issued:　1992-1995

U.S.:	**$325.00**
Can.:	**$400.00**
U.K.:	**£175.00**

HN 2779
Private, 1ˢᵗ Georgia Regiment,
1777
Designer:　E. J. Griffiths
Height:　11", 27.9 cm
Colour:　Light brown
Issued:　1975 in a limited
　　　　edition of 350
Series:　Soldiers of the
　　　　Revolution

U.S.:	**$1,600.00**
Can.:	**$2,000.00**
U.K.:	**£　900.00**

HN 2780
Corporal, 1ˢᵗ New Hampshire
Regiment, 1778
Designer:　E. J. Griffiths
Height:　13", 33.0 cm
Colour:　Green
Issued:　1975 in a limited
　　　　edition of 350
Series:　Soldiers of the
　　　　Revolution

U.S.:	**$1,600.00**
Can.:	**$2,000.00**
U.K.:	**£　900.00**

HN 2781
The Lifeguard
Designer: W. K. Harper
Height: 9 ½", 24.1 cm
Colour: Red, black and white
Issued: 1992-1995

   U.S.:   **$350.00**
   Can.:   **$425.00**
   U.K.:   **£200.00**

HN 2782
The Blacksmith
Style One
Designer: W. K. Harper
Height: 9", 22.9 cm
Colour: Brown, white and grey
Issued: 1987-1991

   U.S.:   **$350.00**
   Can.:   **$425.00**
   U.K.:   **£200.00**

HN 2783
Good Friends
Designer: W. K. Harper
Height: 9", 22.9 cm
Colour: Blue and brown
Issued: 1985-1990

   U.S.:   **$350.00**
   Can.:   **$425.00**
   U.K.:   **£200.00**

HN 2784
The Guardsman
Designer: W. K. Harper
Height: 9 ¾", 24.8 cm
Colour: Red, black and white
Issued: 1992-1995

   U.S.:   **$350.00**
   Can.:   **$425.00**
   U.K.:   **£200.00**

HN 2785 - 2787 not issued.

HN 2788
Marjorie
Designer: M. Davies
Height: 5 ¼", 13.3 cm
Colour: Pale blue
Issued: 1980-1984

   U.S.:   **$350.00**
   Can.:   **$425.00**
   U.K.:   **£200.00**

HN 2789
Kate
Style One
Designer: M. Davies
Height: 7 ½", 19.1 cm
Colour: Flowered white dress
Issued: 1978-1987

   U.S.:   **$250.00**
   Can.:   **$300.00**
   U.K.:   **£135.00**

HN 2790
June
Style Three
Designer: M. Davies
Height: 7 ¾", 19.7 cm
Colour: White and pink
   dress with roses
Issued: 1987-1987
Varieties: Also called 'Gillian'
   (Style Three) HN 3742
Series: Figure of the Month

   U.S.:   **$225.00**
   Can.:   **$275.00**
   U.K.:   **£125.00**

HN 2791
Elaine
Style One
Designer: M. Davies
Height: 7 ½", 19.1 cm
Colour: Blue
Issued: 1980-2000
Varieties: HN 3307, 3741, 4130

   U.S.:   **$300.00**
   Can.:   **$400.00**
   U.K.:   **£175.00**

HN 2792
Christine
Style Two
Designer: M. Davies
Height: 7 ½", 19.1 cm
Colour: Flowered blue and
             white dress
Issued: 1978-1994
Varieties: HN 3172

  U.S.:   **$300.00**
  Can.:   **$375.00**
  U.K.:   **£175.00**

HN 2793
Clare
Designer: M. Davies
Height: 7 ½", 19.1 cm
Colour: Flowered lavender
             dress
Issued: 1980-1984

  U.S.:   **$300.00**
  Can.:   **$375.00**
  U.K.:   **£175.00**

HN 2794
July
Style One
Designer: M. Davies
Height: 7 ¾", 19.7 cm
Colour: White dress;
             Forget-me-not flowers
Issued: 1987-1987
Varieties: Also called 'Gillian'
             (Style Three) HN 3742
Series: Figure of the Month

  U.S.:   **$225.00**
  Can.:   **$275.00**
  U.K.:   **£125.00**

HN 2795
French Horn
Designer: M. Davies
Height: 6", 15.2 cm
Colour: Purple and turquoise
Issued: 1976 in a limited
             edition of 750
Series: Lady Musicians

  U.S.:   **$1,100.00**
  Can.:   **$1,350.00**
  U.K.:   **£ 600.00**

HN 2796
Hurdy Gurdy
Designer: M. Davies
Height: 6", 15.2 cm
Colour: Turquoise and white
Issued: 1975 in a limited
             edition of 750
Series: Lady Musicians

  U.S.:   **$1,100.00**
  Can.:   **$1,350.00**
  U.K.:   **£ 600.00**

HN 2797
Viola d'Amore
Designer: M. Davies
Height: 6", 15.2 cm
Colour: Pale blue and yellow
Issued: 1976 in a limited
             edition of 750
Series: Lady Musicians

  U.S.:   **$1,100.00**
  Can.:   **$1,350.00**
  U.K.:   **£ 600.00**

HN 2798
Dulcimer
Designer: M. Davies
Height: 6 ½", 16.5 cm
Colour: Lavender and cream
Issued: 1975 in a limited
             edition of 750
Series: Lady Musicians

  U.S.:   **$1,100.00**
  Can.:   **$1,350.00**
  U.K.:   **£ 600.00**

HN 2799
Ruth
Style One
Designer: M. Davies
Height: 6", 15.2 cm
Colour: Green
Issued: 1976-1981
Series: Kate Greenaway

  U.S.:   **$325.00**
  Can.:   **$400.00**
  U.K.:   **£175.00**

HN 2800
Carrie
Designer: M. Davies
Height: 6", 15.2 cm
Colour: Turquoise
Issued: 1976-1981
Series: Kate Greenaway

U.S.:	**$300.00**
Can.:	**$375.00**
U.K.:	**£165.00**

HN 2801
Lori
Designer: M. Davies
Height: 5 ¾", 14.6 cm
Colour: Yellow-cream
Issued: 1976-1987
Series: Kate Greenaway

U.S.:	**$300.00**
Can.:	**$375.00**
U.K.:	**£165.00**

HN 2802
Anna
Style One
Designer: M. Davies
Height: 5 ¾", 14.6 cm
Colour: Purple and white
Issued: 1976-1982
Series: Kate Greenaway

U.S.:	**$300.00**
Can.:	**$375.00**
U.K.:	**£165.00**

HN 2803
First Dance
Designer: M. Davies
Height: 7 ¼", 18.4 cm
Colour: Pale blue
Issued: 1977-1992
Varieties: Also called 'Samantha' (Style Two) HN 3304

U.S.:	**$250.00**
Can.:	**$300.00**
U.K.:	**£135.00**

HN 2804
Nicola
Designer: M. Davies
Height: 7", 17.8 cm
Colour: Red and lilac
Issued: 1987-1987
Varieties: HN 2839; also called 'Tender Moment' (Style One) HN 3303
Series: M. Doulton Events

U.S.:	**$325.00**
Can.:	**$400.00**
U.K.:	**£175.00**

HN 2805
Rebecca
Style One
Designer: M. Davies
Height: 7 ¼", 18.4 cm
Colour: Pale blue and lavender
Issued: 1980-1996

U.S.:	**$500.00**
Can.:	**$600.00**
U.K.:	**£275.00**

HN 2806
Jane
Style Two
Designer: M. Davies
Height: 8", 20.3 cm
Colour: Yellow
Issued: 1982-1986

U.S.:	**$300.00**
Can.:	**$375.00**
U.K.:	**£175.00**

HN 2807
Stephanie
Style One
Designer: M. Davies
Height: 7 ¼", 18.4 cm
Colour: Gold
Issued: 1977-1982
Varieties: HN 2811

U.S.:	**$250.00**
Can.:	**$300.00**
U.K.:	**£135.00**

HN 2808
Balinese Dancer
Designer: M. Davies
Height: 8 ¾", 22.2 cm
Colour: Green and yellow
Issued: 1982 in a limited
                   edition of 750
Series: Dancers of the World
   U.S.: $ 900.00
   Can.: $1,100.00
   U.K.:   £ 500.00

HN 2809
North American Indian Dancer
Designer: M. Davies
Height: 8 ½", 21.6 cm
Colour: Yellow
Issued: 1982 in a limited
                   edition of 750
Series: Dancers of the World
   U.S.: $ 900.00
   Can.: $1,100.00
   U.K.:   £ 500.00

HN 2810
Solitude
Designer: M. Davies
Height: 5 ½", 14.0 cm
Colour: Cream, blue
                   and orange
Issued: 1977-1983
   U.S.: $450.00
   Can.: $550.00
   U.K.:   £250.00

HN 2811
Stephanie
Style One
Designer: M. Davies
Height: 7 ¼", 18.4 cm
Colour: Red and white
Issued: 1983-1994
Varieties: HN 2807
   U.S.: $300.00
   Can.: $375.00
   U.K.:   £175.00

HN 2812 - 2813 not issued.

HN 2814
Eventide
Designer: W. K. Harper
Height: 7 ¾", 19.7 cm
Colour: Blue, white, red,
                   yellow and green
Issued: 1977-1991
   U.S.: $275.00
   Can.: $350.00
   U.K.:   £150.00

HN 2815
Sergeant, 6th Maryland
Regiment, 1777
Designer: E. J. Griffiths
Height: 13 ¾", 34.9 cm
Colour: Light grey
Issued: 1976 in a limited
                   edition of 350
Series: Soldiers of the
                   Revolution
   U.S.: $1,600.00
   Can.: $2,000.00
   U.K.:   £ 900.00

HN 2816
Votes for Women
Designer: W. K. Harper
Height: 9 ¾", 24.7 cm
Colour: Gold and grey
Issued: 1978-1981
   U.S.: $350.00
   Can.: $425.00
   U.K.:   £200.00

HN 2817 not issued.

HN 2818
Balloon Girl
Designer: W. K. Harper
Height: 6 ½", 16.5 cm
Colour: Green, white,
                   grey and red
Issued: 1982-1997
   U.S.: $400.00
   Can.: $500.00
   U.K.:   £225.00

HN 2819 - 2823 not issued.

HN 2824
Harmony
Style One
Designer: R. Jefferson
Height: 8", 20.3 cm
Colour: Grey
Issued: 1978-1984

U.S.: $325.00
Can.: $400.00
U.K.: £175.00

HN 2825
Lady and the Unicorn
Designer: R. Jefferson
Height: 8 ¾", 22.2 cm
Colour: Blue, white and red
Issued: 1982 in a limited
edition of 300
Series: Myths and Maidens

U.S.: $2,250.00
Can.: $2,750.00
U.K.: £1,200.00

HN 2826
Leda and the Swan
Designer: R. Jefferson
Height: 9 ¾", 24.7 cm
Colour: Yellow, green,
red and blue
Issued: 1983 in a limited
edition of 300
Series: Myths and Maidens

U.S.: $2,250.00
Can.: $2,750.00
U.K.: £1,200.00

HN 2827
Juno and the Peacock
Designer: R. Jefferson
Height: 11", 27.9 cm
Colour: Turquoise, lavender
and gold
Issued: 1984 in a limited
edition of 300
Series: Myths and Maidens

U.S.: $2,250.00
Can.: $2,750.00
U.K.: £1,200.00

HN 2828
Europa and the Bull
Style Two
Designer: R. Jefferson
Height: 10 ½", 26.5 cm
Colour: Yellow, orange, white
and lavender
Issued: 1985 in a limited
edition of 300
Series: Myths and Maidens

U.S.: $2,250.00
Can.: $2,750.00
U.K.: £1,200.00

HN 2829
Diana the Huntress
Designer: R. Jefferson
Height: 11 ¼", 28.6 cm
Colour: Green and gold
Issued: 1986 in a limited
edition of 300
Series: Myths and Maidens

U.S.: $2,250.00
Can.: $2,750.00
U.K.: £1,200.00

HN 2830
Indian Temple Dancer
Designer: M. Davies
Height: 9 ¼", 23.5 cm
Colour: Gold
Issued: 1977 in a limited
edition of 750
Series: Dancers of the World

U.S.: $1,400.00
Can.: $1,675.00
U.K.: £ 750.00

HN 2831
Spanish Flamenco Dancer
Designer: M. Davies
Height: 9 ½", 24.1 cm
Colour: Red and white
Issued: 1977 in a limited
edition of 750
Series: Dancers of the World

U.S.: $1,750.00
Can.: $2,100.00
U.K.: £ 950.00

HN 2832
Fair Lady
Style One
Designer:	M. Davies
Height:	7 ¼", 18.4 cm
Colour:	Red and white
Issued:	1977-1996
Varieties:	HN 2193, 2835; also called 'Kay' HN 3340

U.S.:	**$225.00**
Can.:	**$275.00**
U.K.:	**£125.00**

HN 2833
Sophie
Style One
Designer:	M. Davies
Height:	6", 15.2 cm
Colour:	Red and grey
Issued:	1977-1987
Series:	Kate Greenaway

U.S.:	**$325.00**
Can.:	**$400.00**
U.K.:	**£175.00**

HN 2834
Emma
Style One
Designer:	M. Davies
Height:	5 ¾", 14.6 cm
Colour:	Pink and white
Issued:	1977-1981
Series:	Kate Greenaway

U.S.:	**$350.00**
Can.:	**$450.00**
U.K.:	**£200.00**

HN 2835
Fair Lady
Style One
Designer:	M. Davies
Height:	7 ¼", 18.4 cm
Colour:	Peach
Issued:	1977-1996
Varieties:	HN 2193, 2832; also called 'Kay' HN 3340

U.S.:	**$225.00**
Can.:	**$275.00**
U.K.:	**£125.00**

HN 2836
Polish Dancer
Designer:	M. Davies
Height:	9 ½", 24.1 cm
Colour:	Multicoloured
Issued:	1980 in a limited edition of 750
Series:	Dancers of the World

U.S.:	**$ 950.00**
Can.:	**$1,150.00**
U.K.:	**£ 525.00**

HN 2837
Awakening
Style Two
Designer:	M. Davies
Height:	8 ½", 21.6 cm
Colour:	Black
Issued:	1981-1997
Varieties:	HN 2875
Series:	Images

U.S.:	**$150.00**
Can.:	**$175.00**
U.K.:	**£ 85.00**

Also known in Flambé

HN 2838
Sympathy
Designer:	M. Davies
Height:	11 ¾", 29.8 cm
Colour:	Black
Issued:	1981-1986
Varieties:	HN 2876
Series:	Images

U.S.:	**$200.00**
Can.:	**$250.00**
U.K.:	**£110.00**

HN 2839
Nicola
Designer:	M. Davies
Height:	7", 17.8 cm
Colour:	Flowered lavender dress
Issued:	1978-1995
Varieties:	HN 2804; also called 'Tender Moment' HN 3303

U.S.:	**$350.00**
Can.:	**$450.00**
U.K.:	**£200.00**

CHARACTER FIGURES

HN 2217
Old King Cole
1963-1967

HN 2250
The Toymaker
1959-1973

HN 2253
The Puppetmaker
1962-1973

HN 2204
Long John Silver
Style One, 1957-1965

HN 2205
Master Sweep
1957-1962

HN 2226
The Cellist
1960-1967

CHARACTER FIGURES

HN 2042
Owd Willum
1949-1973

HN 2043
The Poacher
1949-1959

HN 2068
Calumet
1950-1953

HN 2053
The Gaffer
1950-1959

HN 2118
Good King Wenceslas
Style One, 1953-1976

HN 2119
Town Crier
Style One, 1953-1976

CHARACTER FIGURES

HN 2171
The Fiddler
1956-1962

HN 2163
In The Stocks
Style Two, 1955-1959

HN 2161
The Hornpipe
1955-1962

HN 2172
Jolly Sailor
1956-1965

HN 2173
The Organ Grinder
1956-1965

HN 2174
The Tailor
1956-1959

QUEENS

HN 4073
Margaret of Anjou
Style Two
1998 Limited edition of 5,000

HN 4066
Philippa of Hainault
Style Two
1998 Limited edition of 5,000

HN 3957
Eleanor of Aquitaine
1997 Limited edition of 5,000

HN 4074
Sophia Dorothea
1998 Limited edition of 2,500

HN 4266
Anne of Denmark
(Wife of James I)
2001 Limited edition of 2,500

KINGS

HN 4022
William III
1998 Limited edition of 1,500

HN 3824
Charles I
1997 Limited edition of 1,500

HN 4263
Edward VI
2000 Limited edition of 5,000

HN 3822
James I
1996 Limited edition of 1,500

HN 3825
Charles II
1996 Limited edition of 1,500

REFLECTIONS

HN 2992
Golfer
1988-1991

HN 3039
Reflection
1987-1991

HN 3083
Sheikh
1987-1989

HN 3160
Shepherd, Style Five
1988-1989

HN 3161
The Gardener
1988-1991

HN 3185
Traveller's Tale
1988-1989

CLOWNS

HN 3293
Tip-Toe
1990-1994

HN 3119
Partners
1990-1992

HN 2277
Slapdash
1990-1994

HN 2252
The Joker, Style Two
1990-1992

HN 3196
The Joker, Style One
1988-1990

HN 3275
Will He, Won't He
1990-1994

HN 3283
Tumbling
1990-1994

FLAMBÉ FIGURINES

HN 2999
The Genie

HN 3229
The Geisha
Style Three, 1989-1989

HN 3277
The Carpet Seller
Style Three, 1990-1995

HN 3278
Lamp Seller
1990-1995

HN 3314
Confucius
1990-1995

HN 3402
Samurai Warrior
1992 Limited edition of 950

HN 2840
Chinese Dancer
Designer: M. Davies
Height: 9", 22.9 cm
Colour: Red, green, purple
and lavender
Issued: 1980 in a limited
edition of 750
Series: Dancers of the World
U.S.: $ 950.00
Can.: $1,150.00
U.K.: £ 525.00

HN 2841
Mother and Daughter
Style One
Designer: E. J. Griffiths
Height: 8 ½", 21.6 cm
Colour: White
Issued: 1981-1997
Varieties: HN 2843; also known
in flambé
Series: Images
U.S.: $200.00
Can.: $250.00
U.K.: £110.00

HN 2842
Innocence
Style One
Designer: E. J. Griffiths
Height: 7 ½", 19.1 cm
Colour: Red
Issued: 1979-1983
U.S.: $225.00
Can.: $300.00
U.K.: £125.00

HN 2843
Mother and Daughter
Style One
Designer: E. J. Griffiths
Height: 8 ½", 21.6 cm
Colour: Black
Issued: 1981-1992
Varieties: HN 2841
Series: Images
U.S.: $200.00
Can.: $250.00
U.K.: £110.00

Also known in flambé

HN 2844
Sergeant, Virginia 1st Regiment Continental Light Dragoons, 1777
Designer: E. J. Griffiths
Height: 14 ¼", 36.1 cm
Colour: Brown and green
Issued: 1978 in a limited
edition of 350
Series: Soldiers of the
Revolution
U.S.: $5,000.00
Can.: $6,500.00
U.K.: £3,000.00

HN 2845
Private, Connecticut Regiment, 1777
Designer: E. J. Griffiths
Height: 11 ¼", 28.5 cm
Colour: Brown and cream
Issued: 1978 in a limited
edition of 350
Series: Soldiers of the
Revolution
U.S.: $1,600.00
Can.: $2,000.00
U.K.: £ 900.00

HN 2846
Private, Pennsylvania Rifle Battalion, 1776
Designer: E. J. Griffiths
Height: 8", 20.3 cm
Colour: Grey
Issued: 1978 in a limited
edition of 350
Series: Soldiers of the
Revolution
U.S.: $1,600.00
Can.: $2,000.00
U.K.: £ 900.00

HN 2847 - 2850 not issued.

HN 2851
Christmas Parcels
Style One
Designer: W. K. Harper
Height: 8 ¾", 22.2 cm
Colour: Black
Issued: 1978-1982
U.S.: $350.00
Can.: $425.00
U.K.: £195.00

HN 2852 - 2854 not issued.

HN 2855
Embroidering
Designer: W. K. Harper
Height: 7 ¼", 18.4 cm
Colour: Grey
Issued: 1980-1990

U.S.:	**$375.00**
Can.:	**$450.00**
U.K.:	**£210.00**

HN 2856
St. George
Style Three
Designer: W. K. Harper
Height: 16", 40.6 cm
Colour: Cream and grey
Issued: 1978-1994

U.S.:	**$7,000.00**
Can.:	**$9,000.00**
U.K.:	**£4,000.00**

HN 2857
Covent Garden
Style Two
Designer: W. K. Harper
Height: 10", 25.4 cm
Colour: Pale blue and white
Issued: 1988-1990
Series: Reflections

U.S.:	**$275.00**
Can.:	**$325.00**
U.K.:	**£150.00**

HN 2858
The Doctor
Style One
Designer: W. K. Harper
Height: 7 ½", 19.1 cm
Colour: Black and grey
Issued: 1979-1992

U.S.:	**$300.00**
Can.:	**$375.00**
U.K.:	**£165.00**

HN 2859
The Statesman
Designer: W. K. Harper
Height: 9", 22.9 cm
Colour: Black and grey
Issued: 1988-1990
Varieties: Also called 'Sir John
            A. MacDonald'
            HN 2860

U.S.:	**$250.00**
Can.:	**$300.00**
U.K.:	**£150.00**

HN 2860
Sir John A. MacDonald
Designer: W. K. Harper
Height: 9", 22.9 cm
Colour: Black and grey
Issued: 1987-1987
Varieties: Also called 'The
            Statesman' HN 2859

U.S.:	**$300.00**
Can.:	**$350.00**
U.K.:	**£165.00**

HN 2861
**George Washington
at Prayer**
Designer: L. Ispanky
Height: 12 ½", 31.7 cm
Colour: Blue and tan
Issued: 1977 in a limited
            edition of 750

U.S.:	**$2,850.00**
Can.:	**$3,750.00**
U.K.:	**£1,650.00**

HN 2862
First Waltz
Designer: M. Davies
Height: 7 ¼", 18.4 cm
Colour: Red
Issued: 1979-1983

U.S.:	**$375.00**
Can.:	**$450.00**
U.K.:	**£210.00**

HN 2863
Lucy
Style One
Designer: M. Davies
Height: 6", 15.2 cm
Colour: Blue and white
Issued: 1980-1984
Series: Kate Greenaway

U.S.: $300.00
Can.: $350.00
U.K.: £165.00

HN 2864
Tom
Designer: M. Davies
Height: 5 ¾", 14.6 cm
Colour: Blue and yellow
Issued: 1978-1981
Series: Kate Greenaway

U.S.: $400.00
Can.: $475.00
U.K.: £215.00

HN 2865
Tess
Designer: M. Davies
Height: 5 ¾", 14.6 cm
Colour: Green
Issued: 1978-1983
Series: Kate Greenaway

U.S.: $300.00
Can.: $350.00
U.K.: £165.00

HN 2866
Mexican Dancer
Designer: M. Davies
Height: 8 ¼", 21.0 cm
Colour: Gold and white
Issued: 1979 in a limited
edition of 750
Series: Dancers of the World

U.S.: $ 950.00
Can.: $1,150.00
U.K.: £ 525.00

HN 2867
Kurdish Dancer
Designer: M. Davies
Height: 8 ¼", 21.0 cm
Colour: Blue
Issued: 1979 in a limited
edition of 750
Series: Dancers of the World

U.S.: $ 950.00
Can.: $1,150.00
U.K.: £ 525.00

HN 2868
Cleopatra
Style One
Designer: M. Davies
Height: 7 ¼", 18.4 cm
Colour: White, blue and black
Issued: 1979 in a limited
edition of 750
Series: Les Femmes Fatales

U.S.: $1,900.00
Can.: $2,300.00
U.K.: £1,100.00

HN 2869
Louise
Style One
Designer: M. Davies
Height: 6", 15.2 cm
Colour: Brown
Issued: 1979-1986
Series: Kate Greenaway

U.S.: $300.00
Can.: $375.00
U.K.: £165.00

HN 2870
Beth
Style One
Designer: M. Davies
Height: 5 ¾", 14.6 cm
Colour: Pink and white
Issued: 1979-1983
Series: Kate Greenaway

U.S.: $425.00
Can.: $500.00
U.K.: £230.00

HN 2871
Beat You To It
Designer: M. Davies
Height: 6 ½", 16.5 cm
Colour: Pink, gold and blue
Issued: 1980-1987

U.S.:	**$375.00**
Can.:	**$450.00**
U.K.:	**£200.00**

HN 2872
Young Master
Designer: M. Davies
Height: 7", 17.8 cm
Colour: Purple, grey
             and brown
Issued: 1980-1989

U.S.:	**$350.00**
Can.:	**$425.00**
U.K.:	**£200.00**

HN 2873
The Bride
Style Three
Designer: M. Davies
Height: 8", 20.3 cm
Colour: White with gold trim
Issued: 1980-1989

U.S.:	**$225.00**
Can.:	**$275.00**
U.K.:	**£125.00**

HN 2874
The Bridesmaid
Style Five
Designer: M. Davies
Height: 5 ¼", 13.3 cm
Colour: White with gold trim
Issued: 1980-1989

U.S.:	**$125.00**
Can.:	**$150.00**
U.K.:	**£ 70.00**

HN 2875
Awakening
Style Two
Designer: M. Davies
Height: 8 ½", 21.6 cm
Colour: White
Issued: 1981-1997
Varieties: HN 2837; also known
             in flambé
Series: Images

U.S.:	**$125.00**
Can.:	**$150.00**
U.K.:	**£ 70.00**

HN 2876
Sympathy
Designer: M. Davies
Height: 11 ¾", 29.8 cm
Colour: White
Issued: 1981-1986
Varieties: HN 2838
Series: Images

U.S.:	**$175.00**
Can.:	**$225.00**
U.K.:	**£100.00**

HN 2877
The Wizard
Style One
Designer: A. Maslankowski
Height: 9 ¾", 24.8 cm
Colour: Blue
Issued: 1979 to the present
Varieties: HN 3121, 4069

U.S.:	**$575.00**
Can.:	**$590.00**
U.K.:	**£170.00**

HN 2878
Her Majesty
Queen Elizabeth II
Style Two
Designer: E. J. Griffiths
Height: 10 ½", 26.7 cm
Colour: Blue, red and cream
Issued: 1983 in a limited
             edition of 2500

U.S.:	**$475.00**
Can.:	**$575.00**
U.K.:	**£250.00**

HN 2879
The Gamekeeper
Designer:	E. J. Griffiths
Height:	7 ¼", 18.4 cm
Colour:	Green, black and tan
Issued:	1984-1992

U.S.:	**$325.00**
Can.:	**$400.00**
U.K.:	**£175.00**

HN 2880
Monique
Designer:	E. J. Griffiths
Height:	12 ½", 31.7 cm
Colour:	Pale green
Issued:	1984-1984
Varieties:	Colourways:
	1. Pale blue
	2. Fawn
	Also called 'Allure'
	HN 3080
Series:	Elegance (Series One)

U.S.:	**$500.00**
Can.:	**$600.00**
U.K.:	**£275.00**

HN 2881
Lord Olivier as Richard III
Designer:	E. J. Griffiths
Height:	11 ½", 29.2 cm
Colour:	Red, blue and black
Issued:	1985 in a limited
	edition of 750

U.S.:	**$ 900.00**
Can.:	**$1,100.00**
U.K.:	**£ 500.00**

HN 2882
HM Queen Elizabeth
The Queen Mother
Style One
Designer:	E. J. Griffiths
Height:	8", 20.3 cm
Colour:	Pink
Issued:	1980 in a limited
	edition of 1500

U.S.:	**$1,000.00**
Can.:	**$1,200.00**
U.K.:	**£ 550.00**

HN 2883
HRH The Prince of Wales
Style One
Designer:	E. J. Griffiths
Height:	8", 20.3 cm
Colour:	Purple, white and
	black
Issued:	1981 in a limited
	edition of 1500

U.S.:	**$750.00**
Can.:	**$900.00**
U.K.:	**£400.00**

HN 2884
HRH The Prince of Wales
Style Two
Designer:	E. J. Griffiths
Height:	8", 20.3 cm
Colour:	Red and black
Issued:	1981 in a limited
	edition of 1500

U.S.:	**$750.00**
Can.:	**$900.00**
U.K.:	**£400.00**

HN 2885
Lady Diana Spencer
Designer:	E. J. Griffiths
Height:	7 ¾", 19.7 cm
Colour:	Blue and white
Issued:	1982 in a limited
	edition of 1500

U.S.:	**$1,400.00**
Can.:	**$1,700.00**
U.K.:	**£ 750.00**

HN 2886 not issued.

HN 2887
HRH The Princess of Wales
Designer:	E. J. Griffiths
Height:	7 ¾", 19.7 cm
Colour:	Cream
Issued:	1982 in a limited
	edition of 1500

U.S.:	**$2,500.00**
Can.:	**$3,000.00**
U.K.:	**£1,350.00**

HN 2888
His Holiness Pope John-Paul II
Designer: E. J. Griffiths
Height: 10", 25.4 cm
Colour: White
Issued: 1982-1992

U.S.:	$300.00
Can.:	$375.00
U.K.:	£165.00

HN 2889
Captain Cook
Designer: W. K. Harper
Height: 8", 20.3 cm
Colour: Black and cream
Issued: 1980-1984
Series: Sea Characters

U.S.:	$500.00
Can.:	$600.00
U.K.:	£275.00

HN 2890
The Clown
Designer: W. K. Harper
Height: 9", 22.9 cm
Colour: Gold and grey
Issued: 1979 to 1988

U.S.:	$400.00
Can.:	$500.00
U.K.:	£225.00

HN 2891
The Newsvendor
Designer: W. K. Harper
Height: 8", 20.3 cm
Colour: Gold and grey
Issued: 1986 in a limited
             edition of 2,500

U.S.:	$325.00
Can.:	$400.00
U.K.:	£175.00

HN 2892
The Chief
Designer: W. K. Harper
Height: 7", 17.8 cm
Colour: Gold
Issued: 1979-1988

U.S.:	$300.00
Can.:	$375.00
U.K.:	£175.00

HN 2894
Balloon Clown
Designer: W. K. Harper
Height: 9 ¼", 23.5 cm
Colour: White and blue
Issued: 1986-1992

U.S.:	$475.00
Can.:	$575.00
U.K.:	£250.00

HN 2895
Morning Ma'am
Designer: W. K. Harper
Height: 9", 23.5 cm
Colour: Pale blue
Issued: 1986-1989

U.S.:	$275.00
Can.:	$325.00
U.K.:	£150.00

HN 2896
Good Day Sir
Designer: W. K. Harper
Height: 8 ½", 21.6 cm
Colour: Purple
Issued: 1986-1989

U.S.:	$275.00
Can.:	$325.00
U.K.:	£150.00

HN 2893 not issued.

HN 2897
Francoise
Designer: W. K. Harper
Height: 12 ½", 31.7 cm
Colour: Fawn
Issued: 1984-1984
Varieties: Colourways:
1. Pale blue
2. Pale green
Series: Elegance (Series One)

U.S.: $500.00
Can.: $600.00
U.K.: £275.00

HN 2898
Ko-Ko
Style Two
Designer: W. K. Harper
Height: 11 ½", 29.2 cm
Colour: Yellow and blue
Issued: 1980-1985
Series: Gilbert and Sullivan

U.S.: $ 950.00
Can.: $1,150.00
U.K.: £ 525.00

HN 2899
Yum-Yum
Style Two
Designer: W. K. Harper
Height: 10 ¾", 27.3 cm
Colour: Green and yellow
Issued: 1980-1985
Series: Gilbert and Sullivan

U.S.: $1,100.00
Can.: $1,350.00
U.K.: £ 600.00

HN 2900
Ruth, The Pirate Maid
Designer: W. K. Harper
Height: 11 ¾", 29.8 cm
Colour: Brown and blue
Issued: 1981-1985
Series: Gilbert and Sullivan

U.S.: $ 950.00
Can.: $1,150.00
U.K.: £ 525.00

HN 2901
The Pirate King
Designer: W. K. Harper
Height: 10", 25.4 cm
Colour: Blue and gold
Issued: 1981-1985
Series: Gilbert and Sullivan

U.S.: $ 950.00
Can.: $1,150.00
U.K.: £ 525.00

HN 2902
Elsie Maynard
Style Two
Designer: W. K. Harper
Height: 12", 30.5 cm
Colour: Green and white
Issued: 1982-1985
Series: Gilbert and Sullivan

U.S.: $ 975.00
Can.: $1,200.00
U.K.: £ 550.00

HN 2903
Colonel Fairfax
Designer: W. K. Harper
Height: 11 ½", 29.2 cm
Colour: Red and gold
Issued: 1982-1985
Series: Gilbert and Sullivan

U.S.: $1,200.00
Can.: $1,500.00
U.K.: £ 650.00

HN 2904 - 2905 not issued.

HN 2906
Paula
Designer: P. Parsons
Height: 7", 17.8 cm
Colour: Yellow with green trim
Issued: 1980-1986
Varieties: HN 3234

U.S.: $325.00
Can.: $400.00
U.K.: £175.00

HN 2907
The Piper
Style One
Designer: M. Abberley
Height: 8", 20.3 cm
Colour: Green
Issued: 1980-1992

U.S.:	$500.00
Can.:	$600.00
U.K.:	£275.00

HN 2908
HMS Ajax
Designer: S. Keenan
Height: 9 ¾", 24.8 cm
Colour: Red, green and gold
Issued: 1980 in a limited
             edition of 950
Series: Ships Figureheads

U.S.:	$650.00
Can.:	$775.00
U.K.:	£350.00

HN 2909
Benmore
Designer: S. Keenan
Height: 9 ¼", 23.5 cm
Colour: Blue, red, white
             and gold
Issued: 1980 in a limited
             edition of 950
Series: Ships Figureheads

U.S.:	$650.00
Can.:	$775.00
U.K.:	£350.00

HN 2910
Lalla Rookh
Designer: S. Keenan
Height: 9", 22.9 cm
Colour: Brown, green with
             gold trim
Issued: 1981 in a limited
             edition of 950
Series: Ships Figureheads

U.S.:	$800.00
Can.:	$975.00
U.K.:	£450.00

HN 2911
Gandalf
Designer: D. Lyttleton
Height: 7", 17.8 cm
Colour: Green and white
Issued: 1980-1984
Series: Middle Earth

U.S.:	$425.00
Can.:	$525.00
U.K.:	£225.00

HN 2912
Frodo
Designer: D. Lyttleton
Height: 4 ½", 11.4 cm
Colour: Black and white
Issued: 1980-1984
Series: Middle Earth

U.S.:	$275.00
Can.:	$325.00
U.K.:	£150.00

HN 2913
Gollum
Designer: D. Lyttleton
Height: 3 ¼", 8.3 cm
Colour: Brown
Issued: 1980-1984
Series: Middle Earth

U.S.:	$375.00
Can.:	$450.00
U.K.:	£200.00

HN 2914
Bilbo
Designer: D. Lyttleton
Height: 4 ½", 11.4 cm
Colour: Brown
Issued: 1980-1984
Series: Middle Earth

U.S.:	$275.00
Can.:	$325.00
U.K.:	£150.00

Lord of the Rings Stand $2,500. U.S.F.

HN 2915
Galadriel
Designer: D. Lyttleton
Height: 5 ½", 14.0 cm
Colour: White
Issued: 1981-1984
Series: Middle Earth

U.S.: $375.00
Can.: $450.00
U.K.: £200.00

HN 2916
Aragorn
Designer: D. Lyttleton
Height: 6 ¼", 15.9 cm
Colour: Brown and green
Issued: 1981-1984
Series: Middle Earth

U.S.: $275.00
Can.: $325.00
U.K.: £150.00

HN 2917
Legolas
Designer: D. Lyttleton
Height: 6 ¼", 15.9 cm
Colour: Cream and tan
Issued: 1981-1984
Series: Middle Earth

U.S.: $300.00
Can.: $375.00
U.K.: £165.00

HN 2918
Boromir
Designer: D Lyttleton
Height: 6 ¾", 17.2 cm
Colour: Brown and green
Issued: 1981-1984
Series: Middle Earth

U.S.: $550.00
Can.: $650.00
U.K.: £300.00

HN 2919
Rachel
Style One
Designer: P. Gee
Height: 7 ½", 19.1 cm
Colour: Gold and green
Issued: 1981-1984
Varieties: HN 2936

U.S.: $275.00
Can.: $325.00
U.K.: £150.00

HN 2920
Yearning
Designer: P. Gee
Height: 11 ¾", 29.8 cm
Colour: White
Issued: 1982-1986
Varieties: HN 2921
Series: Images

U.S.: $175.00
Can.: $225.00
U.K.: £100.00

HN 2921
Yearning
Designer: P. Gee
Height: 11 ¾", 29.8 cm
Colour: Black
Issued: 1982-1986
Varieties: HN 2920
Series: Images

U.S.: $175.00
Can.: $225.00
U.K.: £100.00

HN 2922
Gimli
Designer: D. Lyttleton
Height: 5 ½", 14.0 cm
Colour: Brown and blue
Issued: 1981-1984
Series: Middle Earth

U.S.: $325.00
Can.: $400.00
U.K.: £175.00

HN 2923
Barliman Butterbur
Designer: D. Lyttleton
Height: 5 ¼", 13.3 cm
Colour: Brown, tan and white
Issued: 1982-1984
Series: Middle Earth

U.S.:	**$1,000.00**
Can.:	**$1,200.00**
U.K.:	**£ 575.00**

HN 2924
Tom Bombadil
Designer: D. Lyttleton
Height: 5 ¾", 14.6 cm
Colour: Black and yellow
Issued: 1982-1984
Series: Middle Earth

U.S.:	**$1,150.00**
Can.:	**$1,400.00**
U.K.:	**£ 625.00**

HN 2925
Samwise
Designer: D. Lyttleton
Height: 4 ½", 11.4 cm
Colour: Black and brown
Issued: 1982-1984
Series: Middle Earth

U.S.:	**$1,150.00**
Can.:	**$1,400.00**
U.K.:	**£ 625.00**

HN 2926
Tom Sawyer
Designer: D. Lyttleton
Height: 5 ¼", 13.3 cm
Colour: Blue
Issued: 1982-1985
Series: Characters from
             Children's Literature

U.S.:	**$225.00**
Can.:	**$275.00**
U.K.:	**£125.00**

HN 2927
Huckleberry Finn
Designer: D. Lyttleton
Height: 7", 17.8 cm
Colour: Tan and brown
Issued: 1982-1985
Series: Characters from
             Children's Literature

U.S.:	**$225.00**
Can.:	**$275.00**
U.K.:	**£125.00**

HN 2928
Nelson
Designer: S. Keenan
Height: 8 ¾", 22.2 cm
Colour: Blue, gold and green
Issued: 1981 in a limited
             edition of 950
Series: Ships Figureheads

U.S.:	**$ 925.00**
Can.:	**$1,100.00**
U.K.:	**£ 500.00**

HN 2929
Chieftain
Designer: S. Keenan
Height: 8 ¾", 22.2 cm
Colour: Green and brown
Issued: 1982 in a limited
             edition of 950
Series: Ships Figureheads

U.S.:	**$1,500.00**
Can.:	**$1,750.00**
U.K.:	**£ 800.00**

HN 2930
Pocahontas
Designer: S. Keenan
Height: 8", 20.3 cm
Colour: White, red and gold
Issued: 1982 in a limited
             edition of 950
Series: Ships Figureheads

U.S.:	**$1,500.00**
Can.:	**$1,750.00**
U.K.:	**£ 800.00**

HN 2931
Mary Queen of Scots
Style One
Designer: S. Keenan
Height: 9 ½", 24.1 cm
Colour: Purple, red and white
Issued: 1983 in a limited
edition of 950
Series: Ships Figureheads
U.S.: $2,250.00
Can.: $2,750.00
U.K.: £1,200.00

HN 2932
Hibernia
Designer: S. Keenan
Height: 9 ½", 24.1 cm
Colour: Black, white and gold
Issued: 1983 in a limited
edition of 950
Series: Ships Figureheads
U.S.: $4,000.00
Can.: $4,750.00
U.K.: £2,150.00

HN 2933
Kathleen
Style Two
Designer: S. Keenan
Height: 6 ½", 16.5 cm
Colour: Orange, yellow
and green
Issued: 1983 Canada,
1984 Worldwide -1987
Varieties: HN 3100
U.S.: $275.00
Can.: $350.00
U.K.: £150.00

HN 2934
Balloon Boy
Designer: P. Gee
Height: 7 ½", 19.1 cm
Colour: Green and black
Issued: 1984-1998
U.S.: $400.00
Can.: $475.00
U.K.: £225.00

HN 2935
Balloon Lady
Designer: P. Gee
Height: 8 ¼", 21.0 cm
Colour: Purple, gold and white
Issued: 1984 to the present
U.S.: $245.00
Can.: $550.00
U.K.: £140.00

HN 2936
Rachel
Style One
Designer: P. Gee
Height: 7 ½", 19.1 cm
Colour: Red and cream
Issued: 1985-1997
Varieties: HN 2919
U.S.: $325.00
Can.: $400.00
U.K.: £175.00

HN 2937
Gail
Style One
Designer: P. Gee
Height: 7 ½", 19.1 cm
Colour: Red and cream
Issued: 1986-1997
U.S.: $325.00
Can.: $400.00
U.K.: £175.00

HN 2938
Isadora
Designer: P. Gee
Height: 8", 20.3 cm
Colour: Lavender
Issued: 1986-1992
Varieties: Also called 'Celeste'
(Style Two) HN 3322
U.S.: $325.00
Can.: $400.00
U.K.: £175.00

HN 2939
Donna
Designer: P. Gee
Height: 7 ¾", 19.7 cm
Colour: White
Issued: 1982-1994
Series: Vanity Fair Ladies

U.S.:	**$225.00**
Can.:	**$275.00**
U.K.:	**£125.00**

HN 2940
All Aboard
Designer: R. Tabbenor
Height: 9 ¼", 23.5 cm
Colour: Blue, cream and
           brown
Issued: 1982-1986
Series: Sea characters

U.S.:	**$425.00**
Can.:	**$500.00**
U.K.:	**£225.00**

HN 2941
Tom Brown
Designer: R. Tabbenor
Height: 6 ¾", 17.2 cm
Colour: Blue and cream
Issued: 1983-1985
Series: Characters from
           Children's Literature

U.S.:	**$250.00**
Can.:	**$300.00**
U.K.:	**£135.00**

HN 2942
Prized Possessions
Designer: R. Tabbenor
Height: 6 ½", 16.5 cm
Colour: Cream, purple
           and green
Issued: 1982-1982
Series: RDICC

U.S.:	**$775.00**
Can.:	**$925.00**
U.K.:	**£425.00**

HN 2943
The China Repairer
Designer: R. Tabbenor
Height: 6 ¾", 17.2 cm
Colour: Blue, white and tan
Issued: 1982 Canada,
           1983 Worldwide-1988

U.S.:	**$375.00**
Can.:	**$450.00**
U.K.:	**£200.00**

HN 2944
The Rag Doll Seller
Designer: R. Tabbenor
Height: 7", 17.8 cm
Colour: Green, lavender
           and white
Issued: 1983-1995

U.S.:	**$425.00**
Can.:	**$500.00**
U.K.:	**£225.00**

HN 2945
Pride and Joy
Style One
Designer: R. Tabbenor
Height: 7", 17.8 cm
Colour: Brown, gold and green
Issued: 1984-1984
Series: RDICC

U.S.:	**$550.00**
Can.:	**$650.00**
U.K.:	**£300.00**

HN 2946
Elizabeth
Style One
Designer: B. Franks
Height: 8", 20.3 cm
Colour: Green and yellow
Issued: 1982-1986

U.S.:	**$425.00**
Can.:	**$500.00**
U.K.:	**£225.00**

HN 2947 - 2951 not issued.

HN 2952
Susan
Style Two
Designer: P. Parsons
Height: 8 ½", 21.6 cm
Colour: Blue, black and pink
Issued: 1982-1993
Varieties: HN 3050

U.S.:	**$350.00**
Can.:	**$425.00**
U.K.:	**£200.00**

HN 2953
Sleepy Darling
Designer: P. Parsons
Height: 7 ¼", 18.4 cm
Colour: Pale blue and pink
Issued: 1981-1981
Series: RDICC

U.S.:	**$325.00**
Can.:	**$400.00**
U.K.:	**£175.00**

HN 2954
Samantha
Style One
Designer: P. Parsons
Height: 7", 17.8 cm
Colour: White
Issued: 1982-1984
Series: Vanity Fair Ladies

U.S.:	**$250.00**
Can.:	**$300.00**
U.K.:	**£135.00**

HN 2955
Nancy
Designer: P. Parsons
Height: 7 ½", 19.1 cm
Colour: White
Issued: 1982-1994
Series: Vanity Fair Ladies

U.S.:	**$275.00**
Can.:	**$325.00**
U.K.:	**£150.00**

HN 2956
Heather
Designer: P. Parsons
Height: 6", 15.2 cm
Colour: White
Issued: 1982-2000
Varieties: Also called 'Marie'
(Style Three) HN 3357
Series: Vanity Fair Ladies

U.S.:	**$225.00**
Can.:	**$275.00**
U.K.:	**£125.00**

HN 2957
Edith
Designer: P. Parsons
Height: 5 ¾", 14.6 cm
Colour: Green and white
Issued: 1982-1985
Series: Kate Greenaway

U.S.:	**$425.00**
Can.:	**$500.00**
U.K.:	**£225.00**

HN 2958
Amy
Style One
Designer: P. Parsons
Height: 6", 15.2 cm
Colour: White and blue
Issued: 1982-1987
Series: Kate Greenaway

U.S.:	**$325.00**
Can.:	**$400.00**
U.K.:	**£175.00**

HN 2959
Save Some For Me
Designer: P. Parsons
Height: 7 ¼", 18.4 cm
Colour: Blue and white
Issued: 1982-1985
Series: Childhood Days

U.S.:	**$250.00**
Can.:	**$300.00**
U.K.:	**£135.00**

HN 2960
Laura
Style One
Designer: P. Parsons
Height: 7 ¼", 18.4 cm
Colour: Pale blue and white, yellow flowers
Issued: 1982 Canada, 1984 Worldwide -1994
Varieties: HN 3136
  U.S.: **$275.00**
  Can.: **$330.00**
  U.K.: **£150.00**

HN 2961
Carol
Designer: P. Parsons
Height: 7 ½", 19.1 cm
Colour: White
Issued: 1982-1995
Series: Vanity Fair Ladies
  U.S.: **$250.00**
  Can.: **$300.00**
  U.K.: **£135.00**

HN 2962
Barbara
Style Two
Designer: P. Parsons
Height: 8", 20.3 cm
Colour: White
Issued: 1982-1984
Series: Vanity Fair Ladies
  U.S.: **$275.00**
  Can.: **$325.00**
  U.K.: **£150.00**

HN 2963
It Won't Hurt
Designer: P. Parsons
Height: 7 ½", 19.1 cm
Colour: White, brown and blue
Issued: 1982-1985
Series: Childhood Days
  U.S.: **$250.00**
  Can.: **$300.00**
  U.K.: **£135.00**

HN 2964
Dressing Up
Style One
Designer: P. Parsons
Height: 7 ½", 19.1 cm
Colour: White and blue
Issued: 1982-1985
Series: Childhood Days
  U.S.: **$225.00**
  Can.: **$275.00**
  U.K.: **£125.00**

HN 2965
Pollyanna
Designer: P. Parsons
Height: 6 ½", 16.5 cm
Colour: White, grey and tan
Issued: 1982-1985
Series: Characters from Children's Literature
  U.S.: **$225.00**
  Can.: **$275.00**
  U.K.: **£125.00**

HN 2966
And So To Bed
Designer: P. Parsons
Height: 7 ½", 19.1 cm
Colour: Cream and gold
Issued: 1982-1985
Series: Childhood Days
  U.S.: **$275.00**
  Can.: **$325.00**
  U.K.: **£150.00**

HN 2967
Please Keep Still
Designer: P. Parsons
Height: 4 ½", 11.4 cm
Colour: Yellow and blue
Issued: 1982-1985
Series: Childhood Days
  U.S.: **$275.00**
  Can.: **$325.00**
  U.K.: **£150.00**

HN 2968
Juliet
Style One
Designer: P. Parsons
Height: 7", 17.8 cm
Colour: Blue and white
Issued: 1983-1984
Series: Ladies of Covent
               Garden
Comm.by: Amex
   U.S.:   **$525.00**
   Can.:   **$650.00**
   U.K.:   **£300.00**

HN 2969
Kimberley
Style One
Designer: P. Parsons
Height: 8", 20.3 cm
Colour: Yellow and white
Issued: 1983-1984
Varieties: Also called 'Yours
               Forever' HN 3354
Series: Ladies of Covent
               Garden
Comm.by: Amex
   U.S.:   **$525.00**
   Can.:   **$650.00**
   U.K.:   **£300.00**

HN 2970
And One For You
Designer: A. Hughes
Height: 6 ½", 16.5 cm
Colour: White and brown
Issued: 1982-1985
Series: Childhood Days
   U.S.:   **$200.00**
   Can.:   **$250.00**
   U.K.:   **£110.00**

HN 2971
As Good As New
Designer: A. Hughes
Height: 6 ½", 16.5 cm
Colour: Blue, green and tan
Issued: 1982-1985
Series: Childhood Days
   U.S.:   **$200.00**
   Can.:   **$250.00**
   U.K.:   **£110.00**

HN 2972
Little Lord Fauntleroy
Designer: A. Hughes
Height: 6 ¼", 15.9 cm
Colour: Blue and white
Issued: 1982-1985
Series: Characters from
               Children's Literature
   U.S.:   **$200.00**
   Can.:   **$250.00**
   U.K.:   **£110.00**

HN 2973 not issued.

HN 2974
Carolyn
Style Two
Designer: A. Hughes
Height: 5 ½", 14.0 cm
Colour: Green
Issued: 1982 Canada,
               1984 Worldwide -1986
   U.S.:   **$300.00**
   Can.:   **$375.00**
   U.K.:   **£165.00**

HN 2975
Heidi
Designer: A. Hughes
Height: 4 ½", 11.4 cm
Colour: Green and white
Issued: 1983-1985
Series: Characters from
               Children's Literature
   U.S.:   **$225.00**
   Can.:   **$275.00**
   U.K.:   **£125.00**

HN 2976
I'm Nearly Ready
Designer: A. Hughes
Height: 7 ½", 19.1 cm
Colour: Black, white and brown
Issued: 1983 Canada,
               1984 Worldwide -1985
Series: Childhood Days
   U.S.:   **$275.00**
   Can.:   **$325.00**
   U.K.:   **£150.00**

HN 2977
Magic Dragon
Designer:	A. Hughes
Height:	4 ¾", 12.0 cm
Colour:	Cream
Issued:	1983-1986
Series:	Enchantment
U.S.:	**$225.00**
Can.:	**$275.00**
U.K.:	**£125.00**

HN 2978
The Magpie Ring
Designer:	A. Hughes
Height:	8", 20.3 cm
Colour:	Cream
Issued:	1983-1986
Series:	Enchantment
U.S.:	**$225.00**
Can.:	**$275.00**
U.K.:	**£125.00**

HN 2979
Fairyspell
Designer:	A. Hughes
Height:	5 ¼", 13.3 cm
Colour:	Cream
Issued:	1983-1986
Series:	Enchantment
U.S.:	**$225.00**
Can.:	**$275.00**
U.K.:	**£125.00**

HN 2980
Just One More
Designer:	A. Hughes
Height:	7", 17.8 cm
Colour:	Gold and blue
Issued:	1983 Canada,
	1984 Worldwide -1985
Series:	Childhood Days
U.S.:	**$200.00**
Can.:	**$250.00**
U.K.:	**£115.00**

HN 2981
Stick 'em Up
Designer:	A. Hughes
Height:	7", 17.8 cm
Colour:	Blue and tan
Issued:	1983 Canada,
	1984 Worldwide -1985
Series:	Childhood Days
U.S.:	**$225.00**
Can.:	**$275.00**
U.K.:	**£125.00**

HN 2982 - 2987 not issued.

HN 2988
The Auctioneer
Designer:	R. Tabbenor
Height:	8 ½", 21.6 cm
Colour:	Black, grey and
	brown
Issued:	1986-1986
Series:	RDICC
U.S.:	**$375.00**
Can.:	**$450.00**
U.K.:	**£200.00**

HN 2989
The Genie
Designer:	R. Tabbenor
Height:	9 ¾", 24.7 cm
Colour:	Blue
Issued:	1983-1990
Varieties:	HN 2999
U.S.:	**$275.00**
Can.:	**$325.00**
U.K.:	**£150.00**

HN 2990
Shepherdess
Style Three
Designer:	R. Tabbenor
Height:	8", 20.3 cm
Colour:	Pale blue, white
	and tan
Issued:	1987-1988
Series:	Reflections
U.S.:	**$275.00**
Can.:	**$325.00**
U.K.:	**£150.00**

HN 2991
June
Style Four
Designer: R. Tabbenor
Height: 9", 22.9 cm
Colour: Lavender and red
Issued: 1988-1994
U.S.: $325.00
Can.: $400.00
U.K.: £175.00

HN 2992
Golfer
Designer: R. Tabbenor
Height: 9 ½", 24.1 cm
Colour: Blue, white and
pale brown
Issued: 1988-1991
Series: Reflections
U.S.: $275.00
Can.: $325.00
U.K.: £150.00

HN 2993
Old Father Thames
Designer: R. Tabbenor
Height: 5 ¾", 14.6 cm
Colour: Cream with gold trim
Issued: 1988 in a limited
edition of 500
Comm.by: Thames Water
U.S.: $275.00
Can.: $325.00
U.K.: £150.00

HN 2994
Helen
Style Two
Designer: R. Tabbenor
Height: 5", 12.7 cm
Colour: White
Issued: 1985-1987
Series: Vanity Fair Children
U.S.: $125.00
Can.: $150.00
U.K.: £ 70.00

HN 2995
Julie
Style One
Designer: R. Tabbenor
Height: 5", 12.7 cm
Colour: White
Issued: 1985-1995
Varieties: HN 3407
Series: Vanity Fair Children
U.S.: $125.00
Can.: $150.00
U.K.: £ 70.00

HN 2996
Amanda
Designer: R. Tabbenor
Height: 5 ¼", 13.3 cm
Colour: White and pink
Issued: 1986-2000
Varieties: HN 3406, 3632, 3634,
3635; Also called
'Flower of the Month,
Child'
Series: Vanity Fair Children
U.S.: $125.00
Can.: $150.00
U.K.: £ 70.00

HN 2997
Chic
Designer: R. Tabbenor
Height: 13", 33.0 cm
Colour: Pale blue
Issued: 1987 N. America,
1988 Worldwide -1990
Series: Reflections
U.S.: $375.00
Can.: $450.00
U.K.: £200.00

HN 2998
Aperitif
Designer: P. Gee
Height: 12", 30.5 cm
Colour: Pale green
Issued: 1988-1988
Series: Reflections
Comm.by: Home Shopping
Network, Florida
U.S.: $375.00
Can.: $450.00
U.K.: £200.00

HN 2999
The Genie
Designer: R. Tabbenor
Height: 9 ¾", 24.7 cm
Colour: Red
Issued: 1990-1995
Varieties: HN 2989
Series: Flambé
U.S.:   **$500.00**
Can.:   **$600.00**
U.K.:   **£275.00**

HN 3000
Sweet Bouquet
Style One
Designer: R. Tabbenor
Height: 13", 33.0 cm
Colour: Blue and white
Issued: 1988-1988
Series: Reflections
Comm.by: Home Shopping
           Network, Florida
U.S.:   **$375.00**
Can.:   **$450.00**
U.K.:   **£200.00**

HN 3001
Danielle
Style Two
Designer: P. Gee
Height: 7", 17.8 cm
Colour: Pink and white
Issued: 1990-1995
Varieties: Also called 'Spring
           Song' HN 3446
Series: Vanity Fair Ladies
U.S.:   **$250.00**
Can.:   **$300.00**
U.K.:   **£135.00**

HN 3002
Marilyn
Designer: P. Gee
Height: 7 ¼", 18.4 cm
Colour: White dress
           with flowers
Issued: 1985 Canada,
           1986 Worldwide -1995
U.S.:   **$275.00**
Can.:   **$325.00**
U.K.:   **£150.00**

HN 3003
Lilian In Summer
Designer: P. Gee
Height: 8 ½", 21.6 cm
Colour: White, blue and pink
Issued: 1985
Series: The Seasons
           (Series Three)
Comm.by: Danbury Mint
U.S.:   **$450.00**
Can.:   **$550.00**
U.K.:   **£250.00**

HN 3004
Emily In Autumn
Designer: P. Gee
Height: 8", 20.3 cm
Colour: Yellow and white
Issued: 1986
Series: The Seasons
           (SeriesThree)
Comm.by: Danbury Mint
U.S.:   **$450.00**
Can.:   **$550.00**
U.K.:   **£250.00**

HN 3005
Sarah In Winter
Designer: P. Gee
Height: 8", 20.3 cm
Colour: Pale green and white
Issued: 1986
Series: The Seasons
           (SeriesThree)
Comm.by: Danbury Mint
U.S.:   **$450.00**
Can.:   **$550.00**
U.K.:   **£250.00**

HN 3006
Catherine In Spring
Designer: P. Gee
Height: 8 ½", 21.6 cm
Colour: Pink and white
Issued: 1985
Series: The Seasons
           (Series Three)
Comm.by: Danbury Mint
U.S.:   **$450.00**
Can.:   **$550.00**
U.K.:   **£250.00**

HN 3007
Mary, Countess Howe
Designer: P. Gee
Height: 9 ¼", 23.5 cm
Colour: Pink and blue
Issued: 1990 in a limited
           edition of 5,000
Series: Gainsborough
           Ladies

U.S.:	**$575.00**
Can.:	**$700.00**
U.K.:	**£315.00**

HN 3008
Sophia Charlotte, Lady Sheffield
Designer: P. Gee
Height: 10", 25.4 cm
Colour: Yellow and turquoise
Issued: 1990 in a limited
           edition of 5,000
Series: Gainsborough
           Ladies

U.S.:	**$550.00**
Can.:	**$650.00**
U.K.:	**£300.00**

HN 3009
Honourable Frances Duncombe
Designer: P. Gee
Height: 9 ¾", 24.7 cm
Colour: Blue and yellow
Issued: 1991 in a limited
           edition of 5,000
Series: Gainsborough
           Ladies

U.S.:	**$600.00**
Can.:	**$725.00**
U.K.:	**£325.00**

HN 3010
Isabella, Countess of Sefton
Designer: P. Gee
Height: 9 ¾", 24.7 cm
Colour: Yellow and black
Issued: 1991 in a limited
           edition of 5,000
Series: Gainsborough
           Ladies

U.S.:	**$600.00**
Can.:	**$725.00**
U.K.:	**£325.00**

HN 3011
My Best Friend
Designer: P. Gee
Height: 8", 20.3 cm
Colour: Pink
Issued: 1990-2000

U.S.:	**$375.00**
Can.:	**$450.00**
U.K.:	**£200.00**

HN 3012
Painting
Designer: P. Parsons
Height: 7 ½", 18.4 cm
Colour: Purple
Issued: 1987 in a limited
           edition of 750
Series: Gentle Arts

U.S.:	**$1,400.00**
Can.:	**$1,700.00**
U.K.:	**£ 800.00**

HN 3013
James
Designer: P. Parsons
Height: 6", 15.2 cm
Colour: White
Issued: 1983-1987
Series: Kate Greenaway

U.S.:	**$750.00**
Can.:	**$900.00**
U.K.:	**£425.00**

HN 3014
Nell
Designer: P. Parsons
Height: 4", 10.1 cm
Colour: White and pink
Issued: 1982-1987
Series: Kate Greenaway

U.S.:	**$325.00**
Can.:	**$400.00**
U.K.:	**£185.00**

HN 3015
Adornment
Designer: P. Parsons
Height: 7 ¼", 18.4 cm
Colour: Pink and lavender
             stripes
Issued: 1989 in a limited
             edition of 750
Series: Gentle Arts
   U.S.:   **$1,400.00**
   Can.:   **$1,700.00**
   U.K.:   **£ 800.00**

HN 3016
The Graduate (female)
Style One
Designer: P. Parsons
Height: 8 ¾", 22.2 cm
Colour: Black, pink and yellow
Issued: 1984-1992
   U.S.:   **$300.00**
   Can.:   **$375.00**
   U.K.:   **£165.00**

HN 3017
The Graduate (male)
Style One
Designer: P. Parsons
Height: 9 ¼", 23.5 cm
Colour: Black and grey
Issued: 1984-1992
   U.S.:   **$300.00**
   Can.:   **$375.00**
   U.K.:   **£165.00**

HN 3018
Sisters
Designer: P. Parsons
Height: 8 ½", 21.6 cm
Colour: White
Issued: 1983 to the present
Varieties: HN 3019
Series: Images
   U.S.:   **$125.00**
   Can.:   **$225.00**
   U.K.:   **£ 39.00**

HN 3019
Sisters
Designer: P. Parsons
Height: 8 ½", 21.6 cm
Colour: Black
Issued: 1983-1997
Varieties: HN 3018
Series: Images
   U.S.:   **$150.00**
   Can.:   **$175.00**
   U.K.:   **£ 80.00**

HN 3020
Ellen
Style One
Designer: P. Parsons
Height: 3 ½", 8.9 cm
Colour: Blue and yellow
Issued: 1984-1987
Series: Kate Greenaway
   U.S.:   **$750.00**
   Can.:   **$950.00**
   U.K.:   **£425.00**

HN 3021
Polly Put The Kettle On
Designer: P. Parsons
Height: 8", 20.3 cm
Colour: White and pink
Issued: 1984-1987
Series: Nursery Rhymes
             (Series Two)
   U.S.:   **$225.00**
   Can.:   **$300.00**
   U.K.:   **£125.00**

HN 3022 - 3023 not issued.

HN 3024
April Shower
Designer: R. Jefferson
Height: 4 ¾", 12.0 cm
Colour: Cream
Issued: 1983-1986
Series: Enchantment
   U.S.:   **$225.00**
   Can.:   **$275.00**
   U.K.:   **£125.00**

HN 3025
Rumpelstiltskin
Designer: R. Jefferson
Height: 8", 20.3 cm
Colour: Cream
Issued: 1983-1986
Series: Enchantment
U.S.: $250.00
Can.: $300.00
U.K.: £150.00

HN 3026
Carefree
Style One
Designer: R. Jefferson
Height: 12 ¼", 31.1 cm
Colour: White
Issued: 1986-2001
Varieties: HN 3029
Series: Images
U.S.: $200.00
Can.: $250.00
U.K.: £110.00

HN 3027
Windswept
Designer: R. Jefferson
Height: 12 ¾", 32.0 cm
Colour: Pale blue
Issued: 1985 N. America
1987 Worldwide-1994
Series: Reflections
U.S.: $275.00
Can.: $325.00
U.K.: £150.00

HN 3028
Panorama
Designer: R. Jefferson
Height: 12 ¾", 32.5 cm
Colour: Pale blue
Issued: 1985 N. America,
1987 Worldwide-1988
Series: Reflections
U.S.: $225.00
Can.: $275.00
U.K.: £125.00

HN 3029
Carefree
Style One
Designer: R. Jefferson
Height: 12 ¼", 31.1 cm
Colour: Black
Issued: 1986-1997
Varieties: HN 3026
Series: Images
U.S.: $225.00
Can.: $275.00
U.K.: £125.00

HN 3030
Little Bo Peep
Designer: A. Hughes
Height: 8", 20.3 cm
Colour: White with blue trim
Issued: 1984-1987
Series: Nursery Rhymes
(Series Two)
U.S.: $200.00
Can.: $250.00
U.K.: £110.00

HN 3031
Wee Willie Winkie
Style Two
Designer: A. Hughes
Height: 7 ¾", 19.7 cm
Colour: White and blue
Issued: 1984-1987
Series: Nursery Rhymes
(Series Two)
U.S.: $250.00
Can.: $300.00
U.K.: £135.00

HN 3032
Tom, Tom, the Piper's Son
Designer: A. Hughes
Height: 7", 17.8 cm
Colour: White, yellow
and pink
Issued: 1984-1987
Series: Nursery Rhymes
(Series Two)
U.S.: $200.00
Can.: $250.00
U.K.: £110.00

HN 3033
Springtime
Style Two
Designer: A. Hughes
Height: 8", 20.3 cm
Colour: Yellow, cream
            and green
Issued: 1983-1983
Series: 1. The Seasons
               (Series Four)
            2. RDICC

U.S.: $375.00
Can.: $450.00
U.K.:   £200.00

HN 3034
Little Jack Horner
Style Two
Designer: A. Hughes
Height: 7", 17.8 cm
Colour: White, yellow
            and green
Issued: 1984-1987
Series: Nursery Rhymes
            (Series Two)

U.S.: $200.00
Can.: $250.00
U.K.:   £110.00

HN 3035
Little Boy Blue
Style Two
Designer: A. Hughes
Height: 7 ¾", 19.7 cm
Colour: Blue and white
Issued: 1984-1987
Series: Nursery Rhymes
            (Series Two)

U.S.: $200.00
Can.: $250.00
U.K.:   £110.00

HN 3036
Kerry
Designer: A. Hughes
Height: 5 ¼", 13.3 cm
Colour: White
Issued: 1986-1992
Varieties: HN 3461
Series: Vanity Fair Children

U.S.: $125.00
Can.: $150.00
U.K.:   £ 70.00

HN 3037
Miranda
Style Two
Designer: A. Hughes
Height: 8 ½", 21.5 cm
Colour: Cream, yellow
            and purple
Issued: 1987-1990

U.S.: $325.00
Can.: $400.00
U.K.:   £175.00

HN 3038
Yvonne
Designer: A. Hughes
Height: 8 ½", 21.6 cm
Colour: Turquoise
Issued: 1987-1992

U.S.: $275.00
Can.: $325.00
U.K.:   £150.00

HN 3039
Reflection
Designer: A. Hughes
Height: 8", 20.3 cm
Colour: Pale blue, pale
            brown and white
Issued: 1987-1991
Series: Reflections

U.S.: $275.00
Can.: $325.00
U.K.:   £150.00

HN 3040
Flower Arranging
Designer: D. Brindley
Height: 7 ¼", 18.4 cm
Colour: Green, purple
            and pink
Issued: 1988 in a limited
            edition of 750
Series: Gentle Arts

U.S.: $1,400.00
Can.: $1,700.00
U.K.:   £ 800.00

HN 3041
The Lawyer
Style One
Designer: P. Parsons
Height: 8 ¾", 22.2 cm
Colour: Grey and black
Issued: 1985-1995

U.S.:	$350.00
Can.:	$425.00
U.K.:	£200.00

HN 3042
Gillian
(With shoulder straps)
Style Two
Designer: P. Parsons
Height: 8 ¼", 21.0 cm
Colour: Green
Issued: 1984-Unknown
Varieties: HN 3042A (without shoulder straps)
Series: M. Doulton Events

U.S.:	$300.00
Can.:	$375.00
U.K.:	£175.00

HN 3042A
Gillian
(Without shoulder straps)
Style Two
Designer: P. Parsons
Height: 8 ¼", 21.0 cm
Colour: Green
Issued: Unknown-1990
Varieties: HN 3042 (with shoulder straps)

U.S.:	$225.00
Can.:	$275.00
U.K.:	£125.00

HN 3043
Lynsey
Designer: P. Parsons
Height: 4 ¾", 12.0 cm
Colour: White
Issued: 1985-1995
Series: Vanity Fair Children

U.S.:	$125.00
Can.:	$150.00
U.K.:	£ 70.00

HN 3044
Catherine
Style Two
Designer: P. Parsons
Height: 5", 12.7 cm
Colour: White with blue flowers
Issued: 1985-1996
Varieties: HN 3451
Series: Vanity Fair Children

U.S.:	$125.00
Can.:	$150.00
U.K.:	£ 70.00

HN 3045
Demure
Designer: P. Parsons
Height: 12 ¾", 32.5 cm
Colour: Grey-blue and white
Issued: 1985 N. America, 1987 Worldwide -1988
Series: Reflections

U.S.:	$325.00
Can.:	$400.00
U.K.:	£175.00

HN 3046
Debut
Style One
Designer: P. Parsons
Height: 12 ½", 32.0 cm
Colour: Pale blue , white and green
Issued: 1985 N. America, 1986 Worldwide -1989
Series: Reflections

U.S.:	$325.00
Can.:	$400.00
U.K.:	£175.00

HN 3047
Sharon
Style One
Designer: P. Parsons
Height: 5 ½", 14.0 cm
Colour: White and blue
Issued: 1984-1993
Varieties: HN 3455

U.S.:	$175.00
Can.:	$200.00
U.K.:	£ 95.00

HN 3048
Tapestry Weaving
Designer:	P. Parsons
Height:	7 ½", 19.1 cm
Colour:	Flowered pink dress
Issued:	1985 in a limited edition of 750
Series:	Gentle Arts
U.S.:	**$1,600.00**
Can.:	**$2,000.00**
U.K.:	**£ 860.00**

HN 3049
Writing
Designer:	P. Parsons
Height:	7 ¼", 18.4 cm
Colour:	Flowered yellow dress
Issued:	1986 in a limited edition of 750
Series:	Gentle Arts
U.S.:	**$1,400.00**
Can.:	**$1,700.00**
U.K.:	**£ 800.00**

HN 3050
Susan
Style Two
Designer:	P. Parsons
Height:	8 ½", 21.6 cm
Colour:	Pink and red
Issued:	1986-1995
Varieties:	HN 2952
U.S.:	**$375.00**
Can.:	**$450.00**
U.K.:	**£200.00**

HN 3051
Country Girl
Style One
Designer:	A. Hughes
Height:	7 ¾", 19.7 cm
Colour:	Blue and white
Issued:	1987-1992
Series:	Reflections
U.S.:	**$200.00**
Can.:	**$250.00**
U.K.:	**£110.00**

HN 3052
A Winter's Walk
Designer:	A. Hughes
Height:	12 ¼", 31.1 cm
Colour:	Pale blue and white
Issued:	1987 N. America, 1988 Worldwide -1995
Series:	Reflections
U.S.:	**$650.00**
Can.:	**$775.00**
U.K.:	**£350.00**

HN 3053
Martine
Designer:	A. Hughes
Height:	13 ½", 34.3 cm
Colour:	1. Fawn
	2. Pale blue
	3. Pale green
Issued:	1984
Varieties:	Reissued in 1985 as 'Promenade' (Style Two), HN 3072
Series:	Elegance (Series One)
U.S.:	**$650.00**
Can.:	**$775.00**
U.K.:	**£350.00**

HN 3054
Dominique
Designer:	A. Hughes
Height:	14", 35.6 cm
Colour:	Fawn
Issued:	1984-1984
Varieties:	Colourways:
	1. Pale blue
	2. Pale green;
	Also called 'Paradise' HN 3074
Series:	Elegance (Series One)
U.S.:	**$ 500.00**
Can.:	**$ 600.00**
U.K.:	**£ 275.00**

Photograph
Not
Available

HN 3055
Claudine
Designer:	A. Hughes
Height:	12", 30.5 cm
Colour:	Fawn
Issued:	1984-1984
Varieties:	Colourways:
	1. Pale blue
	2. Pale green
Series:	Elegance (Series One)
U.S.:	**$ 500.00**
Can.:	**$ 600.00**
U.K.:	**£ 275.00**

HN 3056
Danielle
Style One
Designer: A. Hughes
Height: 12", 30.5 cm
Colour: Fawn
Issued: 1984-1984
Varieties: Colourways:
 1. Pale blue
 2. Pale green
Series: Elegance (Series One)
U.S.: **$ 500.00**
Can.: **$ 600.00**
U.K.: **£ 275.00**

HN 3057
Sir Winston Churchill
Style One
Designer: A. Hughes
Height: 10 ½", 26.7 cm
Colour: White
Issued: 1985 to the present
U.S.: **$360.00**
Can.: **$465.00**
U.K.: **£130.00**

HN 3058
Andrea
Style One
Designer: A. Hughes
Height: 5 ¼", 13.3 cm
Colour: Blue and white
Issued: 1985-1995
Series: Vanity Fair Children
U.S.: **$125.00**
Can.: **$150.00**
U.K.: **£ 70.00**

HN 3059
Sophistication
Designer: A. Hughes
Height: 11 ½", 29.2 cm
Colour: Pale blue and white
Issued: 1987 N. America,
 1988 Worldwide-1990
Series: Reflections
U.S.: **$300.00**
Can.: **$375.00**
U.K.: **£175.00**

HN 3060
Wintertime
Style One
Designer: A. Hughes
Height: 8 ½", 21.6 cm
Colour: Red and white
Issued: 1985-1985
Series: 1. The Seasons
 (Series Four)
 2. RDICC
U.S.: **$325.00**
Can.: **$400.00**
U.K.: **£175.00**

HN 3061
Hope
Style One
Designer: S. Mitchell
Height: 8 ¼", 21.0 cm
Colour: Pale blue
Issued: 1984 in a limited
 edition of 9.500
Series: NSPCC Charity
Comm.by: Lawleys By Post
U.S.: **$500.00**
Can.: **$600.00**
U.K.: **£275.00**

HN 3062 - 3065 not issued.

HN 3066
Printemps (Spring)
Designer: R. Jefferson
Height: 11 ¼", 28.6 cm
Colour: White, brown and
 green
Issued: 1987 in a limited
 edition of 300
Series: Les Saisons
U.S.: **$1,500.00**
Can.: **$1,800.00**
U.K.: **£ 850.00**

HN 3067
Ete (Summer)
Designer: R. Jefferson
Height: 11 ¾", 29.8 cm
Colour: Yellow and green
Issued: 1989 in a limited
 edition of 300
Series: Les Saisons
U.S.: **$1,700.00**
Can.: **$2,000.00**
U.K.: **£ 925.00**

HN 3068
Automne (Autumn)
Designer:	R. Jefferson
Height:	11 ½", 29.2 cm
Colour:	Lavender and cream
Issued:	1986 in a limited edition of 300
Series:	Les Saisons
U.S.:	**$1,500.00**
Can.:	**$1,800.00**
U.K.:	**£ 850.00**

HN 3069
Hiver (Winter)
Designer:	R. Jeffferson
Height:	11 ¾", 29.8 cm
Colour:	White
Issued:	1988 in a limited edition of 300
Series:	Les Saisons
U.S.:	**$1,500.00**
Can.:	**$1,800.00**
U.K.:	**£ 850.00**

HN 3070
Cocktails
Designer:	A. Hughes
Height:	11", 28.0 cm
Colour:	Pale brown
Issued:	1985 N. America, 1987 Worldwide -1995
Series:	Reflections
U.S.:	**$325.00**
Can.:	**$400.00**
U.K.:	**£175.00**

HN 3071
Flirtation
Designer:	A. Hughes
Height:	10", 25.4 cm
Colour:	Pale blue
Issued:	1985 N. America, 1987 Worldwide -1995
Series:	Reflections
U.S.:	**$325.00**
Can.:	**$400.00**
U.K.:	**£175.00**

HN 3072
Promenade
Style Two
Designer:	A. Hughes
Height:	13 ¼", 33.5 cm
Colour:	Pale brown
Issued:	1985 N. America, 1987 Worldwide -1995
Varieties:	Also called 'Martine' HN 3053
Series:	Reflections
U.S.:	**$650.00**
Can.:	**$775.00**
U.K.:	**£350.00**

HN 3073
Strolling
Style One
Designer:	A. Hughes
Height:	13 ½", 34.3 cm
Colour:	Pale green and white
Issued:	1985 N. America, 1987 Worldwide -1995
Series:	Reflections
U.S.:	**$650.00**
Can.:	**$775.00**
U.K.:	**£350.00**

HN 3074
Paradise
Designer:	A. Hughes
Height:	14", 35.5 cm
Colour:	Pale brown
Issued:	1985 N. America, 1987 Worldwide -1992
Varieties:	Also called 'Dominique' HN 3054
Series:	Reflections
U.S.:	**$400.00**
Can.:	**$475.00**
U.K.:	**£220.00**

HN 3075
Tango
Designer:	A. Hughes
Height:	13", 33.0 cm
Colour:	Pale blue and cream
Issued:	1985 N. America, 1987 Worldwide -1992
Series:	Reflections
U.S.:	**$375.00**
Can.:	**$450.00**
U.K.:	**£200.00**

HN 3076
Bolero
Designer: A. Hughes
Height: 13 ½", 34.3 cm
Colour: Pale blue and pink
Issued: 1985 N. America,
1987 Worldwide -1992
Series: Reflections
U.S.:	$375.00
Can.:	$450.00
U.K.:	£200.00

HN 3077
Windflower
Style Four
Designer: A. Hughes
Height: 12 ¼", 31.1 cm
Colour: Pale blue
Issued: 1986 N. America,
1987 Worldwide -1992
Series: Reflections
U.S.:	$325.00
Can.:	$400.00
U.K.:	£175.00

HN 3078
Dancing Delight
Designer: A. Hughes
Height: 12 ¾", 32.0 cm
Colour: Pale brown
Issued: 1986 N. America,
1987 Worldwide -1988
Series: Reflections
U.S.:	$375.00
Can.:	$450.00
U.K.:	£200.00

HN 3079
Sleeping Beauty
Style One
Designer: A. Hughes
Height: 4 ½", 11.4 cm
Colour: Green and white
Issued: 1987-1989
U.S.:	$300.00
Can.:	$375.00
U.K.:	£165.00

HN 3080
Allure
Designer: E. J. Griffiths
Height: 12 ½", 32.0 cm
Colour: Pale green
Issued: 1985 N. America
1987 Worldwide-1988
Varieties: Also called 'Monique'
HN 2880
Series: Reflections
U.S.:	$300.00
Can.:	$375.00
U.K.:	£165.00

HN 3082
Faith
Style One
Designer: E. J. Griffiths
Height: 8 ½", 21.6 cm
Colour: Pink
Issued: 1986 in a limited
edition of 9,500
Series: NSPCC Charity
Comm.by: Lawleys By Post
U.S.:	$250.00
Can.:	$325.00
U.K.:	£150.00

HN 3083
Sheikh
Designer: E. J. Griffiths
Height: 9 ¾", 24.7 cm
Colour: White
Issued: 1987-1989
Series: Reflections
U.S.:	$250.00
Can.:	$300.00
U.K.:	£135.00

HN 3084
Harvestime
Designer: E. J. Griffiths
Height: 8", 20.3 cm
Colour: Blue and blue-grey
Issued: 1988-1990
Series: Reflections
U.S.:	$250.00
Can.:	$300.00
U.K.:	£135.00

HN 3081 not issued.

HN 3085
Summer Rose
Style One
Designer: E. J. Griffiths
Height: 8 ½", 21.6 cm
Colour: Blue
Issued: 1987 N. America,
             1988 Worldwide -1992
Series: Reflections
    U.S.: $250.00
    Can.: $300.00
    U.K.:   £135.00

HN 3086
The Duchess of York
Designer: E. J. Griffiths
Height: 8 ¼", 21.0 cm
Colour: Cream
Issued: 1986 in a limited
             edition of 1,500
Comm.by: Lawleys By Post
    U.S.: $ 900.00
    Can.: $1,100.00
    U.K.:   £ 500.00

HN 3087
Charity
Style One
Designer: E. J. Griffiths
Height: 8 ½", 21.6 cm
Colour: Yellow and purple
Issued: 1987 in a limited
             edition of 9,500
Series: NSPCC Charity
Comm.by: Lawleys By Post
    U.S.: $450.00
    Can.: $550.00
    U.K.:   £250.00

HN 3088
Kate Hannigan
Designer: E. J. Griffiths
Height: 9", 22.9 cm
Colour: Light brown
Issued: 1989 in a limited
             edition of 9,500
Comm.by: Lawleys By Post
    U.S.: $450.00
    Can.: $550.00
    U.K.:   £250.00

HN 3089
Grace Darling
Designer: E. J. Griffiths
Height: 9", 22.9 cm
Colour: Blue, yellow and rose
Issued: 1987 in a limited
             edition of 9,500
Comm.by: Lawleys By Post
    U.S.: $350.00
    Can.: $425.00
    U.K.:   £190.00

HN 3090
Charisma
Designer: P. Parsons
Height: 12 ½", 31.7 cm
Colour: Pale blue, white
             and brown
Issued: 1986 N. America,
             1987 Worldwide -1990
Series: Reflections
    U.S.: $300.00
    Can.: $350.00
    U.K.:   £165.00

HN 3091
Summer's Darling
Style One
Designer: P. Parsons
Height: 11 ½", 29.0 cm
Colour: Pale blue
Issued: 1986 N. America,
             1987 Worldwide -1995
Series: Reflections
    U.S.: $300.00
    Can.: $350.00
    U.K.:   £165.00

HN 3092
Cherry Blossom
Designer: P. Parsons
Height: 12 ¾", 32.0 cm
Colour: Pale green and
             pale brown
Issued: 1986 N. America,
             1987 Worldwide -1989
Series: Reflections
    U.S.: $300.00
    Can.: $350.00
    U.K.:   £165.00

HN 3093
Morning Glory
Designer: P. Parsons
Height: 13", 33.0 cm
Colour: Green and blue
Issued: 1986 N. America,
1987 Worldwide-1989
Series: Reflections
U.S.: $300.00
Can.: $350.00
U.K.: £165.00

HN 3094
Sweet Perfume
Designer: P. Parsons
Height: 13", 33.0 cm
Colour: Pale blue and white
Issued: 1986 N. America,
1987 Worldwide-1995
Series: Reflections
U.S.: $300.00
Can.: $350.00
U.K.: £165.00

HN 3095
Happy Birthday
Style One
Designer: P. Parsons
Height: 8 ½", 21.6 cm
Colour: Yellow and white
Issued: 1987-1994
Series: Special Occasions
U.S.: $300.00
Can.: $350.00
U.K.: £165.00

HN 3096
Merry Christmas
Designer: P. Parsons
Height: 8 ½", 21.6 cm
Colour: Green and white
Issued: 1987-1992
Series: Special Occasions
U.S.: $325.00
Can.: $400.00
U.K.: £175.00

HN 3097
Happy Anniversary
Style One
Designer: P. Parsons
Height: 6 ½", 16.5 cm
Colour: Purple and white
Issued: 1987-1993
Series: Special Occasions
U.S.: $300.00
Can.: $350.00
U.K.: £165.00

HN 3098
Dorothy
Designer: P. Parsons
Height: 7", 17.8 cm
Colour: Grey
Issued: 1987-1990
U.S.: $450.00
Can.: $550.00
U.K.: £250.00

HN 3099
Queen Elizabeth I
Designer: P. Parsons
Height: 9", 22.9 cm
Colour: Red and gold
Issued: 1986 U.K.,
1987 Worldwide in a
limited edition of 5,000
Series: Queens of the Realm
U.S.: $750.00
Can.: $900.00
U.K.: £400.00

HN 3100
Kathleen
Style Two
Designer: S. Keenan
Height: 6 ½", 16.5 cm
Colour: Purple, cream
and pink
Issued: 1986-1986
Varieties: HN 2933
Series: M. Doulton Events
U.S.: $325.00
Can.: $400.00
U.K.: £175.00

HN 3101 - 3104 not issued.

HN 3105
The Love Letter
Style Two
Designer: R. Jefferson
Height: 12", 30.5 cm
Colour: Pale blue and
             pale brown
Issued: 1986 N. America,
             1987 Worldwide -1988
Series: Reflections
  U.S.:   **$300.00**
  Can.:   **$350.00**
  U.K.:   **£165.00**

HN 3106
Secret Moment
Designer: R. Jefferson
Height: 12 ¼", 31.1 cm
Colour: Pale blue, green
             flowers
Issued: 1986 N. America,
             1987 Worldwide-1988
Series: Reflections
  U.S.:   **$300.00**
  Can.:   **$350.00**
  U.K.:   **£165.00**

HN 3107
Daybreak
Style One
Designer: R. Jefferson
Height: 11 ¾", 29.8 cm
Colour: White, pale green
             borders with yellow
             flowers
Issued: 1986 N. America,
             1987 Worldwide-1988
Series: Reflections
  U.S.:   **$300.00**
  Can.:   **$350.00**
  U.K.:   **£165.00**

HN 3108
Enchanting Evening
Designer: R. Jefferson
Height: 11 ¾", 29.8 cm
Colour: Pale pink
Issued: 1986 N. America,
             1987 Worldwide -1992
Series: Reflections
  U.S.:   **$325.00**
  Can.:   **$400.00**
  U.K.:   **£175.00**

HN 3109
Pensive
Designer: R. Jefferson
Height: 13", 33.0 cm
Colour: White with yellow
             flowers on skirt
Issued: 1986 N. America,
             1987 Worldwide -1988
Series: Reflections
  U.S.:   **$275.00**
  Can.:   **$325.00**
  U.K.:   **£150.00**

HN 3110
Enigma
Designer: R. Jefferson
Height: 12 ¾", 32.0 cm
Colour: Cream
Issued: 1986 N. America,
             1987 Worldwide -1995
Series: Reflections
  U.S.:   **$275.00**
  Can.:   **$325.00**
  U.K.:   **£150.00**

HN 3111
Robin Hood and Maid Marion
Designer: R. Jefferson
Height: 12 ¾", 33.0 cm
Colour: Blue, green and cream
Issued: 1994 in a limited
             edition of 150
Series: Great Lovers
  U.S.:   **$2,500.00**
  Can.:   **$3,000.00**
  U.K.:   **£1,350.00**

HN 3112
Lancelot and Guinivere
Designer: R. Jefferson
Height: 12 ¾", 33.0 cm
Colour: Lilac, purple, cream,
             green and yellow
Issued: 1996 in a limited
             edition of 150
Series: Great Lovers
  U.S.:   **$2,750.00**
  Can.:   **$3,300.00**
  U.K.:   **£1,500.00**

HN 3113
Romeo and Juliet
Style One
Designer: R. Jefferson
Height: 12", 30.5 cm
Colour: Lilac, purple, cream,
yellow and green
Issued: 1993 in a limited
edition of 150
Series: Great Lovers
U.S.: $2,500.00
Can.: $3,000.00
U.K.: £1,350.00

HN 3114
Antony and Cleopatra
Designer: R. Jefferson
Height: 11 ¾", 29.8 cm
Colour: Pale blue and cream
Issued: 1995 in a limited
edition of 150
Series: Great Lovers
U.S.: $2,750.00
Can.: $3,300.00
U.K.: £1,500.00

HN 3115
Idle Hours
Designer: A. Maslankowski
Length: 12 ¼", 31.1 cm
Colour: Blue-white and
pale green
Issued: 1986 N. America,
1987 Worldwide -1988
Series: Reflections
U.S.: $300.00
Can.: $375.00
U.K.: £165.00

HN 3116
Park Parade
Designer: A. Maslankowski
Height: 11 ¾", 29.8 cm
Colour: Pale green and
pale blue
Issued: 1987 N. America,
1988 Worldwide-1994
Series: Reflections
U.S.: $475.00
Can.: $575.00
U.K.: £260.00

HN 3117
Indian Maiden
Designer: A. Maslankowski
Height: 12", 30.5 cm
Colour: Pale tan and pale blue
Issued: 1987-1990
Series: Reflections
U.S.: $350.00
Can.: $425.00
U.K.: £190.00

HN 3118
Lorraine
Style One
Designer: A. Maslankowski
Height: 7 ¾", 19.7 cm
Colour: Blue
Issued: 1988-1995
U.S.: $375.00
Can.: $450.00
U.K.: £200.00

HN 3119
Partners
Designer: A. Maslankowski
Height: 6 ¾", 17.2 cm
Colour: Black, blue and grey
Issued: 1990-1992
Series: Clowns
U.S.: $400.00
Can.: $500.00
U.K.: £225.00

HN 3120
Spring Walk
Designer: A. Maslankowski
Height: 13", 32.9 cm
Colour: Blue with white poodle
Issued: 1990-1992
Series: Reflections
U.S.: $650.00
Can.: $775.00
U.K.: £350.00

HN 3121
Wizard
Style One
Designer: A. Maslankowski
Height: 10", 25.4 cm
Colour: Flambé
Issued: 1990-1995
Varieties: HN 2877, 4069
Series: Flambé
  U.S.: $650.00
  Can.: $775.00
  U.K.:   £350.00

HN 3122
My First Pet
Designer: A. Maslankowski
Height: 4 ½", 11.4 cm
Colour: Blue and white
Issued: 1991-1997
Series: Vanity Fair Children
  U.S.: $150.00
  Can.: $180.00
  U.K.:   £ 80.00

HN 3123
Sit
Designer: A. Maslankowski
Height: 4 ½", 11.4 cm
Colour: White and yellow
Issued: 1991-2000
Varieties: HN 3430
Series: Vanity Fair Children
  U.S.: $150.00
  Can.: $180.00
  U.K.:   £ 80.00

HN 3124
Thinking of You
Style One
Designer: A. Maslankowski
Height: 6 ¾", 17.1 cm
Colour: White
Issued: 1991-2001
Varieties: HN 3490
Series: Sentiments
  U.S.: $125.00
  Can.: $150.00
  U.K.:   £ 70.00

HN 3125
Queen Victoria
Designer: P. Parsons
Height: 8", 20.3 cm
Colour: Pink and white
Issued: 1987 U.K.,
             1988 Worldwide in a
             limited edition of 5,000
Series: Queens of the Realm
  U.S.: $1,250.00
  Can.: $1,500.00
  U.K.:   £ 700.00

HN 3126
Storytime
Style One
Designer: P. Parsons
Height: 6", 15.2 cm
Colour: Pale blue
Issued: 1987-1992
Series: Reflections
  U.S.: $200.00
  Can.: $250.00
  U.K.:   £110.00

HN 3127
Playmates
Style One
Designer: P. Parsons
Height: 8 ½", 21.6 cm
Colour: Pale blue, green
             and white
Issued: 1987-1992
Series: Reflections
  U.S.: $200.00
  Can.: $250.00
  U.K.:   £110.00

HN 3128
Tomorrow's Dreams
Style One
Designer: P. Parsons
Height: 6 ½", 16.5 cm
Colour: White and green
Issued: 1987-1992
Series: Reflections
  U.S.: $250.00
  Can.: $300.00
  U.K.:   £135.00

HN 3129
Thankful
Designer: P. Parsons
Height: 8 ½", 21.6 cm
Colour: White
Issued: 1987-1999
Varieties: HN 3135
Series: Images

U.S.:	$125.00
Can.:	$150.00
U.K.:	£ 70.00

HN 3130
Sisterly Love
Designer: P. Parsons
Height: 8 ½", 21.6 cm
Colour: Pale blue and white
Issued: 1987-1995
Series: Reflections

U.S.:	$200.00
Can.:	$250.00
U.K.:	£110.00

HN 3131 not issued.

HN 3132
Good Pals
Designer: P. Parsons
Height: 6 ¼", 15.9 cm
Colour: Pale blue and white
Issued: 1987-1992
Series: Reflections

U.S.:	$200.00
Can.:	$250.00
U.K.:	£110.00

HN 3133
Dreaming
Designer: P. Parsons
Height: 9", 22.9 cm
Colour: Pale pink
Issued: 1987-1995
Series: Reflections

U.S.:	$225.00
Can.:	$275.00
U.K.:	£120.00

HN 3134
Ballet Class
Style One
Designer: P. Parsons
Height: 6", 15.2 cm
Colour: White and tan
Issued: 1987 N. America,
1988 Worldwide -1992
Series: Reflections

U.S.:	$225.00
Can.:	$275.00
U.K.:	£120.00

HN 3135
Thankful
Designer: P. Parsons
Height: 8 ½", 21.6 cm
Colour: Black
Issued: 1987-1994
Varieties: HN 3129
Series: Images

U.S.:	$175.00
Can.:	$210.00
U.K.:	£ 95.00

HN 3136
Laura
Style One
Designer: P. Parsons
Height: 7 ¼", 18.4 cm
Colour: Dark blue and white
Issued: 1988-1988
Varieties: HN 2960
Series: M. Doulton Events

U.S.:	$325.00
Can.:	$400.00
U.K.:	£175.00

HN 3137
Summertime
Style One
Designer: P. Parsons
Height: 8", 20.3 cm
Colour: White and blue
Issued: 1987-1987
Series: 1. The Seasons
(Series Four)
2. RDICC

U.S.:	$275.00
Can.:	$350.00
U.K.:	£150.00

HN 3138
Eastern Grace
Designer: P. Parsons
Height: 12", 30.5 cm
Colour: Cream
Issued: 1988-1989
Varieties: HN 3683
Series: Reflections
   U.S.: $350.00
   Can.: $425.00
   U.K.:   £200.00

HN 3139
Free As The Wind
Designer: P. Parsons
Height: 9 ½", 24.1 cm
Colour: Pale blue
Issued: 1988 N. America,
              1989 Worldwide -1995
Series: Reflections
   U.S.: $325.00
   Can.: $400.00
   U.K.:   £175.00

HN 3140
Gaiety
Designer: P. Parsons
Height: 10 ¼", 26.0 cm
Colour: Pale green and
              pale blue
Issued: 1988-1990
Series: Reflections
   U.S.: $325.00
   Can.: $400.00
   U.K.:   £175.00

HN 3141
Queen Anne
Designer: P. Parsons
Height: 9", 22.9 cm
Colour: Green, red and white
Issued: 1988 in a limited
              edition of 5,000
Series: Queens of the Realm
Comm.by: Lawleys By Post
   U.S.: $600.00
   Can.: $725.00
   U.K.:   £325.00

HN 3142
Mary, Queen of Scots
Style Two
Designer: P. Parsons
Height: 9", 22.9 cm
Colour: Blue and purple
Issued: 1989 in a limited
              edition of 5,000
Series: Queens of the Realm
Comm.by: Lawleys By Post
   U.S.: $1,100.00
   Can.: $1,250.00
   U.K.:   £ 600.00

HN 3143
Rosemary
Style Two
Designer: P. Parsons
Height: 7 ½", 19.1 cm
Colour: White dress with
              pink flowers
Issued: 1988-1991
   U.S.: $325.00
   Can.: $400.00
   U.K.:   £175.00

HN 3144
Florence Nightingale
Designer: P. Parsons
Height: 8 ¼", 21.0 cm
Colour: Red
Issued: 1988 in a limited
              edition of 5,000
Comm.by: Lawleys By Post
   U.S.: $1,100.00
   Can.: $1,250.00
   U.K.:   £ 600.00

HN 3145
Rose Arbour
Designer: D. Brindley
Height: 12", 30.5 cm
Colour: Pale blue and white
Issued: 1987 N. America,
              1988 Worldwide -1990
Series: Reflections
   U.S.: $300.00
   Can.: $350.00
   U.K.:   £165.00

HN 3146 - 3154 not issued.

HN 3155
Water Maiden
Designer: A. Hughes
Height: 12", 30.5 cm
Colour: Blue
Issued: 1987-1991
Series: Reflections

U.S.:	**$350.00**
Can.:	**$425.00**
U.K.:	**£200.00**

HN 3156
Bathing Beauty
Style One
Designer: A. Hughes
Height: 9 ¾", 24.7 cm
Colour: Pale grey
Issued: 1987-1989
Series: Reflections

U.S.:	**$550.00**
Can.:	**$650.00**
U.K.:	**£300.00**

HN 3157
Free Spirit
Style One
Designer: A. Hughes
Height: 10 ½", 26.5 cm
Colour: White
Issued: 1987-1992
Varieties: HN 3159
Series: Images

U.S.:	**$200.00**
Can.:	**$250.00**
U.K.:	**£110.00**

HN 3158 not issued.

HN 3159
Free Spirit
Style One
Designer: A. Hughes
Height: 10 ½", 26.5 cm
Colour: Black
Issued: 1987-1992
Varieties: HN 3157
Series: Images

U.S.:	**$200.00**
Can.:	**$250.00**
U.K.:	**£110.00**

HN 3160
Shepherd
Style Five
Designer: A. Hughes
Height: 8 ½", 21.6 cm
Colour: Grey-blue and black
Issued: 1988-1989
Series: Reflections

U.S.:	**$375.00**
Can.:	**$450.00**
U.K.:	**£200.00**

HN 3161
The Gardener
Designer: A. Hughes
Height: 8 ¼", 21.0 cm
Colour: Blue and pale brown
Issued: 1988-1991
Series: Reflection

U.S.:	**$325.00**
Can.:	**$400.00**
U.K.:	**£175.00**

HN 3162
Breezy Day
Designer: A. Hughes
Height: 8 ½", 21.6 cm
Colour: Pale blue, pale
         brown and white
Issued: 1988-1990
Series: Reflections

U.S.:	**$275.00**
Can.:	**$325.00**
U.K.:	**£150.00**

HN 3163
Country Maid
Designer: A. Hughes
Height: 8 ¼", 21.0 cm
Colour: Blue, pink, white
         and black
Issued: 1988-1991

U.S.:	**$375.00**
Can.:	**$450.00**
U.K.:	**£200.00**

HN 3164
Farmer's Wife
Style Two
Designer: A. Hughes
Height: 8 ¾", 22.2 cm
Colour: Brown and blue
Issued: 1988-1991
   U.S.: **$325.00**
   Can.: **$400.00**
   U.K.: **£175.00**

HN 3165
August
Style One
Designer: M. Davies
Height: 7 ¾", 19.7 cm
Colour: White and blue
            dress, poppies
Issued: 1987-1987
Varieties: Also called 'Gillian'
            (Style Three) HN 3742
Series: Figure of the Month
   U.S.: **$225.00**
   Can.: **$275.00**
   U.K.: **£125.00**

HN 3166
September
Style One
Designer: M. Davies
Height: 7 ¾", 19.7 cm
Colour: White and yellow
            dress, michaelmas
            daisies
Issued: 1987-1987
Varieties: Also called 'Gillian'
            (Style Three) HN 3742
Series: Figure of the Month
   U.S.: **$225.00**
   Can.: **$275.00**
   U.K.: **£125.00**

HN 3167
Hazel
Style Two
Designer: M. Davies
Height: 8", 20.3 cm
Colour: Flowered white dress
Issued: 1988-1991
   U.S.: **$350.00**
   Can.: **$425.00**
   U.K.: **£200.00**

HN 3168
Jemma
Designer: M. Davies
Height: 7 ¼", 18.4 cm
Colour: Red and blue
Issued: 1988-1991
   U.S.: **$275.00**
   Can.: **$325.00**
   U.K.: **£150.00**

HN 3169
Jessica
Style One
Designer: M. Davies
Height: 7", 17.8 cm
Colour: White
Issued: 1988-1995
Varieties: HN 3497
Series: Vanity Fair Ladies
   U.S.: **$225.00**
   Can.: **$275.00**
   U.K.: **£125.00**

HN 3170
Caroline
Style One
Designer: M. Davies
Height: 7 ½", 19.1 cm
Colour: White dress with
            blue flowers
Issued: 1988-1992
Varieties: Also called 'Winter
            Welcome' HN 3611
   U.S.: **$275.00**
   Can.: **$325.00**
   U.K.: **£150.00**

HN 3171
Camille
Style Two
Designer: M. Davies
Height: 7 ½", 19.1 cm
Colour: Orange-yellow,
            white and green
Issued: 1987
Varieties: 'Adéle' HN 2480;
            'Margaret' (Style Two)
            HN 2397, 3496
Comm.by: Marks and Spencer
   U.S.: **$325.00**
   Can.: **$400.00**
   U.K.: **£175.00**

HN 3172
Christine
Style Two
Designer: M. Davies
Height: 7 ½", 19.1 cm
Colour: Pink and white
Issued: 1987 in a limited
                 edition of 1,000
Varieties: HN 2792
Comm.by: Guild of Specialist
                 China and Glass
                 Retailers
   U.S.:   **$400.00**
   Can.:   **$475.00**
   U.K.:   **£220.00**

HN 3173
Natalie
Style One
Designer: M. Davies
Height: 8", 20.3 cm
Colour: Yellow and white
Issued: 1988-1996
Varieties: HN 3498
Series: Vanity Fair Ladies
   U.S.:   **$275.00**
   Can.:   **$350.00**
   U.K.:   **£150.00**

HN 3174
Southern Belle
Style Two
Designer: M. Davies
Remodeller: R. Tabbenor
Height: 4", 10.1 cm
Colour: Red and yellow
Issued: 1988-1997
Varieties: HN 3244
Series: Miniatures
   U.S.:   **$200.00**
   Can.:   **$250.00**
   U.K.:   **£110.00**

HN 3175
Sweet Violets
Designer: D. V. Tootle
Height: 10 ¼", 26.0 cm
Colour: Pale blue and white
Issued: 1988-1989
Series: Reflections
   U.S.:   **$250.00**
   Can.:   **$300.00**
   U.K.:   **£135.00**

HN 3176
Young Dreams
Designer: D. V. Tootle
Height: 6 ¼", 15.9 cm
Colour: Pink
Issued: 1988-1992
   U.S.:   **$275.00**
   Can.:   **$325.00**
   U.K.:   **£150.00**

HN 3177
Harriet
Style One
Designer: D. V. Tootle
Height: 7 ¼", 18.4 cm
Colour: Pink
Issued: 1988-1991
   U.S.:   **$400.00**
   Can.:   **$500.00**
   U.K.:   **£225.00**

HN 3178
Polly
Designer: D. V. Tootle
Height: 8", 20.3 cm
Colour: Green and lavender
Issued: 1988-1991
   U.S.:   **$275.00**
   Can.:   **$350.00**
   U.K.:   **£150.00**

HN 3179
Eliza
Style Two
Designer: D. V. Tootle
Height: 7 ½", 19.1 cm
Colour: Red and lilac
Issued: 1988-1992
   U.S.:   **$275.00**
   Can.:   **$350.00**
   U.K.:   **£150.00**

HN 3180
Phyllis
Style Two
Designer: D. V. Tootle
Height: 7 ¼", 18.4 cm
Colour: Red, white and purple
Issued: 1988-1991
   U.S.:   **$350.00**
   Can.:   **$425.00**
   U.K.:   **£200.00**

HN 3181
Moondancer
Designer: D. V. Tootle
Height: 11 ¾", 29.8 cm
Colour: Blue, white and
              pale green
Issued: 1988-1990
Series: Reflections
   U.S.:   **$350.00**
   Can.:   **$425.00**
   U.K.:   **£200.00**

HN 3182
Stargazer
Designer: D. V. Tootle
Height: 10 ½", 26.7 cm
Colour: Blue and pale blue
Issued: 1988-1990
Series: Reflections
   U.S.:   **$350.00**
   Can.:   **$425.00**
   U.K.:   **£200.00**

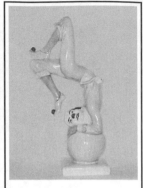

HN 3183
Tumbler
Designer: D. V. Tootle
Height: 9", 22.9 cm
Colour: Pink and yellow
Issued: 1989-1991
Varieties: Also called 'Tumbling'
              HN 3283, 3289
Series: 1. Clowns
              2. Reflections
   U.S.:   **$425.00**
   Can.:   **$525.00**
   U.K.:   **£230.00**

HN 3184
Joy
Style One
Designer: D. V. Tootle
Height: 6 ¾", 17.2 cm
Colour: Blue and pink
Issued: 1988-1990
Series: Reflections
   U.S.:   **$325.00**
   Can.:   **$400.00**
   U.K.:   **£175.00**

HN 3185
Traveller's Tale
Designer: E. J. Griffiths
Height: 9 ¼", 23.5 cm
Colour: Pale blue and
              pale green
Issued: 1988-1990
Series: Reflections
   U.S.:   **$300.00**
   Can.:   **$375.00**
   U.K.:   **£165.00**

HN 3186
Entranced
Designer: E. J. Griffiths
Height: 7 ¼", 18.4 cm
Colour: Green, white and tan
Issued: 1988-1989
Series: Reflections
   U.S.:   **$225.00**
   Can.:   **$275.00**
   U.K.:   **£120.00**

HN 3187
Balloons
Designer: E. J. Griffiths
Height: 9 ¼", 23.5 cm
Colour: Pale blue
Issued: 1988-in a limited
              edition of 1,000
Series: Reflections
Comm.by: Home Shopping
              Network
   U.S.:   **$500.00**
   Can.:   **$600.00**
   U.K.:   **£275.00**

HN 3188
Debutante
Style Two
Designer: E. J. Griffiths
Height: 12", 30.5 cm
Colour: Grey-pink
Issued: 1988 in a limited
edition of 1,000
Series: Reflections
Comm.by: Home Shopping
Network

U.S.:	**$350.00**
Can.:	**$425.00**
U.K.:	**£200.00**

HN 3189
HM Queen Elizabeth,
The Queen Mother
Style Two
Designer: E. J. Griffiths
Height: 8", 20.3 cm
Colour: Lavender, blue
and pink
Issued: 1990 in a limited
edition of 2,500

U.S.:	**$775.00**
Can.:	**$950.00**
U.K.:	**£420.00**

HN 3190
Old Ben
Designer: M. Nicholl
Height: 8 ½", 21.6 cm
Colour: Green, brown and
blue
Issued: 1990 in a limited
edition of 1,500
Comm.by: Newsvendors
Benevolent Society

U.S.:	**$250.00**
Can.:	**$300.00**
U.K.:	**£135.00**

HN 3191
Brothers
Designer: E. J. Griffiths
Height: 8 ¼", 21.0 cm
Colour: White
Issued: 1991 to the present
Series: Images

U.S.:	**$125.00**
Can.:	**$220.00**
U.K.:	**£ 39.00**

HN 3192
Mantilla
Designer: E. J. Griffiths
Height: 11 ½", 29.2 cm
Colour: Red, black and white
Issued: 1992 in a limited
edition of 1992
Varieties: HN 2712

U.S.:	**$450.00**
Can.:	**$550.00**
U.K.:	**£250.00**

Issued to commemorate Expo 92
Seville, Spain
HN 3193 - 3194 not issued.

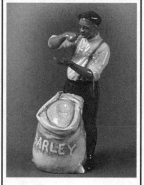

HN 3195
The Farmer
Style One
Designer: A. Hughes
Height: 9", 22.9 cm
Colour: Brown and white
Issued: 1988-1991

U.S.:	**$325.00**
Can.:	**$400.00**
U.K.:	**£175.00**

HN 3196
The Joker
Style One
Designer: A. Hughes
Height: 9 ¼", 23.5 cm
Colour: White and blue
Issued: 1988-1990
Varieties: Also called 'Tip-Toe';
HN 3293
Series: 1. Clowns
2. Reflections

U.S.:	**$425.00**
Can.:	**$500.00**
U.K.:	**£225.00**

HN 3197
Ballerina
Style Two
Designer: A. Hughes
Height: 14", 35.5 cm
Colour: White and beige
Issued: 1988 in a limited
edition of 1,000
Series: Reflections
Comm.by: Home Shopping
Network

U.S.:	**$400.00**
Can.:	**$475.00**
U.K.:	**£225.00**

HN 3198
Vanessa
Style Two
Designer:	A. Hughes
Height:	8 ½", 21.6 cm
Colour:	Green and black
Issued:	1989-1990
U.S.:	**$325.00**
Can.:	**$400.00**
U.K.:	**£175.00**

HN 3199
Maxine
Style One
Designer:	A. Hughes
Height:	8 ½", 21.6 cm
Colour:	Pink and purple
Issued:	1989-1990
U.S.:	**$325.00**
Can.:	**$400.00**
U.K.:	**£175.00**

HN 3200
Gloria
Style Two
Designer:	A. Hughes
Height:	8 ¾", 22.2 cm
Colour:	Pink
Issued:	1989-1990
U.S.:	**$325.00**
Can.:	**$400.00**
U.K.:	**£175.00**

HN 3201
Liberty
Style One
Designer:	A. Hughes
Height:	8 ¼", 21.0 cm
Colour:	White, blue and red
Issued:	1989-1990
U.S.:	**$325.00**
Can.:	**$400.00**
U.K.:	**£175.00**

HN 3202
The Boy Evacuee
Designer:	A. Hughes
Height:	8 ½", 21.6 cm
Colour:	Green and blue
Issued:	1989 in a limited edition of 9,500
Series:	Children of the Blitz
Comm.by:	Lawleys By Post
U.S.:	**$ 925.00**
Can.:	**$1,100.00**
U.K.:	**£ 500.00**

HN 3203
The Girl Evacuee
Designer:	A. Hughes
Height:	8", 20.3 cm
Colour:	Red, blue and brown
Issued:	1989 in a limited edition of 9,500
Series:	Children of the Blitz
Comm.by:	Lawleys By Post
U.S.:	**$ 925.00**
Can.:	**$1,100.00**
U.K.:	**£ 500.00**

HN 3204
Emily
Style One
Designer:	A. Hughes
Height:	8 ¼", 21.0 cm
Colour:	White and blue
Issued:	1989-1994
Series:	Vanity Fair Ladies
U.S.:	**$225.00**
Can.:	**$275.00**
U.K.:	**£125.00**

HN 3205
Veronica
Style Four
Designer:	A. Hughes
Height:	8", 20.3 cm
Colour:	White and pink
Issued:	1989-1992
Series:	Vanity Fair Ladies
U.S.:	**$250.00**
Can.:	**$300.00**
U.K.:	**£135.00**

Exclusive to North America.

HN 3206
Teresa
Style Two
Designer: A. Hughes
Height: 7 ¾", 19.7 cm
Colour: White with flowers
Issued: 1989-1992

U.S.:	**$250.00**
Can.:	**$325.00**
U.K.:	**£135.00**

HN 3207
Louise
Style Two
Designer: A. Hughes
Height: 7 ½", 19.1 cm
Colour: Red
Issued: 1990-1996

U.S.:	**$300.00**
Can.:	**$375.00**
U.K.:	**£165.00**

HN 3208
Emma
Style Two
Designer: A. Hughes
Height: 4 ¼", 10.8 cm
Colour: Red
Issued: 1990-1998
Series: Miniatures

U.S.:	**$200.00**
Can.:	**$250.00**
U.K.:	**£110.00**

HN 3209
Claire
Style One
Designer: A. Hughes
Height: 8 ½", 21.6 cm
Colour: Pink and with dress
            with flowers
Issued: 1990-1992

U.S.:	**$225.00**
Can.:	**$275.00**
U.K.:	**£125.00**

HN 3210
Christening Day
Designer: P. A. Northcroft
Height: 8 ½", 21.6 cm
Colour: White, baby's
            shawl blue
Issued: 1988-1990
Varieties: HN 3211
Series: Special Occasions

U.S.:	**$225.00**
Can.:	**$275.00**
U.K.:	**£125.00**

HN 3211
Christening Day
Designer: P. A. Northcroft
Height: 8 ½", 21.6 cm
Colour: White, pink baby's
            shawl
Issued: 1988-1990
Varieties: HN 3210
Series: Special Occasions

U.S.:	**$225.00**
Can.:	**$275.00**
U.K.:	**£120.00**

HN 3212
Christmas Morn
Style Two
Designer: M. Davies
Remodeller: R. Tabbenor
Height: 4", 10.1 cm
Colour: Red and white
Issued: 1988-1998
Varieties: HN 3245
Series: Miniatures

U.S.:	**$175.00**
Can.:	**$225.00**
U.K.:	**£100.00**

HN 3213
Kirsty
Style Two
Designer: M. Davies
Remodeller: P. Gee
Height: 3 ¾", 9.5 cm
Colour: Red
Issued: 1988-1997
Varieties: HN 3246, 3480,
            3743
Series: Miniatures

U.S.:	**$150.00**
Can.:	**$180.00**
U.K.:	**£ 80.00**

HN 3214
Elaine
Style Two
Designer: M. Davies
Remodeller: P. Gee
Height: 4", 10.1 cm
Colour: Blue
Issued: 1988-1998
Varieties: HN 3247, 3900
Series: Miniatures

U.S.:	**$175.00**
Can.:	**$225.00**
U.K.:	**£100.00**

HN 3215
Ninette
Style Two
Designer: M. Davies
Remodeller: P. Gee
Height: 3 ½", 8.9 cm
Colour: Cream and lavender
Issued: 1988-1997
Varieties: HN 3248, 3901
Series: Miniatures

U.S.:	**$175.00**
Can.:	**$225.00**
U.K.:	**£100.00**

HN 3216
Fair Lady
Style Two
Designer: M. Davies
Remodeller: P. Gee
Height: 3 ¾", 9.5 cm
Colour: Lemon and blue
Issued: 1988-1995
Varieties: HN 3336
Series: Miniatures

U.S.:	**$175.00**
Can.:	**$225.00**
U.K.:	**£100.00**

HN 3217
Joan
Style Two
Designer: M. Davies
Height: 8", 20.3 cm
Colour: Yellow and green
Issued: 1988 in a limited
edition of 2,000
Varieties: Also called 'Adrienne'
HN 2152, 2304;
'Fiona' (Style Four),
HN 3748
Comm.by: Joan's Gift Shop,
Scotland

U.S.:	**$350.00**
Can.:	**$450.00**
U.K.:	**£200.00**

HN 3218
Sunday Best
Style Two
Designer: M. Davies
Remodeller: P. Gee
Height: 3 ¾", 9.5 cm
Colour: Green and blue
Issued: 1988-1993
Varieties: HN 3312
Series: Miniatures

U.S.:	**$175.00**
Can.:	**$225.00**
U.K.:	**£100.00**

HN 3219
Sara
Style Two
Designer: M. Davies
Remodeller: P. Gee
Height: 3 ¾", 9.5 cm
Colour: Pink and green
Issued: 1988-1998
Varieties: HN 3249
Series: Miniatures

U.S.:	**$200.00**
Can.:	**$250.00**
U.K.:	**£110.00**

HN 3220
Fragrance
Style Two
Designer: M. Davies
Remodeller: P. Gee
Height: 3 ¾", 9.5 cm
Colour: Gold
Issued: 1988-1992
Varieties: HN 3250
Series: Miniatures

U.S.:	**$175.00**
Can.:	**$225.00**
U.K.:	**£100.00**

HN 3221
Country Rose
Designer: M. Davies
Height: 8 ½", 21.6 cm
Colour: White dress,
red flowers
Issued: 1989-2000
Varieties: Also called 'Alyssa'
HN 4132

U.S.:	**$325.00**
Can.:	**$400.00**
U.K.:	**£175.00**

HN 3222
Kelly
Style One
Designer: M. Davies
Height: 7 ½", 19.1 cm
Colour: White and blue
Issued: 1989
Varieties: HN 2478
Comm.by: Kay's Mail Order
Catalogue

U.S.:	**$300.00**
Can.:	**$375.00**
U.K.:	**$160.00**

HN 3223
Pamela
Style Two
Designer: M. Davies
Height: 7", 17.8 cm
Colour: Blue and white
Issued: 1989-1989
Varieties: HN 2479
Series: M. Doulton Events

U.S.:	**$275.00**
Can.:	**$375.00**
U.K.:	**£150.00**

HN 3224 - 3227 not issued.

HN 3228
Devotion
Designer: P. Parsons
Height: 9 ½", 24.1 cm
Colour: Pale green
Issued: 1989-1995
Series: Reflections

U.S.:	**$425.00**
Can.:	**$500.00**
U.K.:	**£225.00**

HN 3229
The Geisha
Style Three
Designer: P. Parsons
Height: 9 ½", 24.1 cm
Colour: Flambé
Issued: 1989-1989
Series: 1. Flambé
2. RDICC

U.S.:	**$600.00**
Can.:	**$725.00**
U.K.:	**£325.00**

HN 3230
HM Queen Elizabeth the
Queen Mother as the
Duchess of York
Designer: P. Parsons
Height: 9", 22.9 cm
Colour: Pale blue and pink
Issued: 1989 in a limited
edition of 9,500
Comm.by: Lawleys By Post

U.S.:	**$ 825.00**
Can.:	**$1,000.00**
U.K.:	**£ 450.00**

HN 3231
Autumntime
Style One
Designer: P. Parsons
Height: 8", 20.3 cm
Colour: Golden brown
Issued: 1989-1989
Series: 1. The Seasons
(Series Four)
2. RDICC

U.S.:	**$375.00**
Can.:	**$450.00**
U.K.:	**£200.00**

HN 3232
Anne Bolelyn
Designer: P. Parsons
Height: 8", 20.3 cm
Colour: Red and grey
Issued: 1990 in a limited
edition of 9,500
Series: Six Wives of
Henry VIII
Comm.by: Lawleys By Post

U.S.:	**$ 825.00**
Can.:	**$1,000.00**
U.K.:	**£ 450.00**

HN 3233
Catherine of Aragon
Designer: P. Parsons
Height: 6 ½", 16.5 cm
Colour: Green, blue and
white
Issued: 1990 in a limited
edition of 9,500
Series: Six Wives of
Henry VIII
Comm.by: Lawleys By Post

U.S.:	**$ 825.00**
Can.:	**$1,000.00**
U.K.:	**£ 450.00**

HN 3234
Paula
Designer:	P. Parsons
Height:	7", 17.8 cm
Colour:	White and blue
Issued:	1990-1996
Varieties:	HN 2906
Series:	Vanity Fair Ladies
U.S.:	**$250.00**
Can.:	**$300.00**
U.K.:	**£135.00**

HN 3235
Mother and Child
Style One
Designer:	P. Parsons
Height:	7 ½", 19.1 cm
Colour:	White and blue
Issued:	1991-1993
Varieties:	HN 3348, 3353
U.S.:	**$275.00**
Can.:	**$325.00**
U.K.:	**£150.00**

HN 3236
Falstaff
Style Three
Designer:	C. J. Noke
Remodeller:	R. Tabbenor
Height:	3 ¾", 9.5 cm
Colour:	Brown, yellow and lavender
Issued:	1989-1990
Series:	Miniatures
U.S.:	**$125.00**
Can.:	**$150.00**
U.K.:	**£ 70.00**

HN 3237 - 3243 not issued.

HN 3244
Southern Belle
Style Two
Designer:	M. Davies
Remodeller:	R. Tabbenor
Height:	4", 10.1 cm
Colour:	Turquoise and gold
Issued:	1989-1996
Varieties:	HN 3174
Series:	1. Miniatures
	2. Signature
Comm.by:	Lawleys By Post
U.S.:	**$275.00**
Can.:	**$325.00**
U.K.:	**£150.00**

HN 3245
Christmas Morn
Style Two
Designer:	M. Davies
Remodeller:	R. Tabbenor
Height:	3 ½", 8.9 cm
Colour:	Green, blue and gold
Issued:	1991-1996
Varieties:	HN 3212
Series:	1. Miniatures
	2. Signature
Comm.by:	Lawleys By Post
U.S.:	**$275.00**
Can.:	**$325.00**
U.K.:	**£150.00**

HN 3246
Kirsty
Style Two
Designer:	M. Davies
Remodeller:	P. Gee
Height:	3 ¾", 9.5 cm
Colour:	Purple, gold trim
Issued:	1989-1996
Varieties:	HN 3213, 3480, 3743
Series:	1. Miniatures
	2. Signature
Comm.by:	Lawleys By Post
U.S.:	**$275.00**
Can.:	**$325.00**
U.K.:	**£150.00**

HN 3247
Elaine
Style Two
Designer:	M. Davies
Remodeller:	P. Gee
Height:	4", 10.1 cm
Colour:	Blue, gold trim
Issued:	1989-1996
Varieties:	HN 3214, 3900
Series:	1. Miniatures
	2. Signature
Comm.by:	Lawleys By Post
U.S.:	**$275.00**
Can.:	**$325.00**
U.K.:	**£150.00**

HN 3248
Ninette
Style Two
Designer:	M. Davies
Remodeller:	P. Gee
Height:	3 ½", 8.9 cm
Colour:	Red, green and gold
Issued:	1989-1996
Varieties:	HN 3215, 3901
Series:	1. Miniatures
	2. Signature
U.S.:	**$275.00**
Can.:	**$325.00**
U.K.:	**£150.00**

HN 3249
Sara
Style Two
Designer: M. Davies
Remodeller: P. Gee
Height: 3 ¾", 9.5 cm
Colour: Blue and pink, gold trim
Issued: 1989-1996
Varieties: HN 3219
Series: 1. Miniatures
        2. Signature

U.S.:	$275.00
Can.:	$325.00
U.K.:	£150.00

HN 3250
Fragrance
Style Two
Designer: M. Davies
Remodeller: P. Gee
Height: 3 ¾", 9.5 cm
Colour: Red, gold trim
Issued: 1989-1992
Varieties: HN 3220
Series: 1. Miniatures
        2. Signature
Comm.by: Lawleys By Post

U.S.:	$275.00
Can.:	$325.00
U.K.:	£150.00

HN 3251
May
Style One
Designer: D. V. Tootle
Height: 8", 20.3 cm
Colour: Blue, red and pink
Issued: 1989 in a limited edition of 2,000
Varieties: HN 2746
Comm.by: U.S.A. Direct Mail Service

U.S.:	$325.00
Can.:	$400.00
U.K.:	£175.00

HN 3252
Fiona
Style Three
Designer: D. V. Tootle
Height: 7", 17.8 cm
Colour: Red
Issued: 1989-1992

U.S.:	$325.00
Can.:	$400.00
U.K.:	£175.00

HN 3253
Cheryl
Designer: D. V. Tootle
Height: 7 ½", 19.1 cm
Colour: Red and white
Issued: 1989-1994

U.S.:	$375.00
Can.:	$450.00
U.K.:	£210.00

HN 3254
Happy Anniversary
Style Two
Designer: D. V. Tootle
Height: 12", 30.5 cm
Colour: White
Issued: 1989 to the present
Series: Images

U.S.:	$240.00
Can.:	$345.00
U.K.:	£110.00

HN 3255
Madeleine
Designer: D. V. Tootle
Height: 7 ½", 19.1 cm
Colour: Blue, pink and cream
Issued: 1989-1992

U.S.:	$275.00
Can.:	$350.00
U.K.:	£150.00

HN 3256
Queen Victoria and Prince Albert
Designer: D. V. Tootle
Height: 9 ¼", 20.3 cm
Colour: Yellow-pink, cream and red
Issued: 1990 in a limited edition of 2,500
Comm.by: Lawleys By Post

U.S.:	$1,100.00
Can.:	$1,300.00
U.K.:	£ 600.00

HN 3257
Sophie
Style Two
Designer: D. V. Tootle
Height: 8", 20.3 cm
Colour: Blue and red
Issued: 1990-1992
  U.S.:   **$350.00**
  Can.:   **$425.00**
  U.K.:   **£200.00**

HN 3258
Dawn
Style Two
Designer: D. V. Tootle
Height: 8", 20.3 cm
Colour: Purple, red and white
Issued: 1990-1992
  U.S.:   **$300.00**
  Can.:   **$400.00**
  U.K.:   **£175.00**

HN 3259
Ann
Style Two
Designer: D. V. Tootle
Height: 8", 20.3 cm
Colour: Pink, green and blue
Issued: 1990-1996
Varieties: Also called 'Lauren'
             (Style One) HN 3290
  U.S.:   **$375.00**
  Can.:   **$450.00**
  U.K.:   **£210.00**

HN 3260
Jane
Style Three
Designer: D. V. Tootles
Height: 7 ¾", 19.7 cm
Colour: Green, blue and
             yellow
Issued: 1990-1993
  U.S.:   **$325.00**
  Can.:   **$425.00**
  U.K.:   **£180.00**

HN 3261
The Town Crier
Style Two
Designer: M. Davies
Remodeller: R. Tabbenor
Height: 4", 10.1 cm
Colour: Purple, green
             and black
Issued: 1989-1991
Series: Miniatures
  U.S.:   **$175.00**
  Can.:   **$200.00**
  U.K.:   **£ 95.00**

HN 3262
Good King Wenceslas
Style Two
Designer: M. Davies
Remodeller: R. Tabbenor
Height: 4", 10.1 cm
Colour: Black and purple
Issued: 1989-1992
Series: Miniatures
  U.S.:   **$175.00**
  Can.:   **$200.00**
  U.K.:   **£ 95.00**

HN 3263
Beatrice
Designer: M. Davies
Height: 7", 17.8 cm
Colour: Blue flowered dress
Issued: 1989-1998
Varieties: HN 3631; also called
             'Kathryn' (Style One)
             HN 3413, 'Lucy' (Style
             Two) HN 3653,
             'Summer Serenade'
             HN 3610; 'Wildflower
             of the Month'
  U.S.:   **$225.00**
  Can.:   **$275.00**
  U.K.:   **£120.00**

HN 3264
Alison
Style One
Designer: M. Davies
Height: 7 ½", 19.1 cm
Colour: White and pastel pink
Issued: 1989-1993
Varieties: HN 2336
  U.S.:   **$225.00**
  Can.:   **$275.00**
  U.K.:   **£120.00**

HN 3265
Lisa
Style One
Designer: M. Davies
Height: 7 ½", 19.1 cm
Colour: White and rose
Issued: 1989-1995
Varieties: HN 2310, 2394

U.S.:	**$225.00**
Can.:	**$275.00**
U.K.:	**£125.00**

HN 3266
Diana
Style Two
Designer: M. Davies
Height: 8", 20.3 cm
Colour: Pink and white
Issued: 1990-1990
Varieties: HN 2468
Series: M. Doulton Events

U.S.:	**$300.00**
Can.:	**$400.00**
U.K.:	**£180.00**

HN 3267
Salome
Style Two
Designer: M. Davies
Height: 9 ½", 24.1cm
Colour: Red, blue, lavender
and green
Issued: 1990 in a limited
edition of 1,000

U.S.:	**$1,200.00**
Can.:	**$1,500.00**
U.K.:	**£ 650.00**

HN 3268
Buttercup
Style Two
Designer: M. Davies
Remodeller: R. Tabbenor
Height: 4", 10.1 cm
Colour: Green
Issued: 1990-1998
Varieties: HN 3908
Series: Miniatures

U.S.:	**$200.00**
Can.:	**$250.00**
U.K.:	**£110.00**

HN 3269
Christine
Style Three
Designer: M. Davies
Remodeller: P. Gee
Height: 3 ¾", 9.5 cm
Colour: Orange and pink
Issued: 1990-1994
Varieties: HN 3337
Series: Miniatures

U.S.:	**$200.00**
Can.:	**$250.00**
U.K.:	**£110.00**

HN 3270
Karen
Style Three
Designer: M. Davies
Remodeller: R. Tabbenor
Height: 4", 10.1 cm
Colour: Red
Issued: 1990-1995
Varieties: HN 3338, 3749
Series: Miniatures

U.S.:	**$200.00**
Can.:	**$250.00**
U.K.:	**£110.00**

HN 3271
Guy Fawkes
Style Two
Designer: C. J. Nokes
Remodeller: P. Gee
Height: 4", 10.1 cm
Colour: Red and black
Issued: 1989-1991
Series: Miniatures

U.S.:	**$150.00**
Can.:	**$175.00**
U.K.:	**£ 80.00**

HN 3272
Dick Turpin
Style One
Designer: G. Tongue
Height: 12", 30.5 cm
Colour: Brown and black
Issued: 1989 in a limited
edition of 5,000
Comm.by: Lawleys By Post

U.S.:	**$1,000.00**
Can.:	**$1,200.00**
U.K.:	**£ 525.00**

HN 3273
Annabel
Style One
Designer: R. Tabbenor
Height: 6", 15.2 cm
Colour: White and blue
Issued: 1989-1992

U.S.:	**$325.00**
Can.:	**$400.00**
U.K.:	**£175.00**

HN 3274
Over The Threshold
Designer: R. Tabbenor
Height: 12", 30.5 cm
Colour: White
Issued: 1989-1998
Series: Images

U.S.:	**$250.00**
Can.:	**$300.00**
U.K.:	**£135.00**

HN 3275
Will He, Won't He
Designer: R. Tabbenor
Height: 9", 22.9 cm
Colour: Green
Issued: 1990-1994
Series: Clowns

U.S.:	**$400.00**
Can.:	**$475.00**
U.K.:	**£215.00**

HN 3276
Teeing Off
Designer: R. Tabbenor
Height: 9", 22.9 cm
Colour: Yellow and green
Issued: 1990-1997

U.S.:	**$350.00**
Can.:	**$425.00**
U.K.:	**£200.00**

HN 3277
The Carpet Seller
(Seated)
Style Three
Designer: R. Tabbenor
Height: 7 ½", 19.0 cm
Colour: Red
Issued: 1990-1995
Series: Flambé

U.S.:	**$625.00**
Can.:	**$750.00**
U.K.:	**£350.00**

HN 3278
Lamp Seller
Designer: R. Tabbenor
Height: 9", 22.9 cm
Colour: Red
Issued: 1990-1995
Series: Flambé

U.S.:	**$725.00**
Can.:	**$900.00**
U.K.:	**£425.00**

HN 3279
Winning Put
Designer: R. Tabbenor
Height: 8", 20.3 cm
Colour: Blue and yellow
Issued: 1991-1995

U.S.:	**$325.00**
Can.:	**$400.00**
U.K.:	**£175.00**

HN 3280
Bridesmaid
Style Six
Designer: R. Tabbenor
Height: 8 ½", 21.6 cm
Colour: White
Issued: 1991-1999
Series: Images

U.S.:	**$125.00**
Can.:	**$150.00**
U.K.:	**£ 65.00**

HN 3281
Bride and Groom
Designer: R. Tabbenor
Height: 6 ¼", 15.9 cm
Colour: White
Issued: 1991-2000
Series: Images

U.S.:	**$125.00**
Can.:	**$150.00**
U.K.:	**£ 70.00**

HN 3282
First Steps
Style Two
Designer: R. Tabbenor
Height: 9 ½", 24.0 cm
Colour: White
Issued: 1991-2001
Series: Images

U.S.:	**$225.00**
Can.:	**$275.00**
U.K.:	**£125.00**

HN 3283
Tumbling
Designer: D. V. Tootle
Height: 8 ¾", 22.2 cm
Colour: White, yellow,
           blue and green
Issued: 1990-1994
Varieties: 3289; also called
           'Tumbler' HN 3183
Series: Clowns

U.S.:	**$450.00**
Can.:	**$550.00**
U.K.:	**£250.00**

HN 3284
The Bride
Style Four
Designer: D. V. Tootle
Height: 8 ¼", 21.0 cm
Colour: White
Issued: 1990-1997
Varieties: HN 3285

U.S.:	**$275.00**
Can.:	**$325.00**
U.K.:	**£150.00**

HN 3285
The Bride
Style Four
Designer: D. V. Tootle
Height: 8 ¼", 21.0 cm
Colour: Ivory
Issued: 1990-1996
Varieties: HN 3284

U.S.:	**$275.00**
Can.:	**$325.00**
U.K.:	**£150.00**

HN 3286
Alexandra
Style Two
Designer: D. V. Tootle
Height: 7 ¾", 19.7 cm
Colour: Yellow and peach
Issued: 1990-2000
Varieties: HN 3292

U.S.:	**$375.00**
Can.:	**$450.00**
U.K.:	**£200.00**

HN 3287
Harlequin
Style Two
Designer: D. V. Tootle
Height: 12 ½", 31.7 cm
Colour: Black, gold and
           yellow
Issued: 1993-1993
Varieties: HN 2737, 4058
Comm.by: Harrods

U.S.:	**$2,200.00**
Can.:	**$2,600.00**
U.K.:	**£1,200.00**

HN 3288
Columbine
Style Three
Designer: D. V. Tootle
Height: 12 ½", 31.7 cm
Colour: Red, yellow, black
           and gold
Issued: 1993-1993
Varieties: HN 2738, 4059
Comm.by: Harrods

U.S.:	**$2,200.00**
Can.:	**$2,600.00**
U.K.:	**£1,200.00**

HN 3289
Tumbling
Designer: D. V. Tootle
Height: 8 ¾", 22.2 cm
Colour: Pink and blue
Issued: 1991 in a limited
            edition of 2,500
Varieties: HN 3283; also called
            'Tumbler' HN 3183
Series: Clowns
Comm.by: National Playing
            Fields Association

U.S.: $450.00
Can.: $550.00
U.K.:   £250.00

HN 3290
Lauren
Style One
Designer: D. V. Tootle
Height: 8", 20.3 cm
Colour: Mauve and yellow
Issued: 1992-1992
Varieties: Also called 'Ann'
            (Style Two), HN 3259
Comm.by: Great Universal
            Stores

U.S.: $425.00
Can.: $500.00
U.K.:   £225.00

HN 3291
Tracy
Designer: D.V. Toole
Height: 7 ½", 19.1 cm
Colour: White and pink
Issued: 1993-1999
Varieties: HN 2736

U.S.: $250.00
Can.: $300.00
U.K.:   £135.00

Exclusive t o U.S.A.

HN 3292
Alexandra
Style Two
Designer: D. V. Tootle
Height: 7 ¾", 19.7 cm
Colour: Pink and white
Issued: 1994-2002
Varieties: HN 3286

U.S.: $350.00
Can.: $425.00
U.K.: $200.00

HN 3293
Tip-Toe
Designer: A. Hughes
Height: 9", 22.9 cm
Colour: Black, white and yellow
Issued: 1990-1994
Varieties: Also called 'Joker'
            (Style One) HN 3196
Series: Clowns

U.S.: $450.00
Can.: $550.00
U.K.:   £250.00

HN 3294
Daddy's Joy
Designer: A. Hughes
Height: 8", 20.3 cm
Colour: Pink, yellow and
            white
Issued: 1990 in a limited
            edition of 12,500
Comm.by: Lawleys By Post

U.S.: $425.00
Can.: $500.00
U.K.:   £225.00

HN 3295
The Homecoming
Designer: A. Hughes
Height: 7", 17.8 cm
Colour: Blue, pink and green
Issued: 1990 in a limited
            edition of 9,500
Series: Children of the Blitz
Comm.by: Lawleys By Post

U.S.: $650.00
Can.: $775.00
U.K.:   £350.00

HN 3296
Fantasy
Designer: A. Hughes
Height: 12 ½", 31.7 cm
Colour: White
Issued: 1990-1992
Series: Reflections

U.S.: $750.00
Can.: $900.00
U.K.:   £400.00

HN 3297
Milestone
Designer: A. Hughes
Height: 7 ¼", 18.4 cm
Colour: Red and blue
Issued: 1990-1994

   U.S.: $550.00
   Can.: $650.00
   U.K.:   £300.00

HN 3298
Hold Tight
Designer: A. Hughes
Height: 8 ½", 21.6 cm
Colour: Red, blue and green
Issued: 1990-1993

   U.S.: $750.00
   Can.: $900.00
   U.K.:   £400.00

HN 3299
Welcome Home
Designer: A. Hughes
Height: 8 ½", 21.6 cm
Colour: Grey and turquoise
Issued: 1991 in a limited
            edition of 9,500
Series: Children of the Blitz
Comm.by: Lawleys By Post

   U.S.: $650.00
   Can.: $775.00
   U.K.:   £350.00

HN 3300
Dressing Up
Style Two
Designer: A. Hughes
Height: 6 ¾", 17.5 cm
Colour: Yellow and blue
Issued: 1991 in a limited
            edition of 9,500
Comm.by: Lawleys By Post

   U.S.: $425.00
   Can.: $500.00
   U.K.:   £225.00

HN 3301
Santa's Helper
Designer: A. Hughes
Height: 6 ½", 16.5 cm
Colour: Green, red and white
Issued: 1991-1995
Comm.by: Lawleys By Post

   U.S.: $450.00
   Can.: $550.00
   U.K.:   £250.00

HN 3302
Please Sir
Designer: A. Hughes
Height: 8", 20.3 cm
Colour: Blue, grey and beige
Issued: 1992 in a limited
            edition of 7,500
Comm.by: Lawleys By Post
            'National Children's
            Home'

   U.S.: $450.00
   Can.: $550.00
   U.K.:   £250.00

HN 3303
Tender Moment
Style One
Designer: M. Davies
Height: 7", 17.8 cm
Colour: Pink
Issued: 1990-1997
Varieties: Also called 'Nicola'
            HN 2804, 2839
Series: Vanity Fair Ladies

   U.S.: $250.00
   Can.: $300.00
   U.K.:   £135.00

HN 3304
Samantha
Style Two
Designer: M. Davies
Height: 7 ½", 19.1 cm
Colour: White-green dress,
            flowered border
Issued: 1990-1996
Varieties: Also called 'First
            Dance' HN 2803

   U.S.: $275.00
   Can.: $325.00
   U.K.:   £150.00

HN 3305
Kathy
Style Two
Designer: M. Davies
Height: 7 ¼", 18.4 cm
Colour: Blue-white dress,
           flowered border
Issued: 1990-1996
Varieties: Also called 'Lynne'
           (Style One) HN 2329,
           3740

U.S.:	**$275.00**
Can.:	**$350.00**
U.K.:	**£150.00**

HN 3306
Megan
Style One
Designer: M. Davies
Height: 7 ½", 19.0 cm
Colour: White and yellow
Issued: 1991-1994
Series: Vanity Fair Ladies

U.S.:	**$200.00**
Can.:	**$250.00**
U.K.:	**£110.00**

HN 3307
Elaine
Style One
Designer: M. Davies
Height: 7 ¼", 18.4 cm
Colour: Pink
Issued: 1990-2000
Varieties: HN 2791, 3741, 4130

U.S.:	**$325.00**
Can.:	**$400.00**
U.K.:	**£175.00**

HN 3308
Sara
Style One
Designer: M. Davies
Height: 7 ¾", 19.7 cm
Colour: Blue, pink and white
Issued: 1990-1996
Varieties: HN 2265

U.S.:	**$350.00**
Can.:	**$425.00**
U.K.:	**£200.00**

HN 3309
Summer Rose
Style Two
Designer: M. Davies
Height: 7 ½", 19.1 cm
Colour: White with
           pink flowers
Issued: 1991-1997
Varieties: Also called 'Denise'
           (Style Three) HN 2477

U.S.:	**$250.00**
Can.:	**$300.00**
U.K.:	**£135.00**

HN 3310
Diana
Style Three
Designer: M. Davies
Remodeller: D. Frith
Height: 4 ¼", 10.8 cm
Colour: Pale pink and blue
Issued: 1991-1995
Series: Miniatures

U.S.:	**$200.00**
Can.:	**$250.00**
U.K.:	**£110.00**

HN 3311
Fragrance
Style One
Designer: M. Davies
Height: 7 ¼", 18.4 cm
Colour: Red
Issued: 1991-1991
Varieties: HN 2334
Series: M. Doulton Events

U.S.:	**$300.00**
Can.:	**$350.00**
U.K.:	**£165.00**

HN 3312
Sunday Best
Style Two
Designer: M. Davies
Remodeller: P. Gee
Height: 3", 7.6 cm,
Colour: Green, blue, gold
Issued: 1991-1993
Varieties: HN 3218
Series: 1. Miniatures
           2. Signature
Comm.by: Lawleys By Post

U.S.:	**$275.00**
Can.:	**$350.00**
U.K.:	**£150.00**

HN 3313
Morning Breeze
Designer: P. Gee
Height: 8", 20.3 cm
Colour: Mottled blue
and orange
Issued: 1990-1994

U.S.:	$325.00
Can.:	$400.00
U.K.:	£175.00

HN 3314
Confucius
Designer: P. Gee
Height: 9", 22.9 cm
Colour: Flambé
Issued: 1990-1995
Series: Flambé

U.S.:	$650.00
Can.:	$775.00
U.K.:	£350.00

HN 3315
Waiting For A Train
Designer: P. Gee
Height: 8 ½", 21.6 cm
Colour: Cashmere coat, black
hat, 'biscuit' finish
Issued: 1991 in a limited
edition of 9,500
Comm.by: Lawleys By Post

U.S.:	$450.00
Can.:	$550.00
U.K.:	£250.00

HN 3316
Amy
Style Two
Designer: P. Gee
Height: 8", 20.3 cm
Colour: Blue and rose
Issued: 1991-1991
Series: Figure of the Year

U.S.:	$ 950.00
Can.:	$1,150.00
U.K.:	£ 525.00

HN 3317
Countess of Harrington
Designer: P. Gee
Height: 9 ½", 24.3 cm
Colour: Pale green
Issued: 1992 in a limited
edition of 5,000
Series: Reynolds Ladies

U.S.:	$750.00
Can.:	$900.00
U.K.:	£400.00

HN 3318
Lady Worsley
Designer: P. Gee
Height: 9 ½", 24.3 cm
Colour: Red, black and gold
Issued: 1991 in a limited
edition of 5,000
Series: Reynolds Ladies

U.S.:	$525.00
Can.:	$650.00
U.K.:	£300.00

HN 3319
Mrs. Hugh Bonfoy
Designer: P. Gee
Height: 9 ½", 24.3 cm
Colour: Blue-pink
Issued: 1992 in a limited
edition of 5,000
Series: Reynolds Ladies

U.S.:	$525.00
Can.:	$650.00
U.K.:	£300.00

HN 3320
Countess Spencer
Designer: P. Gee
Height: 9 ½", 24.3 cm
Colour: Red, blue and white
Issued: 1993 in a limited
edition of 5,000
Series: Reynolds Ladies

U.S.:	$550.00
Can.:	$650.00
U.K.:	£300.00

HN 3321
Gail
Style Two
Designer:	P. Gee
Height:	3 ¾", 9.5 cm
Colour:	Red and white
Issued:	1992-1997
Series:	Miniatures
U.S.:	**$200.00**
Can.:	**$250.00**
U.K.:	**£110.00**

HN 3322
Celeste
Style Two
Designer:	P. Gee
Height:	8", 20.3 cm
Colour:	Yellow
Issued:	1992-1992
Varieties:	Also called 'Isadora' HN 2938
Comm.by:	Great Universal Stores
U.S.:	**$350.00**
Can.:	**$425.00**
U.K.:	**£200.00**

HN 3323
June
Style Five
Designer:	R. Tabbenor
Height:	5 ¼", 13.3 cm
Colour:	White, pink flowers
Issued:	1990-2004
Varieties:	Also called 'Amanda' HN 2996, 3406, 3632, 3634, 3635
Series:	Flower of the Month, Child
U.S.:	**$50.00**
Can.:	**$60.00**
U.K.:	**£30.00**

HN 3324
July
Style Two
Designer:	R. Tabbenor
Height:	5 ¼", 13.3 cm
Colour:	White, blue flowers
Issued:	1990-2004
Varieties:	Also called 'Amanda' HN 2996, 3406, 3632, 3634, 3635
Series:	Flower of the Month, Child
U.S.:	**$50.00**
Can.:	**$60.00**
U.K.:	**£30.00**

HN 3325
August
Style Two
Designer:	R. Tabbenor
Height:	5 ¼", 13.3 cm
Colour:	White, purple flowers
Issued:	1990-2004
Varieties:	Also called 'Amanda' HN 2996, 3406, 3632, 3634, 3635
Series:	Flower of the Month, Child
U.S.:	**$50.00**
Can.:	**$60.00**
U.K.:	**£30.00**

HN 3326
September
Style Two
Designer:	R. Tabbenor
Height:	5 ¼", 13.3 cm
Colour:	White, lilac flowers
Issued:	1990-2004
Varieties:	Also called 'Amanda' HN 2996, 3406, 3632, 3634, 3635
Series:	Flower of the Month, Child
U.S.:	**$50.00**
Can.:	**$60.00**
U.K.:	**£30.00**

HN 3327
October
Style Two
Designer:	R. Tabbenor
Height:	5 ¼", 13.3 cm
Colour:	White, lilac/white flowers
Issued:	1990-2004
Varieties:	Also called 'Amanda' HN 2996, 3406, 3632, 3634, 3635
Series:	Flower of the Month, Child
U.S.:	**$50.00**
Can.:	**$60.00**
U.K.:	**£30.00**

HN 3328
November
Style Two
Designer:	R. Tabbenor
Height:	5 ¼", 13.3 cm
Colour:	White, lilac flowers
Issued:	1990-2004
Varieties:	Also called 'Amanda' HN 2996, 3406, 3632, 3634, 3635
Series:	Flower of the Month, Child
U.S.:	**$50.00**
Can.:	**$60.00**
U.K.:	**£30.00**

HN 3329
December
Style Two
Designer: R. Tabbenor
Height: 5 ¼", 13.3 cm
Colour: White, holly berries
Issued: 1990-2004
Varieties: Also called 'Amanda'
            HN 2996, 3406, 3632,
            3634, 3635
Series: Flower of the Month,
            Child

U.S.:	**$50.00**
Can.:	**$60.00**
U.K.:	**£30.00**

HN 3330
January
Style Two
Designer: R. Tabbenor
Height: 5 ¼", 13.3 cm
Colour: White, yellow flowers
Issued: 1990-2004
Varieties: Also called 'Amanda'
            HN 2996, 3406, 3632,
            3634, 3635
Series: Flower of the Month,
            Child

U.S.:	**$50.00**
Can.:	**$60.00**
U.K.:	**£30.00**

HN 3331
February
Style Two
Designer: R. Tabbenor
Height: 5 ¼", 13.3 cm
Colour: White, blue flowers
Issued: 1990-2004
Varieties: Also called 'Amanda'
            HN 2996, 3406, 3632,
            3634, 3635
Series: Flower of the Month,
            Child

U.S.:	**$50.00**
Can.:	**$60.00**
U.K.:	**£30.00**

HN 3332
March
Style Two
Designer: R. Tabbenor
Height: 5 ¼", 13.3 cm
Colour: White, purple flowers
Issued: 1990-2004
Varieties: Also called 'Amanda'
            HN 2996, 3406, 3632,
            3634, 3635
Series: Flower of the Month,
            Child

U.S.:	**$50.00**
Can.:	**$60.00**
U.K.:	**£30.00**

HN 3333
April
Style Two
Designer: R. Tabbenor
Height: 5 ¼", 13.3 cm
Colour: White, purple flowers
Issued: 1990-2004
Varieties: Also called 'Amanda'
            HN 2996, 3406, 3632,
            3634, 3635
Series: Flower of the Month,
            Child

U.S.:	**$50.00**
Can.:	**$60.00**
U.K.:	**£30.00**

HN 3334
May
Style Three
Designer: R. Tabbenor
Height: 5 ¼", 13.3 cm
Colour: White with lily-of-
            the-valley flowers
Issued: 1990-2004
Varieties: Also called 'Amanda'
            HN 2996, 3406, 3632,
            3634, 3635
Series: Flower of the Month,
            Child

U.S.:	**$50.00**
Can.:	**$60.00**
U.K.:	**£30.00**

HN 3335
Jester
Style Three
Designer: C. J. Noke
Remodeller: R. Tabbenor
Height: 4", 10.1 cm
Colour: Brown and purple
Issued: 1990-1990
Series: 1. Miniatures
             2. RDICC

U.S.:	**$175.00**
Can.:	**$200.00**
U.K.:	**£ 95.00**

HN 3336
Fair Lady
Style Two
Designer: M. Davies
Remodeller: P. Gee
Height: 3 ½", 8.9 cm
Colour: Red, purple, gold
Issued: 1991-1994
Varieties: HN 3216
Series: 1. Miniatures
             2. Signature
Comm.by: Lawleys By Post

U.S.:	**$275.00**
Can.:	**$350.00**
U.K.:	**£150.00**

HN 3337
Christine
Style Three
Designer: M. Davies
Remodeller: P. Gee
Height: 3 ½", 8.9 cm
Colour: Yellow, black, gold
Issued: 1991-1994
Varieties: HN 3269
Series: 1. Miniatures
2. Signature
Comm.by: Lawleys By Post

U.S.:	**$275.00**
Can.:	**$325.00**
U.K.:	**£150.00**

HN 3338
Karen
Style Three
Designer: M. Davies
Remodeller: R. Tabbenor
Height: 3 ½", 8.9 cm
Colour: Purple, gold trim
Issued: 1991-1994
Varieties: HN 3270, 3749
Series: 1. Miniatures
2. Signature
Comm.by: Lawleys By Post

U.S.:	**$275.00**
Can.:	**$325.00**
U.K.:	**£150.00**

HN 3339
Olivia
Style Two
Designer: M. Davies
Height: 8", 20.3 cm
Colour: Red
Issued: 1992
Varieties: Also called 'Ninette' (Style One) HN 2379, 3417
Comm.by: Great Universal Stores

U.S.:	**$375.00**
Can.:	**$450.00**
U.K.:	**£200.00**

HN 3340
Kay
Designer: M. Davies
Height: 7 ¼", 18.4 cm
Colour: Dark blue and white
Issued: 1991
Varieties: Also called 'Fair Lady' (Style One) HN 2193, 2832, 2835
Comm.by: Sears, Canada

U.S.:	**$250.00**
Can.:	**$300.00**
U.K.:	**£135.00**

HN 3341
January - Style Three
Designer: M. Davies
Height: 7 ½", 19.0 cm
Colour: White/blue, snowdrops
Issued: 1991-1991
Varieties: Also called 'Beatrice' HN 3263, 3631; 'Kathryn' (Style One) HN 3413; 'Lucy' HN 3653; 'Summer Serenade' HN 3610
Series: Wildflower / Month

U.S.:	**$225.00**
Can.:	**$275.00**
U.K.:	**£125.00**

HN 3342
February - Style Three
Designer: M. Davies
Height: 7 ½", 19.0 cm
Colour: White/pink, anemones
Issued: 1991-1991
Varieties: 'Beatrice' HN 3263, 3631; 'Kathryn' HN 3413; 'Lucy' HN 3653; 'Summer Serenade' HN 3610
Series: Wildflower / Month

U.S.:	**$225.00**
Can.:	**$275.00**
U.K.:	**£125.00**

HN 3343
March - Style Three
Designer: M. Davies
Height: 7 ½", 19.0 cm
Colour: White, violet flowers
Issued: 1991-1991
Varieties: 'Beatrice' HN 3263, 3631; 'Kathryn' HN 3413; 'Lucy' HN 3653; 'Summer Serenade' HN 3610
Series: Wildflower / Month

U.S.:	**$225.00**
Can.:	**$275.00**
U.K.:	**£125.00**

HN 3344
April - Style Three
Designer: M. Davies
Height: 7 ½", 19.0 cm
Colour: White, primroses
Issued: 1991-1991
Varieties: 'Beatrice' HN 3263, 3631; 'Kathryn' HN 3413; 'Lucy' HN 3653; 'Summer Serenade' HN 3610
Series: Wildflower / Month

U.S.:	**$225.00**
Can.:	**$275.00**
U.K.:	**£125.00**

HN 3345
May - Style Four
Designer: M. Davies
Height: 7 ½", 19.0 cm
Colour: White, lady's smock
Issued: 1991-1991
Varieties: 'Beatrice' HN 3263, 'Kathryn' HN 3653; 'Lucy' HN 3653; 3631; 'Summer Serenade' HN 3610
Series: Wildflower / Month

U.S.:	$225.00
Can.:	$275.00
U.K.:	£125.00

HN 3346
June - Style Six
Designer: M. Davies
Height: 7 ½", 19.0 cm
Colour: White, briar roses
Issued: 1991-1991
Varieties: 'Beatrice' HN 3263, 3631; 'Kathryn' HN 3653; 'Lucy' HN 3653; 'Summer Serenade' HN 3610
Series: Wildflower / Month

U.S.:	$225.00
Can.:	$275.00
U.K.:	£125.00

HN 3347
July - Style Three
Designer: M. Davies
Height: 7 ½", 19.0 cm
Colour: White, hare bells
Issued: 1991-1991
Varieties: 'Beatrice' HN 3263, 3631; 'Kathryn' HN 3413; 'Lucy' HN 3653; 'Summer Serenade' HN 3610
Series: Wildflower / Month

U.S.:	$225.00
Can.:	$275.00
U.K.:	£125.00

HN 3348
Mother and Child
Style One
Designer: P. Parsons
Height: 7 ½", 19.0 cm
Colour: White and pink
Issued: 1991-1993
Varieties: HN 3235, 3353

U.S.:	$275.00
Can.:	$325.00
U.K.:	£150.00

HN 3349
Jane Seymour
Designer: P. Parsons
Height: 9", 22.9 cm
Colour: Orange and blue
Issued: 1991 in a limited edition of 9,500
Series: Six Wives of Henry VIII
Comm.by: Lawleys By Post

U.S.:	$1,000.00
Can.:	$1,300.00
U.K.:	£ 550.00

HN 3350
Henry VIII
Style Three
Designer: P. Parsons
Height: 9 ½", 24.0 cm
Colour: Gold-brown and red
Issued: 1991 in a limited edition of 1991
Comm.by: Lawleys By Post

U.S.:	$2,700.00
Can.:	$3,500.00
U.K.:	£1,500.00

HN 3351
Congratulations
Designer: P. Gee
Height: 11", 27.9 cm
Colour: White
Issued: 1991 to the present
Series: Images

U.S.:	N/I
Can.:	$345.00
U.K.:	£ 69.00

HN 3353
Mother and Child
Style One
Designer: P. Parsons
Height: 7 ½", 19.0 cm
Colour: White
Issued: 1992-1999
Varieties: HN 3235, 3348
Series: Vanity Fair Series

U.S.:	$275.00
Can.:	$325.00
U.K.:	£150.00

HN 3352 not issued.

HN 3354
Yours Forever
Designer: P. Parsons
Height: 8", 20.3 cm
Colour: Yellow and pink
Issued: 1992 Canada,
1993 Worldwide-1997
Varieties: Also called 'Kimberley'
(Style One) HN 2969
Series: Vanity Fair Ladies
U.S.: $225.00
Can.: $275.00
U.K.: £125.00

HN 3355
Just For You
Style One
Designer: P. Parsons
Height: 8 ¼", 21 cm
Colour: White
Issued: 1992-1998
Series: Vanity Fair Ladies
U.S.: $225.00
Can.: $275.00
U.K.: £125.00

HN 3356
Anne of Cleves
Designer: P. Parsons
Height: 6 ¼", 15.9 cm
Colour: Green and gold
Issued: 1991 in a limited
edition of 9,500
Series: Six Wives of
Henry VIII
Comm.by: Lawleys By Post
U.S.: $1,100.00
Can.: $1,300.00
U.K.: £ 550.00

HN 3357
Marie
Style Three
Designer: P. Parson
Height: 6", 15.2 cm
Colour: Pink and yellow
Issued: 1992
Varieties: Also called 'Heather'
HN 2956
Comm.by: Great Universal
Stores
U.S.: $300.00
Can.: $350.00
U.K.: £165.00

HN 3358
Loyal Friend
Style One
Designer: V. Annand
Height: 8 ¼", 20.9 cm
Colour: Pale green and white
Issued: 1991-1995
U.S.: $450.00
Can.: $550.00
U.K.: £250.00

HN 3359
L'Ambitieuse
Designer: V. Annand
Height: 8 ¼", 20.9 cm
Colour: Rose and pale blue
Issued: 1991 in a limited
edition of 5,000
Series: RDICC
U.S.: $450.00
Can.: $550.00
U.K.: £250.00

HN 3360
Katie
Style One
Designer: V. Annand
Height: 8 ¼", 21.0 cm
Colour: Yellow and pink
Issued: 1992-1997
U.S.: $350.00
Can.: $425.00
U.K.: £200.00

HN 3361
First Steps
Style Three
Designer: V. Annand
Height: 5", 12.7 cm
Colour: Pink
Issued: 1992
Series: Little Cherubs
Comm.by: Lawleys By Post
U.S.: $200.00
Can.: $250.00
U.K.: £110.00

HN 3362
Well Done
Designer:	V. Annand
Height:	4", 10.1 cm
Colour:	Pink
Issued:	1992
Series:	Little Cherubs
Comm.by:	Lawleys By Post

U.S.:	**$200.00**
Can.:	**$250.00**
U.K.:	**£110.00**

HN 3363
Peek a Boo
Designer:	V. Annand
Height:	2 ½", 6.4 cm
Colour:	Pink
Issued:	1992
Series:	Little Cherubs
Comm.by:	Lawleys By Post

U.S.:	**$200.00**
Can.:	**$250.00**
U.K.:	**£110.00**

HN 3364
What Fun
Designer:	V. Annand
Height:	3 ¾", 9.5 cm
Colour:	Pink
Issued:	1992
Series:	Little Cherubs
Comm.by:	Lawleys By Post

U.S.:	**$200.00**
Can.:	**$250.00**
U.K.:	**£110.00**

HN 3365
Patricia
Style Four
Designer:	V. Annand
Height:	8 ½", 21.6 cm
Colour:	Red and black
Issued:	1993-1993
Series:	Figure of the Year

U.S.:	**$425.00**
Can.:	**$525.00**
U.K.:	**£225.00**

HN 3366
Wimbledon
Designer:	V. Annand
Height:	7 ¾", 19.8 cm
Colour:	Cream, pink and green
Issued:	1995 in a limited edition of 5,000
Series:	British Sporting Heritage

U.S.:	**$700.00**
Can.:	**$850.00**
U.K.:	**£380.00**

HN 3367
Henley
Designer:	V. Annand
Height:	8", 20.3 cm
Colour:	Green and pink
Issued:	1993 in a limited edition of 5,000
Series:	British Sporting Heritage

U.S.:	**$575.00**
Can.:	**$700.00**
U.K.:	**£300.00**

HN 3368
Alice
Style Two
Designer:	N. Pedley
Height:	8 ¼", 21.0 cm
Colour:	Light blue and pink
Issued:	1991-1996

U.S.:	**$375.00**
Can.:	**$450.00**
U.K.:	**£200.00**

HN 3369
Hannah
Style One
Designer:	N. Pedley
Height:	8 ¼", 19.0 cm
Colour:	Pale pink, yellow and blue
Issued:	1991-1996
Varieties:	HN 3655

U.S.:	**$375.00**
Can.:	**$450.00**
U.K.:	**£200.00**

HN 3370
Bunny's Bedtime
Designer: N. Pedley
Height: 6", 15.2 cm
Colour: Pale blue, pink ribbon
Issued: 1991 in a limited
            edition of 9,500
Series: RDICC
   U.S.: $375.00
   Can.: $550.00
   U.K.:   £200.00

HN 3371
Puppy Love
Designer: N. Pedley
Height: 7 ½", 19.0 cm
Colour: Yellow-orange
            and brown
Issued: 1991 in a limited
            edition of 9,500
Series: Age of Innocence
   U.S.: $450.00
   Can.: $525.00
   U.K.:   £250.00

HN 3372
Making Friends
Designer: N. Pedley
Height: 5 ½", 14.0 cm
Colour: Pink-yellow and white
Issued: 1991 in a limited
            edition of 9,500
Series: Age of Innocence
   U.S.: $450.00
   Can.: $525.00
   U.K.:   £250.00

HN 3373
Feeding Time
Designer: N. Pedley
Height: 7", 17.8 cm
Colour: Yellow and white
Issued: 1991 in a limited
            edition of 9,500
Series: Age of Innocence
   U.S.: $450.00
   Can.: $525.00
   U.K.:   £250.00

HN 3374
Linda
Style Three
Designer: N. Pedley
Height: 8 ¼", 21.0 cm
Colour: Turquoise and white
Issued: 1990 Canada
            1991 Worldwide -1995
   U.S.: $375.00
   Can.: $450.00
   U.K.:   £200.00

HN 3375
Mary
Style Two
Designer: N. Pedley
Height: 8 ½", 21.6 cm
Colour: Blue and white
Issued: 1992-1992
Series: Figure of the Year
   U.S.: $750.00
   Can.: $925.00
   U.K.:   £400.00

HN 3376
Single Red Rose
Designer: N. Pedley
Height: 8", 20.3 cm
Colour: Red
Issued: 1992-1995
   U.S.: $300.00
   Can.: $375.00
   U.K.:   £165.00

HN 3377
First Outing
Designer: N. Pedley
Height: 7 ½", 19.0 cm
Colour: Peach and white
Issued: 1992 in a limited
            edition of 9,500
Series: Age of Innocence
   U.S.: $450.00
   Can.: $525.00
   U.K.:   £250.00

HN 3378
Summer's Day
Style Two
Designer: T. Potts
Height: 8 ½", 21.6 cm
Colour: Rose and white
Issued: 1991-1996
U.S.:   **$325.00**
Can.:   **$400.00**
U.K.:   **£175.00**

HN 3379
Kimberley
Style Two
Designer: T. Potts
Height: 8 ½", 21.6 cm
Colour: White and blue
Issued: 1992-1997
Varieties: HN 3382, 3864
Series: Vanity Fair Ladies
U.S.:   **$300.00**
Can.:   **$375.00**
U.K.:   **£165.00**

HN 3380
Sarah
Style One
Designer: T. Potts
Height: 8", 20.3 cm
Colour: Yellow and pink
Issued: 1993-1993
Series: M. Doulton Events
U.S.:   **$375.00**
Can.:   **$450.00**
U.K.:   **£200.00**

HN 3381
Maria
Designer: T. Potts
Height: 8", 20.3 cm
Colour: White and yellow
Issued: 1993-1999
Series: 1. Roadshow Events
            2. Vanity Fair Ladies
U.S.:   **$250.00**
Can.:   **$300.00**
U.K.:   **£135.00**

HN 3382
Kimberley
Style Two
Designer: T. Potts
Height: 8 ½", 21.6 cm
Colour: Yellow, pink and white
Issued: 1993-1996
Varieties: HN 3379, 3864
U.S.:   **$300.00**
Can.:   **$375.00**
U.K.:   **£165.00**

Exclusive to U.S.A.

HN 3383
Sally
Style Two
Designer: T. Potts
Height: 8 ¼", 21.0 cm
Colour: Red
Issued: 1995-1997
Varieties: HN 3851, 4160
Comm.by: Freemans
U.S.:   **$275.00**
Can.:   **$350.00**
U.K.:   **£150.00**

HN 3384
Sarah
Style Two
Designer: T. Potts
Height: 8", 20.3 cm
Colour: Red and pink
Issued: 1995-2000
Varieties: HN 3852, 3857
U.S.:   **$350.00**
Can.:   **$450.00**
U.K.:   **£200.00**

HN 3385 - 3387 not issued.

HN 3388
Forget Me Not
Style Two
Designer: A. Maslankowski
Height: 6", 15.2 cm
Colour: White
Issued: 1999-2002
Series: Sentiments
U.S.:   **$100.00**
Can.:   **$125.00**
U.K.:   **£ 55.00**

HN 3389
Loving You
Designer: A. Maslankowski
Height: 6 ¼", 15.8 cm
Colour: White
Issued: 1991-2004
Series: Sentiments

U.S.:	**$100.00**
Can.:	**$125.00**
U.K.:	**£ 55.00**

HN 3390
Thank You
Style Two
Designer: A. Maslankowski
Height: 6 ¼", 15.8 cm
Colour: White
Issued: 1991-2004
Varieties: Also called 'Thank
You Mother' HN 4251
Series: Sentiments

U.S.:	**$100.00**
Can.:	**$125.00**
U.K.:	**£ 55.00**

HN 3391
Reward
Designer: A. Maslankowski
Height: 4 ½", 11.4 cm
Colour: White and pink
Issued: 1992-1996
Series: Vanity Fair Children

U.S.:	**$150.00**
Can.:	**$175.00**
U.K.:	**£ 80.00**

HN 3392
Christopher Columbus
Designer: A. Maslankowski
Height: 12", 30.5 cm
Colour: Green, brown and red
Issued: 1992 in a limited
edition of 1,492

U.S.:	**$1,400.00**
Can.:	**$1,700.00**
U.K.:	**£ 750.00**

HN 3393
With Love
Style One
Designer: A. Maslankowski
Height: 6", 15.2 cm
Colour: White
Issued: 1992-2004
Varieties: HN 3492
Series: Sentiments

U.S.:	**$100.00**
Can.:	**$125.00**
U.K.:	**£ 55.00**

HN 3394
Sweet Dreams
Style Two
Designer: A. Maslankowski
Height: 6", 15.2 cm
Colour: White
Issued: 1992-1998
Series: Sentiments

U.S.:	**$100.00**
Can.:	**$125.00**
U.K.:	**£ 55.00**

HN 3395
Little Ballerina
Designer: A. Maslankowski
Height: 6", 15.2 cm
Colour: White; pink slippers
Issued: 1992-2003
Varieties: HN 3431

U.S.:	**$125.00**
Can.:	**$150.00**
U.K.:	**£ 65.00**

HN 3396
Buddies
Style Two
Designer: A. Maslankowski
Height: 4 ¼", 10.8 cm
Colour: Pink and beige
Issued: 1992-1996
Series: Vanity Fair Children

U.S.:	**$150.00**
Can.:	**$180.00**
U.K.:	**£ 80.00**

HN 3397
Let's Play
Designer: A. Maslankowski
Height: 4", 10.0 cm
Colour: Pale green and white
Issued: 1992-1996
Series: Vanity Fair Children

U.S.:	**$150.00**
Can.:	**$180.00**
U.K.:	**£ 80.00**

HN 3398
The Ace
Designer: R. Tabbenor
Height: 10", 25.4 cm
Colour: White
Issued: 1991-1995

U.S.:	**$250.00**
Can.:	**$325.00**
U.K.:	**£150.00**

HN 3399
Father Christmas
Designer: R. Tabbenor
Height: 9", 22.9 cm
Colour: Red and white
Issued: 1992-1999

U.S.:	**$375.00**
Can.:	**$450.00**
U.K.:	**£200.00**

HN 3400
God Bless You
Designer: R. Tabbenor
Height: 8", 20.3 cm
Colour: White
Issued: 1992 to the present
Series: Images

U.S.:	**N/I**
Can.:	**$160.00**
U.K.:	**£ 29.00**

HN 3401
Gardening Time
Designer: R. Tabbenor
Height: 5", 12.7 cm
Colour: Yellow, blue and green
Issued: 1992-1994

U.S.:	**$275.00**
Can.:	**$325.00**
U.K.:	**£150.00**

HN 3402
Samurai Warrior
Designer: R. Tabbenor
Height: 9", 22.7 cm
Colour: Red
Issued: 1992 in a limited
           edition of 950
Series: Flambé

U.S.:	**$650.00**
Can.:	**$775.00**
U.K.:	**£350.00**

HN 3403
Lt. General Ulysses S. Grant
Designer: R. Tabbenor
Height: 11 ¾", 29.8 cm
Colour: Blue and brown
Issued: 1993 in a limited
           edition of 5,000

U.S.:	**$1,400.00**
Can.:	**$1,700.00**
U.K.:	**£ 775.00**

HN 3404
General Robert E. Lee
Designer: R. Tabbenor
Height: 11 ½", 29.2 cm
Colour: Grey and brown
Issued: 1993 in a limited
           edition of 5,000

U.S.:	**$1,400.00**
Can.:	**$1,700.00**
U.K.:	**£ 775.00**

HN 3405
Field Marshall Montgomery
Designer: R. Tabbenor
Height: 11 ¾", 29.2 cm
Colour: Browns
Issued: 1994 in a limited
edition of 1,944

U.S.: $1,400.00
Can.: $1,700.00
U.K.: £ 775.00

HN 3406
Amanda
Designer: R. Tabbenor
Height: 5 ¼", 13.3 cm
Colour: White and pink
Issued: 1993-1999
Varieties: HN 2996, 3632,
3634, 3635; also
called Flower of
the Month, Child
Series: Vanity Fair Children

U.S.: $125.00
Can.: $150.00
U.K.: £ 70.00

Exclusive to U.S.A.

HN 3407
Julie
Style One
Designer: R. Tabbenor
Height: 5", 12.7 cm
Colour: White and blue
Issued: 1993-1999
Varieties: HN 2995

U.S.: $125.00
Can.: $150.00
U.K.: £ 70.00

Exclusive to U.S.A.

HN 3408
August
Style Three
Designer: M. Davies
Height: 7 ½", 19.1 cm
Colour: White, poppies
Issued: 1991-1991
Varieties: 'Beatrice' HN 3263,
3631; 'Kathryn'
HN 3413; 'Lucy'
HN 3653; 'Summer
Serenade' HN 3610
Series: Wildflower / Month

U.S.: $225.00
Can.: $275.00
U.K.: £125.00

HN 3409
September
Style Three
Designer: M. Davies
Height: 7 ½", 19.1 cm
Colour: White, blue flowers
Issued: 1991-1991
Varieties: 'Beatrice' HN 3263,
3631; 'Kathryn'
HN 3413; 'Lucy'
HN 3653; 'Summer
Serenade' HN 3610
Series: Wildflower / Month

U.S.: $225.00
Can.: $275.00
U.K.: £125.00

HN 3410
October
Style Three
Designer: M. Davies
Height: 7 ½", 19.1 cm
Colour: White, buttercups
Issued: 1991-1991
Varieties: 'Beatrice' HN 3263,
3631; 'Kathryn'
HN 3413; 'Lucy'
HN 3653; 'Summer
Serenade' HN 3610
Series: Wildflower / Month

U.S.: $225.00
Can.: $275.00
U.K.: £125.00

HN 3411
November
Style Three
Designer: M. Davies
Height: 7 ½", 19.1 cm
Colour: White, pink flowers
Issued: 1991-1991
Varieties: 'Beatrice' HN 3263,
3631; 'Kathryn'
HN 3413; 'Lucy'
HN 3653; 'Summer
Serenade' HN 3610
Series: Wildflower / Month

U.S.: $225.00
Can.: $275.00
U.K.: £125.00

HN 3412
December
Style Three
Designer: M. Davies
Height: 7 ½", 19.1 cm
Colour: White, Christmas roses
Issued: 1991-1991
Varieties: 'Beatrice' HN 3263,
3631; 'Kathryn'
HN 3413; 'Lucy'
HN 3653; 'Summer
Serenade' HN 3610
Series: Wildflower / Month

U.S.: $225.00
Can.: $275.00
U.K.: £125.00

HN 3413
Kathryn
Style One
Designer: M. Davies
Height: 7", 17.8 cm
Colour: Blue and white
Issued: 1992-1992
Varieties: 'Beatrice' HN 3263,
            3631; 'Lucy' HN 3653;
            'Summer Serenade'
            HN 3610; Wildflower
            of the Month

    U.S.:   **$225.00**
    Can.:   **$275.00**
    U.K.:   **£125.00**

HN 3414
Rebecca
Style Two
Designer: M. Davies
Remodeller: D. Frith
Height: 3 ½", 8.9 cm
Colour: Pale blue and pink
Issued: 1992-1997
Series: Miniatures

    U.S.:   **$175.00**
    Can.:   **$215.00**
    U.K.:   **£ 95.00**

HN 3415
Janette
Designer: M. Davies
Height: 7 ½:, 19.1 cm
Colour: Blue and green
Issued: 1992-1992
Varieties: Also called 'Kirsty'
            (Style One) HN 2381
Comm.by: Great Universal
            Stores

    U.S.:   **$350.00**
    Can.:   **$425.00**
    U.K.:   **£200.00**

HN 3416
Victoria
Style One
Designer: M. Davies
Height: 6 ½", 16.5 cm
Colour: Blue and rose
            with gold trim
Issued: 1992-1992
Varieties: HN 2471
Series: Roadshow Events

    U.S.:   **$475.00**
    Can.:   **$575.00**
    U.K.:   **£260.00**

HN 3417
Ninette
Style One
Designer: M. Davies
Height: 7 ½", 19.1 cm
Colour: Orange and green
            dress, with gold trim
Issued: 1992-1992
Varieties: HN 2379; also called
            'Olivia' (Style Two)
            HN 3339
Series: Roadshow Events

    U.S.:   **$475.00**
    Can.:   **$575.00**
    U.K.:   **£260.00**

HN 3418
Bedtime
Style Two
Designer: N. Pedley
Height: 7 ¼", 18.4 cm
Colour: Pink-yellow
Issued: 1992 in a limited
            edition of 9,000
Comm.by: Lawleys By Post

    U.S.:   **$300.00**
    Can.:   **$350.00**
    U.K.:   **£165.00**

HN 3419
Angela
Style Three
Designer: N. Pedley
Height: 8 ½", 21.6 cm
Colour: Blue, pink and white
Issued: 1992-1992
Series: M. Doulton Events

    U.S.:   **$350.00**
    Can.:   **$425.00**
    U.K.:   **£200.00**

HN 3420
Ashley
Designer: N. Pedley
Height: 8", 20.3 cm
Colour: Lavender
Issued: 1992-1999
Series: Vanity Fair Ladies

    U.S.:   **$250.00**
    Can.:   **$300.00**
    U.K.:   **£135.00**

HN 3421
Nicole
Style One
Designer: N. Pedley
Height: 7 ½", 19.1 cm
Colour: Pink and cream
Issued: 1993-1997
Varieties: HN 3686

U.S.:	**$250.00**
Can.:	**$325.00**
U.K.:	**£135.00**

HN 3422
Joanne
Style Two
Designer: N. Pedley
Height: 7 ½", 19.1 cm
Colour: White and pink dress flowered border
Issued: 1993-1998
Varieties: Also called 'Annabelle' HN 4090

U.S.:	**$275.00**
Can.:	**$350.00**
U.K.:	**£150.00**

HN 3423
Birthday Girl
Designer: N. Pedley
Height: 6", 15.2 cm
Colour: White
Issued: 1993-2000
Series: Vanity Fair Children

U.S.:	**$150.00**
Can.:	**$180.00**
U.K.:	**£ 80.00**

HN 3424
My First Figurine
Designer: N. Pedley
Height: 4 ¼", 10.8 cm
Colour: Red and pink
Issued: 1993-1998

U.S.:	**$150.00**
Can.:	**$180.00**
U.K.:	**£ 80.00**

HN 3425
Almost Grown
Designer: N. Pedley
Height: 4 ½", 11.4 cm
Colour: White and pale green
Issued: 1993-1997

U.S.:	**$125.00**
Can.:	**$150.00**
U.K.:	**£ 70.00**

HN 3426
Best Wishes
Style One
Designer: N. Pedley
Height: 6", 15.2 cm
Colour: Red and white
Issued: 1993-1995

U.S.:	**$225.00**
Can.:	**$275.00**
U.K.:	**£125.00**

HN 3427
Gift of Love
Style One
Designer: N. Pedley
Height: 7 ½", 19.1 cm
Colour: White, yellow and pink
Issued: 1993-2000
Series: Vanity Fair Ladies

U.S.:	**$225.00**
Can.:	**$300.00**
U.K.:	**£125.00**

HN 3428
Discovery
Designer: A. Munslow
Height: 12", 30.5 cm
Colour: Matte white
Issued: 1992-1992
Series: RDICC

U.S.:	**$200.00**
Can.:	**$250.00**
U.K.:	**£110.00**

HN 3429
Napoleon at Waterloo
Designer: A. Maslankowski
Height: 11 ½", 29.2 cm
Colour: Black, cream and green
Issued: 1992 in a limited edition of 1,500

U.S.:	**$1,650.00**
Can.:	**$2,000.00**
U.K.:	**£ 900.00**

HN 3430
Sit
Designer: A. Maslankowski
Height: 4 ½", 11.4 cm
Colour: Pink and white
Issued: 1992-1996
Varieties: HN 3123
Series: Vanity Fair Children

U.S.:	**$150.00**
Can.:	**$180.00**
U.K.:	**£ 80.00**

Exclusive to North America

HN 3431
Little Ballerina
Designer: A. Maslankowski
Height: 6", 15.2 cm
Colour: Pink
Issued: 1993 in a limited edition of 2,000
Varieties: HN 3395

U.S.:	**$150.00**
Can.:	**$180.00**
U.K.:	**£ 80.00**

Exclusive to North America

HN 3432
Duke of Wellington
Designer: A. Maslankowski
Height: 12", 30.5 cm
Colour: Dark blue and cream
Issued: 1993 in a limited edition of 1,500

U.S.:	**$1,650.00**
Can.:	**$2,000.00**
U.K.:	**£ 900.00**

HN 3433
Winston S. Churchill
Style Two
Designer: A. Maslankowski
Height: 12", 30.5 cm
Colour: Black and grey
Issued: 1993 in a limited edition of 5,000

U.S.:	**$1,000.00**
Can.:	**$1,200.00**
U.K.:	**£ 550.00**

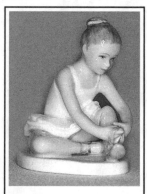

HN 3434
Ballet Shoes
Designer: A. Maslankowski
Height: 3 ¾", 9.5 cm
Colour: White
Issued: 1993-2001

U.S.:	**$150.00**
Can.:	**$180.00**
U.K.:	**£ 80.00**

HN 3435
Daddy's Girl
Designer: A. Maslankowski
Height: 4 ½", 11.4 cm
Colour: Pink and white
Issued: 1993-1998
Series: Vanity Fair Children

U.S.:	**$150.00**
Can.:	**$180.00**
U.K.:	**£ 80.00**

HN 3436
HM Queen Elizabeth II
Style Three
Designer: A. Maslankowski
Height: 8 ¼", 21.0 cm
Colour: Lilac and yellow
Issued: 1992 in a limited edition of 2,500
Comm.by: Lawleys By Post

U.S.:	**$1,575.00**
Can.:	**$1,900.00**
U.K.:	**£ 850.00**

HN 3437
Mary
Style Three
Designer: A. Maslankowski
Height: 3 ¼", 8.3 cm
Colour: White
Issued: 1993-1996
Varieties: HN 3485
Series: Holy Family

U.S.:	**$100.00**
Can.:	**$125.00**
U.K.:	**£ 55.00**

Exclusive to North America

HN 3438
Joseph
Style One
Designer: A. Maslankowski
Height: 5 ¾", 14.6 cm
Colour: White
Issued: 1993-1996
Varieties: HN 3486
Series: Holy Family

U.S.:	**$100.00**
Can.:	**$125.00**
U.K.:	**£ 55.00**

Exclusive to North America

HN 3439
The Skater
Style Two
Designer: P. Gee
Height: 8", 20.3 cm
Colour: Red
Issued: 1992-1997

U.S.:	**$450.00**
Can.:	**$550.00**
U.K.:	**£250.00**

HN 3440
HM Queen Elizabeth II
Style Four
Designer: P. Gee
Height: 7 ½", 19.0 cm
Colour: Yellow and pink
Issued: 1992 in a limited
            edition of 3,500

U.S.:	**$550.00**
Can.:	**$650.00**
U.K.:	**£300.00**

HN 3441
Barbara
Style Three
Designer: P. Gee
Height: 8", 20.3 cm
Colour: Pink and lavender
Issued: 1993 in a limited
            edition of 9,500
Series: RDICC

U.S.:	**$600.00**
Can.:	**$725.00**
U.K.:	**£325.00**

HN 3442
Eliza Farren,
Countess of Derby
Designer: P. Gee
Height: 8 ¾", 22.2 cm
Colour: Pale blue, white
            and beige
Issued: 1993 in a limited
            edition of 5,000
Series: RDICC

U.S.:	**$375.00**
Can.:	**$450.00**
U.K.:	**£200.00**

HN 3443
Gift of Freedom
Designer: P. Gee
Height: 9 ¾", 24.8 cm
Colour: White
Issued: 1993 to the present
Series: Images

U.S.:	**$125.00**
Can.:	**$245.00**
U.K.:	**£ 59.00**

HN 3444
Piper
Style Two
Designer: P. Gee
Height: 9 ¼", 23.4 cm
Colour: Black, red and green
Issued: 1993 in a limited
            edition of 750
Comm.by: Site of the Green

U.S.:	**$525.00**
Can.:	**$625.00**
U.K.:	**£275.00**

HN 3445
Amy's Sister
Designer: P. Gee
Height: 8", 20.3 cm
Colour: Red, cream and blue
Issued: 1993-1996
U.S.: **$275.00**
Can.: **$325.00**
U.K.: **£150.00**

HN 3446
Spring Song
Designer: P. Gee
Height: 7 ¼", 18.4 cm
Colour: Yellow and white
Issued: 1993-1996
Varieties: Also called 'Danielle'
 (Style Two), HN 3001
Series: The Seasons
 (Series Five)
U.S.: **$200.00**
Can.: **$250.00**
U.K.: **£110.00**

HN 3447
Jennifer
Style Three
Designer: P. Gee
Height: 7 ¼", 18.4 cm
Colour: Deep pink
Issued: 1994-1994
Series: Figure of the Year
U.S.: **$450.00**
Can.: **$550.00**
U.K.: **£250.00**

HN 3448
Charles Dickens
Designer: P. Gee
Height: 4", 10.1 cm
Colour: Black and grey
Issued: 1994 in a limited
 edition of 1,500
Comm.by: Pascoe & Company
U.S.: **$175.00**
Can.: **$210.00**
U.K.: **£100.00**

HN 3449
Catherine Howard
Designer: P. Parsons
Height: 8 ¼", 21.0 cm
Colour: Purple
Issued: 1992 in a limited
 edition of 9,500
Series: Six Wives of
 Henry VIII
Comm.by: Lawleys By Post
U.S.: **$ 925.00**
Can.: **$1,100.00**
U.K.: **£ 500.00**

HN 3450
Catherine Parr
Designer: P. Parsons
Height: 6 ¼", 15.9 cm
Colour: Red
Issued: 1992 in a limited
 edition of 9,500
Series: Six Wives of
 Henry VIII
Comm.by: Lawleys By Post
U.S.: **$ 925.00**
Can.: **$1,100.00**
U.K.: **£ 500.00**

HN 3451
Catherine
Style Two
Designer: P. Parsons
Height: 5", 12,7 cm
Colour: White and lemon
Issued: 1993-1999
Varieties: HN 3044
U.S.: **$125.00**
Can.: **$150.00**
U.K.: **£ 70.00**

Exclusive to U.S.A.

HN 3452
Our First Christmas
Designer: P. Parsons
Height: 11 ½", 29.2 cm
Colour: White
Issued: 1993-1998
Series: Images
U.S.: **$175.00**
Can.: **$225.00**
U.K.: **£100.00**

HN 3453
Juliet
Style Two
Designer: P. Parsons
Height: 6", 15.2 cm
Colour: Red, pink and green
Issued: 1994 in a limited
             edition of 5,000
Series: Shakespearean
             Ladies
Comm.by: Lawleys By Post
  U.S.:   **$650.00**
  Can.:   **$775.00**
  U.K.:   **£350.00**

HN 3454
Flowers For Mother
Designer: P. Parsons
Height: 5 ¾", 14.6 cm
Colour: White and pink
Issued: 1994-1997
  U.S.:   **$150.00**
  Can.:   **$180.00**
  U.K.:   **£ 80.00**

HN 3455
Sharon
Style One
Designer: P. Parsons
Height: 5 ½", 14.0 cm
Colour: White dress
             with pink flowers
Issued: 1994-1999
Varieties: HN 3047
  U.S.:   **$175.00**
  Can.:   **$215.00**
  U.K.:   **£ 95.00**

HN 3456
Grandpa's Story
Designer: P. Parsons
Height: 6", 15.2 cm
Colour: Green, blue and pink
Issued: 1994-2000
  U.S.:   **$450.00**
  Can.:   **$550.00**
  U.K.:   **£250.00**

HN 3457
When I Was Young
Designer: P. Parsons
Height: 5 ½", 14.0 cm
Colour: Pink, green and purple
Issued: 1994-2000
  U.S.:   **$450.00**
  Can.:   **$550.00**
  U.K.:   **£250.00**

HN 3458
Henry VIII
Style Four
Designer: P. Parsons
Height: 9 ¼", 23.5 cm
Colour: Browns, black
             and white
Issued: 1994 in a limited
             edition of 9,500
Comm.by: Lawleys By Post
  U.S.:   **$1,000.00**
  Can.:   **$1,200.00**
  U.K.:   **£ 550.00**

HN 3459
King Charles
Designer: C. J. Noke and
             H. Tittensor
Height: 16 ¾", 42.5 cm
Colour: Red, dark blue,
             purple and white
Issued: 1992 in a limited
             edition of 350
Varieties: HN 404, 2084
  U.S.:   **$3,250.00**
  Can.:   **$4,000.00**
  U.K.:   **£1,750.00**

HN 3460
Brother and Sister
Designer: A. Hughes
Height: 8", 20.3 cm
Colour: White
Issued: 1993 to the present
Series: Images
  U.S.:   **$125.00**
  Can.:   **$220.00**
  U.K.:   **£ 39.00**

HN 3461
Kerry
Designer: A. Hughes
Height: 5 ¼", 13.3 cm
Colour: White and green
Issued: 1993-1999
Varieties: HN 3036

U.S.: $125.00
Can.: $150.00
U.K.: £ 70.00

Exclusive to U.S.A.

HN 3462
Boy Scout
Designer: A. Hughes
Height: 7 ¾", 19.7 cm
Colour: Brown and black
Issued: 1994 in a limited
edition of 9,500
Comm.by: Lawleys By Post

U.S.: $475.00
Can.: $575.00
U.K.: £260.00

HN 3463 - 3469 Animal and Bird
figures, except HN 3465 and 3469
not issued.

HN 3470
Croquet
Designer: V. Annand
Height: 8 ½", 21.6 cm
Colour: Red and blue
Issued: 1994 in a limited
edition of 5,000
Series: British Sporting
Heritage

U.S.: $700.00
Can.: $850.00
U.K.: £375.00

HN 3471
Ascot
Style Two
Designer: V. Annand
Height: 8 ½", 21.6 cm
Colour: Pink and purple
Issued: 1994 in a limited
edition of 5,000
Series: British Sporting
Heritage

U.S.: $700.00
Can.: $850.00
U.K.: £375.00

HN 3472
La Loge
Designer: V. Annand
Height: 8 ½", 21.6 cm
Colour: White and black
Issued: 1992 in a limited
edition of 7,500
Comm.by: Lawleys By Post

U.S.: $ 850.00
Can.: $1,050.00
U.K.: £ 475.00

HN 3473
Les Parapluies
Designer: V. Annand
Height: 8 ¼", 21.0 cm
Colour: Blue
Issued: 1993 in a limited
edition of 7,500
Comm.by: Lawleys By Post

U.S.: $ 925.00
Can.: $1,175.00
U.K.: £ 550.00

HN 3474
Lise
Designer: V. Annand
Height: 8 ½", 21.6 cm
Colour: Lavender and purple
Issued: 1994 in a limited
edition of 7,500
Comm.by: Lawleys By Post

U.S.: $650.00
Can.: $775.00
U.K.: £350.00

HN 3475
Marie Sisley
Designer: V. Annand
Height: 8 ½", 21.6 cm
Colour: Red, yellow and grey
Issued: 1994 in a limited
edition of 7,500
Comm.by: Lawleys By Post

U.S.: $750.00
Can.: $950.00
U.K.: £425.00

HN 3476
Bridesmaid
Style Seven
Designer: V. Annand
Height: 5 ½", 13.3 cm
Colour: Pink
Issued: 1994-1997
Varieties: Also called 'Flowergirl'
             (Style One) HN 3479

U.S.:	**$175.00**
Can.:	**$225.00**
U.K.:	**£100.00**

HN 3477
Springtime
Style Three
Designer: V. Annand
Height: 8", 20.3 cm
Colour: Pink and cream
Issued: 1993-1996
Series: The Seasons
             (Series Six)

U.S.:	**$475.00**
Can.:	**$575.00**
U.K.:	**£260.00**

HN 3478
Summertime
Style Two
Designer: V. Annand
Height: 8 ½", 21.6 cm
Colour: Lilac and green
Issued: 1994-1996
Series: The Seasons
             (Series Six)

U.S.:	**$450.00**
Can.:	**$550.00**
U.K.:	**£250.00**

HN 3479
Flowergirl
Style One
Designer: V. Annand
Height: 5", 12.7 cm
Colour: White and pink
Issued: 1994-1997
Varieties: Also called
             'Bridesmaid' (Style
             Seven) HN 3476

U.S.:	**$175.00**
Can.:	**$225.00**
U.K.:	**£100.00**

Exclusive to North America

HN 3480
Kirsty
Style Two
Designer: M. Davies
Remodeller: P. Gee
Height: 3 ¾", 9.5 cm
Colour: Blue
Issued: 1993-1997
Varieties: HN 3213, 3246, 3743
Series: Miniatures

U.S.:	**$175.00**
Can.:	**$225.00**
U.K.:	**£100.00**

Exclusive to Canada

HN 3481
Lavender Rose
Designer: M. Davies
Height: 6", 15.2 cm
Colour: White, pink flowers
Issued: 1993-1995
Varieties: 'Debbie' HN 2385,
             2400; 'Moonlight Rose'
             HN 3483; 'Old Country
             Roses' (Style One)
             HN 3482; 'Memory
             Lane' HN 3746;
             'Tranquility', HN 3747

U.S.:	**$125.00**
Can.:	**$150.00**
U.K.:	**£ 70.00**

HN 3482
Old Country Roses - Style One
Designer: M. Davies
Height: 6", 15.2 cm
Colour: White, red flowers
Issued: 1993-1995
Varieties: 'Debbie' HN 2385,
             2400; 'Lavender Rose'
             HN 3481; 'Moonlight
             Roses' HN 3483;
             'Memory Lane'
             HN 374;6 'Tranquillity'
             HN 3747

U.S.:	**$125.00**
Can.:	**$150.00**
U.K.:	**£ 70.00**

HN 3483
Moonlight Rose
Designer: M. Davies
Height: 6", 15.2 cm
Colour: White, blue flowers
Issued: 1993-1995
Varieties: Also called 'Debbie'
             HN 2385, 2400;
             'Lavender Rose' HN 3481;
             'Old Country Roses'
             (Style One) HN 3482;
             'Memory Lane' HN3746
             'Tranquillity' HN 3747

U.S.:	**$125.00**
Can.:	**$150.00**
U.K.:	**£ 70.00**

HN 3484
Jesus
Style One
Designer: A. Maslankowski
Width: 2 ½", 6.4 cm
Colour: White
Issued: 1993-1996
Varieties: HN 3487
Series: Holy Family

U.S.:	**$75.00**
Can.:	**$95.00**
U.K.:	**£40.00**

Exclusive to North America

HN 3485
Mary
Style Three
Designer: A. Maslankowski
Height: 3 ¼", 8.3 cm
Colour: Blue and white
Issued: 1993-1996
Varieties: HN 3437
Series: Holy Family

U.S.:	**$100.00**
Can.:	**$125.00**
U.K.:	**£ 60.00**

Exclusive to North America

HN 3486
Joseph
Style One
Designer: A. Maslankowski
Height: 5 ¾", 14.6 cm
Colour: Brown and white
Issued: 1993-1996
Varieties: HN 3438
Series: Holy Family

U.S.:	**$100.00**
Can.:	**$125.00**
U.K.:	**£ 60.00**

Exclusive to North America

HN 3487
Jesus
Style One
Designer: A. Maslankowski
Width: 2 ½", 6.4 cm
Colour: White and brown
Issued: 1993-1996
Varieties: HN 3484
Series: Holy Family

U.S.:	**$75.00**
Can.:	**$95.00**
U.K.:	**£40.00**

Exclusive to North America

HN 3488
Christmas Day
Designer: A. Maslankowski
Height: 6", 15.2 cm
Colour: White
Issued: 1993-1999
Varieties: HN 4062
Series: Sentiments

U.S.:	**$125.00**
Can.:	**$150.00**
U.K.:	**£ 70.00**

HN 3489
Vice Admiral Lord Nelson
Designer: A. Maslankowski
Height: 12 ½", 31.7 cm
Colour: Dark blue, gold and cream
Issued: 1993 in a limited edition of 950

U.S.:	**$1,600.00**
Can.:	**$2,000.00**
U.K.:	**£ 900.00**

HN 3490
Thinking of You
Style One
Designer: A. Maslankowski
Height: 6 ¾", 17.2 cm
Colour: White with pink sash
Issued: 1993-1993
Varieties: HN 3124
Series: 1. Roadshow Events
2. Sentiments

U.S.:	**$150.00**
Can.:	**$180.00**
U.K.:	**£ 80.00**

HN 3491
Friendship
Designer: A. Maslankowski
Height: 6", 15.2 cm
Colour: White
Issued: 1994-2004
Series: Sentiments

U.S.:	**$100.00**
Can.:	**$125.00**
U.K.:	**£ 55.00**

HN 3492
With Love
Style One
Designer: A. Maslankowski
Height: 5 ¾", 14.6 cm
Colour: White dress and sash
Issued: 1994-1997
Varieties: HN 3393
Series: Sentiments

   U.S.:   **$100.00**
   Can.:   **$125.00**
   U.K.:   **£ 55.00**

Exclusive to Canada

HN 3493
Christmas Parcels
Style Two
Designer: A. Maslankowski
Height: 6", 15.2 cm
Colour: White
Issued: 1994-1998
Varieties: HN 4063
Series: Sentiments

   U.S.:   **$100.00**
   Can.:   **$125.00**
   U.K.:   **£ 55.00**

HN 3494
Tina
Designer: M. Davies
Height: 7 ½", 19.1 cm
Colour: Blue and white
Issued: 1993
Varieties: Also called 'Maureen'
            (Style Three);
            HN 2481
Comm.by: Great Universal
            Stores

   U.S.:   **$175.00**
   Can.:   **$225.00**
   U.K.:   **£ 90.00**

HN 3495
Annette
Style Two
Designer: M. Davies
Height: 8", 20.3 cm
Colour: Pale green
Issued: 1993-1993
Varieties: Also called 'Sandra'
            HN 2275, 2401

   U.S.:   **$400.00**
   Can.:   **$475.00**
   U.K.:   **£225.00**

HN 3496
Margaret
Style Two
Designer: M. Davies
Height: 7 ½", 19.1 cm
Colour: White and green
Issued: 1993-1999
Varieties: HN 2397; 'Adele'
            HN 2480; 'Camille'
            (Style Two) HN 3171

   U.S.:   **$275.00**
   Can.:   **$325.00**
   U.K.:   **£150.00**

Exclusive to U.S.A.

HN 3497
Jessica
Style One
Designer: M. Davies
Height: 7", 17.8 cm
Colour: White and blue
Issued: 1993
Varieties: HN 3169

   U.S.:   **$225.00**
   Can.:   **$275.00**
   U.K.:   **£125.00**

Exclusive to North America.

HN 3498
Natalie
Style One
Designer: M. Davies
Height: 8", 20.3 cm
Colour: White and lemon
Issued: 1993-1999
Varieties: HN 3173

   U.S.:   **$250.00**
   Can.:   **$300.00**
   U.K.:   **£135.00**

Exclusive to U.S.A.

HN 3499
Top o' the Hill
Style Two
Designer: L. Harradine
Remodeller: P. Gee
Height: 3 ¾", 9.5 cm
Colour: Red
Issued: 1993-1998
Varieties: HN 2126
Series: Miniatures

   U.S.:   **$250.00**
   Can.:   **$300.00**
   U.K.:   **£135.00**

HN 3500 - 3552 Animal and Bird
figures, except HN 3537 not issued;
HN 3553 - 3599 not issued.

HN 3600
Dawn
Style Three
Designer: N. Pedley
Height: 7 ½", 19.1 cm
Colour: White and pink
Issued: 1993-1998
Series: Vanity Fair Ladies

U.S.:	**$250.00**
Can.:	**$300.00**
U.K.:	**£135.00**

HN 3601
Helen
Style Three
Designer: N. Pedley
Height: 8 ¼", 21.0 cm
Colour: Blue and white
Issued: 1993-2003
Varieties: HN 3687, 3763, 3886
            Also called 'Miss Kay'
            HN 3659

U.S.:	**$300.00**
Can.:	**$350.00**
U.K.:	**£150.00**

HN 3602
Flowergirl
Style Two
Designer: N. Pedley
Height: 5 ¼", 13.3. cm
Colour: Pink and cream
Issued: 1993-1996

U.S.:	**$125.00**
Can.:	**$150.00**
U.K.:	**£ 70.00**

HN 3603
Sharon
Style Two
Designer: N. Pedley
Height: 8 ¾", 22.2 cm
Colour: Peach, cream
            and blue
Issued: 1994-1994
Series: M. Doulton Events

U.S.:	**$275.00**
Can.:	**$350.00**
U.K.:	**£150.00**

HN 3604
Diane
Designer: N. Pedley
Height: 8 ½", 21.6 cm
Colour: Pink and blue
Issued: 1994-1994
Series: RDICC

U.S.:	**$325.00**
Can.:	**$400.00**
U.K.:	**£175.00**

HN 3605
First Performance
Designer: N. Pedley
Height: 6", 15.2 cm
Colour: White and pink
Issued: 1994-1998

U.S.:	**$175.00**
Can.:	**$200.00**
U.K.:	**£ 95.00**

HN 3606
A Posy For You
Designer: N. Pedley
Height: 4 ¼", 10.8 cm
Colour: Blue and white
Issued: 1994-1997

U.S.:	**$150.00**
Can.:	**$180.00**
U.K.:	**£ 80.00**

HN 3607
Special Friend
Designer: N. Pedley
Height: 4 ¼", 10.8 cm
Colour: Blue and white
Issued: 1994-1998

U.S.:	**$150.00**
Can.:	**$180.00**
U.K.:	**£ 80.00**

HN 3608
Good Companion
Designer: N. Pedley
Height: 8 ½", 21.6 cm
Colour: Pink and white
Issued: 1994-1999
Series: Vanity Fair Ladies
U.S.:   **$250.00**
Can.:   **$300.00**
U.K.:   **£135.00**

HN 3609
Kathleen
Style Three
Designer: N. Pedley
Height: 8 ½", 21.6 cm
Colour: White and yellow
Issued: 1994-2000
Varieties: HN 3880; Also called
           'Brianna' HN 4126
Series: Vanity Fair Ladies
U.S.:   **$250.00**
Can.:   **$300.00**
U.K.:   **£135.00**

HN 3610
Summer Serenade
Designer: M. Davies
Height: 7", 17.8 cm
Colour: Blue and white
Issued: 1993-1996
Varieties: Also called 'Beatrice'
           HN 3263, 3631;
           'Kathryn' HN 3413;
           'Lucy' HN 3653;
           Wildflower / Month
Series: Seasons (Series Five)
U.S.:   **$250.00**
Can.:   **$300.00**
U.K.:   **£135.00**

HN 3611
Winter Welcome
Designer: M. Davies
Height: 7 ½", 19.1 cm
Colour: Rust and white
Issued: 1993-1996
Varieties: Also called 'Caroline'
           (Style One) HN 3170
Series: The Seasons
           (Series Five)
U.S.:   **$250.00**
Can.:   **$300.00**
U.K.:   **£135.00**

HN 3612
Autumn Attraction
Designer: M. Davies
Height: 6 ¾", 17.2 cm
Colour: Gold and white
Issued: 1993-1996
Varieties: Also called 'Michele'
           HN 2234
Series: The Seasons
           (Series Five)
U.S.:   **$250.00**
Can.:   **$300.00**
U.K.:   **£135.00**

HN 3613
Darling
Style Two
Designer: C. Vyse
Height: 5 ¼", 13.3 cm
Colour: Pale blue
Issued: 1993
Varieties: HN 1985
U.S.:   **$150.00**
Can.:   **$180.00**
U.K.:   **£ 80.00**

HN 3614 - 3616 not issued.

HN 3617
Monica
Style One
Designer: L. Harradine
Height: 4 ¼", 10.8 cm
Colour: Rose, lemon and white
Issued: 1993-1999
Varieties: HN 1458, 1459, 1467
U.S.:   **$175.00**
Can.:   **$215.00**
U.K.:   **£ 95.00**

HN 3618
Dinky Doo
Designer: L. Harradine
Height: 4 ½", 11.9 cm
Colour: White and blue
Issued: 1994-2002
Varieties: HN 1678, 2120
U.S.:   **$125.00**
Can.:   **$150.00**
U.K.:   **£ 70.00**

HN 3619 not issued.

HN 3620
Valerie
Style One
Designer: M. Davies
Height: 5 ¼", 13.3 cm
Colour: Blue, pink and white
Issued: 1994-1999
Varieties: HN 2107

U.S.: $150.00
Can.: $180.00
U.K.:   £ 80.00

HN 3621
Autumntime
Style Two
Designer: V. Annand
Height: 8 ¾", 22.2 cm
Colour: Turquoise and brown
Issued: 1994-1996
Series: The Seasons
             (Series Six)

U.S.: $500.00
Can.: $600.00
U.K.:   £275.00

HN 3622
Wintertime
Style Two
Designer: Valerie Annand
Height: 8 ½", 21.6 cm
Colour: Red, white and green
Issued: 1995-1996
Series: The Seasons
             (Series Six)

U.S.: $500.00
Can.: $600.00
U.K.:   £275.00

HN 3623
Lady Eaton
Designer: V. Annand
Height: 7 ½", 19.1 cm
Colour: Blue, white and yellow
Issued: 1994 in a limited
             edition of 2,500
Varieties: Also called 'Janice'
             (Style Two) HN 3624

U.S.: $600.00
Can.: $725.00
U.K.:   £325.00

HN 3624
Janice
Style Two
Designer: V. Annand
Height: 7 ½", 19.1 cm
Colour: Blue, pink, white
             and yellow
Issued: 1994-1997
Varieties: Also called 'Lady
             Eaton' HN 3623
Comm.by: Great Universal
             Stores

U.S.: $500.00
Can.: $600.00
U.K.:   £270.00

HN 3625
Anniversary
Designer: V. Annand
Height: 8 ¾", 22.2 cm
Colour: Blue, black and pink
Issued: 1994-1998

U.S.: $600.00
Can.: $725.00
U.K.:   £325.00

HN 3626
Lily
Style Two
Designer: V. Annand
Height: 9 ½", 24.0 cm
Colour: Mauve and yellow
Issued: 1995-1995
Series: 1. Lady Doulton 1995
             2. M. Doulton Events

U.S.: $350.00
Can.: $450.00
U.K.:   £200.00

HN 3627
England
Designer: V. Annand
Height: 8", 20.3 cm
Colour: Blue and pink
Issued   1996-1998
Series: Ladies of the
             British Isles

U.S.: $500.00
Can.: $600.00
U.K.:   £275.00

HN 3628
Ireland
Designer: V. Annand
Height: 7 ¾", 19.7 cm
Colour: Green and white
Issued: 1996-1998
Series: Ladies of the
British Isles

U.S.: $600.00
Can.: $725.00
U.K.:   £325.00

HN 3629
Scotland
Designer: V. Annand
Height: 7 ¾", 19.7 cm
Colour: Green, white and
pink
Issued: 1995-1998
Series::   Ladies of the
British Isles

U.S.: $600.00
Can.: $725.00
U.K.:   £325.00

HN 3630
Wales
Designer: V. Annand
Height: 8 ½", 21.6 cm
Colour: Red, white and green
Issued: 1995-1998
Varieties: Also called 'Welsh
Lady' HN 4712
Series: Ladies of the
British Isles

U.S.: $600.00
Can.: $725.00
U.K.:   £325.00

HN 3631
Beatrice
Designer: M. Davies
Height: 7", 17.8 cm
Colour: White
Issued: 1994-1998
Varieties: HN 3263; also called
'Kathryn' HN 3413;
'Lucy' HN 3653;
'Summer Serenade'
HN 3610; Wildflower
of the Month

U.S.: $250.00
Can.: $300.00
U.K.:   £135.00

HN 3632
Amanda
Designer: R. Tabbenor
Height: 5 ¼", 13.3 cm
Colour: White and pink
Issued: 1994-1996
Varieties: HN 2996, 3406,
3634, 3635; also
called 'Flower of the
Month, Child'
Series: Vanity Fair Children

U.S.: $125.00
Can.: $150.00
U.K.:   £ 70.00

HN 3633
Shakespeare
Designer: R. Tabbenor
Height: 11 ¾", 29.8 cm
Colour: Browns and cream
Issued: 1994 in a limited
edition of 1,564
Comm.by: Lawleys By Post

U.S.: $1,500.00
Can.: $1,800.00
U.K.:   £ 800.00

HN 3634
Amanda
Designer: R. Tabbenor
Height: 5 ¼", 13.3 cm
Colour: White and blue
Issued: 1995
Varieties: HN 2996, 3406, 3632,
3635; also called
'Flower of The
Month, Child'
Comm.by: Youngs, Canada

U.S.: $125.00
Can.: $150.00
U.K.:   £ 70.00

HN 3635
Amanda
Designer: R. Tabbenor
Height: 5 ¼", 13.3 cm
Colour: White and pink
Issued: 1995-1995
Series: R.D.I.C.C.
Varieties: HN 2996, 3406, 3632,
3634; also called
'Flower of The Month,
Child'

U.S.: $125.00
Can.: $150.00
U.K.:   £ 70.00

HN 3636
Captain Hook
Designer:	R. Tabbenor
Height:	9 ¼", 23.5 cm
Colour:	Red, blue and brown
Issued:	1993-1996
Series:	Character Sculptures
U.S.:	**$300.00**
Can.:	**$375.00**
U.K.:	**£160.00**

Resin

HN 3637
Dick Turpin
Style Two
Designer:	R. Tabbenor
Height:	9", 22.9 cm
Colour:	Brown, black, red and white
Issued:	1993-1996
Series:	Character Sculptures
U.S.:	**$300.00**
Can.:	**$375.00**
U.K.:	**£160.00**

Resin

HN 3638
D'Artagnan
Style One
Designer:	R. Tabbenor
Height:	9", 22.9 cm
Colour:	Maroon, black, blue and brown
Issued:	1993-1996
Series:	Character Sculptures
U.S.:	**$300.00**
Can.:	**$375.00**
U.K.:	**£160.00**

Resin

HN 3639
Sherlock Holmes
Designer:	R. Tabbenor
Height:	7 ½", 19.1 cm
Colour:	Brown and grey
Issued:	1995-1996
Series:	Character Sculptures
U.S.:	**$300.00**
Can.:	**$375.00**
U.K.:	**£160.00**

Resin

HN 3640
W. G. Grace
Designer:	R. Tabbenor
Height:	8", 20.3 cm
Colour:	White, beige and red
Issued:	1995 in a limited edition of 9,500
Comm.by:	Lawleys By Post
U.S.:	**$375.00**
Can.:	**$450.00**
U.K.:	**£200.00**

HN 3641
Robert Burns
Style Two
Designer:	R. Tabbenor
Height:	7 ½", 19.1 cm
Colour:	Green and brown
Issued:	1996-1998
U.S.:	**$600.00**
Can.:	**$725.00**
U.K.:	**£325.00**

HN 3642
The Moor
Designer:	C.J. Noke
Height:	13 ½", 34.3 cm
Colour:	Flambé
Issued:	1994-1995
Varieties:	HN 1308, 1366, 1425, 1657, 2082, 3926; also called 'An Arab' HN 33, 343, 378
Series:	Flambé
U.S.:	**$3,250.00**
Can.:	**$4,000.00**
U.K.:	**£1,750.00**

HN 3643
Pauline
Style Three
Designer:	N. Pedley
Height:	7 ¼", 18.4 cm
Colour:	Red and white
Issued:	1994-1994
Varieties:	HN 3656
Series:	Roadshow Events
U.S.:	**$300.00**
Can.:	**$350.00**
U.K.:	**£160.00**

HN 3644
Deborah
Style Two
Designer: N. Pedley
Height: 7 ½", 19.1 cm
Colour: Yellow and white
Issued: 1995-1995
Series: Figure of the Year

U.S.: $325.00
Can.: $400.00
U.K.:   £175.00

HN 3645
Lindsay
Designer: N. Pedley
Height: 8", 20.3 cm
Colour: White, blue
            and cream
Issued: 1994-1998
Varieties: Also called 'Katie'
            (Style Two) HN 4123

U.S.: $275.00
Can.: $330.00
U.K.:   £150.00

HN 3646
Claire
Style Two
Designer: N. Pedley
Height: 8", 20.3 cm
Colour: White and blue
Issued: 1994-2000
Varieties: Also called 'Kaitlyn'
            HN 4128; 'Molly'
            HN 4091; 'Rosemary'
            (Style Three)
            HN 3691, 3698

U.S.: $250.00
Can.: $300.00
U.K.:   £135.00

HN 3647
Holly
Designer: N. Pedley
Height: 8", 20.3 cm
Colour: Green and red
Issued: 1994-2000

U.S.: $425.00
Can.: $500.00
U.K.:   £225.00

HN 3648
Sweet Sixteen
Style Two
Designer: N. Pedley
Height: 8", 20.3 cm
Colour: Dark pink and white
Issued: 1994-1998
Varieties: Also called 'Angela'
            (Style Four) HN 3690;
            'Kelly' (Style Two)
            HN 3912

U.S.: $250.00
Can.: $300.00
U.K.:   £135.00

HN 3649
Hannah
Style Two
Designer: N. Pedley
Height: 4", 10.1 cm
Colour: Pink, yellow and blue
Issued: 1994-1998
Varieties: HN 3870
Series: Miniatures

U.S.: $175.00
Can.: $225.00
U.K.:   £100.00

HN 3650
Mother's Helper
Designer: N. Pedley
Height: 4 ½", 11.4 cm
Colour: White, pink
            and yellow
Issued: 1994-2000

U.S.: $150.00
Can.: $180.00
U.K.:   £ 80.00

HN 3651
Hello Daddy
Designer: N. Pedley
Height: 5 ¾", 14.6 cm
Colour: White and green
Issued: 1994-2000

U.S.: $200.00
Can.: $250.00
U.K.:   £110.00

HN 3652
First Recital
Designer: N. Pedley
Height: 4 ½", 11.4 cm
Colour: Blue, pink and white
Issued: 1994-1996

U.S.:	**$150.00**
Can.:	**$180.00**
U.K.:	**£ 80.00**

HN 3653
Lucy
Style Two
Designer: M. Davies
Height: 7", 17.8 cm
Colour: White
Issued: 1994-1997
Varieties: 'Beatrice' HN 3263,
3631; 'Kathryn'
HN 3413; 'Lucy'
HN 3653; 'Summer
Serenade' HN 3610;
Wildflower / Month
Comm.by: Great Univ. Stores

U.S.:	**$250.00**
Can.:	**$300.00**
U.K.:	**£135.00**

HN 3654
Young Melody
Designer: N. Pedley
Height: 4 ¼", 10.8 cm
Colour: Yellow and white
Issued: 1994-1996

U.S.:	**$150.00**
Can.:	**$180.00**
U.K.:	**£ 80.00**

HN 3655
Hannah
Style One
Designer: N. Pedley
Height: 8 ¼", 19.0 cm
Colour: Blue
Issued: 1995-1995
Varieties: HN 3369

U.S.:	**$325.00**
Can.:	**$400.00**
U.K.:	**£175.00**

HN 3656
Pauline
Style Three
Designer: N. Pedley
Height: 7 ¼", 18.4 cm
Colour: Red and white
Issued: 1994-1994
Varieties: HN 3643
Comm.by: Littlewoods

U.S.:	**$300.00**
Can.:	**$350.00**
U.K.:	**£160.00**

HN 3657
Quiet, They're Sleeping
Designer: N. Pedley
Height: 5 ½", 14.0 cm
Colour: Blue, pink and white
Issued: 1994-1997
Comm.by: Lawleys By Post

U.S.:	**$225.00**
Can.:	**$275.00**
U.K.:	**£125.00**

HN 3658
Charlotte
Style Two
Designer: N. Pedley
Height: 8", 20.3 cm
Colour: Blue
Issued: 1995-1996
Comm.by: Littlewoods

U.S.:	**$275.00**
Can.:	**$330.00**
U.K.:	**£150.00**

HN 3659
Miss Kay
Designer: N. Pedley
Height: 8 ¼", 21.0 cm
Colour: Pink
Issued: 1994
Varieties: Also called 'Helen'
(Style Three),
HN 3601, 3687,
3763, 3886
Comm.by: Kay's Catalogue
Company

U.S.:	**$275.00**
Can.:	**$330.00**
U.K.:	**£150.00**

HN 3660
Happy Birthday
Style Two
Designer: N. Pedley
Height: 8", 20.3 cm
Colour: Green
Issued: 1995-1999

U.S.:	**$275.00**
Can.:	**$350.00**
U.K.:	**£150.00**

HN 3661
Gemma
Designer: N. Pedley
Height: 8", 20.3 cm
Colour: Green and pink
Issued: 1995-1998

U.S.:	**$275.00**
Can.:	**$350.00**
U.K.:	**£150.00**

HN 3662
Take Me Home
Designer: N. Pedley
Height: 8", 20.3 cm
Colour: White dress, pink roses
Issued: 1995-1999

U.S.:	**$300.00**
Can.:	**$360.00**
U.K.:	**£165.00**

HN 3663
Special Treat
Designer: N. Pedley
Height: 6", 15.0 cm
Colour: Pink and white
Issued: 1995-1997

U.S.:	**$175.00**
Can.:	**$225.00**
U.K.:	**£100.00**

HN 3664
Wistful
Style Two
Designer: P. Gee
Height: 12 ¼", 31.1 cm
Colour: White
Issued: 1994-2002
Series: Images

U.S.:	**$175.00**
Can.:	**$225.00**
U.K.:	**£100.00**

HN 3665
Tomorrow's Dreams
Style Two
Designer: P. Gee
Height: 8 ½", 21.6 cm
Colour: White
Issued: 1995 to the present
Series: Images

U.S.:	**$ 70.00**
Can.:	**$170.00**
U.K.:	**£ 39.00**

HN 3666 - 3673 not issued.

HN 3674
Ophelia
Designer: P. Parsons
Height: 7", 17.8 cm
Colour: Rose, yellow, white
Issued: 1995 in a limited
                edition of 5,000
Series: Shakespearean
                Ladies
Comm.by: Lawleys By Post

U.S.:	**$550.00**
Can.:	**$650.00**
U.K.:	**£300.00**

HN 3675
Richard the Lionheart
Designer: P. Parsons
Height: 10", 25.4 cm
Colour: Grey and white
Issued: 1995-2002

U.S.:	**$750.00**
Can.:	**$900.00**
U.K.:	**£375.00**

HN 3676
Desdemona
Designer: P. Parsons
Height: 9", 22.9 cm
Colour: Blue, orange and
           white
Issued: 1995 in a limited
           edition of 5,000
Series: Shakespearean
           Ladies
Comm.by: Lawleys By Post
   U.S.:   **$550.00**
   Can.:   **$650.00**
   U.K.:   **£300.00**

HN 3677
Cinderella
Style One
Designer: P. Parsons
Height: 8", 20.3 cm
Colour: Blue and white
Issued: 1995 in a limited
           edition of 2,000
Series: The Disney Princess
           Collection
   U.S.:   **$450.00**
   Can.:   **$550.00**
   U.K.:   **£250.00**

HN 3678
Snow White
Designer: P. Parsons
Height: 8 ¼", 21.0 cm
Colour: Yellow, blue and red
Issued: 1995 in a limited
           edition of 2,000
Series: The Disney Princess
           Collection
   U.S.:   **$525.00**
   Can.:   **$650.00**
   U.K.:   **£300.00**

HN 3679
Titania
Designer: P. Parsons
Height: 8 ¾", 22.2 cm
Colour: Rose-yellow and blue
Issued: 1995 in a limited
           edition of 5,000
Series: Shakespearean
           Ladies
Comm.by: Lawleys By Post
   U.S.:   **$650.00**
   Can.:   **$775.00**
   U.K.:   **£350.00**

HN 3680
Lady Jane Grey
Designer: P. Parsons
Height: 8 ¼", 19.0 cm
Colour: Green and gold
Issued: 1995 in a limited
           edition of 5,000
Series: Tudor Roses
Comm.by: Lawleys By Post
   U.S.:   **$1,000.00**
   Can.:   **$1,200.00**
   U.K.:   **£ 550.00**

HN 3681
Joan of Arc
Designer: P. Parsons
Height: 10", 25.4 cm
Colour: Cream and blue
Issued: 1996-1998
   U.S.:   **$650.00**
   Can.:   **$775.00**
   U.K.:   **£350.00**

HN 3682
Princess Elizabeth
Designer: P. Parsons
Height: 8 ½", 21.6 cm
Colour: Red and pink
Issued: 1996 in a limited
           edition of 5,000
Series: Tudor Roses
Comm.by: Lawleys By Post
   U.S.:   **$ 900.00**
   Can.:   **$1,100.00**
   U.K.:   **£ 500.00**

HN 3683
Eastern Grace
Designer: P. Parsons
Height: 12 ½", 31.7 cm
Colour: Flambé
Issued: 1995 in a limited
           edition of 2,500
Varieties: HN 3138
Series: Flambé
   U.S.:   **$625.00**
   Can.:   **$750.00**
   U.K.:   **£375.00**

HN 3684
What's The Matter?
Designer: N. Pedley
Height: 5 ½", 14.0 cm
Colour: Yellow and white
Issued: 1995-1998
U.S.:	**$200.00**
Can.:	**$250.00**
U.K.:	**£110.00**

HN 3685
Hometime
Designer: N. Pedley
Height: 6", 15.0 cm
Colour: White and blue
Issued: 1995-1997
U.S.:	**$200.00**
Can.:	**$250.00**
U.K.:	**£110.00**

HN 3686
Nicole
Style One
Designer: N. Pedley
Height: 7 ½", 19.1 cm
Colour: Pink and cream
Issued: 1995
Varieties: HN 3421
Comm.by: Birks, Canada
U.S.:	**$250.00**
Can.:	**$325.00**
U.K.:	**£135.00**

HN 3687
Helen
Style Three
Designer: N. Pedley
Height: 7 ½", 19.1 cm
Colour: Green
Issued: 1995-1996
Varieties: HN 3601, 3763,
             3886; also called
             'Miss Kay' HN 3659
Comm.by: Express Gifts
U.S.:	**$300.00**
Can.:	**$350.00**
U.K.:	**£150.00**

HN 3688
Emily
Style Two
Designer: N. Pedley
Height: 8 ¼", 21.0 cmm
Colour: Blue and yellow
Issued: 1995-1995
Series: RDICC
U.S.:	**$325.00**
Can.:	**$400.00**
U.K.:	**£175.00**

HN 3689
Jacqueline
Style Three
Designer: N. Pedley
Height: 8", 20.3 cm
Colour: White and green
Issued: 1995-1995
Series: Roadshow Events
U.S.:	**$250.00**
Can.:	**$300.00**
U.K.:	**£135.00**

HN 3690
Angela
Style Four
Designer: N. Pedley
Height: 8", 20.3 cm
Colour: Yellow and white
Issued: 1995-1997
Varieties: 'Kelly' (Style Two)
             HN 3912; 'Sweet
             Sixteen' (Style Two)
             HN 3648
Comm.by: Great Univ. Studios
U.S.:	**$275.00**
Can.:	**$325.00**
U.K.:	**£150.00**

HN 3691
Rosemary
Style Three
Designer: N. Pedley
Height: 8", 20.3 cm
Colour: Mauve and yellow
Issued: 1995 U.K.,
             1996 Canada-1997
Varieties: HN 3698; 'Claire'
             (Style Two) HN 3646;
             'Kaitlyn' HN 4128;
             'Molly' HN 4091
U.S.:	**$325.00**
Can.:	**$400.00**
U.K.:	**£175.00**

HN 3692
Old Country Roses
Style Two
Designer: N. Pedley
Height: 8", 20.3 cm
Colour: Red, white and yellow
Issued: 1995-1999
U.S.: $400.00
Can.: $500.00
U.K.: £225.00

HN 3693
April
Style Four
Designer: N. Pedley
Height: 8", 20.3 cm
Colour: Green, yellow and white
Issued: 1995-1997
U.S.: $350.00
Can.: $425.00
U.K.: £200.00

HN 3694
Caroline
Style Two
Designer: N. Pedley
Height: 8", 20.3 cm
Colour: Pink and yellow
Issued: 1995-1998
U.S.: $325.00
Can.: $400.00
U.K.: £175.00

HN 3695
Storytime
Style Two
Designer: N. Pedley
Height: 4", 10.1 cm
Colour: White dress with red flowers
Issued: 1995-1998
U.S.: $200.00
Can.: $250.00
U.K.: £110.00

HN 3696
Faithful Friend
Designer: N. Pedley
Height: 6", 15.0 cm
Colour: Rose-pink, yellow and white
Issued: 1995-1997
U.S.: $200.00
Can.: $250.00
U.K.: £110.00

HN 3697
Home at Last
Designer: N. Pedley
Height: 5 ¾", 14.6 cm
Colour: Green and cream
Issued: 1995-1999
U.S.: $200.00
Can.: $250.00
U.K.: £110.00

HN 3698
Rosemary
Style Three
Designer: N. Pedley
Height: 8", 20.3 cm
Colour: Mauve and yellow
Issued: 1995-1997
Varieties: HN 3691; 'Claire' (Style Two) HN 3646; 'Kaitlyn' HN 4128; 'Molly' HN 4091
U.S.: $325.00
Can.: $400.00
U.K.: £175.00

HN 3699
Grace
Style Two
Designer: N. Pedley
Height: 8", 20.3 cm
Colour: Green
Issued: 1996-2001
Series: Vanity Fair Ladies
U.S.: $300.00
Can.: $350.00
U.K.: £160.00

HN 3700
Forget-Me-Nots
Designer: V. Annand
Height: 9", 22.9 cm
Colour: Lavender
Issued: 1995-1998
Series: Flowers of Love

U.S.:	$500.00
Can.:	$600.00
U.K.:	£270.00

HN 3701
Camellias
Designer: V. Annand
Height: 8 ½", 21.6 cm
Colour: Pink
Issued: 1995-1998
Series: Flowers of Love

U.S.:	$500.00
Can.:	$600.00
U.K.:	£270.00

HN 3702
Le Bal
Designer: V. Annand
Height: 8 ½", 21.6 cm
Colour: Yellow and pink
Issued: 1995 in a limited
            edition of 5,000
Series: RDICC

U.S.:	$550.00
Can.:	$650.00
U.K.:	£300.00

HN 3703
Belle
Style Three
Designer: V. Annand
Height: 8", 20.3 cm
Colour: Red and gold
Issued: 1996-1996
Series: Figure of the year

U.S.:	$450.00
Can.:	$550.00
U.K.:	£250.00

HN 3704
First Violin
Designer: V. Annand
Height: 9", 22.9 cm
Colour: Grey, yellow ribbon
Issued: 1995 in a limited
            edition of 1,500
Series: Edwardian String
            Quartet
Comm.by: Lawleys By Post

U.S.:	$700.00
Can.:	$850.00
U.K.:	£375.00

HN 3705
Second Violin
Designer: V. Annand
Height: 9", 22.9 cm
Colour: Grey, pink ribbon
Issued: 1995 in a limited
            edition of 1,500
Series: Edwardian String
            Quartet
Comm.by: Lawleys By Post

U.S.:	$700.00
Can.:	$850.00
U.K.:	£375.00

HN 3706
Viola
Designer: V. Annand
Height: 8 ¾", 22.2 cm
Colour: Grey, green ribbon
Issued: 1995 in a limited
            edition of 1,500
Series: Edwardian String
            Quartet
Comm.by: Lawleys By Post

U.S.:	$700.00
Can.:	$850.00
U.K.:	£375.00

HN 3707
Cello
Style Two
Designer: V. Annand
Height: 7", 17.8 cm
Colour: Grey, blue ribbon
Issued: 1995 in a limited
            edition of 1,500
Series: Edwardian String
            Quartet
Comm.by: Lawleys By Post

U.S.:	$700.00
Can.:	$850.00
U.K.:	£375.00

HN 3708
Katherine
Style Two
Designer: V. Annand
Height: 9", 22.9 cm
Colour: Peach
Issued: 1996-1996
Series: Lady Doulton, 1996
U.S.: $375.00
Can.: $450.00
U.K.: £200.00

HN 3709
Rose
Style Two
Designer: V. Annand
Height: 8 ½", 21.6 cm
Colour: Peach and white
Issued: 1996-2000
Series: Flowers of Love
U.S.: $500.00
Can.: $600.00
U.K.: £270.00

HN 3710
Primrose
Designer: V. Annand
Height: 9", 22.9 cm
Colour: Yellow and pink
Issued: 1996-1998
Series: Flowers of Love
U.S.: $500.00
Can.: $600.00
U.K.: £270.00

HN 3711
Jane
Style Four
Designer: V. Annand
Height: 9", 22.9 cm
Colour: White, green and red
Issued: 1997 in a limited
edition of 1997
Series: Lady Doulton, 1997
U.S.: $250.00
Can.: $300.00
U.K.: £135.00

HN 3712
New Baby
Designer: V. Annand
Height: 2", 5.0 cm
Colour: White with pink
highlights
Issued: 1997-2002
Varieties: HN 3713
Series: Name Your Own
U.S.: $125.00
Can.: $150.00
U.K.: £ 70.00

Metal plaque on base for engraved name.

HN 3713
New Baby
Designer: V. Annand
Height: 2", 5.0 cm
Colour: White with blue
highlights
Issued: 1997-2002
Varieties: HN 3712
Series: Name Your Own
U.S.: $125.00
Can.: $150.00
U.K.: £ 70.00

Metal plaque on base for engraved name.

HN 3714
Emma
Style Three
Designer: V. Annand
Height: 8 ½", 21.6 cm
Colour: Red
Issued: 1997-2003
Varieties: Also called 'Madison'
HN 4204
Series: In Vogue
U.S.: $250.00
Can.: $300.00
U.K.: £135.00

HN 3715
Sophie
Style Four
Designer: V. Annand
Height: 8 ¾", 22.2 cm
Colour: Green dress, yellow
scarf and gloves
Issued: 1997-2001
Series: In Vogue
U.S.: $250.00
Can.: $300.00
U.K.: £135.00

HN 3716
Isabel
Style One
Designer: V. Annand
Height: 8 ½", 21.6 cm
Colour: Pale blue dress,
            pink scarf
Issued: 1997-2001
Series: Chelsea

U.S.:	$250.00
Can.:	$300.00
U.K.:	£135.00

HN 3717
Olivia
Style Three
Designer: V. Annand
Height: 8 ¾", 22.2 cm
Colour: Pale blue
Issued: 1997-2002
Varieties" Also called 'Brittany'
            HN 4206
Series: Chelsea

U.S.:	$225.00
Can.:	$275.00
U.K.:	£100.00

HN 3718
The Charge of the Light Brigade
Stsyle One
Designer: A. Maslankowski
Height: 17", 43.2 cm
Colour: Dark blue, brown
            and black
Issued: 1995 to the present
Series: Prestige

U.S.:	$19,250.00
Can.:	$19,300.00
U.K.:	£10,500.00

HN 3719
Long John Silver
Style Two
Designer: A. Maslankowski
Height: 8 ¾", 22.2 cm
Colour: Browns and yellow
Issued: 1993-1996
Series: Character Sculptures

U.S.:	$325.00
Can.:	$400.00
U.K.:	£175.00

Resin

HN 3720
Robin Hood
Style Two
Designer: A. Maslankowski
Height: 10 ½", 26.7 cm
Colour: Greens and browns
Issued: 1993-1996
Series: Character Sculptures

U.S.:	$400.00
Can.:	$500.00
U.K.:	£225.00

Resin

HN 3721
Pied Piper
Style Two
Designer: A. Maslankowski
Height: 8 ¾", 22.2 cm
Colour: Red, yellow and black
Issued: 1993-1996
Series: Character Sculptures

U.S.:	$325.00
Can.:	$400.00
U.K.:	£175.00

Resin

HN 3722
The Wizard
Style Two
Designer: A. Maslankowski
Height: 10", 25.4 cm
Colour: Blue
Issued: 1994-1996
Varieties: HN 3732
Series: Character Sculptures

U.S.:	$375.00
Can.:	$450.00
U.K.:	£200.00

Resin

HN 3723
Au Revoir
Style One
Designer: A. Maslankowski
Height: 7 ¾", 19.7 cm
Colour: Cream with gold trim
Issued: 1995-1998
Varieties: Also called 'Fond
            Farewell' HN 3815
Series: Elegance (Series Two)

U.S.:	$225.00
Can.:	$275.00
U.K.:	£125.00

HN 3724
Summer Breeze
Style One
Designer: A. Maslankowski
Height: 7 ¾", 19.7 cm
Colour: Cream with gold trim
Issued: 1995-1998
Varieties: Also called 'Moonlight
Stroll' HN 3954
Series: Elegance (Series Two)
  U.S.: **$225.00**
  Can.: **$275.00**
  U.K.: **£125.00**

HN 3725
Spring Morning
Style Two
Designer: A. Maslankowski
Height: 7 ¾", 19.7 cm
Colour: Cream with gold trim
Issued: 1995-1998
Varieties: Also called 'Summer
Scent' HN 3955
Series: Elegance (Series Two)
  U.S.: **$225.00**
  Can.: **$275.00**
  U.K.: **£125.00**

HN 3726
Dinnertime
Designer: A. Maslankowski
Height: 4 ½", 11.9 cm
Colour: White and green
Issued: 1995-1998
Series: Vanity Fair Children
  U.S.: **$125.00**
  Can.: **$150.00**
  U.K.: **£ 70.00**

HN 3727
Christmas Carols
Designer: A. Maslankowski
Height: 6", 15.0 cm
Colour: White
Issued: 1995-1999
Varieties: HN 4061
Series: Sentiments
  U.S.: **$125.00**
  Can.: **$150.00**
  U.K.: **£ 70.00**

HN 3728
Free Spirit
Style Two
Designer: A. Maslankowski
Height: 7 ½", 19.1 cm
Colour: Cream with gold trim
Issued: 1995-1998
Varieties: Also called 'Spring
Serenade' HN 3956
Series: Elegance (Series Two)
  U.S.: **$225.00**
  Can.: **$275.00**
  U.K.: **£125.00**

HN 3729
Au Revoir
Style Two
Designer: A. Maslankowski
Height: 6 ½", 16.5 cm
Colour: White
Issued: 1996-1999
Series: Sentiments
  U.S.: **$125.00**
  Can.: **$150.00**
  U.K.: **£ 70.00**

HN 3730
Innocence
Style Two
Designer: A. Maslankowski
Height: 3 ½", 8.9 cm
Colour: Pink and white
Issued: 1996-2000
  U.S.: **$125.00**
  Can.: **$150.00**
  U.K.: **£ 70.00**

HN 3731
Ballet Class
Style Two
Designer: A. Maslankowski
Height: 6", 15.0 cm
Colour: White, yellow slippers
Issued: 1996-2003
Series: Images
  U.S.: **$125.00**
  Can.: **$150.00**
  U.K.: **£ 70.00**

HN 3732
The Wizard
Style Two
Designer:	A. Maslankowski
Height:	10", 25.4 cm
Colour:	Blue and orange
Issued:	1995-1996
Varieties:	HN 3722
Series:	Character Sculptures
Comm.by:	Lawleys By Post
U.S.:	**$375.00**
Can.:	**$450.00**
U.K.:	**£200.00**

Resin

HN 3733
Christmas Angel
Designer:	A. Maslankowski
Height:	5 ¾", 14.6 cm
Colour:	White
Issued:	1996-1998
Varieties:	HN 4060
Series:	Sentiments
U.S.:	**$125.00**
Can.:	**$150.00**
U.K.:	**£ 70.00**

HN 3734
Top o' the Hill
Style Two
Designer:	L. Harradine
Remodeller:	P. Gee
Height:	3 ¾", 9.5 cm
Colour:	Red, white, gold trim
Issued:	1995-1996
Varieties:	HN 2126, 3499
Series:	1. Signature
	2. Miniatures
Comm.by:	Lawleys By Post
U.S.:	**$275.00**
Can.:	**$325.00**
U.K.:	**£150.00**

HN 3735
Victoria
Style Two
Designer:	M. Davies
Remodeller:	P. Gee
Height:	3 ½", 8.9 cm
Colour:	Purple
Issued:	1995-1996
Varieties:	HN 3744, 3909
Series:	1. Signature
	2. Miniatures
Comm.by:	Lawleys By Post
U.S.:	**$275.00**
Can.:	**$325.00**
U.K.:	**£150.00**

HN 3735A
Top o' the Hill
Style One
Designer:	L. Harradine
Height:	7", 17.8 cm
Colour:	Dark blue
Issued:	1997 in a limited edition of 3,500
Varieties:	HN 1833, 1834, 1849, 2127
U.S.:	**$425.00**
Can.:	**$525.00**
U.K.:	**£230.00**

HN 3736
Autumn Breezes
Style One
Designer:	L. Harradine
Height:	7 ½", 19.1 cm
Colour:	Blue and yellow
Issued:	1997-1998
Varieties:	HN 1911,1913, 1934, 2131, 2147
Series:	M. Doulton Events
U.S.:	**$400.00**
Can.:	**$475.00**
U.K.:	**£225.00**

HN 3737
Old Balloon Seller
Style One
Designer:	L. Harradine
Height:	7 ½", 19.1 cm
Colour:	Purple, blue, white, yellow and green
Issued:	1999-1999
Varieties:	HN 1315
Series:	M. Doulton Events
U.S.:	**$400.00**
Can.:	**$475.00**
U.K.:	**£225.00**

Serial Numbered
HN 3738 - 3739 not issued.

HN 3740
Lynne
Style One
Designer:	M. Davies
Height:	7", 17.8 cm
Colour:	Multicoloured with gold trim
Issued:	1995-1995
Varieties:	HN 2329; also called 'Kathy' (Style Two) HN 3305
Series:	Roadshow Events
U.S.:	**$475.00**
Can.:	**$575.00**
U.K.:	**£250.00**

HN 3741
Elaine
Style One
Designer: M. Davies
Height: 7 ½", 19.1 cm
Colour: Red with gold trim
Issued: 1995-1995
Varieties: HN 2791, 3307, 4130
Series: Roadshow Events

   U.S.:   **$475.00**
   Can.:   **$575.00**
   U.K.:   **£250.00**

HN 3742
Gillian
Style Three
Designer: M. Davies
Height: 7 ¾", 19.7 cm
Colour: White and pink
Issued: 1995-1997
Varieties: Also called 'Figure of
          the Month'
Comm.by: Great Universal
          Studios

   U.S.:   **$225.00**
   Can.:   **$275.00**
   U.K.:   **£125.00**

HN 3743
Kirsty
Style Two
Designer: M. Davies
Remodeller: P. Gee
Height: 3 ¾", 9.5 cm
Colour: Yellow
Issued: 1995
Varieties: HN 3213, 3246, 3480
Series: Miniatures
Comm.by: Great Universal
          Studios

   U.S.:   **$175.00**
   Can.:   **$200.00**
   U.K.:   **£ 95.00**

HN 3744
Victoria
Style Two
Designer: M. Davies
Remodeller: P. Gee
Height: 3 ½", 8.9 cm
Colour: Patterned pink dress
Issued: 1995-1998
Varieties: HN 3735, 3909
Series: Miniatures

   U.S.:   **$200.00**
   Can.:   **$250.00**
   U.K.:   **£110.00**

HN 3745 not issued.

HN 3746
Memory Lane
Designer: M. Davies
Height: 5 ½", 14.0 cm
Colour: White with blue flowers
Issued: c.1996
Varieties: 'Debbie',HN 2385,
          2400; 'Lavender Rose',
          HN 3481; 'Moonlight
          Roses', HN 3483; 'Old
          Country Roses', (Style
          One) HN 3842;
          'Tranquillity' HN 3747

   U.S.:   **$125.00**
   Can.:   **$150.00**
   U.K.:   **£ 70.00**

HN 3747
Tranquillity
Designer: M. Davies
Height: 5 ½", 14.0 cm
Colour: White with pink flowers
Issued: c.1996
Varieties: 'Debbie'; HN 2385,
          2400; 'Lavender Rose',
          HN 3481; 'Moonlight
          Roses' HN 3483; 'Old
          Country Roses', (Style
          One) HN 3842;
          'Memory Lane' HN
          3746

   U.S.:   **$125.00**
   Can.:   **$150.00**
   U.K.:   **£ 70.00**

HN 3748
Fiona
Style Four
Designer: M. Davies
Height: 7 ½", 19.1 cm
Colour: Lemon, tartan shawl
Issued: 1996-2002
Varieties: Adrienne HN 2152,
          2304; Joan (Style Two)
          HN 3217

   U.S.:   **$225.00**
   Can.:   **$275.00**
   U.K.:   **£125.00**

HN 3749
Karen
Style Three
Designer: M. Davies
Remodeller: R. Tabbenor
Height: 4", 10.1 cm
Colour: White with gold trim
Issued: 1997
Varieties: HN 3270, 3338
Series: Miniatures

   U.S.:   **$275.00**
   Can.:   **$325.00**
   U.K.: :   **£150.00**

HN 3750
Gulliver
Designer: D. Biggs
Height: 8 ½", 21.6 cm
Colour: Blue, yellow,
              green and red
Issued: 1995-1996
Series: Character Sculptures

U.S.:	**$300.00**
Can.:	**$375.00**
U.K.:	**£175.00**

Resin

HN 3751
Cyrano de Bergerac
Designer: D. Biggs
Height: 8 ½", 21.6 cm
Colour: Red, blue, black
              and brown
Issued: 1995-1996
Series: Character Sculptures

U.S.:	**$300.00**
Can.:	**$375.00**
U.K.:	**£175.00**

Resin

HN 3752
Fagin
Style Two
Designer: A. Dobson
Height: 8 ½", 21.6 cm
Colour: Browns, black and
              green
Issued: 1995-1996
Series: Character Sculptures

U.S.:	**$300.00**
Can.:	**$375.00**
U.K.:	**£175.00**

Resin
HN 3753 not issued.

HN 3754
For You
Designer: T. Potts
Height: 8 ½", 21.6 cm
Colour: Blue
Issued: 1996-2003
Varieties: HN 3863
Series: Name Your Own

U.S.:	**$225.00**
Can.:	**$275.00**
U.K.:	**£120.00**

Metal plaque on base for engraved
name.

HN 3755
Strolling
Style Two
Designer: T. Potts
Height: 8", 20.3 cm
Colour: Red and yellow
Issued: 1996-1999

U.S.:	**$275.00**
Can.:	**$350.00**
U.K.:	**£150.00**

HN 3756
Pamela
Style Three
Designer: T. Potts
Height: 8", 20.3 cm
Colour: Blue and pink
Issued: 1996-1996
Series: RDICC

U.S.:	**$325.00**
Can.:	**$400.00**
U.K.:	**£175.00**

HN 3757
Jean
Style Three
Designer: T. Potts
Height: 6 ¾", 17.2 cm
Colour: White and blue
Issued: 1996-1997
Varieties: HN 3862
Comm.by: Kay's Mail Order
              Catalogue

U.S.:	**$225.00**
Can.:	**$275.00**
U.K.:	**£125.00**

HN 3758
Bride of the Year
Designer: T. Potts
Height: 8", 20.3 cm
Colour: White and peach
Issued: 1996
Varieties: Also called 'Wedding
              Morn' (Style Two)
              HN 3853
Comm.by: Kay's Mail Order
              Catalogue

U.S.:	**$300.00**
Can.:	**$375.00**
U.K.:	**£175.00**

HN 3759
Stephanie
Style Two
Designer: T. Potts
Height: 8 ¼", 21.0 cm
Colour: Pink and lavender
Issued: 1996-1996
Series: Roadshow Events

U.S.:	**$225.00**
Can.:	**$275.00**
U.K.:	**£125.00**

HN 3760
Laura
Style Two
Designer: N. Pedley
Height: 8", 20.3 cm
Colour: White and blue
Issued: 1996-1999

U.S.:	**$225.00**
Can.:	**$275.00**
U.K.:	**£125.00**

HN 3761
Sleepyhead
Style Two
Designer: N. Pedley
Height: 4", 10.1 cm
Colour: White, green
and brown
Issued: 1996-1998

U.S.:	**$200.00**
Can.:	**$250.00**
U.K.:	**£110.00**

HN 3762
Time For Bed
Designer: N. Pedley
Height: 5 ¼", 13.3 cm
Colour: Pink
Issued: 1996-1998

U.S.:	**$200.00**
Can.:	**$250.00**
U.K.:	**£110.00**

HN 3763
Helen
Style Three
Designer: N. Pedley
Height: 8 ¼", 21.0 cm
Colour: Pink
Issued: 1996
Varieties: HN 3601, 3687,
3886; also called
'Miss Kay' HN 3659
Comm.by: Sears, Canada

U.S.:	**$275.00**
Can.:	**$325.00**
U.K.:	**£150.00**

HN 3764
Welcome
Designer: N. Pedley
Height: 5 ¾", 14.6 cm
Colour: White
Issued: 1996-1996
Series: Club Membership
Figure

U.S.:	**$125.00**
Can.:	**$150.00**
U.K.:	**£ 70.00**

HN 3765
Kate
Style Two
Designer: N. Pedley
Height: 8", 20.3 cm
Colour: Rose pink bodice,
white flowered skirt
Issued: 1996
Varieties: HN 3882
Comm.by: Kay's Mail Order
Catalogue

U.S.:	**$275.00**
Can.:	**$325.00**
U.K.:	**£150.00**

HN 3766
Anita
Designer: N. Pedley
Height: 8", 20.3 cm
Colour: White, yellow
and green
Issued: 1996
Comm.by: Kay's Mail Order
Catalogue

U.S.:	**$200.00**
Can.:	**$250.00**
U.K.:	**£110.00**

HN 3767
Christine
Style Four
Designer: N. Pedley
Height: 8", 20.3 cm
Colour: Blue
Issued: 1996-1998
  U.S.: **$300.00**
  Can.: **$375.00**
  U.K.: **£175.00**

HN 3768
Off to School
Designer: N. Pedley
Height: 5 ¼", 13.3 cm
Colour: Navy and grey
Issued: 1996-1998
  U.S.: **$225.00**
  Can.: **$275.00**
  U.K.: **£125.00**

HN 3769
Winter's Day
Designer: N. Pedley
Height: 7 ¾", 19.7 cm
Colour: Red and white
Issued: 1996-1997
Series: RDICC
  U.S.: **$350.00**
  Can.: **$425.00**
  U.K.: **£200.00**

HN 3770
Sir Francis Drake
Designer: D. Biggs
Height: 8 ½", 21.6 cm
Colour: Red, yellow, brown
and green
Issued: 1996-1996
Series: Character Sculptures
  U.S.: **$300.00**
  Can.: **$375.00**
  U.K.: **£175.00**

Resin
HN 3771 - 3779 not issued.

HN 3780
The Bowls Player
Designer: J. Jones
Height: 6", 15.0 cm
Colour: Yellow, white
and green
Issued: 1996-1996
Series: Character Sculptures
  U.S.: **$300.00**
  Can.: **$375.00**
  U.K.: **£175.00**

Resin
HN 3781 - 3784 not issued.

HN 3785
Bill Sikes
Designer: A. Dobson
Height: 9", 22.9 cm
Colour: Brown
Issued: 1996-1996
Series: Character Sculptures
  U.S.: **$325.00**
  Can.: **$400.00**
  U.K.: **£175.00**

Resin

HN 3786
Oliver Twist and
The Artful Dodger
Designer: A. Dobson
Height: 8", 20.3 cm
Colour: Browns, blue
and black
Issued: 1996-1996
Series: Character Sculptures
  U.S.: **$375.00**
  Can.: **$450.00**
  U.K.: **£200.00**

Resin
HN 3787 - 3789 not issued.

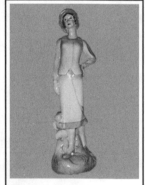

HN 3790
Sophie
Style Three
Designer: A. Maslankowski
Height: 9 ½", 24.1 cm
Colour: Cream and green
Issued: 1996-1997
Varieties: HN 3791, 3792, 3793
Series: Charleston
  U.S.: **$225.00**
  Can.: **$275.00**
  U.K.: **£125.00**

HN 3791
Sophie
Style Three
Designer: A. Maslankowski
Height: 9 ½", 24.1 cm
Colour: Cream and blue
Issued: 1996-1997
Varieties: HN 3790, 3792, 3793
Series: Charleston

U.S.:	$225.00
Can.:	$275.00
U.K.:	£125.00

HN 3792
Sophie
Style Three
Designer: A. Maslankowski
Height: 9 ½", 24.1 cm
Colour: Cream and pink
Issued: 1996-1997
Varieties: HN 3790, 3791, 3793
Series: Charleston

U.S.:	$225.00
Can.:	$275.00
U.K.:	£125.00

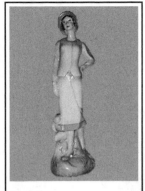

HN 3793
Sophie
Style Three
Designer: A. Maslankowski
Height: 9 ½", 24.1 cm
Colour: Ivory and gold
Issued: 1996-1997
Varieties: HN 3790, 3791, 3792
Series: Charleston

U.S.:	$225.00
Can.:	$275.00
U.K.:	£125.00

HN 3794
Harriet
Style Two
Designer: A. Maslankowski
Height: 9 ¼", 23.5 cm
Colour: Cream and green
Issued: 1996-1997
Varieties: HN 3795, 3796, 3797
Series: Charleston

U.S.:	$325.00
Can.:	$400.00
U.K.:	£175.00

HN 3795
Harriet
Style Two
Designer: A. Maslankowski
Height: 9 ¼", 23.5 cm
Colour: Cream and blue
Issued: 1996-1997
Varieties: HN 3794, 3796, 3797
Series: Charleston

U.S.:	$325.00
Can.:	$400.00
U.K.:	£175.00

HN 3796
Harriet
Style Two
Designer: A. Maslankowski
Height: 9 ¼", 23.5 cm
Colour: Cream and pink
Issued: 1996-1997
Varieties: HN 3794, 3795, 3797
Series: Charleston

U.S.:	$325.00
Can.:	$400.00
U.K.:	£175.00

HN 3797
Harriet
Style Two
Designer: A. Maslankowski
Height: 9 ¼", 23.5 cm
Colour: Cream, ivory and gold
Issued: 1996-1997
Varieties: HN 3794, 3795, 3796
Series: Charleston

U.S.:	$325.00
Can.:	$400.00
U.K.:	£175.00

HN 3798
Eliza
Style Three
Designer: A. Maslankowski
Height: 9 ½", 24.1 cm
Colour: Cream and green
Issued: 1996-1997
Varieties: HN 3799, 3800, 3801
Series: Charleston

U.S.:	$250.00
Can.:	$300.00
U.K.:	£125.00

HN 3799
Eliza
Style Three
Designer: A. Maslankowski
Height: 9 ½", 24.1 cm
Colour: Cream and blue
Issued: 1996-1997
Varieties: HN 3798, 3800, 3801
Series: Charleston

U.S.:	$250.00
Can.:	$300.00
U.K.:	£125.00

HN 3800
Eliza
Style Three
Designer: A. Maslankowski
Height: 9 ½", 24.1 cm
Colour: Cream and pink
Issued: 1996-1997
Varieties: HN 3798, 3799, 3801
Series: Charleston

U.S.:	$250.00
Can.:	$300.00
U.K.:	£125.00

HN 3801
Eliza
Style Three
Designer: A. Maslankowski
Height: 9 ½", 24.1 cm
Colour: Ivory and gold
Issued: 1996-1997
Varieties: HN 3798, 3799, 3800
Series: Charleston

U.S.:	$250.00
Can.:	$300.00
U.K.:	£125.00

HN 3802
Daisy
Style Two
Designer: A. Maslankowski
Height: 9 ¼", 23.5 cm
Colour: Cream and green
Issued: 1996-1997
Varieties: HN 3803, 3804, 3805
Series: Charleston

U.S.:	$325.00
Can.:	$400.00
U.K.:	£175.00

HN 3803
Daisy
Style Two
Designer: A. Maslankowski
Height: 9 ¼", 23.5 cm
Colour: Cream and blue
Issued: 1996-1997
Varieties: HN 3802, 3804, 3805
Series: Charleston

U.S.:	$325.00
Can.:	$400.00
U.K.:	£175.00

HN 3804
Daisy
Style Two
Designer: A. Maslankowski
Height: 9 ¼", 23.5 cm
Colour: Cream and pink
Issued: 1996-1997
Varieties: HN 3802, 3803, 3805
Series: Charleston

U.S.:	$325.00
Can.:	$400.00
U.K.:	£175.00

HN 3805
Daisy
Style Two
Designer: A. Maslankowski
Height: 9 ¼", 23.5 cm
Colour: Ivory and gold
Issued: 1996-1997
Varieties: HN 3802, 3803, 3804
Series: Charleston

U.S.:	$325.00
Can.:	$400.00
U.K.:	£175.00

HN 3806
Emily
Style Three
Designer: A. Maslankowski
Height: 9", 22.9 cm
Colour: Cream and green
Issued: 1996-1997
Varieties: HN 3807, 3808, 3809
Series: Charleston

U.S.:	$300.00
Can.:	$350.00
U.K.:	£150.00

HN 3807
Emily
Style Three
Designer: A. Maslankowski
Height: 9", 22.9 cm
Colour: Cream and blue
Issued: 1996-1997
Varieties: HN 3806, 3808, 3809
Series: Charleston

U.S.:	**$300.00**
Can.:	**$350.00**
U.K.:	**£150.00**

HN 3808
Emily
Style Three
Designer: A. Maslankowski
Height: 9", 22.9 cm
Colour: Cream and pink
Issued: 1996-1997
Varieties: HN 3806, 3807, 3809
Series: Charleston

U.S.:	**$300.00**
Can.:	**$350.00**
U.K.:	**£150.00**

HN 3809
Emily
Style Three
Designer: A. Maslankowski
Height: 9", 22.9 cm
Colour: Ivory and gold
Issued: 1996-1997
Varieties: HN 3806. 3807, 3808
Series: Charleston

U.S.:	**$300.00**
Can.:	**$350.00**
U.K.:	**£150.00**

HN 3810
Charlotte
Style Three
Designer: A. Maslankowski
Height: 9 ¼", 23.5 cm
Colour: Cream and green
Issued: 1996-1997
Varieties: HN 3811, 3812, 3813
Series: Charleston

U.S.:	**$400.00**
Can.:	**$475.00**
U.K.:	**£215.00**

HN 3811
Charlotte
Style Three
Designer: A. Maslankowski
Height: 9 ¼", 23.5 cm
Colour: Cream and blue
Issued: 1996-1997
Varieties: HN 3810, 3812, 3813
Series: Charleston

U.S.:	**$400.00**
Can.:	**$475.00**
U.K.:	**£215.00**

HN 3812
Charlotte
Style Three
Designer: A. Maslankowski
Height: 9 ¼", 23.5 cm
Colour: Cream and pink
Issued: 1996-1997
Varieties: HN 3810, 3811, 3813
Series: Charleston

U.S.:	**$400.00**
Can.:	**$475.00**
U.K.:	**£215.00**

HN 3813
Charlotte
Style Three
Designer: A. Maslankowski
Height: 9 ¼", 23.5 cm
Colour: Ivory and gold
Issued: 1996-1997
Varieties: HN 3810, 3811, 3812
Series: Charleston

U.S.:	**$400.00**
Can.:	**$475.00**
U.K.:	**£215.00**

HN 3814
The Cricketer
Style One
Designer: A. Maslankowski
Height: 8 ¼", 21.0 cm
Colour: White
Issued: 1996-1996

U.S.:	**$250.00**
Can.:	**$300.00**
U.K.:	**£135.00**

HN 3815
Fond Farewell
Designer: A. Maslankowski
Height: 8", 20.3 cm,
Colour: Red
Issued: 1997-1999
Varieties: Also called 'Au Revoir'
            (Style One) HN 3723

U.S.:	**$325.00**
Can.:	**$400.00**
U.K.:	**£180.00**

HN 3816
Ellen
Style Two
Designer: A. Maslankowski
Height: 8 ¾", 22.2 cm
Colour: Blue
Issued: 1997-1997
Varieties: HN 3819
Series: Charleston

U.S.:	**$225.00**
Can.:	**$275.00**
U.K.:	**£125.00**

HN 3817 - 3818 not issued.

HN 3819
Ellen
Style Two
Designer: A. Maslankowski
Height: 8 ¾", 22.2 cm
Colour: Ivory with gold
            highlights
Issued: 1997-1997
Varieties: HN 3816
Series: Charleston

U.S.:	**$225.00**
Can.:	**$275.00**
U.K.:	**£125.00**

HN 3820
Lillie Langtry
Designer: D. V. Tootle
Height: 8 ¾", 22.2 cm
Colour: Pink
Issued: 1996 in a limited
            edition of 5,000
Series: Victorian and
            Edwardian actresses
Comm.by: Lawleys By Post

U.S.:	**$500.00**
Can.:	**$600.00**
U.K.:	**£275.00**

HN 3821
Alfred The Great
Designer: D. V. Tootle
Height: 9 ¼", 23.5 cm
Colour: Gold, red and green
Issued: 1996-1997

U.S.:	**$650.00**
Can.:	**$775.00**
U.K.:	**£350.00**

HN 3822
James I
(1603-1625)
Designer: D. V. Tootle
Height: 9", 22.9 cm
Colour: Red, grey, gold trim
Issued: 1996 in a limited
            edition of 1,500
Series: Stuart Kings
Comm.by: Lawleys By Post

U.S.:	**$ 900.00**
Can.:	**$1,100.00**
U.K.:	**£ 480.00**

HN 3823 not issued.

HN 3824
Charles I
(1625-1649)
Designer: Douglas Tootle
Height: 10", 25.4 cm
Colour: Green and white
Issued: 1997 in a limited
            edition of 1,500
Series: Stuart Kings
Comm.by: Lawleys By Post

U.S.:	**$1,200.00**
Can.:	**$1,500.00**
U.K.:	**£ 650.00**

HN 3825
Charles II
(1660-1685)
Designer: D.V. Tootle
Height: 9", 22.9 cm
Colour: Purple and beige
Issued: 1996 in a limited
            edition of 1,500
Series: Stuart Kings
Comm.by: Lawleys By Post

U.S.:	**$ 900.00**
Can.:	**$1,100.00**
U.K.:	**£ 475.00**

HN 3826
Ellen Terry
Designer: D.V. Tootle
Height: 9", 22.9 cm
Colour: Blue and yellow
Issued: 1996 in a limited
edition of 5,000
Series: Victorian and
Edwardian Actresses
Comm.by: Lawleys By Post
U.S.: $650.00
Can.: $775.00
U.K.: £350.00

HN 3827
The Performance
Designer: D.V. Tootle
Height: 10 ¼", 26.0 cm
Colour: White
Issued: 1997-2001
Series: Images
U.S.: $275.00
Can.: $350.00
U.K.: £150.00

HN 3828
The Ballerina
Style Three
Designer: D.V. Tootle
Height: 5 ½", 14.0 cm
Colour: White
Issued: 1997-2001
Series: Images
U.S.: $150.00
Can.: $175.00
U.K.: £ 80.00

HN 3829
Happy Birthday
Style Three
Designer: D.V. Tootle
Height: 7 ½", 19.1 cm
Colour: White
Issued: 1997-2002
Series: Images
U.S.: $125.00
Can.: $150.00
U.K.: £ 80.00

HN 3830
Belle
Style Four
Designer: P. Parsons
Height: 8", 20.3 cm
Colour: Yellow
Issued: 1996 in a limited
edition of 2,000
Series: The Disney Princess
Collection
U.S.: $425.00
Can.: $500.00
U.K.: £230.00

HN 3831
Ariel
Designer: P. Parsons
Height: 8 ¼", 21.0 cm
Colour: White
Issued: 1996 in a limited
edition of 2,000
Series: The Disney Princess
Collection
U.S.: $425.00
Can.: $500.00
U.K.: £230.00

HN 3832
Jasmine
Style Two
Designer: P. Parsons
Height: 7 ½", 19.1 cm
Colour: Lilac dress
Issued: 1996 in a limited
edition of 2,000
Series: The Disney Princess
Collection
U.S.: $425.00
Can.: $500.00
U.K.: £230.00

HN 3833
Aurora
Designer: P. Parsons
Height: 7 ½", 19.1 cm
Colour: Blue dress
Issued: 1996 in a limited
edition of 2,000
Series: The Disney Princess
Collection
U.S.: $275.00
Can.: $350.00
U.K.: £150.00

HN 3834
Mary Tudor
Designer: P. Parsons
Height: 6 ¼", 15.9 cm
Colour: Purple and peach-
             yellow dress
Issued: 1997 in a limited
             edition of 5,000
Series: Tudor Roses
Comm.by: Lawleys By Post

U.S.:	$700.00
Can.:	$850.00
U.K.:	£375.00

HN 3835
Scheherazade
Designer: P. Parsons
Height: 10 ½", 26.7 cm
Colour: Red and green
Issued: 1996 in a limited
             edition of 1,500
Series: Fabled Beauties
Comm.by: Lawleys By Post

U.S.:	$700.00
Can.:	$850.00
U.K.:	£375.00

HN 3836
Queen Elizabeth II and
The Duke of Edinburgh
Designer: P. Parsons
Height: 9 ¼", 23.5 cm
Colour: White wedding dress,
             navy naval uniform
Issued: 1997 in a limited
             edition of 750

U.S.:	$ 900.00
Can.:	$1,100.00
U.K.:	£ 475.00

Issued to celebrate their golden
wedding anniversary.
HN 3837 not issued.

HN 3838
Margaret Tudor
Designer: P. Parsons
Height: 6 ½", 16.5 cm
Colour: Green and gold dress
Issued: 1997 in a limited
             edition of 5,000
Series: Tudor Roses
Comm.by: Lawleys By Post

U.S.:	$700.00
Can.:	$850.00
U.K.:	£375.00

HN 3839
Cruella De Vil
Designer: P. Parsons
Height: 8", 20.3 cm
Colour: Black dress, white
             coat
Issued: 1997 in a limited
             edition of 2,000
Series: Disney Villains

U.S.:	$450.00
Can.:	$550.00
U.K.:	£250.00

HN 3840
Maleficent
Designer: P. Parsons
Height: 8", 20.3 cm
Colour: Black and purple
Issued: 1997 in a limited
             edition of 2,000
Series: Disney Villains

U.S.:	$450.00
Can.:	$550.00
U.K.:	£250.00

HN 3841
Rapunzel
Designer: P. Parsons
Height: 10", 25.4 cm
Colour: Purple and yellow
Issued: 1998 in a limited
             edition of 1,500
Series: Fabled Beauties
Comm.by: Lawleys By Post

U.S.:	$700.00
Can.:	$850.00
U.K.:	£375.00

HN 3842
Jane Eyre
Designer: P. Parsons
Height: 8 ¼", 21.0 cm
Colour: Blue dress with pale
             blue collar, white dog
             with black patches
Issued: 1997 in a limited
             edition of 3,500
Series: Literary Heroines
Comm.by: Lawleys by Post

U.S.:	$600.00
Can.:	$725.00
U.K.:	£325.00

HN 3843
Emma
Style Four
Designer: P. Parsons
Height: 8 ¼", 21.0 cm
Colour: Light yellow dress
 and hat, red bows
Issued: 1997 in a limited
 edition of 3,500
Series: Literary Heroines
Comm.by: Lawleys By Post

U.S.:	**$450.00**
Can.:	**$550.00**
U.K.:	**£250.00**

HN 3844
Nefertiti
Designer: P. Parsons
Height: 10 ½", 26.7 cm
Colour: Cream
Issued: 1998 in a limited
 edition of 950
Series: Egyptian Queens
Comm.by: Lawleys By Post

U.S.:	**$750.00**
Can.:	**$900.00**
U.K.:	**£400.00**

HN 3845
Elizabeth Bennet
Designer: P. Parsons
Height: 8 ¾", 22.2 cm
Colour: Browns
Issued: 1998 in a limited
 edition of 3,500
Series: Literary Heroines
Comm.by: Lawleys By Post

U.S.:	**$550.00**
Can.:	**$650.00**
U.K.:	**£300.00**

HN 3846
Tess of the D'Urbervilles
Designer: P. Parsons
Height: 8 ¼", 21.0 cm
Colour: Tan, cream and white
Issued: 1998 in a limited
 edition of 3,500
Series: Literary Heroines
Comm.by: Lawleys By Post

U.S.:	**$550.00**
Can.:	**$650.00**
U.K.:	**£300.00**

HN 3847
The Queen
Designer: P. Parsons
Height: 8 ¾", 22.2 cm
Colour: Black, white, purple,
 red and yellow
Issued: 1998 in a limited
 edition of 2,000
Series: Disney Villains

U.S.:	**$350.00**
Can.:	**$425.00**
U.K.:	**£200.00**

HN 3848
The Witch
Style One
Designer: P. Parsons
Height: 7", 17.8 cm
Colour: Black and white
Issued: 1998 in a limited
 edition of 2,000
Series: Disney Villains

U.S.:	**$350.00**
Can.:	**$425.00**
U.K.:	**£200.00**

HN 3849
Moll Flanders
Designer: P. Parsons
Height: 8½", 21.5 cm
Colour: Red, cream and white
Issued: 1999 in a limited
 edition of 3,500
Series: Literary Heroines

U.S.:	**$525.00**
Can.:	**$625.00**
U.K.:	**£275.00**

HN 3850
Jessica
Style Two
Designer: N. Pedley
Height: 8", 20.3 cm
Colour: Light purple dress
Issued: 1997-1997
Series: Figure of the year

U.S.:	**$300.00**
Can.:	**$350.00**
U.K.:	**£150.00**

HN 3851
Sally
Style Two
Designer: T. Potts
Height: 8 ¼", 21.0 cm
Colour: Blue
Issued: 1996-1998
Varieties: HN 3383, 4160

U.S.:	**$300.00**
Can.:	**$350.00**
U.K.:	**£160.00**

HN 3852
Sarah
Style Two
Designer: T. Potts
Height: 8", 20.3 cm
Colour: Green
Issued: 1996-1999
Varieties: HN 3384, 3857

U.S.:	**$350.00**
Can.:	**$450.00**
U.K.:	**£200.00**

HN 3853
Wedding Morn
Style Two
Designer: T. Potts
Height: 8", 20.3 cm
Colour: Ivory, gold highlights
Issued: 1996-1999
Varieties: Also called 'Bride of
            the Year' HN 3758

U.S.:	**$325.00**
Can.:	**$400.00**
U.K.:	**£175.00**

HN 3854
Amy
Style Three
Designer: T. Potts
Height: 8", 20.3 cm
Colour: Pink
Issued: 1996-1999

U.S.:	**$300.00**
Can.:	**$350.00**
U.K.:	**£160.00**

HN 3855
Lambing Time
Style Two
Designer: T. Potts
Height: 8", 20.3 cm
Colour: Ivory, gold highlights
Issued: 1996-1998
Series: Elegance (Series Two)

U.S.:	**$250.00**
Can.:	**$300.00**
U.K.:	**£125.00**

HN 3856
Country Girl
Style Two
Designer: T. Potts
Height: 8", 20.3 cm
Colour: Ivory, gold highlights
Issued: 1996-1998
Series: Elegance (Series Two)

U.S.:	**$250.00**
Can.:	**$300.00**
U.K.:	**£125.00**

HN 3857
Sarah
Style Two
Designer: T. Potts
Height: 8", 20.3 cm
Colour: Pink
Issued: 1996 in a limited
            edition of 1,996
Varieties: HN 3384, 3852
Series   Visitor Centre

U.S.:	**$350.00**
Can.:	**$450.00**
U.K.:	**£200.00**

To commemorate the opening of the
Royal Doulton Visitors Centre

HN 3858
Lucy
Style Three
Designer: T. Potts
Height: 8 ½", 21.6 cm
Colour: Pale pink and white
            dress, white cat with
            black patches
Issued: 1997-1999

U.S.:	**$325.00**
Can.:	**$400.00**
U.K.:	**£175.00**

HN 3859
Sweet Bouquet
Style Two
Designer: T. Potts
Height: 8", 20.3 cm
Colour: Ivory, gold highlights
Issued: 1997 in a special
   edition of 250
Series: Elegance (Series Two)
   U.S.:   **$250.00**
   Can.:   **$300.00**
   U.K.:   **£135.00**

HN 3860
Morning Walk
Designer: T. Potts
Height: 8", 20.3 cm
Colour: Ivory, gold highlights
Issued: 1997-1998
Series: Elegance (Series Two)
   U.S.:   **$325.00**
   Can.:   **$400.00**
   U.K.:   **£175.00**

HN 3861
Centre Stage
Designer: T. Potts
Height: 8", 20.3 cm
Colour: Blue
Issued: 1996
Varieties: 'Courtney' HN 3869
Comm.by: Great Universal
   Stores
   U.S.:   **$275.00**
   Can.:   **$330.00**
   U.K.:   **£140.00**

HN 3862
Jean
Style Three
Designer: T. Potts
Height: 6 ¾", 17.2 cm
Colour: White and blue
Issued: 1997 in a special
   edition of 350
Varieties: HN 3757
Comm.by: Seaway China
   U.S.:   **$225.00**
   Can.:   **$275.00**
   U.K.:   **£125.00**

HN 3863
For You
Designer: T. Potts
Height: 8", 20.3 cm
Colour: Pink
Issued: 1997-1999
Varieties: HN 3754
Series: Name Your Own
   U.S.:   **$225.00**
   Can.:   **$275.00**
   U.K.:   **£125.00**

Metal plaque on base for engraved
name.

HN 3864
Kimberley
Style Two
Designer: T. Potts
Height: 8 ½", 21.6 cm
Colour: White, pink and light
   yellow dress, brown
   and white cat
Issued: 1997 in a limited
   edition of 2,000
Varieties: HN 3379, 3382
Series: Visitor Centre
   U.S.:   **$325.00**
   Can.:   **$400.00**
   U.K.:   **£175.00**

HN 3865
Anna of the Five Towns
Designer: T. Potts
Height: 8", 20.3 cm
Colour: Dark and light brown
   dress and hat
Issued: 1997-1998
Series: 1. Arnold Bennett
   2. Visitor Centre
   U.S.:   **$300.00**
   Can.:   **$375.00**
   U.K.:   **£165.00**

HN 3866
Bon Voyage
Designer: T. Potts
Height: 9", 22.9 cm
Colour: Pink and white dress
Issued: 1998-2001
   U.S.:   **$300.00**
   Can.:   **$375.00**
   U.K.:   **£165.00**

HN 3867
The Countess of Chell
Designer:	T. Potts
Height:	8 ½", 21.6 cm
Colour:	Pale pink dress with gold highlights
Issued:	1998-1998
Series:	1. Arnold Bennett
	2. Visitor Centre

U.S.:	**$275.00**
Can.:	**$325.00**
U.K.:	**£150.00**

HN 3868
Danielle
Style Three	
Designer:	T. Potts
Height:	8 ¾", 22.2 cm
Colour:	Orange
Issued:	1998
Comm.by:	Great Universal Stores

U.S.:	**$275.00**
Can.:	**$325.00**
U.K.:	**£150.00**

HN 3869
Courtney
Designer:	N. Pedley
Height:	8", 20.3 cm
Colour:	Blue
Issued:	1999 in a special edition of 250
Varieties:	Also called 'Centre Stage' HN 3861
Comm.by:	Seaway China

U.S.:	**$275.00**
Can.:	**$330.00**
U.K.:	**£140.00**

HN 3870
Hannah
Style Two	
Designer:	N. Pedley
Height:	4", 10.1 cm
Colour:	Red dress, pink ruffles, gold trim
Issued:	1995-1996
Varieties:	HN 3649
Series:	1. Signature
	2. Miniatures

U.S.:	**$250.00**
Can.:	**$300.00**
U.K.:	**£135.00**

HN 3871
Susan
Style Three	
Designer:	N. Pedley
Height:	8", 20.3 cm
Colour:	Rose pink and white dress
Issued:	1997-1997
Series:	RDICC

U.S.:	**$325.00**
Can.:	**$400.00**
U.K.:	**£175.00**

HN 3872
Lauren
Style Two	
Designer:	N. Pedley
Height:	9", 22.9 cm
Colour:	Cream dress, pink and yellow sash
Issued:	1997-1997
Series:	Roadshow Events

U.S.:	**$275.00**
Can.:	**$325.00**
U.K.:	**£150.00**

HN 3873 - 3874 not issued.

HN 3875
Joy
Style Two	
Designer:	N. Pedley
Height:	5 ¼", 13.3 cm
Colour:	White dress
Issued:	1997-1997
Series:	Club Membership Figure

U.S.:	**$125.00**
Can.:	**$150.00**
U.K.:	**£ 65.00**

HN 3876
Kitty
Style Two	
Designer:	N. Pedley
Height:	4 ½", 11.9 cm
Colour:	White and blue dress, ginger and white cat
Issued:	1997-2000

U.S.:	**$150.00**
Can.:	**$180.00**
U.K.:	**£ 80.00**

HN 3877
On The Beach
Designer: N. Pedley
Height: 3 ½", 8.9 cm
Colour: Pink dress, yellow
 ribbons and pail
Issued: 1997-1999
 U.S.: **$175.00**
 Can.: **$225.00**
 U.K.: **£ 95.00**

HN 3878
Julie
Style Two
Designer: N. Pedley
Height: 8", 20.3 cm
Colour: Pink and white
Issued: 1997-2001
 U.S.: **$225.00**
 Can.: **$275.00**
 U.K.: **£120.00**

HN 3879
Linda
Style Four
Designer: N. Pedley
Height: 8", 20.3 cm
Colour: Deep gold dress,
 red check shawl
Issued: 1997
Comm.by: Great Universal Stores
 U.S.: **$275.00**
 Can.: **$325.00**
 U.K.: **£150.00**

HN 3880
Kathleen
Style Three
Designer: N. Pedley
Height: 8 ½", 21.6 cm
Colour: Pink
Issued: 1997
Varieties: HN 3609; also called
 'Brianna' HN 4126
Comm.by: Great Universal Stores
 U.S.: **$225.00**
 Can.: **$275.00**
 U.K.: **£120.00**

HN 3881 not issued.

HN 3882
Kate
Style Two
Designer: N. Pedley
Height: 8", 20.3 cm
Colour: Rose pink jacket,
 flowered white skirt
Issued: 1997
Varieties: HN 3765
Comm.by: Pascoe & Company
 U.S.: **$275.00**
 Can.: **$325.00**
 U.K.: **£150.00**

HN 3883
Chloe
Style Three
Designer: N. Pedley
Height: 8" 20.3 cm
Colour: Lemon
Issued: 1997-1998
Varieties: HN 3914; also called
 'Amber' HN 4125
Comm.by: Index Catalogue Co.
 U.S.: **$225.00**
 Can.: **$275.00**
 U.K.: **£120.00**

HN 3884 not issued.

HN 3885
Melissa
Style Two
Designer: N. Pedley
Height: 8 ¼", 21.0 cm
Colour: Purple dress,
 cream hat
Issued: 1997-1999
 U.S.: **$250.00**
 Can.: **$300.00**
 U.K.: **£130.00**

HN 3886
Helen
Style Three
Designer: N. Pedley
Height: 8", 20.3 cm
Colour: Red and cream
Issued: 1997-1999
Varieties: HN 3601, 3687, 3763;
 also called 'Miss Kay'
 HN 3659
 U.S.: **$350.00**
 Can.: **$425.00**
 U.K.: **£185.00**

HN 3887
Megan
Style Two
Designer:　N. Pedley
Height:　8", 20.3 cm
Colour:　White and light blue
Issued:　1997-2000
Varieties:　Also called 'Jasmine'
　　　　(Style Three) HN 4127;
　　　　'Millie' HN 4212
Series:　Vanity Fair Ladies

U.S.:	$200.00
Can.:	$250.00
U.K.:	£110.00

HN 3888
Louise
Style Three
Designer:　N. Pedley
Height:　8", 20.3 cm
Colour:　White dress with
　　　　flowered border
Issued:　1997-2000

U.S.:	$225.00
Can.:	$275.00
U.K.:	£120.00

HN 3889
Flowers For You
Designer:　N. Pedley
Height:　5 ¾", 14.5 cm
Colour:　Yellow dress
Issued:　1997-1999

U.S.:	$125.00
Can.:	$150.00
U.K.:	£ 70.00

HN 3890
Geoffrey Boycott
Designer:　R. Tabbenor
Height:　9 ½", 24.0 cm
Colour:　White
Issued:　1996 in a limited
　　　　edition of 8,114
Comm.by:　Lawleys By Post

U.S.:	$325.00
Can.:	$400.00
U.K.:	£175.00

HN 3891
Sir Henry Doulton
Designer:　R. Tabbenor
Height:　8 ¾", 22.2 cm
Colour:　Grey suit, black
　　　　overcoat, hat and
　　　　umbrella
Issued:　1997 in a limited
　　　　edition of 1,997

U.S.:	$425.00
Can.:	$500.00
U.K.:	£230.00

HN 3892 - 3899 Animal and Birds
figures, except HN 3892, 3897 and
3899 not issued.

HN 3900
Elaine
Style Two
Designer:　M. Davies
Remodeller: P. Gee
Height:　4", 10.1 cm
Colour:　White and gold
Issued:　1997
Varieties:　HN 3214, 3247
Series:　Miniatures
Comm.by:　Great Universal
　　　　Stores

U.S.:	$175.00
Can.:	$200.00
U.K.:	£ 95.00

HN 3901
Ninette
Style Two
Designer:　M. Davies
Remodeller: P. Gee
Height:　3 ½", 8.9 cm
Colour:　Yellow and white
Issued:　1997
Varieties:　HN 3215, 3248
Series:　Miniatures
Comm.by:　Index Catalogue Co.

U.S.:	$175.00
Can.:	$200.00
U.K.:	£ 95.00

HN 3902
Lily
Style Three
Designer:　M. Davies
Height:　7 ¾", 19.7 cm
Colour:　Light and dark
　　　　green dress
Issued:　1998-1998
Series:　Peggy Davies
　　　　Collection

U.S.:	$275.00
Can.:	$350.00
U.K.:	£150.00

HN 3903
Mary
Style Four
Designer: M. Davies
Height: 7", 17.8 cm
Colour: Red and pink dress
Issued: 1998-1998
Series: Peggy Davies
Collection

U.S.: $275.00
Can.: $350.00
U.K.: £150.00

HN 3904
Valerie
Style Two
Designer: M. Davies
Height: 7 ¾", 19.7 cm
Colour: Blue and pink dress
Issued: 1998-1998
Series: Peggy Davies
Collection

U.S.: $275.00
Can.: $350.00
U.K.: £150.00

HN 3905
Christine
Style Five
Designer: M. Davies
Height: 7 ½", 19.1 cm
Colour: White flowered dress,
pink overskirt
Issued: 1998-1998
Series: Peggy Davies
Collection

U.S.: $275.00
Can.: $350.00
U.K.: £150.00

HN 3906
Eleanor
Style One
Designer: M. Davies
Height: 8", 20.3 cm
Colour: Pink and yellow dress
Issued: 1998-1998
Series: Peggy Davies
Collection

U.S.: $275.00
Can.: $350.00
U.K.: £150.00

HN 3907
Patricia
Style Five
Designer: M. Davies
Height: 7 ¾", 19.7 cm
Colour: Peach, yellow and
white dress
Issued: 1998-1998
Series: Peggy Davies
Collection

U.S.: $275.00
Can.: $350.00
U.K.: £150.00

HN 3908
Buttercup
Style Two
Designer: M. Davies
Remodeller: P. Gee
Height: 3 ½", 8.9 cm
Colour: Pink
Issued: 1998
Varieties: HN 3268
Series: Miniatures
Comm.by: Great Universal
Stores

U.S.: $175.00
Can.: $200.00
U.K.: £ 95.00

HN 3909
Victoria
Style Two
Designer: M. Davies
Remodeller: P. Gee
Height: 3 ½", 8.9 cm
Colour: Pale blue
Issued: 1998
Varieties: HN 3735, 3744
Series: Miniatures
Comm.by: Index Catalogue Co.

U.S.: $150.00
Can.: $175.00
U.K.: £ 80.00

HN 3910 not issued.

HN 3911
First Prize
Designer: N. Pedley
Height: 5 ¼", 13.3 cm
Colour: White shirt, brown
jodhpurs, black hat,
dark blue coat
Issued: 1997-1999

U.S.: $200.00
Can.: $250.00
U.K.: £110.00

HN 3912
Kelly
Style Two
Designer: N. Pedley
Height: 8", 20.3 cm
Colour: Pink
Issued: 1997-1998
Varieties: Also called 'Angela'
(Style Four) HN 3690;
'Sweet Sixteen'
(Style Two) HN 3648
Comm.by: Home Shopping

U.S.:	$225.00
Can.:	$275.00
U.K.:	£120.00

HN 3913
First Bloom
Designer: N. Pedley
Height: 8", 20.3 cm
Colour: Royal blue
Issued: 1997-1997
Varieties: Also called 'Mackenzie'
HN 4109
Series: Roadshow Events

U.S.:	$250.00
Can.:	$300.00
U.K.:	£135.00

HN 3914
Chloe
Style Three
Designer: N. Pedley
Height: 8", 20.3 cm
Colour: Pink
Issued: 1997-2002
Varieties: HN 3883; also called
"Amber" HN 4125

U.S.:	$275.00
Can.:	$350.00
U.K.:	£150.00

Exclusive to Canada

HN 3915
Colleen
Designer: N. Pedley
Height: 8", 20.3 cm
Colour: White and pale
yellow dress
Issued: 1997-2002

U.S.:	$275.00
Can.:	$350.00
U.K.:	£150.00

Exclusive to Canada

HN 3916
Spring Posy
Designer: N. Pedley
Height: 8 ¾", 22.2 cm
Colour: Dark and light
green dress
Issued: 1997
Series: The Seasons
(Series Seven)
Comm.by: Guild of Specialist
China and Glass
Retailers

U.S.:	$250.00
Can.:	$300.00
U.K.:	£135.00

HN 3917
Summer Blooms
Style One
Designer: N. Pedley
Height: 8 ¾", 22.2 cm
Colour: Light blue dress
Issued: 1997
Series: The Seasons
(Series Seven)
Comm.by: Guild of Specialist
China and Glass
Retailers

U.S.:	$250.00
Can.:	$300.00
U.K.:	£135.00

HN 3918
Autumn Flowers
Designer: N. Pedley
Height: 8 ½", 21.5 cm
Colour: Red and yellow dress
Issued: 1997
Series: The Seasons
(Series Seven)
Comm.by: Guild of Specialist
China and Glass
Retailers

U.S.:	$250.00
Can.:	$300.00
U.K.:	£135.00

HN 3919
Winter Bouquet
Designer: N. Pedley
Height: 8 ¾", 22.2 cm
Colour: Red dress
Issued: 1997
Series: The Seasons
(Series Seven)
Comm.by: Guild of Specialist
China and Glass
Retailers

U.S.:	$250.00
Can.:	$300.00
U.K.:	£135.00

HN 3920
Jack Point
Designer: C. J. Noke
Height: 17", 43.2 cm
Colour: Blue, gold and red
Issued: 1996 in a limited
            edition of 250
Varieties: HN 85, 91, 99, 2080,
            3925

U.S.:	**$4,500.00**
Can.:	**$5,500.00**
U.K.:	**£2,500.00**

HN 3921
Princess Badoura
Style One
Designer: H. Tittensor, Harry
            E. Stanton and
            F. Van Allen Phillips
Height: 20", 50.8 cm
Colour: Blue, gold and red
Issued: 1996-1999
Varieties: HN 2081
Series: Prestige

U.S.:	**$20,000.00**
Can.:	**$25,000.00**
U.K.:	**£11,000.00**

HN 3922
A Jester (Parian)
Style One
Designer: C. J. Noke
Height: 10 ½", 26.7 cm
Colour: Pink, green and gold
Issued: 1997 limited to 950
Varieties: HN 45, 71, 71A,
            320, 367, 412, 426,
            446, 552, 616, 627,
            1295, 1702, 2016
Comm.by: Lawleys By Post

U.S.:	**$575.00**
Can.:	**$700.00**
U.K.:	**£300.00**

HN 3923 not issued.

HN 3924
Lady Jester (Parian)
Style Three
Designer: W. K. Harper
Height: 9 ½", 24.0 cm
Colour: Green and pink
Issued: 1998 in a limited
            edition of 950
Comm.by: Lawleys By Post

U.S.:	**$575.00**
Can.:	**$700.00**
U.K.:	**£300.00**

HN 3925
Jack Point
Designer: C. J. Noke
Height: 16 ¼", 41.2 cm
Colour: Purple, green and
            lavender
Issued: 1998 in a limited
            edition of 85
Varieties: HN 85, 91, 99, 2080,
            3920

U.S.:	**$5,000.00**
Can.:	**$6,000.00**
U.K.:	**£2,750.00**

HN 3926
The Moor
Designer: C. J. Noke
Height: 17 ½", 44.0 cm
Colour: Black and purple
Issued: 1999 in a limited
            edition of 99
Varieties: HN 1308, 1366, 1425
            1657, 2082, 3642;
            also called 'An Arab'
            HN 33, 343, 378
Series: RDICC

U.S.:	**$4,500.00**
Can.:	**$5,500.00**
U.K.:	**£2,500.00**

HN 3927 - 3929 not issued.

HN 3930
Constance
Style Two
Designer: A. Maslankowski
Height: 8 ¾", 22.2 cm
Colour: Blue
Issued: 1997-1997
Varieties: HN 3933
Series: Charleston

U.S.:	**$250.00**
Can.:	**$300.00**
U.K.:	**£125.00**

HN 3931 - 3932 not issued.

HN 3933
Constance
Style Two
Designer: A. Maslankowski
Height: 8 ¾", 22.2 cm
Colour: Ivory, gold highlights
Issued: 1997-1997
Varieties: HN 3930
Series: Charleston

U.S.:	**$250.00**
Can.:	**$300.00**
U.K.:	**£125.00**

HN 3934
Across the Miles
Designer: A. Maslankowski
Height: 4", 10.1 cm
Colour: White
Issued: 1997-1999
Series: Sentiments
U.S.: $100.00
Can.: $125.00
U.K.: £ 55.00

HN 3935
Best Friends
Style One
Designer: A. Maslankowski
Height: 3", 7.6 cm
Colour: White shirt, blue
trousers, black and
white dog
Issued: 1997-1999
U.S.: $150.00
Can.: $200.00
U.K.: £ 80.00

HN 3936
Goose Girl
Style Three
Designer: A. Maslankowski
Height: 11", 27.9 cm
Colour: White
Issued: 1997-1998
Series: Images
U.S.: $150.00
Can.: $200.00
U.K.: £ 80.00

HN 3937 not issued.

HN 3938
Mother and Child
Style Two
Designer: A. Maslankowski
Height: 11 ½", 29.2 cm
Colour: White
Issued: 1997 to the present
Series: Images
U.S.: $140.00
Can.: $245.00
U.K.: £ 49.00

HN 3939 not issued.

HN 3940
Angel
Designer: A. Maslankowski
Height: 11 ½", 29.2 cm
Colour: White
Issued: 1997-1999
Series: Images
U.S.: $150.00
Can.: $200.00
U.K.: £ 80.00

HN 3941 not issued.

HN 3942
Graduation (female)
Designer: A. Maslankowski
Height: 11 ½", 29.2 cm
Colour: White
Issued: 1997-2002
Series: Images
U.S.: $150.00
Can.: $200.00
U.K.: £ 80.00

HN 3943 not issued.

HN 3944
HM Queen Elizabeth
The Queen Mother
Style Three
Designer: A. Maslankowski
Height: 10 ½", 26.7 cm
Colour: Light purple suit and
hat
Issued: 1997 in a limited
edition of 5,000
Comm.by: Lawleys By Post
U.S.: $550.00
Can.: $675.00
U.K.: £300.00

HN 3945
Millie
Style One
Designer: A. Maslankowski
Height: 8 ¾", 22.2 cm
Colour: Green
Issued: 1997-1997
Varieties: HN 3946
Series: Charleston
U.S.: $300.00
Can.: $375.00
U.K.: £160.00

HN 3946
Millie
Style One
Designer: A. Maslankowski
Height: 8 ¾", 22.2 cm
Colour: Ivory, gold highlights
Issued: 1997-1997
Varieties: HN3945
Series: Charleston

U.S.:	**$300.00**
Can.:	**$375.00**
U.K.:	**£160.00**

HN 3947
Henry V at Agincourt
Designer: A. Maslankowski
Height: 20", 50.8 cm
Colour: Blue, grey, red and gold
Issued: 1997 to the present
Series: Prestige

U.S.:	**$18,300.00**
Can.:	**$31,800.00**
U.K.:	**£11,500.00**

HN 3948
Loving Thoughts
Style One
Designer: A. Maslankowski
Height: 6 ¼", 15.9 cm
Colour: White
Issued: 1997-1999
Series: Sentiments

U.S.:	**$125.00**
Can.:	**$150.00**
U.K.:	**£ 65.00**

HN 3949
Forever Yours
Style One
Designer: A. Maslankowski
Height: 3 ¾", 9.5 cm
Colour: White
Issued: 1998-2001
Series: Sentiments

U.S.:	**$125.00**
Can.:	**$150.00**
U.K.:	**£ 65.00**

HN 3950
Star Performer
Designer: A. Maslankowski
Height: 4", 10.1 cm
Colour: White, pink slippers
Issued: 1997-2003
Series: Images

U.S.:	**$125.00**
Can.:	**$150.00**
U.K.:	**£ 65.00**

HN 3951
Stage Struck
Designer: A. Maslankowski
Height: 3 ¾", 9.5 cm
Colour: White, blue slippers
Issued: 1997-2003
Series: Images

U.S.:	**$125.00**
Can.:	**$150.00**
U.K.:	**£ 65.00**

HN 3952
The Messiah
Designer: A. Maslankowski
Height: 11", 27.9 cm
Colour: White
Issued: 1997-1999
Series: Images

U.S.:	**$200.00**
Can.:	**$250.00**
U.K.:	**£110.00**

HN 3953
Christmas Lantern
Designer: A. Maslankowski
Height: 6", 15.0 cm
Colour: White
Issued: 1997-1998
Series: Sentiments

U.S.:	**$125.00**
Can.:	**$150.00**
U.K.:	**£ 65.00**

HN 3954
Moonlight Stroll
Designer: A. Maslankowski
Height: 7 ¾", 19.7 cm
Colour: Deep blue dress,
             flowered cream scarf
             and hat
Issued: 1997-1999
Varieties: Also called 'Summer
             Breeze' (Style One)
             HN 3724
   U.S.:   **$300.00**
   Can.:   **$400.00**
   U.K.:   **£175.00**

HN 3955
Summer Scent
Designer: A. Maslankowski
Height: 7 ¾", 19.7 cm
Colour: Pink and cream
             dress, blue scarf
Issued: 1997-1999
Varieties: Also called 'Spring
             Morning' (Style Two)
             HN 3725
   U.S.:   **$275.00**
   Can.:   **$350.00**
   U.K.:   **£150.00**

HN 3956
Spring Serenade
Designer: A. Maslankowski
Height: 7 ½", 19.1 cm
Colour: Green dress,
             flowered cream scarf
Issued: 1997-1999
Varieties: Also called 'Free Spirit'
             (Style Two) HN 3728
   U.S.:   **$300.00**
   Can.:   **$400.00**
   U.K.:   **£175.00**

HN 3957
Eleanor of Aquitaine
(1122-1204)
Designer: A. Maslankowski
Height: 9", 22.9 cm
Colour: Blue, gold and brown
Issued: 1997 in a limited
             edition of 5,000
Series: Plantagenet Queens
Comm.by: Lawleys By Post
   U.S.:   **$1,100.00**
   Can.:   **$1,300.00**
   U.K.:   **£ 600.00**

HN 3958
Country Girl
Style Three
Designer: A. Maslankowski
Height: 10 ¾", 27.8 cm
Colour: White
Issued: 1998-1999
Series: Images
   U.S.:   **$150.00**
   Can.:   **$180.00**
   U.K.:   **£ 80.00**

HN 3959
The Graduate (male)
Style Two
Designer: A. Maslankowski
Height: 11 ½", 29.2 cm
Colour: White
Issued: 1998-2001
Series: Images
   U.S.:   **$150.00**
   Can.:   **$180.00**
   U.K.:   **£ 80.00**

HN 3960 - 3969 not issued.

HN 3970
Flower of Love
Designer: J. Bromley
Height: 7 ¼", 18.4 cm
Colour: Red
Issued: 1996-1997
Varieties: HN 2460; also called
             'Fleur' (Style One)
             HN 2368, 2369
   U.S.:   **$350.00**
   Can.:   **$425.00**
   U.K.:   **£190.00**

HN 3971
Best Wishes
Style Two
Designer: J. Bromley
Height: 8 ¾", 22.2 cm
Colour: Deep green
Issued: 1998-2004
Varieties: Also called 'Kate'
             (Style Three) HN 4233;
             'Forever Yours' (Style Two)
             HN 4501; 'Especially
             For You' HN 4750
Series: Name Your Own
   U.S.:   **$225.00**
   Can.:   **$425.00**
   U.K.:   **£125.00**
Metal plaque on base for engraved name.

HN 3972
Sweet Lilac
Designer: J. Bromley
Height: 8 ¾", 22.2 cm
Colour: Lilac bodice with white
frill and mauve panel
with cream floral skirt
Issued: 2000-2000
Series: RDICC

U.S.:	**$325.00**
Can.:	**$400.00**
U.K.:	**£175.00**

HN 3973 - 3974 not issued.

HN 3975
Lauren
Style Three
Designer: D. Hughes
Height: 9", 23.0 cm
Colour: Rose-pink dress
Issued: 1999-1999
Series: Figure of the Year

U.S.:	**$325.00**
Can.:	**$400.00**
U.K.:	**£175.00**

HN 3976
Rachel
Style Two
Designer: D. Hughes
Height: 8 ¼", 21.0 cm
Colour: Lilac, pink and cream
Issued: 2000-2000
Series: Figure of the Year

U.S.:	**$275.00**
Can.:	**$350.00**
U.K.:	**£150.00**

HN 3977
Melissa
Style Three
Deisgner: D. Hughes
Height: 8 ½", 22.2 cm
Colour: Blue
Issued: 2001-2001
Series: Figure of the Year

U.S.:	**$250.00**
Can.:	**$325.00**
U.K.:	**£135.00**

HN 3978
Sarah
Style Three
Designer: D. Hughes
Height: 8 ¼", 21.0 cm
Colour: Dark green
Issued: 2002-2002
Series: Figure of the Year

U.S.:	**$250.00**
Can.:	**$325.00**
U.K.:	**£135.00**

HN 3979 - 3990 not issued.

HN 3991
Cinderella
Style Two
Modeller: J. Bromley
Height: 10", 25.4 cm
Colour: 1. Pink
2. Blue
Issued: 1. Pink: 1997 in limited
edition of 2,950
2. Blue: 2000 in limited
edition of 2,000
Series: Fairytale Princesses
Comm.by: Compton/Woodhouse

U.S.:	**$450.00**
Can.:	**$550.00**
U.K.:	**£225.00**

HN 3992
Ellen
Style Three
Designer: J. Bromley
Height: 8 ¼", 21.0 cm
Colour: Rose pink dress,
beige hat
Issued: 1997-1997
Series: Lady of the Year
Comm.by: Compton/Woodhouse

U.S.:	**$300.00**
Can.:	**$375.00**
U.K.:	**£160.00**

HN 3993
Carmen
Style Three
Designer: M. Halson
Height: 9 ½", 24.0 cm
Colour: Red dress with
gold highlights
Issued: 1997 in a limited
edition of 12,500
Comm.by: Compton/Woodhouse

U.S.:	**$450.00**
Can.:	**$550.00**
U.K.:	**£240.00**

HN 3994
Red Red Rose
Designer: R. Hughes
Modeller: J. Bromley
Height: 9", 22.9 cm
Colour: Pink dress, gold
            highlights
Issued: 1997 in a limited
            edition of 12,500
Series: Language of Love
Comm.by: Compton/Woodhouse

U.S.:	**$400.00**
Can.:	**$475.00**
U.K.:	**£215.00**

HN 3995
Sophie
Style Five
Designer: J. Bromley
Height: 8 ¼", 21.0 cm
Colour: Pink dress, gold
            highlights
Issued: 1998-1998
Series: Lady of the Year
Comm.by: Compton/Woodhouse

U.S.:	**$300.00**
Can.:	**$375.00**
U.K.:	**£165.00**

HN 3996
Miss Violet
Designer: M. Evans
Height: 5 ½", 14.0 cm
Colour: Dark and light purple
Issued: 1998 in a limited
            edition of 12,500
Series: Pretty Maids
Comm.by: Compton/Woodhouse

U.S.:	**$225.00**
Can.:	**$275.00**
U.K.:	**£120.00**

HN 3997
Miss Maisie
Designer: M. Evans
Height: 5 ½", 14.0 cm
Colour: Green, blue and pink
Issued: 1998 in a limited
            edition of 12,500
Series: Pretty Maids
Comm.by: Compton/Woodhouse

U.S.:	**$225.00**
Can.:	**$275.00**
U.K.:	**£120.00**

HN 3998
Miss Tilly
Designer: M. Evans
Height: 5 ½", 14.0 cm
Colour: Pink and green
Issued: 1998 in a limited
            edition of 12,500
Series: Pretty Maids
Comm.by: Compton/Woodhouse

U.S.:	**$225.00**
Can.:	**$275.00**
U.K.:	**£120.00**

HN 3999
Shall I Compare Thee To A
Summer's Day
Designer: J. Bromley
Height: 9", 22.9 cm
Colour: White dress, blue
            accents, gold highlights
Issued: 1998 in a limited
            edition of 12,500
Series: Language of Love
Comm.by: Compton/Woodhouse

U.S.:	**$400.00**
Can.:	**$475.00**
U.K.:	**£200.00**

HN 4000
Sleeping Beauty
Style Two
Designer: S. Curzon
Modeller: J. Bromley
Height: 7 ½", 19.1 cm
Colour: White, tan and gold
Issued: 1998 in a limited
            edition of 4,950
Series: Fairytale Princesses
Comm.by: Compton/Woodhouse

U.S.:	**$400.00**
Can.:	**$475.00**
U.K.:	**£200.00**

HN 4001
My True Love
Designer: J. Bromley
Height: 9", 22.9 cm
Colour: White dress with pink
            flowers; dark red
            bodice
Issued: 1999 in a limited
            edition of 12,500
Comm.by: Compton/Woodhouse

U.S.:	**$400.00**
Can.:	**$475.00**
U.K.:	**£200.00**

HN 4002 not issued.

HN 4003
Alice
Style Four
Designer: J. Bromley
Height: 8 ¾, 22.2 cm
Colour: Red and yellow
Issued: 1999-1999
Series: Lady of the Year
Comm.by: Compton/Woodhouse

U.S.:	**$400.00**
Can.:	**$475.00**
U.K.:	**£200.00**

HN 4004 - 4014 not issued.

HN 4015
Eleanor
Style Two
Designer: J. Bromley
Height: 9", 22.9 cm
Colour: Green and cream
Issued: 2001-2001
Series: Lady of the Year
Comm.by: Compton/Woodhouse

U.S.:	**$400.00**
Can.:	**$475.00**
U.K.:	**£200.00**

HN 4016
A Love So Tender
Designer: M. Halson
Height: 9", 22.9 cm
Colour: White
Issued: 2001 in a limited edition of 7,500
Series: Images

U.S.:	**$200.00**
Can.:	**$250.00**
U.K.:	**£100.00**

HN 4017
Ellie
Style Two
Designer: J. Bromley
Height: 8 ¾", 22.2 cm
Colour: Dark and light purple
Issued: 2003-2003
Series: Lady of the Year
Comm. by: Compton/Woodhouse

U.S.:	**$400.00**
Can.:	**$475.00**
U.K.:	**£200.00**

HN 4019 - 4020 not issued.

HN 4018
Alison
Style Two
Designer: J. Bromley
Height: 8 ½", 21.6 cm
Colour: Green and yellow
Issued: 2004-2004
Comm. by: Compton/Woodhouse Charity Figurine of the Year

U.S.:	**$400.00**
Can.:	**$475.00**
U.K.:	**£200.00**

HN 4021
Amen
Designer: D. V. Tootle
Height: 4 ¼", 10.8 cm
Colour: White
Issued: 1997 to the present
Series: Images

U.S.:	**$ 62.50**
Can.:	**$140.00**
U.K.:	**£ 29.00**

HN 4022
William III (1650-1702)
Designer: D. V. Tootle
Height: 10 ¼", 26.0 cm
Colour: Red, white, beige and gold
Issued: 1998 in a limited edition of 1,500
Series: Stuart Kings
Comm.by: Lawleys By Post

U.S.:	**$1,400.00**
Can.:	**$1,700.00**
U.K.:	**£ 750.00**

HN 4023
Sarah Bernhardt
Designer: D. V. Tootle
Height: 9", 22.9 cm
Colour: Green dress, flowered cream scarf and fan
Issued: 1998 in a limited edition of 5,000
Series: Victorian and Edwardian Actresses
Comm.by: Lawleys By Post

U.S.:	**$650.00**
Can.:	**$775.00**
U.K.:	**£350.00**

HN 4024
Prima Ballerina
Designer:	D. V. Tootle
Height:	8 ¼", 21.0 cm
Colour:	White
Issued:	1998-2000
Series:	Images
U.S.:	**$175.00**
Can.:	**$200.00**
U.K.:	**£ 95.00**

HN 4025
The Dance
Style One
Designer:	D. V. Tootle
Height:	7", 17.8 cm
Colour:	White
Issued:	1998-2002
Series:	Images
U.S.:	**$175.00**
Can.:	**$200.00**
U.K.:	**£ 95.00**

HN 4026
Best Friends
Style Two
Designer:	D. V. Tootle
Height:	7", 17.8 cm
Colour:	White
Issued:	1998-1998
Series:	Images Figure of the Year
U.S.:	**$175.00**
Can.:	**$200.00**
U.K.:	**£ 95.00**

HN 4027
The Ballet Dancer
Designer:	D. V. Tootle
Height:	9 ¼", 23.5 cm
Colour:	White
Issued:	1998-2000
Series:	Images
U.S.:	**$175.00**
Can.:	**$200.00**
U.K.:	**£ 95.00**

HN 4028
Ballet Lesson
Designer:	D. V. Tootle
Height:	5", 13.0 cm
Colour:	White
Issued:	1998-2001
Series:	Images
U.S.:	**$150.00**
Can.:	**$175.00**
U.K.:	**£ 80.00**

HN 4029 not issued.

HN 4030
Leap-Frog
Designer:	D. V. Tootle
Height:	8 ½", 21.5 cm
Colour:	White
Issued:	1999-2001
Series:	Images
U.S.:	**$150.00**
Can.:	**$175.00**
U.K.:	**£ 80.00**

HN 4031
Carol Singer (Boy)
Designer:	D. V. Tootle
Height:	6", 15.2 cm
Colour:	White
Issued:	1999 in a limited edition of 6,000
Series:	1. Christmas Choir Collection
	2. Images
U.S.:	**$100.00**
Can.:	**$125.00**
U.K.:	**£ 55.00**

HN 4032
Carol Singer (Girl)
Designer:	D. V. Tootle
Height:	5", 12.0 cm
Colour:	White
Issued:	1999 in a limited edition of 6,000
Series:	1. Christmas Choir Collection
	2. Images
U.S.:	**$100.00**
Can.:	**$125.00**
U.K.:	**£ 55.00**

HN 4033
The Promise
Designer: D. V. Tootle
Height: 6 ¼", 16.0 cm
Colour: White
Issued: 1999-1999
Series: Images of the Year
U.S.: $175.00
Can.: $225.00
U.K.: £100.00

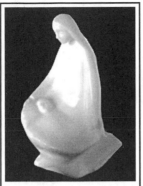

HN 4034
Mary and Jesus
Designer: D. V. Tootle
Height: Unknown
Colour: White
Issued: 1999 in a limited
edition of 2,000
Series: 1. Images: The
Christmas Story
2. Millennium
U.S.: $300.00
Can.: $375.00
U.K.: £170.00 set price

Note: 10 items sold as set

HN 4035
Joseph
Style Two
Designer: D. V. Tootle
Height: Unknown
Colour: White
Issued: 1999 in a limited
edition of 2,000
Series: 1. Images: The
Christmas Story
2. Millennium
U.S.: $300.00
Can.: $375.00
U.K.: £170.00 set price

Note: 10 items sold as set.

HN 4036
Balthazar
Style One
Designer: D. V. Tootle
Height: Unknown
Colour: White
Issued: 1999 in a limited
edition of 2,000
Series: 1. Images: The
Christmas Story
2. Millennium
U.S.: $300.00
Can.: $375.00
U.K.: £170.00 set price

Note: 10 items sold as set

HN 4037
Melchior
Style One
Designer: D. V. Tootle
Height: Unknown
Colour: White
Issued: 1999 in a limited
edition of 2,000
Series: 1. Images: The
Christmas Story
2. Millennium
U.S.: $300.00
Can.: $375.00
U.K.: £170.00 set price

Note: 10 items sold as set

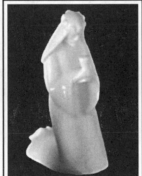

HN 4038
Caspar
Designer: D. V. Tootle
Heieght: Unknown
Colour: White
Issued: 1999 in a limited
edition of 2,000
Series: 1. Images: The
Christmas Story
2. Millennium
U.S.: $300.00
Can.: $375.00
U.K.: £170.00 set price

Note: 10 items sold as set

HN 4039
Boy Shepherd
Designer: D. V. Tootle
Height: Unknown
Colour: White
Issued: 1999 in a limited
edition of 2,000
Series: 1. Images: The
Christmas Story
2. Millennium
U.S.: $300.00
Can.: $375.00
U.K.: £170.00 set price

Note: 10 items sold as set

HN 4040
Kathryn
Style Two
Designer: V. Annand
Height: 8 ½", 21.6 cm
Colour: Light yellow dress
Issued: 1997-2003
Varieties: Also called 'Alexis'
HN 4205
Series: Chelsea
U.S.: $200.00
Can.: $250.00
U.K.: £110.00

HN 4041
Rebecca
Style Three
Designer: V. Annand
Height: 9", 22.9 cm
Colour: Blue dress,
           yellow ribbons
Issued: 1998-1998
Series: Figure of the Year

U.S.:	$375.00
Can.:	$450.00
U.K.:	£200.00

HN 4042
Janet
Style Four
Designer: V. Annand
Height: 9", 22.9 cm
Colour: Rose pink and white
Issued: 1998-1998
Series: RDICC

U.S.:	$375.00
Can.:	$450.00
U.K.:	£200.00

HN 4043
Samantha
Style Three
Designer: V. Annand
Height: 8 ¼", 21.0 cm
Colour: Blue and white
Issued: 1998-1998
Series: Roadshow Events

U.S.:	$325.00
Can.:	$400.00
U.K.:	£175.00

HN 4044
Abigail
Style One
Designer: V. Annand
Height: 8 ¼", 21.0 cm
Colour: Light blue and
           cream dress
Issued: 1998-2001
Series: In Vogue

U.S.:	$225.00
Can.:	$275.00
U.K.:	£125.00

HN 4045
Blossomtime
Designer: V. Annand
Height: 8", 20.3 cm
Colour: Pink
Issued: 1998-1998
Series: Annabelle Doulton
           Collection
Comm.by: Lawleys By Post

U.S.:	$ 800.00
Can.:	$1,000.00
U.K.:	£ 475.00

HN 4046
Ellie
Style One
Designer: V. Annand
Height: 8 ¼", 21.0 cm
Colour: Pale pink dress with
           lemon scarf
Issued: 1998-2001
Varieties: Also called 'Allison'
           HN 4207
Series: Chelsea

U.S.:	$225.00
Can.:	$275.00
U.K.:	£125.00

HN 4047
Georgina
Style Two
Designer: V. Annand
Height: 8 ¼", 21.0 cm
Colour: Peach dress
Issued: 1998-2001
Series: Chelsea

U.S.:	$225.00
Can.:	$275.00
U.K.:	£125.00

HN 4048
Natalie
Style Two
Designer: V. Annand
Height: 8 ¼", 21.0 cm
Colour: Pink and cream dress;
           blue purse
Issued: 1999-2001
Series: In Vogue

U.S.:	$250.00
Can.:	$300.00
U.K.:	£135.00

HN 4049
Jessica
Style Three
Designer: V. Annand
Height: 8 ½", 21.6 cm
Colour: Yellow dress with
           peach shading
Issued: 1999-2001
Series: In Vogue

U.S.:	**$250.00**
Can.:	**$300.00**
U.K.:	**£135.00**

HN 4050
Hannah
Style Three
Designer: V. Annand
Height: 8 ¾", 22.2 cm
Colour: Blue and pink
Issued: 1998 in a special
           edition of 250
Varieties: HN 4051, 4052
Comm.by: Hadleigh

U.S.:	**$350.00**
Can.:	**$425.00**
U.K.:	**£200.00**

Note: HN 4050, 4051, 4053 - only
variation is backstamp.

HN 4051
Hannah
Style Three
Designer: V. Annand
Height: 8 ¾", 22.2 cm
Colour: Blue and pink
Issued: 1998 in a special
           edition of 250
Varieties: HN 4050, 4052
Comm.by: Collectibles

U.S.:	**$350.00**
Can.:	**$425.00**
U.K.:	**£200.00**

Note: HN 4050, 4051, 4053 - only
variation is backstamp.

HN 4052
Hannah
Style three
Designer: V. Annand
Height: 8 ½", 21.6 cm
Colour: Blue and pink
Issued: 1999-2000
Varieties: HN 4050, 4051

U.S.:	**$350.00**
Can.:	**$425.00**
U.K.:	**£200.00**

Note: HN 4050, 4051, 4052 - only
variation is backstamp.

HN 4053
Joy
Style Three
Designer: V. Annand
Height: 8", 20.0 cm
Colour: Pink and white
Issued: 1999-2000
Varieties: HN 4054

U.S.:	**$350.00**
Can.:	**$425.00**
U.K.:	**£200.00**

HN 4054
Joy
Style Three
Designer: V. Annand
Height: 8", 20.0 cm
Colour: Red
Issued: 1999-2000
Varieties: HN 4053

U.S.:	**$350.00**
Can.:	**$425.00**
U.K.:	**£200.00**

HN 4055
Kneeling Shepherd
Designer: D. V. Tootle
Height: Unknown
Colour: White
Issued: 1999 in a limited
           edition of 2,000
Series: 1. Images: The
              Christmas Story
           2. Millennium

U.S.:	**$300.00**
Can.:	**$375.00**
U.K.:	**£170.00 set price**

Note: 10 items sold as set.

HN 4056
Standing Shepherd
Designer: D. V. Tootle
Height: Unknown
Colour: White
Issued: 1999 in a limited
           edition of 2,000
Series: 1. Images: The
              Christmas Story
           2. Millennium

U.S.:	**$300.00**
Can.:	**$375.00**
U.K.:	**£170.00 set price**

Note: 10 items sold as set

HN 4057
Romeo and Juliet
Style Two
Designer: D. V. Tootle
Height: 12", 30.5 cm
Colour: Pink and white
Issued: 1999 in a limited
            edition of 300
Series: Prestige

U.S.:	**$3,000.00**
Can.:	**$3,750.00**
U.K.:	**£1,600.00**

HN 4058
Harlequin
Style Two
Designer: D. V. Tootle
Height: 12 ½", 31.7 cm
Colour: Multicoloured pastels
Issued: 1999 in a limited
            ediiton of 200
Variations: HN 2737, 3287
Series: 1. Millennium
            2. Prestige
Comm. by: Lawleys By Post

U.S.:	**$2,250.00**
Can.:	**$2,750.00**
U.K.:	**£1,250.00**

HN 4059
Columbine
Style Three
Designer: D. V. Tootle
Height: 12 ½", 31.7 cm
Colour: Flowered pink dress
Issued: 1999 in a limited
            edition of 200
Varieties: HN2738, 3288
Series: 1. Millennium
            2. Prestige
Comm. by: Lawleys By Post

U.S.:	**$2,250.00**
Can.:	**$2,750.00**
U.K.:	**£1,250.00**

HN 4060
Christmas Angel
Designer: A. Maslankowski
Height: 5 ¾", 14.6 cm
Colour: White
Issued: 1997-1998
Varieties: HN 3733
Series: Sentiments

U.S.:	**$125.00**
Can.:	**$150.00**
U.K.:	**£ 65.00**

Gold backstamp edition for Canada

HN 4061
Christmas Carols
Designer: A. Maslankowski
Height: 6", 15.0 cm
Colour: White
Issued: 1997-1998
Varieties: HN 3727
Series: Sentiments

U.S.:	**$125.00**
Can.:	**$150.00**
U.K.:	**£ 65.00**

Gold backstamp edition for Canada

HN 4062
Christmas Day
Designer: A. Maslankowski
Height: 6", 15.2 cm
Colour: White
Issued: 1997-1998
Varieties: HN 3488
Series: Sentiments

U.S.:	**$125.00**
Can.:	**$150.00**
U.K.:	**£ 65.00**

Gold backstamp edition for Canada

HN 4063
Christmas Parcels
Style Two
Designer: A. Maslankowski
Height: 6", 15.2 cm
Colour: White
Issued: 1997-1998
Varieties: HN 3493
Series: Sentiments

U.S.:	**$125.00**
Can.:	**$150.00**
U.K.:	**£ 65.00**

Gold backstamp edition for Canada

HN 4064
The Kiss (boy)
Designer: A. Maslankowski
Height: 6 ¼", 15.9 cm
Colour: White
Issued: 1998-2003
Series: Images

U.S.:	**$ 75.00**
Can.:	**$100.00**
U.K.:	**£ 40.00**

ROSE GARDEN

HN 4559

The *Rose Garden* is one of Royal Doulton's most complex figurines,
limited to 250 pieces.

FIGURE OF THE YEAR

HN 3850
Jessica
Style Two, 1997

HN 4041
Rebecca
Style Three, 1998

HN 3975
Lauren
Style Three, 1999

HN 3976
Rachel
Style Two, 2000

HN 3977
Melissa
Style Three, 2001

HN 3978
Sarah
Style Three, 2002

HN 4426
Elizabeth
Style Three, 2003

HN 4532
Susan
Style Five, 2004

CHRISTMAS DAY FIGURES

HN 4214
Christmas Day 1999

HN 4242
Christmas Day 2000

HN 4315
Christmas Day 2001

HN 4422
Christmas Day 2002

HN 4552
Christmas Day 2003

HN 4558
Christmas Day 2004

IMPRESSIONS

HN 4194
Summer Blooms
Style Two, 1999-2003

HN 4193
Sweet Dreams
Style Three, 1999-2002

HN 4261
Tender Greetings
2000-2002

HN 4195
Summer Fragrance
1999-2000

HN 4196
Daybreak
Style Two, 1999-2003

HN 4197
Secret Thoughts
Style Two, 1999-2003

HN 4192
Tender Moment
Style Two, 1999-2003

HN 4262
In Loving Arms
2000-2002

RECENT RELEASES

HN 4583
Jessica
Style Four, 2003-2004

HN 4603
Dawn
Style Four, 2004-2004

HN 4665
Laura
2004-2004

HN 4620
Sophie
Style Six, 2004-2004

HN 4580
Irish Charm
2004-2004

HN 4621
True Love
2004-2004

RECENT RELEASES

HN 4286
Doctor
Style Two, 2001-2002

HN 4424
Antique Dealer, 2002-Current

HN 4287
Nurse, 2001-Current

HN 4651
Town Veterinary
2004-Current

HN 4570
Lifeboat Man
Style Two, 2003-Current

HN 4650
Country Veterinary
2004-Current

LADY GODIVA

HN 4641
2004 In a Limited Edition of 50

COMPTON & WOODHOUSE LTD. EXCLUSIVES

HN 3999
**Shall I Compare Thee To
A Summer's Day**
1998 Limited to 12,500

HN 4001
My True Love
1999 Limited to 12,500

HN 4003
Alice
Style Four-1999

HN 4201A
Chloe, Style Four
2000, Limited edition of 2,000

HN 4538
A Winter's Morn
2004 Limited to 7,500

HN 4018A
Alison
2004 Charity Figure of the Year

HN 4065
The Kiss (girl)
Designer: A. Maslankowski
Height: 6", 15.0 cm
Colour: White
Issued: 1998-2003
Series: Images
  U.S.: $ 75.00
  Can.: $100.00
  U.K.: £ 40.00

HN 4066
Philippa of Hainault
(1314-1369)
Style Two
Designer: A. Maslankowski
Height: 7", 17.8 cm
Colour: Red and green
Issued: 1998 in a limited
    edition of 5,000
Series: Plantagenet Queens
Comm.by: Lawleys By Post
  U.S.: $650.00
  Can.: $775.00
  U.K.: £350.00

HN 4067
Christmas Garland
Designer: A. Maslankowski
Height: 6", 15.0 cm
Colour: White
Issued: 1998-2000
Series: Sentiments
  U.S.: $125.00
  Can.: $150.00
  U.K.: £ 65.00

HN 4068
Happy Anniversary
Style Three
Designer: A. Maslankowski
Height: 5 ¾", 14.5 cm
Colour: White
Issued: 1998-2004
Series: Sentiments
  U.S.: $ 90.00
  Can.: $110.00
  U.K.: £ 45.00

HN 4069
Wizard (Parian)
Style One
Designer: A. Maslankowski
Height: 10", 25.4 cm
Colour: Green and pink
Issued: 1998 in a limited
    edition of 1,500
Varieties: HN 2877, 3121
Comm.by: Lawleys By Post
  U.S.: $400.00
  Can.: $500.00
  U.K.: £225.00

HN 4070
Good Luck
Designer: A. Maslankowski
Height: 6", 15.0 cm
Colour: White
Issued: 1999-2004
Series: Sentiments
  U.S.: $ 90.00
  Can.: $110.00
  U.K.: £ 45.00

HN 4071
Heathcliff and Cathy
Designer: A. Maslankowski
Height: 12 ½", 31.5 cm
Colour: Blue, cream, green
    and brown
Issued: 1999 in a limited
    edition of 750
Series: Literary Loves
  U.S.: $1,650.00
  Can.: $2,000.00
  U.K.: £ 875.00

HN 4072 not issued.

HN 4073
Margaret of Anjou
(1430-1482)
Style Two
Designer: A. Maslankowski
Height: 7 ½", 19.1 cm
Colour: Purple and white
Issued: 1998 in a limited
    edition of 5,000
Series: Plantagenet Queens
Comm.by: Lawleys By Post
  U.S.: $500.00
  Can.: $600.00
  U.K.: £250.00

HN 4074
Sophia Dorothea
(1666-1726)
Designer: A. Maslankowski
Height: 9 ½", 24.0 cm
Colour: Red, pink and white
Issued: 1998 in a limited
edition of 2,500
Series: Georgian Queens
Comm.by: Lawleys By Post
U.S.: $500.00
Can.: $600.00
U.K.: £250.00

HN 4075 not issued.

HN 4076
Missing You
Designer: A. Maslankowski
Height: 6", 15.5 cm
Colour: White
Issued: 1999-2001
Series: Sentiments
U.S.: $100.00
Can.: $125.00
U.K.: £ 55.00

HN 4077
Kindred Spirits
Designer: A. Maslankowski
Height: 6", 15.5 cm
Colour: White
Issued: 2000-2000
Series: Image of the Year
U.S.: $150.00
Can.: $200.00
U.K.: £ 85.00

HN 4078
Aurora, Goddess of the Dawn
Designer: A. Maslankowski
Height: 18", 45.0 cm
Colour: White Parian body;
gold base
Issued: 1999 in a limited
edition of 250
Series: The Immortals and
Aurora
U.S.: $2,500.00
Can.: $3,000.00
U.K.: £1,350.00

HN 4079
Hebe, Handmaiden to the Gods
Designer: A. Maslankowski
Height: 14", 35.0 cm
Colour: White Parian body;
gold base
Issued: 1999 in a limited
edition of 250
Series: The Immortals and
Aurora
U.S.: $1,300.00
Can.: $1,500.00
U.K.: £ 700.00

HN 4080
Ceres, Goddess of Plenty
Designer: A. Maslankowski
Height: 14", 35.0 cm
Colour: White Parian body;
gold base
Issued: 1999 in a limited
edition of 250
Series: The Immortals and
Aurora
U.S.: $1,300.00
Can.: $1,500.00
U.K.: £ 700.00

HN 4081
Artemis, Goddess of the Hunt
Designer: A. Maslankowski
Height: 14", 35.0 cm
Colour: White Parian body;
gold base
Issued: 1999 in a limited
edition of 250
Series: The Immortals and
Aurora
U.S.: $1,300.00
Can.: $1,500.00
U.K.: £ 700.00

HN 4082
Erato, The Parnassian Muse
Designer: A. Maslankowski
Height: 14", 35.0 cm
Colour: White Parian body;
gold base
Issued: 1999 in a limited
edition of 250
Series: The Immortals and
Aurora
U.S.: $1,450.00
Can.: $1,750.00
U.K.: £ 750.00

HN 4083
Wisdom
Style One
Designer: A. Maslankowski
Height: Unknown
Colour: White
Issued: 1999-2001
Series: Sentiments
Comm.By. Great Universal
Stores

U.S.:	$100.00
Can.:	$125.00
U.K.:	£ 55.00

HN 4084
Noel
Designer: A. Maslankowski
Height: 6", 15.2 cm
Colour: White
Issued: 1999-1999
Series: Christmas Sentiments

U.S.:	$125.00
Can.:	$150.00
U.K.:	$ 65.00

Exclusive to Canada

HN 4085
Remembering You
Designer: A. Maslankowski
Height: 6", 15.5 cm
Colour: White
Issued: 2000-2002
Series: Sentiments

U.S.:	$ 90.00
Can.:	$110.00
U.K.:	£ 45.00

HN 4086
H.M. Queen Elizabeth
The Queen Mother
Style Four
Designer: A. Maslankowski
Height: 9", 22.9 cm
Colour: Pale blue
Issued: 2000 in a limited
edition of 2,000

U.S.:	$550.00
Can.:	$650.00
U.K.:	£300.00

HN 4087 Bird figure.

HN 4088
Storytime (Boy)
Designer: A. Maslankowski
Length: 4", 10.4 cm
Colour: White
Issued: 2000-2003
Series: Images

U.S.:	$ 85.00
Can.:	$100.00
U.K.:	£ 45.00

HN 4089
Storytime (Girl)
Designer: A. Maslankowski
Height: 4 ¼", 11.0 cm
Colour: White
Issued: 2000 to the present
Series: Images

U.S.:	N/I
Can.:	$130.00
U.K.:	£ 35.00

HN 4090
Annabelle
Designer: N. Pedley
Height: 7 ½", 19.1 cm
Colour: Pink dress with
flowered border
Issued: 1998 in a special
edition of 2,500
Varieties: Also called 'Joanne'
(Style Two) HN 3422

U.S.:	$275.00
Can.:	$350.00
U.K.:	$150.00

Exclusive to QVC, U.S.A.

HN 4091
Molly
Designer: N. Pedley
Height: 8", 20.3 cm
Colour: Red and yellow dress
Issued: 1997-2003
Varieties: Also called 'Claire'
(Style Two) HN 3646;
'Kaitlyn' HN 4128;
'Rosemary' (Style
Three) HN 3691,
3698
Comm.by: Debenhams

U.S.:	$250.00
Can.:	$300.00
U.K.:	£125.00

HN 4092
Charlotte
Style Four
Designer: N. Pedley
Height: 8 ½", 21.6 cm
Colour: Blue and white
Issued: 1998-2002
Varieties: HN 4303

U.S.:	$250.00
Can.:	$300.00
U.K.:	£125.00

HN 4093
Emily
Style Four
Designer: N. Pedley
Height: 8 ¼", 21.0 cm
Colour: Green and white
Issued: 1998-2004
Varieties: Also called 'Patricia'
                   (Style Six) HN 4738

U.S.:	$150.00
Can.:	$175.00
U.K.:	£ 80.00

HN 4094
Rosie
Designer: N. Pedley
Height: 8", 20.3 cm
Colour: Rose pink
Issued: 1998-2004
Varieties: Also called 'Special
                   Gift' (Style Two)
                   HN 4744

U.S.:	$150.00
Can.:	$175.00
U.K.:	£ 80.00

HN 4095
Anna
Style Two
Designer: N. Pedley
Height: 6 ¾", 17.2 cm
Colour: White and pink dress
Issued: 1998-2000
Series: Vanity Fair Ladies

U.S.:	$200.00
Can.:	$250.00
U.K.:	£110.00

HN 4096
Harmony
Style Two
Designer: N. Pedley
Height: 5 ¾", 14.6 cm
Colour: White
Issued: 1998-1998
Series: Club Membership
                   Figure

U.S.:	$100.00
Can.:	$125.00
U.K.:	£ 55.00

HN 4097
Hope
Style Two
Designer: N. Pedley
Height: 8 ½", 21.6 cm
Colour: Pink
Issued: 1998-1999
Series: Charity (Breast Cancer)

U.S.:	$325.00
Can.:	$425.00
U.K.:	£175.00

HN 4098
Suzanne
Style One
Designer: N. Pedley
Height: 8 ½", 21.6 cm
Colour: Lilac
Issued: 1998-2001
Series: Vanity Fair Ladies

U.S.:	$250.00
Can.:	$325.00
U.K.:	£135.00

HN 4099
Ruth
Style Two
Designer: N. Pedley
Height: 8", 20.3 cm
Colour: Rose pink
Issued: 1998-2001

U.S.:	$250.00
Can.:	$325.00
U.K.:	£135.00

HN 4100
Special Occasion
Designer: N. Pedley
Height: 8¼", 21.0 cm
Colour: Red and yellow
Issued: 1998-2002
    U.S.: $300.00
    Can.: $375.00
    U.K.:   £170.00

HN 4101
Kirsten
Designer: N. Pedley
Height: 8", 20.3 cm
Colour: Blue
Issued: 1998-2000
Series: Vanity Fair Ladies
    U.S.: $250.00
    Can.: $300.00
    U.K.:   £125.00

HN 4102
Pride and Joy
Style Two
Designer: N. Pedley
Height: 4 ½", 11.9 cm
Colour: White shirt, light blue
              overalls, red hat,
              black and white ball
Issued: 1998-2004
Series: Name Your Own
    U.S.: $175.00
    Can.: $225.00
    U.K.:   £ 75.00

Metal plaque on base for engraved
name.

HN 4103
Sugar and Spice
Designer: N. Pedley
Height: 4 ¼", 10.8 cm
Colour: Pink dress, brown
              teddy bear
Issued: 1998-2003
Series: Name Your Own
    U.S.: $175.00
    Can.: $225.00
    U.K.:   £ 75.00

Metal plaque on base for engraved
name.
HN 4104 - 4108 not issued.

HN 4109
Mackenzie
Designer: N. Pedley
Height: 8", 20.3 cm
Colour: Blue
Issued: 1998 in a special
              edition of 350
Varieties: Also called 'First
              Bloom' HN 3913
Comm.by: Seaway China
    U.S.: $250.00
    Can.: $300.00
    U.K.:   £135.00

HN 4110
Jane
Style Five
Designer: N. Pedley
Height: 8¼", 21.0 cm
Colour: Pink
Issued: 1998
Comm.by: Great Universal
              Stores
    U.S.: $225.00
    Can.: $275.00
    U.K.:   £120.00

HN 4111
Alice
Style Three
Designer: N. Pedley
Height: 8 ¼", 21.0 cm
Colour: Pink and white
Issued: 1998-2001
Comm.by: Index Mail Order
              Catalogue
    U.S.: $225.00
    Can.: $275.00
    U.K.:   £120.00

HN 4112
Nicole
Style Two
Designer: N. Pedley
Height: 8", 20.0 cm
Colour: Red, cream and green
Issued: 1999-1999
Series: RDICC
    U.S.: $450.00
    Can.: $550.00
    U.K.:   £240.00

HN 4113
Sweet Poetry
Designer: N. Pedley
Height: 8", 20.0 cm
Colour: Lilac and pink
Issued: 1999-2002
  U.S.:   **$325.00**
  Can.:   **$400.00**
  U.K.:   **£175.00**

HN 4114
Mary
Style Five
Designer: N. Pedley
Height: 8 ½", 21.5 cm
Colour: Red and lilac
Issued: 1999-2002
  U.S.:   **$275.00**
  Can.:   **$375.00**
  U.K.:   **£150.00**

HN 4115
Brenda
Designer: N. Pedley
Height: 8 ½", 21.5 cm
Colour: White dress with
           pink shading
Issued: 1999-2003
Series: Vanity Fair Ladies
  U.S.:   **$250.00**
  Can.:   **$300.00**
  U.K.:   **£125.00**

Exclusive to Canada

HN 4116
Barbara
Style Four
Designer: N. Pedley
Height: 8 ¼", 21.0 cm
Colour: White and pale green
           dress; pink purse and
           ribbon
Issued: 1999-2003
Series: Vanity Fair Ladies
  U.S.:   **$250.00**
  Can.:   **$300.00**
  U.K.:   **£125.00**

Exclusive to Canada

HN 4117
Melody
Style Two
Designer: N. Pedley
Height: 5 ½", 14.0 cm
Colour: White and blue
Issued: 1999-1999
Series: Club Membership
           Figure
  U.S.:   **$125.00**
  Can.:   **$150.00**
  U.K.:   **£ 70.00**

HN 4118
Special Gift
Style One
Designer: N. Pedley
Height: 5 ½", 14.0 cm
Colour: White dress; pink sash
Issued: 1999-1999
Varieties: HN 4129
  U.S.:   **$125.00**
  Can.:   **$150.00**
  U.K.:   **£ 70.00**

Exclusive to Canada
HN 4119 - 4122 not issued.

HN 4123
Katie
Style Two
Designer: N. Pedley
Height: 8", 20.3 cm
Colour: Blue and white
Issued: 1998-2002
Varieties: Also called 'Lindsay'
           HN 3645
Comm.by: Debenhams
  U.S.:   **$250.00**
  Can.:   **$300.00**
  U.K.:   **£125.00**

HN 4124
Julia
Style Two
Designer: N. Pedley
Height: 8", 20.3 cm
Colour: Pink
Issued: 1999-1999
Series: M. Doulton Events
  U.S.:   **$250.00**
  Can.:   **$300.00**
  U.K.:   **£125.00**

HN 4125
Amber
Designer:	N. Pedley
Height:	8", 20.3 cm
Colour:	White dress with yellow shading
Issued:	1999-2003
Varieties:	Also called 'Chloe' (Style Three) HN 3883, 3914
U.S.:	**$250.00**
Can.:	**$300.00**
U.K.:	**£125.00**

Exclusive to U.S.A

HN 4126
Brianna
Designer:	N. Pedley
Height:	8 ½", 21.6 cm
Colour:	White dress with dark green accents
Issued:	1999-2003
Varieties:	Also called 'Kathleen' (Style Three) HN 3609, 3880
U.S.:	**$225.00**
Can.:	**$275.00**
U.K.:	**£120.00**

Exclusive to U.S.A

HN 4127
Jasmine
Style Three
Designer:	N. Pedley
Height:	8", 20.3 cm
Colour:	White and pink
Issued:	1999-2003
Varieties:	Also called 'Megan' (Style Two) HN 3887; 'Millie' (Style Two) HN 4212
U.S.:	**$225.00**
Can.:	**$275.00**
U.K.:	**£120.00**

Exclusive to U.S.A

HN 4128
Kaitlyn
Designer:	N. Pedley
Height:	8", 20.3 cm
Colour:	White and peach
Issued:	1999-2003
Varieties:	Also called 'Claire' (Style Two) HN 3646; 'Molly' HN 4091; 'Rosemary' (Style Three) HN 3691, 3698
U.S.:	**$225.00**
Can.:	**$275.00**
U.K.:	**£120.00**

Exclusive to U.S.A

HN 4129
Special Gift
Style One
Designer:	N. Pedley
Height:	5 ½" 14.0 cm
Colour:	Peach
Issued:	1999-2000
Varieties:	HN 4118
Series:	Visitor Centre
U.S.:	**$125.00**
Can.:	**$150.00**
U.K.:	**£ 65.00**

HN 4130
Elaine
Style One
Designer:	M. Davies
Height:	7 ¼", 18.4 cm
Colour:	Red
Issued:	1998 in a limited edition of 2,500
Varieties:	HN 2791, 3307, 3741
Comm.by:	Great Universal Stores
U.S.:	**$350.00**
Can.:	**$425.00**
U.K.:	**£185.00**

HN 4131
Elyse
Designer:	M. Davies
Height:	5 ¾", 14.6 cm
Colour:	Rose-pink
Issued:	1998 in a limited edition of 2,500
Varieties:	HN 2429, 2474
Comm.by:	Great Universal Stores
U.S.:	**$350.00**
Can.:	**$425.00**
U.K.:	**£185.00**

HN 4132
Alyssa
Designer:	M. Davies
Height:	8 ½", 21.6 cm
Colour:	White and pale blue
Issued:	1999-2003
Varieties:	Also called 'Country Rose' HN 3221
U.S.:	**$225.00**
Can.:	**$275.00**
U.K.:	**£120.00**

Exclusive to U.S.A.
HN 4133 - 4139 not issued.

HN 4140
Darling
Style One
Designer: C. Vyse
Remodeller: W. K. Harper
Height: 7 ¾", 19.5 cm
Colour: Pale blue
Issued: 1998 in a limited
edition of 1,913
Varieties: HN 1, 1319, 1371,
1372
Comm.by: Lawleys By Post

U.S.:	$200.00
Can.:	$250.00
U.K.:	£110.00

HN 4141
The Mask
Style Two
Designer: L. Harradine
Modeller: W. K. Harper
Height: 9 ½", 24.0 cm
Colour: Blue, black and pink
Issued: 1999 in a limited
edition of 1,500
Comm.by: Lawleys By Post

U.S.:	$450.00
Can.:	$550.00
U.K.:	£250.00

HN 4142 - 4150 not issued.

HN 4151
Faith
Style Two
Designer: N. Pedley
Height: 8 ¼", 21.0 cm
Colour: Pale blue and
dusky pink
Issued: 1999-2000
Series: Charity (Breast Cancer)

U.S.:	$275.00
Can.:	$350.00
U.K.:	£150.00

HN 4152
Madeline
Designer: N. Pedley
Height: 8 ¼", 21.0 cm
Colour: Yellow and white
Issued: 1999-2003

U.S.:	$250.00
Can.:	$350.00
U.K.:	£125.00

HN 4153
Marianne
Style Two
Designer: N. Pedley
Height: 8 ¼", 21.0 cm
Colour: Red and white
Issued: 1999-2003
Varieties: Also called 'Jayne'
(Style One) HN 4210

U.S.:	$300.00
Can.:	$375.00
U.K.:	£160.00

HN 4154
Natasha
Designer: N. Pedley
Height: 8 ¼", 21.0 cm
Colour: Yellow and white
Issued: 1999-2001

U.S.:	$550.00
Can.:	$650.00
U.K.:	£300.00

HN 4155
Lynne
Style Two
Designer: N. Pedley
Height: 8 ¼", 21.0 cm
Colour: Rose and pale pink
Issued: 1999-2002

U.S.:	$275.00
Can.:	$350.00
U.K.:	£140.00

HN 4156
Beth
Style Two
Designer: N. Pedley
Height: 8 ¼", 21.0 cm
Colour: Lilac
Issued: 1999-2003
Varieties: Also called 'Lydia'
(Style Two) HN 4211

U.S.:	$250.00
Can.:	$350.00
U.K.:	£125.00

HN 4157
Kelly
Style Three
Designer: N. Pedley
Height: 8 ¼", 21.0 cm
Colour: Green and white
Issued: 1999-2004
  U.S.: **$150.00**
  Can.: **$175.00**
  U.K.: **£ 80.00**

HN 4158
Michelle
Designer: N. Pedley
Height: 8 ¼", 21.0 cm
Colour: Blue and white
Issued: 1999-2002
  U.S.: **$250.00**
  Can.: **$300.00**
  U.K.: **£125.00**

HN 4159 not issued.

HN 4160
Sally
Style Two
Designer: T. Potts
Height: 8 ¼", 21.0 cm
Colour: Rose pink jacket, turquoise skirt
Issued: 1998 in a limited edition of 1,500
Varieties: HN 3383, 3851
Series: Visitor Centre
  U.S.: **$300.00**
  Can.: **$375.00**
  U.K.: **£160.00**

HN 4161
The Open Road
Designer: T. Potts
Height: 9", 23.0 cm
Colour: Pink
Issued: 1999-2001
  U.S.: **$350.00**
  Can.: **$425.00**
  U.K.: **£190.00**

HN 4162
Clara Hamps
Designer: T. Potts
Height: 8 ½", 21.5 cm
Colour: Blue and white
Issued: 1999-2001
Series: 1. Arnold Bennett
       2. Visitor Centre
  U.S.: **$350.00**
  Can.: **$425.00**
  U.K.: **£190.00**

HN 4163
Ecstasy
Deisgner: T. Potts
Height: 17", 43.2 cm
Colour: Fleshtone; brown and gold
Issued: 1999 in a limited edition of 500
Series: Art Deco
  U.S.: **$1,500.00**
  Can.: **$1,800.00**
  U.K.: **£ 800.00**

HN 4164
Destiny
Designer: T. Potts
Height: 19", 48.0 cm
Colour: Fleshtone; brown and gold
Issued: 1999 in a limited edition of 500
Series: Art Deco
  U.S.: **$1,500.00**
  Can.: **$1,800.00**
  U.K.: **£ 800.00**

HN 4165
Optimism
Designer: T. Potts
Height: 16", 40.6 cm
Colour: Fleshtone, brown and gold
Issued: 1999 in a limited edition of 500
Series: Art Deco
  U.S.: **$1,500.00**
  Can.: **$1,800.00**
  U.K.: **£ 800.00**

HN 4166
Wisdom
Style Two
Designer: T. Potts
Height: 19", 48.0 cm
Colour: Fleshtone, brown
             and gold
Issued: 1999 in a limited
             edition of 500
Series: Art Deco
  U.S.:   **$1,500.00**
  Can.:   **$1,800.00**
  U.K.:   **£ 800.00**

HN 4167
Sophia Baines
Designer: T. Potts
Height: 8", 20.3 cm
Colour: Blue and white
Issued: 2000-2001
Series: 1. Arnold Bennett
             2. Visitor Centre
  U.S.:   **$375.00**
  Can.:   **$450.00**
  U.K.:   **£200.00**

HN 4168
Gladys
Second Version
Designer: L. Harradine
Remodeller: T. Potts
Height: 4 ¼", 11.0 cm
Colour: Sage green
Issued: 2000 in a limited
             edition of 2,000
Comm.by: Lawleys By Post
  U.S.:   **$225.00**
  Can.:   **$275.00**
  U.K.:   **£125.00**

HN 4169
Vera
Second Version
Designer: L. Harradine
Remodeller: T. Potts
Height: 4 ¼", 11.0 cm
Colour: Pink and white
Issued: 2000 in a limited
             edition of 2,000
Comm.by: Lawleys By Post
  U.S.:   **$225.00**
  Can.:   **$275.00**
  U.K.:   **£125.00**

HN 4170 - 4173 Animal figures.

HN 4174
The Land of Nod
Second Version
Designer: H. Tittensor
Remodeller: R. Tabbenor
Height: 7 ¾, 19.7 cm
Colour: Pale blue nightgown;
             white and tan owl;
             tan base
Issued: 2000 in a limited
             edition of 2,500
Comm.by: Lawleys By Post
  U.S.:   **$250.00**
  Can.:   **$325.00**
  U.K.:   **£135.00**

HN 4175
Santa Claus
Style Two
Designer: R. Tabbenor
Height: 9 ½", 24.0 cm
Colour: Red and white suit;
             black belt and boots
Issued: 2000-2003
  U.S.:   **$350.00**
  Can.:   **$450.00**
  U.K.:   **£190.00**

HN 4176 - 4178 Animal figures.

HN 4179
Princess Badoura
Style Two
Designer: R, Tabbenor
Height: 7 ½", 19.1 cm
Colour: Pink, brown, red,
             blue and grey
Issued: 2001 In a limited
             edition of 500
Series: Prestige
  U.S.:   **$1,000.00**
  Can.:   **$1,500.00**
  U.K.:   **£ 600.00**

HN 4180 - 4189 not issued, except
HN 4181, 4182 and 4184 Animal
figures.

HN 4190
Ankhesenamun
Designer: P. Parsons
Height: 10 ½", 26.7 cm
Colour: Green
Issued: 1998 in a limited
             edition of 950
Series: Egyptian Queens
Comm.by: Lawleys By Post
  U.S.:   **$800.00**
  Can.:   **$975.00**
  U.K.:   **£400.00**

HN 4191
Hatshepsut
Designer: P. Parsons
Height: 10 ½", 26.7 cm
Colour: Cream, blue, brown,
            rust and gold
Issued: 1999 in a limited
            edition of 950
Series: Egyptian Queens
Comm.by: Lawleys By Post
   U.S.:   **$ 775.00**
   Can.:   **$1,000.00**
   U.K.:   **£ 425.00**

HN 4192
Tender Moment
Style Two
Designer: P. Parsons
Height: 12", 31.5 cm
Colour: Lilac and cream
Issued: 1999-2003
Series: Impressions
   U.S.:   **$275.00**
   Can.:   **$350.00**
   U.K.:   **£150.00**

HN 4193
Sweet Dreams
Style Three
Designer: P. Parsons
Height: 12", 30.5 cm
Colour: Yellow and cream
Issued: 1999-2002
Series: Impressions
   U.S.:   **$300.00**
   Can.:   **$375.00**
   U.K.:   **£160.00**

HN 4194
Summer Blooms
Style Two
Designer: P. Parsons
Height: 13", 33.0 cm
Colour: Lilac, cream,
            green and tan
Issued: 1999-2003
Series: Impressions
   U.S.:   **$275.00**
   Can.:   **$350.00**
   U.K.:   **£150.00**

Variation exists with arms in a more
downward position.

HN 4195
Summer Fragrance
Designer: P. Parsons
Height: 12", 30.5 cm
Colour: Pink, cream and
            green
Issued: 1999-2000
Series: Impressions
   U.S.:   **$300.00**
   Can.:   **$400.00**
   U.K.:   **£175.00**

HN 4196
Daybreak
Style Two
Designer: P. Parsons
Height: 13", 33.0 cm
Colour: Blue and cream
Issued: 1999-2003
Series: Impressions
   U.S.:   **$275.00**
   Can.:   **$350.00**
   U.K.:   **£150.00**

HN 4197
Secret Thoughts
Style Two
Designer: P. Parsons
Height: 13", 32.5 cm
Colour: Pink and cream
Issued: 1999-2003
Series: Impressions
   U.S.:   **$275.00**
   Can.:   **$350.00**
   U.K.:   **£150.00**

HN 4198
Sunset
Designer: P. Parsons
Height: 7", 17.8 cm
Colour: Blue and cream
Issued: 2000-2003
Series: Impressions
   U.S.:   **$300.00**
   Can.:   **$375.00**
   U.K.:   **£150.00**

HN 4199
Sunrise
Designer:	P. Parsons
Height:	7", 17.8 cm
Colour:	Yellow
Issued:	2000-2003
Series:	Impressions
U.S.:	**$300.00**
Can.:	**$375.00**
U.K.:	**£150.00**

HN 4200
Scarlett O'Hara
Designer:	V. Annand
Height:	9", 22.9 cm
Colour:	Dark green overdress, green-gold underskirt
Issued:	1999-2000
Series:	Classic Movies
U.S.:	**$550.00**
Can.:	**$650.00**
U.K.:	**£295.00**

Serial numbered edition.

HN 4201A
Chloe
Style Four
Designer:	J. Bromley
Height:	8 ½", 21.6 cm
Colour:	Rose pink and cream
Issued:	2000 in a limited edition of 2000
Series:	Millennium Lady of the Year
Comm.by:	Compton/Woodhouse
U.S.:	**$325.00**
Can.:	**$400.00**
U.K.:	**£175.00**

HN 4201B
Millennium Celebration
Designer:	V. Annand
Height:	8 ¼", 21.0 cm
Colour:	Turquoise and yellow
Issued:	1999-2001
Varieties:	HN 4321, 4325
Comm.by:	Great Universal Store
U.S.:	**$275.00**
Can.:	**$325.00**
U.K.:	**£150.00**

HN 4202
Joanne
Style Three
Designer:	V. Annand
Height:	9", 22.9 cm
Colour:	Mint green dress
Issued:	2000-2003
Series:	In Vogue
U.S.:	**$250.00**
Can.:	**$300.00**
U.K.:	**£135.00**

HN 4203
Rebecca
Style Four
Designer:	V. Annand
Height:	9", 22.9 cm
Colour:	Pale pink skirt, red flowers on cream bodice
Issued:	2000-2002
Series:	In Vogue
U.S.:	**$250.00**
Can.:	**$300.00**
U.K.:	**£135.00**

HN 4204
Madison
Designer:	V. Annand
Height:	8 ½", 21.6 cm
Colour:	Pale green and white
Issued:	2000-2003
Varieties:	Also called 'Emma' (Style Three) HN 3714
U.S.:	**$225.00**
Can.:	**$275.00**
U.K.:	**£120.00**

Exclusive to U.S.A.

HN 4205
Alexis
Designer:	V. Annand
Height:	8 ½", 21.6 cm
Colour:	Pale yellow
Issued:	2000-2003
Varieties:	Also called 'Kathryn' (Style Two) HN 4040
U.S.:	**$225.00**
Can.:	**$275.00**
U.K.:	**£120.00**

Exclusive to U.S.A.

HN 4206
Brittany
Designer: V. Annand
Height: 8 ¾", 22.2 cm
Colour: Pale pink dress
Issued: 2000-2003
Varieties: Also called 'Olivia'
             (Style Three) HN 3717

U.S.:	**$225.00**
Can.:	**$275.00**
U.K.:	**£120.00**

Exclusive to U.S.A.

HN 4207
Allison
Designer: V. Annand
Height: 8 ¼", 21.0 cm
Colour: Pale blue dress
Issued: 2000-2003
Varieties: Also called 'Ellie'
             HN 4046

U.S.:	**$225.00**
Can.:	**$275.00**
U.K.:	**£120.00**

Exclusive to U.S.A.

HN 4208
Zoe
Designer: V. Annand
Height: 8 ¼", 21.0 cm
Colour: Lilac
Issued: 2000-2003
Series: Chelsea

U.S.:	**$225.00**
Can.:	**$275.00**
U.K.:	**£120.00**

HN 4209
Melinda
Designer: V. Annand
Height: 8 ¼", 21.0 cm
Colour: Peach
Issued: 2000-2003
Series: Chelsea

U.S.:	**$225.00**
Can.:	**$275.00**
U.K.:	**£120.00**

HN 4210
Jayne
Style One
Designer: N. Pedley
Height: 8¼", 21.0 cm
Colour: Pale blue and yellow
Issued: 1999-2001
Varieties: 'Marianne'
             (Style Two) HN 4153
Comm.by: Great Universal
             Store

U.S.:	**$275.00**
Can.:	**$325.00**
U.K.:	**£150.00**

HN 4211
Lydia
Style Two
Designer: N. Pedley
Height: 8 ¼", 21.0 cm
Colour: Red
Issued: 1999-2001
Varieties: Also called 'Beth'
             (Style Two) HN 4156
Comm.by: Great Universal
             Store

U.S.:	**$275.00**
Can.:	**$325.00**
U.K.:	**£150.00**

HN 4212
Millie
Style Two
Designer: N. Pedley
Height: 8", 20.3 cm
Colour: Pink and white
Issued: 1999
Varieties: Also known as
             'Jasmine' HN 4127;
             'Megan' HN 3887
Comm.by: Debenham

U.S.:	**$275.00**
Can.:	**$325.00**
U.K.:	**£150.00**

HN 4213
With All My Love
Designer: N. Pedley
Height: 5", 12.7 cm
Colour: White and blue
Issued: 2000 in a limited
             edition of 2,500
Varieties: HN 4241

U.S.:	**$225.00**
Can.:	**$275.00**
U.K.:	**£120.00**

Exclusive to Canada

HN 4214
Christmas Day 1999
Designer: N. Pedley
Height: 8", 20.3 cm
Colour: Red dress and hat;
            ivory jacket; ermine
            trim and muff
Issued: 1999-1999
Series: Christmas Figures
U.S.: $425.00
Can.: $500.00
U.K.:   £225.00

HN 4215
Happy Birthday 2000
Designer: N. Pedley
Height: 8 ¾", 22.0 cm
Colour: Pink
Issued: 2000-2000
Series: Happy Birthday
U.S.: $225.00
Can.: $275.00
U.K.:   £120.00

HN 4216
Wedding Celebration
Designer: N. Pedley
Height: 8 ¾", 22.0 cm
Colour: Ivory dress with
            pale pink panel;
            pink flowers
Issued: 2000-2002
Varieties: HN 4229
Series: Name Your Own
U.S.: $225.00
Can.: $275.00
U.K.:   £120.00

Metal plaque on base for engraved
name.
HN 4217 - 4219 not issued.

HN 4220
Camilla
Style Two
Designer: N. Pedley
Height: 8 ½", 21.5 cm
Colour: Pink dress with
            white trim
Issued: 2000-2002
U.S.: $275.00
Can.: $325.00
U.K.:   £150.00

HN 4221
Susannah
Designer: N. Pedley
Height: 8", 20.3 cm
Colour: Cream cardigan;
            cream skirt decorated
            with gold flowers
Issued: 2000-2003
Series: Vanity Fair
U.S.: $250.00
Can.: $325.00
U.K.:   £125.00

HN 4222
Fair Maid
Designer: N. Pedley
Height: 8", 21.0 cm
Colour: Blue and lemon
Issued: 2000-2002
Series: Country Maids
U.S.: $250.00
Can.: $325.00
U.K.:   £125.00

HN 4223
Josephine
Designer: N. Pedley
Height: 8 ½", 21.5 cm
Colour: Blue and white
Issued: 2000-2003
Varieties: Also called 'Caroline'
            (Style three) HN 4395
Series: Vanity Fair
U.S.: $200.00
Can.: $275.00
U.K.:   £100.00

HN 4224 not issued.

HN 4225
Summer Duet
Designer: N. Pedley
Height: 6", 15.0
Colour: Ivory and gold
Issued: 1999 in a limited
            edition of 1,500
Series: Ivory and Gold
Comm.by: Lawleys By Post
U.S.: $150.00
Can.: $175.00
U.K.:   £ 80.00

HN 4226
After the Rain
Designer: N. Pedley
Height: 6", 15.0
Colour: Ivory and gold
Issued: 1999 in a limited
           edition of 1,500
Series: Ivory and Gold
Comm.by: Lawleys By Post

U.S.:	**$150.00**
Can.:	**$175.00**
U.K.:	**£ 80.00**

HN 4227
Off to the Pond
Designer: N. Pedley
Height: 6", 15.0
Colour: Ivory and gold
Issued: 1999 in a limited
           edition of 1,500
Series: Ivory and Gold
Comm.by: Lawleys By Post

U.S.:	**$150.00**
Can.:	**$175.00**
U.K.:	**£ 80.00**

HN 4228
Helping Mother
Designer: N. Pedley
Height: 6", 15.0
Colour: Ivory and gold
Issued: 1999 in a limited
           edition of 1,500
Series: Ivory and Gold
Comm.by: Lawleys By Post

U.S.:	**$150.00**
Can.:	**$175.00**
U.K.:	**£ 80.00**

HN 4229
Wedding Celebration
Designer: N. Pedley
Height: 8 ¾", 22.0 cm
Colour: White with pink
           highlights
Issued: 2000-2002
Varieties: HN 4216
Series: Name Your Own

U.S.:	**$225.00**
Can.:	**$275.00**
U.K.:	**£120.00**

HN 4230
Susan
Style Four
Designer: J. Bromley
Height: 8 ½", 21.6 cm
Colour: Yellow and pink
Issued: 2000-2000
Series: M. Doulton Events

U.S.:	**$325.00**
Can.:	**$400.00**
U.K.:	**£175.00**

Serial numbered.

HN 4231
Ellen
Style Four
Designer: J. Bromley
Height: 8 ½", 21.6 cm
Colour: Red dress; pink
           shawl with red
           flowers
Issued: 2000-2003

U.S.:	**$325.00**
Can.:	**$400.00**
U.K.:	**£175.00**

HN 4232
Specially For You
Designer: J. Bromley
Height: 8 ½", 21.6 cm
Colour: Green jacket; mauve
           skirt and bonnet;
           ermine trim and muff
Issued: 2000-2004

U.S.:	**$250.00**
Can.:	**$300.00**
U.K.:	**£130.00**

HN 4233
Kate
Style Three
Designer: J. Bromley
Height: 8 ½", 21.6 cm
Colour: Dusky rose
Issued: 2000-2000
Varieties: See also HN 3971,
           4501, 4750
Series: Charity figure 2000
Comm.by: Compton/Woodhouse

U.S.:	**$300.00**
Can.:	**$375.00**
U.K.:	**£160.00**

Brass plaque on base for engraving.

HN 4234
Special Celebration
Designer: J. Bromley
Height: 8 ¾", 22.2 cm
Colour: Purple and cream
Issued: 2001-2004
Varieties: Also called 'Treasured
            Moments' HN 4745

U.S.:	**$275.00**
Can.:	**$330.00**
U.K.:	**£145.00**

HN 4235
Belle
Style Five
Designer: J. Bromley
Height: 8 ½", 21.6 cm
Colour: Purple gown with
            ermine trim
Issued: 2001-2004

U.S.:	**$275.00**
Can.:	**$330.00**
U.K.:	**£145.00**

HN 4236
Just For You
Style Two
Designer: J. Bromley
Height: 8 ¾", 22.2 cm
Colour: Deep pink
Issued: 2002-2004
Varieties: Also called 'With Love'
            (Style Two) HN 4746

U.S.:	**$250.00**
Can.:	**$300.00**
U.K.:	**£130.00**

HN 4237
Georgina
Style Three
Designer: J. Bromley
Height: 9 ¼", 23.5 cm
Colour: Pink and white
Issued: 2002-2002
Series: Lady of the Year
Comm.by: Compton/Woodhouse

U.S.:	**$275.00**
Can.:	**$350.00**
U.K.:	**£150.00**

HN 4238
Francesca
Style One
Designer: D. Hughes
Height: 8 ½", 21.5 cm
Colour: Red
Issued: 2001 in a limited
            edition of 2,500
Comm.by: Home Shopping Ltd.

U.S.:	**$275.00**
Can.:	**$350.00**
U.K.:	**£150.00**

HN 4240
Flower of Scotland
Designer: N. Pedley
Height: 9", 22.9 cm
Colour: Blue and white dress,
            pale green plaid shawl
Issued: 2000-2004

U.S.:	**$200.00**
Can.:	**$250.00**
U.K.:	**£ 95.00**

HN 4241
With All My Love
Designer: N. Pedley
Height: 5", 12.7 cm
Colour: White and pink
Issued: 2000-2001
Varieties: HN 4213
Series: Visitor Centre

U.S.:	**$125.00**
Can.:	**$150.00**
U.K.:	**£ 65.00**

HN 4242
Christmas Day 2000
Designer: N. Pedley
Height: 8 ¼", 21.0 cm
Colour: Dark green dress
            and hat; red jacket;
            ermine trim and muff
Issued: 2000-2000
Series: Christmas Day

U.S.:	**$300.00**
Can.:	**$375.00**
U.K.:	**£160.00**

HN 4239 not issued.

HN 4243
Charity
Style Two
Designer: N. Pedley
Height: 8 ¼", 21.0 cm
Colour: Pink
Issued: 2000-2001
Series: Charity Breast Cancer
U.S.: **$300.00**
Can.: **$375.00**
U.K.: **£160.00**

HN 4244
The Bather
Style One, Second Version
Designer: L. Harradine
Remodeller: N. Pedley
Height: 7 ¼", 18.4 cm
Colour: Royal blue robe
Issued: 2000 in a limited
edition of 2,000
Series: Bathers
U.S.: **$525.00**
Can.: **$630.00**
U.K.: **£285.00**

HN 4245
The Sunshine Girl
Second Version
Designer: L.Harradine
Remodeller: N. Pedley
Height: 4 ½", 11.5 cm
Colour: Green, red and white
Issued: 2000 in a limited
edition of 2,000
Series: Bathers
U.S.: **$525.00**
Can.: **$630.00**
U.K.: **£285.00**

HN 4246
The Swimmer
Second Version
Designer: L. Harradine
Remodeller: N. Pedley
Height: 7 ¼", 18.4 cm
Colour: Dark blue, red
and black
Issued: 2000 in a limited
edition of 2,000
Series: Bathers
U.S.: **$525.00**
Can.: **$600.00**
U.K.: **£285.00**

HN 4247
Lido Lady
Second Version
Designer: L. Harradine
Remodeller: N. Pedley
Height: 6 ¾", 17.2 cm
Colour: Pink
Issued: 2000-2001
Series: 1. Bathers
2. RDICC
U.S.: **$350.00**
Can.: **$425.00**
U.K.: **£185.00**

HN 4248
Jennifer
Style Four
Designer: N. Pedley
Height: 8 ¼", 21.0 cm
Colour: Yellow
Issued: 2000-2004
U.S.: **$175.00**
Can.: **$200.00**
U.K.: **£ 90.00**

HN 4249
Dairy Maid
Designer: N. Pedley
Height: 8 ¼", 21.0 cm
Colour: Lemon, white and pink
Issued: 2000-2002
Series: Country Maids
U.S.: **$250.00**
Can.: **$325.00**
U.K.: **£135.00**

HN 4250
Greetings
Designer: A. Maslankowski
Height: 5 ¾", 14.6 cm
Colour: White and yellow
Issued: 2000-2000
Series: 1. Club Membership
Gift
2. Sentiments
U.S.: **$100.00**
Can.: **$125.00**
U.K.: **$ 55.00**

HN 4251
Thank You Mother
Designer: A. Maslankowski
Height: 6 ¼", 15.8 cm
Colour: White with violet sash
Issued: 2000-2003
Varieties: Also called 'Thank You'
            (Style Two) HN 3390
Series: Sentiments

U.S.:	$125.00
Can.:	$150.00
U.K.:	£ 70.00

Exclusive to Canada

HN 4252
The Sorcerer
Designer: A. Maslankowski
Height: 9 ¼", 23.5 cm
Colour: Purple, red, white,
            gold and yellow
Issued: 2000-2002
Series: Mystical Figures

U.S.:	$550.00
Can.:	$650.00
U.K.:	£300.00

HN 4253
The Sorceress
Designer: A. Maslankowski
Height: 9 ½", 24.0 cm
Colour: Purple, red, yellow
            and gold
Issued: 2000-2002
Series: Mystical Figures

U.S.:	$500.00
Can.:	$600.00
U.K.:	£270.00

HN 4254
Many Happy Returns
Designer: A. Maslankowski
Height: 5 ¾", 14.6 cm
Colour: White
Issued: 2000-2004
Series: Sentiments

U.S.:	$100.00
Can.:	$125.00
U.K.:	£ 45.00

HN 4255
Happy Christmas
Designer: A. Maslankowski
Height: 6 ¼", 15.9 cm
Colour: White
Issued: 2000-2003
Series: Sentiments

U.S.:	$100.00
Can.:	$125.00
U.K.:	£ 45.00

HN 4256
Carol Singer with Lantern
Designer: D. V. Tootle
Height: 6 ¼", 15.9 cm
Colour: White
Issued: 2000 in a limited
            edition of 6,000
Series: 1. Images
            2. Christmas Choir
               Collection

U.S.:	$75.00
Can.:	$95.00
U.K.:	£40.00

HN 4257
Special Friends
Designer: A. Maslankowski
Height: 6 ¾", 17.2 cm
Colour: White
Issued: 2001-2001
Series: Image of the Year

U.S.:	$175.00
Can.:	$225.00
U.K.:	£100.00

HN 4258
Embrace
Designer: A. Maslankowski
Height: 6", 15.0 cm
Colour: White
Issued: 2001-2001
Series: Club Membership
            Figure

U.S.:	$100.00
Can.:	$125.00
U.K.:	£ 50.00

HN 4259 not issued.

HN 4260
Henrietta-Maria
(Wife of Charles I)
Style Two
Designer: P. Parsons
Height: 9", 22.9 cm
Colour: Red, yellow, white and blue
Issued: 2000 in a limited edition of 2,500
Series: Stuart Queens
Comm.by: Doulton Direct
U.S.: $500.00
Can.: $600.00
U.K.: £250.00

HN 4261
Tender Greetings
Designer: P. Parsons
Height: 11", 27.9 cm
Colour: Mint green overdress; cream underskirt with floral design
Issued: 2000-2002
Series: Impressions
U.S.: $300.00
Can.: $375.00
U.K.: £160.00

HN 4262
In Loving Arms
Designer: P. Parsons
Height: 12", 30.5 cm
Colour: Pink overdress; cream underskirt
Issued: 2000-2002
Series: Impressions
U.S.: $300.00
Can.: $375.00
U.K.: £160.00

HN 4263
Edward VI
Designer: P. Parsons
Height: 8 ¼", 21.0 cm
Colour: Red, cream, black, gold and brown
Issued: 2000 in a limited edition of 5,000
Comm.by: Lawleys By Post
U.S.: $ 850.00
Can.: $1,000.00
U.K.: £ 425.00

HN 4264
Cleopatra
Style Two
Designer: P. Parsons
Height: 10", 25.4 cm
Colour: Pale blue, turquoise, yellow, light brown and red
Issued: 2001 In a limited edition of 950
Series: Egyptian Queens
Comm.by: Doulton-Direct
U.S.: $800.00
Can.: $950.00
U.K.: £425.00

HN 4265
Cherished Memories
Designer: P. Parsons
Height: 12 ¾", 32.4 cm
Colour: Pale yellow
Issued: 2001-2002
Series: 1. ICC
2. Impressions
U.S.: $300.00
Can.: $400.00
U.K.: £160.00

HN 4266
Anne of Denmark
(Wife of James I)
Designer: P. Parsons
Height: 9", 23.0 cm
Colour: Green, white and red
Issued: 2001 in a limited edition of 2,500
Series: Stuart Queens
Comm.by: Doulton-Direct
U.S.: $500.00
Can.: $600.00
U.K.: £250.00

HN 4267
Catherine of Braganza
(Wife of Charles II)
Designer: P. Parsons
Height: 9", 23.0 cm
Colour: Orange and white dress, brown chair, green cushion
Issued: 2001 In a limited edition of 2,500
Series: Stuart Queens
Comm.by: Doulton-Direct
U.S.: $500.00
Can.: $600.00
U.K.: £250.00

HN 4268 - 4269 not issued.

HN 4270
Spring
Style Five
Designer:　M. King
Height:　8 ½", 21.6 cm
Colour:　Yellow and white
Issued:　2000 in a limited
　　　　edition of 2,000
Series:　The Seasons
　　　　(Series Eight)
Comm.by:　Compton/Woodhouse

　U.S.:　$425.00
　Can.:　$500.00
　U.K.:　£225.00

HN 4271
Summer
Style Three
Designer:　M. King
Height:　8 ½", 21.6 cm
Colour:　Blue, yellow and white
Issued:　2000 in a limited
　　　　edition of 2,000
Series:　The Seasons
　　　　(Series Eight)
Comm.by:　Compton/Woodhouse

　U.S.:　$425.00
　Can.:　$500.00
　U.K.:　£225.00

HN 4272
Autumn
Style Three
Designer:　M. King
Height:　8 ½", 21.6 cm
Colour:　Purple
Issued:　2000 in a limited
　　　　edition of 2,000
Series:　The Seasons
　　　　(Series Eight)
Comm.by:　Compton/Woodhouse

　U.S.:　$425.00
　Can.:　$500.00
　U.K.:　£225.00

HN 4273
Winter
Style Three
Designer:　M. King
Height:　8 ½", 21.6 cm
Colour:　Red
Issued:　2000 in a limited
　　　　edition of 2,000
Series:　The Seasons
　　　　(Series Eight)
Comm.by:　Compton/Woodhouse

　U.S.:　$425.00
　Can.:　$500.00
　U.K.:　£225.00

HN 4274 - 4279 not issued.

HN 4280
Love Everlasting
Designer:　A. Hughes
Height:　6 ½", 16.5 cm
Colour:　White
Issued:　2000 to the present
Series:　Images

　U.S.:　$125.00
　Can.:　$175.00
　U.K.:　£ 39.00

HN 4281
Debut
Style Two
Designer:　A. Hughes
Height:　9", 22.9 cm
Colour:　White
Issued:　2000 in a limited
　　　　edition of 2,000
Series:　Images
Comm.by:　Lawleys By Post

　U.S.:　$125.00
　Can.:　$150.00
　U.K.:　£ 65.00

HN 4282
Encore
Style Two
Designer:　A. Hughes
Height:　9", 22.9 cm
Colour:　White
Issued:　2000 in a limited
　　　　edition of 2,000
Series:　Images
Comm.by:　Lawleys By Post

　U.S.:　$125.00
　Can.:　$150.00
　U.K.:　£ 65.00

HN 4283
Trumpet Player
Designer:　A. Hughes
Height:　9 ½", 24.0 cm
Colour:　White
Issued:　2000 in a limited
　　　　edition of 1,500
Series:　The Age of Jazz
Comm.by:　Lawleys By Post

　U.S.:　$125.00
　Can.:　$150.00
　U.K.:　£ 65.00

HN 4284
Saxophone Player
Designer: A. Hughes
Height: 9 ½", 24.0 cm
Colour: White
Issued: 2000 in a limited
edition of 1,500
Series: The Age of Jazz
Comm.by: Lawleys By Post
U.S.: $125.00
Can.: $150.00
U.K.: £ 65.00

HN 4285
The Age of Swing
Designer: A. Hughes
Height: 8", 20.3 cm
Colour: White
Issued: 2000 in a limited
edition of 1,500
Comm.by: Lawleys By Post
U.S.: $125.00
Can.: $150.00
U.K.: £ 65.00

HN 4286
Doctor
Style Two
Designer: A. Hughes
Height: 9 ¼", 23.5 cm
Colour: Brown suit, black
waistcoat and bag
Issued: 2001-2002
U.S.: $400.00
Can.: $500.00
U.K.: £220.00

HN 4287
Nurse
Designer: A. Hughes
Height: 8 ½", 21.6 cm
Colour: White, blue and red
uniform
Issued: 2001 to the present
U.S.: $395.00
Can.: $695.00
U.K.: £230.00

HN 4288 not issued.

HN 4289
Lawyer
Style Two
Designer: A. Hughes
Height: 8 ¾", 22.2 cm
Colour: Black robes, white
collar, red book
brown stand
Issued: 2001-2003
U.S.: $250.00
Can.: $300.00
U.K.: £125.00

HN 4290
Carol Singer (Brother)
Designer: D. V. Tootle
Height: 6 ¼", 15.9 cm
Colour: White
Issued: 2000 in a limited
edition of 6,000
Series: 1. Christmas Choir
2. Images
U.S.: $75.00
Can.: $95.00
U.K.: £40.00

HN 4291
Carol Singer (Sister)
Designer: D. V. Tootle
Height: 6 ¼", 15.9 cm
Colour: White
Issued: 2000 in a limited
edition of 6,000
Series: 1. Christmas Choir
2. Images
U.S.: $75.00
Can.: $95.00
U.K.: £40.00

HN 4292 - 4299 not issued.

HN 4300
Bells Across the Valley
Designer: N. Pedley
Height: 8 ½", 21.5 cm
Colour: Lilac
Issued: 1999-2004
U.S.: $250.00
Can.: $300.00
U.K.: £125.00

HN 4301
Lorraine
Style Two
Designer: N. Pedley
Height: 8 ¼", 21.0 cm
Colour: Cream jacket,
           aqua skirt and hat
Issued: 2000-2004
U.S.: $130.00
Can.: $160.00
U.K.:   £ 70.00

HN 4302
Sweet Music
Designer: N. Pedley
Height: 8 ½", 21.6 cm
Colour: Pink and white
Issued: 2001-2004
U.S.: $150.00
Can.: $180.00
U.K.:   £ 80.00

HN 4303
Charlotte
Style Four
Designer: N. Pedley
Height: 8 ½", 21.6 cm
Colour: Green and white
Issued: 2000-2001
Varieties: HN 4092
Comm.by: Great Universal
           Store
U.S.: $200.00
Can.: $250.00
U.K.:   £110.00

HN 4304
Catherine
Style Three
Designer: N. Pedley
Height: 8 ½", 21.5 cm
Colour: White and pale blue
Issued: 2001-2004
U.S.: $160.00
Can.: $200.00
U.K.:   £ 85.00

HN 4305
Milk Maid
Style Three
Designer: N. Pedley
Height: 8", 20.3 cm
Colour: Soft mint green, cream,
           white and pale pink
Issued: 2001-2003
Series: Country Maids
U.S.: $225.00
Can.: $300.00
U.K.:   £120.00

HN 4306
Congratulations To You
Designer: N. Pedley
Height: 8", 20.3 cm
Colour: Pink and lilac
Issued: 2000-2004
Series: Name Your Own
U.S.: $250.00
Can.: $325.00
U.K.:   £130.00

Metal plaque on base for engraved
name.

HN 4307
Christine
Style Six
Designer: N. Pedley
Height: 8 ½", 21.0 cm
Colour: Red dress, yellow hat
Issued: 2001-2001
Series: M. Doulton Events
U.S.: $275.00
Can.: $375.00
U.K.:   £150.00

HN 4308
Happy Birthday 2001
Designer: N. Pedley
Height: 8", 21.0 cm
Colour: Light green
Issued: 2001-2001
Series: Happy Birthday
U.S.: $200.00
Can.: $250.00
U.K.:   £110.00

HN 4309
Jacqueline
Style Four
Designer: N. Pedley
Height: 8 ½", 21.6 cm
Colour: Cherry blossom
pink and yellow
Issued: 2001-2001
Series: ICC

U.S.:	$300.00
Can.:	$375.00
U.K.:	£170.00

HN 4310
Janet
Style Five
Designer: N. Pedley
Height: 8", 20.3 cm
Colour: Pale blue
Issued: 2001-2002

U.S.:	$225.00
Can.:	$300.00
U.K.:	£125.00

HN 4311
Margaret
Style Three
Designer: N. Pedley
Height: 8 ½", 21.6 cm
Colour: Pink and white
Issued: 2001-2004
Series: Vanity Fair

U.S.:	$200.00
Can.:	$250.00
U.K.:	£100.00

HN 4312
Pretty As A Picture
Designer: N. Pedley
Height: 5 ¾", 14.6 cm
Colour: White dress with
pale pink trim
Issued: 2001-2004
Series: Name Your Own

U.S.:	$100.00
Can.:	$165.00
U.K.:	£ 55.00

HN 4313
For Your Special Day
Designer: N. Pedley
Height: 6", 15.2 cm
Colour: Lemon-white
Issued: 2001-2003
Varieties: Also called 'Sweet
Delight' HN 4398

U.S.:	$100.00
Can.:	$125.00
U.K.:	£ 60.00

Exclusive to Canada

HN 4314
New Dawn
Designer: N. Pedley
Height: 8 ½", 21.0 cm
Colour: Lilac and pink
Issued: 2001-2002
Series: Charity (Breast Cancer)

U.S.:	$250.00
Can.:	$350.00
U.K.:	£130.00

Seven models of "New Dawn" were
painted in different colourways and
auctioned with the proceeds going to
breast cancer research.

HN 4315
Christmas Day 2001
Designer: N. Pedley
Height: 8 ¾", 22.2 cm
Colour: Dark green dress and
hat, red cape, all
trimmed with ermine
Issued: 2001-2001
Series: Christmas Figures

U.S.:	$250.00
Can.:	$350.00
U.K.:	£130.00

HN 4316
Maid of the Meadow
Designer: N. Pedley
Height: 8 ½", 21.0 cm
Colour: Tan, white and yellow
Issued: 2001-2003
Series: Country Maids

U.S.:	$250.00
Can.:	$350.00
U.K.:	£130.00

HN 4317
Gentle Breeze
Designer: N. Pedley
Height: 8 ½", 21.6 cm
Colour: Pink, red and white
Issued: 2001-2003
U.S.: **$275.00**
Can.: **$350.00**
U.K.: **£150.00**

HN 4318
Loving Thoughts
Style Two
Designer: N. Pedley
Height: 8", 20.3 cm
Colour: Green dress, tan hat
Issued: 2001-2004
U.S.: **$175.00**
Can.: **$225.00**
U.K.: **£ 95.00**

HN 4319
Sweetheart
Designer: N. Pedley
Height: 8", 20.3 cm
Colour: Pink
Issued: 2001-2004
U.S.: **$175.00**
Can.: **$225.00**
U.K.: **£ 95.00**

HN 4320
Claudia
Designer: V. Annand
Height: 8 ¼", 21.0 cm
Colour: Pale blue
Issued: 2000-2003
Varieties: Also called 'Amelia'
HN 4327; 'Gift of Love'
(Style Two) HN 4751
Series: In Vogue
U.S.: **$225.00**
Can.: **$275.00**
U.K.: **£120.00**

HN 4321
Millennium Celebration
Designer: V. Annand
Height: 8 ¼", 21.0 cm
Colour: Turquoise and yellow
Issued: 2000
Varieites: HN 4201B, 4325
U.S.: **$275.00**
Can.: **$325.00**
U.K.: **£150.00**

Australian backstamp

HN 4322
Becky
Style Two
Designer: V. Annand
Height: 8 ¾", 22.2 cm
Colour: Pale lilac
Issued: 2001-2004
Series: Chelsea
Varieties: Also called 'Annabel
Vision in Red' HN 4493
U.S.: **$150.00**
Can.: **$180.00**
U.K.: **£ 75.00**

HN 4323
Katie
Style Three
Designer: V. Annand
Height: 8", 20.5 cm
Colour: Blue
Issued: 2001-2004
Series: Chelsea
U.S.: **$150.00**
Can.: **$180.00**
U.K.: **£ 75.00**

HN 4324
The Bride
Style Five
Designer: V. Annand
Height: 8 ½", 21.5 cm
Colour: White and pink
Issued: 2000-2003
Series: In Vogue
U.S.: **$225.00**
Can.: **$275.00**
U.K.: **£120.00**

HN 4325
Millennium Celebration
Designer: V. Annand
Height: 8 ¼", 21.0 cm
Colour: Turquoise and yellow
Issued: 2000-2000
Varieties: HN 4201B, 4321

U.S.:	**$275.00**
Can.:	**$325.00**
U.K.:	**£150.00**

Canadian backstamp

HN 4326
Bethany
Designer: V. Annand
Height: 8 ¾", 22.2 cm
Colour: Yellow and white
Issued: 2001-2003
Series: Chelsea

U.S.:	**$225.00**
Can.:	**$300.00**
U.K.:	**£120.00**

HN 4327
Amelia
Designer: V. Annand
Height: 8 ½", 21.5 cm
Colour: Black with silver trim
Issued: 2002-2004
Varieties: Also called 'Claudia'
HN 4320; 'Gift of Love'
(Style Two) HN 4751
Series: In Vogue

U.S.:	**$175.00**
Can.:	**$225.00**
U.K.:	**£ 90.00**

HN 4328
Applause
Designer: V. Annand
Height: 8 ½", 21.5 cm
Colour: Yellow, white,
burnt orange edging
Issued: 2002-2002
Series: ICC

U.S.:	**$300.00**
Can.:	**$400.00**
U.K.:	**£160.00**

HN 4329
Finishing Touch
Designer: V. Annand
Height: 9", 22.5 cm
Colour: White skirt, dark
blue bodice
Issued: 2002-2004
Series: In Vogue

U.S.:	**$175.00**
Can.:	**$225.00**
U.K.:	**£ 90.00**

HN 4330 - 4349 not issued.

HN 4350
Christmas Eve
Designer: A. Maslankowski
Height: 5 ¾", 14.6 cm
Colour: White
Issued: 2000-2002
Series: Sentiments

U.S.:	**$125.00**
Can.:	**$150.00**
U.K.:	**£ 70.00**

Exclusive to Canada

HN 4351
Sweetheart (Boy)
Designer: A. Maslankowski
Height: 6", 15.0 cm
Colour: White
Issued: 2000-2003
Series: Images

U.S.:	**$55.00**
Can.:	**$65.00**
U.K.:	**£30.00**

HN 4352
Sweetheart (Girl)
Designer: A. Maslankowski
Height: 6 ½", 16.5 cm
Colour: White
Issued: 2000-2003
Series: Images

U.S.:	**$55.00**
Can.:	**$65.00**
U.K.:	**£30.00**

HN 4353
Liberty
Style Two
Designer: A. Maslankowski
Height: 10 ¼", 26 cm
Colour: Fleshtones and brown
Issued: 2000 in a limited
             edition of 1,500
Comm.by: Lawleys By Post

U.S.:	**$400.00**
Can.:	**$500.00**
U.K.:	**£200.00**

HN 4354
Felicity
Designer: A. Maslankowski
Height: 10 ¼", 26.0 cm
Colour: Fleshtones and brown
Issued: 2000 in a limited
             edition of 1,500
Comm.by: Lawleys By Post

U.S.:	**$400,00**
Can.:	**$500,00**
U.K.:	**£200.00**

HN 4355 not issued.

HN 4356
Sister and Brother
Designer: A. Maslankowski
Height: 7 ½", 19.0 cm
Colour: White
Issued: 2001 to the present
Series: Images

U.S.:	**$ 99.00**
Can.:	**$190.00**
U.K.:	**£ 39.00**

HN 4357
Perfect Pose
Designer: A. Maslankowski
Height: 6 ¼", 15.9 cm
Colour: White
Issued: 2001-2003
Series: Images

U.S.:	**$100.00**
Can.:	**$125.00**
U.K.:	**£ 50.00**

HN 4358
First Lesson
Designer: A. Maslankowski
Height: 6 ¼", 15.9 cm
Colour: White
Issued: 2001-2003
Series: Images

U.S.:	**$60.00**
Can.:	**$70.00**
U.K.:	**£30.00**

HN 4359 not issued.

HN 4360
Arnold Bennett
Designer: T. Potts
Height: 8 ½", 21.6 cm
Colour: Dark grey suit, brown
             waistcoat, white shirt,
             black shoes
Issued: 2001
Series: 1. Arnold Bennett
             2. Visitor Centre

U.S.:	**$300.00**
Can.:	**$400.00**
U.K.:	**£175.00**

HN 4361
Land Girl
Designer: T. Potts
Height: 8 ¾", 22.2 cm
Colour: Tan pants, black shirt
             and boots, yellow
             collar, brown basket
Issued: 2001 In a limited
             edition of 2,500
Series: Nostalgia
Comm.by.:   Doulton-Direct

U.S.:	**$425.00**
Can.:	**$500.00**
U.K.:	**£175.00**

HN 4362
Moonlight Gaze
Designer: T. Potts
Height: 8", 20.5 cm
Colour: Blue
Issued: 2002-2002
Series: Lady of the Year
Comm.by: Doulton-Direct

U.S.:	**$275.00**
Can.:	**$350.00**
U.K.:	**£160.00**

HN 4363
Farewell Daddy
Designer:	T. Potts
Height:	10 ½", 26.7 cm
Colour:	Khaki
Issued:	2002 in a limited edition of 2,500
Series:	Nostalgia
Comm.by:	Doulton-Direct
U.S.:	**$500.00**
Can.:	**$600.00**
U.K.:	**£250.00**

HN 4364
Women's Land Army
Designer:	T. Potts
Height:	8 ¾", 22.2 cm
Colour:	Green and brown
Issued:	2002 in a limited edition of 2,500
Series:	Nostalgia
Comm.by:	Doulton-Direct
U.S.:	**$425.00**
Can.:	**$500.00**
U.K.:	**£250.00**

HN 4365 not issued.

HN 4366
The Batsman
Designer:	T. Potts
Height:	8 ¾", 22.2 cm
Colour:	Cream
Issued:	2003 in a limited edition of 2,500
Comm.by:	Doulton-Direct
U.S.:	**$400.00**
Can.:	**$475.00**
U.K.:	**£200.00**

HN 4367 - 4369 not issued.

HN 4370
Skating
Designer:	A. Maslankowski
Height:	6 ¼", 15.9 cm
Colour:	White
Issued:	2001-2002
Series:	Sentiments
U.S.:	**$150.00**
Can.:	**$200.00**
U.K.:	**£ 85.00**

Exclusive to Canada

HN 4371
St. George
Style Four
Designer:	A. Maslankowski
Height:	17", 43.2 cm
Colour:	Charcoal, white, red and yellow
Issued:	2001 in a limited edition of 50
Series:	Prestige
U.S.:	**$17,950.00**
Can.:	**$26,000.00**
U.K.:	**£10,000.00**

HN 4372
HM Queen Elizabeth II
Style Five
Designer:	A. Maslankowski
Height:	8 ½", 21.0 cm
Colour:	White with gold trim
Issued:	2001 in a limited edition of 1,500
U.S.:	**$525.00**
Can.:	**$700.00**
U.K.:	**£275.00**

HN 4373
Bridesmaid
Style Eight
Designer:	A. Maslankowski
Height:	6 ½", 16.5 cm
Colour:	White
Issued:	2001 to the present
Series:	Images
U.S.:	**$ 65.00**
Can.:	**$120.00**
U.K.:	**£ 29.00**

HN 4374
Pageboy
Designer:	A. Maslankowski
Height:	6 ¼", 16.0 cm
Colour:	White
Issued:	2001-2003
Series:	Images
U.S.:	**$60.00**
Can.:	**$70.00**
U.K.:	**£30.00**

HN 4375
Independence
Designer: A. Maslankowski
Height: 9 ", 22.9 cm
Colour: White
Issued: 2002-2002
Series: 1. Images
             2. Save the Children
                Charity
    U.S.: $150.00
    Can.: $200.00
    U.K.:   £ 80.00

HN 4376
Surprise
Designer: A. Maslankowski
Height: 7 ¼", 18.5 cm
Colour: White
Issued: 2001-2003
Series: Images
    U.S.: $ 75.00
    Can.: $100.00
    U.K.:   £ 45.00

HN 4377
Keep In Touch
Designer: A. Maslankowski
Height: 7", 17.8 cm
Colour: White
Issued: 2002-2002
Series: Image of the Year
    U.S.: $150.00
    Can.: $200.00
    U.K.:   £ 80.00

HN 4378
Prayers
Designer: A. Maslankowski
Height: 6", 15.0 cm
Colour: White
Issued: 2002 to the present
Series: Images
    U.S.: $ 62.50
    Can.: $120.00
    U.K.:   £ 29.00

HN 4379
Wedding Vows
Styel Two
Designer: A. Maslankowski
Height: 10 ¼", 26.0 cm
Colour: White
Issued: 2002 to the present
Series: Images
    U.S.: $135.00
    Can.: $245.00
    U.K.:   £ 59.00

HN 4380
From This Day Forward
Designer: N. Lee
Height: 10", 25.4 cm
Colour: White
Issued: 2000
Series: Images
Comm.by.:   Compton/Woodhouse
    U.S.: $175.00
    Can.: $225.00
    U.K.:   £100.00

HN 4390
Julia
Style Three
Designer: N. Pedley
Height: 8 ½", 21.6 cm
Colour: Lavender and peach
Issued: 2001-2003
    U.S.: $250.00
    Can.: $300.00
    U.K.:   £140.00

HN 4391
Anna
Stsyle Three
Designer: N. Pedley
Height: 8 ¼", 21.0 cm
Colour: Pale blue and white
Issued: 2001-2004
Series: Vanity Fair
    U.S.: $200.00
    Can.: $275.00
    U.K.:   £ 90.00

HN 4381 - 4389 not issued.

HN 4392
My Love
Style Two
Designer: N. Pedley
Height: 8 ¼", 21.0 cm
Colour: Red
Issued: 2001-2004
Varieties: Also called 'Loyal
           Friend' (Style Two)
           HN 4736
Series: Name Your Own
U.S.:   **$250.00**
Can.:   **$325.00**
U.K.:   **£120.00**

HN 4393
Happy Birthday 2002
Designer: N. Pedley
Height: 8 ¼", 21.0 cm
Colour: Pale blue
Issued: 2002-2002
Series: Happy Birthday
  U.S.: **$200.00**
  Can.: **$275.00**
  U.K.: **£100.00**

HN 4394 not issued.

HN 4395
Caroline
Style Three
Designer: N. Pedley
Height: 8 ¼", 21.0 cm
Colour: Yellow
Issued: 2001
Varieties: Also called
           'Josephine' HN 4223
Comm.by.: Great Universal
           Store
  U.S.: **$200.00**
  Can.: **$250.00**
  U.K.: **£100.00**

HN 4396
Serenity
Style One
Designer: N. Pedley
Height: 8 ¼", 21.0 cm
Colour: Dark blue bodice,
           pale blue skirt
Issued: 2001-2003
  U.S.: **$160.00**
  Can.: **$200.00**
  U.K.: **£ 85.00**

HN 4397
Thoughts For You
Designer: N. Pedley
Height: 8 ¼", 21.0 cm
Colour: Blue, white and
           yellow
Issued: 2001
Series: Name Your Own
Comm.by.: Great Universal
           Store
  U.S.: **$200.00**
  Can.: **$250.00**
  U.K.: **£100.00**

HN 4398
Sweet Delight
Designer: N. Pedley
Height: 6", 15.2 cm
Colour: Pink
Issued: 2001-2004
Varieties: Also called 'For Your
           Special Day' HN 4313
Series: Visitor Centre
  U.S.: **N/I**
  Can.: **N/I**
  U.K.: **£48.00**

HN 4399
Bathing Beauty
Style Two
Designer: N. Pedley
Height: 7 ¼", 18.5 cm
Colour: Flesh tones, dark blue
           and yellow towel
Issued: 2001 in a limited
           edition of 1,000
Varieties: HN 4599
Series: Leslie Harradine
           Tribute
  U.S.: **$300.00**
  Can.: **$375.00**
  U.K.: **£150.00**

HN 4400
Brighton Belle
Designer: N. Pedley
Height: 7", 17.8 cm
Colour: Flesh tones, pink
           bathing suit
Issued: 2001 in a limited
           edition of 1,000
Varieties: HN 4600
Series: Leslie Harradine
           Tribute
  U.S.: **$300.00**
  Can.: **$375.00**
  U.K.: **£150.00**

HN 4401
Summer's Darling
Style Two
Designer: N. Pedley
Height: 4 ¼", 10.8 cm
Colour: Flesh tones, dark
          green robe
Issued: 2001 in a limited
          edition of 1,000
Varieties: HN 4601
Series: Leslie Harradine
          Tribute

   U.S.:   **$300.00**
   Can.:   **$375.00**
   U.K.:   **£150.00**

HN 4402
Taking The Waters
Designer: N. Pedley
Height: 6 ¼", 16.0 cm
Colour: Flesh tones, purple
          bathing suit
Issued: 2001 in a limited
          edition of 1,000
Varieties: HN 4602
Series: Leslie Harradine
          Tribute

   U.S.:   **$300.00**
   Can.:   **$375.00**
   U.K.:   **£150.00**

HN 4403
Samantha
Style Four
Designer: N. Pedley
Height: 8 ½", 21.6 cm
Colour: Lilac
Issued: 2002-2004

   U.S.:   **$170.00**
   Can.:   **$200.00**
   U.K.:   **£ 90.00**

HN 4404
Gillian
Style Four
Designer: N. Pedley
Height: 8 ¼", 21.0 cm
Colour: Pale green, white
          and yellow
Issued: 2002-2003
Varieties: Also called 'Christine',
          (Style seven) HN 4526

   U.S.:   **$160.00**
   Can.:   **$200.00**
   U.K.:   **£ 85.00**

HN 4405
Angela
Style Five
Designer: N. Pedley
Height: 8", 20.5 cm
Colour: White and mint green
Issued: 2002-2003

   U.S.:   **$160.00**
   Can.:   **$200.00**
   U.K.:   **£ 85.00**

HN 4406
Summer Stroll
Designer: N. Pedley
Height: 8 ¼", 21.0 cm
Colour: White, yellow and pink
Issued: 2002-2004

   U.S.:   **$160.00**
   Can.:   **$200.00**
   U.K.:   **£ 85.00**

HN 4407
Hannah
Style Four
Designer: N. Pedley
Height: 8 ¼", 21.0 cm
Colour: Blue, yellow and white
Issued: 2002-2004

   U.S.:   **$170.00**
   Can.:   **$200.00**
   U.K.:   **£ 90.00**

HN 4408
Scarlett
Designer: N. Pedley
Height: 8 ½", 20.5 cm
Colour: Red
Issued: 2002-2004
Varieties: Also called 'All My
          Love' HN 4747

   U.S.:   **$250.00**
   Can.:   **$300.00**
   U.K.:   **£125.00**

HN 4409
Perfect Gift
Designer:	N. Pedley
Height:	8", 20.3 cm
Colour:	Pale pink
Issued:	2002-2004
Series:	Name Your Own
U.S.:	**$225.00**
Can.:	**$325.00**
U.K.:	**£120.00**

HN 4410
Policeman
Designer:	A. Hughes
Height:	8 ¾", 22.2 cm
Colour:	Dark blue uniform
Issued:	2001-2003
U.S.:	**$350.00**
Can.:	**$450.00**
U.K.:	**£175.00**

HN 4411
Fireman
Designer:	A. Hughes
Height:	8", 20.0 cm
Colour:	Dark blue uniform, yellow helmet
Issued:	2002 - 2003
U.S.:	**$350.00**
Can.:	**$450.00**
U.K.:	**£175.00**

HN 4412
Judge
Style Two
Designer:	A. Hughes
Height:	7", 17.5 cm
Colour:	Red and white robes, brown chair
Issued:	2002 to the present
U.S.:	**$395.00**
Can.:	**$695.00**
U.K.:	**£205.00**

HN 4413
Sleepyhead
Style Three
Designer:	A. Hughes
Height:	6", 15.0 cm
Colour:	White
Issued:	2002 to the present
Series:	Images
U.S.:	**$ 62.50**
Can.:	**$120.00**
U.K.:	**£ 29.00**

HN 4414
Athos
Designer:	A. Hughes
Height:	8 ¾", 22.2 cm
Colour:	Black, white and cream
Issued:	2001 In a limited edition of 950
Comm.by.:	Doulton-Direct
U.S.:	**$450.00**
Can.:	**$550.00**
U.K.:	**£250.00**

HN 4415
Aramis
Designer:	A. Hughes
Height:	9 ¼", 23.0 cm
Colour:	Dark navy and white
Issued:	2001 In a limited edition of 950
Comm.by.:	Doulton-Direct
U.S.:	**$450.00**
Can.:	**$550.00**
U.K.:	**£250.00**

HN 4416
Porthos
Designer:	A. Hughes
Height:	9 ½", 24.0 cm
Colour:	Browns, white and black
Issued:	2001 In a limited edition of 950
Comm.by.:	Doulton-Direct
U.S.:	**$450.00**
Can.:	**$550.00**
U.K.:	**£250.00**

HN 4417
D'Artagnan
Style Two
Designer: A. Hughes
Height: 8 ¾", 22.5 cm
Colour: Browns and white
Issued: 2001 In a limited
            edition of 950
Comm.by.:   Doulton-Direct

U.S.:	$450.00
Can.:	$550.00
U.K.:	£250.00

HN 4418
Railway Sleeper
Designer: T. Potts
Height: 7", 17.5 cm
Colour: Brown uniform with
            green shading, black
            hat and trunk
Issued: 2001 In a limited
            edition of 2,500
Series: Nostalgia
Comm.by.:   Doulton-Direct

U.S.:	$375.00
Can.:	$450.00
U.K.:	£200.00

HN 4419 not issued.

HN 4420
Prince Albert, Duke of York
(Wedding Day)
Designer: V. Annand
Height: 9", 22.5 cm
Colour: Dark blueuniform,
            gold trim
Issued: 2002 in a limited
            edition of 1,000
Series: Prestige

U.S.:	$ 715.00
Can.:	$1,350.00
U.K.:	£ 400.00 pair

Sold as a pair with HN 4421

HN 4421
Elizabeth Bowes-Lyon
(Wedding Day)
Designer: V. Annand
Height: 8 ¼", 21.0 cm
Colour: White
Issued: 2002 in a limited
            edition of 1,000
Series: Prestige

U.S.:	$ 715.00
Can.:	$1,350.00
U.K.:	£ 400.00 pair

Sold as pair with HN 4420

HN 4422
Christmas Day 2002
Designer: V. Annand
Height: 8 ¼", 21.0 cm
Colour: Green, cream, white
            and red
Issued: 2002-2002
Series: Christmas Figures

U.S.:	$300.00
Can.:	$400.00
U.K.:	£150.00

HN 4423
Jenny
Designer: V. Annand
Height: 8", 20.3 cm
Colour: Pink
Issued: 2002-2004
Varieties: Also called 'Alexandra'
            (Style Three) HN 4557;
            Chloe (Style Six)
            HN 4727
Series: Chelsea

U.S.:	$150.00
Can.:	$175.00
U.K.:	£ 70.00

HN 4424
Antique Dealer
Designer: V. Annand
Height: 6 ¾", 17.0 cm
Colour: Dark grey, light
            and dark brown
Issued: 2002 to the present

U.S.:	$350.00
Can.:	$695.00
U.K.:	£205.00

HN 4425 not issued.

HN 4426
Elizabeth
Style Three
Designer: J. Bromley
Height: 8 ¼", 21.0 cm
Colour: Peach
Issued: 2003-2003
Series: Figure of the Year

U.S.:	$250.00
Can.:	$300.00
U.K.:	£125.00

HN 4427
Baby's First Christmas
Designer: V. Annand
Height: 4", 10.1 cm
Colour: White, green and red
Issued: 2002-2003

U.S.:	**$150.00**
Can.:	**$175.00**
U.K.:	**£ 65.00**

HN 4428
Here A Little Child I Stand
Second Version
Designer: V. Annand
Height: 4 ¾", 12.2 cm
Colour: Blue-grey, flesh tones
                 dark green and pink
                 base
Issued: 2002 in a limited
                 edition of 1,000
Series: Leslie Harradine Tribute

U.S.:	**$250.00**
Can.:	**$300.00**
U.K.:	**£125.00**

HN 4429
Do You Wonder Where
The Fairies Are
Second Version
Designer: V. Annand
Height: 4 ¾", 12.2 cm
Colour: Blue-grey pants,
                 flesh tones, yellow,
                 green base
Issued: 2002 in a limited
                 edition of 1,000
Series: Leslie Harradine Tribute

U.S.:	**$250.00**
Can.:	**$300.00**
U.K.:	**£125.00**

HN 4430
Special Moments
Designer: C. Froud
Height: 9", 22.9 cm
Colour: Pink
Issued: 2002-2004

U.S.:	**$175.00**
Can.:	**$225.00**
U.K.:	**£ 95.00**

HN 4431
Jasmine
Style Four
Designer: C. Froud
Height: 8", 20 cm
Colour: Red
Issued: 2002-2004

U.S.:	**$225.00**
Can.:	**$275.00**
U.K.:	**£115.00**

HN 4432 - 4439 not issued;
HN 4440 - 4441 Animal Figures.

HN 4442
Cherish
Designer: A. Maslankowski
Height: 6", 15.0 cm
Colour: White
Issued: 2002-2002
Series: 1. Club Membership
                    Figure
                 2. Sentiments

U.S.:	**$75.00**
Can.:	**$90.00**
U.K.:	**£40.00**

HN 4443
Happy Holidays
Designer: A. Maslankowski
Height: 6 ¼", 15.5 cm
Colour: White
Issued: 2002-2003
Series: Sentiments

U.S.:	**$100.00**
Can.:	**$125.00**
U.K.:	**£ 60.00**

Exclusive to Canada

HN 4444
Witch
Style Two
Designer: A. Maslankowski
Height: 10", 25.4 cm
Colour: Dark red, dark blue
                 and black
Issued: 2002-2003

U.S.:	**$500.00**
Can.:	**$600.00**
U.K.:	**£250.00**

HN 4445
Charmed
Designer: A. Maslankowski
Height: 5 ½", 14.0 cm
Colour: White
Issued: 2003-2003
Series: 1. Club Membership
                Figure
             2. Sentiments
    U.S.:   **$75.00**
    Can.:   **$90.00**
    U.K.:   **£40.00**

HN 4446
Gift of Friendship
Designer: A. Maslankowski
Height: 5 ½", 14.0 cm
Colour: White
Issued: 2003-2003
Series: Images of the Year
    U.S.:   **$100.00**
    Can.:   **$150.00**
    U.K.:   **£ 55.00**

HN 4447
Christmas Dreams
Designer: A. Maslankowski
Height: 6", 15.0 cm
Colour: White
Issued: 2002-2003
Series: Images
    U.S.:   **$100.00**
    Can.:   **$130.00**
    U.K.:   **£ 30.00**

HN 4448
Father and Son
Designer: A. Maslankowski
Height: 8 ¾", 22.2 cm
Colour: White
Issued: 2002-2003
Series: Images
    U.S.:   **$200.00**
    Can.:   **$275.00**
    U.K.:   **£ 70.00**

HN 4449
A Gift For You
Designer: A. Maslankowski
Height: 6", 15 cm
Colour: White
Issued: 2002 to the present
Series: Images
    U.S.:   **N/I**
    Can.:   **$140.00**
    U.K.:   **£ 29.00**

HN 4450
Linda
Style Five
Designer: N. Pedley
Height: 8 ¼", 21.0 cm
Colour: Light and dark blue
Issued: 2002-2002
Series: M. Doulton Events
    U.S.:   **$325.00**
    Can.:   **$400.00**
    U.K.:   **£175.00**

HN 4451
Spring Morning
Style Three
Designer: N. Pedley
Height: 8", 20.0 cm
Colour: White and green
Issued: 2002-2003
Series: Charity (Breast Cancer)
    U.S.:   **$275.00**
    Can.:   **$350.00**
    U.K.:   **£140.00**

HN 4452
Suzanne
Style Two
Designer: N. Pedley
Height: 8 ¼", 21.0 cm
Colour: Yellow
Issued: 2002
    U.S.:   **$300.00**
    Can.:   **$375.00**
    U.K.:   **£150.00**

Exclusive to U.K. Mail Order and
Canada

HN 4453
Pride of Scotland
Designer: N. Pedley
Height: 8 ¼", 21.0 cm
Colour: White, mauve,
and purple
Issued: 2002-2004
Varieties: HN 4310 Janet (Style
Five)

U.S.: $175.00
Can.: $200.00
U.K.:   £ 90.00

HN 4454
From The Heart
Designer: N. Pedley
Height: 5 ¾", 14.6 cm
Colour: Pale blue
Issued: 2002-2003

U.S.: $125.00
Can.: $150.00
U.K.:   £ 70.00

Exclusive to Canada
HN 4455 not issued.

HN 4456
Chloe
Style Five
Designer: N. Pedley
Height: 8", 20.0 cm
Colour: White with green
bodice
Issued: 2002-2004

U.S.: $150.00
Can.: $175.00
U.K.:   £ 75.00

HN 4457
Georgia
Designer: N. Pedley
Height: 8", 20.0 cm
Colour: Yellow
Issued: 2002-2004

U.S.: $150.00
Can.: $180.00
U.K.:   £ 80.00

HN 4458
Isabel
Style Two
Designer: N. Pedley
Height: 8 ¼", 21.0 cm
Colour: Light and dark blue
Issued: 2002-2004
Varieties: Also called 'Deborah'
(Style Four) HN 4735

U.S.: $175.00
Can.: $200.00
U.K.:   £ 90.00

HN 4459
Lucy
Style Four
Designer: N. Pedley
Height: 8", 20.0 cm
Colour: Lilac and white
Issued: 2002-2004
Varieties: Also called 'Love Song'
HN 4737

U.S.: $160.00
Can.: $200.00
U.K.:   £ 85.00

HN 4460 not issued.

HN 4461
Stephanie
Style Three
Designer: N. Pedley
Height: 8", 20.0 cm
Colour: Pale green, white
with yellow fan
Issued: 2002-2004

U.S.: $160.00
Can.: $200.00
U.K.:   £ 85.00

HN 4462 not issued.

HN 4463
Eleanor
Style Three
Designer: N. Pedley
Height: 8 ¼", 21.0 cm
Colour: Green
Issued: 2003-2003
Series: M. Doulton Events

U.S.: $225.00
Can.: $300.00
U.K.:   £130.00

HN 4464
Happy Birthday 2003
Designer: N. Pedley
Height: 8 ¼", 21.0 cm
Colour: Yellow and lilac
Issued: 2003-2003
Series: Happy Birthday
   U.S.:   **$175.00**
   Can.:   **$250.00**
   U.K.:   **£100.00**

HN 4465
Lights Out
Style Two
Designer: N. Pedley
Height: 6 ¼", 15.9 cm
Colour: Pale blue and white
            pyjamas
Issued: 2003-2003
Series: ICC
   U.S.:   **$175.00**
   Can.:   **$225.00**
   U.K.:   **£ 95.00**

HN 4466
The Recital
Designer: N. Pedley
Height: 8 ¼", 21.0 cm
Colour: Purple dress; cream
            shawl
Issued: 2003-2003
Series: ICC
   U.S.:   **$300.00**
   Can.:   **$375.00**
   U.K.:   **£165.00**

HN 4467
Katrina
Style Two
Designer: N. Pedley
Height: 8", 20.0 cm
Colour: White and yellow
Issued: 2002-2004
Series: Vanity Fair Ladies
   U.S.:   **$175.00**
   Can.:   **$250.00**
   U.K.:   **£ 95.00**

HN 4468
Deborah
Style Three
Designer: N. Pedley
Height: 8 ¼", 21.0 cm
Colour: Light and dark blue
Issued: 2002-2004
   U.S.:   **$150.00**
   Can.:   **$180.00**
   U.K.:   **£ 80.00**

HN 4469
Spirit of Scotland
Designer: N. Pedley
Height: 8 ¼", 21.0 cm
Colour: Lilac
Issued: 2003-2004
   U.S.:   **$160.00**
   Can.:   **$200.00**
   U.K.:   **£ 85.00**

Exclusive to Scotland 2003.

HN 4470
For Someone Special
Designer: N. Pedley
Height: 5 ½", 14.0 cm
Colour: Pale blue and white
Issued: 2003-2003
   U.S.:   **$150.00**
   Can.:   **$175.00**
   U.K.:   **£ 75.00**

Canadian exclusive.
HN 4471 - 4473 not issued.

HN 4474
Queen Mary II
(Wife of William of Orange)
Designer: P. Parsons
Height: 8 ¾", 22.2 cm
Colour: Pale blue and purple
            dress, red and gold
            tablecloth
Issued: 2002 in a limited
            edition of 2,500
Series: Stuart Queens
Comm.by: Doulton-Direct
   U.S.:   **$550.00**
   Can.:   **$675.00**
   U.K.:   **£275.00**

HN 4475
Young Queen Victoria
Designer: P. Parsons
Height: 5 ½", 14.0 cm
Colour: Purple
Issued: 2003 in a limited
edition of 950
Comm.by: Doulton-Direct
U.S.: $550.00
Can.: $650.00
U.K.: £275.00

HN 4476
H.M. Queen Elizabeth II Coronation
Designer: P. Parsons
Height: 7 ¾", 19.7 cm
Colour: White, purple
brown and gold
Issued: 2003 in a limited
edition of 2,000
Series: Prestige
Comm.by: Doulton-Direct
U.S.: $600.00
Can.: $750.00
U.K.: £300.00

HN 4477 - 4480 not issued.

HN 4481
Alexander the Great
Designer: A. Maslankowski
Height: 18 ¼", 46.0 cm
Colour: Mauve toga, black
horse, tiger skin
Issued: 2002 in a limited
edition of 50
Series: Prestige
U.S.: $17,950.00
Can.: $30,000.00
U.K.: £12,000.00

HN 4482
Clever Boy
Designer: A. Maslankowski
Height: 6 ¼", 16.0 cm
Colour: White
Issued: 2003 to the present
Series: Images
U.S.: N/I
Can.: $140.00
U.K.: £ 29.00

HN 4483
Clever Girl
Designer: A. Maslankowski
Height: 6 ¼", 16.0 cm
Colour: White
Issued: 2003 to the present
Series: Images
U.S.: N/I
Can.: $140.00
U.K.: £ 29.00

HN4484
Father and Daughter
Designer: A. Maslankowski
Height: 8 ¼", 21.0 cm
Colour: White
Issued: 2003 to the present
Series: Images
U.S.: N/I
Can.: $245.00
U.K.: £ 75.00

HN 4485
Unity
Designer: A. Maslankowski
Height: 6 ¾", 17.2 cm
Colour: White
Issued: 2003-2003
Series: 1. Images
2. Save the Children
Charity
U.S.: $175.00
Can.: $225.00
U.K.: £100.00

HN 4486
Charge of the Light Brigade
Style Two
Designer: A. Maslankowski
Height: 8", 20.3 cm
Colour: Blues, grey, brown
and green
Issued: 2002 in a limited
edition of 500
Series: Prestige
U.S.: $1,600.00
Can.: $2,700.00
U.K.: £ 900.00

HN 4487
Farmer
Style Two
Designer: A. Hughes
Height: 8 ¼", 21.0 cm
Colour: White, brown, and black
Issued: 2003 to the present

U.S.:	**$345.00**
Can.:	**$695.00**
U.K.:	**£205.00**

HN 4488
Blacksmith
Style Two
Designer: T. Potts
Height: 8 ¾", 22.2 cm
Colour: White, grey and dark brown
Issued: 2003 to the present

U.S.:	**$345.00**
Can.:	**$695.00**
U.K.:	**£205.00**

HN 4489 - 4490 not issued.

HN 4491
Little Child So Rare And Sweet
Style Three
Designer: V. Annand
Height: 4 ¾", 12.1 cm
Colour: Pink, mottled pink and purple base
Issued: 2002 in a limited editin of 1,000
Series: Leslie Harradine Tribute
Comm.by: Doulton-Direct

U.S.:	**$250.00**
Can.:	**$300.00**
U.K.:	**£125.00**

HN 4492
Dancing Eyes and Sunny Hair
Style Two
Designer: V. Annand
Height: 4 ¾", 12.1 cm
Colour: Pale green
Issued: 2002 in a limited edition of 1,000
Series: Leslie Harradine Tribute
Comm.by: Doulton-Direct

U.S.:	**$250.00**
Can.:	**$300.00**
U.K.:	**£125.00**

HN 4493
Annabel Vision in Red
Designer: V. Annand
Height: 8 ¼", 21.0 cm
Colour: Red
Issued: 2003 to the present
Varieties: Also called 'Becky' HN 4322
Series: Chelsea

U.S.:	**N/I**
Can.:	**$425.00**
U.K.:	**N/I**

Exclusive to Canada

HN 4494
Home Guard
Designer: V. Annand
Height: 8 ¾", 22.2 cm
Colour: Khaki
Issued: 2002 in a limited edition of 2,500
Series: Nostalgia
Comm.by: Doulton-Direct

U.S.:	**$500.00**
Can.:	**N/I**
U.K.:	**£195.00**

HN 4495
Auxiliary Territorial Service
Designer: V. Annand
Height: 8 ¾", 22.2 cm
Colour: Khaki
Issued: 2002 in a limited edition of 2,500
Series: Nostalgia
Comm.by: Doulton-Direct

U.S.:	**$500.00**
Can.:	**N/I**
U.K.:	**£195.00**

HN 4496
Taylor
Designer: V. Annand
Height: 8 ¼", 21.0 cm
Colour: Blue and lemon
Issued: 2003-2004
Series: In Vogue

U.S.:	**$175.00**
Can.:	**$225.00**
U.K.:	**£ 90.00**

HN 4497
Helen of Troy
Style Two
Designer:	V. Annand
Height:	9 ¾", 24.7 cm
Colour:	White, pink, green, yellow and beige
Issued:	2002 in a limited edition of 950
Series:	1. Greek Mythology 2. Prestige
Comm.by:	Doulton-Direct
U.S.:	**$400.00**
Can.:	**$500.00**
U.K.:	**£200.00**

HN 4498
Women's Royal Navy Service
Designer:	V. Annand
Height:	9", 22.9 cm
Colour:	Navy uniform, brown bags
Issued:	2003 in a limited edition of 2,500
Series:	Nostalgia
Comm.by:	Doulton-Direct
U.S.:	**$500.00**
Can.:	**N/I**
U.K.:	**£195.00**

HN 4499
Alana
Designer:	V. Annand
Height:	8 ½", 21.5 cm
Colour:	Black
Issued:	2003-2004
Series:	In Vogue
U.S.:	**$130.00**
Can.:	**$160.00**
U.K.:	**£ 70.00**

HN 4500
Nadine
Style Two
Designer:	V. Annand
Height:	8 ½", 21.5 cm
Colour:	Black
Issued:	2003-2004
Series:	In Vogue
U.S.:	**$130.00**
Can.:	**$160.00**
U.K.:	**£ 70.00**

HN 4501
Forever Yours, Style Two
Designer:	J. Bromley
Height:	8 ¾", 22.2 cm
Colour:	Pink
Issued:	2002-2003
Varieties:	Also called 'Best Wishes' (Style Two) HN 3971; 'Especially For You' HN 4750; 'Kate' (Style Three) HN 4233
U.S.:	**$375.00**
Can.:	**$450.00**
U.K.:	**£150.00**

Canadian and U.K. Catalogue
HN 4502 - 4509 not issued.

HN 4510
The Pilot Skipper
Designer:	Unknown
Height:	6 ¾", 17.2 cm
Colour:	Brown, grey, white and yellow
Issued:	2002
Comm.by:	Pilot Insurance
U.S.:	
Can.:	**Very rare**
U.K.:	

HN 4511
Fisherman
Designer:	M. Alcock
Height:	7", 17.8 cm
Colour:	Brown, grey and green
Issued:	2003 to the present
U.S.:	**$325.00**
Can.:	**$695.00**
U.K.:	**£195.00**

HN 4515-4516 Teddy Bears

HN 4517
Footballer
Designer:	M. Alcock
Height:	8 ¼", 21.0 cm
Colour:	White
Issued:	2004 to the present
Series:	Images
U.S.:	**N/I**
Can.:	**$175.00**
U.K.:	**£ 54.00**

HN 4518
Cricketer
Style Two
Designer: M. Alcock
Height: 8", 20.3 cm
Colour: White
Issued: 2004 to the present
Series: Images
  U.S.:   **N/I**
  Can.:   **175.00**
  U.K.:   **£ 49.00**

HN 4519
Hockey Player
Designer: M. Alcock
Height: 5", 12.7 cm
Colour: White
Issued: 2004 to the present
Series: Images
  U.S.:   **N/I**
  Can.:   **$120.00**
  U.K.:   **£ 49.00**

HN 4520
April
Style Five
Designer: N. Pedley
Height: 8 ½", 21.6 cm
Colour: Pink and white
Issued: 2003-2004
  U.S.:   **$200.00**
  Can.:   **$250.00**
  U.K.:   **£100.00**

HN 4521
Ruby
Style Two
Designer: N. Pedley
Height: 8 ¼", 21.0 cm
Colour: Red
Issued: 2003-2004
Varieties: Also called 'Rachel'
          (Style Four) HN 4742
  U.S.:   **$175.00**
  Can.:   **$225.00**
  U.K.:   **£ 95.00**

HN 4522
Anne Marie
Designer: N. Pedley
Height: 8 ¼", 21.0 cm
Colour: Pale green and white
Issued: 2003-2004
  U.S.:   **$150.00**
  Can.:   **$180.00**
  U.K.:   **£ 80.00**

HN 4523
Faye
Designer: N. Pedley
Height: 8 ½", 21.6 cm
Colour: Pale green, and white
Issued: 2003-2004
  U.S.:   **$150.00**
  Can.:   **$180.00**
  U.K.:   **£ 75.00**

HN 4524
Jayne
Style Two
Designer: N. Pedley
Height: 8", 20.3 cm
Colour: Pink and white
Issued: 2003-2004
Series: Vanity Fair
  U.S.:   **$165.00**
  Can.:   **$250.00**
  U.K.:   **£ 95.00**

HN 4525
Lisa
Style Two
Designer: N. Pedley
Height: 8 ¼", 21.0 cm
Colour: Lemon and white
Issued: 2003-2004
Varieties: Also called 'Eileen'
          HN 4730
  U.S.:   **$185.00**
  Can.:   **$275.00**
  U.K.:   **£ 95.00**

HN 4526
Christine
Style Seven
Designer: N. Pedley
Height: 8 ¼", 21.0 cm
Colour: Dark and light blue, and white
Issued: 2003-2003
Varieties: Also called 'Gillian' (Style Four) HN 4404
Comm.by: G.U.S.

U.S.:	**$225.00**
Can.:	**$275.00**
U.K.:	**£115.00**

HN 4527
Nicole
Style Three
Designer: N. Pedley
Height: 8 ¼", 21.0 cm
Colour: Purple and pink
Issued: 2003-2004

U.S.:	**$275.00**
Can.:	**$375.00**
U..K.:	**£150.00**

HN 4528
Happy Birthday 2004
Designer: N. Pedley
Height: 8 ¼", 21.0 cm
Colour: Yellow
Issued: 2004-2004
Series: Happy Birthday

U.S.:	**$175.00**
Can.:	**$370.00**
U.K.:	**£100.00**

HN 4529
Love of Life
Designer: N. Pedley
Height: 8 ¾", 22.2 cm
Colour: Pink and white
Issued: 2003-2004
Series: Charity (Breast Cancer)

U.S.:	**$225.00**
Can.:	**$350.00**
U.K.:	**£130.00**

HN 4530
Moonlight Serenade
Designer: J. Bromley
Height: 8 ¾", 22.2 cm
Colour: Blue and mottled grey
Issued: 2003-2004
Varieties: Also called 'Special Wishes' HN 4749

U.S.:	**$275.00**
Can.:	**$450.00**
U.K.:	**£150.00**

HN 4531
Message of Love
Designer: J. Bromley
Height: 9 ¼", 23.5 cm
Colour: Pink
Issued: 2003-2004

U.S.:	**$325.00**
Can.:	**$500.00**
U.K.:	**£175.00**

HN 4532
Susan
Style Five
Designer: J. Bromley
Height: 9", 22.9 cm
Colour: Dark and light blue and white
Issued: 2004-2004
Series: Figure of the Year

U.S.:	**$250.00**
Can.:	**$300.00**
U.K.:	**£120.00**

HN 4533
Beautiful Blossom
Designer: J. Bromley
Height: 8 ¾", 22.2 cm
Colour: Lilac
Issued: 2003-2004

U.S.:	**$275.00**
Can.:	**$375.00**
U.K.:	**£150.00**

HN 4534 not issued.

HN 4534
Francesca
Style Two
Designer: J. Bromley
Height: 11", 27.9 cm
Colour: White evening gown
Issued: 2004 to the present
Series: The Sensual Collection
U.S.:   N/I
Can.: $550.00
U.K.:   £135.00

HN 4535
Simone
Style Two
Designer: J. Bromley
Height: 11", 27.9 cm
Colour: White evening gown
              and gloves
Issued: 2004 to the present
Series: The Sensual Collection
Comm.by: Home Shopping
U.S.:   N/I
Can.:   N/I
U.K.:   £135.00

HN 4536
Charlotte
Style Five
Designer: J. Bromley
Height: 11", 27.9 cm
Colour: White evening gown
Issued: 2004 to the present
Series: The Sensual Collection
U.S.:   N/I
Can.:   N/I
U.K.:   £135.00

HN 4537
Kristine
Designer: J. Bromley
Height: 11", 27.9 cm
Colour: White evening gown
Issued: 2004 to the present
Series: The Sensual Collection
U.S.:   N/I
Can.:   N/I
U.K.:   £135.00

HN 4538
A Winter's Morn
Designer: J. Bromley
Height: 8 ¾", 22.2 cm
Colour: Red coat; white dress,
              ermine hat and muff,
              gold highlights
Issued: 2004 in a limited
              edition of 7,500
Varieties: HN 4622
Comm.by: Compton/Woodhouse
U.S.:   N/I
Can.:   N/I
U.K.:   £165.00

HN 4539
Megan
Style Three
Designer: J. Bromley
Height: 8 ¾", 22.2 cm
Colour: Purple and lilac dress
              with white trim
Issued: 2004-2004
Series: Lady of the Year
Comm.by: Compton/Woodhouse
U.S.: $400.00
Can.: $500.00
U.K.:   £200.00

HN 4540
Merlin
Designer: S. Ridge
Height: 9 ¾", 24.7 cm
Colour: Green, yellow, brown
              and grey
Issued: 2003 in a limited
              edition of 950
Comm.by: Doulton-Direct
U.S.: $500.00
Can.: $600.00
U.K.:   £250.00

HN 4541
King Arthur
Designer: S. Ridge
Height: 9", 22.9 cm
Colour: Light brown, blue,
              light and dark grey
              and brown
Issued: 2003 in a limited
              edition of 950
Series: Prestige
U.S.: $600.00
Can.: $725.00
U.K.:   £300.00

HN 4542
Graduate Female
Style Two
Designer: S. Ridge
Height: 8", 20.3 cm
Colour: White
Issued: 2004 to the present
Series: Images

U.S.:	N/I
Can.:	$150.00
U.K.:	£ 39.00

HN 4543
Graduate Male
Style Three
Designer: S. Ridge
Height: 8", 20.3 cm
Colour: White
Issued: 2004 to the present
Series: Images

U.S.:	N/I
Can.:	$150.00
U.K.:	£ 39.00

HN 4544 - 4549 not issued.

HN 4550
Mikaela
Designer: V. Annand
Height: 8 ½", 21.6 cm
Colour: Black
Issued: 2003-2004
Series: In Vogue

U.S.:	$130.00
Can.:	$160.00
U.K.:	£ 70.00

HN 4551
Daniella
Designer: V. Annand
Height: 8 ½", 21.5 cm
Colour: Black
Issued: 2003-2004
Series: In Vogue

U.S.:	$130.00
Can.:	$160.00
U.K.:	£ 70.00

HN 4552
Christmas Day 2003
Designer: V. Annand
Height: 8 ¾", 22.2 cm
Colour: Red and white
Issued: 2003-2003
Series: Christmas Figures

U.S.:	$400.00
Can.:	$500.00
U.K.:	£150.00

HN 4553
The Dance
Style Two
Designer: V. Annand
Height: 8 ¾", 22.2 cm
Colour: Pale blue, pale pink and white
Issued: 2004-2004
Series: ICC

U.S.:	$300.00
Can.:	$375.00
U.K.:	£150.00

HN 4554
Women's Auxiliary Air Force
Designer: V. Annand
Height: 8 ¼", 21.0 cm
Colour: Navy uniform, brown satchel and cases
Issued: 2003 in a limited edition of 2,500
Series: Nostalgia
Comm.by: Doulton-Direct

U.S.:	$400.00
Can.:	$450.00
U.K.:	£195.00

HN 4555
Air Raid Precaution Warden
Designer: V. Annand
Height: 5 ½", 14.0 cm
Colour: Green jacket; grey trousers, hat and base; brown seat and bag
Issued: 2003 in a limited edition of 2,500
Series: Nostalgia
Comm.by: Doulton-Direct

U.S.:	$400.00
Can.:	$450.00
U.K.	£195.00

HN 4556
Hayley
Designer: V. Annand
Height: 8 ½", 21.5 cm
Colour: Pale green and lemon
Issued: 2003-2004
Series: Chelsea Collection
U.S.: $175.00
Can.: $225.00
U.K.: £ 95.00

HN 4557
Alexandra
Style Three
Designer: V. Annand
Height: 8", 20.3 cm
Colour: Dark blue
Issued: 2003
Varieties: Also called 'Chloe'
(Style Six) HN 4727;
'Jenny' HN 4423
Comm.by: G.U.S.
U.S.: $250.00
Can.: $275.00
U.K.: £115.00

HN 4558
Christmas Day 2004
Designer: V. Annand
Height: 8 ¼", 21.0 cm
Colour: Purple and white
Issued: 2004-2004
Varieties: Also called 'Victorian
Christmas' HN 4675
Series: Christmas Day
U.S.: $275.00
Can.: $425.00
U.K.: £150.00

HN 4559
Rose Garden
Designer: V. Annand
Height: 9 ½", 24.0 cm
Width: 13 ¾", 34.9 cm
Depth: 12", 30.5 cm
Colour: Blues, greens, pinks,
yellows and white
Issued: 2004 in a limited
edition of 250
Series: Prestige
U.S.: N/I
Can.: $4,500.00
U.K.: £1,600.00

HN 4560
The Secret
Designer: A. Maslankowski
Height: 6 ¼", 15.9 cm
Colour: White
Issued: 2004-2004
Series: Image of the Year
U.S.: $120.00
Can.: $175.00
U.K.: £ 60.00

HN 4561
Hercules
Designer: A. Maslankowski
Height: 16 ¼", 41.2 cm
Colour: Light brown, brown,
flesh tones, white,
grey base
Issued: 2003 in a limited
edition of 50
Series: Prestige
U.S.: $17,500.00
Can.: $27,000.00
U.K.: £10,000.00

HN 4562
Mother and Daughter
Style Two
Designer: A. Maslankowski
Height: 7 ½", 19.1 cm
Colour: White
Issued: 2003 to the present
Series: Images
U.S.: N/I
Can.: $245.00
U.K.: £65.00

HN 4563
Studious Boy
Designer: A. Maslankowski
Height: 3 ¼", 8.3 cm
Colour: White
Issued: 2003 to the present
Series: Images
U.S.: N/I
Can.: $130.00
U.K.: £ 39.00

HN 4564
Studious Girl
Designer: A. Maslankowski
Height: 3 ¼", 8.3 cm
Colour: White
Issued: 2003 to the present
Series: Images

U.S.:	N/I
Can.:	$130.00
U.K.:	£ 39.00

HN 4565
Hope
Style Three
Designer: A. Maslankowski
Height: 6", 15.2 cm
Colour: White with ermine trim
Issued: 2003-2004
Series: 1. Holiday Collection
2. Sentiments

U.S.:	$100.00
Can.:	$150.00
U.K.:	£ 60.00

Exclusive to Canada

HN 4566
Matador and Bull
Style Two
Designer: A. Maslankowski
Height: 7", 17.8 cm
Colour: Black, yellow, pink and gold
Issued: 2004 in a limited edition of 250
Series: Prestige

U.S.:	$1,000.00
Can.:	N/A
U.K.:	£ 795.00

HN 4567
Harmony
Style Three
Designer: A. Maslankowski
Height: 7 ¾", 19.7 cm
Colour: White
Issued: 2004-2004
Series: 1. Images
2. Save The Children Charity

U.S.:	$200.00
Can.:	$340.00
U.K.:	£ 99.00

HN 4568
Peace
Style Two
Designer: A. Maslankowski
Height: 6 ¼", 15.9 cm
Colour: White
Issued: July 2006
Series: 1. Holiday Collection
2. Sentiments

U.S.:	To be
Can.:	issued
U.K.:	July 2006

Exclusive to Canada

HN 4569
Joy
Style Four
Designer: A. Maslankowski
Height: 6 ¼", 15.9 cm
Colour: White
Issued: 2004-2005
Series: 1. Holiday Collection
2. Sentiments

U.S.:	N/I
Can.:	$140.00
U.K.:	N/I

Exclusive to Canada

HN 4570
Lifeboat Man
Style Two
Designer: A. Hughes
Height: 9", 22.9 cm
Colour: Yellow and brown
Issued: 2003 to the present

U.S.:	$325.00
Can.:	$695.00
U.K.:	£195.00

HN 4571 - 4579 not issued.

HN 4580
Irish Charm
Designer: N. Pedley
Height: 8 ¼", 21.0 cm
Colour: Green and white
Issued: 2004-2004

U.S.:	$275.00
Can.:	$350.00
U.K.:	£130.00

HN 4581
Rose
Style Three
Designer: N. Pedley
Height: 8 ¼", 21.0 cm
Colour: Pale yellow gown with orange trim
Issued: 2004-2004
Series: M. Doulton Event

U.S.:	**$250.00**
Can.:	**$400.00**
U.K.:	**£130.00**

HN 4582
Sweet Memories
Designer: N. Pedley
Height: 8 ¼", 21.0 cm
Colour: Rose-pink
Issued: 2003-2004

U.S.:	**$175.00**
Can.:	**$225.00**
U.K.:	**£ 90.00**

HN 4583
Jessica
Style Four
Designer: N. Pedley
Height: 8 ½", 21.6 cm
Colour: Red and white
Issued: 2003-2004

U.S.:	**$225.00**
Can.:	**$275.00**
U.K.:	**£120.00**

HN 4584
Andrea
Style Two
Designer: N. Pedley
Height: 8 ¼", 21.0 cm
Colour: Green
Issued: 2003-2004

U.S.:	**$175.00**
Can.:	**$225.00**
U.K.:	**£ 90.00**

HN 4585
Thinking of You
Style Two
Designer: N. Pedley
Height: 8 ½", 21.6 cm
Colour: Pale yellow
Issued: 2003-2004
Series: Name Your Own

U.S.:	**$225.00**
Can.:	**$300.00**
U.K.:	**£120.00**

HN 4586
Springtime
Style Four
Designer: N. Pedley
Height: 6", 15.0 cm
Colour: Lemon yellow
Issued: 2004-2004
Series: 1. Club Membership Figure
2. Seasons (Series Nine)

U.S.:	**$60.00**
Can.:	**$75.00**
U.K.:	**£30.00**

HN 4587
Summer
Style Four
Designer: N. Pedley
Height: 6 ¼", 15.9 cm
Colour: Pink, lilac and white
Issued: 2005-2005
Series: 1. ICC Complimentary Figure
2. Seasons (Series Nine)

U.S.:	**Membership**
Can.:	**Figure**
U.K.:	**2005**

HN 4588
Autumn
Style Four
Designer: N. Pedley
Height: 6", 15.0 cm
Colour: Orange and lemon
Issued: 2006-2006
Series: 1. ICC Complimentary Figure
2. Seasons (Series Nine)

U.S.:	**Complimentary**
Can.:	**Figure**
U.K.:	**2006**

HN 4589
Winter
Style Four
Designer: N. Pedley
Height: 6 ¼", 15.9 cm
Colour: Red, green and white
Issued: 2007-2007
Series: 1. ICC Complimentary
            Figure
            2. Seasons (Series
            Nine)

U.S.:   **Complimentary**
Can.:   **Figure**
U.K.:   **2007**

HN 4590 - 4595 not issued

HN 4596
Queen Alexandra Nurse
Designer: M. Alcock
Height: 8 ¼", 21.0 cm
Colour: Blue, white, red
            and brown
Issued: 2004 in a limited
            edition of 2,500
Comm. by: Doulton-Direct

U.S.:   **$295.00**
Can.:   **N/I**
U.K.:   **£195.00**

HN 4597 - 4598 not issued

HN 4599
Bathing Beauty
Designer: N. Pedley
Height: 7 ¼", 18.5 cm
Colour: Flesh tones; red towel
Issued: 2003 in a limited
            edition of 200
Varieties: HN 4399
Series: Leslie Harradine
            Tribute
Comm.by: Sinclairs

U.S.:   **$350.00**
Can.:   **$425.00**
U.K.:   **£175.00**

HN 4600
Brighton Belle
Designer: N. Pedley
Height: 7", 17.8 cm
Colour: Flesh tones; yellow
            bathing suit
Issued: 2003 in a limited
            edition of 200
Varieties: HN 4400
Series: Leslie Harradine
            Tribute
Comm.by: Sinclairs

U.S.:   **$350.00**
Can.:   **$425.00**
U.K.:   **£175.00**

HN 4601
Summer's Darling
Designer: N. Pedley
Height: 4 ¼", 10.8 cm
Colour: Flesh tones;
            purple towel
Issued: 2003 in a limited
            edition of 200
Varieties: HN 4401
Series: Leslie Harradine
            Tribute
Comm.by: Sinclairs

U.S.:   **$350.00**
Can.:   **$425.00**
U.K.:   **£175.00**

HN 4602
Taking the Waters
Designer: N. Pedley
Height: 6 ¼", 16.0 cm
Colour: Flesh tones; royal
            blue bathing suit
Issued: 2003 in a limited
            edition of 200
Varieties: HN 4402
Series: Leslie Harradine
            Tribute
Comm.by: Sinclairs

U.S.:   **$350.00**
Can.:   **$425.00**
U.K.:   **£175.00**

HN 4603
Dawn
Style Four
Designer: N. Pedley
Height: 8 ¼", 21.0 cm
Colour: Rose pink and white
Issued: 2004-2004

U.S.:   **$200.00**
Can.:   **$250.00**
U.K.:   **£100.00**

HN 4604
Happy Anniversary
Style Four
Designer: N. Pedley
Height: 8 ¼", 21.0 cm
Colour: Pale blue skirt;
            silver bodice;
            dark blue sleeves
Issued: 2004-2004
Varieties: HN 4605, 4606
Series: Name Your Own

U.S.:   **$275.00**
Can.:   **$375.00**
U.K.:   **£135.00**

HN 4605
Happy Anniversary
Style Four
Designer: N. Pedley
Height: 8 ¼", 21.0 cm
Colour: Pale green skirt; pearl bodice; dark green sleeves
Issued: 2004-2004
Varieties: HN 4604, 4606
Series: Name Your Own

U.S.:	**$275.00**
Can.:	**$375.00**
U.K.:	**£135.00**

HN 4606
Happy Anniversary
Style Four
Designer: N. Pedley
Height: 8 ¼", 21.0 cm
Colour: Pink dress with ruby bodice
Issued: 2004-2004
Varieties: HN 4604, 4605
Series: Name Your Own

U.S.:	**$275.00**
Can.:	**$375.00**
U.K.:	**£135.00**

HN 4607
Magical Moments
Designer: N. Pedley
Height: 5 ¾", 14.6 cm
Colour: Pink
Issued: 2004 to the present

U.S.:	**N/I**
Can.:	**$160.00**
U.K.:	**N/I**

Exclusive to Canada.

HN 4608
Heart of Scotland
Designer: N. Pedley
Height: 8", 20.3 cm
Colour: Dark green dress; red tartan scarf
Issued: 2004 to the present

U.S.:	**N/I**
Can.:	**$425.00**
U.K.:	**£120.00**

Exclusive to Scotland for 2004.
General release 2005.

HN 4609
Free Spirit
Style Three
Designer: N. Pedley
Height: 5 ¾", 14.6 cm
Colour: Dark and pale purple
Issued: 2004-2005
Series: Charity (Breast Cancer)

U.S.:	**N/A**
Can.:	**$200.00**
U.K.:	**£ 90.00**

HN 4610
Daybreak
Style Three
Designer: N. Welch
Height: 8 ¼", 21.0 cm
Colour: White dress
Issued: 2004 to the present

U.S.:	**N/I**
Can.:	**N/I**
U.K.:	**£110.00**

HN 4611
Moonlight
Designer: N. Welch
Height: 8 ¼", 21.0 cm
Colour: Pale blue-grey dress
Issued: 2004 to the present

U.S.:	**N/I**
Can.:	**N/I**
U.K.:	**£110.00**

HN 4612 - 4619 not issued.

HN 4620
Sophie
Style Six
Designer: J. Bromley
Height: 8 ¼", 21.0 cm
Colour: Dark blue
Issued: 2004-2004

U.S.:	**$300.00**
Can.:	**$400.00**
U.K.:	**£165.00**

HN 4621
True Love
Designer: J. Bromley
Height: 8 ¼", 21.0 cm
Colour: Purple and gold dress,
            grey shawl
Issued: 2004-2004

U.S.:   **$300.00**
Can.:   **$400.00**
U.K.:   **£165.00**

HN 4622
A Winter's Morn
Designer: J. Bromley
Height: 8 ¾", 22.2 cm
Colour: White, gold trim
Issued: 2004 in a limited
            edition of 7,500
Varieties: HN 4538
Comm.by: Compton/Woodhouse

U.S.:   **N/I**
Can.:   **N/I**
U.K.:   **£99.00**

HN 4623
Victoria
Style Four
Designer: J. Bromley
Height: 8 ½", 21.6 cm
Colour: Purple
Issued: 2005-2005
Series: Figure of the Year

U.S.:   **N/A**
Can.:   **$350.00**
U.K.:   **£125.00**

HN 4624
Eleanor
Style Four
Designer: J. Bromley
Height: 8 ¾", 22.2 cm
Colour: Purple and pink
Issued: 2004-2004

U.S.:   **$300.00**
Can.:   **$375.00**
U.K.:   **£165.00**

HN 4625
Sweet Devotion
Designer: J. Bromley
Height: 8 ½", 21.6 cm
Colour: Purple and pink
Issued: 2004 in a limited
            edition of 2,000
Comm.by: Home Shopping

U.S.:   **N/I**
Can.:   **N/I**
U.K.:   **N/A**

HN 4626
Summer Breeze
Style Two
Designer: J. Bromley
Height: 8 ½", 21.6 cm
Colour: White with gold trim
Issued: 2005 in a limited
            edition of 7,500
Varieties: HN 4627
Comm.by: Compton/Woodhouse

U.S.:   **N/I**
Can.:   **N/I**
U.K.:   **£165.00**

HN 4627
Summer Breeze
Style Two
Designer: J. Bromley
Height: 8 ½", 21.6 cm
Colour: Blue with gold trim
Issued: 2005 in a limited
            edition of 7,500
Varieties: HN 4626
Comm.by: Compton/Woodhouse

U.S.:   **N/I**
Can.:   **N/I**
U.K.:   **£165.00**

HN 4628 - 4629 not issued
HN 4630 - 4631 Animal figures

HN 4632
Sailor
Designer: S. Ridge
Height: 8 ¼", 21.0 cm
Colour: Navy, white and brown
Issued: 2004 in a limited
            edition of 2,500
Comm. by: Doulton-Direct

U.S.:   **$295.00**
Can.:   **N/I**
U.K.:   **£195.00**

HN 4633 - 4634 not issued

HN 4635
Bowler
Designer: T. Potts
Height: 8 ¾", 22.2 cm
Colour: White; green base
Issued: 2003 in a limited
             edition of 2,500
Comm.by: Doulton-Direct
  U.S.:   **$300.00**
  Can.:   **$350.00**
  U.K.:   **£150.00**

HN 4636 - 4639 not issued

HN 4640
Love
Designer: A. Maslankowski
Height: 6 ¼", 15.9 cm
Colour: White
Issued: July 2005
Series: 1. Holiday Collection
             2. Sentiments
  U.S.:   **To be**
  Can.:   **issued**
  U.K.:   **July 2005**

Exclusive to Canada

HN 4641
Lady Godiva
Designer: A. Maslankowski
Height: 13 ¾", 34.9 cm
Colour: Fleshtones, grey,
             brown, red and gold
Issued: 2004 in a limited
             edition of 50
Series: Prestige
  U.S.:   **N/I**
  Can.:   **$27,000.00**
  U.K.:   **£ 8,000.00**

HN 4642 not issued

HN 4643
Best Friends
Style Three
Designer: A. Maslankowski
Height: 8 ¼", 21.0 cm
Colour: White
Issued: 2004 to the present
Series: Images
  U.S.:   **N/I**
  Can.:   **$175.00**
  U.K.:   **£60.00**

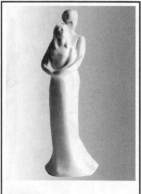

HN 4644
Two Become One
Designer: A. Maslankowski
Height: 10 ¼", 26.0 cm
Colour: White
Issued: 2004 to the present
Series: Images
  U.S.:   **N/I**
  Can.:   **$175.00**
  U.K.:   **£60.00**

HN 4645
Family
Style Two
Designer: A. Maslankowski
Height: 10 ¼", 26.0 cm
Colour: White
Issued: 2004 to the present
Series: Images
  U.S.:   **N/I**
  Can.:   **$175.00**
  U.K.:   **£60.00**

HN 4646-4649 not issued

HN 4650
Country Veterinary
Designer: M. Alcock
Height: 9", 22.9 cm
Colour: Brown, dark and
             light grey and black
Issued: 2004 to the present
  U.S.:   **$280.00**
  Can.:   **$650.00**
  U.K.:   **£215.00**

HN 4651
Town Veterinary
Designer: M. Alcock
Height: 5 ½", 14.0 cm
Colour: White, brown,
             grey and black
Issued: 2004 to the present
  U.S.:   **$280.00**
  Can.:   **$650.00**
  U.K.:   **£175.00**

HN 4652-4659 not issued

HN 4660
Summer's Dream
Designer: N. Pedley
Height: 8 ¼", 21.0 cm
Colour: Rust and cream
Issued: 2004-2005
Series: Charity (Breast Cancer)

U.S.:	$225.00
Can.:	$350.00
U.K.:	£150.00

HN 4661
Naomi
Designer: N. Pedley
Height: 8 ¼", 21.0 cm
Colour: Pink
Issued: 2004-2004
Series: Vanity Fair

U.S.:	$210.00
Can.:	$300.00
U.K.:	£130.00

HN 4662
Rosemary
Style Four
Designer: N. Pedley
Height: 8 ¼", 21.0 cm
Colour: Pale blue and pink
Issued: 2004-2004

U.S.:	$215.00
Can.:	$300.00
U.K.:	£135.00

HN 4663
Fleur
Style Two
Designer: N. Pedley
Height: 8", 20.3 cm
Colour: Rose pink
Issued: 2004-2004

U.S.:	$200.00
Can.:	$375.00
U.K.:	£125.00

HN 4664
Abigail
Style Two
Designer: N. Pedley
Height: 8 ¼", 21.0 cm
Colour: Red
Issued: 2004-2004

U.S.:	$175.00
Can.:	$300.00
U.K.:	£110.00

HN 4665
Laura
Style Three
Designer: N. Pedley
Height: 8 ¼", 21.0 cm
Colour: Green and white
Issued: 2004-2004

U.S.:	$225.00
Can.:	$325.00
U.K.:	£140.00

HN 4666
Caitlyn
Designer: N. Pedley
Height: 8 ¼", 21.0 cm
Colour: Black and purple
Issued: 2004-2004

U.S.:	$215.00
Can.:	$325.00
U.K.:	£135.00

HN 4667
Alison
Style Three
Designer: N. Pedley
Height: 8 ½", 21.6 cm
Colour: Orange and gold
Issued: 2004
Comm.by: Home Shopping

U.S.:	N/I
Can.:	N/I
U.K.:	N/A

HN 4675
Victorian Christmas
Designer: V. Annand
Height: 8 ¼", 21.0 cm
Colour: Red, white and green
Issued: 2004-2004
Varieties: Also called 'Christmas
             Day 2004' HN 4558
U.S.: $275.00
Can.: $400.00
U.K.:   £150.00

HN 4680
Mother and Son
Designer: Unknown
Height: 10 ½", 26.7 cm
Colour: White
Issued: 2005 to the present
Series: Images
U.S.:   N/A
Can.: $280.00
U.K.:   £ 45.00

HN 4681
First Kiss
Designer: Unknown
Height: 6 ¼", 15.9 cm
Colour: White
Issued: 2005 to the present
Series: Images
U.S.:   N/A
Can.: $280.00
U.K.:   £ 35.00

HN 4682
Playmates
Style Two
Designer: Unknown
Height: 7 ¼", 18.4 cm
Colour: White
Issued: 2005 to the present
Series: Images
U.S.:   N/A
Can.: $280.00
U.K.:   £ 35.00

HN 4683
Carefree
Style Two
Designer: M. Alcock
Height: 7 ¼", 18.4 cm
Colour: White
Issued: 2005-2005
Series: Image of the Year
U.S.:   N/A
Can.: $280.00
U.K.:   £ 45.00

HN 4684-4685

HN 4686
Autumn Stroll
Designer: John Bromley
Height: 9", 22.9 cm
Colour: Purple and white
Issued: 2004 in a limited
             edition of 7,500
Comm. by: Compton/Woodhouse
U.S.:   N/I
Can.:   N/I
U.K.:   £175.00

HN 4687-4699

HN 4700
Mary
Style Six
Designer: Unknown
Height: 5 ½", 14.0 cm
Colour: Pink, blue, white
             and gold
Issued: 2004 to the present
Series: Nativity Collection
U.S.: $143.00 set
Can.:   N/I
U.K.:   N/I

Exclusive to the U.S.A.
Sold as a set with HN 4701 and
HN 4707.

HN 4701
Joseph
Style Three
Designer: Unknown
Height: 8 ½", 21.6 cm
Colour: Brown, tan and gold
Issued: 2004 to the present
Series: Nativity Collection
U.S.: $143.00 set
Can.:   N/I
U.K.:   N/I

Exclusive to the U.S.A.
Sold as a set with HN 4700 and
HN 4707.

HN 4702
Melchior
Style Two
Designer: Unknown
Height: 6", 15.0 cm
Colour: Green, rose-pink, white
               and gold
Issued: 2004 to the present
Series: Nativity Collection
   U.S.:   **$58.00**
   Can.:   **N/I**
   U.K.:   **N/I**

Exclusive to the U.S.A.

HN 4703
Balthazar
Style Two
Designer: Unknown
Height: 9", 22.9 cm
Colour: Blue, yellow, black
               and gold
Issued: 2004 to the present
Series: Nativity Collection
   U.S.:   **$58.00**
   Can.:   **N/I**
   U.K.:   **N/I**

Exclusive to the U.S.A.

HN 4704
Gaspar
Designer: Unknown
Height: 6 ½", 16.5 cm
Colour: Green, purple,
               brown and gold
Issued: 2004 to the present
Series: Nativity Collection
   U.S.:   **$58.00**
   Can.:   **N/I**
   U.K.:   **N/I**

Exclusive to the U.S.A.

HN 4705 - 4706 Animals

HN 4707
Jesus
Style Two
Designer: Unknown
Height: 3 ½", 8.9 cm
Colour: White clothing;
               brown manger
Issued: 2004 to the present
Series: Nativity Collection
   U.S.:   **$143.00 set**
   Can.:   **N/I**
   U.K.:   **N/I**

Exclusive to the U.S.A.
Sold as a set with HN 4700 and
HN 4701.
HN 4708 - 4710

HN 4711
Joanna
Designer: A. Maslankowski
Height: 8 ¼", 21.0 cm
Colour: Gold and cream, with
               gilt highlights
Issued: 2005-2005
Series: ICC Lady of the Year
   U.S.:   **N/A**
   Can.:   **$390.00**
   U.K.:   **£125.00**

HN 4712
Welsh Lady
Designer: V. Annand
Height: 8 ½", 21.6 cm
Colour: Red, white, pale blue
               and black
Issued: 2004 in a limited
               edition of 600
Varieties: Also called 'Wales'
               HN 3630
Comm.by: 1. J.H. Williams & Sons
               2. Place Settings
   U.S.:   **N/I**
   Can.:   **N/I**
   U.K.:   **N/A**

HN 4713
Rooftop Santa
Designer: Unknown
Height: 9", 22.9 cm
Colour: Red, brown, green,
               white and gold
Issued: 2004 in a limited
               edition of 2,000
   U.S.:   **$115.00**
   Can.:   **$140.00**
   U.K.:   **N/A**

HN 4714
Santa Claus
Style Three
Designer: Unknown
Height: 4 ¼", 10.8 cm
Colour: Red, white, green,
               black, tan and gold
Issued: 2004 in a limited
               edition of 600
Comm.by: Pascoe & Company
   U.S.:   **$58.00**
   Can.:   **N/I**
   U.K.:   **N/I**

HN 4715
Santa Claus
Style Four
Designer: Unknown
Height: 3 ¾", 9.5 cm
Colour: Red, white, yellow, green, gold, black and pink
Issued: 2004 in a limited edition of 600
Comm.by: Pascoe & Company
U.S.: $50.00
Can.: N/I
U.K.: N/I

HN 4716
Autumn Breezes
Style Three
Designer: L. Harradine
Height: 6 ¾", 17.2 cm
Colour: Rose pink, lilac and green
Issued: 2004 to the present
Series: Petite
U.S.: $ 80.00
Can.: $185.00
U.K.: £ 50.00

HN 4717
Ninette
Style Four
Designer: M. Davies
Height: 6 ¾", 17.2 cm
Colour: Yellow
Issued: 2004 to the present
Series: Petite
U.S.: $ 80.00
Can.: $185.00
U.K.: £ 50.00

HN 4718
Elaine
Style Four
Designer: M. Davies
Height: 6 ¾", 17.2 cm
Colour: Dark blue
Issued: 2004 to the present
Series: Petite
U.S.: $ 80.00
Can.: $185.00
U.K.: £ 50.00

HN 4719
Fair Lady
Style Three
Designer: M. Davies
Height: 6 ¾" 17.2 cm
Colour: Green, yellow and white
Issued: 2004 to the present
Series: Petite
U.S.: $ 80.00
Can.: $185.00
U.K.: £ 50.00

HN 4720
Sara
Style Three
Designer: M. Davies
Height: 6 ¾", 17.2 cm
Colour: Dark blue and rose pink
Issued: 2004 to the present
Series: Petite
U.S.: $ 80.00
Can.: $185.00
U.K.: £ 50.00

HN 4721
Christmas Celebration
Designer: V. Annand
Height: 6 ¾", 17.2 cm
Colour: Red and white
Issued: 2004 to the present
Series: Petite
U.S.: $ 95.00
Can.: $185.00
U.K.: £ 60.00

Petite version of Christmas Day 2003

HN 4722
Happy Birthday 2005
Designer: N. Pedley
Height: 8 ½", 21.6 cm
Colour: Rose pink with gold highlights
Issued: 2005-2005
Series: Happy Birthday
U.S.: N/A
Can.: $280.00
U.K.: £125.00

HN 4723-4726

HN 4727
Chloe
Style Six
Designer: V. Annand
Height: 8", 20.3 cm
Colour: Peach
Issued: 2005 to the present
Varieties: Also called 'Alexandra'
(Style Three) HN 4557;
'Jenny' HN 4423

  U.S.: **N/A**
  Can.: **$330.00**
  U.K.: **£125.00**

HN 4728-4729

HN 4730
Eileen
Designer: N. Pedley
Height: 8 ¼", 21.0 cm
Colour: Red dress with pale
yellow trim
Issued: 2005 to the present
Varieties: Also called 'Lisa'
(Style Two) HN 4525

  U.S.: **N/A**
  Can.: **$330.00**
  U.K.: **£125.00**

HN 4731-4734

HN 4735
Deborah
Style Four
Designer: N. Pedley
Height: 8 ¼", 21.0 cm
Colour: Red and white
Issued: 2005 to the present
Varieties: Also called 'Isabel'
(Style Two) HN 4458

  U.S.: **N/A**
  Can.: **$330.00**
  U.K.: **£125.00**

HN 4736
Loyal Friend
Style Two
Designer: N. Pedley
Height: 8 ¼", 21.0 cm
Colour: Blue
Issued: 2005 to the present
Varieties: Also called 'My Love'
(Style Two) HN 4392

  U.S.: **N/A**
  Can.: **$330.00**
  U.K.: **£125.00**

HN 4737
Love Song
Designer: N. Pedley
Height: 8", 20.3 cm
Colour: Light and dark
turquoise
Issued: 2005 to the present
Varieties: Also called 'Lucy'
(Style Four) HN 4459

  U.S.: **N/A**
  Can.: **$330.00**
  U.K.: **£125.00**

HN 4738
Patricia
Style Six
Designer: N. Pedley
Height: 8 ¼", 21.0 cm
Colour: Orange-yellow, white
and pink
Issued: 2005 to the present
Varieties: Also called 'Emily'
Style Four) HN 4093

  U.S.: **N/A**
  Can.: **$390.00**
  U.K.: **£125.00**

HN 4739 - 4741

HN 4742
Rachel
Style Four
Designer: N. Pedley
Height: 8 ¼", 21.0 cm
Colour: Lavender
Issued: 2005 to the present
Varieties: Also called 'Ruby'
(Style Two) HN 4521

  U.S.: **N/A**
  Can.: **$330.00**
  U.K.: **£125.00**

HN 4743

HN 4744
Special Gift
Style Two
Designer: N. Pedley
Height: 8", 20.3 cm
Colour: Dark and light purple,
white and beige
Issued: 2005 to the present
Varieties: Also called 'Rosie'
HN 4094

  U.S.: **N/A**
  Can.: **$390.00**
  U.K.: **£125.00**

HN 4745
Treasured Moments
Designer: J. Bromley
Height: 8 ¾", 22.2 cm
Colour: Red dress; pale pink shawl
Issued: 2005 to the present
Varieties: Also called 'Special Celebration' HN 4234

U.S.: N/A
Can.: $390.00
U.K.: £150.00

HN 4746
With Love
Style Two
Designer: J. Bromley
Height: 8 ¾", 22.2 cm
Colour: Red. pink and white
Issued: 2005 to the present
Varieties: Also called 'Just For You' (Style Two) HN 4236

U.S.: N/A
Can.: $390.00
U.K.: £150.00

HN 4747
All My Love
Designer: N. Pedley
Height: 8", 20.3 cm
Colour: Pink, red and white
Issued: 2005 to the present
Varieties: Also called 'Scarlett' HN 4408

U.S.: N/A
Can.: $390.00
U.K.: £150.00

HN 4748

HN 4749
Special Wishes
Designer: J. Bromley
Height: 8 ¾", 22.2 cm
Colour: Black dress, mottled grey shawl
Issued: 2005 to the present
Varieties: Also called 'Moonlight Serenade' HN 4530

U.S.: N/A
Can.: $390.00
U.K.: £150.00

HN 4750
Especially For You
Designer: J. Bromley
Height: 8 ¾", 22.2 cm
Colour: Rose pink and white
Issued: 2005 to the present
Varieties: Also called 'Best Wishes' (Style Two) HN 3971; 'Forever Yours' (Style Two) HN 4501; 'Kate' (Style Three) HN 4233

U.S.: N/I
Can.: $330.00
U.K.: £125.00

HN 4751
Gift of Love
Style Two
Designer: V. Annand
Height: 8", 20.3 cm
Colour: Blue with silver highlights
Issued: 2005 to the present
Varieties: Also called 'Claudia' HN 4320; 'Amelia' HN4327

U.S.: N/I
Can.: $330.00
U.K.: £125.00

HN 4752-4754

HN 4755
Autumn Days
Style Four
Designer: L. Harradine
Height: 6 ¾", 17.2 cm
Colour: Purple, pink and white
Issued: 2005 to the present
Varieties: Also called 'Top o' the Hill' HN 4778

U.S.: N/I
Can.: $390.00
U.K.: £150.00

HN 4756-4757

HN 4758
Charlotte
Style Six
Designer: N. Pedley
Height: 8 ¼", 21.0 cm
Colour: Pale blue and white with silver highlights
Issued: 2005-2005
Series: M. Doulton Exclusive

U.S.: N/A
Can.: $280.00
U.K.: £125.00

HN 4759
A Moment in Time
Designer: Unknown
Height: 6 ¾", 17.2 cm
Colour: Purple
Issued: 2005-2005
Series: 1. Best of the Classics
2. Petite

U.S.:	N/I
Can.:	$140.00
U.K.:	N/I

Exclusive to Canada

HN 4760
Amy
Style Four
Designer: N. Pedley
Height: 8 ½", 21.6 cm
Colour: Dark blue dress with silver design
Issued: 2005 to the present

U.S.:	N/A
Can.:	$390.00
U.K.:	£125.00

HN 4761
Contemplation
Style Two
Designer: N. Walsh
Height: 6 ¼", 15.9 cm
Colour: Pale pink dress; light brown chair
Issued: 2005 to the present
Series: Natural Beauty Collection

U.S.:	N/A
Can.:	$250.00
U.K.:	£99.00

HN 4762
Courtney
Style Two
Designer: V. Annand
Height: 8", 20.3 cm
Colour: Red, white and black
Issued: 2005 to the present
Series: Chic Trends

U.S.:	N/A
Can.:	$280.00
U.K.:	£125.00

HN 4763
Jessie
Designer: V. Annand
Height: 8 ¼", 21.0 cm
Colour: Blue, pale green and red
Issued: 2005 to the present
Series: Chic Trends

U.S.:	N/A
Can.:	$280.00
U.K.:	£125.00

HN 4764
Diana
Style Four
Designer: J. Bromley
Height: 8 ¾", 22.2 cm
Colour: Emerald green dress; white shawl
Issued: 2005 to the present

U.S.:	N/A
Can.:	$330.00
U.K.:	£125.00

HN 4765
Midnight Premier
Designer: J. Bromley
Height: 8 ¼", 21.0 cm
Colour: Red dress; yellow fan
Issued: 2005 to the present

U.S.:	N/A
Can.:	$390.00
U.K.:	£125.00

HN 4766
Olivia
Style Four
Designer: N. Pedley
Height: 8 ¾", 22.2 cm
Colour: Pink dress with silver accents
Issued: 2005 to the present

U.S.:	N/A
Can.:	$330.00
U.K.:	£125.00

HN 4767
Paige
Designer: V. Annand
Height: 8 ¼", 21.0 cm
Colour: Blue outfit with pink
           decoration on vest;
           pink boot and jewellery
Issued: 2005 to the present
Series: Chic Trends

U.S.:   N/A
Can.: $280.00
U.K.:   £125.00

HN 4768
Rebecca
Style Five
Designer: J. Bromley
Height: 8 ¾", 22.2 cm
Colour: Orange-peach dress;
           pink roses
Issued: 2005 to the present

U.S.:   N/A
Can.: $330.00
U.K.:   £125.00

HN 4769
Serenity
Style Two
Designer: N. Walsh
Height: 8", 20.3 cm
Colour: Pale pink
Issued: 2005 to the present
Series: Natural Beauty
           Collection

U.S.:   N/A
Can.: $250.00
U.K.:   £ 99.00

HN 4770
Tranquility
Style Two
Designer: N. Walsh
Height: 6", 15.0 cm
Colour: Pale turquoise
Issued: 2005 to the present
Series: Natural Beauty
           Collection

U.S.:   N/A
Can.: $250.00
U.K.:   £99.00

HN 4771
Tiffany
Designer: V. Annand
Height: 8 ¼", 21.0 cm
Colour: Pink, white and tan
Issued: 2005 to the present
Series: Chic Trends

U.S.:   N/A
Can.: $280.00
U.K.:   £125.00

HN 4777
Susan
Style Seven
Designer: P. Parsons
Height: 6 ¾", 17.2 cm
Colour: Blue, black and pink
Issued: 2005 to the present
Series: 1. Best of the Classics
           2. Petite

U.S.:   N/A
Can.: $185.00
U.K.:   £ 50.00

HN 4778
Top o' The Hill
Style Four
Designer: L. Harradine
Height: 6 ¾", 17.2 cm
Colour: Red and white
Issued: 2005 to the present
Varieties: Also called 'Autumn
           Days' HN 4755
Series: 1. Best of the Classics
           2. Petite

U.S.:   N/A
Can.: $185.00
U.K.:   £ 50.00

HN 4779
Karen
Style Five
Designer: M. Davies
Height: 6 ¾", 17.2 cm
Colour: Red and white
Issued: 2005 to the present
Series: 1. Best of the Classics
           2. Petite

U.S.:   N/A
Can.: $185.00
U.K.:   £ 50.00

HN 4772 - 4776

HN 4780
Rachel
Style Five
Designer: P. Gee
Height: 6 ¾", 17.2 cm
Colour: Gold and green
Issued: 2005 to the present
Series: 1. Best of the Classics
           2. Petite

U.S.:	N/A
Can.:	$185.00
U.K.:	£ 50.00

HN 4781
Buttercup
Style Four
Designer: M. Davies
Height: 6 ¾", 17.2 cm
Colour: Green and yellow
Issued: 2005 to the present
Series: 1. Best of the Classics
           2. Petite

U.S.:	N/A
Can.:	$185.00
U.K.:	£ 50.00

HN 4782
Amy
Style Five
Designer: P. Gee
Height: 6 ¾", 17.2 cm
Colour: Blue and rose
Issued: 2005-2005
Series: 1. Best of the Classics
           2. Petite Figure of the
              Year

U.S.:	N/A
Can.:	$200.00
U.K.:	£ 60.00

HN
A Winter's Walk
Designer: J. Bromley
Height: 9", 22.9 cm
Colour: Blue
Issued: 2004 in a limited
           edition of 7,500
Comm. by: Compton/Woodhouse

U.S.:	N/I
Can.:	N/I
U.K.:	£145.00

HN
A Winter's Walk
Designer: J. Bromley
Height: 9", 22.9 cm
Colour: Red
Issued: 2004 in a limited
           edition of 7,500
Comm. by: Compton/Woodhouse

U.S.:	N/I
Can.:	N/I
U.K.:	£145.00

HN
Autumn Stroll
Designer: John Bromley
Height: 9", 22.9 cm
Colour: White
Issued: 2004 in a limited
           edition of 7,500
Varieties: HN 4686
Comm. by: Compton/Woodhouse

U.S.:	N/I
Can.:	N/I
U.K.:	£99.00

Paige HN 4767 from the 2005 Chic Trends Series

ART IS LIFE SERIES

AIL1
Kiss
Designer:	A. Maslankowski
Height:	14 ¾, 37.5 cm
Colour:	White Parian
Issued:	2000 in a limited edition of 950
Series:	Art Is Life
U.S.:	**$375.00**
Can.:	**$450.00**
U.K.:	**£200.00**

Note: A limited edition of sixteen coloured models were auctioned in 2004.

AIL2
Love
Designer:	A. Maslankowski
Height:	11 ¼, 28.5 cm
Colour:	White Parian
Issued:	2000 in a limited edition of 950
Series:	Art Is Life
U.S.:	**$375.00**
Can.:	**$450.00**
U.K.:	**£200.00**

Note: A limited edition of four coloured models were auctioned in 2004.

AIL6
Girl Stretching
Designer:	A. Maslankowski
Height:	11 ¼", 28.5 cm
Colour:	White Parian
Issued:	2000 in a limited edition of 2,000
Series:	Art Is Life
U.S.:	**$325.00**
Can.:	**$400.00**
U.K.:	**£175.00**

AIL7
Girl With Pony Tail
Designer:	A. Maslankowski
Height:	10 ¾, 27.9 cm
Colour:	White Parian
Issued:	2000 in a limited edition of 2,000
Series:	Art Is Life
U.S.:	**$325.00**
Can.:	**$400.00**
U.K.:	**£175.00**

AIL8
Girl on Rock
Designer:	A. Maslankowski
Height:	9", 22.9 cm
Colour:	White Parian
Issued:	2000 in a limited edition of 2,000
Series:	Art Is Life
U.S.:	**$300.00**
Can.:	**$375.00**
U.K.:	**£150.00**

Note: A limited edition of six coloured models were auctioned in 2004.

AIL9
Ballerina
Designer:	A. Maslankowski
Height:	12", 30.5 cm
Colour:	White Parian
Issued:	2000 in a limited edition of 1,250
Series:	Art Is Life
U.S.:	**$400.00**
Can.:	**$475.00**
U.K.:	**£200.00**

AIL10
Ballet Dancer
Designer:	A. Maslankowski
Height:	14", 35.5 cm
Colour:	White Parian
Issued:	2000 in a limited edition of 1,250
Series:	Art Is Life
U.S.:	**$400.00**
Can.:	**$475.00**
U.K.:	**£200.00**

Note: A limited edition of five coloured models were auctioned in 2004.

CLASSIQUE SERIES

CL 3980
Isobel
Designer: T. Potts
Height: 10 ½", 26.7 cm
Colour: Yellow and blue
Issued: 1997-1999
Varieties: Also called 'Annabel'
CL 3981

U.S.: **$250.00**
Can.: **$300.00**
U.K.: **£125.00**

CL 3981
Annabel
Designer: T. Potts
Height: 10 ½", 26.7 cm
Colour: Black and yellow
Issued: 1997-2001
Varieties: Also called 'Isobel'
CL 3980

U.S.: **$250.00**
Can.: **$300.00**
U.K.: **£125.00**

CL 3982
Susanne
Designer: T. Potts
Height: 10 ½", 26.7 cm
Colour: Yellow dress and hat,
peach scarf
Issued: 1997-1998
Varieties: Also called 'Lucinda'
CL 3983

U.S.: **$250.00**
Can.: **$300.00**
U.K.: **£125.00**

CL 3983
Lucinda
Designer: T. Potts
Height: 10 ½", 26.7 cm
Colour: Green skirt and hat,
beige blouse
Issued: 1997-2001
Varieties: Also called 'Susanne'
CL 3982

U.S.: **$250.00**
Can.: **$300.00**
U.K.: **£125.00**

CL 3984
Faye
Designer: T. Potts
Height: 10 ½", 26.7 cm
Colour: Green flowered dress
Issued: 1997-2002
Varieties: Also called 'Stephanie'
CL 3985

U.S.: **$250.00**
Can.: **$300.00**
U.K.: **£125.00**

CL 3985
Stephanie
Designer: T. Potts
Height: 10 ½", 26.7 cm
Colour: Rose pink with gold
highlights
Issued: 1997-2001
Varieties: Also called 'Faye'
CL 3984

U.S.: **$250.00**
Can.: **$300.00**
U.K.: **£125.00**

CL 3986
Felicity
Designer: T. Potts
Height: 10 ½", 26.7 cm
Colour: Light brown, rose
and yellow
Issued: 1997-1999
Varieties: Also called 'Bethany'
CL 3987; CL 4103

U.S.: **$250.00**
Can.: **$300.00**
U.K.: **£125.00**

CL 3987
Bethany
Designer: T. Potts
Height: 10 ½", 26.7 cm
Colour: Yellow flowered dress
Issued: 1997-1998
Varieties: Also called 'Felicity'
CL 3986; CL 4103

U.S.: **$250.00**
Can.: **$300.00**
U.K.: **£125.00**

CL 3988
Penelope

Designer: T. Potts
Height: 10 ½", 26.7 cm
Colour: Pink with gold
highlights
Issued: 1997-1999
Varieties: Also called 'Vanessa'
CL 3989

U.S.:	**$250.00**
Can.:	**$300.00**
U.K.:	**£125.00**

CL 3989
Vanessa

Designer: T. Potts
Height: 10 ½", 26.7 cm
Colour: White and brown
Issued: 1997-2001
Varieties: Also called 'Penelope'
CL 3988

U.S.:	**$250.00**
Can.:	**$300.00**
U.K.:	**£125.00**

CL 3990
From This Day Forth

Designer: T. Potts
Height: 10 ½", 26.7 cm
Colour: White dress
Issued: 1997-1999

U.S.:	**$250.00**
Can.:	**$300.00**
U.K.:	**£125.00**

CL 3991
Christina

Designer: T. Potts
Height: 11 ¼", 28.5 cm
Colour: Pink and cream
Issued: 1998-2001
Varieties: Also called 'Theresa'
CL 3992

U.S.:	**$250.00**
Can.:	**$300.00**
U.K.:	**£125.00**

CL 3992
Theresa

Designer: T. Potts
Height: 11 ¼", 28.5 cm
Colour: Yellow and blue
Issued: 1998-2000
Varieties: Also called 'Christina'
CL 3991

U.S.:	**$250.00**
Can.:	**$300.00**
U.K.:	**£125.00**

CL 3993
Julia

Designer: T. Potts
Height: 11", 27.9 cm
Colour: Pink dress and pearls
Issued: 1998-2001
Varieties: Also called 'Chloe'
CL 4017; 'Helena'
CL 3994

U.S.:	**$250.00**
Can.:	**$300.00**
U.K.:	**£125.00**

CL 3994
Helena

Designer: T. Potts
Height: 11", 27.9 cm
Colour: Peach lustre dress
and pearls
Issued: 1998-2001
Varieties: Also called 'Chloe'
CL 4017; 'Julia'
CL 3993;

U.S.:	**$250.00**
Can.:	**$300.00**
U.K.:	**£125.00**

CL 3995
Kate

Designer: T. Potts
Height: 11", 27.9 cm
Colour: Green and pink
Issued: 1998-2000
Varieties: Also called 'Naomi'
CL 3996

U.S.:	**$275.00**
Can.:	**$350.00**
U.K.:	**£150.00**

CL 3996
Naomi
Designer: T. Potts
Height: 11", 27.9 cm
Colour: Cream and pink
Issued: 1998-2001
Varieties: Also called 'Kate'
           CL 3995

U.S.:	**$275.00**
Can.:	**$350.00**
U.K.:	**£150.00**

CL 3997
Lorna
Designer: T. Potts
Height: 10 ½", 26.7 cm
Colour: Pink and brown
Issued: 1998-1999
Varieties: Also called 'Harriet'
           CL 3998

U.S.:	**$250.00**
Can.:	**$300.00**
U.K.:	**£125.00**

CL 3998
Harriet
Designer: T. Potts
Height: 10 ½", 26.7 cm
Colour: Green and brown
Issued: 1998-2001
Varieties: Also called 'Lorne'
           CL 3997

U.S.:	**$250.00**
Can.:	**$300.00**
U.K.:	**£125.00**

CL 3999
Virginia
Designer: T. Potts
Height: 10 ½", 26.7 cm
Colour: Blue dress
Issued: 1998-1999
Varieties: Also called 'Nicola'
           CL 4000

U.S.:	**$250.00**
Can.:	**$300.00**
U.K.:	**£125.00**

CL 4000
Nicola
Designer: T. Potts
Height: 10 ½", 26.7 cm
Colour: Gold dress
Issued: 1998-2000
Varieties: Also called 'Virginia'
           CL 3999

U.S.:	**$250.00**
Can.:	**$300.00**
U.K.:	**£125.00**

CL 4001
Frances
Designer: T. Potts
Height: 8 ½", 21.6 cm
Colour: Pale pink and yellow
Issued: 1998-1999
Varieties: Also called 'Eve'
           CL 4002

U.S.:	**$250.00**
Can.:	**$300.00**
Ster:	**£125.00**

CL 4002
Eve
Designer: T. Potts
Height: 8 ½", 21.6 cm
Colour: Green
Issued: 1998-2001
Varieties: Also called 'Frances'
           CL 4001

U.S.:	**$250.00**
Can.:	**$300.00**
U.K.:	**£125.00**

CL 4003
To Love and To Cherish
Designer: T. Potts
Height: 11 ½", 29.2 cm
Colour: Cream
Issued: 1999-2001

U.S.:	**$250.00**
Can.:	**$300.00**
U.K.:	**$125.00**

CL 4004
Simone
Designer: T. Potts
Height: 11 ½", 29.2 cm
Colour: Rose-pink dress; lemon collar; light and dark brown coat
Issued: 1999-2001
U.S.: $250.00
Can.: $300.00
U.K.: £125.00

CL 4005
Bernadette
Designer: T. Potts
Height: 11", 27.9 cm
Colour: Orange flowers on white dress; white coat; light grey cuffs and collar
Issued: 1999-2001
U.S.: $275.00
Can.: $350.00
U.K.: £150.00

CL 4006
Tanya
Designer: T. Potts
Height: 11", 27.9 cm
Colour: Red dress and shoes; white gloves
Issued: 1999-2001
U.S.: $250.00
Can.: $300.00
U.K.: £125.00

CL 4007
Anyone For Tennis ?
Designer: T. Potts
Height: 10", 25.4 cm
Colour: White and lilac
Issued: 1999-2001
U.S.: $250.00
Can.: $300.00
U.K.: £125.00

CL 4008
To The Fairway
Designer: T. Potts
Height: 10", 25.4 cm
Colour: Green skirt with red, yellow and blue check; yellow jumper; blue coat; red golf bag
Issued: 1999-2001
U.S.: $275.00
Can.: $350.00
U.K.: £150.00

CL 4009
Elizabeth
Designer: T. Potts
Height: 10", 25.4 cm
Colour: Blue
Issued: 2000-2002
U.S.: $250.00
Can.: $300.00
U.K.: £125.00

Serial numbered

CL 4010
Philippa
Designer: T. Potts
Height: 10", 25.4 cm
Colour: Silver grey dress; grey shoes; white cat
Issued: 2000-2002
U.S.: $250.00
Can.: $300.00
U.K.: £125.00

CL 4011
Celebration
Designer: T. Potts
Height: 10", 25.4 cm
Colour: Silver and gold gown; white gloves
Issued: 2000-2002
U.S.: $250.00
Can.: $300.00
U.K.: £125.00

CL 4012
Gabrielle
Designer: T. Potts
Height: 10", 25.4 cm
Colour: Mottled purple top
           and scarf; peach
           trousers
Issued: 2000-2001

U.S.:   **$250.00**
Can.:   **$300.00**
U.K.:   **£125.00**

CL 4013
Taking the Reins
Designer: T. Potts
Height: 11 ½", 28.5 cm
Colour: Lilic blouse with
           purple bow, beige
           trousers, black and
           brown boots and hat
Issued: 2001-2002

U.S.:   **$250.00**
Can.:   **$300.00**
U.K.:   **£125.00**

CL 4014
At the Races
Designer: T. Potts
Height: 11 ¾", 29.8 cm
Colour: Pale pink
Issued: 2001-2002

U.S.:   **$250.00**
Can.:   **$300.00**
U.K.:   **£125.00**

CL 4016
Victoria
Designer: T. Potts
Height: 11 ¼", 28.5 cm
Colour: Blue dress with
           gold trim; light
           brown dogs
Issued: 2001-2002

U.S.:   **$275.00**
Can.:   **$350.00**
U.K.:   **£150.00**

CL 4017
Chloe
Designer: T. Potts
Height: 10 ¾", 27.8 cm
Colour: Black and silver
Issued: 2001-2002
Varieties: Also called 'Helena'
           CL 3994; 'Julia'
           CL 3993
Comm.by: Compton/Woodhouse

U.S.:   **$250.00**
Can.:   **$300.00**
U.K.:   **£125.00**

CL 4103
Felicity
Designer: T. Potts
Height: 10 ½", 26.7 cm
Colour: Bronze
Issued: c.2000
Varieties: CL 3986; Also called
           'Bethany' CL 3987

U.S.:   **$250.00**
Can.:   **$300.00**
U.K.:   **£125.00**

M SERIES

M 1
Victorian Lady
Style Two
Designer: L. Harradine
Height: 3 ¾", 9.5 cm
Colour: Pink and green
Issued: 1932-1945
Varieties: M 2, 25

U.S.:	**$700.00**
Can.:	**$850.00**
U.K.:	**£375.00**

M 2
Victorian Lady
Style Two
Designer: L. Harradine
Height: 3 ¾", 9.5 cm
Colour: Lavender and green
Issued: 1932-1945
Varieties: M 1, 25

U.S.:	**$575.00**
Can.:	**$725.00**
U.K.:	**£300.00**

M 3
Paisley Shawl
Style Two
Designer: L. Harradine
Height: 4", 10.1 cm
Colour: Lavender
Issued: 1932-1938
Varieties: M 4, 26

U.S.:	**$650.00**
Can.:	**$800.00**
U.K.:	**£350.00**

M 4
Paisley Shawl
Style Two
Designer: L. Harradine
Height: 4", 10.1 cm
Colour: Purple and green
Issued: 1932-1945
Varieties: M 3, 26

U.S.:	**$450.00**
Can.:	**$550.00**
U.K.:	**£250.00**

M 5
Sweet Anne
Style Two
Designer: L. Harradine
Height: 4", 10.1 cm
Colour: Lavender and green
Issued: 1932-1945
Varieties: HN 6, 27

U.S.:	**$500.00**
Can.:	**$600.00**
U.K.:	**£275.00**

M 6
Sweet Anne
Style Two
Designer: L. Harradine
Height: 4", 10.1 cm
Colour: Blue
Issued: 1932-1945
Varieties: HN 5, 27

U.S.:	**$500.00**
Can.:	**$600.00**
U.K.:	**£275.00**

M 7
Patricia
Style Two
Designer: L. Harradine
Height: 4", 10.1 cm
Colour: Pink and green
Issued: 1932-1945
Varieties: HN 8, 28

U.S.:	**$650.00**
Can.:	**$800.00**
U.K.:	**£350.00**

M 8
Patricia
Style Two
Designer: L. Harradine
Height: 4", 10.1 cm
Colour: Orange and yellow
Issued: 1932-1938
Varieties: HN 7, 28

U.S.:	**$650.00**
Can.:	**$800.00**
U.K.:	**£350.00**

M 9
Chloe
Style Two
Designer:	L. Harradine
Height:	2 ¾", 7.0 cm
Colour:	Pink
Issued:	1932-1945
Varieties:	HN 10, 29
U.S.:	**$600.00**
Can.:	**$725.00**
U.K.:	**£325.00**

M 10
Chloe
Style Two
Designer:	L. Harradine
Height:	2 ¾", 7.0 cm
Colour:	Lavender
Issued:	1932-1945
Varieties:	HN 9, 29
U.S.:	**$600.00**
Can.:	**$725.00**
U.K.:	**£325.00**

M 11
Bridesmaid
Style Two
Designer:	L. Harradine
Height:	3 ¾", 9.5 cm
Colour:	Pink and lavender
Issued:	1932-1938
Varieties:	M 12, 30
U.S.:	**$600.00**
Can.:	**$725.00**
U.K.:	**£325.00**

M 12
Bridesmaid
Style Two
Designer:	L. Harradine
Height:	3 ¾", 9.5 cm
Colour:	Yellow and lavender
Issued:	1932-1945
Varieties:	M 11, 30
U.S.:	**$500.00**
Can.:	**$600.00**
U.K.:	**£275.00**

M 13
Priscilla
Style Two
Designer:	L. Harradine
Height:	4", 10.1 cm
Colour:	Green and yellow
Issued:	1932-1938
Varieties:	M 14, 24
U.S.:	**$ 800.00**
Can.:	**$1,000.00**
U.K.:	**£ 400.00**

M 14
Priscilla
Style Two
Designer:	L. Harradine
Height:	4", 10.1 cm
Colour:	Lavender and pink
Issued:	1932-1945
Varieties:	M 13, 24
U.S.:	**$ 800.00**
Can.:	**$1,000.00**
U.K.:	**£ 400.00**

M 15
Pantalettes
Style Two
Designer:	L. Harradine
Height:	3 ¾", 9.5 cm
Colour:	Lavender
Issued:	1932-1945
Varieties:	M 16, 31
U.S.:	**$650.00**
Can.:	**$800.00**
U.K.:	**£350.00**

M 16
Pantalettes
Style Two
Designer:	L. Harradine
Height:	3 ¾", 9.5 cm
Colour:	Pink
Issued:	1932-1945
Varieties:	M 15, 31
U.S.:	**$650.00**
Can.:	**$800.00**
U.K.:	**£350.00**

M 17
Shepherd
Style Two
Designer: Unknown
Height: 3 ¾", 9.5 cm
Colour: Purple, pink
         and green
Issued: 1932-1938
Varieties: HN 709, M 19

U.S.:	$3,750.00
Can.:	$4,500.00
U.K.:	£2,000.00

M 18
Shepherdess
Style One
Designer: Unknown
Height: 3 ½", 8.9 cm
Colour: Green and lavender
Issued: 1932-1938
Varieties: HN 708, M 20

U.S.:	$3,750.00
Can.:	$4,500.00
U.K.:	£2,000.00

M 19
Shepherd
Style Two
Designer: Unknown
Height: 3 ¾", 9.5 cm
Colour: Purple, green
         and brown
Issued: 1932-1938
Varieties: HN 709, M 17

U.S.:	$3,750.00
Can.:	$4,500.00
U.K.:	£2,000.00

M 20
Shepherdess
Style One
Designer: Unknown
Height: 3 ¾", 9.5 cm
Colour: Yellow
Issued: 1932-1938
Varieties: HN 708, M 18

U.S.:	$3,750.00
Can.:	$4,500.00
U.K.:	£2,000.00

M 21
Polly Peachum
Style Three
Designer: L. Harradine
Height: 2 ¼", 5.7 cm
Colour: Pink
Issued: 1932-1945
Varieties: HN 698, 699, 757,
          758, 759, 760, 761,
          762, M 22, 23

U.S.:	$ 900.00
Can.:	$1,100.00
U.K.:	£ 450.00

M 22
Polly Peachum
Style Three
Designer: L. Harradine
Height: 2 ¼", 5.7 cm
Colour: Red and blue
Issued: 1932-1938
Varieties: HN 698, 699, 757,
          758, 759, 760, 761,
          762, M 21, 23

U.S.:	$1,650.00
Can.:	$2,000.00
U.K.:	£ 850.00

M 23
Polly Peachum
Style Three
Designer: L. Harradine
Height: 2 ¼", 5.7 cm
Colour: Purple, pink
         and white
Issued: 1932-1938
Varieties: HN 698, 699, 757,
          758, 759, 760, 761,
          762, M 21, 22

U.S.:	$1,650.00
Can.:	$2,000.00
U.K.:	£ 850.00

M 24
Priscilla
Style Two
Designer: L. Harradine
Height: 3 ¾", 9.5 cm
Colour: Red
Issued: 1932-1945
Varieties: M 13, 14

U.S.:	$600.00
Can.:	$750.00
U.K.:	£325.00

M 25
Victorian Lady
Style Two
Designer: L. Harradine
Height: 3 ¾", 9.5 cm
Colour: Lavender and pink
Issued: 1932-1945
Varieties: M 1, 2

U.S.:	**$625.00**
Can.:	**$775.00**
U.K.:	**£325.00**

M 26
Paisley Shawl
Style Two
Designer: L. Harradine
Height: 3 ¾", 9.5 cm
Colour: Green
Issued: 1932-1945
Varieties: M 3, 4

U.S.:	**$650.00**
Can.:	**$800.00**
U.K.:	**£350.00**

M 27
Sweet Anne
Style Two
Designer: L. Harradine
Height: 4", 10.1 cm
Colour: Red, blue and yellow
Issued: 1932-1945
Varieties: M 5, 6

U.S.:	**$625.00**
Can.:	**$775.00**
U.K.:	**£325.00**

M 28
Patricia
Style Two
Designer: L. Harradine
Height: 4", 10.1 cm
Colour: Lavender
Issued: 1932-1945
Varieties: M 7, 8

U.S.:	**$650.00**
Can.:	**$800.00**
U.K.:	**£350.00**

M 29
Chloe
Style Two
Designer: L. Harradine
Height: 2 ¾", 7.0 cm
Colour: Pink and yellow
Issued: 1932-1945
Varieties: M 9, 10

U.S.:	**$675.00**
Can.:	**$825.00**
U.K.:	**£350.00**

M 30
Bridesmaid
Style Two
Designer: L. Harradine
Height: 3 ¾", 9.5 cm
Colour: Pink and lavender
Issued: 1932-1945
Varieties: M 11, 12

U.S.:	**$625.00**
Can.:	**$775.00**
U.K.:	**£325.00**

M 31
Pantalettes
Style Two
Designer: L. Harradine
Height: 4", 10.1 cm
Colour: Green and blue
Issued: 1932-1945
Varieties: M 15, 16

U.S.:	**$750.00**
Can.:	**$900.00**
U.K.:	**£400.00**

M 32
Rosamund
Style Three
Designer: L. Harradine
Height: 4 ¼", 10.8 cm
Colour: Yellow
Issued: 1932-1945
Varieties: M 33

U.S.:	**$1,250.00**
Can.:	**$1,500.00**
U.K.:	**£ 675.00**

M 33
Rosamund
Style Three
Designer: L. Harradine
Height: 4", 10.1 cm
Colour: Red
Issued: 1932-1945
Varieties: M 32

  U.S.: $1,150.00
  Can.: $1,350.00
  U.K.: £   600.00

M 34
Denise
Style One
Designer: L. Harradine
Height: 4 ½", 11.4 cm
Colour: Green, red and blue
Issued: 1933-1945
Varieties: M 35

  U.S.: $1,400.00
  Can.: $1,750.00
  U.K.: £   700.00

M 35
Denise
Style One
Designer: L. Harradine
Height: 4 ½", 11.4 cm
Colour: Blue and pink
Issued: 1933-1945
Varieties: M 34

  U.S.: $1,650.00
  Can.: $2,000.00
  U.K.: £   850.00

M 36
Norma
Designer: L. Harradine
Height: 4 ½", 11.4 cm
Colour: Red and green
Issued: 1933-1945
Varieties: M 37

  U.S.: $1,450.00
  Can.: $1,750.00
  U.K.: £   750.00

M 37
Norma
Designer: L. Harradine
Height: 4 ½", 11.4 cm
Colour: Blue, red
        and white
Issued: 1933-1945
Varieties: M 36

  U.S.: $1,650.00
  Can.: $2,000.00
  U.K.: £   900.00

M 38
Robin
Designer: L. Harradine
Height: 2 ½", 6.4 cm
Colour: Pink and lavender
Issued: 1933-1945
Varieties: M 39

  U.S.: $ 925.00
  Can.: $1,150.00
  U.K.: £   500.00

M 39
Robin
Designer: L. Harradine
Height: 2 ½", 6.4 cm
Colour: Blue and green
Issued: 1933-1945
Varieties: M 38

  U.S.: $ 925.00
  Can.: $1,150.00
  U.K.: £   500.00

M 40
Erminie
Designer: L. Harradine
Height: 4", 10.1 cm
Colour: White and pink
Issued: 1933-1945

  U.S.: $1,150.00
  Can.: $1,500.00
  U.K.: £   625.00

M 41
Mr. Pickwick
Style One
Designer: L. Harradine
Height: 4", 10.1 cm
Colour: Yellow and black
Issued: 1932-1983
Varieties: HN 529
Series: Dickens (Series One)

U.S.:	**$115.00**
Can.:	**$150.00**
U.K.:	**£ 65.00**

■

M 42
Mr. Micawber
Style One
Designer: L. Harradine
Height: 4", 10.1 cm
Colour: Yellow and black
Issued: 1932-1983
Varieties: HN 532
Series: Dickens (Series One)

U.S.:	**$115.00**
Can.:	**$150.00**
U.K.:	**£ 65.00**

Prices are based on bone china
bodies for Dickens (Series One).

M 43
Pecksniff
Style One
Designer: L. Harradine
Height: 4 ¼", 10.8 cm
Colour: Black
Issued: 1932-1982
Varieties: HN 535
Series: Dickens (Series One)

U.S.:	**$115.00**
Can.:	**$150.00**
U.K.:	**£ 65.00**

M 44
Fat Boy
Style One
Designer: L. Harradine
Height: 4 ¼", 10.8 cm
Colour: Blue and white
Issued: 1932-1983
Varieties: HN 530
Series: Dickens (Series One)

U.S.:	**$125.00**
Can.:	**$150.00**
U.K.:	**£ 65.00**

M 45
Uriah Heep
Style One
Designer: L. Harradine
Height: 4", 10.1 cm
Colour: Black
Issued: 1932-1983
Varieties: HN 545
Series: Dickens (Series One)

U.S.:	**$115.00**
Can.:	**$150.00**
U.K.:	**£ 65.00**

M 46
Sairey Gamp
Style One
Designer: L. Harradine
Height: 4", 10.1 cm
Colour: Green
Issued: 1932-1983
Varieties: HN 533
Series: Dickens (Series One)

U.S.:	**$115.00**
Can.:	**$150.00**
U.K.:	**£ 65.00**

M 47
Tony Weller
Style Two
Designer: L. Harradine
Height: 4", 10.1 cm
Colour: Green, black,
             red and yellow
Issued: 1932-1981
Varieties: HN 544
Series: Dickens (Series One)

U.S.:	**$115.00**
Can.:	**$150.00**
U.K.:	**£ 65.00**

M 48
Sam Weller
Designer: L. Harradine
Height: 4", 10.1 cm
Colour: Yellow and
             brown
Issued: 1932-1981
Varieties: HN 531
Series: Dickens (Series One)

U.S.:	**$125.00**
Can.:	**$150.00**
U.K.:	**£ 65.00**

M 49
Fagin
Style One
Designer: L. Harradine
Height: 4", 10.1 cm
Colour: Brown
Issued: 1932-1983
Varieties: HN 534
Series: Dickens (Series One)

  U.S.:   **$125.00**
  Can.:   **$150.00**
  U.K.:   **£ 65.00**

M 50
Stiggins
Designer: L. Harradine
Height: 4", 10.1 cm
Colour: Black
Issued: 1932-1981
Varieties: HN 536
Series: Dickens (Series One)

  U.S.:   **$115.00**
  Can.:   **$150.00**
  U.K.:   **£ 65.00**

M 51
Little Nell
Designer: L. Harradine
Height: 4 ¼", 10.8 cm
Colour: Pink
Issued: 1932-1983
Varieties: HN 540
Series: Dickens (Series One)

  U.S.:   **$125.00**
  Can.:   **$150.00**
  U.K.:   **£ 65.00**

M 52
Alfred Jingle
Designer: L. Harradine
Height: 3 ¾", 9.5 cm
Colour: Black and white
Issued: 1932-1981
Varieties: HN 541
Series: Dickens (Series One)

  U.S.:   **$125.00**
  Can.:   **$150.00**
  U.K.:   **£ 65.00**

M 53
Buz Fuz
Designer: L. Harradine
Height: 4", 10.1 cm
Colour: Black and red
Issued: 1932-1983
Varieties: HN 538
Series: Dickens (Series One)

  U.S.:   **$125.00**
  Can.:   **$150.00**
  U.K.:   **£ 65.00**

M 54
Bill Sykes
Designer: L. Harradine
Height: 4 ¼", 10.8 cm
Colour: Black and brown
Issued: 1932-1981
Varieties: HN 537
Series: Dickens (Series One)

  U.S.:   **$125.00**
  Can.:   **$150.00**
  U.K.:   **£ 65.00**

M 55
Artful Dodger
Designer: L. Harradine
Height: 4 ¼", 10.8 cm
Colour: Black and brown
Issued: 1932-1983
Varieties: HN 546
Series: Dickens (Series One)

  U.S.:   **$125.00**
  Can.:   **$150.00**
  U.K.:   **£ 65.00**

M 56
Tiny Tim
Designer: L. Harradine
Height: 3 ¾", 9.5 cm
Colour: Black and brown
Issued: 1932-1983
Varieties: HN 539
Series: Dickens (Series One)

  U.S.:   **$115.00**
  Can.:   **$150.00**
  U.K.:   **£ 65.00**

M 64
Veronica
Style Two
Designer: L. Harradine
Height: 4 ½", 10.8 cm
Colour: Pink
Issued: 1934-1949
Varieties: M 70

U.S.:	**$1,100.00**
Can.:	**$1,350.00**
U.K.:	**£ 600.00**

M 65
June
Style Two
Designer: L. Harradine
Height: 4 ¼", 10.8 cm
Colour: Pink and lavender
Issued: 1935-1949
Varieties: M 71

U.S.:	**$1,000.00**
Can.:	**$1,300.00**
U.K.:	**£ 600.00**

M 66
Monica
Style Two
Designer: L. Harradine
Height: 3", 7.6 cm
Colour: Blue and pink
Issued: 1935-1949
Varieties: M 72

U.S.:	**$1,200.00**
Can.:	**$1,500.00**
U.K.:	**£ 675.00**

M 67
Dainty May
Style Two
Designer: L. Harradine
Height: 4", 10.1 cm
Colour: Turquoise and pink
Issued: 1935-1949
Varieties: M 73

U.S.:	**$1,200.00**
Can.:	**$1,500.00**
U.K.:	**£ 675.00**

M 68
Mirabel
Style Two
Designer: L. Harradine
Height: 4", 10.1 cm
Colour: Pink and green
Issued: 1936-1949
Varieties: M 74

U.S.:	**$1,000.00**
Can.:	**$1,250.00**
U.K.:	**£ 600.00**

M 69
Janet
Style Two
Designer: L. Harradine
Height: 4", 10.1 cm
Colour: Blue and white
Issued: 1936-1949
Varieties: M 75

U.S.:	**$ 900.00**
Can.:	**$1,100.00**
U.K.:	**£ 450.00**

M 70
Veronica
Style Two
Designer: L. Harradine
Height: 4 ¼", 10.8 cm
Colour: Green
Issued: 1936-1949
Varieties: M 64

U.S.:	**$1,400.00**
Can.:	**$1,700.00**
U.K.:	**£ 775.00**

M 71
June
Style Two
Designer: L. Harradine
Height: 4 ¼", 10.8 cm
Colour: Lavender and green
Issued: 1936-1949
Varieties: M 65

U.S.:	**$1,350.00**
Can.:	**$1,600.00**
U.K.:	**£ 725.00**

M 72
Monica
Style Two
Designer: L. Harradine
Height: 3", 7.6 cm
Colour: Blue and white
Issued: 1936-1949
Varieties: M 66

U.S.:	**$1,400.00**
Can.:	**$1,700.00**
U.K.:	£ 775.00

M 73
Dainty May
Style Two
Designer: L. Harradine
Height: 4", 10.1 cm
Colour: Pink and turquoise
Issued: 1936-1949
Varieties: M 67

U.S.:	**$1,400.00**
Can.:	**$1,750.00**
U.K.:	£ 775.00

M 74
Mirabel
Style Two
Designer: L. Harradine
Height: 4", 10.1 cm
Colour: Turquoise and red
Issued: 1936-1949
Varieties: M 68

U.S.:	**$1,200.00**
Can.:	**$1,500.00**
U.K.:	£ 650.00

M 75
Janet
Style Two
Designer: L. Harradine
Height: 4", 10.1 cm
Colour: Purple
Issued: 1936-1949
Varieties: M 69

U.S.:	**$1,000.00**
Can.:	**$1,250.00**
U.K.:	£ 600.00

M 76
Bumble
Designer: L. Harradine
Height: 4", 10.1 cm
Colour: Green and red
Issued: 1939-1982
Series: Dickens (Series One)

U.S.:	**$115.00**
Can.:	**$150.00**
U.K.:	£ 65.00

M 77
Captain Cuttle
Designer: L. Harradine
Height: 4", 10.1 cm
Colour: Yellow and black
Issued: 1939-1982
Series: Dickens (Series One)

U.S.:	**$115.00**
Can.:	**$150.00**
U.K.:	£ 65.00

M 78
Windflower
Style Three
Designer: L. Harradine
Height: 4", 10.1 cm
Colour: Red and pink
Issued: 1939-1949
Varieties: M 79

U.S.:	**$1,400.00**
Can.:	**$1,750.00**
U.K.:	£ 750.00

M 79
Windflower
Style Three
Designer: L. Harradine
Height: 4", 10.1 cm
Colour: Blue and green
Issued: 1939-1949
Varieties: M 78

U.S.:	**$1,400.00**
Can.:	**$1,750.00**
U.K.:	£ 750.00

M 80
Goody Two Shoes
Style Two
Designer: L. Harradine
Height: 4", 10.1 cm
Colour: Pink and blue
Issued: 1939-1949
Varieties: M 81

U.S.:	**$1,500.00**
Can.:	**$1,750.00**
U.K.:	**£ 800.00**

M 81
Goody Two Shoes
Style Two
Designer: L. Harradine
Height: 4", 10.1 cm
Colour: Lavender and pink
Issued: 1939-1949
Varieties: M 80

U.S.:	**$1,500.00**
Can.:	**$1,800.00**
U.K.:	**£ 800.00**

M 82
Bo-Peep
Style Three
Designer: L. Harradine
Height: 4", 10.1 cm
Colour: Pink
Issued: 1939-1949
Varieties: M 83

U.S.:	**$1,500.00**
Can.:	**$1,800.00**
U.K.:	**£ 750.00**

M 83
Bo-Peep
Style Three
Designer: L. Harradine
Height: 4", 10.1 cm
Colour: Purple
Issued: 1939-1949
Varieties: M 82

U.S.:	**$1,500.00**
Can.:	**$1,800.00**
U.K.:	**£ 750.00**

M 84
Maureen
Style Two
Designer: L. Harradine
Height: 4", 10.1 cm
Colour: Pink
Issued: 1939-1949
Varieties: M 85

U.S.:	**$1,400.00**
Can.:	**$1,750.00**
U.K.:	**£ 750.00**

M 85
Maureen
Style Two
Designer: L. Harradine
Height: 4", 10.1 cm
Colour: Purple
Issued: 1939-1949
Varieties: M 84

U.S.:	**$1,400.00**
Can.:	**$1,750.00**
U.K.:	**£ 750.00**

M 86
Mrs. Bardell
Designer: L. Harradine
Height: 4 ¼", 10.8 cm
Colour: Green
Issued: 1949-1982
Series: Dickens (Series One)

U.S.:	**$125.00**
Can.:	**$150.00**
U.K.:	**£ 65.00**

M 87
Scrooge
Designer: L. Harradine
Height: 4", 10.1 cm
Colour: Brown
Issued: 1949-1982
Series: Dickens (Series One)

U.S.:	**$125.00**
Can.:	**$150.00**
U.K.:	**£ 65.00**

M 88
David Copperfield
Designer:	L. Harradine
Height:	4 ¼", 10.8 cm
Colour:	Black and tan
Issued:	1949-1983
Series:	Dickens (Series One)
U.S.:	**$125.00**
Can.:	**$150.00**
U.K.:	**£ 65.00**

M 89
Oliver Twist
Designer:	L. Harradine
Height:	4 ¼", 10.8 cm
Colour:	Black and tan
Issued:	1949-1983
Series:	Dickens (Series One)
U.S.:	**$125.00**
Can.:	**$150.00**
U.K.:	**£ 65.00**

M 90
Dick Swiveller
Designer:	L. Harradine
Height:	4 ¼", 10.8 cm
Colour:	Black and tan
Issued:	1949-1981
Series:	Dickens (Series One)
U.S.:	**$125.00**
Can.:	**$150.00**
U.K.:	**£ 65.00**

M 91
Trotty Veck
Designer:	L. Harradine
Height:	4 ¼", 10.8 cm
Colour:	Black and brown
Issued:	1949-1982
Series:	Dickens (Series One)
U.S.:	**$125.00**
Can.:	**$150.00**
U.K.:	**£ 65.00**

M 200
Christine
Style Eight
Designer:	M. Davies
Remodeller:	Unknown
Height:	2", 5.0 cm
Colour:	White, pink, pale blue and yelllow
Issued:	2004 to the present
U.S.:	**$30.00**
Can.:	**$39.95**
U.K.:	**£15.00**

M 201
Elaine
Style Three
Designer:	M. Davies
Remodeller:	Unknown
Height:	2", 5.0 cm
Colour:	Blue and white
Issued:	2004 to the present
U.S.:	**$30.00**
Can.:	**$39.95**
U.K.:	**£15.00**

M 202
Elizabeth
Style Four
Designer:	B. Franks
Remodeller:	Unknown
Height:	2", 5.0 cm
Colour:	White, yellow and green
Issued:	2004 to the present
U.S.:	**$30.00**
Can.:	**$39.95**
U.K.:	**£15.00**

M 203
Jane
Style Six
Designer:	D. V. Tootles
Remodeller:	Unknown
Height:	2", 5.0 cm
Colour:	Blue-green, blue, white and yellow
Issued:	2004 to the present
U.S.:	**$30.00**
Can.:	**$39.95**
U.K.:	**£15.00**

M 204
Karen
Style Four
Designer: M. Davies
Remodeller: Unknown
Height: 2", 5.0 cm
Colour: Red, white and black
Issued: 2004 to the present

U.S.: $30.00
Can.: $39.95
U.K.: £15.00

M 205
Margaret
Style Four
Designer: M. Davies
Remodeller: Unknown
Height: 2", 5.0 cm
Colour: White dress; pale blue sash
Issued: 2004 to the present

U.S.: $30.00
Can.: $39.95
U.K.: £15.00

M 206
Ninette
Style Three
Designer: M. Davies
Remodeller: Unknown
Height: 2", 5.0 cm
Colour: Yellow dress; white ruffles; pink shading
Issued: 2004 to the present

U.S.: $30.00
Can.: $39.95
U.K.: £15.00

M 207
Rachel
Style Three
Designer: P. Gee
Remodeller: Unknown
Height: 2", 5.0 cm
Colour: Red cloak with white trim; pale lemon dress
Issued: 2004 to the present

U.S.: $30.00
Can.: $39.95
U.K.: £15.00

M 208
Susan
Style Six
Designer: P. Parsons
Remodeller: Unknown
Height: 2", 5.0 cm
Colour: White, pink and black
Issued: 2004 to the present

U.S.: $30.00
Can.: $39.95
U.K.: £15.00

M 209
Victoria
Style Three
Designer: M. Davies
Remodeller: Unknown
Height: 2", 5.0 cm
Colour: Red, pink and white
Issued: 2004 to the present

U.S.: $30.00
Can.: $39.95
U.K.: £15.00

M 210
Bess
Style Two
Designer: L. Harradine
Remodeller: Unknown
Height: 2", 5.0 cm
Colour: Blue cloak with red lining; pink and white dress
Issued: 2004 to the present

U.S.: $30.00
Can.: $39.95
U.K.: £15.00

M 211
Buttercup
Style Three
Designer: M. Davies
Remodeller: Unknown
Height: 2", 5.0 cm
Colour: Green and yellow
Issued: 2004 to the present

U.S.: $30.00
Can.: $39.95
U.K.: £15.00

M 212
Gail
Style Three
Designer: P. Gee
Remodeller: Unknown
Height: 2", 5.0 cm
Colour: Red, white, black
               and gold
Issued: 2004 to the present

U.S.:	**$30.00**
Can.:	**$39.95**
U.K.:	**£15.00**

M 213
Helen
Style Four
Designer: N. Pedley
Remodeller: Unknown
Height: 2", 5.0 cm
Colour: Blue, white, yellow
               and green
Issued: 2004 to the present

U.S.:	**$30.00**
Can.:	**$39.95**
U.K.:	**£15.00**

M 214
Laura
Style Four
Designer: P. Parsons
Remodeller: Unknown
Height: 2", 5.0 cm
Colour: Dark blue, white,
               black and red
Issued: 2004 to the present

U.S.:	**$30.00**
Can.:	**$39.95**
U.K.:	**£15.00**

M 215
Soiree
Style Two
Designer: M. Davies
Remodeller: Unknown
Height: 2", 5.0 cm
Colour: Dark and light green
               white and cream
Issued: 2004 to the present

U.S.:	**$30.00**
Can.:	**$39.95**
U.K.:	**£15.00**

M 216
Stephanie
Style Four
Designer: M. Davies
Remodeller: Unknown
Height: 2", 5.0 cm
Colour: Gold and white
Issued: 2004 to the present

U.S.:	**$30.00**
Can.:	**$39.95**
U.K.:	**£15.00**

M 217
Top o' the Hill
Style Three
Designer: L. Harradine
Remodeller: Unknown
Height: 2", 5.0 cm
Colour: Red dress; mottled
               pink and green shawl
               and petticoats
Issued: 2004 to the present

U.S.:	**$30.00**
Can.:	**$39.95**
U.K.:	**£15.00**

M 218
Annabel
Style Two
Designer: R. Tabbenor
Remodeller: Unknown
Height: 2", 5.0 cm
Colour: White, blue, rose pink
               and beige
Issued: 2004 to the present

U.S.:	**$30.00**
Can.:	**$39.95**
U.K.:	**£15.00**

M 219
Barbara
Style Five
Designer: P. Gee
Remodeller: Unknown
Height: 2", 5.0 cm
Colour: Pink, blue and white
Issued: 2004 to the present

U.S.:	**$30.00**
Can.:	**$39.95**
U.K.:	**£15.00**

COLLECTING BY TYPE OR SERIES

AGE OF CHIVALRY

Sir Edward	HN 2370
Sir Ralph	HN 2371
Sir Thomas	HN 2372

AGE OF INNOCENCE

Feeding Time	HN 3373
First Outing	HN 3377
Making Friends	HN 3372
Puppy Love	HN 3371

AGE OF JAZZ

Saxophone Player	HN 4284
Trumpet Player	HN 4283

ART DECO

Destiny	HN 4164
Ecstasy	HN 4163
Optimism	HN 4165
Wisdom (Style Two)	HN 4166

ART IS LIFE

Ballerina	AIL 9
Ballet Dancer	AIL 10
Girl On Rock	AIL 8
Girl Stretching	AIL 6
Girl With Pony Tail	AIL 7
Kiss	AIL 1
Love	AIL 2

BATHERS COLLECTION

Bather (Second Version)	HN 4244
Lido Lady (Second Version)	HN 4247
Sunshine Girl (Second Version)	HN 4245
Swimmer, Style Two (Second Version)	HN 4246

BEGGAR'S OPERA

Beggar (Style One)	HN 526, 591
Beggar (Style Two)	HN 2175
Captain MacHeath	HN 464, 590, 1256
Highwayman	HN 527, 592, 1257
Lucy Lockett (Style One)	HN 485
Lucy Lockett (Style Two)	HN 524
Lucy Lockett (Style Three)	HN 695, 696
Polly Peachum (Style One)	HN 463, 465, 550, 589, 614, 680, 693
Polly Peachum (Style Two)	HN 489, 549, 620, 694, 734
Polly Peachum (Style Three)	HN 698, 699, 757, 758, 759, 760, 761, 762, M21, 22, 23

ARNOLD BENNETT

Anna of the Five Towns	HN 3865
Arnold Bennett	HN 4360
Clara Hamps	HN 4162
Countess of Chell	HN 3867
Sophia Baines	HN 4167

BEST OF THE CLASSICS

A Moment in Time	HN 4759
Amy (Style Five)	HN 4782
Buttercup (Style Four)	HN 4781
Karen (Style Five)	HN 4779
Rachel (Style Five)	HN 4780
Susan (Style Seven)	HN 4777
Top o' the Hill (Style Four)	HN 4778

BRITISH SPORTING HERITAGE

Ascot (Style Two)	HN 3471
Croquet	HN 3470
Henley	HN 3367
Wimbledon	HN 3366

CHARACTER SCULPTURES (RESIN)

Bill Sikes	HN 3785
Bowls Player	HN 3780
Captain Hook	HN 3636
Cyrano de Bergerac	HN 3751
D'Artagnan (Style One)	HN 3638
Dick Turpin (Style Two)	HN 3637
Fagin (Style Two)	HN 3752
Gulliver	HN 3750
Long John Silver (Style Two)	HN 3719
Oliver Twist and The Artful Dodger	HN 3786
Pied Piper (Style Two)	HN 3721
Robin Hood (Style Two)	HN 3720
Sherlock Holmes	HN 3639
Sir Francis Drake	HN 3770
Wizard, (Style Two)	HN 3722, 3732

CHARACTERS FROM CHILDREN'S LITERATURE

Heidi	HN 2975
Huckleberry Finn	HN 2927
Little Lord Fauntleroy	HN 2972
Pollyanna	HN 2965
Tom Brown	HN 2941
Tom Sawyer	HN 2926

CHARITIES
Breast Cancer

1998 Hope (Style Two)	HN 4097
1999 Faith (Style Two)	HN 4151
2000 Charity (Style Two)	HN 4243
2001 New Dawn	HN 4314
2002 Spring Morning (Style Three)	HN 4451
2003 Love of Life	HN 4529
2004 Free Spirit (Style Three)	HN 4609
2004 Summer's Dream	HN 4660

Compton & Woodhouse

2000 Kate (Style Three)	HN 4233

Save The Children

Harmony (Style Three)	HN 4567
Independence	HN 4375
Unity	HN 4485

CHARLESTON

Charlotte (Style Three)	HN 3810, 3811, 3812, 3813
Constance (Style Two)	HN 3930, 3933
Daisy (Style Three)	HN 3802, 3803, 3804, 3805
Eliza (Style Three)	HN 3798, 3799, 3800, 3801
Ellen (Style Two)	HN 3816, 3819
Emily (Style Three)	HN 3806, 3807, 3808, 3809
Harriet (Style Two)	HN 3794, 3795, 3796, 3997
Millie (Style One)	HN 3945, 3946
Sophie (Style Three)	HN 3790, 3791, 3792, 3793

CHELSEA

Annabel Vision in Red	HN 4493
Becky (Style Two)	HN 4322
Bethany	HN 4326
Ellie (Style One)	HN 4046
Georgina (Style Two)	HN 4047
Hayley	HN 4556
Isabel (Style One)	HN 3716
Jenny	HN 4423

Katie (Style Three)	HN 4323
Kathryn (Style Two)	HN 4040
Melinda	HN 4209
Olivia (Style Three)	HN 3717
Zoe	HN 4208

CHIC TRENDS

Courtney (Style Two)	HN 4762
Jessie	HN 4763
Paige	HN 4767
Tiffany	HN 4771

CHILDHOOD DAYS

And One For You	HN 2970
And So To Bed	HN 2966
As Good As New	HN 2971
Dressing Up (Style One)	HN 2964
I'm Nearly Ready	HN 2976
It Won't Hurt	HN 2963
Just One More	HN 2980
Please Keep Still	HN 2967
Save Some For Me	HN 2959
Stick 'em Up	HN 2981

CHILDREN OF THE BLITZ

Boy Evacuee	HN 3202
Girl Evacuee	HN 3203
Homecoming	HN 3295
Welcome Home	HN 3299

CHRISTMAS CHOIR COLLECTION

Carol Singer (Boy)	HN 4031
Carol Singer (Brother)	HN 4290
Carol Singer (Girl)	HN 4032
Carol Singer (Sister)	HN 4291
Carol Singer With Lantern	HN 4256

CHRISTMAS FIGURES

Christmas Day 1999	HN 4214
Christmas Day 2000	HN 4242
Christmas Day 2001	HN 4315
Christmas Day 2002	HN 4422
Christmas Day 2003	HN 4552
Christmas Day 2004	HN 4558

CLASSIC MOVIES

Scarlett O'Hara	HN 4200

CLOWNS

Joker (Style One)	HN 3196
Joker (Style Two)	HN 2252
Partners	HN 3119
Slapdash	HN 2277
Tip-Toe	HN 3293
Tumbler	HN 3183
Tumbling	HN 3283, 3289
Will He, Won't He	HN 3275

CLUB MEMBERSHIP FIGURE

1996 Welcome	HN 3764
1997 Joy (Style Two)	HN 3875
1998 Harmony (Style Two)	HN 4096
1999 Melody (Style Two)	HN 4117
2000 Greetings	HN 4250
2002 Cherish	HN 4442
2003 Charmed	HN 4445
2004 Springtime (Style Four)	HN 4586
2005 Summer (Style Four)	HN 4587
2006 Autumn (Style Four)	HN 4588
2007 Winter (Style Four)	HN 4589

COUNTRY MAIDS

Dairy Maid	HN 4249
Fair Maid	HN 4222
Maid of the Meadow	HN 4316
Milk Maid (Style Three)	HN 4305

DANCERS OF THE WORLD

Balinese Dancer	HN 2808
Breton Dancer	HN 2383
Chinese Dancer	HN 2840
Indian Temple Dancer	HN 2830
Kurdish Dancer	HN 2867
Mexican Dancer	HN 2866
North American Indian Dancer	HN 2809
Philippine Dancer	HN 2439
Polish Dancer	HN 2836
Scottish Highland Dancer	HN 2436
Spanish Flamenco Dancer	HN 2831
West Indian Dancer	HN 2384

DICKENS
Series One

Alfred Jingle	HN 541, M52
Artful Dodger	HN 546, M55
Bill Sykes	HN 537, M54
Bumble	M76
Buz Fuz	HN 538, M53
Captain Cuttle	M77
David Copperfield	M88
Dick Swiveller	M90
Fagin (Style One)	HN 534, M49
Fat Boy (Style One)	HN 530, M44
Little Nell	HN 540, M51
Mr. Micawber (Style One)	HN 532, M42
Mr. Pickwick (Style One)	HN 529, M41
Mrs. Bardell	M86
Oliver Twist	M89
Pecksniff (Style One)	HN 535, M43
Sairey Gamp (Style One)	HN 533, M46
Sam Weller	HN 531, M48
Scrooge	M87
Stiggins	HN 536, M50
Tiny Tim	HN 539, M56
Tony Weller (Style Two)	HN 544, M47
Trotty Veck	M91
Uriah Heep (Style One)	HN 545, M45

Series Two

Fat Boy (Style Two)	HN 555, 1893
Mr. Micawber (Style Two)	HN 557, 1895
Mr. Pickwick (Style Two)	HN 556, 1894
Pecksniff (Style Two)	HN 553, 1891
Sairey Gamp (Style Two)	HN 558, 1896
Uriah Heep (Style Two)	HN 554, 1892

Series Three

Fat Boy (Style Three)	HN 2096
Mr. Micawber (Style Three)	HN 2097
Mr. Pickwick (Style Three)	HN 2099
Pecksniff (Style Three)	HN 2098
Sairey Gamp (Style Three)	HN 2100
Uriah Heep (Style Three)	HN 2101

DISNEY PRINCESS COLLECTION

Ariel	HN 3831
Aurora	HN 3833
Belle (Style Four)	HN 3830
Cinderella (Style One)	HN 3677
Jasmine (Style Two)	HN 3832
Snow White	HN 3678

DISNEY VILLAINS

Cruella De Vil	HN 3839
Maleficent	HN 3840
Queen	HN 3847
Witch	HN 3848

DOULTON COLLECTORS ROADSHOW EVENTS

1992 Ninette (Style One)	HN 3417
1992 Victoria (Style One)	HN 3416
1993 Maria	HN 3381
1993 Thinking of You	HN 3490
1994 Pauline (Style Three)	HN 3643
1995 Elaine (Style One)	HN 3741
1995 Jacqueline (Style Three)	HN 3689
1995 Lynne (Style One)	HN 3740
1996 Stephanie (Style Two)	HN 3759
1997 First Bloom	HN 3913
1997 Lauren (Style Two)	HN 3872
1998 Samantha (Style Three)	HN 4043

EDWARDIAN STRING QUARTET

Cello (Style Two)	HN 3707
First Violin	HN 3704
Second Violin	HN 3705
Viola	HN 3706

EGYPTIAN QUEENS

Ankhesenamun	HN 4190
Cleopatra (Style Two)	HN 4264
Hatshepsut	HN 4191
Nefertiti	HN 3844

ELEGANCE
Series One

Claudine	HN 3055
Danielle (Style One)	HN 3056
Dominique	HN 3054
Francoise	HN 2897
Martine	HN 3053
Monique	HN 2880

Series Two

Au Revoir (Style One)	HN 3723
Country Girl (Style Two)	HN 3856
Free Spirit (Style Two)	HN 3728
Lambing Time (Style Two)	HN 3855
Morning Walk	HN 3860
Spring Morning (Style Two)	HN 3725
Summer Breeze(Style One)	HN 3724
Sweet Bouquet (Style Two)	HN 3859

ENCHANTMENT

April Shower	HN 3024
Fairyspell	HN 2979
Lyric	HN 2757
Magic Dragon	HN 2977
Magpie Ring	HN 2978
Musicale	HN 2756
Queen of the Dawn	HN 2437
Queen of the Ice	HN 2435
Rumpelstiltskin	HN 3025
Serenade	HN 2753
Sonata	HN 2438

ENTERTAINERS

Charlie Chaplin	HN 2771
Groucho Marx	HN 2777
Oliver Hardy	HN 2775
Stan Laurel	HN 2774

FABLED BEAUTIES

Rapunzel	HN 3841
Scheherazade	HN 3835

FAIRYTALE PRINCESSES

Cinderella (Style Two)	HN 3991
Sleeping Beauty (Style Two)	HN 4000

FIGURE OF THE MONTH

January (Style One)	HN 2697
February (Style One)	HN 2703
March (Style One)	HN 2707
April (Style One)	HN 2708
May (Style Two)	HN 2711
June (Style Three)	HN 2790
July (Style One)	HN 2794
August (Style One)	HN 3165
September (Style One)	HN 3166
October (Style One)	HN 2693
November (Style One)	HN 2695
December (Style One)	HN 2696

FIGURE OF THE YEAR

1991 Amy (Style Two)	HN 3316
1992 Mary (Style Two)	HN 3375
1993 Patricia (Style Four)	HN 3365
1994 Jennifer (Style Three)	HN 3447
1995 Deborah (Style Two)	HN 3644
1996 Belle (Style Three)	HN 3703
1997 Jessica (Style Two)	HN 3850
1998 Rebecca (Style Three)	HN 4041
1999 Lauren (Style Three)	HN 3975
2000 Rachel (Style Two)	HN 3976
2001 Melissa (Style Three)	HN 3977
2002 Sarah (Style Three)	HN 3978
2003 Elizabeth (Style Three)	HN 4426
2004 Susan (Style Five)	HN 4532
2005 Victoria (Style Four)	HN 4623

FIGURES OF WILLIAMSBURG

Blacksmith of Williamsburg	HN 2240
Boy From Williamsburg	HN 2183
Child From Williamsburg	HN 2154
Gentleman From Williamsburg	HN 2227
Hostess of Williamsburg	HN 2209
Lady From Williamsburg	HN 2228
Royal Governor's Cook	HN 2233
Silversmith of Williamsburg	HN 2208
Wigmaker of Williamsburg	HN 2239

FLAMBÉ

Carpet Seller (Style Three)	HN 3277
Carpet Seller (Style Two)	HN 2776
Confucius	HN 3314
Eastern Grace	HN 3683
Geisha (Style Three)	HN 3229
Genie	HN 2999
Lamp Seller	HN 3278
Moor	HN 3642
Samurai Warrior	HN 3402
Wizard (Style One)	HN 3121

FLOWERS OF LOVE

Camellias	HN 3701
Forget-Me-Nots	HN 3700
Primrose	HN 3710
Rose (Style Two)	HN 3709

FLOWER OF THE MONTH, CHILD

January (Style Two)	HN 3330
February (Style Two)	HN 3331
March (Style Two)	HN 3332
April (Style Two)	HN 3333
May (Style Three)	HN 3334
June (Style Five)	HN 3323
July (Style Two)	HN 3324
August (Style Two)	HN 3325
September (Style Two)	HN 3326
October (Style Two)	HN 3327
November (Style Two)	HN 3328
December (Style Two)	HN 3329

GAINSBOROUGH LADIES

Honourable Frances Duncombe	HN 3009
Isabella, Countess of Sefton	HN 3010
Mary, Countess Howe	HN 3007
Sophia Charlotte, Lady Sheffield	HN 3008

GENTLE ARTS

Adornment	HN 3015
Flower Arranging	HN 3040
Painting	HN 3012
Spinning	HN 2390
Tapestry Weaving	HN 3048
Writing	HN 3049

GEORGIAN QUEENS

Sophia Dorothea (1666-1726)	HN 4074

GILBERT AND SULLIVAN

Colonel Fairfax	HN 2903
Elsie Maynard (Style Two)	HN 2902
Ko-Ko (Style Two)	HN 2898
Pirate King,	HN 2901
Ruth, The Pirate Maid,	HN 2900
Yum-Yum (Style Two),	HN 2899

GREAT LOVERS

Antony and Cleopatra	HN 3114
Lancelot and Guinivere	HN 3112
Robin Hood and Maid Marion	HN 3111
Romeo and Juliet	HN 3113

GREEK MYTHOLOGY

Helen of Troy (Style Two)	HN 4497

HAPPY BIRTHDAY

Happy Birthday 2000	HN 4215
Happy Birthday 2001	HN 4308
Happy Birthday 2002	HN 4393
Happy Birthday 2003	HN 4464
Happy Birthday 2004	HN 4528
Happy Birthday 2005	HN 4722

HAUTE ENSEMBLE

A la Mode	HN 2544
Boudoir	HN 2542
Carmen (Style Two)	HN 2545
Eliza (Style One)	HN 2543, 2543A
Mantilla	HN 2712

HOLIDAY COLLECTION

Hope (Style Three)	HN 4565
Joy (Style Four)	HN 4569
Love	HN 4640
Peace (Style Two)	HN 4568

HOLY FAMILY

Jesus (Style One)	HN 3484, 3487
Joseph (Style One)	HN 3438, 3486
Mary (Style Three)	HN 3437, 3485

IMAGES

Amen	HN 4021
Angel	HN 3940
Awakening (Style Two)	HN 2837, 2875
Ballerina (Style Three)	HN 3828
Ballet Class	HN 3731
Ballet Dancer	HN 4027
Ballet Lesson	HN 4028
Best Friends	HN 4643
Bride and Groom	HN 3281
Bridesmaid (Style Five)	HN 3280
Bridesmaid (Style Eight)	HN 4373
Brother and Sister	HN 3460
Brothers	HN 3191
Carefree (Style One)	HN 3026, 3029
Clever Boy	HN 4482
Clever Girl	HN 4483
Christmas Dreams	HN 4447
Congratulations	HN 3351
Contemplation (Style One)	HN 2213, 2241
Country Girl (Style Three)	HN 3958
Cricketer	HN 4518
Dance (Style One)	HN 4025
Debut (Style Two)	HN 4281
Encore (Style Two)	HN 4282
Father and Daughter	HN 4484
Father and Son	HN 4448
Family (Style One)	HN 2720, 2721
Family (Style Two)	HN 4645
First Kiss	HN 4681
First Lesson	HN 4358
First Love	HN 2747
First Steps (Style Two)	HN 3282
Footballer	HN 4517
Free Spirit (Style One)	HN 3157, 3159
From This Day Forward	HN 4380
Gift For You, A	HN 4449
Gift of Freedom	HN 3443
God Bless You	HN 3400
Goose Girl (Style Three)	HN 3936
Graduate [Female] (Style Two)	HN 4542
Graduate, [Male] (Style Two)	HN 3959
Graduate [Male] (Style Three)	HN 4543
Graduation (Female)	HN 3942
Happy Anniversary (Style Two)	HN 3254
Happy Birthday (Style Three)	HN 3829
Harmony (Style Three)	HN 4567
Hockey Player	HN 4519
Independence	HN 4375
Kiss (Boy)	HN 4064
Kiss (Girl)	HN 4065
Leap-frog	HN 4030
Love Everlasting	HN 4280
Lovers	HN 2762, 2763
Messiah	N 3952
Mother and Child (Style Two)	HN 3938
Mother and Daughter (Style One)	HN 2841, 2843
Mother and Daughter (Style Two)	HN 4562
Mother and Son	HN 4680
Our First Christmas	HN 3452
Over the Threshold	HN 3274
Pageboy	HN 4374
Peace (Style One)	HN 2433, 2470
Perfect Pose	HN 4357
Performance	HN 3827
Playmates	HN 4682
Prima Ballerina	HN 4024
Prayers	HN 4378
Sister and Brother	HN 4356
Sisters	HN 3018, 3019
Sleepyhead (Style Three)	HN 4413
Stage Struck	HN 3951
Star Performer	HN 3950

Storytime (Boy)	HN 4088
Storytime (Girl)	HN 4089
Studious Boy	HN 4563
Studious Girl	HN 4564
Surprise	HN 4376
Sweatheart (Boy)	HN 4351
Sweatheart (Girl)	HN 4352
Sympathy	HN 2838, 2876
Tenderness	HN 2713, 2714
Thankful	HN 3129, 3135
Tomorrow's Dreams	HN 3665
Tranquility (Style One)	HN 2426, 2469
Two Become One	HN 4644
Unity	HN 4485
Wedding Day	HN 2748
Wedding Vows (Style Two)	HN 4379
Wistful (Style Two)	HN 3664
Yearning	HN 2920, 2921

IMAGES
Christmas Choir

Carol Singer (Boy)	HN 4031
Carol Singer (Brother)	HN 4290
Carol Singer (Girl)	HN 4032
Carol Singer (Sister)	HN 4291
Carol Singer With Lantern	HN 4256

The Christmas Story

Balthazar (Style One)	HN 4036
Boy Shepherd	HN 4039
Caspar	HN 4038
Joseph (Style Two)	HN 4035
Kneeling Shepherd	HN 4055
Mary and Jesus	HN 4034
Melchior (Style One)	HN 4037
Standing Shepherd	HN 4056

Figure of the Year

1998 Best Friends (Style Two)	HN 4026
1999 Promise	HN 4033
2000 Kindred Spirits	HN 4077
2001 Special Friends	HN 4257
2002 Keep In Touch	HN 4377
2003 Gift of Friendship	HN 4446
2004 Secret (The)	HN 4560
2005 Carefree (Style Two)	HN 4683

IMMORTALS AND AURORA

Artemis, Goddess of the Hunt	HN 4081
Aurora, Goddess of the Dawn	HN 4078
Ceres, Goddess of Plenty	HN 4080
Erato, The Parnassian Muse	HN 4082
Hebe, Handmaiden to the Gods	HN 4079

IMPRESSIONS

Cherished Memories	HN 4265
Daybreak (Style Two)	HN 4196
In Loving Arms	HN 4262
Secret Thoughts (Style Two)	HN 4197
Summer Blooms (Style Two)	HN 4194
Summer Fragrance	HN 4195
Sunrise	HN 4199
Sunset	HN 4198
Sweet Dreams (Style Three)	HN 4193
Tender Greetings	HN 4261
Tender Moment (Style Two)	HN 4192

IN VOGUE

Abigail (Style One)	HN 4044
Alana	HN 4499
Amelia	HN 4327
Bride (Style Five)	HN 4324

Claudia	HN 4320
Daniella	HN 4551
Emma (Style Three)	HN 3714
Finishing Touch	HN 4329
Jessica (Style Three)	HN 4049
Joanne (Style Three)	HN 4202
Mikaela	HN 4550
Nadine	HN 4500
Natalie (Style Two)	HN 4048
Rebecca (Style Four)	HN 4203
Sophie (Style Four)	HN 3715
Taylor	HN 4496

IVORY AND GOLD

After The Rain	HN 4226
Helping Mother	HN 4228
Off To The Pond	HN 4227
Summer Duet	HN 4225

KATE GREENAWAY

Amy (Style One)	HN 2958
Anna (Style One)	HN 2802
Beth (Style One)	HN 2870
Carrie	HN 2800
Edith	HN 2957
Ellen (Style One)	HN 3020
Emma (Style One)	HN 2834
Georgina (Style One)	HN 2377
James	HN 3013
Kathy (Style One)	HN 2346
Lori	HN 2801
Louise (Style One)	HN 2869
Lucy (Style One)	HN 2863
Nell	HN 3014
Ruth (Style One)	HN 2799
Sophie (Style One)	HN 2833
Tess	HN 2865
Tom	HN 2864

LADIES OF COVENT GARDENS

Catherine (Style One)	HN 2395
Deborah (Style One)	HN 2701
Juliet (Style One)	HN 2968
Kimberley (Style One)	HN 2969

LADIES OF THE BRITISH ISLES

England	HN 3627
Ireland	HN 3628
Scotland	HN 3629
Wales	HN 3630

LADY DOULTON

1995 Lily (Style Two)	HN 3626
1996 Katherine (Style Two)	HN 3708
1997 Jane (Style Four)	HN 3711

LADY MUSICIANS

Cello (Style One)	HN 2331
Chitarrone	HN 2700
Cymbals	HN 2699
Dulcimer	HN 2798
Flute	HN 2483
French Horn	HN 2795
Harp	HN 2482
Hurdy Gurdy	HN 2796
Lute	HN 2431
Viola d'Amore	HN 2797
Violin	HN 2432
Virginals	HN 2427

LADY OF THE YEAR
(Compton and Woodhouse)

1997 Ellen (Style Three)	HN 3992
1998 Sophie (Style Five)	HN 3995
1999 Alice (Style Four)	HN 4003
2000 Chloe (Style Four)	HN 4201
2001 A Love So Tender	HN 4016
2001 Eleanor (Style Two)	HN 4015
2002 Georgina (Style Three)	HN 4237
2003 Ellie (Style Two)	HN 4017
2004 Megan (Style Three)	HN 4539

LANGUAGE OF LOVE

Red Red Rose	HN 3994
Shall I Compare Thee To A Summer's Day	HN 3999

LES FEMMES FATALES

Cleopatra (Style One)	HN 2868
Eve	HN 2466
Helen of Troy (Style One)	HN 2387
Lucrezia Borgia	HN 2342
Queen of Sheba	HN 2328
T'zu-hsi, Empress Dowager	HN 2391

LESLIE HARRADINE TRIBUTE

Bathing Beauty (Style Two)	HN 4399, 4599
Brighton Belle	HN 4400, 4600
Dancing Eyes and Sunny Hair (Style Two)	HN 4492
Do You Wonder Where The Fairies Are (Second Version)	HN 4429
Here A Little Child I Stand (Second Version)	HN 4428
Little Child So Rare and Sweet (Style Three)	HN 4491
Summer's Darling (Style Two)	HN 4401, 4601
Taking The Waters	HN 4402, 4602

LES SAISONS

Automne (Autumn)	HN 3068
Ete (Summer)	HN 3067
Hiver (Winter)	HN 3069
Printemps (Spring)	HN 3066

LITERARY HEROINES

Elizabeth Bennet	HN 3845
Emma (Style Four)	HN 3843
Jane Eyre	HN 3842
Moll Flanders	HN 3849
Tess of the D'Urbervilles	HN 3846

LITERARY LOVES

Heathcliff and Cathy	HN 4071

LITTLE CHERUBS

First Steps (Style Three)	HN 3361
Peek A Boo	HN 3363
Well Done	HN 3362
What Fun	HN 3364

MICHAEL DOULTON EVENTS

1984 Gillian (Style Two)	HN 3042
1985 Wistful (Style One)	HN 2472
1986 Kathleen (Style Two)	HN 3100
1987 Last Waltz	HN 2316
1987 Nicola	HN 2804
1988 Laura (Style One)	HN 3136
1989 Pamela (Style Two)	HN 3223
1990 Diana (Style Two)	HN 3266
1991 Fragrance (Style One)	HN 3311

1992 Angela (Style Three)	HN 3419
1993 Sarah (Style One)	HN 3380
1994 Sharon (Style Two)	HN 3603
1995 Lily (Style Two)	HN 3626
1997 Autumn Breezes (Style One)	HN 3736
1999 Julia (Style Two)	HN 4124
1999 Old Balloon Seller	HN 3737
2000 Susan (Style Four)	HN 4230
2001 Christine (Style Six)	HN 4307
2002 Linda (Style Five)	HN 4450
2003 Eleanor (Style Three)	HN 4463
2004 Rose (Style Three)	HN 4581
2005 Charlotte (Style Six)	HN 4758

MICHAEL DOULTON
SIGNATURE COLLECTION

Autumn Breezes (Style Two)	HN 2180
Christine (Style Three)	HN 3337
Christmas Morn (Style Two)	HN 3245
Elaine (Style Two)	HN 3247
Fair Lady (Style Two)	HN 3336
Fragrance (Style Two)	HN 3250
Hannah (Style Two)	HN 3870
Karen (Style Three)	HN 3338
Kirsty (Style Two)	HN 3246
Ninette (Style Two)	HN 3248
Sara (Style Two)	HN 3249
Southern Belle (Style Two)	HN 3244
Sunday Best (Style Two)	HN 3312
Top o' The Hill (Style Two)	HN 3734
Victoria (Style Two)	HN 3735

MIDDLE EARTH

Aragorn	HN 2916
Barliman Butterbur	HN 2923
Bilbo	HN 2914
Boromir	HN 2918
Frodo	HN 2912
Galadriel	HN 2915
Gandalf	HN 2911
Gimli	HN 2922
Gollum	HN 2913
Legolas	HN 2917
Samwise	HN 2925
Tom Bombadil	HN 2924

MILLENNIUM

Balthazar (Style One)	HN 4036
Boy Shepherd	HN 4039
Caspar	HN 4038
Columbine (Style Three)	HN 4059
Harlequin (Style Two)	HN 4058
Joseph (Style Two)	HN 4035
Kneeling Shepherd	HN 4055
Mary and Jesus	HN 4034
Melchior (Style One)	HN 4037
Standing Shepherd	HN 4056

MINIATURES
Character Studies

Balloon Seller	HN 2130
Falstaff (Style Three)	HN 3236
Good King Wenceslas (Style Two)	HN 3262
Guy Fawkes (Style Two)	HN 3271
Jester (Style Three)	HN 3335
Old Balloon Seller	HN 2129
Town Crier, The (Style Two)	HN 3261

Ladies

Annabel (Style Two)	M 218
Autumn Breezes (Style Two)	HN 2176, 2180
Barbara (Style Five)	M 219
Bess (Style Two)	M 210

Buttercup (Style Two)   HN 3268, 3908
Buttercup (Style Three)   M 211
Christine (Style Three)   HN 3269, 3337
Christine (Style Eight)   M 200
Christmas Morn (Style Two)   HN 3212, 3245
Diana (Style Three)   HN 3310
Elaine (Style Two)   HN 3214, 3247, 3900
Elaine (Style Three)   M 201
Elizabeth (Style Four)   M 202
Emma (Style Two)   HN 3208
Fair Lady (Style Two)   HN 3216, 3336
Fragrance (Style Two)   HN 3220, 3250
Gail (Style Two)   HN 3321
Gail (Style Three)   M 212
Hannah (Style Two)   HN 3649, 3876
Helen (Style Four)   M 213
Jane (Style Six)   M 203
Karen (Style Three)   HN 3270, 3338, 3749
Karen (Style Four)   M 204
Kirsty (Style Two)   HN 3213, 3246, 3480, 3743
Laura (Style Four)   M 214
Margaret (Style Four)   M 205
Ninette (Style Two)   HN 3215, 3248, 3901
Ninette (Style Three)   M 206
Rachel (Style Three)   M 207
Rebecca (Style Two)   HN 3414
Sara (Style Two)   HN 3219, 3249
Soiree (Style Two)   M 215
Southern Belle (Style Two)   HN 3174, 3244
Stephanie (Style Four)   M 216
Sunday Best (Style Two)   HN 3218, 3312
Susan (Style Six)   M 208
Top o' the Hill (Style Two)   HN 2126, 3499, 3734
Top o' the Hill (Style Three)   M 217
Victoria (Style Two)   HN 3735, 3744, 3909
Victoria (Style Three)   M 209

MYSTICAL FIGURES

Sorcerer   HN 4252
Sorceress   HN 4253

MYTHS AND MAIDENS

Diana the Huntress   HN 2829
Europa and the Bull (Style Two)   HN 2828
Juno and the Peacock   HN 2827
Lady and the Unicorn   HN 2825
Leda and the Swan   HN 2826

NAME YOUR OWN

Baby's First Christmas   HN 4427
Best Wishes   HN 3971
Congratulations to You   HN 4306
For You   HN 3754, 3863
Happy Anniversary (Style Four) HN 4604, 4605, 4606
My Love (Style Two)   HN 4392
New Baby   HN 3712, 3713
Perfect Gift   HN 4409
Pretty As A Picture   HN 4312
Pride and Joy (Style Two)   HN 4102
Sugar and Spice   HN 4103
Thinking of You (Style Two)   HN 4585
Thoughts For You   HN 4397
Wedding Celebration   HN 4216, 4229

NATIONAL SOCIETY FOR THE PREVENTION OF CRUELTY TO CHILDREN CHARITY

Charity (Style One)   HN 3087
Faith (Style One)   HN 3082
Hope (Style One)   HN 3061

NATIVITY COLLECTION

Balthazar (Style Two)   HN 4703
Gaspar   HN 4704
Jesus (Style Two)   HN 4707
Joseph (Style Three)   HN 4701
Mary (Style Six)   HN 4700
Melchior (Style Two)   HN 4702

NATURAL BEAUTY COLLECTION

Contemplation (Style Two)   HN 4761
Serenity (Style Two)   HN 4769
Tranquility (Style Two)   HN 4770

NOSTALGIA

Air Raid Precaution Warden   HN 4555
Auxiliary Territorial Service   HN 4495
Farewell Daddy   HN 4363
Home Guard   HN 4494
Land Girl   HN 4361
Railway Sleeper   HN 4418
Women's Auxiliary Air Force   HN 4554
Women's Land Army   HN 4364
Women's Royal Naval Service   HN 4498

NURSERY RHYMES
Series One

Curly Locks   HN 2049
He Loves Me   HN 2046
Jack   HN 2060
Jill   HN 2061
Little Boy Blue (Style One)   HN 2062
Little Jack Horner (Style One)   HN 2063
Mary Had a Little Lamb   HN 2048
Mary, Mary   HN 2044
My Pretty Maid   HN 2064
Once Upon a Time   HN 2047
She Loves Me Not   HN 2045
Wee Willie Winkie (Style One)   HN 2050

Series Two

Little Bo Peep   HN 3030
Little Boy Blue (Style Two)   HN 3035
Little Jack Horner (Style Two)   HN 3034
Little Miss Muffet   HN 2727
Polly Put the Kettle On   HN 3021
Tom, Tom, The Piper's Son   HN 3032
Wee Willie Winkie (Style Two)   HN 3031

PEGGY DAVIES COLLECTION

Christine (Style Five)   HN 3905
Eleanor (Style One)   HN 3906
Lily (Style Three)   HN 3902
Mary (Style Four)   HN 3903
Patricia (Style Five)   HN 3907
Valerie (Style Two)   HN 3904

PERIOD FIGURES IN ENGLISH HISTORY

Eleanor of Provence   HN 2009
Henrietta Maria (Style One)   HN 2005
Lady Anne Nevill   HN 2006
Margaret of Anjou (Style One)   HN 2012
Matilda   HN 2011
Mrs. Fitzherbert   HN 2007
Philippa of Hainault (Style One)   HN 2008
Young Miss Nightingale   HN 2010

PETITE

A Moment in Time   HN 4759
Amy (Style Five)   HN 4782
Autumn Breezes(Style Three)   HN 4716
Buttercup (Style Four)   HN 4781
Christmas Celebration   HN 4721
Elaine (Style Four)   HN 4718
Fair Lady (Style Three)   HN 4719
Karen (Style Five)   HN 4779
Ninette (Style Four)   HN 4717
Rachel (Style Five)   HN 4780
Sara (Style Three)   HN 4720
Susan (Style Seven)   HN 4777
Top o' the Hill (Style Four)   HN 4778

PLANTAGENET QUEENS

Eleanor of Aquitaine (1122-1204)   HN 3957
Margaret of Anjou [1430-1482] (Style Two)   HN 4073
Phillipa of Hainault [1314-1369] (Style Two) HN 4066

PRESTIGE

Alexander The Great   HN 4481
Charge of the Light Brigade (Style One)   HN 3718
Charge of the Light Brigade (Style Two)   HN 4486
Columbine (Style Three)   HN 2738, 3288, 4059
Harlequin (Style Two)   HN 2737, 3287, 4058
Helen of Troy (Style Two)   HN 4497
Henry V at Agincourt   HN 3947
Hercules   HN 4561
H.M. Queen Elizabeth II   HN 4476
Jack Point   HN 2080
King Arthur   HN 4541
Lady Godiva   HN 4641
Matador and Bull   HN 4566
Moor, The   HN 2082
Princess Badoura (Style One)   HN 2081, 3921
Princess Badoura (Style Two)   HN 4179
Rose Garden   HN 4559
St. George (Style Four)   HN 4371

QUEENS OF THE REALM

Mary, Queen of Scots (Style Two)   HN 3142
Queen Anne   HN 3141
Queen Elizabeth I   HN 3099
Queen Victoria   HN 3125

REFLECTIONS

Allure   HN 3080
Aperitif   HN 2998
Autumn Glory   HN 2766
Ballerina (Style Two)   HN 3197
Ballet Class (Style One)   HN 3134
Balloons   HN 3187
Bathing Beauty (Style One)   HN 3156
Bolero   HN 3076
Breezy Day   HN 3162
Charisma   HN 3090
Cherry Blossom   HN 3092
Chic   HN 2997
Cocktails   HN 3070
Country Girl (Style One)   HN 3051
Covent Garden (Style Two)   HN 2857
Dancing Delight   HN 3078
Daybreak (Style One)   HN 3107
Debut (Style One)   HN 3046
Debutante (Style Two)   HN 3188
Demure (Style One)   HN 3045
Devotion   HN 3228
Dreaming   HN 3133
Eastern Grace   HN 3138
Enchanting Evening   HN 3108
Encore (Style One)   HN 2751
Enigma   HN 3110
Entranced   HN 3186

Fantasy HN 3296
Flirtation HN 3071
Free As The Wind HN 3139
Gaiety HN 3140
Gardener HN 3161
Golfer HN 2992
Good Pals HN 3132
Harvestime HN 3084
Idle Hours HN 3115
Indian Maiden HN 3117
Joker, The (Style One) HN 3196
Joy (Style One) HN 3184
Love Letter, The (Style Two) HN 3105
Moondancer HN 3181
Morning Glory HN 3093
Panorama HN 3028
Paradise HN 3074
Park Parade HN 3116
Pensive HN 3109
Playmates HN 3127
Promenade (Style Two) HN 3072
Reflection HN 3039
Rose Arbour HN 3145
Secret Moment HN 3106
Sheikh HN 3083
Shepherd (Style Five) HN 3160
Shepherdess (Style Three) HN 2990
Sisterly Love HN 3130
Sophistication HN 3059
Spring Walk HN 3120
Stargazer HN 3182
Storytime (Style One) HN 3126
Strolling (Style One) HN 3073
Summer Rose (Style One) HN 3085
Summer's Darling HN 3091
Sweet Bouquet (Style One) HN 3000
Sweet Perfume HN 3094
Sweet Violets HN 3175
Tango HN 3075
Tomorrow's Dreams HN 3128
Traveller's Tale HN 3185
Tumbler HN 3183
Water Maiden HN 3155
Windflower (Style Four) HN 3077
Windswept HN 3027
Winter's Walk, A HN 3052

REYNOLDS LADIES

Countess of Harrington HN 3317
Countess Spencer HN 3320
Lady Worsley HN 3318
Mrs. Hugh Bonfoy HN 3319

ROYAL DOULTON INTERNATIONAL COLLECTORS CLUB

Applause HN 4328
Auctioneer HN 2988
Autumntime (Style One) HN 3231
Barbara (Style Three) HN 3441
Bunny's Bedtime HN 3370
Cherished Memories HN 4265
Dance (Style Two) HN 4553
Diane HN 3604
Discovery HN 3428
Eliza Farren, Countess of Derby HN 3442
Emily (Style Two) HN 3688
Geisha, The (Style Three) HN 3229
Jacqueline (Style Four) HN 4309
Janet (Style Four) HN 4042
Jester (Style Three) HN 3335
Joanna HN 4711
L'Ambitieuse HN 3359
Le Bal HN 3702
Lido Lady (Second Version) HN 4247
Lights Out (Style Two) HN 4465
Moor HN 3926
Nicole (Style Two) HN 4112

Pamela (Style Three) HN 3756
Pride and Joy HN 2945
Prized Possessions HN 2942
Recital, The HN 4466
Sleepy Darling HN 2953
Springtime (Style Two) HN 3033
Summertime (Style One) HN 3137
Susan (Style Three) HN 3871
Sweet Lilac HN 3972
Top o' the Hill (Style Two) HN 2126
Winter's Day HN 3769
Wintertime (Style One) HN 3060

SEA CHARACTERS

All Aboard HN 2940
Boatman 'Pilot' HN 2417A
Boatman 'Skylark' HN 2417
Captain (Style Two) HN 2260
Captain Cook HN 2889
Good Catch, A HN 2258
Helmsman HN 2499
Lifeboat Man HN 2764
Lobster Man HN 2317, 2323
Officer of the Line HN 2733
Sailor's Holiday HN 2442
Sea Harvest HN 2257
Seafarer HN 2455
Shore Leave HN 2254
Song of the Sea HN 2729
Tall Story HN 2248

SEASONS
Series One

Autumn (Style One) HN 314, 474
Spring (Style One) HN 312, 472
Summer (Style One) HN 313, 473
Winter (Style One) HN 315, 475

Series Two

Autumn (Style Two) HN 2087
Spring (Style Four) HN 2085
Summer (Style Two) HN 2086
Winter (Style Two) HN 2088

Series Three

Catherine in Spring HN 3006
Emily in Autumn HN 3004
Lilian in Summer HN 3003
Sarah in Winter HN 3005

Series Four

Autumntime (Style One) HN 3231
Springtime (Style Two) HN 3033
Summertime (Style One) HN 3137
Wintertime (Style One) HN 3060

Series Five

Autumn Attraction HN 3612
Spring Song HN 3446
Summer Serenade HN 3610
Winter Welcome HN 3611

Series Six

Autumntime (Style Two) HN 3621
Springtime (Style Three) HN 3477
Summertime (Style Two) HN 3478
Wintertime (Style Two) HN 3622

Series Seven

Autumn Flowers HN 3918
Spring Posy HN 3916
Summer Blooms HN 3917
Winter Bouquet HN 3919

Series Eight

Autumn (Style Three) HN 4272
Spring (Style Five) HN 4270
Summer (Style Three) HN 4271
Winter (Style Three) HN 4273

Series Nine

Autumn (Style Four) HN 4588
Springtime (Style Four) HN 4586
Summer (Style Four) HN 4587
Winter (Style Four) HN 4589

THE SENSUAL COLLECTION

Charlotte (Style Five) HN 4536
Francesca (Style Two) HN 4534
Kristine HN 4537
Simone (Style Two) HN 4535

SENTIMENTS

Across the Miles HN 3934
Au Revoir (Style Two) HN 3729
Charmed HN 4445
Cherish HN 4442
Christmas Angel HN 3733, 4060
Christmas Carols HN 3727, 4061
Christmas Day HN 3488, 4062
Christmas Eve HN 4350
Christmas Garland HN 4067
Christmas Lantern HN 3953
Christmas Parcels (Style Two) HN 3493, 4063
Forever Yours (Style One) HN 3949
Forget Me Not (Style Two) HN 3388
Friendship HN 3491
Good Luck HN 4070
Greetings HN 4250
Happy Anniversary (Style Three) HN 4068
Happy Christmas HN 4255
Happy Holidays HN 4443
Hope (Style Three) HN 4565
Joy (Style Four) HN 4569
Love HN 4640
Loving Thoughts HN 3948
Loving You HN 3389
Many Happy Returns HN 4254
Missing You HN 4076
Noel HN 4084
Peae (Style Two) HN 4568
Remembering You HN 4085
Skating HN 4370
Sweet Dreams (Style Two) HN 3394
Thank You (Style Two) HN 3390
Thank You Mother HN 4251
Thinking of You HN 3124, 3490
Wisdom (Style One) HN 4083
With All My Love HN 4213
With Love (Style One) HN 3393, 3492

SHAKESPEAREAN LADIES

Desdemona HN 3676
Juliet (Style Two) HN 3453
Ophelia HN 3674
Titania HN 3679

SHIPS FIGUREHEADS

Benmore	HN 2909
Chieftain	HN 2929
Hibernia	HN 2932
HMS Ajax	HN 2908
Lalla Rookh	HN 2910
Mary Queen of Scots (Style One)	HN 2931
Nelson	HN 2928
Pocahontas	HN 2930

SIX WIVES OF HENRY VIII

Anne Bolelyn	HN 3232
Anne of Cleves	HN 3356
Catherine Howard	HN 3449
Catherine of Aragon	HN 3233
Catherine Parr	HN 3450
Jane Seymour	HN 3349

SOLDIERS OF THE REVOLUTION

Captain, 2nd New York Regiment, 1775	HN 2755
Corporal, 1st New Hamshire Regiment, 1778	HN 2780
Major, 3rd New Jersey Regiment, 1776	HN 2752
Private, 1st Georgia Regiment, 1777	HN 2779
Private, 2nd South Carolina Regiment, 1781	HN 2717
Private, 3rd North Carolina Regiment, 1778	HN 2754
Private, Connecticut Regiment, 1777	HN 2845
Private, Delaware Regiment, 1776	HN 2761
Private, Massachusetts Regiment, 1778	HN 2760
Private, Pennsylvania Rifle Battalion, 1776	HN 2846
Private, Rhode Island Regiment, 1781	HN 2759
Sergeant, 6th Maryland Regiment, 1777	HN 2815
Sergeant, Virginia 1st Regiment Continental Light Dragoons, 1777	HN 2844

SPECIAL OCCASIONS

Christening Day	HN 3210, 3211
Happy Anniversary (Style One)	HN 3097
Happy Birthday (Style One)	HN 3095
Merry Christmas	HN 3096

STUART KINGS

Charles I (1625-1649)	HN 3824
Charles II (1660-1685)	HN 3825
James I (1603-1625)	HN 3822
William III (1650-1702)	HN 402

STUART QUEENS

Anne of Denmark	HN 4266
Catherine of Braganza	HN 4267
Henrietta-Maria	HN 4260
Queen Mary II	HN 4474

SWEET AND TWENTIES

Deauville	HN 2344
Monte Carlo	HN 2332

TEENAGERS

Columbine (Style Two)	HN 2185
Faraway	HN 2133
Harlequin (Style One)	HN 2186
Melody (Style One)	HN 2202
Sea Sprite (Style Two)	HN 2191
Sweet Sixteen (Style One)	HN 2231
Teenager	HN 2203
Wood Nymph	HN 2192

TUDOR ROSES

Lady Jane Grey	HN 3680
Margaret Tudor	HN 3838
Mary Tudor	HN 3834
Princess Elizabeth	HN 3682

VANITY FAIR CHILDREN

Amanda	HN 2996, 3406, 3632
Andrea	HN 3058
Birthday Girl	HN 3423
Buddies (Style Two)	HN 3396
Catherine (Style Two)	HN 3044
Daddy's Girl	HN 3435
Dinnertime	HN 3726
Helen (Style Two)	HN 2994
Julie (Style One)	HN 2995
Kerry	HN 3036
Let's Play	HN 3397
Lynsey	HN 3043
My First Pet	HN 3122
Reward	HN 3391
Sit	HN 3123, 3430

VANITY FAIR LADIES

Angela (Style Two)	HN 2389
Ann (Style One)	HN 2739
Anna (Style Two)	HN 4095
Anna (Style Three)	HN 4391
Ashley	HN 3420
Barbara (Style Four)	HN 4116
Barbara (Style Two)	HN 2962
Brenda	HN 4115
Carol	HN 2961
Danielle (Style Two)	HN 3001
Dawn (Style Three)	HN 3600
Denise (Style Three)	HN 2477
Donna	HN 2939
Emily (Style One)	HN 3204
Flower of Love	HN 2460
Gift of Love	HN 3427
Good Companion	HN 3608
Grace (Style Two)	HN 3699
Heather	HN 2956
Jayne (Style Two)	HN 4524
Jean (Style Two)	HN 2710
Jessica (Style One)	HN 3169
Joanne (Style One)	HN 2373
Josephine	HN 4223
Just For You	HN 3355

Kathleen (Style Three)	HN 3609
Katrina (Style Two)	HN 4467
Kimberley (Style Two)	HN 3379
Kirsten	HN 4101
Linda (Style Two)	HN 2758
Margaret (Style Two)	HN 2397
Maria	HN 3381
Margaret (Style Three)	HN 4311
Mary (Style One)	HN 2374
Maureen (Style Three)	HN 2481
Megan (Style One)	HN 3306
Megan (Style Two)	HN 3887
Mother and Child (Style One)	HN 3353
Nancy	HN 2955
Naomi	HN 4661
Natalie (Style One)	HN 3173
Pamela (Style Two)	HN 2479
Patricia (Style Three)	HN 2715
Paula	HN 3234
Samantha (Style One)	HN 2954
Susannah	HN 4221
Suzanne (Style One)	HN 4098
Tender Moment	HN 3303
Tracy	HN 2736
Veronica (Style Four)	HN 3205
Yours Forever	HN 3354

VICTORIAN AND EDWARDIAN ACTRESSES

Ellen Terry	HN 3826
Lillie Langtry	HN 3820
Sarah Bernhardt	HN 4023

VISITOR CENTRE

Anna of the Five Towns	HN 3865
Arnold Bennett	HN 4360
Clara Hamps	HN 4162
Countess of Chell	HN 3867
Kimberley (Style One)	HN 3864
Sally (Style Two)	HN 4160
Sarah (Style Two)	HN 3857
Sophia Baines	HN 4167
Special Gift (Style One)	HN 4129
Sweet Delight	HN 4398
With All My Love	HN 4241

WILDFLOWER OF THE MONTH

January (Style Three)	HN 3341
February (Style Three)	HN 3342
March (Style Three)	HN 3343
April (Style Three)	HN 3344
May (Style Four)	HN 3345
June (Style Six)	HN 3346
July (Style Three)	HN 3347
August (Style Three)	HN 3408
September (Style Three)	HN 3409
October (Style Three)	HN 3410
November (Style Three)	HN 3411
December (Style Three)	HN 3412

ALPHABETICAL
INDEX

A

A la Mode, HN 2544
A Moment in Time, HN 4759
A Winter's Morn, HN 4538, 4622
Abdullah, HN 1410, 2104
Abigail (Style One), HN 4044
Abigail (Style Two), HN 4664
Ace, HN 3398
A'Courting, HN 2004
Across The Miles, HN 3934
Adele, HN 2480; also called Camille (Style Two),
    HN 3171; Margaret (Style Two), HN 2397, 3496
Adornment, HN 3015
Adrienne, HN 2152, 2304; also called Fiona (Style
    Four), HN 3748; Joan (Style Two), HN 3217
Affection, HN 2236
After The Rain, HN 4226
Afternoon Call: see Lady With an Ermine Muff
Afternoon Tea, HN 1747, 1748
Age of Swing, HN 4285
Aileen, HN 1645, 1664, 1803
Air Raid Precaution Warden, HN 4555
Ajax, HMS, HN 2908
Alana, HN 4499
Alchemist, HN 1259, 1282
Alexander the Great, HN 4481
Alexandra (Style One), HN 2398
Alexandra (Style Two), HN 3286, 3292
Alexandra (Style Three), HN 4557; also called
    Chloe (Style Six) HN 4727
Alexis, HN 4205; also called Kathryn (Style Two)
    HN 4040
Alfred Jingle, HN 541, M 52
Alfred the Great, HN 3821
Alice (Style One), HN 2158
Alice (Style Two), HN 3368
Alice (Style Three), HN 4111
Alice (Style Four), HN 4003
Alison (Style One), HN 2336, 3264
Alison (Style Two), HN 4018
Alison (Style Three) HN 4667
All Aboard, HN 2940
All My Love, HN 4747; also called Scarlett HN 4508
All-A-Blooming, HN 1457, 1466
Allison, HN 4207; also called Ellie, HN 4046
Allure, HN 3080; also called Monique, HN 2880
Almost Grown, HN 3425
Alyssa, HN 4132; also called Country Rose,
    HN 3221
Amanda, HN 2996, 3406, 3632, 3634, 3635;
    also called Flower of the Month, Child
Amber, HN 4125; also called Chloe (Style Three)
    HN 3883, 3914
Amelia, HN 4327; also called Claudia, HN 4320;
    Gift of Love (Style Two) HN 4751
Amen, HN 4021
Amy (Style One), HN 2958
Amy (Style Two), HN 3316
Amy (Style Three), HN 3854
Amy (Style Four), HN 4760
Amy (Style Five), HN 4782
Amy's Sister, HN 3445
And One For You, HN 2970
And So To Bed, HN 2966
Andrea (Style One), HN 3058
Andrea (Style Two), HN 4584

Angel, HN 3940
Angela (Style One), HN 1204, 1303;
    also called Fanny
Angela (Style Two), HN 2389
Angela (Style Three), HN 3419
Angela (Style Four), HN 3690; also called Kelly
    (Style Two), HN 3912; Sweet Sixteen (Style Two),
    HN 3648 Angela (Style Five), HN 4405
Angelina, HN 2013
Anita, HN 3766
Ankhesenamun, HN 4190
Ann (Style One), HN 2739
Ann (Style Two), HN 3259; also called Lauren,
    HN 3290
Anna (Style One), HN 2802
Anna (Style Two), HN 4095
Anna (Style Three), HN 4391
Anna of the Five Towns, HN 3865
Annabel (Style One), HN 3273
Annabel (Style Two), M218
Annabel, CL 3981
Annabel Vision in Red, HN 4493; also called
    Becky (Style Two), HN 4322
Annabella, HN 1871, 1872, 1875
Annabelle, HN 4090; also called Joanne
    (Style Two), HN 3422
Anne Bolelyn, HN 3232
Anne Marie, HN 4522
Anne of Cleves, HN 3356
Anne of Denmark, HN 4266
Annette (Style One), HN 1471, 1472, 1550
Annette (Style Two), HN 3495; also called Sandra,
    HN 2275, 2401
Anniversary, HN 3625
Anthea, HN 1526, 1527, 1669
Antique Dealer, HN 4424
Antoinette (Style One), HN 1850, 1851
Antoinette (Style Two), HN 2326; also called
    My Love, HN 2339
Antony and Cleopatra, HN 3114
Any Old Lavender: see Sweet Lavender
Anyone For Tennis, CL 4007
Aperitif, HN 2998
Applause, HN 4328
Apple Maid, HN 2160
April (Style One), HN 2708; also called Gillian
    (Style Three), HN 3742
April (Style Two), HN 3333; also called Amanda
    HN 2996, 3406, 3632, 3634, 3635
April (Style Three), HN 3344; also called Beatrice
    HN 3263, 3631; Kathryn (Style One), HN 3413;
    Lucy (Style Two) HN 3653; Summer Serenade,
    HN 3610
April (Style Four), HN 3693
April (Style Five), HN 4520
April Shower, HN 3024
Arab, HN 33, 343, 378; also called The Moor,
    HN 1308, 1366, 1425, 1657, 2082, 3642, 3926
Aragorn, HN 2916
Aramis, HN 4415
Ariel, HN 3831
Arnold Bennett, HN 4360
Artemis, Goddess of the Hunt, HN 4081
Artful Dodger, HN 546, M 55
As Good As New, HN 2971
Ascot (Style One), HN 2356

Ascot (Style Two), HN 3471
Ashley, HN 3420
At Ease, HN 2473
At the Races, CL 4014
Athos, HN 4414
Attentive Scholar: see Diligent Scholar
Auctioneer, HN 2988
August (Style One), HN 3165; also called
    Gillian (Style Three), HN 3742
August (Style Two), HN 3325; also called Amanda,
    HN 2996, 3406, 3632, 3634, 3635
August (Style Three), HN 3408; also called Beatrice,
    HN 3263, 3631; Kathryn (Style One), HN 3413;
    Lucy (Style Two), HN 3653; Summer Serenade,
    HN 3610
Au Revoir (Style One), HN 3723; also called
    Fond Farewell, HN 3815
Au Revoir (Style Two), HN 3729
Aurora, HN 3833
Aurora, Goddess of the Dawn, HN 4078
Automne (Autumn), HN 3068
Autumn (Style One), HN 314, 474
Autumn (Style Two), HN 2087
Autumn (Style Three), HN 4272
Autumn (Style Four) , HN 4588
Autumn Attraction, HN 3612; also called
    Michele, HN 2234
Autumn Breezes (Style One), HN 1911, 1913, 1934,
    2131, 2147, 3736
Autumn Breezes (Style Two), HN 2176, 2180
Autumn Breezes (Style Three) 4716
Autumn Days, HN 4755; also called Top o'the Hill
    HN 4778
Autumn Flowers, HN 3918
Autumn Glory, HN 2766
Autumn Stroll, HN 4686
Autumntime (Style One), HN 3231
Autumntime (Style Two), HN 3621
Auxiliary Territorial Service, HN 4495
Awakening (Style One), HN 1927
Awakening (Style Two), HN 2837, 2875

B

Baba, HN 1230, 1243-1248
Babette, HN 1423, 1424
Babie, HN 1679, 1842, 2121
Baby, HN 12
Baby Bunting, HN 2108
Baby's First Christmas, HN 4427
Bachelor, HN 2319
Balinese Dancer, HN 2808
Ballad Seller, HN 2266
Ballerina, AIL 9
Ballerina (Style One), HN 2116
Ballerina (Style Two), HN 3197
Ballerina (Style Three), HN 3828
Ballet Class (Style One), HN 3134
Ballet Class (Style Two), HN 3731
Ballet Dancer, AIL 10
Ballet Dancer, HN 4027
Ballet Lesson, HN 4028
Ballet Shoes, HN 3434
Balloon Boy, HN 2934
Balloon Clown, HN 2894
Balloon Girl, HN 2818
Balloon Lady, HN 2935

Balloon Man, HN 1954
Balloon Seller (Style One), HN 479, 486, 548, 583, 697; also called The Balloon Woman
Balloon Seller (Style Two), HN 2130
Balloon Woman: see Balloon Seller (Style One)
Balloons, HN 3187
Balthazar (Style One), HN 4036
Balthazar (Style Two), HN 4703
Barbara (Style One), HN 1421, 1432, 1461
Barbara (Style Two), HN 2962
Barbara (Style Three), HN 3441
Barbara (Style Four), HN 4116
Barbara (Style Five), M219
Barliman Butterbur, HN 2923
Basket Weaver, HN 2245
Bather (Style One, First Version), HN 597, 687, 781, 782, 1238, 1708
Bather (Style One, Second Version), HN 4244
Bather (Style Two), HN 773, 774, 1227
Bathing Beauty (Style One), HN 3156
Bathing Beauty (Style Two), HN 4399, 4599
Batsman, HN 4366
Beachcomber, HN 2487
Beat You To It, HN 2871
Beatrice, HN 3263, 3631; also called Kathryn (Style One), HN 3413; Lucy (Style Two), HN 3653; Summer Serenade, HN 3610; Wildflower of the Month
Beautiful Blossom, HN 4533
Becky (Style One), HN 2740
Becky (Style Two), HN 4322; also called Annabel Vision in Red; HN 4493
Bedtime (Style One), HN 1978, 2219
Bedtime (Style Two), HN 3418
Bedtime Story, HN 2059
Beethoven, HN 1778
Beggar (Style One), HN 526, 591
Beggar (Style Two), HN 2175
Belle (Style One), HN 754, 776
Belle (Style Two), HN 2340
Belle (Style Three), HN 3703
Belle (Style Four), HN 3830
Belle (Style Five), HN 4235
Belle o' the Ball, HN 1997
Bells Across the Valley, HN 4300
Benmore, HN 2909
Bernadette, CL 4005
Bernice, HN 2071
Bess (Style One), HN 2002, 2003
Bess (style Two), M210
Best Friends (Style One), HN 3935
Best Friends (Style Two), HN 4026
Best Friends (Style Three), HN 4643
Best Wishes (Style One), HN 3426
Best Wishes (Style Two), HN 3971; also called Especially For You HN 4750; Forever Yours (Style Two) HN 4501; Kate (Style Three), HN 4233
Beth (Style One), HN 2870
Beth (Style Two), HN 4156; also called Lydia (Style Two), HN 4211
Bethany, CL 3987; also called 'Felicity' CL 3986, CL 4103
Bethany, HN 4326
Betsy, HN 2111
Betty (Style One), HN 402, 403, 435, 438, 477, 478
Betty (Style Two), HN 1404, 1405, 1435, 1436

Biddy, HN 1445, 1500, 1513
Biddy Penny Farthing, HN 1843
Bilbo, HN 2914
Bill Sikes, HN 3785
Bill Sykes, HN 537, M 54
Birthday Girl, HN 3423
Black Cat: see Pussy
Blacksmith (Style One), HN 2782
Blacksmith (Style Two), HN 4488
Blacksmith of Williamsburg, HN 2240
Blighty, HN 323
Blithe Morning, HN 2021, 2065
Blossom, HN 1667
Blossomtime, HN 4045
Blue Beard (Style One), HN 75, 410
Blue Bird, HN 1280
Bluebeard (Style Two), HN 1528, 2105
Boatman, HN 2417, 2417A
Bobby, HN 2778
Bolero, HN 3076
Bon Appetit, HN 2444
Bon Jour, HN 1879, 1888
Bon Voyage, HN 3866
Bonnie Lassie, HN 1626
Bo-Peep (Style One), HN 777, 1202, 1327, 1328
Bo-Peep (Style Two), HN 1810, 1811
Bo-Peep (Style Three), M 82, 83
Boromir, HN 2918
Boudoir, HN 2542
Bouquet, HN 406, 414, 422, 428, 429, 567, 794; also called The Nosegay
Bow (The): see Flounced Skirt
Bowler, HN 4635
Bowls Player, HN 3780
Boy Evacuee, HN 3202
Boy from Williamsburg, HN 2183
Boy on Crocodile, HN 373
Boy on Pig, HN 1369
Boy Scout, HN 3462
Boy Shepherd, HN 4039
Boy with Turban, HN 586, 587, 661, 662, 1210, 1212, 1213, 1214, 1225
Breezy Day, HN 3162
Brenda, HN 4115
Breton Dancer, HN 2383
Brianna, HN 4126; also called Kathleen (Style Three) HN 3609, 3880
Bride (Style One), HN 1588, 1600, 1762, 1841
Bride (Style Two), HN 2166
Bride (Style Three), HN 2873
Bride (Style Four), HN 3284, 3285
Bride (Style Five), HN 4324
Bride and Groom, HN 3281
Bride of the Year, HN 3758; also called Wedding Morn, (Style Two), HN 3853
Bridesmaid (Style One), HN 1433, 1434, 1530
Bridesmaid (Style Two), M 11, 12, 30
Bridesmaid (Style Three), HN 2148
Bridesmaid (Style Four), HN 2196
Bridesmaid (Style Five), HN 2874
Bridesmaid (Style Six), HN 3280
Bridesmaid (Style Seven), HN 3476; also called Flowergirl (Style One), HN 3479
Bridesmaid (Style Eight), HN 4373
Bridget, HN 2070
Brighton Belle, HN 4400, 4600

Brittany, HN 4206; also called Olivia (Style Three) HN 3717
Broken Lance, HN 2041
Brother and Sister, HN 3460
Brothers, HN 3191
Buddies (Style One), HN 2546
Buddies (Style Two), HN 3396
Bumble, M 76
Bunny, HN 2214
Bunny's Bedtime, HN 3370
Buttercup (Style One), HN 2309, 2399
Buttercup (Style Two), HN 3268, 3908
Buttercup (Style Three), M211
Buttercup (Style Four) HN 4781
Butterfly, HN 719, 720, 730, 1203; also called Butterfly Woman, HN 1456
Butterfly Woman, HN 1456; also called Butterfly, HN 719, 720, 730, 1203
Buz Fuz, HN 538, M 53

C

Caitlyn, HN 4666
Called Love, A Little Boy, HN 1545
Calumet, HN 1428, 1689, 2068
Camellia, HN 2222
Camellias, HN 3701
Camilla (Style One), HN 1710, 1711
Camilla (Style Two), HN 4220
Camille (Style One), HN 1586, 1648, 1736
Camille (Style Two), HN 3171; also called Adele, HN 2480; Margaret (Style Two), HN 2397, 3496
Captain (Style One), HN 778
Captain (Style Two), HN 2260
Captain Cook, HN 2889
Captain Cuttle, M 77
Captain Hook, HN 3636
Captain MacHeath, HN 464, 590, 1256
Captain, 2nd New York Regiment, 1775, HN 2755
Carefree (Style One), HN 3026, 3029
Carefree (Style Two), HN 4683
Carmen (Style One), HN 1267, 1300
Carmen (Style Two), HN 2545
Carmen (Style Three), HN 3993
Carnival, HN 1260, 1278
Carol, HN 2961
Carol Singer (Boy), HN 4031
Carol Singer (Brother), HN 4290
Carol Singer (Girl), HN 4032
Carol Singer (Sister), HN 4291
Carol Singer With Lantern, HN 4256
Caroline (Style One), HN 3170; also called Winter Welcome, HN 3611
Caroline (Style Two), HN 3694
Caroline (Style Three), HN 4395; also called Josephine, HN 4223
Carolyn (Style One), HN 2112
Carolyn (Style Two), HN 2974
Carpenter, HN 2678
Carpet Seller (Style One), HN 1464, 1464A
Carpet Seller (Style Two), HN 2776
Carpet Seller (Style Three), HN 3277
Carpet Vendor (Style One), HN 38, 76, 350
Carpet Vendor (Style Two), HN 38A, 348
Carrie, HN 2800
Caspar, HN 4038
Cassim (Style One), HN 1231, 1232

Cassim (Style Two), HN 1311, 1312
Catherine (Style One), HN 2395
Catherine (Style Two), HN 3044, 3451
Catherine (Style Three), HN 4304
Catherine Howard, HN 3449
Catherine In Spring, HN 3006
Catherine of Aragon, HN 3233
Catherine of Braganza, HN 4267
Catherine Parr, HN 3450
Cavalier (Style One), HN 369
Cavalier (Style Two), HN 2716
Celebration, CL 4011
Celeste (Style One), HN 2237
Celeste (Style Two), HN 3322; also called Isadora, HN 2938
Celia, HN 1726, 1727
Cellist, HN 2226
Cello (Style One), HN 2331
Cello (Style Two), HN 3707
Centre Stage, HN 3861; also called Courtney, (Style One) HN 3869
Centurion, HN 2726
Ceres, Goddes of Plenty, HN 4080
Cerise, HN 1607
Charge of the Light Brigade (Style One), HN 3718
Charge of the Light Brigade (Style Two), HN 4486
Charisma, HN 3090
Charity (Style One), HN 3087
Charity (Style Two), HN 4243
Charles I (1625-1649), HN 3824
Charles II (1660-1685), HN 3825
Charles Dickens, HN 3448
Charley's Aunt (Style One), HN 35, 640
Charley's Aunt (Style Two), HN 1411, 1554
Charley's Aunt (Style Three), HN 1703
Charlie Chaplin, HN 2771
Charlotte (Style One), HN 2421, 2423
Charlotte (Style Two), HN 3658
Charlotte (Style Three), HN 3810, 3811, 3812, 1813
Charlotte (Style Four), HN 4092, 4303
Charlotte (Style Five), HN 4536
Charlotte (Style Six), HN 4758
Charmed, HN 4445
Charmian HN 1568, 1569, 1651
Chelsea Pair (man), HN 579, 580
Chelsea Pair (woman), HN 577, 578
Chelsea Pensioner, HN 689
Cherie, HN 2341
Cherish, HN 4442
Cherished Memories, HN 4265
Cherry Blossom, HN 3092
Cheryl, HN 3253
Chic, HN 2997
Chief, HN 2892
Chieftain, HN 2929
Child from Williamsburg, HN 2154
Child on Crab, HN 32
Child Study (Style One), HN 603A, 603B, 1441
Child Study (Style Two), HN 604A, 604B, 1442, 1443
Child Study (Style Three), HN 605A, 605B
Child's Grace, HN 62, 62A, 510
China Repairer, HN 2943
Chinese Dancer, HN 2840
Chinese Mandarin: see Mandarin (Style One)

Chitarrone, HN 2700
Chloe, CL 4017
Chloe (Style One), HN 1470, 1476, 1479, 1498, 1765, 1956
Chloe (Style Two), M 9, 10, 29
Chloe (Style Three), HN 3883, 3914; also called Amber, HN 4125
Chloe (Style Four), HN 4201A
Chloe (Style Five), HN 4456
Chloe (Style Six), HN 4727; also called Alexandra (Style Three) HN 4557
Choice, HN 1959, 1960
Choir Boy, HN 2141
Chorus Girl, HN 1401
Christening Day, HN 3210, 3211
Christina, CL 3991
Christine (Style One), HN 1839, 1840
Christine (Style Two), HN 2792, 3172
Christine (Style Three), HN 3269, 3337
Christine (Style Four), HN 3767
Christine (Style Five), HN 3905
Christine (Style Six), HN 4307
Christine (Style Seven), HN 4526; also called Gillian (Style Four) HN 4404
Christine (Style Eight), M 200
Christmas Angel, HN 3733, 4060
Christmas Carols, HN 3727, 4061
Christmas Celebration, HN 4721
Christmas Day, HN 3488, 4062
Christmas Day 1999, HN 4214
Christmas Day 2000, HN 4242
Christmas Day 2001, HN 4315
Christmas Day 2002, HN 4422
Christmas Day 2003, HN 4552
Christmas Day 2004, HN 4558; also called Victoria Christmas HN 4675
Christmas Dreams, HN 4447
Christmas Eve, HN 4350
Christmas Garland, HN 4067
Christmas Lantern, HN 3953
Christmas Morn (Style One), HN 1992
Christmas Morn (Style Two), HN 3212, 3245
Christmas Parcels (Style One), HN 2851
Christmas Parcels (Style Two), HN 3493, 4063
Christmas Time, HN 2110
Christopher Columbus, HN 3392
Chu Chin Chow (Style One), HN 450, 460, 461
Chu Chin Chow (Style Two): see One of the Forty, HN 423A - F
Cicely, HN 1516
Cinderella (Style One), HN 3677
Cinderella (Style Two), HN 3991
Circe, HN 1249, 1250, 1254, 1255
Cissie, HN 1808, 1809
Claire (Style One), HN 3209
Claire (Style Two), HN 3646; also called Kaitlyn, HN 4128; Molly, HN 4091; Rosemary (Style Three), HN 3691, 3698
Clara Hamps, HN 4162
Clare, HN 2793
Claribel, HN 1950, 1951
Clarinda, HN 2724
Clarissa (Style One), HN 1525, 1687
Clarissa (Style Two), HN 2345
Claudia, HN 4320; also called Amelia, HN 4327; Gift of Love (Style Two) HN 4751

Claudine, HN 3055
Clemency, HN 1633, 1634, 1643
Cleopatra (Style One), HN 2868
Cleopatra (Style Two), HN 4264
Clever Boy, HN 4482
Clever Girl, HN 4483
Clockmaker, HN 2279
Clothilde, HN 1598, 1599
Cloud, HN 1831
Clown, HN 2890
Clownette, HN 1263; also called Lady Clown, HN 717, 718, 738, 770
Coachman, HN 2282
Cobbler (Style One), HN 542, 543, 682
Cobbler (Style Two), HN 681, 1251, 1283
Cobbler (Style Three), HN 1705, 1706
Cocktails, HN 3070
Colleen, HN 3915
Collinette, HN 1998, 1999
Colonel Fairfax, HN 2903
Columbine (Style One), HN 1296, 1297, 1439
Columbine (Style Two), HN 2185
Columbine (Style Three), HN 2738, 3288, 4059
Coming of Spring, HN 1722, 1723
Confucious, HN 3314
Congratulations, HN 3351
Congratulations To You, HN 4306
Constance (Style One), HN 1510, 1511
Constance (Style Two), HN 3930, 3933
Contemplation (Style One), HN 2213, 2241
Contemplation (Style Two), HN 4761
Contentment, HN 395, 396, 421, 468, 572, 685, 686, 1323
Cookie, HN 2218
Coppelia, HN 2115
Coquette, HN 20, 20A, 37
Coralie, HN 2307
Corinthian, HN 1973
Corporal, 1st, New Hampshire Regiment, 1778, HN 2780
Countess of Chell, HN 3867
Countess of Harrington, HN 3317
Countess Spencer, HN 3320
Country Girl (Style One), HN 3051
Country Girl (Style Two), HN 3856
Country Girl (Style Three), HN 3958
Country Lass, HN 1991A; also called Market Day, HN 1991
Country Love, HN 2418
Country Maid, HN 3163
Country Rose, HN 3221
Country Veterinary, HN 4650
Court Shoemaker, HN 1755
Courtier, HN 1338
Courtney (Style One), HN 3869; also called Centre Stage, HN 3861
Courtney (Style Two), HN 4762
Covent Garden (Style One), HN 1339
Covent Garden (Style Two), HN 2857
Cradle Song, HN 2246
Craftsman, HN 2284
Cricketer (Style One), HN 3814
Cricketer (Style Two), HN 4518
Crinoline, HN 8, 9, 9A, 21, 21A, 413, 566, 628
Crinoline Lady, HN 650, 651, 652, 653, 654, 655
Croquet, HN 3470

Crouching Nude, HN 457
Cruella De Vil, HN 3839
Cup of Tea, HN 2322
Curly Knob, HN 1627
Curly Locks, HN 2049
Curtsey, HN 57, 57B, 66A, 327, 334, 363, 371,
    518, 547, 629, 670
Cymbals, HN 2699
Cynthia (Style One), HN 1685, 1686, 1686A
Cynthia (Style Two), HN 2440
Cyrano de Bergerac, HN 3751

D

D'Artagnan (Style One), HN 3638
D'Artagnan (Style Two), HN 4417
Daddy's Girl, HN 3435
Daddy's Joy, HN 3294
Daffy-Down-Dilly, HN 1712, 1713
Dainty May (Style One), HN 1639, 1656
Dainty May (Style Two), M 67, 73
Dairy Maid, HN 4249
Daisy (Style One), HN 1575, 1961
Daisy (Style Two), HN 3802, 3803, 3804, 3805
Damaris, HN 2079
Dance (Style One), HN 4025
Dance (Style Two), HN 4553
Dancing Delight, HN 3078
Dancing Eyes and Sunny Hair (Style One), HN 1543
Dancing Eyes and Sunny Hair (Style Two), HN 4492
Dancing Figure, HN 311
Dancing Years, HN 2235
Dandy, HN 753
Daniella, HN 4551
Danielle (Style One), HN 3056
Danielle (Stye Two), HN 3001; also called
    Spring Song, HN 3446
Danielle (Style Three), HN 3868
Daphne, HN 2268
Dapple Grey, HN 2521
Darby, HN 1427, 2024
Darling (Style One), HN 1, 1319, 1371, 1372, 4140
Darling (Style Two), HN 1985, 3613
David Copperfield, M 88
Dawn (Style One), HN 1858, 1858A
Dawn (Style Two), HN 3258
Dawn (Style Three), HN 3600
Dawn (Style Four) HN 4603
Daybreak (Style One), HN 3107
Daybreak (Style Two), HN 4196
Daybreak (Style Three), HN 4610
Daydreams, HN 1731, 1732, 1944
Deauville, HN 2344
Debbie, HN 2385, 2400; also called Lavender Rose,
    HN 3481; Moonlight Rose, HN 3483;
    Old Country Roses (Style One), HN 3482;
    Memory Lane, HN 3746; Tranquillity, HN 3747
Deborah (Style One), HN 2701
Deborah (Style Two), HN 3644
Deborah (Style Three), HN 4468
Deborah (Style Four), HN 4735; also called
    Isabel (Style Two) HN 4458
Debut (Style One), HN 3046
Debut (Style Two), HN 4281
Debutante (Style One), HN 2210
Debutante (Style Two), HN 3188

December (Style One), HN 2696; also called
    Gillian (Style Three), HN 3742
December (Style Two), HN 3329; also called
    Amanda, HN 2996, 3406, 3632, 3634, 3635
December (Style Three), HN 3412; also called
    Beatrice, HN 3263, 3631; Kathryn (Style One),
    HN 3413; Lucy (Style Two), HN 3653;
    Summer Serenade, HN 3610
Deidre, HN 2020
Delicia, HN 1662, 1663, 1681
Delight, HN 1772, 1773
Delphine, HN 2136
Demure, HN 3045
Denise (Style One), M 34, 35
Denise (Style Two), HN 2273
Denise (Style Three), HN 2477; also called
    Summer Rose (Style Two), HN 3309
Derrick, HN 1398
Desdemona, HN 3676
Despair, HN 596
Destiny, HN 4164
Detective, HN 2359
Devotion, HN 3228
Diana (Style One), HN 1716, 1717, 1986
Diana (Style Two), HN 2468, 3266
Diana (Style Three), HN 3310
Diana (Style Four), HN4764
Diana the Huntress, HN 2829
Diane, HN 3604
Dick Swiveller, M 90
Dick Turpin (Style One), HN 3272
Dick Turpin (Style Two), HN 3637
Digger (Australian), HN 322, 353
Digger (New Zealand), HN 321
Diligent Scholar, HN 26; also called
    The Attentive Scholar
Dimity, HN 2169
Dinky Doo, HN 1678, 2120, 3618
Dinnertime, HN 3726
Discovery, HN 3428
Do You Wonder... (First Version), HN 1544
Do You Wonder... (Second Version), HN4429
Doctor (Style One), HN 2858
Doctor (Style Two), HN 4286
Dolly (Style One), HN 355
Dolly (Style Two), HN 389, 390; also called
    The Little Mother (Style One), HN 469
Dolly Vardon, HN 1514, 1515
Dominique, HN 3054; also called Paradise, HN 3074
Donna, HN 2939
Dorcas, HN 1490, 1491, 1558
Doreen, HN 1363, 1389, 1390
Doris Keene as Cavallini (Style One), HN 90, 467
Doris Keene as Cavallini (Style Two), HN 96, 345;
    also called Romance
Dorothy, HN 3098
Double Jester, HN 365
Double Spook: see Spooks
Dreaming, HN 3133
Dreamland, HN 1473, 1481
Dreamweaver, HN 2283
Dressing Up (Style One), HN 2964
Dressing Up (Style Two), HN 3300
Drummer Boy, HN 2679
Dryad of the Pines, HN 1869
Duchess of York, HN 3086

Duke of Wellington, HN 3432
Dulcie, HN 2305
Dulcimer, HN 2798
Dulcinea, HN 1343, 1419
Dunce, HN 6, 310, 357

E

Easter Day, HN 1976, 2039
Eastern Grace, HN 3138, 3683
Ecstasy, HN 4163
Edith, HN 2957
Edward VI, HN 4263
Eileen, HN 4730; also called Lisa (Style Two)
    HN 4525
Elaine (Style One), HN 2791, 3307, 3741, 4130
Elaine (Style Two), HN 3214, 3247, 3900
Elaine (Style Three), M 201
Elaine (Style Four), HN 4718
Eleanor (Style One), HN 3906
Eleanor (Style Two), HN 4015
Eleanor (Style Three), HN 4463
Eleanor (Style Four), HN 4624
Eleanor of Aquitaine (1122-1204), HN 3957
Eleanor of Provence, HN 2009
Eleanore, HN 1753, 1754
Elegance, HN 2264
Elfreda, HN 2078
Eliza (Style One), HN 2543, 2543A
Eliza (Style Two), HN 3179
Eliza (Style Three), HN 3798, 3799, 3800, 3801
Eliza Farren, Countess of Derby, HN 3442
Elizabeth, CL 4009
Elizabeth (Style One), HN 2946
Elizabeth (Style Two), HN 2465
Elizabeth (Style Three), HN 4426
Elizabeth (Style Four), M 202
Elizabeth Bennet, HN 3845
Elizabeth Bowes-Lyon, HN 4421
Elizabeth Fry, HN 2, 2A
Elizabethan Lady (Style One): see Lady of the
    Elizabethan Period (Style One)
Elizabethan Lady (Style Two), HN 309; also called
    A Lady of the Elizabethan Period (Style Two)
Ellen (Style One), HN 3020
Ellen (Style Two), HN 3816, 3819
Ellen (Style Three), HN 3992
Ellen (Style Four), HN 4231
Ellen Terry, HN 3826
Ellen Terry as Queen Catherine, HN 379
Ellie (Style One), HN 4046; also called Allison,
    HN 4207
Ellie (Style Two), HN 4017
Elsie Maynard (Style One), HN 639
Elsie Maynard (Style Two), HN 2902
Elyse, HN 2429, 2474, 4131
Embrace, HN 4258
Embroidering, HN 2855
Emily (Style One), HN 3204
Emily (Style Two), HN 3688
Emily (Style Three), HN 3806, 3807, 3808, 3809
Emily (Style Four), HN 4093; also called Patricia
    (Style Six) HN 4738
Emily In Autumn, HN 3004
Emir, HN 1604, 1605; also called Ibrahim, HN 2095
Emma (Style One), HN 2834
Emma (Style Two), HN 3208

Emma (Style Three), HN 3714; also called Madison, HN 4204

Emma (Style Four), HN 3843

Enchanting Evening, HN 3108

Enchantment, HN 2178

Encore (Style One), HN 2751

Encore (Style Two), HN 4282

England, HN 3627

Enigma, HN 3110

Entranced, HN 3186

Erato, The Parnassian Muse, HN 4082

Ermine Coat, HN 1981

Ermine Muff, HN 54, 332, 671; also called Lady Ermine; Lady With Ermine Muff

Erminie, M 40

Esmeralda, HN 2168

Especially For You, HN 4750; also called Best Wishes (Style Two) HN 3971; Forever Yours (Style Two) HN 4501; Kate (Style Three) HN 4233

Estelle, HN 1566, 1802

Ete (Summer), HN 3067

Eugene, HN 1520, 1521

Europa and the Bull (Style One), HN 95

Europa and the Bull (Style Two), HN 2828

Eve, CL 4002

Eve, HN 2466

Evelyn, HN 1622, 1637

Eventide, HN 2814

F

Fagin (Style One), HN 534, M 49

Fagin (Style Two), HN 3752

Fair Lady (Style One), HN 2193, 2832, 2835; also called Kay, HN 3340

Fair Lady (Style Two), HN 3216, 3336

Fair Lady (Style Three), HN 4719

Fair Maid, HN 4222

Fair Maiden, HN 2211, 2434

Fairy (Style One), HN 1324

Fairy (Style Two), HN 1374, 1380, 1532

Fairy (Style Three), HN 1375, 1395, 1533

Fairy (Style Four), HN 1376, 1536

Fairy (Style Five), HN 1377

Fairy (Style Six), HN 1378, 1396, 1535

Fairy (Style Seven), HN 1379, 1394, 1534

Fairy (Style Eight), HN 1393

Fairyspell, HN 2979

Faith (Style One), HN 3082

Faith (Style Two), HN 4151

Faithful Friend, HN 3696

Falstaff (Style One), HN 571, 575, 608, 609, 619, 638, 1216, 1606

Falstaff (Style Two), HN 618, 2054

Falstaf (Style Three), HN 3236

Family (Style One), HN 2720, 2721

Family (Style Two), HN 4645

Family Album, HN 2321

Fanny: see Angela (Style One)

Fantasy, HN 3296

Faraway, HN 2133

Farewell Daddy, HN 4363

Farmer (Style One), HN 3195

Farmer (Style Two), HN 4487

Farmer's Boy, HN 2520

Farmer's Wife (Style One), HN 2069

Farmer's Wife (Style Two), HN 3164

Fat Boy (Style One), HN 530, M44

Fat Boy (Style Two), HN 555, 1893

Fat Boy (Style Three), HN 2096

Father and Daughter, HN 4484

Father and Son, HN 4448

Father Christmas, HN 3399

Favourite, HN 2249

Faye, CL 3984

Faye, HN 4523

February (Style One), HN 2703; also called Gillian (Style Three), HN 3742; February (Style Two), HN 3331; also called Amanda, HN 2996, 3406, 3632, 3634, 3635

February (Style Three), HN 3342; also called Beatrice, HN 3263, 3631; Kathryn (Style One), HN 3413; Lucy (Style Two), HN 3653; Summer Serenade, HN 3610

Feeding Time, HN 3373

Felicity, CL 3986, CL 4103; also called 'Bethany' CL 3987

Felicity, HN 4354

Female Study, HN 606A, 606B

Fiddler, HN 2171

Field Marshall Montgomery, HN 3405

Figure of the Month; HN 2693, 2695, 2696, 2697, 2703, 2707, 2708, 2711, 2790, 2794, 3165, 3166; also called Gillian (Style Three), HN 3742

Finishing Touch, HN 4329

Fiona (Style One), HN 1924, 1925, 1933

Fiona (Style Two), HN 2694

Fiona (Style Three), HN 3252

Fiona (Style Four), HN 3748; also called Adrienne, HN 2152, 2304; Joan (Style Two), HN 3217

Fireman, HN 4411

First Bloom, HN 3913; also called Mackenzie, HN 4109

First Dance, HN 2803; also called Samantha (Style Two), HN 3304

First Kiss, HN 4681

First Lesson, HN 4358

First Love, HN 2747

First Outing, HN 3377

First Performance, HN 3605

First Prize, HN 3911

First Recital, HN 3652

First Steps (Style One), HN 2242

First Steps (Style Two), HN 3282

First Steps (Style Three), HN 3361

First Violin, HN 3704

First Waltz, HN 2862

Fisherman, HN 4511

Fisherwomen, HN 80, 349, 359, 631; also called Looking for the Boats; Waiting for the Boats

Fleur (Style One), HN 2368, 2369; also called Flower of Love, HN 2460, 3970

Fleur (Style Two), HN 4663

Fleurette, HN 1587

Flirtation, HN 3071

Flora, HN 2349

Florence, HN 2745

Florence Nightingale, HN 3144

Flounced Skirt, HN 57A, 66, 77, 78, 333; also called The Bow

Flower Arranging, HN 3040

Flower of Love, HN 2460, 3970; also called Fleur, HN 2368, 2369

Flower of the Month, Child; HN 3323, 3324, 3325, 3326, 3327, 3328, 3329, 3330, 3331, 3332, 3333, 3334; also called Amanda, HN 2996, 3406, 3632, 3634, 3635

Flower of Scotland, HN 4240

Flower Seller, HN 789

Flower Seller's Children, HN 525, 551, 1206, 1342, 1406

Flowergirl (Style One), HN 3479; also called Bridesmaid (Style Seven), HN 3476

Flowergirl (Style Two), HN 3602

Flowers for Mother, HN 3454

Flowers for You, HN 3889

Flute, HN 2483

Foaming Quart, HN 2162

Folly, HN 1335, 1750

Fond Farewell, HN 3815; also called Au Revoir (Style One), HN 3723

Footballer, HN 4517

For Someone Special, HN 4470

For You, HN 3754, 3863

For Your Special Day, HN 4313; also called Sweet Delight, HN 4398

Forever Yours (Style One), HN 3949

Forever Yours (Style Two), HN 4501; also called Best Wishes (Style Two), HN 3971; Especially For You HN 4750; Forever Yours (Style Two) HN 4501; Kate (Style Three), HN 4233

Forget-Me-Not (Style One), HN 1812, 1813

Forget Me Not (Style Two), HN 3388

Forget-Me-Nots, HN 3700

Fortune Teller, HN 2159

Forty Winks, HN 1974

Four O'Clock, HN 1760

Fragrance (Style One), HN 2334, 3311

Fragrance (Style Two), HN 3220, 3250

Frances, CL 4001

Francesca (Style One), HN 4238

Francesca (Style Two), HN 4534

Francine, HN 2422, 2422A

Francoise, HN 2897

Frangçon, HN 1720, 1721

Free As The Wind, HN 3139

Free Spirit (Style One), HN 3157, 3159

Free Spirit (Style Two), HN 3728; also called Spring Serenade, HN 3956

Free Spirit (Style Three), HN 4609

French Horn, HN 2795

French Peasant, HN 2075

Friar Tuck, HN 2143

Friendship, HN 3491

Frodo, HN 2912

From the Heart, HN 4454

From This Day Forth, CL 3990

From This Day Forward, HN 4380

Fruit Gathering, HN 449, 476, 503, 561, 562, 706, 707

G

Gabrielle, CL 4012

Gaffer, HN 2053

Gaiety, HN 3140

Gail (Style One), HN 2937

Gail (Style Two), HN 3321

Gail (Style Three), M212

Gainsborough Hat, HN 46, 46A, 47, 329, 352, 383, 453, 675, 705
Galadriel, HN 2915
Gamekeeper, HN 2879
Gandalf, HN 2911
Gardener, HN 3161
Gardening Time, HN 3401
Gaspar, HN 4704
Gay Morning, HN 2135
Geisha (Style One), HN 354, 376, 376A, 387, 634, 741, 779, 1321, 1322; also called The Japanese Lady
Geisha (Style Two), HN 1223, 1234, 1292, 1310
Geisha (Style Three), HN 3229
Gemma, HN 3661
General Robert E. Lee, HN 3404
Genevieve, HN 1962
Genie, HN 2989, 2999
Gentle Breeze, HN 4317
Gentleman from Williamsburg, HN 2227
Gentlewoman, HN 1632
Geoffrey Boycott, HN 3890
George Washington at Prayer, HN 2861
Georgia, HN 4457
Georgiana, HN 2093
Georgina (Style One), HN 2377
Georgina (Style Two), HN 4047
Georgina (Style Three), HN 4237
Geraldine, HN 2348
Gift For You, HN 4449
Gift of Freedom, HN 3443
Gift of Friendship, HN 4446
Gift of Love (Style One), HN 3427
Gift of Love (Style Two), HN 4751; also called Amelia HN 4327; Claudia HN 4320
Gillian (Style One), HN 1670, 1670A
Gillian (Style Two), HN 3042, 3042A
Gillian (Style Three), HN 3742; also called Figure of the Month, HN 2693, 2695, 2696, 2697, 2703, 2707, 2708, 2711, 2790, 2794, 3165, 3166
Gillian (Style Four), HN4404; also called Christine (Style Seven), HN 4526
Gimli, HN 2922
Girl Evacuee, HN 3203
Girl on Rock, AIL 8
Girl Stretching, AIL 6
Girl With Ponytail, AIL 7
Giselle, HN 2139
Giselle, The Forest Glade, HN 2140
Gladys (First Version), HN 1740, 1741
Gladys (Second Version), HN 4168
Gleaner, HN 1302
Gloria (Style One), HN 1488, 1700
Gloria (Style Two), HN 3200
Gnome, HN 319, 380, 381
God Bless You, HN 3400
Golden Days, HN 2274
Golfer, HN 2992
Gollum, HN 2913
Gollywog, HN 1979, 2040
Good Catch, HN 2258
Good Companion, HN 3608
Good Day Sir, HN 2896
Good Friends, HN 2783
Good King Wenceslas (Style One), HN 2118
Good King Wenceslas (Style Two), HN 3262
Good Luck, HN 4070

Good Morning, HN 2671
Good Pals, HN 3132
Goody Two Shoes (Style One), HN 1889, 1905, 2037
Goody Two Shoes (Style Two), M 80, 81
Goosegirl (Style One), HN 425, 436, 437, 448, 559, 560
Goose Girl (Style Two), HN 2419
Goose Girl (Style Three), HN 3936
Gossips, HN 1426, 1429, 2025
Grace (Style One), HN 2318
Grace (Style Two), HN 3699
Grace Darling, HN 3089
Grace, W.G., HN 3640
Graduate [female] (Style One), HN 3016
Graduate [female] (Style Two), HN 4542
Graduate [male] (Style One), HN 3017
Graduate [male] (Style Two), HN 3959
Graduate [male] (Style Three), HN 4543
Graduation [female], HN 3942
Grand Manner, HN 2723
Grandma, HN 2052, 2052A
Grandpa's Story, HN 3456
Granny, HN 1804, 1832
Granny's Heritage, HN 1873, 1874, 2031
Granny's Shawl, HN 1642, 1647
Greetings, HN 4250
Greta, HN 1485
Gretchen, HN 1397, 1562
Grief, HN 595
Griselda, HN 1993
Grizel, HN 1629
Grossmith's 'Tsang Ihang' Perfume of Tibet, HN 582
Groucho Marx, HN 2777
Guardsman, HN 2784
Gulliver, HN 3750
Guy Fawkes (Style One), HN 98, 347, 445
Guy Fawkes (Style Two), HN 3271
Gwendolen, HN 1494, 1503, 1570
Gwynneth, HN 1980
Gypsy Dance (Style One), HN 2157
Gypsy Dance (Style Two), HN 2230

H

Hannah (Style One), HN 3369, 3655
Hannah (Style Two), HN 3649, 3870
Hannah (Style Three), HN 4050, 4051, 4052
Hannah (Style Four), HN 4407
Happy Anniversary (Style One), HN 3097
Happy Anniversary (Style Two), HN 3254
Happy Anniversary (Style Three), HN 4068
Happy Anniversary (Style Four), HN 4604, 4605, 4606
Happy Birthday (Style One), HN 3095
Happy Birthday (Style Two), HN 3660
Happy Birthday (Style Three), HN 3829
Happy Birthday 2000, HN 4215
Happy Birthday 2001, HN 4308
Happy Birthday 2002, HN 4393
Happy Birthday 2003, HN 4464
Happy Birthday 2004, HN 4528
Happy Birthday 2005, HN 4722
Happy Christmas, HN 4255
Happy Joy, Baby Boy, HN 1541
Happy Holidays, HN 4443
Harlequin (Style One), HN 2186

Harlequin (Style Two), HN 2737, 3287, 4058
Harlequinade, HN 585, 635, 711, 780
Harlequinade Masked, HN 768, 769, 1274, 1304
Harmony (Style One), HN 2824
Harmony (Style Two), HN 4096
Harmony (Style Three), HN 4567
Harp, HN 2482
Harriet, CL 3998
Harriet (Style One), HN 3177
Harriet (Style Two), HN 3794, 3795, 3796, 3797
Harvestime, HN 3084
Hatshepsut, HN 4191
Hayley, HN 4556
Hazel (Style One), HN 1796, 1797
Hazel (Style Two), HN 3167
He Loves Me, HN 2046
Heart of Scotland, HN 4608
Heart to Heart, HN 2276
Heathcliff and Cathy, HN 4071
Heather, HN 2956; also called Marie (Style Three), HN 3357
Hebe, Handmaiden to the Gods, HN 4079
Heidi, HN 2975
Helen (Style One), HN 1508, 1509, 1572
Helen (Style Two), HN 2994
Helen (Style Three), HN 3601, 3687, 3763, 3886; also called Miss Kay, HN 3659
Helen (Style Four), M213
Helen of Troy (Style One), HN 2387
Helen of Troy (Style Two), HN 4497
Helena, CL 3994
Hello Daddy, HN 3651
Helmsman, HN 2499
Helping Mother, HN 4228
Henley, HN 3367
Henrietta Maria (Style One), HN 2005
Henrietta-Maria (Style Two), HN 4260
Henry Irving As Cardinal Wolsey, HN 344
Henry Lytton As Jack Point, HN 610
Henry V at Agincourt, HN 3947
Henry VIII (Style One), HN 370, 673
Henry VIII (Style Two), HN 1792
Henry VIII (Style Three), HN 3350
Henry VIII (Style Four), HN 3458
Her Ladyship, HN 1977
Here A Little Child I Stand... (First Version), HN 1546
Here A Little Child I Stand... (Second Version), HN 4428
Herminia, HN 1644, 1646, 1704
Hermione, HN 2058
Hercules, HN 4561
Hibernia, HN 2932
Highwayman, HN 527, 592, 1257
Hilary, HN 2335
Hinged Parasol, HN 1578, 1579
His Holiness Pope John-Paul II, HN 2888
Hiver (Winter), HN 3069
HM Queen Elizabeth, The Queen Mother (Style One), HN 2882
HM Queen Elizabeth, The Queen Mother (Style Two), HN 3189
HM Queen Elizabeth, The Queen Mother (Style Three), HN 3944
HM Queen Elizabeth, The Queen Mother (Style Four), HN 4086
HM Queen Elizabeth, The Queen Mother As The Duchess of York, HN 3230

HM Queen Elizabeth II (Style One), HN 2502
HM Queen Elizabeth II (Style Two), HN 2878
HM Queen Elizabeth II (Style Three), HN 3436
HM Queen Elizabeth II (Style Four), HN 3440
HM Queen Elizabeth II (Style Five), HN 4372
HM Queen Elizabeth II Coronation, HN 4476
Hockey Player, HN 4519
Hold Tight, HN 3298
Holly, HN 3647
Home Again, HN 2167
Home at Last, HN 3697
Home Guard, HN 4494
Homecoming, HN 3295
Hometime, HN 3685
Honey, HN 1909, 1910, 1963
Honourable Frances Duncombe, HN 3009
Hope (Style One), HN 3061
Hope (Style Two), HN 4097
Hope (Style Three), HN 4565
Hornpipe, HN 2161
Hostess of Williamsburg, HN 2209
HRH Prince Philip, Duke of Edinburgh, HN 2386
HRH The Prince of Wales (Style One), HN 2883
HRH The Prince of Wales (Style Two), HN 2884
HRH The Princess of Wales, HN 2887
Huckleberry Finn, HN 2927
Hunting Squire, HN 1409; also called Squire,
    HN 1814
Hunts Lady, HN 1201
Huntsman (Style One), HN 1226
Huntsman (Style Two), HN 1815; also called
    John Peel, HN 1408
Huntsman (Style Three), HN 2492
Hurdy Gurdy, HN 2796

I

I'm Nearly Ready, HN 2976
Ibrahim, HN 2095; also called Emir, HN 1604, 1605
Idle Hours, HN 3115
In Grandma's Days, HN 339, 340 388, 442;
    also called Lilac Shawl HN 44, 44A;
    Poke Bonnet HN 362, 612, 765
In Loving Arms, HN 4262
In The Stocks (Style One), HN 1474, 1475; also
    called Love in the Stocks; Love Locked In
In The Stocks (Style Two), HN 2163
Independence, HN 4375
Indian Brave, HN 2376
Indian Maiden, HN 3117
Indian Temple Dancer, HN 2830
Innocence (Style One), HN 2842
Innocence (Style Two), HN 3730
Invitation, HN 2170
Iona, HN 1346
Ireland, HN 3628
Irene, HN 1621, 1697, 1952
Irish Charm, HN 4580
Irish Colleen, HN 766, 767
Irishman, HN 1307
Isabel (Style One), HN 3716
Isabel (Style Two), HN 4458; also called Deborah
    (Style Four) HN 4735
Isabella, Countess of Sefton, HN 3010
Isadora, HN 2938; also called Celeste (Style Two),
    HN 3322
Isobel, CL 3980

It Won't Hurt, HN 2963
Ivy, HN 1768, 1769

J

Jack, HN 2060
Jack Point, HN 85, 91, 99, 2080, 3920, 3925
Jacqueline (Style One), HN 2000, 2001
Jacqueline (Style Two), HN 2333
Jacqueline (Style Three), HN 3689
Jacqueline (Style Four), HN 4309
James, HN 3013
James I (1603-1625), HN 3822
Jane (Style One), HN 2014
Jane (Style Two), HN 2806
Jane (Style Three), HN 3260
Jane (Style Four), HN 3711
Jane (Style Five), HN 4110
Jane (Style Six), M 203
Jane Eyre, HN 3842
Jane Seymour, HN 3349
Janet (Style One), HN 1537, 1538, 1652, 1737
Janet (Style Two), M 69, 75
Janet (Style Three), HN 1916, 1964
Janet (Style Four), HN 4042
Janet (Style Five), HN 4310; also called Pride of
    Scotland HN 4453
Janette, HN 3415; also called Kirsty (Style One),
    HN 2381
Janice (Style One), HN 2022, 2165
Janice (Style Two), HN 3624; also called
    Lady Eaton HN 3623
Janine, HN 2461
January (Style One), HN 2697; also called
    Gillian (Style Three), HN 3742
January (Style Two), HN 3330; also called Amanda,
    HN 2996, 3406, 3632, 3634, 3635
January (Style Three), HN 3341; also called Beatrice,
    HN 3263, 3631; Kathryn (Style One), HN 3413;
    Lucy (Style Two), HN 3653; Summer Serenade,
    HN 3610
Japanese Fan, HN 399, 405, 439, 440
Japanese Lady: see A Geisha (Style One)
Jasmine (Style One), HN 1862, 1863, 1876
Jasmine (Style Two), HN 3832
Jasmine (Style Three), HN 4127; also called
    Megan (Style Two) HN 3887
Jasmine (Style Four), HN 4431
Jayne (Style One), HN 4210; also called Marianne
    (Style Two), HN 4153
Jayne (Style Two), HN 4524
Jean (Style One), HN 1877, 1878, 2032
Jean (Style Two), HN 2710
Jean (Style Three), HN 3757, 3862
Jemma, HN 3168
Jennifer (Style One), HN 1484
Jennifer (Style Two), HN 2392
Jennifer (Style Three), HN 3447
Jennifer (Style Four), HN 4248
Jenny, HN 4423; also called Alexandra (Style Three)
    HN 4557; Chloe (Style Six) HN 4727
Jersey Milkmaid, HN 2057; also called The Milkmaid
    (Style Two), HN 2057A
Jessica (Style One), HN 3169, 3497
Jessica (Style Two), HN 3850
Jessica (Style Three), HN 4049
Jessica (Style Four), HN 4583

Jessie, HN 4763
Jester (Style One), HN 45, 71, 71A, 320, 367, 412,
    426, 446, 552, 616, 627, 1295, 1702, 2016,
    3922
Jester (Style Two), HN 45A, 45B, 55, 308, 630,
    1333
Jester (Style Three), HN 3335
Jesus (Style One), HN 3484, 3487
Jesus (Style Two), HN 4707
Jill, HN 2061
Joan (Style One), HN 1422, 2023
Joan (Style Two), HN 3217; also called Adrienne,
    HN 2152, 2304; Fiona (Style Four), HN 3748
Joan of Arc, HN 3681
Joanna, HN 4711
Joanne (Style One), HN 2373
Joanne (Style Two), HN 3422; also called
    Annabelle, HN 4090
Joanne (Style Three), HN 4202
John Peel, HN 1408; also called Huntsman
    (Style Two), HN 1815
Joker (Style One), HN 3196; also called Tip-Toe,
    HN 3293
Joker (Style Two), HN 2252
Jolly Sailor, HN 2172
Joseph (Style One), HN 3438, 3486
Joseph (Style Two), HN 4035
Joseph (Style Three), HN 4701
Josephine, HN 4223; also called Caroline
    (Style Three), HN 4395
Jovial Monk, HN 2144
Joy (Style One), HN 3184
Joy (Style Two), HN 3875
Joy (Style Three), HN 4053, 4054
Joy (Style Four), HN 4568
Judge (Style One), HN 2443, 2443A
Judge (Style Two), HN 4412
Judge and Jury, HN 1264
Judith (Style One), HN 2089
Judith (Style Two), HN 2278, 2313
Julia, CL 3993
Julia (Style One), HN 2705, 2706
Julia (Style Two), HN 4124
Julia (Style Three), HN 4390
Julie (Style One), HN 2995, 3407
Julie (Style Two), HN 3878
Juliet (Style One), HN 2968
Juliet (Style Two), HN 3453
July (Style One), HN 2794; also called Gillian
    (Style Three), HN 3742
July (Style Two), HN3324; also called Amanda,
    HN 2996, 3406, 3632, 3634, 3635
July (Style Three), HN 3347; also called Beatrice,
    HN 3263, 3631; Kathryn (Style One), HN 3413;
    Lucy (Style Two), HN 3653; Summer Serenade,
    HN 3610
June (Style One), HN 1690, 1691, 1947, 2027
June (Style Two), M 65, 71
June (Style Three), HN 2790; also called Gillian
    (Style Three), HN 3742
June (Style Four), HN 2991
June (Style Five), HN 3323; also called Amanda,
    HN 2996, 3406, 3632, 3634, 3635
June (Style Six), HN 3346; also called Beatrice,
    HN 3263, 3631; Kathryn (Style One), HN 3413;
    Lucy (Style Two), HN 3653; Summer Serenade,
    HN 3610

Juno and the Peacock, HN 2827
Just For You (Style One), HN 3355
Just For You (Style Two), HN 4236; also called
    With Love (Style Two) HN 4746
Just One More, HN 2980

K

Kaitlyn, HN 4128; also called Claire (Style Two),
    HN 3646; Molly, HN 4091; Rosemary (Style
    Three), HN 3691, 3698
Karen (Style One), HN 1994
Karen (Style Two), HN 2388
Karen (Style Three), HN 3270, 3338, 3749
Karen (Style Four), M 204
Kate, CL 3995
Kate (Style One), HN 2789
Kate (Style Two), HN 3765, 3882
Kate (Style Three), HN 4233; also called Best Wishes
    (Style Two), HN 3971, Especially For You
    HN 4650; Forever Yours, HN 4501
Kate (Style Five), HN 4779
Kate Hannigan, HN 3088
Kate Hardcastle, HN 1718, 1719, 1734, 1861,
    1919, 2028
Katie (Style One), HN 3360
Katie (Style Two), HN 4123; also called Lindsay,
    HN 3645
Katie (Style Three), HN 4323
Katharine (Style One), HN 61, 74, 341, 471, 615,
    793
Katherine (Style Two), HN 3708
Kathleen (Style One), HN 1252, 1253, 1275, 1279,
    1291, 1357, 1512
Kathleen (Style Two), HN 2933, 3100
Kathleen (Style Three), HN 3609, 3880;
    also called Brianna, HN 4126
Kathryn (Style One), HN 3413; also called Beatrice,
    HN 3263, 3631; Lucy (Style Two), HN 3653;
    Summer Serenade, HN 3610; Wildflower of the
    Month
Kathryn (Style Two), HN 4040; also called Alexis,
    HN 4205
Kathy (Style One), HN 2346
Kathy (Style Two), HN 3305; also called Lynne
    (Style One), HN 2329, 3740
Katrina (Style One), HN 2327
Katrina (Style Two), HN 4467
Kay, HN 3340; also called Fair Lady (Style One),
    HN 2193, 2832, 2835
Keep In Touch, HN 4377
Kelly (Style One), HN 2478, 3222
Kelly (Style Two), HN 3912; also called Angela
    (Style Four), HN 3690; Sweet Sixteen (Style Two),
    HN 3648
Kelly (Style Three), HN 4157
Kerry, HN 3036, 3461
Kimberley (Style One), HN 2969; also called
    Yours Forever, HN 3354
Kimberley (Style Two), HN 3379, 3382, 3864
Kindred Spirits, HN 4077
King Arthur, HN 4541
King Charles, HN 404, 2084, 3459
Kirsten, HN 4101
Kirsty (Style One), HN 2381; also called Janette,
    HN 3415

Kirsty (Style Two), HN 3213, 3246, 3480, 3743
Kiss, AIL 1
Kiss [boy], HN 4064
Kiss [girl], HN 4065
Kitty (Style One), HN 1367
Kitty (Style Two), HN 3876
Kneeling Shepherd, HN 4055
Ko-Ko (Style One), HN 1266, 1286
Ko-Ko (Style Two), HN 2898
Kristine, HN 4537
Kurdish Dancer, HN 2867

L

L'Ambitieuse, HN 3359
La Loge, HN 3472
La Sylphide, HN 2138
Lady and Blackamoor (Style One), HN 374
Lady and Blackamoor (Style Two), HN 375, 377, 470
Lady and the Unicorn, HN 2825
Lady Anne, HN 83, 87, 93
Lady Anne Nevill, HN 2006
Lady April, HN 1958, 1965
Lady Betty, HN 1967
Lady Charmian, HN 1948, 1949
Lady Clare, HN 1465
Lady Clown, HN 717, 718, 738, 770; also called
    Clownette, HN 1263
Lady Diana Spencer, HN 2885
Lady Eaton, HN 3623; also called Janice (Style Two),
    HN 3624
Lady Ermine: see The Ermine Muff
Lady Fayre, HN 1265, 1557
Lady from Williamsburg, HN 2228
Lady Godiva, HN 4641
Lady Jane Grey, HN 3680
Lady Jester (Style One), HN 1221, 1222, 1332
Lady Jester (Style Two), HN 1284, 1285
Lady Jester (Style Three), HN 3924
Lady of the Elizabethan Period (Style One), HN 40,
    40A, 73, 411; also called Elizabethan Lady
    (Style One)
Lady of the Elizabethan Period (Style Two): see
    Elizabethan Lady (Style Two)
Lady of the Fan, HN 48, 52, 53, 53A, 335, 509
Lady of the Georgian Period, HN 41, 331, 444, 690,
    702
Lady of the Snows, HN 1780, 1830
Lady Pamela, HN 2718
Lady with an Ermine Muff, HN 82; also called
    Afternoon Call; Making a Call
Lady with Rose, HN 48A, 52A, 68, 304, 336, 515,
    517, 584, 624
Lady with Shawl, HN 447, 458, 626, 678, 679
Lady Worsley, HN 3318
Ladybird, HN 1638, 1640
Laird, HN 2361, 2361A
Lalla Rookh, HN 2910
Lambeth Walk, HN 1880, 1881
Lambing Time (Style One), HN 1890
Lambing Time (Style Two), HN 3855
Lamp Seller, HN 3278
Lancelot and Guinivere, HN 3112
Land Girl, HN 4361
Land of Nod (First Version), HN 56, 56A, 56B
Land of Nod (Second Version), HN 4174
Last Waltz, HN 2315, 2316

Laura (Style One), HN 2960, 3136
Laura (Style Two), HN 3760
Laura (Style Three), HN 4665
Laura (Style Four), M214
Lauren (Style One), HN 3290; also called Ann
    (Style Two), HN 3259
Lauren (Style Two), HN 3872
Lauren (Style Three), HN 3975
Laurianne, HN 2719
Lavender Rose, HN 3481; also called Debbie,
    HN 2385, 2400; Memory Lane, HN 3746;
    Moonlight Rose, HN 3483; Old Country Roses
    (Style One), HN 3482; Tranquillity, HN 3747
Lavender Woman, HN 22, 23, 23A, 342, 569, 744
Lavinia, HN 1955
Lawyer (Style One), HN 3041
Lawyer (Style Two), HN 4289
Leading Lady, HN 2269
Leap-Frog, HN 4030
Le Bal, HN 3702
Leda and the Swan, HN 2826
Legolas, HN 2917
Leisure Hour, HN 2055
Les Parapluies, HN 3473
Lesley, HN 2410
Let's Play, HN 3397
Liberty (Style One), HN 3201
Liberty (Style Two), HN 4353
Lido Lady (First Version), HN 1220, 1229
Lido Lady (Second Version), HN 4247
Lifeboat Man (Style One), HN 2764
Lifeboat Man (Style Two), HN 4570
Lifeguard, HN 2781
Lights Out (Style One), HN 2262
Lights Out (Style Two), HN 4465
Lilac Shawl, HN 44, 44A; also called In Grandma's
    Days, HN 339, 340, 388, 442; The Poke Bonnet,
    HN 362, 612, 765
Lilac Time, HN 2137
Lilian In Summer, HN 3003
Lillie Langtry, HN 3820
Lily (Style One), HN 1798, 1799
Lily (Style Two), HN 3626
Lily (Style Three), HN 3902
Linda (Style One), HN 2106
Linda (Style Two), HN 2758
Linda (Style Three), HN 3374
Linda (Style Four), HN 3879
Linda (Style Five), HN 4450
Lindsay, HN 3645; also called Katie (Style Two),
    HN 4123
Lisa (Style One), HN 2310, 2394, 3265
Lisa (Style Two), HN4525; also called Eileen
    HN 4730
Lise, HN 3474
Lisette, HN 1523, 1524, 1684
Little Ballerina, HN 3395, 3431
Little Bo Peep, HN 3030
Little Boy Blue (Style One), HN 2062
Little Boy Blue (Style Two), HN 3035
Little Bridesmaid: see Bridesmaid (Style One)
Little Child So Rare And Sweet (Style One), HN 1540
Little Child So Rare And Sweet (Style Two), HN 1542
Little Child So Rare And Sweet (Style Three),
    HN 4491
Little Jack Horner (Style One), HN 2063
Little Jack Horner (Style Two), HN 3034

Little Lady Make Believe, HN 1870
Little Land, HN 63, 67
Little Lord Fauntleroy, HN 2972
Little Miss Muffet, HN 2727
Little Mistress, HN 1449
Little Mother (Style One), HN 469; also called
　Dolly (Style Two), HN 389, 390
Little Mother (Style Two), HN 1418, 1641;
　also called Young Widow, HN 1399
Little Nell, HN 540, M 51
Lizana, HN 1756, 1761
Lizzie, HN 2749
Lobster Man, HN 2317, 2323
London Cry, Strawberries, HN 749, 772
London Cry, Turnips and Carrots, HN 752, 771
Long John Silver (Style One), HN 2204
Long John Silver (Style Two), HN 3719
Looking for the Boats: see Fisherwomen
Lord Olivier as Richard III, HN 2881
Loretta, HN 2337
Lori, HN 2801
Lorna, HN 2311
Lorna, CL 3997
Lorraine (Style One), HN 3118
Lorraine (Style Two), HN 4301
Louise (Style One), HN 2869
Louise (Style Two), HN 3207
Louise (Style Three), HN 3888
Love, AIL 2
Love Everlasting, HN 4280
Love In The Stocks: see In The Stocks (Style One)
Love Letter (Style One), HN 2149
Love Letter (Style Two), HN 3105
Love Locked In: see In The Stocks (Style One)
Love of Life, HN 4529
Love So Tender, HN 4016
Love Song, HN 4737; also called Lucy (Style Four)
　HN 4459
Lovers, HN 2762, 2763
Loving Thoughts (Style One), HN 3948
Loving Thoughts (Style Two), HN 4318
Loving You, HN 3389
Loyal Friend (Style One), HN 3358
Loyal Friend (Style Two), HN 4736; also called
　My Love (Style Two) HN 4392
Lt. General Ulysses S. Grant, HN 3403
Lucinda, CL 3983
Lucrezia Borgia, HN 2342
Lucy (Style One), HN 2863
Lucy (Style Two), HN 3653; also called Beatrice,
　HN 3263, 3631; Kathryn (Style One), HN 3413;
　Lucy (Style Two), HN 3653; Summer Serenade,
　HN 3610; Wildflower of the Month
Lucy (Style Three), HN 3858
Lucy (Style Four), HN 4459; also called Love Song
　HN 4737
Lucy Ann, HN 1502, 1565
Lucy Lockett (Style One), HN 485
Lucy Lockett (Style Two), HN 524
Lucy Lockett (Style Three), HN 695, 696
Lunchtime, HN 2485
Lute, HN 2431
Lydia (Style One), HN 1906, 1907, 1908
Lydia (Style Two), HN 4211; also called Beth
　(Style Two) HN 4156
Lynne (Style One), HN 2329, 3740; also called
　Kathy (Style Two), HN 3305

Lynne (Style Two), HN 4155
Lynsey, HN 3043
Lyric, HN 2757

M

Macaw, HN 1779, 1829
Mackenzie, HN 4109; also called First Bloom,
　HN 3913
Madaleine, HN 3255
Madeline, HN 4152
Madison, HN 4204; also called Emma (Style Three),
　HN 3714
Madonna of the Square, HN 10, 10A, 11, 14, 27,
　326, 573, 576, 594, 613, 764, 1968, 1969,
　2034
Magic Dragon, HN 2977
Magical Moments, HN 4607
Magpie Ring, HN 2978
Maid of the Meadow, HN 4316
Maisie, HN 1618, 1619
Major, 3rd New Jersey Regiment, 1776, HN 2752
Make Believe, HN 2224, 2225
Making A Call: see Lady With an Ermine Muff
Making Friends, HN 3372
Maleficent, HN 3840
Mam'selle, HN 658, 659, 724, 786
Man in Tudor Costume, HN 563
Mandarin (Style One), HN 84, 316, 318, 382, 611,
　746, 787, 791; also called Chinese Mandarin;
　Mikado
Mandarin (Style Two), HN 366, 455, 641
Mandarin (Style Three), HN 601
Mandy, HN 2476
Mantilla, HN 2712, 3192
Many Happy Returns, HN 4254
March (Style One), HN 2707; also called
　Gillian (Style Three), HN 3742
March (Style Two), HN 3332; also called Amanda,
　HN 2996, 3406, 3632, 3634, 3635
March (Style Three), HN 3343; also called Beatrice,
　HN 3263, 3631; Kathryn (Style One), HN 3413;
　Lucy (Style Two), HN 3653; Summer Serenade,
　HN 3610
Margaret (Style One), HN 1989
Margaret (Style Two), HN 2397, 3496; also called
　Adele, HN 2480; Camille (Style Two), HN 3171
Margaret (Style Three), HN 4311
Margaret (Style Four), M 205
Margaret of Anjou (Style One), HN 2012
Margaret of Anjou (Style Two), HN 4073
Margaret Tudor, HN 3838
Margery, HN 1413
Margot, HN 1628, 1636, 1653
Marguerite, HN 1928, 1929, 1930, 1946
Maria, HN 3381
Marianne (Style One), HN 2074
Marianne (Style Two), HN 4153; also called Jane
　(Style Six), HN 4210
Marie (Style One), HN 401, 434, 502, 504, 505,
　506
Marie (Style Two), HN 1370, 1388, 1417, 1489,
　1531, 1635, 1655
Marie (Style Three), HN 3357; also called
　Heather, HN 2956
Marie Sisley, HN 3475
Marietta, HN 1341, 1446, 1699

Marigold, HN 1447, 1451, 1555
Marilyn, HN 3002
Marion, HN 1582, 1583
Mariquita, HN 1837
Marjorie, HN 2788
Market Day, HN 1991; also called Country Lass,
　HN 1991A
Marriage of Art and Industry, HN 2261
Martine, HN 3053; also called Promenade
　(Style Two), HN 3072
Mary (Style One), HN 2374
Mary (Style Two), HN 3375
Mary (Style Three), HN 3437, 3485
Mary (Style Four), HN 3903
Mary (Style Five), HN 4114
Mary (Style Six), HN 4700
Mary and Jesus, HN 4034
Mary, Countess Howe, HN 3007
Mary Had A Little Lamb, HN 2048
Mary Jane, HN 1990
Mary, Mary, HN 2044
Mary Queen of Scots (Style One), HN 2931
Mary Queen of Scots (Style Two), HN 3142
Mary Tudor, HN 3834
Mask (Style One), HN 656, 657, 729, 733, 785,
　1271
Mask (Style Two), HN 4141
Mask Seller, HN 1361, 2103
Masque, HN 2554, 2554A
Masquerade [man] (Style One), HN 599, 636, 683
Masquerade [woman] (Style One), HN 600, 637,
　674
Masquerade (Style Two), HN 2251, 2259
Master, HN 2325
Master Sweep, HN 2205
Matador and Bull (Style One), HN 2324
Matador and Bull (Style Two), HN 4566
Matilda, HN 2011
Maureen (Style One), HN 1770, 1771
Maureen (Style Two), M 84, 85
Maureen (Style Three), HN 2481; also called
　Tina, HN 3494
Maxine, HN 3199
May (Style One), HN 2746, 3251
May (Style Two), HN 2711; also called Gillian
　(Style Three), HN 3742
May (Style Three), HN 3334; also called Amanda,
　HN 2996, 3406, 3632, 3634, 3635
May (Style Four), HN 3345; also called Beatrice,
　HN 3263, 3631; Kathryn (Style One), HN 3413;
　Lucy (Style Two), HN 3653; Summer Serenade,
　HN 3610
Mayor, HN 2280
Maytime, HN 2113
Meditation, HN 2330
Meg, HN 2743
Megan (Style One), HN 3306
Megan (Style Two), HN 3887; also called Jasmine
　(Style Three), HN 4127
Megan (Style Three), HN 4539
Melanie, HN 2271
Melchior (Style One), HN 4037
Melchior (Style Two), HN 4702
Melinda, HN 4209
Melissa (Style One), HN 2467
Melissa (Style Two), HN 3885
Melissa (Style Three), HN 3977

Melody (Style One), HN 2202
Melody (Style Two), HN 4117
Memories, HN 1855, 1856, 1857, 2030
Memory Lane, HN 3746 also called Debbie,
    HN 2385, 2400; Lavender Rose, HN 3481;
    Moonlight Roses, HN 3483; Old Country Roses
    (Style One), HN 3842
Mendicant, HN 1355, 1365
Mephisto, HN 722, 723
Mephistopheles and Marguerite, HN 755, 775
Meriel, HN 1931, 1932
Merlin, HN 4540
Mermaid, HN 97, 300
Merry Christmas, HN 3096
Meryll, HN 1917; also called Toinette, HN 1940
Message of Love, HN 4531
Messiah, HN 3952
Mexican Dancer, HN 2866
Michele, HN 2234; also called Autumn Attraction,
    HN 3612
Michelle, HN 4158
Midinette (Style One), HN 1289, 1306
Midinette (Style Two), HN 2090
Midnight Premier, HN 4765
Midsummer Noon, HN 1899, 1900, 2033
Mikado: see A Mandarin (Style One)
Mikaela, HN 4550
Milady, HN 1970
Milestone, HN 3297
Milking Time, HN 3, 306
Milkmaid (Style One): see Shepherdess (Style Two)
Milkmaid (Style Two), HN 2057A; also called Jersey
Milkmaid, HN 2057
Milkmaid (Style Three), HN 4305
Millennium Celebration, HN 4201B, 4321, 4325
Millicent, HN 1714, 1715, 1860
Millie (Style One), HN 3945, 3946
Millie (Style Two), HN 4212
Minuet, HN 2019, 2066
Mirabel (Style One), HN 1743, 1744
Mirabel (Style Two), M 68, 74
Miranda (Style One), HN 1818, 1819
Miranda (Style Two), HN 3037
Mirror, HN 1852, 1853
Miss 1926, HN 1205, 1207
Miss Demure, HN 1402, 1440, 1463, 1499, 1560
Miss Fortune, HN 1897, 1898
Miss Kay, HN 3659; also called Helen (Style Three),
    HN 3601, 3687, 3763, 3886
Miss Maisie, HN 3997
Miss Muffet, HN 1936, 1937
Miss Tilly, HN 3998
Miss Violet, HN 3997
Miss Winsome, HN 1665, 1666
Missing You, HN 4076
M'Ladys Maid, HN 1795, 1822
Modena, HN 1845, 1846
Modern Piper, HN 756
Modesty, HN 2744
Moira, HN 1347
Moll Flanders, HN 3849
Molly, HN 4091; also called Claire (Style Two),
    HN 3646; Kaitlyn, HN 4128; Rosemary
    (Style Three) HN 3691, 3698
Molly Malone, HN 1455
Monica (Style One), HN 1458, 1459, 1467, 3617
Monica (Style Two), M 66, 72

Monique, HN 2880; also called Allure, HN 3080
Monte Carlo, HN 2332
Moondancer, HN 3181
Moonlight, HN 4611
Moonlight Gaze, HN4362
Moonlight Rose, HN 3483; also called Debbie,
    HN 2385, 2400; Lavender Rose, HN 3481,
    Memory Lane, HN 3746; Old Country Roses
    (Style One), HN 3482; Tranquillity, HN 3747
Moonlight Serenade, HN 4530; also called
    Special Wished HN 4749
Moonlight Stroll, HN 3954; also called
    Summer Breeze, HN 3724
Moor, HN 1308, 1366, 1425, 1657, 2082, 3642,
    3926; also called An Arab, HN 33, 343, 378
Moorish Minstrel, HN 34, 364, 415, 797
Moorish Piper Minstrel, HN 301, 328, 416
Morning Breeze, HN 3313
Morning Glory, HN 3093
Morning Ma'am, HN 2895
Morning Walk, HN 3860
Mother and Child (Style One), HN 3235, 3348,
    3353
Mother and Child (Style Two), HN 3938
Mother and Daughter (Style One), HN 2841, 2843
Mother and Daughter (Style Two), HN 4562
Mother and Son, HN 4680
Motherhood (Style One), HN 28, 30, 303
Motherhood (Style Two), HN 462, 570, 703, 743
Mother's Help, HN 2151
Mother's Helper, HN 3650
Mr. Micawber (Style One), HN 532, M 42
Mr. Micawber (Style Two), HN 557, 1895
Mr. Micawber (Style Three), HN 2097
Mr. Pickwick (Style One), HN 529, M 41
Mr. Pickwick (Style Two), HN 556, 1894
Mr. Pickwick (Style Three), HN 2099
Mrs. Bardell, M 86
Mrs. Fitzherbert, HN 2007
Mrs. Hugh Bonfoy, HN 3319
Musicale, HN 2756
My Best Friend, HN 3011
My First Figurine, HN 3424
My First Pet, HN 3122
My Love (Style One), HN 2339; also called
    Antoinette (Style Two), HN 2326
My Love (Style Two), HN 4392; also called
    Loyal Friend (Style Two) HN 4736
My Pet, HN 2238
My Pretty Maid, HN 2064
My Teddy, HN 2177
My True Love, HN 4001
Myfanwy Jones, HN 39, 92, 456, 514, 516, 519,
    520, 660, 668, 669, 701, 792; also called
    The Welsh Girl

N

Nadine (Style One), HN 1885, 1886
Nadine (Style Two), HN 4500
Nana, HN 1766, 1767
Nancy, HN 2955
Nanny, HN 2221
Naomi, CL 3996
Naomi, HN 4661
Napoleon at Waterloo, HN 3429
Natalie (Style One), HN 3173, 3498

Natalie (Style Two), HN 4048
Natasha, HN 4154
Necklace, HN 393, 394
Nefertiti, HN 3844
Negligee, HN 1219, 1228, 1272, 1273, 1454
Nell, HN 3014
Nell Gwynn, HN 1882, 1887
Nelson, HN 2928
New Baby, HN 3712, 3713
New Bonnet, HN 1728, 1957
New Companion, HN 2770
New Dawn, HN 4314
Newhaven Fishwife, HN 1480
Newsboy, HN 2244
Newsvendor, HN 2891
Nicola, CL 4000
Nicola, HN 2804, 2839; also called Tender Moment,
    HN 3303
Nicole (Style One), HN 3421, 3686
Nicole (Style Two), HN 4112
Nicole (Style Three), HN 4527
Nina, HN 2347
Ninette (Style One), HN 2379, 3417; also called
    Olivia (Style Two), HN 3339
Ninette (Style Two), HN 3215, 3248, 3901
Ninette (Style Three), M 206
Ninette (Style Four), HN 4717
Noel, HN 4084
Noelle, HN 2179
Norma, M 36, 37
North American Indian Dancer, HN 2809
Nosegay: see The Bouquet
November (Style One), HN 2695; also called
    Gillian (Style Three), HN 3742
November (Style Two), HN 3328; also called
    Amanda, HN 2996, 3406, 3632, 3634, 3635
November (Style Three), HN 3411; also called
    Beatrice, HN 3263, 3631; Kathryn (Style One),
    HN 3413; Lucy (Style Two), HN 3653;
    Summer Serenade, HN 3610
Nude on Rock, HN 593
Nurse, HN 4287

O

October (Style One), HN 2693; also called
    Gillian (Style Three), HN 3742
October (Style Two), HN 3327; also called Amanda,
    HN 2996, 3406, 3632, 3634, 3635
October (Style Three), HN 3410; also called
    Beatrice, HN 3263, 3631; Kathryn (Style One),
    HN 3413; Lucy (Style Two), HN 3653; Summer
    Serenade, HN 3610
Odds and Ends, HN 1844
Off To School, HN 3768
Off To The Pond, HN 4227
Officer of the Line, HN 2733
Old Balloon Seller (Style One), HN 1315, 3737
Old Balloon Seller (Style Two), HN 2129
Old Balloon Seller and Bulldog, HN 1791, 1912
Old Ben, HN 3190
Old Country Roses (Style One), HN 3482; also called
    Debble, HN 2385, 2400; Lavender Rose,
    HN 3481; Memory Lane, HN 3746; Moonlight
    Rose, HN 3483; Tranquillity, HN 3747
Old Country Roses (Style Two), HN 3692
Old Father Thames, HN 2993

Old King, HN 358, 623, 1801, 2134
Old King Cole, HN 2217
Old Lavender Seller, HN 1492, 1571
Old Man, HN 451
Old Meg, HN 2494
Old Mother Hubbard, HN 2314
Olga, HN 2463
Oliver Hardy, HN 2775
Oliver Twist, M 89
Oliver Twist and The Artful Dodger, HN 3786
Olivia (Style One), HN 1995
Olivia (Style Two), HN 3339; also called Ninette
   (Style One), HN 2379, 3417
Olivia (Style Three), HN 3717; also called
   Britanny, HN 4206
Olivia (Style Four), HN 4766
Omar Khayyam (Style One), HN 408, 409
Omar Khayyam (Style Two), HN 2247
Omar Khayyam and the Beloved (Style One),
   HN 407
Omar Khayyam and the Beloved (Style Two)
   419, 459, 598
On the Beach, HN 3877
Once Upon a Time, HN 2047
One of the Forty (Style One), HN 417, 490, 495,
   501, 528, 648, 677, 1351, 1352
One of the Forty (Style Two), HN 418, 494, 498,
   647, 666, 704, 1353
One of the Forty (Style Three), HN 423
One of the Forty (Style Four), HN 423A
One of the Forty (Style Five), HN 423B
One of the Forty (Style Six), HN 423C
One of the Forty (Style Seven), HN 423D
One of the Forty (Style Eight), HN 423E
One of the Forth (Style Nine), HN 423F
One of the Forty (Style Ten), HN 427
One of the Forty (Style Eleven), HN 480, 493, 497,
   499, 664, 714
One of the Forty (Style Twelve), HN 481, 483, 491,
   646, 667, 712, 1336, 1350
One of the Forty (Style Thirteen), HN 482, 484, 492,
   645, 663, 713
One of the Forty (Style Fourteen), HN 496, 500,
   649, 665, 1354
One That Got Away, HN 2153
Ophelia, HN 3674
Open Road, HN 4161
Optimism, HN 4165
Orange Lady, HN 1759, 1953
Orange Seller, HN 1325
Orange Vendor, HN 72, 508, 521, 1966
Organ Grinder, HN 2173
Our First Christmas, HN 3452
Out for a Walk, HN 86, 443, 748
Over the Threshold, HN 3274
Owd Willum, HN 2042

P

Pageboy, HN 4374
Paige, HN 4767
Painting, HN 3012
Paisley Shawl (Style One), HN 1392, 1460, 1707,
   1739, 1987
Paisley Shawl (Style Two), M 3, 4, 26
Paisley Shawl (Style Three), HN 1914, 1988
Palio, HN 2428

Pamela (Style One), HN 1468, 1469, 1564
Pamela (Style Two), HN 2479, 3223
Pamela (Style Three), HN 3756
Pan on Rock, HN 621, 622
Panorama, HN 3028
Pantalettes (Style One), HN 1362, 1412, 1507,
   1709
Pantalettes (Style Two), M 15, 16, 31
Paradise, HN 3074; also called Dominique, HN 3054
Parisian, HN 2445
Park Parade, HN 3116
Parson's Daughter, HN 337, 338, 441, 564, 790,
   1242, 1356, 2018
Partners, HN 3119
Past Glory, HN 2484
Patchwork Quilt, HN 1984
Patricia (Style One), HN 1414, 1431, 1462, 1567
Patricia (Style Two), M7, 8, 28
Patricia (Style Three), HN 2715
Patricia (Style Four), HN 3365
Patricia (Style Five), HN 3907
Patricia (Style Six), HN 4738; also called Emily
   (Style Four) HN 4093
Paula, HN 2906, 3234
Pauline (Style One), HN 1444
Pauline (Style Two), HN 2441
Pauline (Style Three), HN 3643, 3656
Pavlova, HN 487, 676; also called Swan Song
Peace (Style One), HN 2433, 2470
Peace (Style Two), HN 4568
Pearly Boy (Style One), HN 1482, 1547
Pearly Boy (Style Two), HN 2035
Pearly Boy (Style Three), HN 2767
Pearly Girl (Style One), HN 1483, 1548
Pearly Girl (Style Two), HN 2036
Pearly Girl (Style Three), HN 2769
Pecksniff (Style One), HN 535, M43
Pecksniff (Style Two), HN 553, 1891
Pecksniff (Style Three), HN 2098
Pedlar Wolf, HN 7
Peek a Boo, HN 3363
Peggy, HN 1941, 2038
Penelope, CL 3988
Penelope, HN 1901, 1902
Penny, HN 2338, 2424
Penny's Worth, A, HN 2408
Pensive, HN 3109
Pensive Moments, HN 2704
Perfect Gift, HN 4409
Perfect Pair, HN 581
Perfect Pose, HN 4357
Performance, HN 3827
Philippa, CL 4010
Philippa of Hainault (Style One), HN 2008
Philippa of Hainault (Style Two), HN 4066
Philippine Dancer, HN 2439
Phyllis (Style One), HN 1420, 1430, 1486, 1698
Phyllis (Style Two), HN 3180
Picardy Peasant (man), HN 13, 17, 19
Picardy Peasant (woman), HN 4, 5, 17A, 351, 513
Picnic, HN 2308
Pied Piper (Style One), HN 1215, 2102
Pied Piper (Style Two), HN 3721
Pierrette (Style One), HN 642, 643, 644, 691, 721,
   731, 732, 784
Pierrette (Style Two), HN 795, 796
Pierrette (Style Three), HN 1391, 1749

Pillow Fight, HN 2270
Pilot Skipper, HN 4510
Pinkie, HN 1552, 1553
Piper (Style One), HN 2907
Piper (Style Two), HN 3444
Pirate King, HN 2901
Pirouette, HN 2216
Playmates (Style One), HN 3127
Playments (Style Two), HN 4682
Please Keep Still, HN 2967
Please Sir, HN 3302
Poacher, HN 2043
Pocahontas, HN 2930
Poke Bonnet, HN 362, 612, 765; also called In
   Grandma's Days, HN 339, 340, 388, 442;
   Lilac Shawl HN 44, 44A
Policeman, HN 4410
Polish Dancer, HN 2836
Polka, HN 2156
Polly, HN 3178
Polly Peachum (Style One), HN 463, 465, 550, 589,
   614, 680, 693
Polly Peachum (Style Two), HN 489, 549, 620, 694,
   734
Polly Peachum (Style Three), HN 698, 699, 757-762,
   M 21, 22, 23
Polly Put The Kettle On, HN 3021
Pollyanna, HN 2965
Porthos, HN 4416
Posy For You, A, HN 3606
Potter, HN 1493, 1518, 1522
Prayers, HN 4378
Premiere, HN 2343, 2343A
Pretty As A Picture, HN 4312
Pretty Lady, HN 69, 70, 302, 330, 361, 384, 565,
   700, 763, 783
Pretty Polly, HN 2768
Pride and Joy (Style One), HN 2945
Pride and Joy (Style Two), HN 4102
Pride of Scotland HN 4453; also called Janet
   (Style Five) HN 4310
Prima Ballerina, HN 4024
Primrose, HN 3710
Primroses, HN 1617
Prince Albert, Duke of York, HN 4420
Prince of Wales, HN 1217
Princess, HN 391, 392, 420, 430, 431, 633
Princess Badoura (Style One), HN 2081, 3921
Princess Badoura (Style Two), HN 4179
Princess Elizabeth, HN 3682
Printemps (Spring), HN 3066
Priscilla (Style One), HN 1337, 1340, 1495, 1501,
   1559
Priscilla (Style Two), M 13, 14, 24
Private, 1st Georgia Regiment, 1777, HN 2779
Private, 2nd South Carolina Regiment, 1781,
   HN 2717
Private, 3rd North Carolina Regiment, 1778,
   HN 2754
Private, Connecticut Regiment, 1777, HN 2845
Private, Delaware Regiment, 1776, HN 2761
Private, Massachusetts Regiment, 1778, HN 2760
Private, Pennsylvania Rifle Battalion, 1776, HN 2846
Private, Rhode Island Regiment, 1781, HN 2759
Prized Possession, HN 2942
Professor, HN 2281
Promenade (Style One), HN 2076

Promenade (Style Two), HN 3072; also called Martine, HN 3053
Promise, HN 4033
Proposal (man), HN 725, 1209
Proposal (woman), HN 715, 716, 788
Prudence, HN 1883, 1884
Prue, HN 1996
Puff and Powder, HN 397, 398, 400, 432, 433
Punch and Judy Man, HN 2765
Puppetmaker, HN 2253
Puppy Love, HN 3371
Pussy, HN 18, 325, 507; also called The Black Cat
Pyjamas, HN 1942

Q

Quality Street, HN 1211, 1211A
Queen, HN 3847
Queen Alexandra Nurse, HN 4596
Queen Anne, HN 3141
Queen Elizabeth I, HN 3099
Queen Elizabeth II and The Duke of Edinburgh, HN 3836
Queen Mary II, HN 4474
Queen of Sheba, HN 2328
Queen of the Dawn, HN 2437
Queen of the Ice, HN 2435
Queen Sophia, HN 4074
Queen Victoria, HN 3125
Queen Victoria and Prince Albert, HN 3256
Quiet, They're Sleeping, HN 3657

R

R.C.M.P. 1873, HN 2555
R.C.M.P. 1973, HN 2547
Rachel (Style One), HN 2919, 2936
Rachel (Style Two), HN 3976
Rachel (Style Three), M 207
Rachel (Style Four), HN 4742; also called Ruby (Style Two) HN 4521
Rachel (Style Five), HN 4780
Rag Doll, HN 2142
Rag Doll Seller, HN 2944
Railway Sleeper, HN 4418
Rapunzel, HN 3841
Rebecca (Style One), HN 2805
Rebecca (Style Two), HN 3414
Rebecca (Style Three), HN 4041
Rebecca (Style Four), HN 4203
Rebecca (Style Five), HN 4768
Recital, HN 4466
Red Red Rose, HN 3994
Reflection, HN 3039
Reflections, HN 1820, 1821, 1847, 1848
Regal Lady, HN 2709
Regency, HN 1752
Regency Beau, HN 1972
Remembering You, HN 4085
Rendezvous, HN 2212
Repose, HN 2272
Rest Awhile, HN 2728
Return of Persephone, HN 31
Reverie, HN 2306
Reward, HN 3391
Rhapsody, HN 2267
Rhoda, HN 1573, 1574, 1688

Rhythm, HN 1903, 1904
Richard the Lionheart, HN 3675
Rita, HN 1448, 1450
Ritz Bell Boy, HN 2772
River Boy, HN 2128
Robert Burns (Style One), HN 42
Robert Burns (Style Two), HN 3641
Robin, M 38, 39
Robin Hood (Style One), HN 2773
Robin Hood (Style Two), HN 3720
Robin Hood and Maid Marion, HN 3111
Rocking Horse, HN 2072
Rooftop Santa, HN 4713; also called Santa Claus (Style Four) HN 4715
Romance (Style Two), HN 2430
Romance (Style One): see Doris Keene as Cavallini (Style Two)
Romany Sue, HN 1757, 1758
Romeo and Juliet (Style One), HN 3113
Romeo and Juliet (Style Two), HN 4057
Rosabell, HN 1620
Rosalind, HN 2393
Rosamund (Style One), HN 1320
Rosamund (Style Two), HN 1497, 1551
Rosamund (Style Three), M 32, 33
Rose (Style One), HN 1368, 1387, 1416, 1506, 1654, 2123
Rose (Style Two), HN 3709
Rose (Style Three), HN 4581
Rose Arbour, HN 3145
Rose Garden, HN 4559
Roseanna, HN 1921, 1926
Rosebud (Style One), HN 1580, 1581
Rosebud (Style Two), HN 1983
Rosemary (Style One), HN 2091
Rosemary (Style Two), HN 3143
Rosemary (Style Three), HN 3691, 3698; also called Claire (Style Two), HN 3646; Kaitlyn, HN 4128; Molly, HN 4091
Rosemary (Style Four), HN 4662
Rosie, HN 4094; also called Special Gift (Style Two) HN 4744
Rosina, HN 1358, 1364, 1556
Rowena, HN 2077
Royal Governor's Cook, HN 2233
Ruby (Style One), HN 1724, 1725
Ruby (Style Two), HN 4521; also called Rachel (Style Four) HN 4742
Rumpelstiltskin, HN 3025
Rustic Swain, HN 1745, 1746
Ruth (Style One), HN 2799
Ruth (Style Two), HN 4099
Ruth, The Pirate Maid, HN 2900

S

Sabbath Morn, HN 1982
Sailor, HN 4632
Sailor's Holiday, HN 2442
Sairey Gamp (Style One), HN 533, M 46
Sairey Gamp (Style Two), HN 558, 1896
Sairey Gamp (Style Three), HN 2100
Sally (Style One), HN 2741
Sally (Style Two), HN 3383, 3851, 4160
Salome (Style One), HN 1775, 1828
Salome (Style Two), HN 3267
Sam Weller, HN 531, M 48

Samantha (Style One), HN 2954
Samantha (Style Two), HN 3304; also called First Dance, HN 2803
Samantha (Style Three), HN 4043
Samantha (Style Four), HN 4403
Samurai Warrior, HN 3402
Samwise, HN 2925
Sandra, HN 2275, 2401; also called Annette (Style Two), HN 3495
Santa Claus (Style One), HN 2725
Santa Claus (Style Two), HN 4175
Santa Claus (Style Three), HN 4714
Santa Clause (Style Four), HN 4715
Santa's Helper, HN 3301
Sara (Style One), HN 2265, 3308
Sara (Style Two), HN 3219, 3249
Sara (Style Three), HN 4720
Sarah (Style One), HN 3380
Sarah (Style Two), HN 3384, 3852, 3857
Sarah (Style Three), HN 3978
Sarah Bernhardt, HN 4023
Sarah In Winter, HN 3005
Saucy Nymph, HN 1539
Save Some For Me, HN 2959
Saxaphone Player, HN 4284
Scarlett, HN 4408; also called All My Love HN 4747
Scarlett O'Hara, HN 4200
Scheherazade, HN 3835
Schoolmarm, HN 2223
Scotch Girl, HN 1269
Scotland, HN 3629
Scotties, HN 1281, 1349
Scottish Highland Dancer, HN 2436
Scribe, HN 305, 324, 1235
Scrooge, M 87
Sea Harvest, HN 2257
Sea Sprite (Style One), HN 1261
Sea Sprite (Style Two), HN 2191
Seafarer, HN 2455
Seashore, HN 2263
Second Violin, HN 3705
Secret The, HN 4560
Secret Moment, HN 3106
Secret Thoughts (Style One), HN 2382
Secret Thoughts (Style Two), HN 4197
Sentimental Pierrot, HN 36, 307
Sentinel, HN 523
September (Style One), HN 3166; also called Gillian (Style Three), HN 3742
September (Style Two), HN 3326; also called Amanda, HN 2996, 3406, 3632, 3634, 3635
September (Style Three), HN 3409; also called Beatrice, HN 3263, 3631; Kathryn (Style One), HN 3413; Lucy (Style Two), HN 3653; Summer Serenade, HN 3610
Serena, HN 1868
Serenade, HN 2753
Serenity (Style One), HN 4396
Serenity (Style Two), HN 4769
Sergeant, 6th Maryland Regiment, 1777, HN 2815
Sergeant, Virginia 1st Regiment Continental Light Dragoons, 1777, HN 2844
Shakespeare, HN 3633
Shall I Compare Thee To A Summer's Day, HN 3999
Sharon (Style One), HN 3047, 3455
Sharon (Style Two), HN 3603
She Loves Me Not, HN 2045

Sheikh, HN 3083
Sheila, HN 2742
Shepherd (Style One), HN 81, 617, 632
Shepherd (Style Two), HN 709, M 17, 19
Shepherd (Style Three), HN 751
Shepherd (Style Four), HN 1975
Shepherd (Style Five), HN 3160
Shepherdess (Style One), HN 708, M 18, 20
Shepherdess (Style Two), HM 735, 750;
    also called The Milkmaid (Style One)
Shepherdess (Style Three), HN 2990
Shepherdess (Style Four), HN 2420
Sherlock Holmes, HN 3639
Shirley, HN 2702
Shore Leave, HN 2254
Shy Anne, HN 60, 64, 65, 568
Shylock, HN 79, 317
Sibell, HN 1668, 1695, 1735
Siesta, HN 1305
Silks and Ribbons, HN 2017
Silversmith of Williamsburg, HN 2208
Simone, CL 4004
Simone (Style One), HN 2378
Simone (Style Two), HN 4535
Single Red Rose, HN 3376
Sir Edward, HN 2370
Sir Francis Drake, HN 3770
Sir Henry Doulton, HN 3891
Sir John A. MacDonald, HN 2860; also called
    The Statesman, HN 2859
Sir Ralph, HN 2371
Sir Thomas, HN 2372
Sir Thomas Lovell, HN 356
Sir Walter Raleigh, HN 1742, 1751, 2015
Sir Winston Churchill (Style One), HN 3057
Sir Winston Churchill (Style Two), HN 3433
Sister and Brother, HN 4356
Sisterly Love, HN 3130
Sisters, HN 3018, 3019
Sit, HN 3123, 3430
Skater, (Style One), HN 2117
Skater, (Style Two), HN 3439
Skating, HN 4370
Slapdash, HN 2277
Sleep, HN 24, 24A, 25, 25A, 424, 692, 710
Sleeping Beauty (Style One), HN 3079
Sleeping Beauty (Style Two), HN 4000
Sleepy Darling, HN 2953
Sleepy Scholar, HN 15, 16, 29
Sleepyhead (Style One), HN 2114
Sleepyhead (Style Two), HN 3761
Sleepyhead (Style Three), HN 4413
Smiling Buddha, HN 454
Snake Charmer, HN 1317
Snow White, HN 3678
Soiree (Style One), HN 2312
Soiree (Style Two), M215
Solitude, HN 2810
Sonata, HN 2438
Song of the Sea, HN 2729
Sonia, HN 1692, 1738
Sonny, HN 1313, 1314
Sophia Baines, HN 4167
Sophia Charlotte, Lady Sheffield, HN 3008
Sophia Dorothea, HN 4074
Sophie (Style One), HN 2833

Sophie (Style Two), HN 3257
Sophie (Style Three), HN 3790, 3791, 3792, 3793
Sophie (Style Four), HN 3715
Sophie (Style Five), HN 3995
Sophie (Style Six), HN 4620
Sophistication, HN 3059
Sorcerer, HN 4252
Sorceress, HN 4253
Southern Belle (Style One), HN 2229, 2425
Southern Belle (Style Two), HN 3174, 3244
Spanish Flamenco Dancer, HN 2831
Spanish Lady, HN 1262, 1290, 1293, 1294, 1309
Special Celebration, HN 4234; also called
    Treasured Moments HN 4745
Special Friend, HN 3607
Special Friends, HN 4257
Special Gift (Style One), HN 4118, 4129
Special Gift (Style Two), HN 4744; also called
    Rosie HN 4094
Special Moments, HN 4430
Special Occasion, HN 4100
Special Treat, HN 3663
Special Wishes, HN 4749; also called Moonlight
    Serenade HN 4530
Specially For You, HN 4232
Spinning, HN 2390
Spirit of Scotland, HN 4469
Spirit of the Wind, HN 1777, 1825
Spook (Style One), HN 50, 51, 51A, 51B, 58, 512,
    625
Spook (Style Two), HN 1218
Spooks, HN 88, 89, 372; also called Double Spooks
Spring (Style One), HN 312, 472
Spring (Style Two), HN 588
Spring (Style Three), HN 1774, 1827
Spring (Style Four), HN 2085
Spring (Style Five), HN 588
Spring Flowers, HN 1807, 1945
Spring Morning (Style One), HN 1922, 1923
Spring Morning (Style Two), HN 3725;
    also called Summer Scent, HN 3955
Spring Morning (Style Three), HN 4451
Spring Posy, HN 3916
Spring Serenade, HN 3956; also called Free Spirit
    (Style Two), HN 3728
Spring Song, HN 3446; also called Danielle
    (Style Two), HN 3001
Spring Walk, HN 3120
Springtime (Style One), HN 1971
Springtime (Style Two), HN 3033
Springtime (Style Three), HN 3477
Springtime (Style Four), HN 4586
Squire, HN 1814; also called Hunting Squire,
    HN 1409
St. George (Style One), HN 385, 386, 1800, 2067
St. George (Style Two), HN 2051
St. George (Style Three), HN 2856
St. George (Style Four), HN 4371
Stage Struck, HN 3951
Standing Shepherd, HN 4056
Stan Laurel, HN 2774
Stargazer, HN 3182
Star Performer, HN 3950
Statesman, HN 2859; also called Sir John A.
    MacDonald, HN 2860
Stayed At Home, HN 2207

Stephanie, CL 3985
Stephanie (Style One), HN 2807, 2811
Stephanie (Style Two), HN 3759
Stephanie (Style Three), HN 4461
Stephanie (Style Four), M216
Stick 'em Up, HN 2981
Stiggins, HN 536, M 50
Stitch in Time, HN 2352
Stop Press, HN 2683
Storytime (Style One), HN 3126
Storytime (Style Two), HN 3695
Storytime (Boy), HN 4088
Storytime (Girl), HN 4089
Strolling (Style One), HN 3073
Strolling (Style Two), HN 3755
Studious Boy, HN 4563
Studious Girl, HN 4564
Sugar and Spice, HN 4103
Suitor, HN 2132
Summer (Style One), HN 313, 473
Summer (Style Two), HN 2086
Summer (Style Three), HN 4271
Summer (Style Four), HN 4587
Summer Blooms (Style One), HN 3917
Summer Blooms (Style Two), HN 4194
Summer Breeze (Style One), HN 3724;
    also called Moonlight Stroll, HN 3954
Summer Breeze (Style Two), HN 4626, 4627
Summer Duet, HN 4225
Summer Fragrance, HN 4195
Summer Rose (Style One), HN 3085
Summer Rose (Style Two), HN 3309; also called
    Denise (Style Three), HN 2477
Summer Scent, HN 3955; also called Spring Morning
    (Style Two), HN 3725
Summer Serenade, HN 3610; also called Beatrice,
    HN 3263, 3631; Kathryn (Style One), HN 3413;
    Lucy (Style Two) HN 3653
Summer Stroll, HN 4406
Summer's Darling (Style One), HN 3091
Summer's Darling (Style Two), HN 4401, 4601
Summer's Day (Style One), HN 2181
Summer's Day (Style Two), HN 3378
Summer's Dream, HN 4660
Summertime (Style One), HN 3137
Summertime (Style Two), HN 3478
Sunday Best (Style One), HN 2206, 2698
Sunday Best (Style Two), HN 3218, 3312
Sunday Morning, HN 2184
Sunrise, HN 4199
Sunset, HN 4198
Sunshine Girl (First Version), HN 1344, 1348
Sunshine Girl (Second Version), HN 4245
Surprise, HN 4376
Susan (Style One), HN 2056
Susan (Style Two), HN 2952, 3050
Susan (Style Three), HN 3871
Susan (Style Four), HN 4230
Susan (Style Five), HN 4532
Susan (Style Six), M 208
Susan (Style Seven), HN 4777
Susanna, HN 1233, 1288, 1299
Susannah, HN 4221
Susanne, CL 3982
Suzanne (Style One), HN 4098
Suzanne (Style Two), HN 4452

Suzette, HN 1487, 1577, 1585, 1696, 2026
Swan Song: see Pavlova
Sweet and Fair, HN 1864, 1865
Sweet and Twenty (Style One), HN 1298, 1360, 1437, 1438, 1549, 1563,
Sweet and Twenty (Style Two), HN 1589, 1610
Sweet Anne (Style One), HN 1318, 1330, 1331, 1453, 1496, 1631, 1701
Sweet Anne (Style Two), M 5, 6, 27
Sweet April, HN 2215
Sweet Bouquet (Style One), HN 3000
Sweet Bouquet (Style Two), HN 3859
Sweet Delight, HN 4398; also called For Your Special Day, HN 4313
Sweet Devotion, HN 4625
Sweet Dreams (Style One), HN 2380
Sweet Dreams (Style Two), HN 3394
Sweet Dreams (Style Three), HN 4193
Sweet Lavender, HN 1373; also called Any Old Lavender
Sweet Lilac, HN 3972
Sweet Maid (Style One), HN 1504, 1505
Sweet Maid (Style Two), HN 2092
Sweet Memories, HN 4582
Sweet Music, HN 4302
Sweet Poetry, HN 4113
Sweet Perfume, HN 3094
Sweet Seventeen, HN 2734
Sweet Sixteen (Style One), HN 2231
Sweet Sixteen (Style Two), HN 3648; also called Angela (Style Four), HN 3690; Kelly (Style Two), HN 3912
Sweet Suzy, HN 1918
Sweet Violets, HN 3175
Sweetheart, HN 4319
Sweetheart Boy, HN 4351
Sweetheart Girl, HN 4352
Sweeting, HN 1935, 1938
Swimmer (First Version), HN 1270, 1326, 1329
Swimmer (Second Version), HN 4246
Sylvia, HN 1478
Sympathy, HN 2838, 2876
Symphony, HN 2287

T

Tailor, HN 2174
Take Me Home, HN 3662
Taking The Reins, CL 4013
Taking The Waters, HN 4402, 4602
Taking Things Easy, HN 2677, 2680
Tall Story, HN 2248
Tango, HN 3075
Tanya, CL 4006
Tapestry Weaving, HN 3048
Taylor, HN 4496
Teatime, HN 2255
Teeing Off, HN 3276
Teenager, HN 2203
Tender Greetings, HN 4261
Tender Moment (Style One), HN 3303; also called Nicola, HN 2804, 2839
Tender Moment (Style Two), HN 4192
Tenderness, HN 2713, 2714
Teresa (Style One), HN 1682, 1683
Teresa (Style Two), HN 3206
Tess, HN 2865

Tess of the D'Urbervilles, HN 3846
Tete-a-Tete (Style One), HN 798, 799
Tete-a-Tete (Style Two), HN 1236, 1237
Thank You (Style One), HN 2732
Thank You (Style Two), HN 3390; also called Thank You Mother, HN 4251
Thank You Mother, HN 4251; also called Thank You (Style Two), HN 3390
Thankful, HN 3129, 3135
Thanks Doc, HN 2731
Thanksgiving, HN 2446
Theresa, CL 3992
Thinking of You (Style One), HN 3124, 3490
Thinking of You (Style Two), HN 4585
This Little Pig, HN 1793, 1794, 2125
Thoughts For You, HN 4397
Tiffany, HN 4771
Tildy, HN 1576, 1859
Time For Bed, HN 3762
Tina, HN 3494; also called Maureen (Style Three), HN 2481
Tinkle Bell, HN 1677
Tinsmith, HN 2146
Tiny Tim, HN 539, M 56
Tip-Toe, HN 3293; also called Joker (Style One), HN 3196
Titania, HN 3679
To Bed, HN 1805, 1806
To Love and Cherish, CL 4003
To The Fairway, CL 4008
Toinette, HN 1940; also called Meryll, HN 1917
Tom, HN 2864
Tom Bombadil, HN 2924
Tom Brown, HN 2941
Tom Sawyer, HN 2926
Tom, Tom, The Piper's Son, HN 3032
Tomorrow's Dreams (Style One), HN 3128
Tomorrow's Dreams (Style Two), HN 3665
Tony Weller (Style One), HN 346, 368, 684
Tony Weller (Style Two), HN 544, M 47
Tootles, HN 1680
Top o' the Hill (Style One), HN 1833, 1834, 1849, 2127, 3735A
Top o' the Hill (Style Two), HN 2126, 3499, 3734
Top o' the Hill (Style Three), M217
Top o' the Hill (Style Four), HN 4778; also called Autumn Days, HN 4755
Town Crier (Style One), HN 2119
Town Crier (Style Two), HN 3261
Town Veterinary, HN 4651
Toymaker, HN 2250
Toys, HN 1316
Tracy, HN 2736, 3291
Tranquility (Style One), HN 2426, 2469
Tranquility (Style Two), HN 4770
Tranquillity, HN 3747; also called Debbie, HN 2385, 2400; Lavender Rose, HN 3481; Memory Lane, HN 3746; Moonlight Roses, HN 3483; Old Country Roses (Style One), HN 3842
Traveller's Tale, HN 3185
Treasure Island, HN 2243
Treasured Moments, HN 4745; also called Special Celebration HN 4234
Trotty Veck, M 91
True Love, HN 4621
Trumpet Player, HN 4283

Tulips, HN 466, 488, 672, 747, 1334
Tumbler, HN 3183; also called Tumbling, HN 3283, 3289
Tumbling, HN 3283, 3289; also called Tumbler, HN 3183
Tuppence a Bag, HN 2320
Twilight, HN 2256
Two-a-Penny, HN 1359
Two Became One, HN 4644
T'zu-hsi, Empress Dowager, HN 2391

U

Uncle Ned, HN 2094
Under the Gooseberry Bush, HN 49
Unity, HN 4485
Upon Her Cheeks She Wept, HN 59, 511, 522
Uriah Heep (Style One), HN 545, M 45
Uriah Heep (Style Two), HN 554, 1892
Uriah Heep (Style Three), HN 2101

V

Valerie (Style One), HN 2107, 3620
Valerie (Style Two), HN 3904
Vanessa, CL 3989
Vanessa (Style One), HN 1836, 1838
Vanessa (Style Two), HN 3198
Vanity, HN 2475
Veneta, HN 2722
Vera (First Version), HN 1729, 1730
Vera (Second Version), HN 4169
Verena, HN 1835, 1854
Veronica (Style One), HN 1517, 1519, 1650, 1943
Veronica (Style Two), M 64, 70
Veronica (Style Three), HN 1915
Veronica (Style Four), HN 3205
Vice-Admiral Lord Nelson, HN 3489
Victoria, CL 4016
Victoria (Style One), HN 2471, 3416
Victoria (Style Two), HN 3735, 3744, 3909
Victoria (Style Three), M 209
Victoria (Style Four), HN 4623
Victorian Christmas, HN 4675; also called Christmas Day 2004 HN 4558
Victorian Lady (Style One), HN 726, 727, 728, 736, 739, 740, 742, 745, 1208, 1258, 1276, 1277, 1345, 1452, 1529
Victorian Lady (Style Two), M 1, 2, 25
Viking, HN 2375
Viola, HN 3706
Viola d'Amore, HN 2797
Violin, HN 2432
Virginals, HN 2427
Virginia, CL 3999
Virginia, HN 1693, 1694
Vivienne, HN 2073
Votes For Women, HN 2816

W

Waiting For A Train, HN 3315
Waiting For The Boats: see Fisherwomen
Wales, HN 3630; also called Welsh Lady HN 4712
Wandering Minstrel, HN 1224
Wardrobe Mistress, HN 2145
Water Maiden, HN 3155

Wayfarer, HN 2362
Wedding Celebration, HN 4216, 4229
Wedding Day, HN 2748
Wedding Morn (Style One), HN 1866, 1867
Wedding Morn (Style Two), HN 3853; also called
    Bride of the Year, HN 3758
Wedding Vows (Style One), HN 2750
Wedding Vows (Style Two), HN 4379
Wee Willie Winkie (Style One), HN 2050
Wee Willie Winkie (Style Two), HN 3031
Welcome, HN 3764
Welcome Home, HN 3299
Well Done, HN 3362
Welsh Girl, HN 39, 92, 456, 514, 516, 519, 520,
    660, 668, 669, 701, 792; also called Myfanwy
    Jones
Wlesh Lady, HN 4712; also called Wales HN 3630
Wendy, HN 2109
West Indian Dancer, HN 2384
West Wind, HN 1776, 1826
W. G. Grace, HN 3640
What Fun, HN 3364
What's The Matter?, HN 3684
When I Was Young, HN 3457
Wigmaker of Williamsburg, HN 2239
Wildflower of the Month, HN 3341, 3342, 3343,
    3344, 3345, 3346, 3347, 3408, 3409, 3410,
    3411, 3412; also called Beatrice HN 3263,
    3631; Kathryn (Style One), HN 3413; Lucy (Style
    Two), HN 3653, Summer Serenade, HN 3610
Will He, Won't He, HN 3275
William III (1650-1702), HN 4022
Willy-Won't He, HN 1561, 1584, 2150

Wimbledon, HN 3366
Windflower (Style One), HN 1763, 1764, 2029
Windflower (Style Two), HN 1920, 1939
Windflower (Style Three), M 78, 79
Windflower (Style Four), HN 3077
Windmill Lady, HN 1400
Windswept, HN 3027
Winner, HN 1407
Winning Putt, HN 3279
Winsome, HN 2220
Winston S. Churchill (Style One), HN 3057
Winston S. Churchill (Style Two), HN 3433
Winter (Style One), HN 315, 475
Winter (Style Two), HN 2088
Winter (Style Three), HN 4273
Winter (Style Four), HN 4589
Winter Bouquet, HN 3919
Winter Welcome, HN 3611; also called Caroline
    (Style One), HN 3170
Winter's Day, HN 3769
Winter's Morn, HN 4538, 4622
Winter's Walk, HN 3052
Wintertime (Style One), HN 3060
Wintertime (Style Two), HN 3622
Wisdom (Style Two), HN 4166
Wisdom (Style One), HN 4083
Wistful (Style One), HN 2396, 2472
Wistful (Style Two), HN 3664
Witch (Style One), HN 3848
Witch (Style Two), HN 4444
With All My Love, HN 4213, 4241
With Love (Style One), HN 3393, 3492

With Love (Style Two), HN 4746; also called
    Just For You (Style Two) HN 4236
Wizard (Style One), HN 2877, 3121, 4069
Wizard (Style Two), HN 3722, 3732
Woman of the Time of Henry VI, HN 43
Women's Auxiliary Air Force, HN 4554
Women's Royal Navy Service, HN 4498
Women's Land Army, HN 4364
Wood Nymph, HN 2192
Writing, HN 3049

Y

Yearning, HN 2920, 2921
Yeoman of the Guard, HN 688, 2122
Young Dreams, HN 3176
Young Knight, HN 94
Young Love, HN 2735
Young Master, HN 2872
Young Melody, HN 3654
Young Miss Nightingale, HN 2010
Young Mother with Child, HN 1301
Young Queen Victoria , HN 4475
Young Widow, HN 1399; also called Little Mother
    (Style Two), HN 1418, 1641
Yours Forever, HN 3354; also called Kimberley
(Style One), HN 2969
Yum-Yum (Style One), HN 1268, 1287
Yum-Yum (Style Two), HN 2899
Yvonne, HN 3038

Z

Zoe, HN 4208

Collecting Doulton

&

Beswick Collectors Club

The independent magazine for collectors of Royal Doulton and Beswick

If you are a collector of Doulton or Beswick you cannot afford to be without this lively, authoritative and completely independent publication.

If you are a previous subscriber to Collecting Doulton, you may not know how much the magazine has improved over the past few mon~~~

Published six times a year, Collecting Doulton~~~
range of Doulton and Beswick ceramics, inclu~~~

- Latest auction results
- Your questions answered
- Collectors' profiles
- Free wants and for sale small ads

Amongst the subjects regularly covered are La~~~
jugs, Bunnykins, Burslem wares, Doulton and~~~
advertising wares, new discoveries, rarities, Be~~~

Website: www.collectingdoulton.c~~~

Royal Doulton Stores

DOULTON AND COMPANY STORES - UK

Doulton and Company is the new name for Royal Doulton on high street, offering the very best of our three brands plus selected collectables and giftware and homewares from a range of specialist brands.

Doulton and Company Dudley
Unit 52, Merry Hill,
Brierley Hill, Dudley
West Midlands
DY5 1SR

Doulton and Company Outlet Superstore Etruria
Forge Lane, Etrura, Stoke-on-Trent
Staffordshire
ST1 5NN

Doulton and Company Hanley
The Potteries Centre
Hanley, Stoke-on-Trent
Staffordshire
ST1 1PS

Doulton and Company Hereford
19-21 Maylords Street,
Maylord Shopping Centre
Hereford, Herefordshire
HR1 2DS

Doulton and Company HOME
Central 12 Shopping Park
Southport
PR9 0TQ

Doulton and Company Swindon
McArthur Glen Designer Outlet
Great Western, Kemble Drive
Swindon, Wilts
SN2 2DY

LAWLEYS/CHINACAVES - UK

Lawleys Blackpool
Unit 37, Houndshill Shopping Centre,
Fylde, Blackpool
Lancashire
FY1 4HU

Lawleys Carisle
63 Castle Street
Carlisle, Cumbria
CA3 8SL

Lawleys Chelmsford
42 High Chelmer
Chelmsford, Essex
CM1 1XU

Lawleys Derby
Edwards
71 St. Peters Street
Derby, Derbyshire
DE1 2AB

Lawleys Peterborough
7 Bridge Street
Peterborough, Cambridgeshire
PE1 1HJ

Lawleys Reading
21 Queen Victoria Street
Reading, Berkshire
RG1 1SY

Lawleys Torquay
38 Fleet Street
Torquay, Devon
TQ2 5DJ

Chinacave Llandudno
94 Mostyn Street
Llandudno, Gwynedd
LL30 2SB

Chinacave Macclesfield
Unit 1, 25 Castle Street Mall
Macclesfield, Cheshire
SK11 6AF

FACTORY SHOPS AND OUTLETS - UK

Factory Shop Burslem
Nile Street, Burslem
Stoke-on-Trent, Staffordshire
ST6 2AJ

Factory Shop Fenton
Disribution Centre, Victoria Road
Fenton, Stoke-on-Trent
Staffordshire, ST4 2PJ

Factory Shop Regent
Regent Works, Lawley Street
Longton, Stoke-on-Trent
Staffordshire, ST3 1LZ

Factory Shop Stourbridge
Crystal Glass Centre, Churton House
Audnam, Stourbridge
West Midlands, DY8 4AJ

Factory Outlet Bridgend
Unit 66, Welsh Designer Outlet
Village, Bridgend, Shropshire
CF32 9SU

FOR YOUR NEAREST ROYAL DOULTON DEPARTMENT, PLEASE CALL ROYAL DOULTON CONSUMER ENQUIRIES ON 01782 404041

Factory Outlet Colne
Boundary Mill Stores, Burnley Road
Colne, Lancashire
BB8 8LS

Factory Outlet Dover
De Bradelei Wharf
Cambridge Road
Dover, Kent, CT17 9BY

Factory Outlet Ellesmere Port
Unit 106, Cheshire Oaks
Kinsey Road, Ellesmere Port
Cheshire, L65 9LA

ROYAL DOULTON

Visit our website at:
www.royaldoulton.com

Royal Doulton Stores

ROYAL DOULTON STORES – CANADA

Calgary
Market Mall
C2 - 3625 Shaganappi Trail
NW, Calgary, AB T3A 0E2

Cookstown
Cookstown Manufacturers
Outlet, RR1, Cookstown,
ON L0L 1L0

Dartmouth
Micmac Mall, 21 Micmac
Dartmouth, NS B3A 4K7

Edmonton
West Edmonton Mall
8882 - 170th Street
Edmonton, AB T5T 3J7

Fredericton
Regent Mall
1381 Regent Street,
Fredericton, NB
E3C 1A2

London
White Oaks Mall
1105 Wellington Road
London, ON
N6E 1V4

Markham
Markville Shopping Centre
5000 Highway #7
Markham, ON
L3R 4M9

Pickering
Pickering Town Centre
1355 Kingston Road
Pickering, ON
L1V 1B8

Surrey
Guildford Town Centre
Surrey, BC
V3R 7C1

Toronto
Fairview Mall
1800 Sheppard Avenue East
Willowdale, ON
M2J 5A7

Vaughan
Vaughan Mills
Royal Doulton Home
1 Bass Pro Mills Drive
Vaughan, On
L4K 5W4

Waterloo
St. Jacobs Factory Outlet
Mall, 25 Benjamin Road
Waterloo, ON N2V 2G8

Winnipeg
Polo Park Shopping Centre
1485 Portage Ave.
Winnipeg, MA
R3G 0W4

ROYAL DOULTON STORES – UNITED STATES

Burlington
Prime Outlets – Burlington
288 Fashion Way, Store #5
Burlington, WA 98233

Calhoun
Prime Outlets - Colhoun
455 Belwood Rd., Suite 20
Calhoun, GA 30701

Camarillo
Camarillo Premium Outlets
740 Ventura Blvd,
Suite 530
Camarillo, CA 93010

Central Valley
Woodbury Common
Premium Outlets
161 Marigold Court
Central Valley, NY 10917

Ellenton
Gulf Coast Factory Store
5501 Factory Shops Blvd.
Ellenton, Fl 34222

Estero
Miromar Outlets
10801 Corkscrew Rd.
Suite 366, Estero, Fl 33928

Flemington
Liberty Village
Premium Outlets
34 Liberty Village
Flemington, NJ 08822

Gilroy
Premium Outlets – Gilroy
681 Leavesley Road
Suite C290
Gilroy, CA 95020

Jeffersonville
Ohio Factory Shops
8150 Factory Shops Blvd.
Jeffersonville, OH 43128

Kittery
Kittery Outlet Center
Route 1
Kittery, ME 03904-2505

Las Vegas
Belz Factory Outlet World
7400 Las Vegas Blvd.
South Suite 244
Las Vegas, NV 89123

Pigeon Forge
Belz Factory Outlet
2655 Teaster Lane
Suite 26
Pigeon Forge TN 37683

Prince William
Potomac Mills
2700 Potomac Mills Circle
Suite 976
Prince William, VA 22192

San Marcos
Tanger Factory Outlet Centre
4015 Interstate 35 South
Suite 402
San Marcos, TX 78666

St. Augustine
Belz Factory Outlet World
500 Belz Outlet Blvd
Suite 80
St. Augustine, Fl 32084

Vacaville
Factory Stores at Vacaville
336 Nut Tree Rd.
Vacaville CA 95687

Visit our website at:
www.royaldoulton.com

ROYAL DOULTON

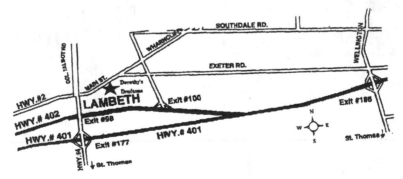